Citizens without Nations

Citizenship is at the heart of our contemporary world, but it is a particular vision of national citizenship forged in the French Revolution. In *Citizens without Nations*, Maarten Prak recovers the much longer tradition of urban citizenship across the medieval and early modern world. Ranging from Europe and the American colonies to China and the Middle East, he reveals how the role of 'ordinary people' in urban politics has been systematically underestimated and how civic institutions such as neighbourhood associations, craft guilds, confraternities and civic militias helped shape local and state politics. By destroying this local form of citizenship, the French Revolution initially made Europe less, rather than more, democratic. Understanding citizenship's longer-term history allows us to change the way we conceive of its future, to rethink what it is that makes some societies more successful than others and to examine whether there are fundamental differences between European and non-European societies.

Maarten Prak is Professor of Social and Economic History at the Department of History and Art History at Utrecht University. He is on the Board of the Royal Netherlands Academy of Arts and Sciences.

Citizens without Nations

Urban Citizenship in Europe and the World, c.1000–1789

Maarten Prak
Utrecht University

CAMBRIDGE
UNIVERSITY PRESS

University Printing House, Cambridge CB2 8BS, United Kingdom

One Liberty Plaza, 20th Floor, New York, NY 10006, USA

477 Williamstown Road, Port Melbourne, VIC 3207, Australia

314–321, 3rd Floor, Plot 3, Splendor Forum, Jasola District Centre, New Delhi – 110025, India

79 Anson Road, #06–04/06, Singapore 079906

Cambridge University Press is part of the University of Cambridge.

It furthers the University's mission by disseminating knowledge in the pursuit of education, learning, and research at the highest international levels of excellence.

www.cambridge.org
Information on this title: www.cambridge.org/9781107104037
DOI: 10.1017/9781316219027

First published 2018

Printed in the United Kingdom by TJ International Ltd. Padstow, Cornwall

A catalogue record for this publication is available from the British Library.

Library of Congress Cataloging-in-Publication Data
NAMES: Prak, Maarten Roy, 1955– author.
TITLE: Citizens without nations : urban citizenship in Europe and the world, c.1000–1789 / Maarten Prak.
DESCRIPTION: Cambridge, United Kingdom ; New York, NY : Cambridge University Press, 2018. | Includes bibliographical references and index.
IDENTIFIERS: LCCN 2018003684| ISBN 9781107104037 (alk. paper) | ISBN 9781107504158 (pbk : alk. paper)
SUBJECTS: LCSH: Citizenship – Europe – History. | Cities and towns, Medieval – Europe. | Cities and towns, Renaissance – Europe. | City and town life – Europe – History.
CLASSIFICATION: LCC JS61 .P73 2018 | DDC 323.6094–dc23
LC record available at https://lccn.loc.gov/2018003684

ISBN 978-1-107-10403-7 Hardback
ISBN 978-1-107-50415-8 Paperback

For Jan Luiten van Zanden.

Contents

Maps

Acknowledgements

Looking back across the arc of my career, I can detect the seeds for this book in my PhD thesis and the book I researched as a postdoc, both during the 1980s. Those were detailed studies of the social history of two Dutch towns in the eighteenth century. The topics I encountered then have continued to fascinate me and inspired subsequent work on European and global history. In this sense, this book has been in the making for more than twenty-five years. That is a long time, but I think it is fair to say that it is also a big topic. In the process I accumulated numerous intellectual and other debts, which cannot be properly settled in a brief acknowledgement. Nevertheless, I want to express my gratitude to a number of people who, willingly or not, have made a contribution to this project.

From early on, I found kindred souls in Jonathan Barry, Antony Black, the late Peter Blickle, Wim Blockmans, Marc Boone, Simona Cerutti, Robert Descimon, Tamar Herzog, Katherine Isaacs, Catharina Lis, Jan Lucassen, Heinz Schilling, Hugo Soly, the late Charles Tilly and, more recently, also Bert De Munck, Patrick Wallis and Phil Withington, all of whom have, in their own work and in conversations we had over those many years, supplied me with ideas and historical examples. In the 1990s, moreover, Robert, Simona, Marc and myself organised several workshops on urban citizenship. I would also like to mention the stimulating influence of the economic historians at the London School of Economics, in particular Debin Ma, Patrick O'Brien and especially the late S. R. (Larry) Epstein.

Various institutions have been hospitable and helpful during the course of this project. The École des Hautes Études en Sciences Sociales in Paris (through the recommendations of Robert Descimon, and later also Simona Cerutti) and the History Department of Exeter University (Jonathan Barry) funded research leaves in 1992, 2004, 2006 and in 1996 and 2002, respectively, all of which proved beneficial for this book, although this may not have been so obvious at the time. I began to collect materials specifically with this book in mind at the London School of Economics in 2008; while a research fellowship at the Zentrum für Niederlande-Studien of the Westfälische-Wilhelms-

Universität in Münster (Friso Wielenga, 2010) allowed me to think about the argument of this book as a whole. In Münster I also made the acquaintance of Christoph Dartmann, who initiated me into medieval Italian history; Michele Campopiano in Utrecht (now in York) taught me the basics of the Italian language when I discovered that it would be impossible to write this book without that skill. Sabbatical leaves, again at the London School of Economics (2011, Janet Hunter) and Christ's College Cambridge (2012, Phil Withington, David Reynolds) enabled me to start writing.

In 2013 the European Commission (EC) decided to award a substantial grant to a consortium of twenty-six universities, led by Utrecht University (Sybe de Vries, Law School), to investigate modern European citizenship. Albeit reluctantly, the EC allowed the inclusion of a historical work package in this bEUcitizen project.[1] Our Work Package 3 team – consisting of Clare Crowston at the University of Illinois at Urbana-Champaign; Christopher Kissane, Chris Minns and Patrick Wallis from the London School of Economics; Bert De Munck and Raoul De Kerf from the University of Antwerp and Marcel Hoogenboom, Ruben Schalk and myself from Utrecht University – was able to collect and analyse data that are used in the first part of this book in particular.

I am deeply indebted to all these colleagues and institutions for the support they have given to my work. This is the third book that I have published with Cambridge University Press. I am grateful to my editor, Michael Watson, for his unflinching support and helpful suggestions throughout these various projects, and this one in particular.

Other significant supporters were much closer to home. My partner, Annelies Bannink, has tolerated my infatuation with the past throughout the more than thirty years that we have been together. My employer, Universiteit Utrecht, has funded most of the work that has gone into this book, and has provided me with a stimulating research environment. I have had many conversations with Josine Blok, professor of ancient history in Utrecht, who was writing her own book on citizenship and gender in ancient Athens. In Utrecht it has been my incredibly good fortune to be part of a magnificent team of economic and social historians. Our projects, conferences, seminars and informal conversations, over lunch and otherwise, have been a source of great personal joy and professional inspiration. I want to thank all the members of the team, past and present, for helping me with this project.

My most important partner in this group, however, and indeed throughout this project, has been Jan Luiten van Zanden, with whom I have shared the chair in social and economic history in Utrecht since 1992. Teaming up with Jan Luiten has been the single most important decision in my scholarly career, and I never have had any reason to regret our collaboration. Together we have published two papers, an edited volume and a monograph on topics related to this book. More importantly, Jan Luiten has encouraged me, and the rest of our team, to think about the Big Issues, and to think about them globally. Dedicating this book to him can only be a small reimbursement for the immense debt of gratitude that I owe him.

Phil Withington suggested the title, Engin Isin invented it.[2] Lars Behrisch, Marc Boone, Christoph Dartmann, Jessica Dijkman, Ewout Frankema, Regina Grafe, Emma Hart, Dariusz Kołodziejczyk, Patrick Lantschner, Marco van Leeuwen, Debin Ma, Gary Nash, Şevket Pamuk, Auke Rijpma, William Rowe, Nico Wilterdink and Phil Withington commented on individual chapters; Jonathan Barry, Bas van Bavel, Oscar Gelderblom, Arie van Steensel, Michael Watson, Jan Luiten van Zanden, and especially Patrick Wallis, as well as three anonymous reviewers commissioned by the publisher, carefully read the entire manuscript. Murray Pearson improved my English; Rex Panneman assisted with the Index. They, and Ami Naramor, all identified errors and forced me to clarify my argument. I thank them for their valuable criticisms and helpful suggestions. I'm sure that at times I have misunderstood them, and at other times found myself incapable of doing them justice. For this and many more reasons, I accept full responsibility for what now appears in print.

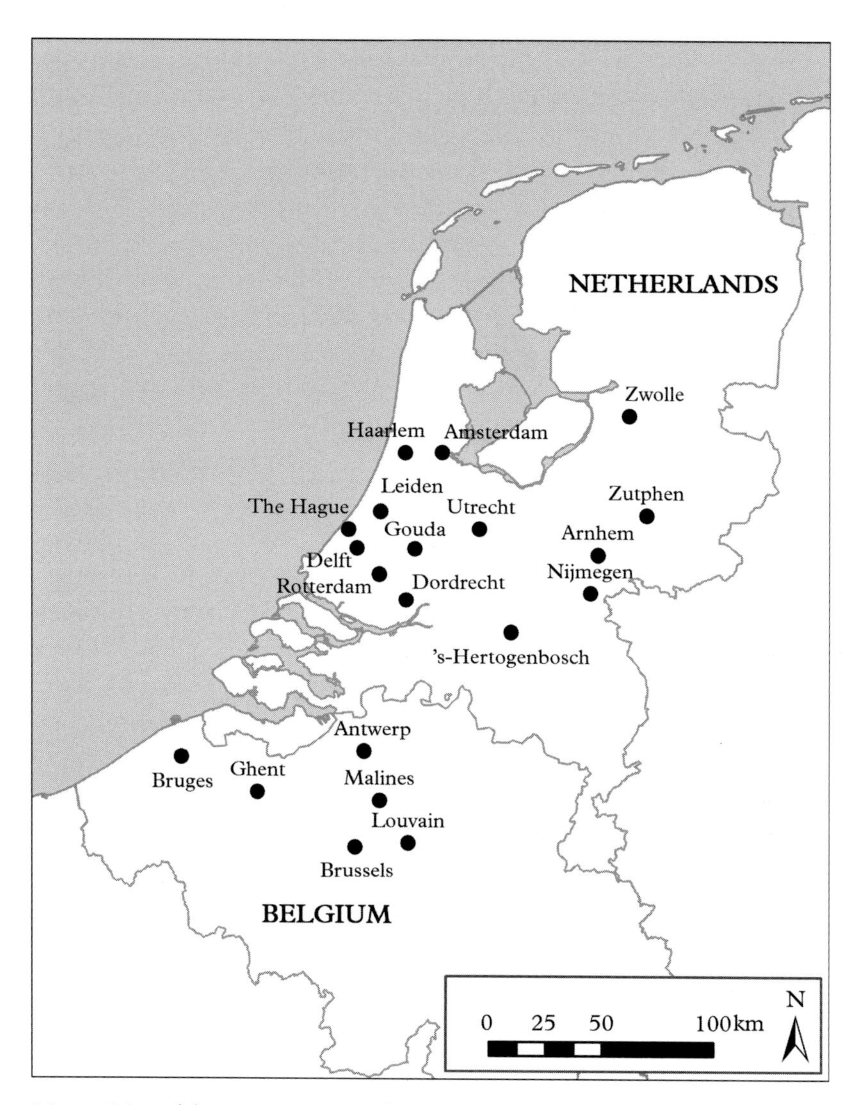

Map 1 Map of the Low Countries, showing locations of cities and towns mentioned frequently in the text. Map produced by Iason Jongepier, GIStorical Antwerp (UAntwerpen/Hercules Foundation)

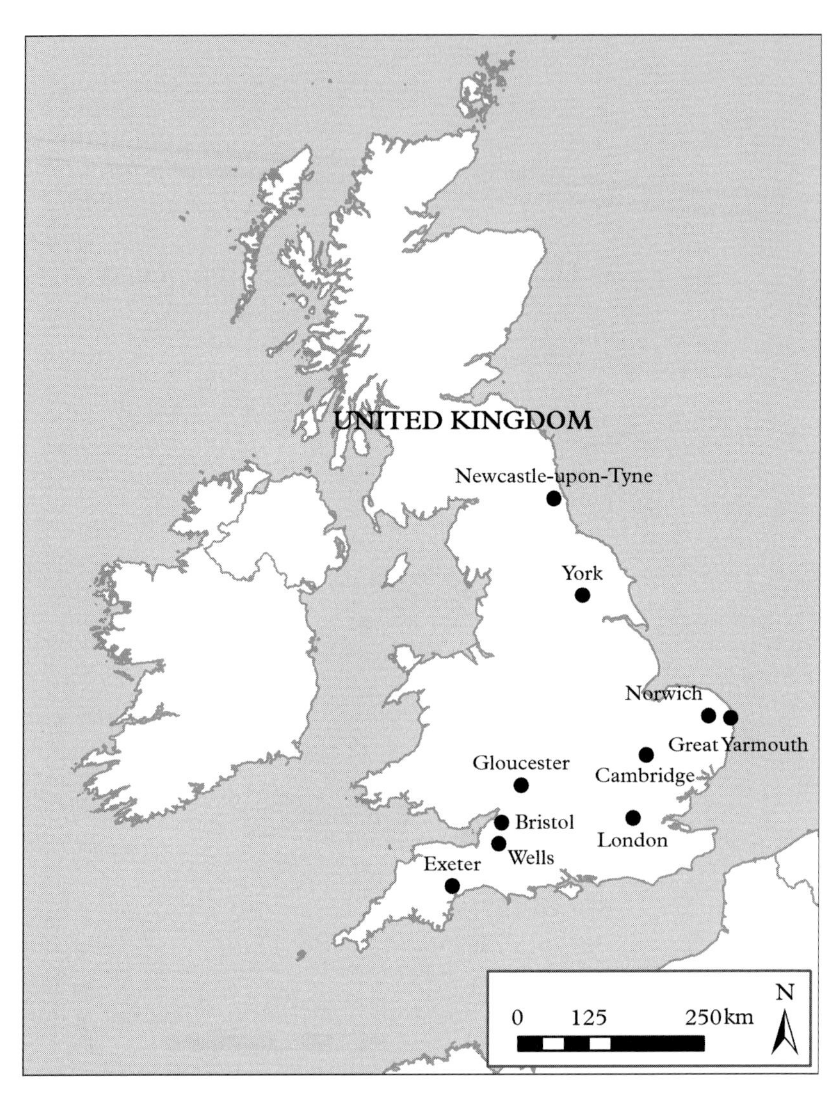

Map 2 Map of the United Kingdom, showing locations of cities and towns mentioned frequently in the text. Map produced by Iason Jongepier, GIStorical Antwerp (UAntwerpen/Hercules Foundation)

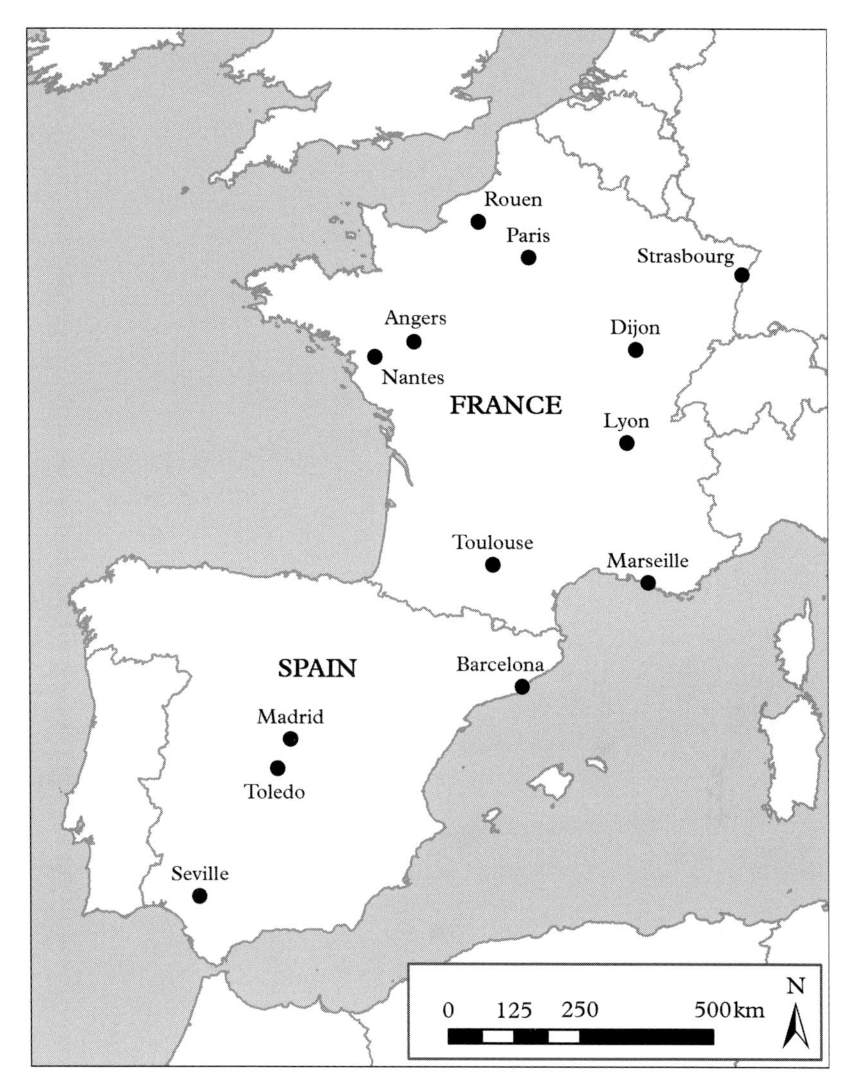

Map 3 Map of Spain and France, showing locations of cities and towns mentioned frequently in the text. Map produced by Iason Jongepier, GIStorical Antwerp (UAntwerpen/Hercules Foundation)

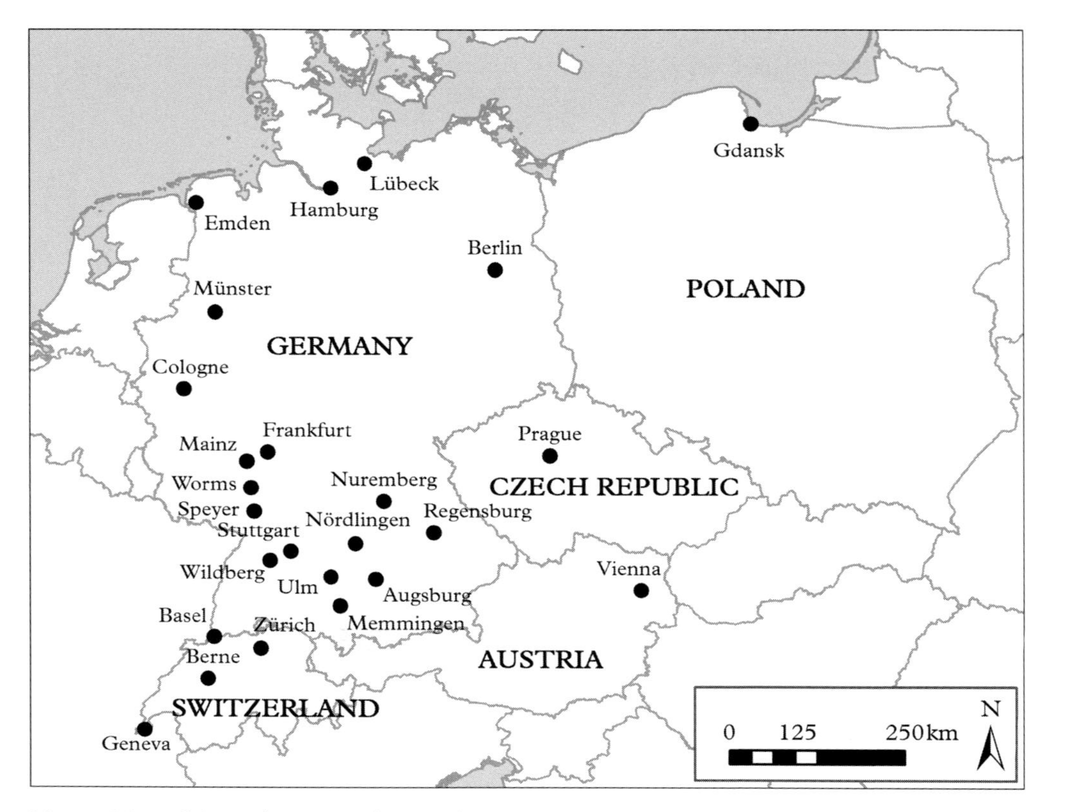

Map 4 Map of Central Europe, showing locations of cities and towns mentioned frequently in the text. Map produced by Iason Jongepier, GIStorical Antwerp (UAntwerpen/Hercules Foundation)

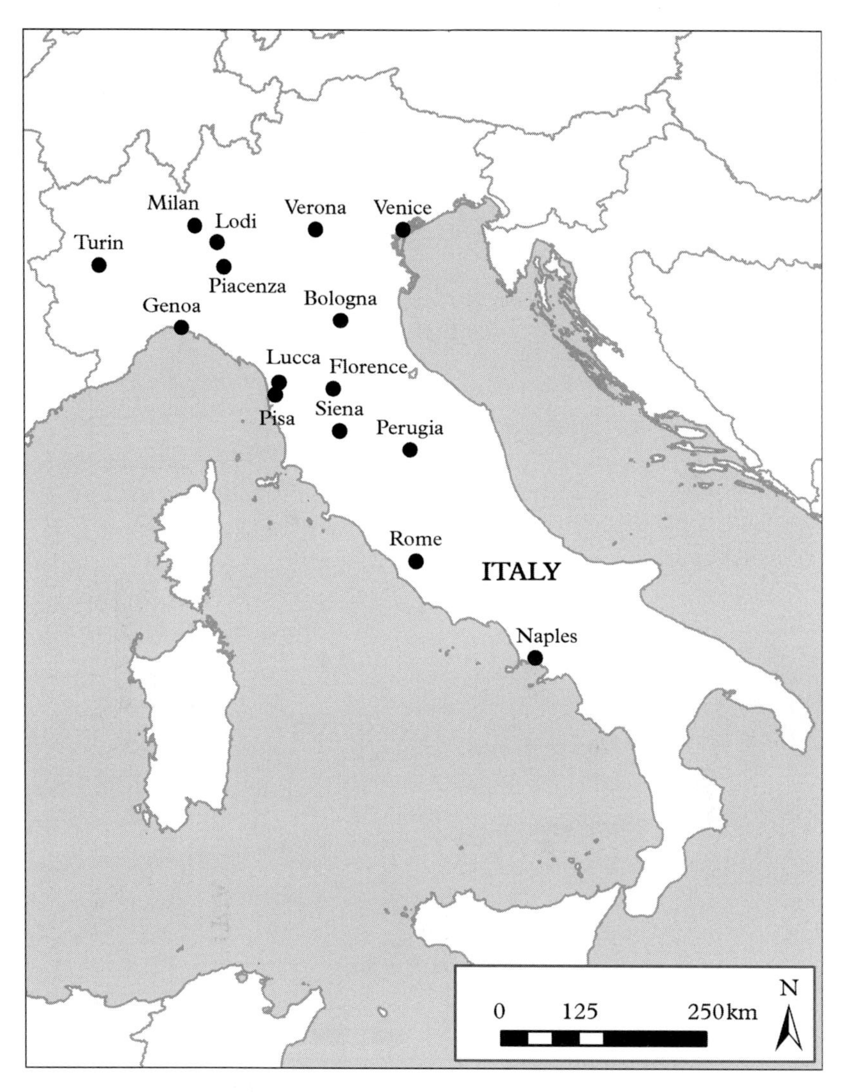

Map 5 Map of Italy, showing locations of cities and towns mentioned frequently in the text. Map produced by Iason Jongepier, GIStorical Antwerp (UAntwerpen/Hercules Foundation)

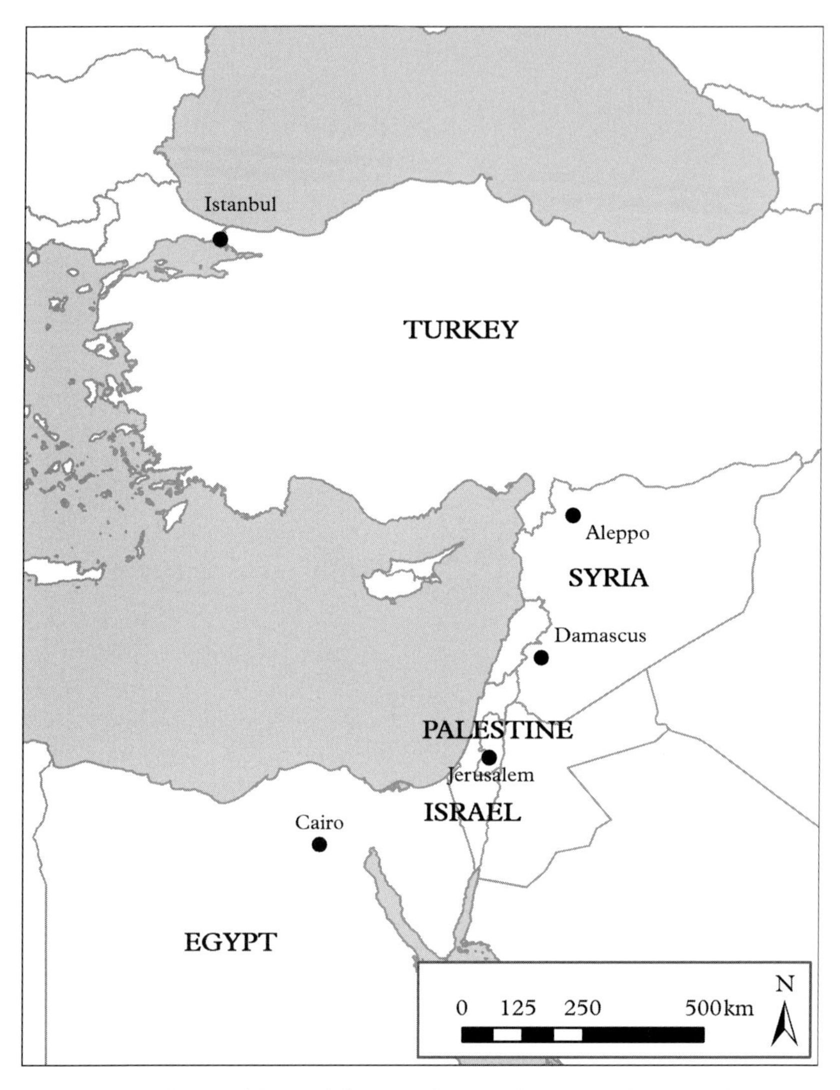

Map 6 Map of part of the Middle East, showing locations of cities and towns mentioned frequently in the text. Map produced by Iason Jongepier, GIStorical Antwerp (UAntwerpen/Hercules Foundation)

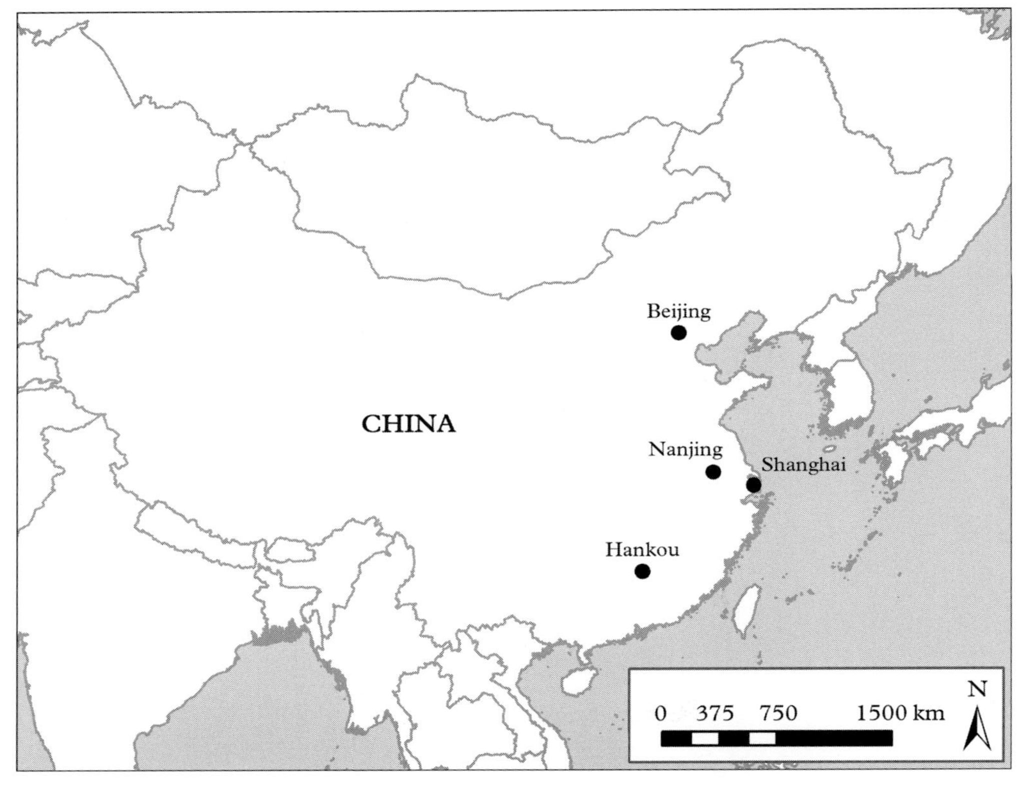

Map 7 Map of China, showing locations of cities and towns mentioned frequently in the text. Map produced by Iason Jongepier, GIStorical Antwerp (UAntwerpen/Hercules Foundation)

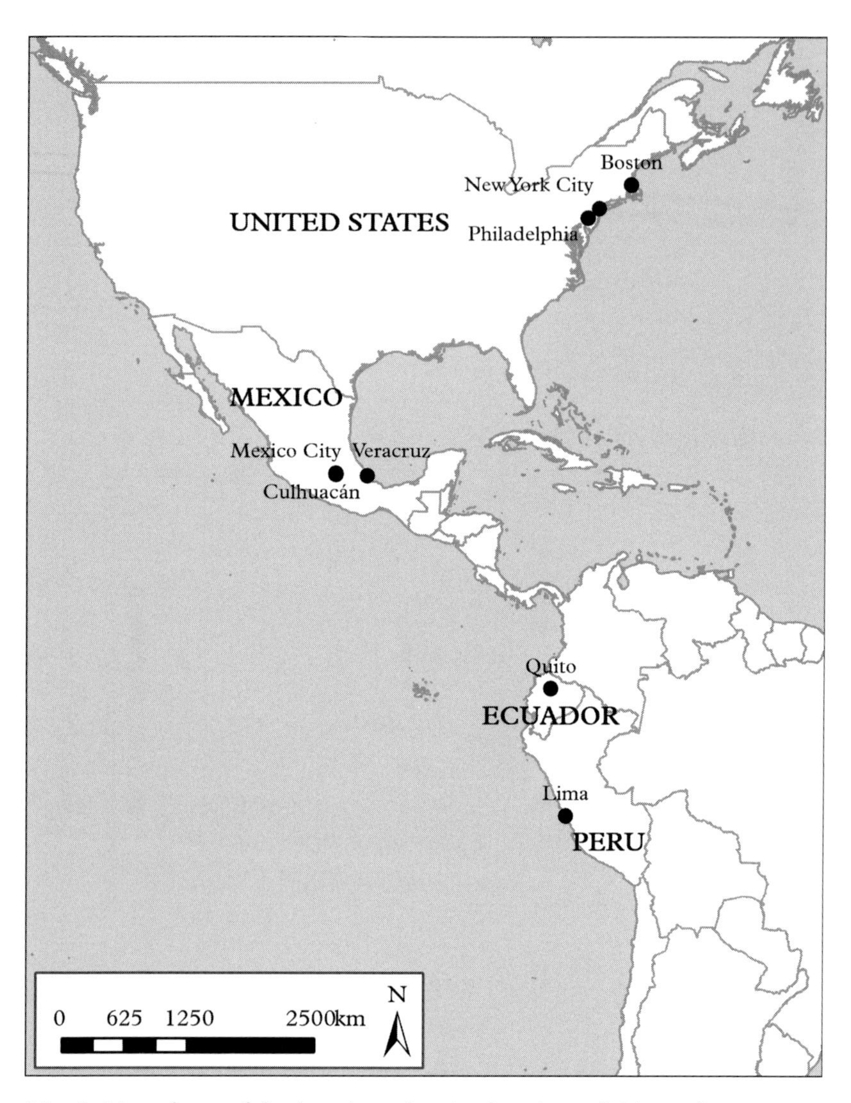

Map 8 Map of part of the Americas, showing locations of cities and towns mentioned frequently in the text. Map produced by Iason Jongepier, GIStorical Antwerp (UAntwerpen/Hercules Foundation)

INTRODUCTION
Worlds of Citizenship

Frankfurt-am-Main, nowadays a financial powerhouse and home to the European Central Bank, was elevated to the rank of imperial city in 1245. Being an imperial city implied that the inhabitants of Frankfurt could acquire citizenship. For some this happened automatically: the sons and daughters of citizen families became citizens too; marrying a citizen gave the immigrant husband or wife citizen status. Citizenship was also available to other immigrants, provided they could demonstrate legitimate birth and that they could make an economic contribution. Immigrants, in fact, made up 56 per cent of all new citizens between 1600 and 1735. Citizens had access to guilds, but were also required to participate in the civic militias and watches, and to perform fire service. Female citizens could not participate in politics, but they could own urban real estate and continue their husbands' businesses after their husbands had died. In the late seventeenth and early eighteenth centuries, legislation was introduced to prevent Calvinists and then Catholics from becoming citizens, but they could bypass such rules by marrying local citizen girls. Jews, however, were completely excluded from citizenship. In 1823, more than half of all Frankfurt households had formal citizen status.[1]

From the fifteenth century, Frankfurt's constitution allowed major citizen participation in all levels of local government; one of the city council's three members was a representative of the guilds. Despite this civic participation, tensions between the patrician elite and broad sections of the population at times erupted into open rebellion – in 1355–68, and again in 1525. Another such rebellion, in 1612–16, led to the complete exclusion of the guilds from politics. Still another uprising, begun in 1705, would ultimately undo this exclusion. The 1732 constitution, the culmination of a series of reforms in previous decades, restored to the citizens of Frankfurt their former broad role in local politics and administration.[2]

The nineteenth century would witness changes of a different order. On 18 January 1806, the imperial city of Frankfurt was occupied by French revolutionary forces determined to bring the benefits of the French Revolution to German citizens. Later that same year the imperial city was converted into the Principality of Frankfurt and a former chancellor of the Holy Roman Empire, Karl Theodor von Dalberg, became Frankfurt's sovereign. The so-called third member of the council, representing the guilds, was soon reduced to a supervisory board for the local economy. In other areas too, citizen participation in local politics and administration was significantly reduced. In 1810 Frankfurt became a territorial Grand-Duchy, the city itself part of a *département* (province). Frankfurt was now a *municipalité* (municipality), subject to the department and the Grand-Duke, and governed by a council that met only twice a year. In 1810 it was stated that from now on, 'all inhabitants of the Grand-Duchy enjoy the same rights'. Among those who benefitted were the local Jews, who in 1812 were at last allowed to acquire formal citizenship.

In 1815, after Napoleon's defeat, Frankfurt's status as an imperial city was restored and as such the city acceded to the *Deutsche Bund*. The third member of the council was restored in its eighteenth-century role. During the years of political shake-up, the percentage of patrician members steadily declined. The same happened to the share of artisan members in the city's political institutions, which went from more than 30 per cent in the years 1727–1806, to more than 40 per cent in the French period (1806–10), to as little as 10 per cent in the Senate of 1866. In Frankfurt – and many other places – the great winners were the professionals.[3] In one sentence, the revolutionary upheavals and subsequent restoration led to more equality in rights, but less equality in representation. And Frankfurt was perhaps lucky with the restoration of its former autonomy.[4]

The story of Frankfurt's citizenship exemplifies two core arguments of this book. On one hand it underlines how, during the premodern era, citizens could be prominent participants in public life. Frankfurt's history shows that citizen participation was not self-evident; the struggle over the role of citizens was not settled permanently, but subject to constant changes, and sometimes dramatic shifts. In this sense, Frankfurt was typical of premodern cities and towns all over Europe, and indeed the rest of the world. Still, citizenship was there, and it was worth fighting over. Frankfurt's history, on the other hand, also demonstrates that the French Revolution and its aftermath did not automatically improve citizens' rights and participation. In very general terms, the French Revolution strengthened the hand of national governments vis-à-vis local authorities. In France itself, and subsequently in territories conquered by the French, local citizenship and such civic organisations as the guilds were abolished. Despite Napoleon's defeat, his programme stuck in many countries where national governments were unwilling to turn back the clock. Instead, they embarked on a programme of political and cultural unification that by 1900 had succeeded in achieving most of its aims. By 2000, however, the downside of this project was becoming increasingly clear. National states had also become bloated bureaucracies, struggling to deliver on their initial promises of political freedom and social equality, and alienating their citizens in the process.

In this book I try to explain why urban autonomy was still popular in 1800, and suggest that it may even offer a (partial) solution to some of the woes of modern societies. This is not an entirely original idea; political scientists have already been toying with similar proposals. They have even invoked the past to underscore their point.[5] These political scientists are, however, poorly served by a historiography that tends to highlight the problems of urban governance and citizenship before the French Revolution and idealises what came after 1789. In the following pages I hope to demonstrate that, compared to the practices of nineteenth-century national citizenship, premodern urban citizenship actually has quite an impressive track record when it comes to political freedom, social equality and inclusiveness; or, to phrase it in the terms of 1789, of *liberté, égalité, fraternité*.

Citizenship remains a key feature of our own societies. Debates about immigration policies, the future of democracy, or how to reform the welfare state immediately touch on issues of citizenship: who is affected by these changes and how? Or, to put it more bluntly: who is 'in' and who is 'out'? Understanding the historical trajectory of citizenship before it morphed into its modern form can help us shape the future, not only through a long-term perspective, but equally by expanding the range of historical possibilities. Citizenship was a crucial element in the modernisation of societies across much of the globe during the centuries referred to in Europe as 'medieval' and 'early modern'. Max Weber made the point almost a century ago when he claimed that self-organisation by urban citizens, as it emerged in medieval Europe, gave them a head start over Asian towns where emperors and clans constrained society. This, he claimed, also helped to explain why Europe has managed to dominate the world over the past half millennium.[6]

Since Weber launched his thesis, however, we have learnt a great deal more about the historical roots and development of citizenship, and the societies in which it emerged. Conceptually, much has changed as well since Weber's time. This book takes a fresh look at the development of citizenship in the premodern era, i.e. before the French Revolution introduced democracy and 'modern' forms of citizenship.[7] Weber's claim, and the accompanying claim that Europe's success on the world stage was predicated on its unique citizenship arrangements, are challenged in this book in two significant ways. First of all, I hope to demonstrate that a remarkable amount of what Weber saw as unique features of European cities can also be found in the cities of the Middle East and China. Secondly, and contrary to Weber's argument, in substantial parts of Europe itself these supposedly unique features of European cities and citizenship failed to deliver the economic dynamism and social well-being promised by his model.

Clearly, another factor was in play. This factor, I argue, was the particular relationship between local, i.e. urban, and national governance. Only where states were organised in such a way that urban institutions could significantly impact state policies did the effects that Weber predicted in fact materialise. To put it the other way around: only those regions where towns were supported by states responsive to their needs did citizenship produce the effect that Weber predicted. Three distinct stages can be distinguished, this book claims, in the emergence of that dynamic state–city interaction. First, in the city-states of Italy during the eleventh to fourteenth centuries, in many ways, city and state were identical. Due to their small sizes, however, city-states were vulnerable to outside pressures. The second stage was the urban federation, as it triumphed in the Low Countries during the sixteenth and seventeenth centuries. In the long run this model too suffered from problems of scale, combined with internal sclerosis. The third stage was parliamentary rule as it evolved in post-Reformation England and ultimately triumphed during the Glorious Revolution of 1689. In all three systems, state policies were to an important extent shaped by urban interests and urban representatives.

In the process of outlining this story of European citizenship, I want to set another record straight. Recent research on premodern towns, within and outside Europe, has been dominated by the social history of elites. Historians of these urban elites have time and again made the point that small oligarchies monopolised urban politics. In the following pages it is argued, however, that the role of ordinary people in urban politics has been systematically underestimated, and that civic institutions directly or indirectly helped shape local politics in most premodern towns. There was, in other words, more 'democracy' before the French Revolution than historians have usually acknowledged, fixated as they have been on national politics. Popular influence was, moreover, greatest where it mattered most: in local institutions, where public services were designed and delivered. By destroying this local form of citizenship, the French Revolution initially made Europe less, rather than more democratic.

Definitions of Citizenship

Before we can explore the historical trajectories of citizenship, we need to know what it is that we are talking about. Like so many concepts that we seem to understand intuitively, citizenship is complex and many-sided. The *Handbook of Citizenship Studies* (2002) provides no fewer than four different definitions of citizenship.[8] The first, and probably most commonly used, focuses on 'political rights to participate in processes of popular self-governance'. This first definition goes back to classical antiquity and its political philosophy. The second concentrates on the legal status of individuals 'as members of a particular, officially sovereign political community'. This definition became predominant in nineteenth-century Europe, after the French Revolution had introduced the modern constitution. A third, which became more popular in the twentieth century, uses a much broader canvas and sees citizens as 'those who belong to any human association'. The final one is broader still, and defines citizenship as 'certain standards of proper conduct'.

The common theme in all four is that citizenship is about the membership of human associations and the standards of behaviour appropriate to that membership. Two out of the four definitions focus on the political domain as distinguishing citizenship from the membership of, say, a sports club or mandolin orchestra. This aspect would therefore seem to be essential to any satisfactory definition. It is also implied in the simple and straightforward definition provided by the world's leading expert in citizenship studies, Engin Isin. Citizenship, he writes, is 'the right to claim rights'.[9] Those rights, one assumes, including the right to claim them, are ultimately provided by the state or some other public authority.

Rights, however, are not homogeneous. In one of the most celebrated discussions of citizenship, the British sociologist T. H. Marshall distinguished three types of rights: civil rights, political rights and social rights. The emergence of these rights in England, according to Marshall, was sequential. In the seventeenth and eighteenth centuries civil rights, the rights to justice and the ownership of property, together with the freedoms of the person, speech and faith, were gradually established. In the nineteenth century political rights were given to many more people with the expansion of the franchise. In the twentieth century, the creation of the welfare state gave people a right to a decent living, through access to education and social services.[10]

Marshall's ideas have been very influential.[11] In at least one area, however, they are no longer accepted. For Marshall, citizenship was self-evidently a national institution and the rights that he talked about were provided by national governments. In the light of developments in the past half-century, this has become much less obvious. Globalisation and the mass migration that is an integral part of it have undermined the nineteenth-century idea of an exclusive relationship with a single national polity. Many people now have dual nationality, or descend from parents of different nationalities, and as a result have strong attachments to more than one state.[12] In Europe, this issue has become more urgent due to the creation of the European Union (EU) and the transfer of sovereign powers from the member states to EU institutions.[13] The EU itself is thinking aloud about the development of an EU citizenship, not as a replacement, of course, but alongside national citizenship.[14]

The identification of citizenship with national states has also left its mark on the historiography of citizenship, which has concentrated very much on two distinct periods: antiquity and the modern age. Greek and Roman antiquity is seen as the cradle of European citizenship, the period starting with the French Revolution as its phase of maturity.[15] The Middle Ages and the early modern period are a problem, because states as we know them either did not exist or failed to provide proper citizenship regulations. Andreas Fahrmeir's textbook on citizenship typically calls this the stage 'before citizenship', and portrays the French Revolution as 'the invention of citizenship'.[16] This gap in the history of citizenship can be bridged by shifting the focus away from states and towards the urban environments where citizenship did exist, both as a formal status and as a set of practices.[17]

This then brings us to a second area where Marshall's definition has been amended: its legal dimension. Underlying Marshall's definition was the assumption that citizens gained rights that would be legally enforceable, because they were established in the constitution or in other laws. Increasingly, students of citizenship have been forced to acknowledge that laws on citizenship can be contradictory and that citizenship practices can exist outside the rules covering formal citizenship, as the product of certain types of behaviour. For example, migrants without formal citizenship can nonetheless participate in local elections after a certain number of years' residence. In these and similar ways, inhabitants become de facto citizens through practices technically reserved for citizens only.[18] This practice-oriented approach, which is used throughout this book, widens the community of 'citizens' far beyond those having formal citizen status. Citizenship therefore is not so much concerned with distinctions between categories of people, but rather with the roles people play in society.[19] Nonetheless, important questions need to be answered about, for example, the gender, cultural or racial distinctions related to formal citizenship. In those areas citizenship status did indeed distinguish between people.

Ruling out the idea of citizenship as an exclusively legal category and abandoning the national perspective on citizenship may add to the problem of definition, but both must be discarded if we wish to compare the development of citizenship across time and space. Therefore I prefer a definition proposed by Charles Tilly. He defined citizenship as[20]

> a continuing series of transactions between persons [i.e. citizens] and agents of a given [polity][21] in which each has enforceable rights and obligations uniquely by virtue of 1. the person's membership in an exclusive category, the native-born plus the

> naturalized, and 2. the agent's relation to the [polity] rather than any other authority the agent may enjoy.

This definition is practice-oriented because it focuses on 'transactions', rather than on the rights and obligations as such, and allows for the possibility that other authorities than the state, for example local institutions, can create citizenship.[22] 'Authority' in this definition should probably be further specified as 'authorities in charge of spatial units', to distinguish them from prison wardens or museum directors. A shorter version, proposed by Richard Bellamy, makes essentially the same point. Bellamy defines citizenship as 'a particular set of political practices involving specific public rights and duties with respect to a given political community'. I agree with the 'political' in community, but think that the practices are broader than merely political. Bellamy too acknowledges that to function properly, political citizenship requires 'social and moral dispositions': in other words, more than politics.[23] Tilly himself proposed a simplified version, defining citizenship as 'a tie entailing mutual obligations between categorically defined persons and agents of a government'.[24] What is lost in this admittedly more elegant formulation, is the interactivity implied in the 'transactions' of his earlier definition. The 'tie' instead foregrounds the legalistic definition that has been a source of so much confusion over this topic in the past.

Citizenship and the 'Quality' of Society

Because it is multifaceted, to some extent voluntary, and touches on several of the crucial dimensions of society – politics, the economy, social arrangements, perhaps also culture – citizenship is clearly an important element of what determines the quality of a society. In recent years, three influential books have strongly suggested a more specific connection between citizenship and economic prosperity. Interestingly, all three have made extensive use of historical data. Only one uses citizenship as such as a key variable, but in a broader sense the other two also touch on the issues discussed in this book.

The most influential of these authors has no doubt been Douglass North, the 1993 Nobel laureate in economics. In a nutshell, North has argued that for market exchanges to proceed smoothly, transaction costs need to be low. Transaction costs include the expenses related to transportation and information gathering, but crucially also the rules and regulations ensuring property rights and contract enforcement. When institutions perform poorly, transaction costs will increase and the economy will be poorer as a result. On the basis of this simple observation, North, together with John Wallis and Barry Weingast, developed a theory of socio-economic development.[25] North, Wallis and Weingast distinguish two basic types of societies; the first they call natural-order societies, the second open-access societies. Natural-order societies are, historically speaking, the commonest type by far. In these societies, elites compete for the largest share of the economic pie. Although this competition is about economic gains, the weapons are political. With the aid of privileges and, if necessary, real weapons, elites help themselves (and their supporters) to whatever they can lay their hands on. In advanced versions of such natural-order societies, elites accept limitations on this sort of rent-seeking, but reluctantly and never permanently. As a result, natural-order societies and their economies are subject to short-term cycles of political upheaval.

North, Wallis and Weingast think that this unholy war of the elites against their subjects first came to an end around 1800 in three countries, through a series of related events.[26] In the British colonies in North America the American Revolution that erupted in 1776 installed a government that was accountable to its citizens. French involvement in this war and its financial consequences then led to the French Revolution of 1789 that toppled the elites in that country. The series of wars against revolutionary France subsequently forced the English elites to follow a path that had already been cleared a century earlier by the Glorious Revolution, which gave power to Parliament. During these three related revolutions, elites were forced to acknowledge the role of citizens in their polities by introducing democratic rule. This finally stopped the endless rounds of rent-seeking and started investments in long-term improvements that would ultimately prove beneficial to all, i.e. citizens and elites alike. The 'open access order' had arrived.

Daron Acemoglu and James Robinson tell a roughly similar story. For them too, the distinction between rich and poor countries is all about 'institutions, institutions, institutions'.[27] They see the Glorious Revolution as the turning point. Parliamentary constraints on the monarch (or the executive) helped secure property rights, changed the fiscal regime and led to improved infrastructure and to a much more aggressive protection of international trade by the British state.[28] This, Acemoglu and Robinson argue, created the foundations to launch the

Industrial Revolution. Institutional reforms, or their absence, then determined which countries were able to follow the British example. Outside Europe, however, the Europeans imposed the sort of institutional regimes that prevented non-European regions from imitating that example. To this day, the distinctions between prosperous and poverty-stricken economies are very much determined by institutional structures and the incentives they generate.

Political scientist Robert Putnam came to the same conclusion in two influential works on civic institutions in Italy and the United States.[29] Of these two, the Italian study is the more interesting for our purposes, because it is historically oriented. In a study of the quality of local government in modern Italy, Putnam and his collaborators found strong evidence of two distinct cultures. In the north, local citizens were very involved in civic organisations; in the south, people were suspicious of public institutions and instead relied on family relations and patronage to get things done. For Italy, Putnam explains this situation as the outcome of long-term historical processes. In the north, city-states created civic institutions and citizenship and promoted general welfare, while in the south, feudal lords excluded their subjects from political participation in order to exploit them. The result, Putnam claimed, was not just poor-quality institutions in southern Italy and better ones in the north but also a serious gap in prosperity between the two regions.[30]

Putnam's claims have not been universally accepted. Scholars of Renaissance Italy have pointed out that he idealised the faction-ridden and often violent political conflicts of the communes and completely ignored the rise of strong-man solutions that saved the city-states from imploding.[31] That, however, is not the point here. Like North, Wallis and Weingast, and like Acemoglu and Robinson, Putnam is convinced that civic involvement in the way society is ruled has long-term beneficial effects.[32]

Putnam explains the impact of civic organisations using the concept of 'social capital'. Membership brought skills and networks that helped people to make their way through life. Amartya Sen has identified 'freedom' as the key factor. Freedom, Sen argues, contributes in itself to people's sense of well-being, but is also positively connected to the improvement of material well-being. The reason is that freedom gives people the opportunities to shape their own lives, and those opportunities will encourage them to work harder and more efficiently. 'Agency', therefore, is both desirable in its own right, and for the positive externalities that it generates.[33] In Besley's 'agency model' citizens can select the most competent politicians through elections, and reward those who deliver on their citizens' preferences by re-electing them.[34]

There are many instances in which effective agency requires that individuals act in unison. Citizenship is a case in point. Defining citizenship as a set of practices more or less automatically implies that citizens themselves can shape and in many ways even create their own citizenship, but that they only do so as part of a collective. The development of citizenship therefore needs to be explained as a form of collective action. Much of the story of this book is concerned with times when states found it very difficult to impose their authority. After the fall of the Roman Empire, most of Europe was plunged into a prolonged period of political anarchy. While the Church and secular princes were trying to figure out who was in charge, towns made their own bid to provide public order, and in many ways this was a bottom-up process. Citizenship, in other words, was created in an environment of collective action, rather than imposed from above, even though that sometimes happened as well.[35]

Collective action is one of the key puzzles of the social sciences and scholars in sociology, anthropology, economics and political science have put forward theories as well as empirical data to demonstrate that collective action can produce durable results. Samuel Bowles and Herbert Gintis, for example, have argued that humans are a naturally 'cooperative species', as a result of their dependence on game. Eating the meat of large animals was possible only when hunters joined forces. Human history is a long series of such combined efforts.[36] Mancur Olson, on the other hand, underlines that collective action can easily produce negative effects. Collectives have to provide incentives for their members to remain loyal to the group and those incentives often take the form of creating insider advantages, or 'rents'. The ways in which modern states defend the interests of their citizens to the exclusion of migrants and refugees are a clear example of how borders create divisions between the established and the outsiders. Collective action, in other words, has winners as well as losers, and rent-seeking behaviour by the insiders is likely to emerge sooner rather than later.[37] Therefore, we cannot take for granted that collective action will automatically produce beneficial effects.

Collective action requires coordinating mechanisms. These can take various forms, starting with the family, but in the public domain the two most important are the market as the coordinator of economic activities, and the state as the coordinator of politics.[38] These two mechanisms are very different. Whereas the market operates, it seems, without an identifiable coordinator, through what Adam Smith called the 'invisible hand' balancing supply and demand, the state can be precisely identified in terms of its personnel. But here is the problem: is it self-evident that what those individuals – the sovereign, the government, a dictator – want to achieve can be imposed upon the people? Too much of the social scientific and historical literature assumes that it can. This book starts from the assumption that this is not at all so, and that huge costs are indeed involved in persuading people to comply with government regulation.[39] The historical record is full of political contestation.[40]

Political scientists Wolfgang Streeck and Philippe Schmitter have suggested that, next to the family, the market and the state, voluntary associations are a fourth type of coordination mechanism. They define them as 'functionally defined interest associations', whose members, through 'inter- and intra-organizational concertation', can ensure 'proportional shares'.[41] From this point of view, civic organisations are effective because they reduce uncertainty and help people to act more effectively.

Claiming that institutions can make societies better is one thing, proving it quite another. This applies especially to the centuries covered by this book, for which reliable statistical data are lacking. Even though much progress has been made in the systematic collection of quantitative data about historical societies, for the time being we still have only two measurements that cover enough countries at sufficient data points to give us more or less reliable indications of the 'quality' of these societies. Those indicators are urbanisation and average national income, or GDP/capita.[42] These are, unfortunately, not even independent indicators, since urbanisation is one of the variables economic historians use to estimate the size of GDP. They are, however, the best we have, and therefore their suitability for the task that they are assigned in this book needs to be briefly discussed.

Many economists see urbanisation as a proxy for premodern economic and social development.[43] Urban economies were predicated on effective farmers who had to feed the town dwellers; urban growth made farmers more productive.[44] Urban trade and industry generally grew faster than agriculture. Recent quantitative research on historical towns in the period covered by this book suggests that citizen participation in local politics and parliamentary representation of urban interests did indeed create 'significant direct positive benefits' for European towns, compared to those of the Middle East and North Africa.[45]

Since World War II, economists have developed increasingly sophisticated tools to establish the size of national income. The results of their calculations nowadays provide a very important instrument for economic policy and a standard for governmental performance. Economic historians have applied the same methodology to past societies. For the nineteenth century good data are available, but for earlier centuries they have to be reconstructed, acknowledging the huge gaps in the historical record and the need, therefore, to estimate and, sometimes, guesstimate missing data. The best-known figures for GDP/capita, and the related concept of living standards, have been produced by the late Angus Maddison.[46] Inevitably, his figures have been challenged, but more importantly, they have also been improved upon by scholars such as Robert Allen, Stephen Broadberry and Bishnupriya Gupta, Paolo Malanima, Bas van Leeuwen and Jan Luiten van Zanden.[47] In combination with improved data on urbanisation, their work allows us to gauge – still crudely, but with greater precision than before – the different trajectories of societies, both within Europe and between Europe and other continents.[48] Where appropriate, but especially in Parts II and III of this book, their figures are used to make claims about the impact of citizenship on the prosperity of societies, and by implication about their overall well-being.

Methodologies for a Comparative History of Citizenship

Methodologically, this book takes its cues from a distinguished series of works on historical sociology.[49] These books share an interest in large topics, such as the rise of the modern state (Charles Tilly, Thomas Ertman) and democratic regimes (Barrington Moore Jr., and North, Wallis and Weingast), the origins of rebellions and revolutions (Tilly again, Theda Skocpol), of the modern world economy (Immanuel Wallerstein), and the emergence of the welfare state (Abram de Swaan).[50] Another characteristic shared by these works is their attempt to mine the historical record for patterns that might help us understand the development of human societies. Most historical sociologists hesitate to apply the word 'theory' to their results, presumably because they have realised that historical processes have certain unique dimensions that make it very difficult to reduce them to statements that can be tested against other evidence.

Historical sociology has been dominated by American social scientists, uninhibited by the historian's natural inclination to see each historical event as somehow unique. Due to the roots of their field in nineteenth-century nationalism, historians moreover tend to be country specialists, reluctant to wander very far outside the area of their expertise. Sociologists, economists and political scientists have felt free to go where they please. I have to admit that I myself, having done a great deal of archival work on the urban history of the Netherlands and relatively little outside it, have often felt intimidated by my lack of first-hand, i.e. archive-based, knowledge of the topics I discuss in this book. I have, however, persuaded myself that at the end of the day it cannot count as a handicap to have at least some experience with the original material, even if that experience is temporally and geographically limited.

Another feature that this book borrows from the historical social scientists is their particular application of the comparative method. In its more sophisticated form, the comparative method requires a precise outcome, or dependent variable, and a limited set of factors (independent variables) that explain the outcome.[51] Given the scope of the present inquiry on one hand, and the incomplete nature of the historical evidence on the other, I allow myself a less restrictive form of narrative, which I reckon will be more accessible to my fellow historians.[52] That narrative is, nonetheless, shaped by two distinct types of comparison, types that Tilly labelled the universalising and variation-finding forms of comparison.[53] The universalising comparison is applied in the first part of this book, which investigates shared features of medieval and early modern European towns. The goal here is to identify characteristics of the legal, political, economic, social and military dimensions of citizenship that were common to most instances, even though the precise details would differ from one town to another. My claim is that between roughly 1000 and 1800 urban citizens all over Europe could tap into a similar set of institutions to shape their lives.

To control for the fact that I use works from a wide range of towns, to capture as much as possible of the variety of individual urban histories, I pay extra attention to four towns in particular: Siena in Italy, Münster in Germany, Utrecht in the Netherlands and York in England. These towns all belonged to the middle-sized category of European towns, with populations that around 1600 all ranged between 10,000 and 15,000 inhabitants. Only Siena, where the population numbered 50,000 at the time of the Black Death, was at some point substantially larger. These four towns crop up time and again in the chapters of Part I of this book.

In the second part, I try to establish why identical local institutions nonetheless did not produce the same beneficial results – in terms of urbanisation or economic growth – throughout Europe. In this part I argue that the different ways in which towns were incorporated into the state's functioning can help explain these variations. Here I apply the variation-finding type of comparison. In Part III I compare Europe's citizenship experience with that of two Asian regions, China and the Middle East, and also the development of citizenship in the Spanish and British colonies in the New World. Again, the aim is to identify variations, in order to understand the emergence, development and impact of citizenship practices.

Max Weber and the 'Great Divergence'

These comparisons between Europe and other continents bring us, inevitably, back to the works of German sociologist Max Weber (1864–1920) – inevitably, because Weber was one of the great sources of inspiration for historical sociology as an intellectual enterprise, but also and more pertinently, because he formulated a thesis that has come to dominate the debate about European citizenship ever since it was first published in 1922. In a nutshell, Weber's argument is that much of the emergence of modern society in Europe is explained by this unique feature of Western society: citizenship.[54] In Weber's definition, towns distinguished themselves from the countryside in five aspects. They had fortifications, markets, their own court of justice, associations of inhabitants and, finally, (partial) self-governance.[55] Weber did not claim that all aspects were found in all European towns. Nor did he claim that all these features were unique to Western towns. Indeed, he acknowledged that Asian towns shared many features with their European counterparts. They had, for instance, occupational organisations that looked very much like guilds. The same was true for the towns of the Middle East. However, these organisations were not bound together in that super-guild that was the European corporate town, with its 'sworn' community and political autonomy.[56]

Corporate status permitted European citizens to develop common policies of their own. They were not, or only to a limited extent, subject to the directives of a central government. The corporation or commune in the West was an alternative to such overarching social structures as the empires, castes and tribes that existed in societies outside Europe.[57] These inhibited the emergence of communes in the non-Western world; their absence was a precondition for the rise of the commune in medieval Italy and subsequently in the rest of Europe.[58] In the original commune, Weber argued, all citizens were equal, even though that did not last very long. The well-to-do were the only citizens with sufficient leisure time to devote to public affairs, and in due course they monopolised municipal offices. In some towns this was formalised by the creation of patrician guilds with an exclusive claim to municipal offices.[59]

It has been suggested that Weber's discussion of the European town was in several dimensions idealised. He emphasised that citizens defended their own towns, but this was not quite true after the Middle Ages, when professional armies took over.[60] His discussion of the rise of the patriciate already casts a huge question mark over his concept of citizenship. If ordinary citizens had so little say in the public affairs of their hometowns, what then did it mean to be a citizen? What was the fundamental difference between being the subject of a prince or a patriciate? Or did he want to say that only the patricians were genuine citizens? He has also been criticised for creating too much of a uniform picture of the Western as well as of the Oriental city.[61] More to the point, perhaps, our knowledge of European urban history has increased massively since Weber wrote his work, which was a development of the argument of his PhD thesis from 1889.[62]

One very influential element of Weber's analysis was his claim that there is a fundamental difference between Western and non-Western societies. It is not very difficult to see how Weber's predilection for 'ideal types' led him into an essentialist position, which assumes that vast areas like Europe, or China, or the Islamic world for that matter, can be captured in certain common, presumably essential, features. The comparison between continents as such is nonetheless valid, and indeed a central feature of this book. It therefore pays to briefly summarise the debate that has preoccupied historians about this issue in recent years, especially since the publication, in 2000, of Kenneth Pomeranz's book *The Great Divergence*, the title of which has carried over into the whole debate.[63]

In a brutally abbreviated form, Pomeranz's argument runs as follows. Around 1900 China and Europe were, economically speaking, two different worlds, whereas in, say, 1600 or even 1700 they had been much more similar. The difference in 1900 therefore was not the result of structural distinctions between these two regions, but of some coincidences that allowed Europe to jump ahead during the eighteenth and nineteenth centuries. One of those coincidences was the availability of cheap calories (sugar, cocoa, etc.) from the colonies; the other one was easily accessible coal that provided – initially inefficient – British steam engines with cheap fuel. To prove his point, Pomeranz systematically compared the most advanced regions in Europe (the British Isles) and China (the Yangzi delta) on a number of points that had been highlighted by other historians as factors explaining the Industrial Revolution. By demonstrating that Britain and the Yangzi delta were perhaps gradually but not radically different, Pomeranz made the point that the Industrial Revolution was not so much the result of structural process of societal transformation, but rather of Fortune favouring the Europeans.

Given the stark outlines of his thesis, critics have naturally been piling on the evidence that would prove Pomeranz wrong.[64] Jan Luiten van Zanden, for example, emphasised how European societies, and especially those around the North Sea, had already during the late Middle Ages developed nuclear households, levels of literacy and corporate institutions, including citizenship, which were all conducive to the development of market economies and economic growth.[65] In other words, it was not so much the level, but the dynamic of economic development that was different in both societies. Jean-Laurent Rosenthal and Bin Wong have combined both arguments. They support Pomeranz in his observation that levels of development were not so different between both societies, but confirm Van Zanden's idea of different trajectories. Rather than the institutions foregrounded by Van Zanden, however, they see warfare as the main area of distinction. The Chinese state, in their picture, was a relatively benign actor, more benign, at least, than its aggressive counterparts in Europe. Paradoxically, warfare led the Europeans to the steam engine.[66] I hope to demonstrate that the history of citizenship can contribute a new and significant angle to this debate about differential development.

About the Contents of This Book

This professes to be a comparative study of different historical forms of citizenship and their impact both in particular polities and on the wider world. Its building blocks are numerous local historical studies, which hold a gold mine of detail on this topic. Unfortunately, even among historians we find a huge gap between the detailed knowledge that has been produced in such studies of individual towns, and the clichés that still abound in textbooks. Those clichés are, inevitably, repeated by social scientists and are as a result firmly embedded in the scholarly literature. Much of that literature, moreover, is still fixated on Weber's ideas from 1922.[67] The problem with those ideas, as we see in the following pages, is not that they were completely wrong. In many respects Weber's intuitions were correct, but they were not entirely correct, and his mistakes have huge implications for the way we have come to think about European institutions and societies, as well as those of other continents.

The aim of this book is to set that historical record straight. With what we have learned about urban societies in the period covered here, it is possible to tell a new story about the development of European societies. This is important for historians, but for the social sciences as well, because citizenship happens to be one of the areas where the social sciences have leaned heavily on knowledge produced by historians. There is an uncanny tendency among social scientists to refer to works that have, frankly, been overtaken by more helpful ideas for some time. Apart from Weber himself one thinks of the continued interest in the works of Belgian historian Henri Pirenne, who died in 1935 and whose work on the medieval city originated as a lecture series in 1922 and was published in 1927.[68] In a way, of course, the historians have only themselves to blame, because they have been reluctant to produce the sort of text that could replace Pirenne as a helpful and up-to-date sampler of the historical literature. The present book seeks to provide that too.

Trying to address this agenda by applying local data to a global questionnaire, this book is in danger of intellectually overstretching itself. Inevitably, I have relied on the case I know best and where

I spent many years in the archives, i.e. the Netherlands, or rather the Dutch Republic, for a substantial chunk of the period covered in these pages. I have tried to avoid the Scylla of portraying the Dutch experience as typical of Europe as a whole, and the Charybdis of saying the exact opposite and making it into a completely unique case, as Dutch historians are at times prone to do. Instead, I try to show in Part II that it was part of a specific trajectory that citizenship in Europe was passing through.

Another limitation is this book's urban setting. Historically, this can be defended by the fact that formal citizenship in the centuries covered in these pages was located in towns. Citizenship in the form of a piece of paper was almost exclusively reserved for the inhabitants of towns – almost, because some regions, notably in Flanders, southern Germany and Switzerland, had so-called *paleburghers*, i.e. villagers who could obtain a special type of citizenship rights in nearby towns.[69] Still, my insistence on citizenship practices rather than formal status implies that villagers too could claim to be citizens. German historian Peter Blickle and his collaborators have provided strong arguments in their work, against the overemphasis on the urban–rural distinction, precisely when it comes to political institutions.[70] I am convinced that a story similar to the one told in this book might also be written about the countryside.

The preceding pages, even though they deal with very complex issues, still suggest a relatively straightforward set of questions for the historian: what was the nature of citizenship prior to the democratic era, and under what circumstances could it have an impact on societal prosperity? To answer these two questions, this book is divided into three parts. The first question is addressed in Part I, the second in Parts II and III. Part I analyses structures rather than developments; Part II turns from these shared experiences to investigate some of the distinctions between various European regions and also suggests a development over time, while Part III compares Europe's trajectory with, on one hand, similar societies in Asia, and, on the other hand, the Spanish and English colonies in the Americas.

Because we have defined citizenship as a set of practices, rather than an idea, Part I concentrates on a systematic analysis of these practices in the political, economic, social and military domains. Each chapter tries to establish how institutions provided citizens with agency, i.e. gave them the capacity to shape their own lives. The purpose of this first part is to show that premodern towns indeed offered many opportunities to their citizens to actively engage in public life and contribute to the development of their communities. To investigate this participation in communal life, we need to focus on some of the institutions that were generally available in premodern towns. For Chapter 2 on politics this is primarily the town council or councils. Many towns had two, some even three councils, with varying degrees of representativeness. Citizens could articulate their political demands through elections, but also through petitions, and if those did not work, through riots and rebellions. Special attention is paid to the role of wards, districts, neighbourhoods – whatever they might be called – the small entities that provided another layer of texture to urban communities. A major question for this chapter is whether urban politics were really dominated by oligarchies, a small number of elite families who presumably monopolised local offices.

Economically, the most important institutions in local communities were the guilds. With very few exceptions, premodern towns had dozens of guilds, each organising tens, hundreds or even thousands of members. A debate has been going on for some time now as to whether guilds contributed to economic growth. In Chapter 3, the focus is much more on their role in the community. We also want to know whether guilds restricted access to urban trades.

Socially, urban welfare agencies looked after those who had problems providing for themselves. Charitable institutions were perhaps even more common, if not more numerous, than guilds. In some places they would be governed by the Church, but very often pious names were a cover for public governance. Charity was simply too important to be left entirely to Churches. Charities were important instruments of communal inclusion and exclusion. The balance between these two is an important topic for Chapter 4.

In modern studies of citizenship, the military aspect tends to be omitted. In the premodern era it was, however, vitally important, as Chapter 5 tries to demonstrate. Large numbers of citizens were drafted in to contribute to the defence of the local community in wartime, but also during periods of peace. In Niccolò Machiavelli's version of citizenship, civic militias allowed citizens to prove their civic virtue. The literature on the Military Revolution has obscured the fact that these forces survived into the early modern era. How and why they did so is a key topic for this chapter.

The first part of this book draws on urban histories from all over Europe and most of the time disregards the variations between towns and regions, and also ignores temporal developments, at least most of the time. The second part does the exact opposite. Here I start to unpack the Weberian idea of a single European urban experience. In the four chapters that make up Part II, I focus on different areas that stood out in the urban and civic landscape. The focus in this second part shifts from the internal workings of citizenship within urban communities to the external relations of those communities with the state in which they were located. I analyse the impact of towns in the wider polity. Three regions, the economically and politically most advanced of their time, are highlighted: medieval Italy (Chapter 6), the early modern Low Countries (Chapter 7) and, finally, England (Chapter 8). The challenge is to explain which types of citizenship arrangements made these three regions so singularly successful – at least for a time. The final chapter (Chapter 9) in this part also looks at other regions, such as the Holy Roman Empire, France and Spain, where towns were embedded in state structures in such ways that urban citizens had less access to the state machinery and national politics.

Part III of this book then widens the inquiry by bringing in evidence from the Middle East and Asia (Chapter 10), as well as from the Spanish and English colonies in the New World (Chapter 11). Here we come to the crux of the Weberian claim concerning the uniqueness of European citizenship and its possible contribution to Europe's precocious economic development since 1800. First we look at endogenous developments in Asia, where urban communities were often as large as they were in Europe. In both the Middle East and China, empires were predominant, a form of government often portrayed as anathema to citizenship. There is no doubt that the concept of citizenship as such was absent from these societies; in this specific sense citizenship was indeed a uniquely European phenomenon. But as we have defined citizenship as a set of practices, we can be more open-minded about the presence or absence of citizenship in Asia. The same aspects of citizenship – urban politics, guilds, social provisioning and civic militias – as in Europe are investigated. Unsurprisingly, we observe both similarities and differences between Europe and Asia. These can, nonetheless, help us to identify the key features that may have distinguished Europe's institutional framework from that of Asian towns and countries.

Whereas the discussion of citizenship in Asia is mostly an endogenous story, turning to the New World forces us to account for the import of institutions by the Spanish and British colonisers. In the Americas, an important debate has been waged about the impact of colonial institutions on long-time economic performance. Spanish colonists left a legacy of 'poor' institutions, it has been argued, whilst the British endowed the United States with 'good' institutions. Historical studies of citizenship in these regions have not been widely undertaken. Still, what we can find out about them seems to contradict this black-and-white contrast between South and North America.

The topic of this book is so enormously complex that it is impossible to 'prove' very much about the role of citizenship in the premodern world. Some readers may also be put off by what they might consider an overly optimistic picture of premodern urban societies painted in the following pages. So am I oblivious to the fact that these premodern towns and cities were pools of vice and violence, that they were regularly ravaged by plague and other diseases, that women and children, not to mention labourers and slaves, were exploited there and that they were often ruled by greedy and corrupt elites? I can assure you that I am aware of all of these things. Yet I am not so sure that in these respects urban environments were worse than rural, or that early modern towns were worse than towns in antiquity, the Middle Ages or even the nineteenth century. Nor do I think that these downsides of urban life help us explain the fact that the percentage of urbanites roughly quadrupled in Europe between the eighth and fifteenth centuries, and had doubled again by 1800.[71]

Instead I hope to persuade the readers of this book that citizenship arrangements could make an important contribution to the promotion of welfare in societies of this period more generally. I also try to show that Asian societies, even if they did not have the concept, nonetheless had citizenship practices which in various dimensions resembled those in Europe. In other words, this book tries to develop a more sophisticated version of Weber's comparison between Asia and Europe. At the same time, it is an attempt to demonstrate that there was much more citizenship and agency in premodern urban populations than textbook histories of the period still usually assume. It is often said that the rise of democracy was a hallmark of the modern era. I hope to show in this book that in many ways nineteenth-century Europe was perhaps less democratic than it had been in previous centuries. To see that, however, we have to let go of the exclusively national perspective that has dominated history-writing since its emergence as an academic discipline in that same nineteenth century.

Part I

DIMENSIONS OF CITIZENSHIP IN EUROPEAN TOWNS

1 FORMAL CITIZENSHIP

On 26 October 1311, Gerino di ser Tano, a native of Casole, a village about twelve miles to the west of Siena in Tuscany, appeared before five Sienese officials to make a formal declaration and a payment.[1] Some hours before, the Nine Governors and Defenders of the Commune and People of Siena – effectively the local government and colloquially known as the Nine – had approved Gerino's petition for citizenship of their community. A document had been drawn up to that effect by their notary and presumably it was this document, handed to Gerino, that prompted him to appear before the treasurer and four *Provvedori* representing the *Biccherna*, the financial council. Gerino paid them the citizenship dues of 100 *soldi* or five pounds. In compliance with a recently introduced ruling he also pledged to build, within a year, a house in Siena worth at least 100 pounds. Five years previously, in an attempt to prevent alien merchants from circumventing the local export duties by acquiring citizenship of the town, the Nine had ruled that henceforth citizens would be required to live in Siena: citizens must be residents. To underwrite his pledge, Gerino was accompanied by two guarantors, Ser Nello di Giovanni, a notary, and Cino di messer Tinaccio, probably also a notary. A second official document was duly produced. Two days later, the city council took the necessary vote to make Gerino a citizen. Of course this too was recorded in an official document. Later that same day the *podestà*, Ranieri di Sasso Gabrielle from Gubbio, who was Siena's formal, albeit temporary head of government, officially granted Gerino the city's citizenship. Immediately

Gerino returned to the treasurer and four *Provvedori*, whom he had met two days before, to register his properties in the tax register.

A year later, on 21 October 1312, Gerino again visited the Palazzo Pubblico, Siena's town hall, to meet with the treasurer and four *Provvedori*, together with his two guarantors. This time it was to declare that he had kept his promise and built a house in the district of San Pietro in Castelvecchio. Its exact location was recorded. Five days later he returned once more and this time handed the *Biccherna* officials a document which stated that he had met all the requirements for citizenship status, and that he submitted his house to the community as security against any debts he might incur in the future and that could otherwise be held against the community as a whole. The next day a document was produced, demonstrating that one month earlier Gerino had acquired the plot on which his house was built. Two other *Biccherna* officials came in to declare that they had inspected the property, and valued it at more than 100 pounds. Yet another document was produced, stating that this declaration had been accepted.

Italian archives of the thirteenth and fourteenth centuries abound with documents relating to the acquisition of citizen status. Most of those documents required citizens to own local real estate and pay taxes; in return citizens were entitled to a fair trial, could join a guild and could participate in public offices.[2] Apart from the fact that a lot of individuals were clearly making a living from writing up official papers in early fourteenth-century Siena and similar towns, Gerino's story also demonstrates that he and many others valued formal citizenship. What was it that they valued, and to what extent did the acquisition of formal citizenship set Gerino and his fellow citizens apart from the other inhabitants in a town like Siena? These are two of the questions this chapter has to answer. In a nutshell, I argue two things. The first is that, at the end of the day, formal citizenship had its greatest impact in two areas: access to the guilds and access to high office. This was relevant, of course, for those aspiring to join a guild or hoping to be elected to high office, but many people either did not have these ambitions or did not expect to achieve them for reasons other than the obstacles they faced to the acquisition of formal citizenship. My second point is that formal citizenship nonetheless turned out to be more accessible than is often assumed on the basis of a narrow set of infamous examples, like Berne or Venice. At the same time, as we shall see, there was much more to citizenship than legal status. In the next chapters I discuss citizenship practices that were available to citizens and non-citizens alike. The final section of this chapter also explores how citizenship became the core element of urban 'imagined communities', in Benedict Anderson's now classic phrase.[3] That imagination could take many forms, but one of the default patterns throughout our period was what I call 'urban republicanism'. Urban republicanism did not care too much about the formal aspects of citizenship; it could easily cover those who were not formal citizens but still participated in citizenship practices.

Citizens' Rights and Duties

Going back to Siena for a moment, it is worth noting that the community that Gerino di ser Tano had joined was a less-than-straightforward sociopolitical sector of society. In Siena citizenship came in a variety of shapes, none entirely clear-cut. First of all, those who, like Gerino, had applied for citizenship needed a two-thirds majority of the city council to approve their applications. Most of these citizens, incidentally, came from non-citizen families already living in Siena, while others had inherited the status from their parents. If their families had been long-established citizens, they would be called *cives antique, veri et naturales* – ancient, genuine and natural citizens. The language made clear that these were elevated, at least in status, above the more recent *cives assidui*. In practice, however, little divided the two categories. A third type of citizen comprised those who resided outside the town's perimeter, the *cives silvestres*, or out-burghers. Finally, Siena had a group of households without citizen status, the *habitatores assidui*, or permanent residents. On paper they were the lowliest sort, but in reality there was not much of a difference between them and the citizens, except that they could not participate in politics and administration. These mere inhabitants were mainly distinguished from the citizens because they were usually workers, whereas the citizens tended to be middle-class artisans and shopkeepers, or upper-class merchants and lawyers. Among the out-burghers no such distinction existed, because often whole villages had been granted citizenship at the same time; it was a way for Siena to buy the loyalty of the *contado*, the hinterland under the control of the city.[4] So when we talk about citizens, we have to be aware that they came in different sorts. On paper it all looked very neat; in practice the distinctions could be quite messy.

This was also true because citizenship arrangements differed from town to town, and from country to country. In German towns, citizens were at one and the same time members of a juridical and privileged community and a sworn association. Swearing the citizens' oath entailed membership in the community.[5] In eighteenth-century Augsburg, and in other towns in southern Germany, the citizens' oath was annually confirmed on the *Schwörtag*, the day of oaths.[6] The citizen swearing the oath in sixteenth-century Cologne confirmed that he was not subject to any other lord, that he did not bring along any debts or other issues that would burden the community; he promised fealty to the city and its council and to uphold the local constitution, and finally to maintain proper relations with the other citizens and inhabitants of the city.[7]

The creation of sworn communities was the result of a long process of urban emancipation that started in Italy and subsequently emerged in other parts of Europe. The Roman Empire had been subdivided into administrative districts called 'civitates'. In later centuries the term had narrowed down to the bishops' sees, a process still captured in the distinction made in English between a city, i.e. the capital of a diocese, and a town. Later still, during the Viking era, walled places also became known as towns. It was among the inhabitants of such places that *coniuratios* were instituted, for the sake of mutual support and protection. In some places, for example, York, these *coniuratios* took the form of a guild, usually a merchant guild.[8] Guilds and urban communities thus became closely related, and in many, probably most, medieval and early modern towns, membership in guilds required citizenship. In some places, all inhabitants were even required to join a guild and thus become citizens.[9]

The community, rather than its individual members, had received various rules and regulations that allowed it to take care of its business. An important element was always the establishment of a local court of justice, regulating conflicts between citizens.[10] Because the judges were themselves citizens, citizenship entailed the right to peer justice. At the same time, the city itself had acquired legal status and permission to create its own regulations and organisations. These organisations are the topic of subsequent chapters, so we need not deal with them in great detail here. Suffice it to say, that for many of them, formal citizen status was a prerequisite for membership. This was most consistently true for merchant and craft guilds, but in the Middle Ages this equally applied to militia guilds, and even to many welfare institutions. As time progressed militias were reformed and thrown open to non-citizens. Similarly, as more general welfare institutions were founded, these were opened to all inhabitants.

Another early privilege all urban communities obtained was the right to rule themselves. That right was always conditional on the approval of the sovereign. Only a handful of European towns were city-states (Venice, Florence and several others in Italy; perhaps Berne in the Swiss Confederacy); the others were ultimately dependent on the goodwill of the crown. That goodwill was certainly not automatically forthcoming.[11]

As formal members of their community, citizens were entitled to participate in local governance. Members of the town council and other high offices were everywhere required to have formal citizen status. Active citizenship, on the other hand, was much more varied. Some towns held elections for the council; in others there was a division between a self-recruiting smaller council that took care of everyday business and a larger council elected by the citizens.[12]

Participation in elections, or even in the administration of the city and its institutions, was perhaps the most important but by no means the only privilege of those holding formal citizenship status.[13] As we see in greater detail in Chapter 3, in most places only citizens had the right to open a shop or workplace, at least if their trade was incorporated. In many German towns, but also sometimes in other regions, the ownership of real estate was restricted to citizens.[14] Urban privileges relieved citizens of various toll duties, although it is not quite clear how significant this was. In Lyon, for example, citizens were exempted from the *taille* on their rural properties, and had the exclusive right to open a wine tavern, or *cabaret bourgeois*.[15] In other French towns, citizens could import their wine without being taxed.[16] Finally, citizens might enjoy social privileges. Amsterdam, for example, had a separate orphanage for citizens' children and another for non-citizens'. Standards of education and provisioning were so much higher in the former that local authorities assumed that these benefits attracted people to apply for citizen status who would otherwise not do so.[17] At the same time, taking up citizen status required one to live locally, pay taxes, assume the burden of office when called upon and assist in the military defence of the town – in other words: support the community.[18] In English towns, the freeman's oath explicitly linked these three elements: the payment of taxes, the participation in local administration and government and the subjection of one's person and property to the local courts.[19]

The rights and duties of citizens thus covered many areas of public life, and could vary across time and space. Not in all of them was the formal distinction between citizens and inhabitants as clear-cut as legal documents suggested.[20] Female citizens in practice did not enjoy the full range of rights and thus were closer to the mere inhabitants; their citizenship has been characterised as 'passive', or 'latent'.[21] On the other hand, those mere inhabitants paid taxes just as much as citizens did, and they served equally in civic militias. In three major European countries, however, much of this distinction did not even apply in legal terms.

In Spain very little distinction was made between town and countryside. On one hand, farmers – and their animals – lived in towns, while on the other hand, even the smallest settlements had urban privileges and their inhabitants were citizens, or *vecinos*.[22] 'He who lives in a settled house in these kingdoms must be considered a citizen', it was said during a discussion in Seville in the 1770s.[23] Local residence did not automatically make one a citizen, however. Immigrants had to marry a citizen, or otherwise purchase citizenship. And even the locals had to petition the council to validate their citizenship. These procedures required the production of various documents proving a legal marriage to a citizen, or indeed proof of one's citizen ancestry. Over the course of the eighteenth century the paperwork increased as urban authorities, in an effort to make citizenship more exclusive, began demanding more documentary evidence. Spanish citizens were expected to pay taxes and to participate in the local meetings called *concejo abierto*, or open council. Women and children were also welcome to these meetings, an extraordinary feature of Spanish law. Women were otherwise limited in the exercise of their citizenship and could not even apply for it unless they were widows.

In many French towns, little distinction was made between citizens and other inhabitants. There were no formal procedures for obtaining citizen status; in most French towns this occurred automatically following residence for a variable number of years.[24] In Paris, which did have a procedure for acquiring citizenship, one became *bourgeois du roi*, rather than a citizen of the city. Only from the sixteenth century onwards do the sources also speak of *bourgeois de Paris*, a status that was primarily attractive because it provided exemption from certain national taxes.[25] French citizenship discourse was oriented towards the state. It had its roots in Roman law, but was also inspired by the ideas developed in Renaissance city-states. One of the arguments deployed by sixteenth-century French jurists who wrote about this topic was that France was really 'one great city', a fiction which allowed them to apply to a national framework ideas about citizenship that were developed in an urban context.[26]

In one way or another, all early modern European states were struggling with this problem: if citizenship as a formal status was a local institution, what did this imply for loyalties to the state and its sovereign? In most countries the relationship between local citizens and the sovereign was mediated by the local authorities, who represented the urban citizen community in national institutions. In France two distinct terms were used: *citoyen* denoted the person's relationship with the sovereign, i.e. the king, whereas *bourgeois* defined his relationship with the local community. The status of *citoyen* was, however, only formalised for foreigners. Like the *bourgeois de Paris*, this institution was primarily tax-driven. The property of foreigners who passed away on French soil would automatically fall to the crown. One could avoid this eventuality by acquiring citizenship, becoming a *citoyen*. On average some fifty individuals a year, overwhelmingly clergymen and merchants residing in France, took out this form of insurance against the possible confiscation of their goods and capital.[27] In a country of twenty million, the *citoyen* was a marginal figure.

In Muscovy, the government insisted on a direct relationship with its citizens and, for instance, organised open assemblies in Moscow where ordinary people were invited to discuss national policies. The authorities likewise encouraged the submission of petitions, and many individuals as well as collectives used that opportunity. In the Russian context, however, there was no idea of freedom in the sense of protection against the power of the state.[28] Nor were there any of the intermediate institutions that embodied those freedoms elsewhere in Europe – even in France.

Citizenship, understood as a legal category, thus meant a variety of things in different parts of Europe. It also changed with time; in some regions (e.g. France) formal citizenship rights became more circumscribed by the state; in other regions (e.g. the Dutch Republic) new possibilities emerged for citizenship. Stated more bluntly: there was no single European model of citizenship. In its most common form, citizenship was a formal status in an urban, i.e. local, context, which provided citizens with a range of rights and duties that spanned the juridical, political, economic and social realms. These local citizens were tied into the wider national community through the relationships between local and national authorities. Local authorities brokered between their own citizens and the state. This model applied in most countries, but France and Russia were major exceptions. In those countries, formal urban citizenship was weakly developed, and national citizenship rights were poorly articulated. Nevertheless, the existence of citizenship as membership in a specific community inevitably created a boundary between insiders and outsiders. So how did one transform from one into the other? And what did it mean for those left in the cold?

Modes of Access

On a European scale there were two main routes into citizenship: birth ('patrimony') and purchase. It is relatively easy to establish the scale of the second route, because records were kept. We therefore also have a better idea of the procedures followed by those who purchased their citizen status. The so-called born citizens seem to have often taken their status for granted. In Frankfurt, for example, the authorities urged citizens' sons to report to the city hall and have their status ratified, but the surviving registers suggest that such summonses were less than completely successful.[29] In Amsterdam people born into citizenship do crop up in the registers, but in such small numbers that they must have constituted a mere fraction of the actual number of people in a position to claim citizen status.[30] Does this mean that such status held little significance? Not necessarily; there could be other explanations for this lack of official registration. One, no doubt, would have been cost-effectiveness on both sides: for many it would be unduly time-consuming to go and register, while the local administration would have found it a laborious task keeping a record of so many names. There were alternative ways of establishing one's citizen status. If the need arose, neighbours and family friends would testify that the individual's parents were citizens, and such testimony was, it seems, accepted as legal proof.[31] In some towns, for example in the Duchy of Brabant, it made no difference whether one's parents were citizens: being born locally sufficed to qualify for citizenship.[32] This may also have been true in Venice.[33]

For immigrants, however, this was not an option; they would have to access citizenship in different ways. One possibility was to marry somebody who already qualified as a citizen. Citizenship was usually passed on through marriage. If there was no opportunity to woo a local lass or lad, the only alternative was to purchase citizenship, an option that is further discussed in the next section. In England, though not in other countries, apprenticeship offered immigrants a cheap route into citizenship; those who completed their apprenticeship in a particular English town qualified almost automatically for local citizenship.[34]

A third possible route into citizenship – in specific cases, at least – was by gift of the local community as a token of respect or gratitude. In the Dutch Republic, for instance, ministers of the official Reformed Church would be granted citizenship in towns where they were asked to take up a position.[35] Perhaps more interesting, urban authorities might bestow free citizenship on refugees or other immigrants whom they wanted to attract to their town or city. Huguenots were given free citizenship in this way in many European towns.[36] In 1745 the Hamburg Chamber of Commerce proposed to give free citizenship to every entrepreneur willing to settle locally.[37] Despite such examples, however, it was unusual to be given citizen status for free, and in terms of numbers citizenship thus acquired remained a marginal phenomenon.[38]

In Frankfurt in 1834 women led a quarter of all citizen households.[39] This was remarkable, not least because in the fourteenth and fifteenth centuries a mere 5 per cent of newly registered citizens in Frankfurt had been female. This had been the normal pattern; only in a handful of towns was more than 10 per cent of newly registered citizens female.[40] It has been claimed that women in the German lands were increasingly marginalised as citizens during the early modern period,[41] but the very low numbers of the late Middle Ages suggest that they had never been substantially represented. In the Dutch towns of the Overijssel region the percentage of registered female citizens likewise varied, but rarely rose above 5 per cent, either in the Middle Ages or subsequently.[42] In Amsterdam 203 out of 6,642 registered citizens in 1636–51 were females, i.e. 3 per cent.[43] These Dutch numbers, however, refer to immigrants rather than natives; among locally born citizens, who inherited their status from their parents, the percentage must have been around fifty.

Immigrants and Obstacles

Demographic historians have claimed that premodern towns were subject to an 'urban graveyard' effect.[44] As a result of overcrowding and poor hygiene, urban populations tended to decrease rather than increase. According to this thesis, immigration was necessary just to maintain a stable population. Obviously, urban growth would have required very substantial numbers of immigrants. Critics of this view have insisted that the effect did not necessarily occur in all premodern towns. Nevertheless, it is now generally accepted that immigration was already a regular feature of urban life in the sixteenth century and probably earlier.[45] Communities would have had to deal with the problem of how to accommodate and integrate these newcomers one way or another, and formal citizenship was part of that process. Middle-sized German towns in the fourteenth and fifteenth centuries routinely registered 1–1.3 per cent of their population stock as new citizens every year. This suggests that immigrants comprised between one fifth and one third of the population – depending on lifespan and the hidden number of non-citizens.[46]

Formal citizenship was not an option for everyone wishing to settle as a newcomer in an urban community.[47] And while some people found themselves excluded, others simply did not bother: if one did not aspire to office, or did not have the means to open one's own business, possession of formal citizenship offered no immediate advantage. Indeed, immigrants faced a range of obstacles. These were invariably financial – but never merely that. One of the most common – albeit very often implicit – requirements was religious conformity. Non-Christians would find it impossible in most premodern towns to obtain citizenship. Even in Amsterdam, with its reputation for tolerance, the earliest Jews were only allowed to apply for citizenship under the pretence that they were indeed Christians.[48] In 1632 Jews were allowed to become full citizens as Jews, without the need for dissimulation. Restrictive conditions did, however, still apply: Jewish citizens could not pass on their citizenship to their children, and they were not permitted to join the guilds, which for others was perhaps the single most important reason to become a citizen in the first place.[49] At least Amsterdam did not discriminate among Christians. In nearby Utrecht, Catholic applicants for citizenship were only considered if they were born within the province of Utrecht. It was later added that exceptions could be made 'for important, particular reasons', i.e. if the candidate was useful to the city. In 1724 Dutch Catholics were declared eligible for citizenship in Utrecht if they could produce a letter of support from a Reformed (!) consistory. Several other Dutch towns introduced similar legislation in the course of the seventeenth century.[50]

In medieval Germany, dozens of towns had a special citizen status for Jews, sometimes remarkably similar to the rights of Christians, at other times a severely restricted version.[51] In the early modern period, some German towns welcomed Portuguese (Sephardic) Jews, but refused to admit Ashkenazi Jews from Central Europe. Frankfurt, however, did the exact opposite in 1609, when a group of Portuguese Jews from Venice was refused residence.[52] In the early seventeenth century, Frankfurt had possibly the largest Jewish community in Germany, but during the so-called Fettmilch Uprising in 1614 the ghetto was plundered and its inhabitants expelled. They were subsequently allowed to return under special imperial protection. In 1694 the Frankfurt ghetto was home to some 260 families.[53] In Spain, only Catholics could become citizens; Jews and Muslims had their own legal framework and were excluded from participating in local affairs.[54] In France, Protestants were likewise excluded from citizenship; they were 'subjects of the king without being citizens', according to a treatise on the marriage of Protestants from 1775. Louis XIV himself had claimed in 1715 that there were no longer any Protestants left in France. Possibly with this fiction in mind, it had been ordered in 1724 that all civil acts, such as the registration of births, marriages and deaths, had to be passed before a parish priest. Only in 1787 did Protestants gain the right to register before either a parish priest or a royal judge. Jews were not included in the legislation of 1787.[55]

The financial obstacles, however, applied everywhere. In German towns it usually took thirty to forty days of unskilled labour to pay for one's citizenship dues. A similar amount was required in most Dutch towns, but in Amsterdam it was in the order of sixty days.[56] Amsterdam's citizenship dues had been quite modest in the early seventeenth century, but they were raised several times before 1650, when they reached fifty guilders. Much of that money went to welfare institutions that had problems coping with the increased demand for support. There is little evidence of any attempt to stem the tide of immigrants, however; it rather appears that Amsterdam was trying to profit from the demand for local citizenship.[57] In some towns in the southern

Netherlands, and even more so in England, purchasing citizenship could be a very expensive process, requiring half a year or more of unskilled wages.[58] Obviously this might have affected immigrant numbers.

Numbers

Formal citizenship arrangements had features of both inclusion and exclusion: inclusion, because they allowed aliens to join the urban community formally, and enjoy its privileges; exclusion, because various sorts of obstacles were usually put in the way of those wanting citizenship. What one wants to know is what effect all of this had on the numbers of people actually acquiring formal citizen status in European towns. Numerical data alone will never resolve the question of which side of the equation was the more dominant factor, but if the percentage of citizens in urban populations could be established, that knowledge would in itself help us to get a sense of the balance between the two. Fortunately, those, like Gerino di ser Tano, aspiring to become citizens had to be registered. As a result of this registration, historians have at their disposal detailed lists of the names, as well as in many cases places of origin, of the new citizens in a great many European towns, often going back well into the Middle Ages. For the historian of citizenship, however, the registers – which at first sight might appear to be a treasure trove – create two formidable problems. The first one is to establish who were actually registered; the second is to transform the 'flow' figures into 'stocks' that allow us to get a sense of the percentage of the urban population included in formal citizenship arrangements.[59]

Given the fact that various modes of access allowed aspiring citizens to join the community, any registration had to deal with that variety. As far as we can tell, urban authorities recorded meticulously those who joined from outside and who, like Gerino, had to pay for their citizenship status. The problems began with those acquiring citizenship under private arrangements, i.e. inheriting it from their citizen parents, or men marrying a daughter from a citizen family. Data from Amsterdam suggest that the registration of these citizens was an erratic affair.[60] In many other towns, the addition of places of origin equally demonstrates that citizenship registers normally dealt with immigrants, and only rarely with locals acquiring citizen status.[61] This makes it more difficult to gauge what part of the citizen community had local roots.

The second problem has to do with the administrative procedure providing our sources of information. New citizens were registered when their applications had been accepted. As a result, we know who joined the community and when – the inflow. What we do not know is when citizens left again, or passed away – the outflow. Clearly, the authorities were not interested in this, and for census purposes (mostly created with taxation in mind), the citizenship status of the population was not seen as a relevant factor. Only rarely do the sources produce a stock of citizens, such as we have for Nuremberg in 1622 when, out of a total of 10,069 registered households, the households of citizens numbered 8,939, i.e. 89 per cent.[62] In other places, we may have population numbers, or the number of households, at specific moments in time, i.e. stock numbers, but for new citizens we may have only the in-flows. A methodology, developed by Chris Minns, has recently enabled us for the first time to transform those flows into stocks of new citizens, which can be divided by the urban population to obtain percentages of citizens and thus give us some sense of the quantitative dimension of formal citizenship. It is important to keep in mind that, given several assumptions required to transform flows into stocks, this methodology does not produce exact numbers, and the percentages quoted here are therefore indications of the approximate size of the citizen share in populations. However, even these indications can give us some clues as to the quantitative impact of formal citizenship. We can calculate these percentages in two ways: by individuals or by households. As the citizen registers only list the heads of households and provide no clues about how many dependants were included in the registration – spouses and newly born children would become citizens automatically (passive citizenship) – I use household rather than individual rates.

Our data are confined to north-west Europe and cover towns and cities in England, the Low Countries and the Holy Roman Empire. In the majority of the ten English towns, nine in the Low Countries and sixteen in the Holy Roman Empire, the majority of households were headed by someone with citizen status. The rates could be as high as 75 per cent or more in places like Antwerp and Ghent throughout the seventeenth and eighteenth centuries, or in Frankfurt during the seventeenth century and Cologne during the eighteenth, and still more than two-thirds in, for example, Bristol (1700–49) and York (1650–99). Some towns registered low figures: Canterbury in the sixteenth century, Berlin in the eighteenth. Classifying these rates in a more systematic way reveals that out of eighty-five half-century observations, forty-three showed rates of 60 per cent and over, twenty-seven fell between 40 and 59 per cent and fifteen fell below the 40 per cent threshold.[63] In other words, in half the observations a clear majority of households were headed by formal citizens, whereas in only a sixth of our observations did citizens constitute a minority of households. These estimates are corroborated by dispersed figures for various German towns: the vast majority of Wetzlar's 2,500 inhabitants were citizens at the end of the seventeenth century; in Augsburg 87 per cent of households were headed by a citizen in 1730, in Hamburg about 60 per cent in 1759, but perhaps just under half in Cologne in 1704.[64] All of this seems to suggest that formal citizenship was accessible to many urban households, but also that this was not the case for all households, nor true for all towns.

It is not clear what gave rise to the distinctions.[65] There was no 'national' pattern, as in each of the four countries investigated here we find both high and low values. There were no dramatic shifts between centuries. It is true that most of the low rates stem from the eighteenth century, but for those towns where we have observations for both the seventeenth and eighteenth centuries, we see no clear downward trend in the percentages of citizen households. The distribution between high and low rates in the second half of the sixteenth century is close to the average. Neither was it the case that large towns made citizenship more accessible than smaller towns: the rates in Amsterdam – around 50 per cent – were much lower than those obtained in middle-sized Utrecht and 's-Hertogenbosch. Similarly, the small town of Nördlingen, site of a famous battle during the Thirty Years' War and only slowly recovering from the combined shocks of warfare and plague, had a much higher percentage of immigrants in its citizen stock than Berlin, capital of the expanding Brandenburg state and itself a city that was rapidly growing.[66] London was very expensive for those wanting to purchase citizenship, but grew nonetheless at a very fast rate during the early modern period. The percentage of citizens declined in London, but this had more to do with the growth of the suburbs, where no formal citizenship was available, than with a decline in the popularity of the institution as such. In the City of London at least three quarters of heads of households were citizens in the early nineteenth century.[67]

Urban Republicanism

Formal citizenship created a legal and political community. At the same time it created an 'imagined community', i.e. an ideological construct that shaped citizens' actions and discourse. That community was not necessarily restricted to those with formal citizenship, but the discourse would have failed without the core elements of formal citizenship. Although citizenship featured as such in this discourse, it was also implicit in all matters of guild membership, which was central to many of the claims arising from the citizens' community, as we can see in the two petitions that were submitted in 1378 by the collective guilds of Louvain to their town council and to the Duke of Brabant, their sovereign.[68] Although the texts were written in Dutch, rather than the French employed in most official documents, the wording clearly displayed the contribution of an author with legal training. In all probability, the petitioners hoped that their proposals might be converted directly into law.

Apart from some minor points, the petitions raised four general concerns. First and foremost, the guilds demanded more transparency in the administration of their town. More specifically, they insisted that the council provide annual public account of its handling of tax receipts, a claim already voiced in an earlier petition in 1360. To be sure, the objective was not to lower taxes, but simply to know how the money had been spent. Their second point was also financial: they insisted on a public inquiry into the size and funding of the town's public debt. This was important, because citizens could be arrested outside Louvain when creditors of the town so demanded. But transparency was also at stake in relation to this point, because there were suspicions that elite families had been manipulating the debt to their own advantage. To ensure such transparency in future, the guilds of Louvain demanded representation on the city council. They insisted that half the aldermen seats go to the 'good folks of the guilds'. Finally, the guilds demanded more autonomy: 'Also, that the guilds of this town can regulate themselves and meet whenever they want in the interest of the town.' Meetings without previous permission from the town council were very unpopular with the elites, because they would almost inevitably create trouble – or even revolution. A century and a half later, when Emperor Charles V sought to curb guild influence in urban constituencies, he made sure that such meetings could only take place after they had been authorised by the council. In Utrecht, moreover, no two guilds were allowed to meet on the same date.[69]

In the mid-fifteenth century, calls for an overhaul of local government were voiced in towns across Europe. In Bruges, not so far from Louvain and at that time a linchpin of early capitalist networks, the guilds were able to restore their dominant role in government in 1477, after a previous revolution, in 1437–38, had resulted in a reduction of their powers. In 1480 the guild deans stated in the Great Council that their opinions were 'by charge of their people [members], who had gathered for that purpose'.[70] Across the North Sea, in York, the guild 'searchers', as the deans were called there, were again the initiators of a series of petitions, and at times of rebellions, to support a 'coherent and feasible political programme', consisting of four core elements. The citizens, united in their guilds, insisted on political and financial accountability and on the defence of urban privileges, including those of the guilds themselves. But uppermost in their minds was, according to the historians who recently investigated these popular movements, their 'unwavering commitment to the city's autonomy'.[71]

In Florence 'guild republicanism', or 'popular republicanism', emerged in the final decade of the thirteenth century.[72] The Florentine Republic, it was claimed in 1343, 'is ruled and governed by the guilds and guildsmen of the same city'.[73] In 1378 the guilds stated that their explicit purpose was to enhance 'the liberty, security, and tranquility of the twenty-one guilds and of each and every guildsman of the city of Florence'.[74] Later that same year a list of recommendations filed on behalf of the guilds requested that reforms be discussed with the Consuls of the guilds, 'so that, if all or parts of these proposals become law, it will have been done with the agreement and consent of the guild Consuls; and then it can truly be said that it has been done with the consent of the whole city'.[75] The ideology that the guilds managed to impose on Florence's electoral system during several brief interludes in the fourteenth century was specifically opposed to the formation of a political elite with its own programme. The latter would develop into civic, or classical republicanism. Whereas the elites aimed at virtual representation, the guilds wanted genuine popular influence, and while the elites insisted that they represented the 'whole people', i.e. on an individual basis, the guilds' conception of the community was corporatist.[76]

This opposition between collective and individual citizenship was echoed in the Dutch Republic at the end of the eighteenth century in debates about political unification. Whilst in the Dutch corporatist tradition 'the people' had been the sum total of local communities, claims were now made in the name of one 'indivisible' nation, whose representatives were no longer the delegate of a single urban community with its citizen membership, but of all Dutch citizens, as individuals.[77] In a similar fashion, the civic opposition in the town of Ulm, in southern Germany, claimed in 1794 that the town's constitution 'is republican'. What this meant for Ulm's citizens, and for similar protesters in other imperial cities in the same region, was an insistence on the fundamental equality between citizens and the towns' officials, on the maintenance of 'liberty' as a fundamental value, and that members of the town council should refrain from pursuing their self-interest.[78] Citizenship was – and still is – at one and the same time an individual status and the membership of a collective. In the wake of the French Revolution this collective identity was transferred from the local to the national level and, in the process, the individual elements in citizenship were foregrounded.[79] In the preceding centuries these individual elements had been much less in evidence.

The consistency of these demands – found in towns great and small, and from the fourteenth to eighteenth centuries – demonstrates that they emanated from a single worldview, or ideology.[80] In terms of theoretical sophistication this view was not particularly well developed, but nonetheless it proved quite persistent. German historian Heinz Schilling has labelled this worldview 'urban republicanism'.[81] The core of urban republicanism, as Schilling defined it, was the citizens' desire to participate in one way or another in the exercise of political power. This was an argument for collective forms of representation, usually through civic organisations, of which the guilds, parishes or neighbourhoods and civic militias were the most obvious. An underlying assumption was that those organisations had mechanisms, for instance general assemblies, in which individual citizens might raise concerns, but at the same time the individual voice was seen as less important than the collective expression of opinions by these corporate organisations. Because of the centrality of corporate organisations, 'urban republicanism' might also be called 'corporatism' or 'communalism'.[82]

Given the importance of representation, urban republicanism had to insist on the collective nature of urban rule. This was connected to two other elements in this ideology: assumptions about the original state of the civic community, and the balancing of interests. On various occasions, petitioners stated that the right to representation went back to the general assemblies of citizens as they had existed in the period immediately after the foundation of the community. As a pamphlet from Leiden added in 1748: when the community grew in size, such assemblies had become impractical and the administration had been delegated to a smaller group of individuals.[83] That group mirrored the community in that it was composed of people who had formal citizen status, and because it should never be dominated by a single individual or family. Collective rule prevented the interests of a small minority from dominating the urban administrative agenda.[84] For the same reason, corporatist ideologues would insist on the rotation of offices: this would return officeholders to the ranks of ordinary citizens and therefore remind them that misbehaviour in office would be corrected, and possibly punished, by the next person in that same office.[85] Delegation, at the same time, did not mean that ordinary citizens had abandoned their right to be informed, for example about public finances. Ultimately, such claims were founded on the citizens' fundamental rights and personal liberties.

This literally popular republican ideology was not necessarily identical with the 'classical republicanism' that has become so fashionable among historians of early modern political ideas.[86] It was 'classical' because its intellectual roots were in Roman law and therefore had a habit of referencing Roman antiquity. Classical republicanism emerged in the Italian city-states of the Renaissance with Marsiglio of Padua (c.1280–1342) and Bartolus of Sassoferrato (1313–57), both writing in the first half of the fourteenth century, but found its most famous voice in Niccolò Machiavelli (1469–1527) from Florence. These authors all shared an interest in the foundations of urban rule, even if Machiavelli's most famous work deals with the prince.[87] Their theories also gained currency beyond the Italian peninsula, in works that either proposed the Italian cities (mainly Venice) as paradigmatic or were influenced by British writings that had developed a northern variety of Italian (mainly Florentine) ideas.[88]

Urban republicanism, on the other hand, did not produce a systematic political philosophy, nor an authoritative statement of its main features. Perhaps its most theoretical articulation was found in the works of Johannes Althusius (c.1553–1638), who was appointed syndic of the German town of Emden in 1604. That appointment was in itself significant. Emden had just experienced a political revolution that started in 1595, when the town rebelled against its sovereign, and the citizen militias – with the help of troops sent by the Dutch – managed to hold out. After further armed conflict in the following years, in 1603 the citizens of Emden forced their sovereign, the Count of East-Frisia, to, in effect, accept Emden's independence.[89] When Althusius was given the job of town syndic, i.e. the most important civil servant of the community, the following year, he came with what might be considered a long testimonial: his *Politica Methodice Digesta* had been published in 1603. A new edition, twice the size of the original, would follow in 1610.

Althusius' *Politica* makes two important claims. The first is that, out of self-interest, individuals and families have no choice but to collaborate. Talents and resources have been unequally distributed across the population, and precisely this makes collective solutions to human needs inevitable. However, these solutions can be reached in a variety of ways and therefore individuals and families – Althusius portrays individuals mainly as representatives of households – can choose how they prefer to collaborate with others. Therefore, the *collegia*, or corporations, that emerge from this collective impulse are bodies 'organised by assembled persons according to their own pleasure and will'.[90] The second claim is that the creation of these *collegia* is not dependent on any sovereign authority. By implication, the state is not the final source of authority – as in Jean Bodin's more or less contemporary theory of sovereignty – but is instead a composite of lower-order corporations, such as towns and villages.[91] In the town, authority 'is entrusted, with the consent of the citizens, to the senatorial collegium', in other words, the town council.[92] Citizens, in Althusius' system, do not act politically as individuals, but always as members of a collective.[93] The popularity of Althusius' work is difficult to gauge, but it would seem that he was merely systematising a practice that had long before emerged in urban environments and would continue to be practised, even without his theoretical blessings.

An important implication of Althusius' version of urban republicanism was its historical character. If corporations were the result of voluntary collaborations, they had to be justified, not from general principles, but from the historically specific conditions of their emergence.[94] The validity of its general claims to equality among citizens, and to representation of the community in the political process, therefore required the support of historical precedents and documents. In 1702 the citizens of Nijmegen, a medium-sized town in the east of the

Dutch Republic, were up in arms after William III of Orange, stadholder of the Duchy of Guelders, had passed away. Their objections to local magistrates, who had been appointed by William without proper consultation with the citizen community (as laid down in the local constitution), were listed at great length in the *Justificatie van het recht, dat de magistraat neffens de gildens en de gemeensluyden der Stadt Nymegen als een vrye Rijks-stadt van-ouds heft gehad, ende als nog competeert, om hare Magistraat, ende vrye keure van dien by haar selfs te doen (etc.)*, i.e. 'Justification of the right that the town council, as well as the guilds and common council of the town of Nijmegen, as an Imperial City, used to have and still has to freely elect its own magistrate'. Its argument was entirely historical. The seventy-one pages of the text, as well as the fifty-five pages of addenda, consisted of an enumeration of old documents, going back to the thirteenth century, that confirmed this right of the community. These documents, it was claimed, demonstrated that Nijmegen had been an autonomous community, and in effect an imperial city, for many centuries and was entitled as such to govern itself. The proper form of government in Nijmegen was, moreover, one in which elites (the town council) and the citizens (guilds and common council) collaborated. Although the parties might disagree at times about the distribution of power between them, they agreed on the fundamental principles underpinning Nijmegen's form of government.[95]

This emphasis on historical trajectories, and more specifically local historical trajectories, was simultaneously the strength and weakness of urban republicanism. On one hand it created a strong sense of local identity; becoming a citizen implied an inclusion in this powerful history of rights gathered in the documents stored in local archives. Indeed, access to those documents was a recurring demand of urban protest movements.[96] By implication, the emphasis on local history provided a sense of place: each town was unique, due to its particular historical trajectory. The other side of the coin, however, was a lack of common ground. Urban republicanism consisted of a set of general principles that implied local specificities. The upshot of this was that urban republicanism resisted the sort of generalisations necessary for a successful political theory. The point of urban republicanism was precisely that it was not generally applicable, but only validated by the specific, i.e. historically determined, trajectory of a particular town – and nowhere else. The strength of urban republicanism was therefore not its theoretical sophistication, nor its applicability in numerous locations, but its powerful social profile: urban republicanism appealed to elites as well as ordinary citizens.

Because urban republicanism was a practical, rather than a theoretical philosophy, its discourse is found primarily in the sort of papers produced by urban institutions and citizens themselves, such as pamphlets and petitions, or urban constitutions and instructions for public officials.[97] The latter routinely referred to ethical standards perfectly compatible with the republican framework that was shaping the political ideals of broad strata of premodern urban populations in Europe. Far into the sixteenth century 'republic' was synonymous with 'commonwealth', and the preservation of the 'bonum commune', or common good, was a key concept in such urban documents.[98] The Nuremberg constitution of 1461, for example, insisted that local government had been entrusted to the council by the kings and emperors of the Holy Roman Empire 'for the values [*wirden*] and honour and the common good of the city'.[99] From a survey of some twenty-five German and Dutch texts, ranging from the late fourteenth century to the early sixteenth, offering counsel to urban officeholders, it appears that keeping the common good always in mind was a central concern in this type of documents. One such work, Johann von Soest's *Wy men wol eyn statt regyrn soll* (*How to Properly Govern a Town*), from 1495, argued: 'The officer should obey the subject; this is self-evident, and he is [in office] for the common good'.[100] Under their 1713 constitution, the Zürich mayors promised to rule in the interest of rich and poor alike, and the document itself stated that 'with good laws our city will experience happy days'.[101]

Urban rebels justified their protest with arguments of 'liberty' and 'justice', precisely because they knew that the local authorities would find these difficult to refute.[102] A similar type of argument was employed in relation to taxation. In 1748, during a major uprising in the towns of Holland, it was argued in an anonymous pamphlet published in Leiden that local rulers were spending the citizens' money, 'emanating from their properties and possessions, or from their profits and labour'. Because it was their money, the citizens should themselves take charge of how it was to be spent. However, given the size of the population – Leiden had some 40,000 inhabitants at the time – this would have been impractical. The town councillors were therefore selected from the midst of the citizens to act 'as trustees and stewards' of the public funds. For this reason, the citizens were entitled to annual public accounting of public expenditures.[103]

Following an argument developed by Jonathan Barry, one could also say that urban citizenship followed not so much a coherent ideology, but a code of conduct, reflecting a set of values. These values encompassed three basic elements: 'charity and mutual benefit', 'antiquity, honour and precedence' and, finally, 'freedom and independence'.[104]

Conclusion

Urban privileges created formalised urban communities. Membership of these communities was of various kinds, but two categories were ubiquitous: full citizenship and mere resident status. Residents, designated as *Beisasse, Einwohner, inwoner, habitant* and so on, were people who resided in the town but had few formal rights. Nevertheless, these people could hope to get a fair trial, could securely own property, could do their jobs, had access to public welfare, and so on. They were usually barred from higher – but not necessarily lower – public offices, and might not participate in policy consultations or elections. In most towns they would be excluded from joining a guild and hence from opening a shop or operating a workshop at their own expense. They were nonetheless required to pay taxes at the same rates as citizens. Citizens had greater political and economic opportunities and were sometimes treated better than mere inhabitants by the local welfare institutions. The contrast looked stark on paper, but in practice the distinctions were blurred in many areas. Although it is probably fair to say that in general most heads of households in the upper classes held formal citizenship and that the inhabitants more likely belonged to the lower classes, this social distinction was cross-cut by a great many exceptions, ranging from resident international merchants without citizen status to paupers who, simply by having been born locally, had automatically acquired formal citizen status.

Precisely because that formal citizenship was not directly connected to social status, the percentage of households headed by a citizen was usually substantial, and may generally be reckoned as between one half and two-thirds, sometimes even higher. Nonetheless, a significant proportion of urban populations, and in one in six towns even a clear majority, consisted of non-citizens. For many of them, not possessing citizenship status reinforced other mechanisms of social exclusion, such as irregular employment, low wages and a lack of opportunities to participate in public and political life. It is not so clear, however, that those other mechanisms were the result of their exclusion from formal citizenship; it was equally possible that the chain of causality ran in the opposite direction. This also applied to women, next to the working classes the most obvious group in society to be negatively affected by formal citizenship. In most towns women were not excluded from citizenship as such, but in practice their citizenship was circumscribed in a variety of ways, excluding them from politics and also from the guilds. This had already been true in the Middle Ages, but in many towns the number of women independently registered as citizens further declined from the sixteenth century.

Perhaps just as important as its formal implications were the ideological consequences of citizenship. Citizens presented themselves as the core of the community, promoted by an urban republican ideology as the best of all worlds. Urban republicanism was a grassroots ideology with very few intellectual advocates, but it was very popular in urban civic society. It was, moreover, an ideology shared by urban elites and the middle classes who, under the umbrella of citizenship, could agree on a number of crucial features of their local societies: the importance of local autonomy, the fundamental equality between citizens, some form of political representation. All this provided a common foundation for, and coherence to, sociopolitical interactions that made urban communities formidable actors in Europe's medieval and early modern societies, often punching well above their population number's weight.

2 URBAN GOVERNANCE
Citizens and Their Authorities

In 1712 Zürich became involved in the Toggenburg War, a domestic conflict between the Catholic and Protestant members of the Swiss Confederation. Zürich's participation had been decided by the town council without consultation with the guilds, even though this was required by the local constitution. It was just one of the political issues dividing Zürich society. Structurally, the guilds, and their middle-class membership, had much reason to feel aggrieved. No artisan had been elected mayor of Zürich since 1601. In 1713, the 212-member *Grosse Rat* (Common Council) had only thirty-four artisan members, while 60 per cent of Zürich's citizens were artisans. Instead, merchants and officials dominated the council. During the 1713 *Zunftbott*, the general meeting of the guilds, members insisted on the maintenance of the original privileges of the town, dating from 1245, and the constitution that had been introduced after a guild revolution in 1336. On 2 September 1713, 600 citizens were mobilised, demanding a '*hochst nöthiger Reformation*', a very necessary reform. A committee of guild deputies was set up to collect the demands from the guilds' members. Ultimately, 115 points were culled from petitions submitted to the committee. In November the committee negotiated with deputies from the council and on 4 December the council accepted a general reform document. Some demands were met, others were rejected, but that is not the point here. What the 1713 events in Zürich demonstrate is how citizens in premodern Europe could invoke a set of political rights to insist on a say in local politics, and how they could, if necessary, use civic organisations like guilds to mobilise support for these demands.

The Zürich events also show a typical mixture of routine and emergency politics.[1]

This type of civic politics has been systematically sidelined in the traditional narrative of European political history. That narrative has a very simple shape, consisting of two stages, separated by the events of the summer of 1789: the Bad Old Days before the French Revolution, and the modern, democratic era that the revolution initiated.[2] The Bad Old Days were the time of oligarchy and corruption; the French Revolution introduced Europe to popular elections, parliamentary control and so on. Almost inevitably, the British version of this story looks slightly different; its own watershed occurred exactly 100 years earlier, in 1689, with the Glorious Revolution and the introduction of parliamentary rule. However, the Bill of Rights was followed by the Age of Oligarchy, which was only overcome with the Reform legislation of the 1830s. At this point, therefore, one need not be unduly concerned about these differences in chronology.

This picture of the division of European political history, created, of course, by the revolutionaries themselves, was reinforced by historical research from the 1960s. Inspired by the work of Lewis Namier, and immortalised as 'prosopography', or more generally the social history of ruling classes, the main gist of this research was to confirm that these ruling classes were self-perpetuating, through the mechanisms of patronage and co-option. Many books and articles were written outlining and detailing the impact of family and wider social networks on the operation of the political system.[3]

Alongside this research on the ruling classes, another line of work developed in the 1960s, which was concerned with the role of ordinary people in politics before the French Revolution. This developed out of a leftist interest in protest movements, kindled by the mass protests of the era itself. Due to its origins in the 1960s, this type of research was mainly preoccupied with 'revel, riot, and rebellion', as the title of David Underdown's celebrated book from 1985 calls it.[4] The least one can say about the achievements of this type of work, is that by now it has become impossible to discuss predemocratic European politics without reference to the role of non-elites. It is today widely accepted that European politics before the French Revolution was much more volatile and variegated than the steady progress from feudalism to absolutism to democracy would suggest. The rise of the modern state was accompanied by the religious wars of the sixteenth century, the civil wars of the seventeenth century and the revolutions of the eighteenth century, and in all those events ordinary people – or, more neutrally, non-elites – were significant participants.[5] Nonetheless, the place of these non-elites in routine political processes is still poorly defined and poorly understood. This is because much of the literature on state formation concentrates on national institutions, in spite of the fact that the issues which would be of importance for the non-elites were mostly local, or at best regional in nature.[6] As a result, the contrast between before and after 1789 continues to be misrepresented. But if we want to evaluate non-elite participation in politics, we need to refocus from the national to these local and regional arenas.

The argument about the importance of participatory institutions has been reinforced by recent interpretations of the effectiveness of early modern states. The traditional narrative assumes that centralisation meant greater effectiveness. Decentralised states, like the Holy Roman Empire, the Dutch Republic and the Swiss Confederacy, were seen as either backward, compared to centralisers like France and England, or exceptional – or simply ignored. The positive evaluation of centralisation was, however, supported by precious little evidence. Historians have for too long taken for granted that more *intendants* in the French provinces was proof in itself of a greater grip of central government on regional politics. This view of absolutism is no longer accepted.[7] Data on interest rates, for example, demonstrate that, until the end of the seventeenth century at least, the 'republican' type of state could borrow more cheaply than absolutist regimes.[8] In other words, these states seem to have commanded greater trust from their citizens than the centralised states.

All of this suggests that we need to rethink fundamentally our ideas of the process of state formation. This chapter proposes that much can be gained by combining the two research traditions of local elite studies and the investigation of ordinary people to see how non-elites, i.e. citizens, were routinely involved in urban politics. What I do in this chapter more particularly is to look at the ways in which urban constitutions left room for the involvement of citizens in day-to-day politics. In other words, we are going to mostly disregard the extraordinary situations of 'revels, riots, and rebellions', and investigate how urban government was organised in quieter times.[9] The purpose is to find out to what extent and in what ways, in the era before democratic rights were formally established, citizens (in the broad definition used in this book) were already participating in local and, more specifically, urban government.

The Origins of Urban Government

Seen from a global perspective, premodern European towns were equipped with a unique feature: a council that was in charge of local affairs. The establishment of this local council was a standard aspect of urban privileges as they were granted by European sovereigns and amounted to a form of power-sharing to the extent that sovereigns allowed local communities a certain amount of autonomy, but always within the confines of the wider set of rules and authority as it applied within the state as such. In this sense, urban privileges were a specific application of feudal principles, with its fragmented authority. Only in a small number of regions, most notably the Italian Peninsula, would urban autonomy move beyond that.[10] Some Italian towns at least achieved sovereign status for themselves, and thus became city-states. In most of Europe, however, urban autonomy was by definition constrained by the presence of a higher authority, which in a variety of ways would monitor, control and interfere with local governance. How these interactions between towns and sovereigns were shaped is discussed in Part II of this book; at this point it is important to keep in mind that sovereigns were almost always lurking somewhere in the background.

In much of Europe the post-Roman urban revival began in the eleventh century.[11] In Italy it was quite a bit earlier, but also in other regions some towns achieved prominence well before 1000 CE. Barcelona was conquered from the Muslims in the spring of 801 by the Frankish armies, to become part of the Spanish March, ruled by a Count. The local bishop evolved into a second power centre, but only seldom was he able to challenge the Count. For several centuries, Barcelona was dominated by nobles. A bailiff acted as the Count's local representative. Citizens were involved in the governance of the municipal domain, but always under the authority of the Count. Only in the second half of the twelfth century did municipal institutions gradually emerge. The bailiff was instrumental in this development, but it was also carried by changes in the composition of local elites. A new group of merchants and bankers was emerging. We might call them 'patricians', but in the sources they are '*prohoms*'. In 1183 the first consuls appeared as representatives of the community, only to make way in the early thirteenth century for other institutions. By 1231 a document referring to '*probi homines, cives, et habitatores Barchinone*', or *prohoms*, citizens and inhabitants of Barcelona, suggests that the local institutions had consolidated and created three distinct categories: mere inhabitants, citizens with formal membership of the community and the *prohoms* who were in charge. Note that the urban constitution was not created at one particular moment, but was the result of a series of minor steps extending over almost a century.[12]

Such a long gestation of municipal institutions was very common. Take Toulouse, in southern France, for example. Once an important Roman settlement and subsequently a Carolingian centre, Toulouse began another cycle of expansion and development in the eleventh and early twelfth centuries. At the time, the Count was the dominant source of authority, having successfully sidetracked the bishop. The Count supervised trade and industry, the judiciary and public finances including feudal services. He was advised by a court, consisting of Good Men who were simultaneously taking care of local affairs and military defence. By the mid-twelfth century the Good Men were known as the 'Common Council of the City and Bourg', i.e. the two elements that together made up the city. This Common Council was subject to the Count, but steadily managed to increase its autonomy. In 1147 the Count devolved his authority over taxation to the Council, and also accepted that the Toulouse civic militia would no longer accompany him on campaigns.[13]

In 1189 the Count lost much of his influence after a rebellion by the city's elites and middling sort. The latter had been encouraged by the Count to organise themselves into guilds; now these same organisations turned against their sovereign. Initially, the elites dominated local politics, but from 1202 merchants and artisans became much more prominent. It was precisely in the decades after 1189 that urban institutions were consolidated and reinforced. Until 1189 the local courts had been mainly concerned with enforcing the Count's ban and maintaining civil order; they offered very little to sort out disputes over property, contracts and so on. Ecclesiastical courts were no help either, so the business community had to rely on informal types of adjudication, by 'friends', 'neighbours' or indeed the Good Men who were now known as consuls. After 1189, and especially after the triumph of the popular party in 1202, much of this informal adjudication was codified and made more transparent. The consuls became an appeals court for those who felt that informal mediation had produced false results.

Representation of the civic community was similarly institutionalised in Toulouse after 1202. In theory the Common Council had been representing all citizens, but in practice it had been the preserve of a relatively small group of families who combined the exploitation of urban and rural real estate with regional and long-distance trade. After 1202 the commercial and industrial sectors of Toulouse society came to power, and they broadened and reinforced the representative character of local government by creating a second council, the General Council. Moreover, for important decisions they called a meeting of all citizens, a *universitas* or public parliament. As this was the time of the Albigensian Crusade, in which Toulouse was heavily implicated, such meetings had to be convened quite often.[14]

The central Middle Ages thus bequeathed a set of urban institutions to subsequent centuries. Even though the number of composite elements was limited, they were cobbled together in endless variety, and both citizens and elites would often attach much value to the specificities of the local assemblage of institutions.

Urban Government – How It Worked

Apart from the way that local government in Europe was established by charters (considered local constitutions), its other special feature was its collective nature. Some of the Italian city-states were transformed into principalities with a single ruler – most notoriously in Florence under the Medici – but this was an exceptional development. By far the most common situation was that in which a council with one or several dozen members acted as the highest local authority. Such councils would normally emerge during the Middle Ages as the consolidated form of a more informal type of meeting, where the local executive sought advice and legitimacy from a group of representatives of the local community. By implication, such town governments had to be accountable, not only to the sovereign, but at the same time also to their own citizens.

So who was the executive, who were these representatives and how did their institutions evolve? The constitutional arrangements in a handful of towns across Europe can help us get a sense of how urban government worked. These arrangements evolved over time, but in many places they were remarkably resilient during the centuries covered in this book.

One example of such continuity can be found in northern England. York became a 'county corporate' in 1396 and until 1835 its governance structure remained more or less the same. As a county, York was represented in Parliament and was not subject to any regional authorities, simply because it had that same status. In 1603 another fifteen provincial towns in England also had county status. York was ruled by its Lord Mayor, twelve aldermen, two sheriffs and a council of twenty-four. The twenty-four were also known as the Privy Council, to distinguish them from the Common Council. The Lord Mayor and the aldermen were together the Justices of the Peace, i.e. the judicial authority in the town. This combination of executive and judicial authority was an almost universal phenomenon in Europe's late medieval and early modern towns. The Lord Mayor was elected for one year and usually came from the ranks of the recently appointed aldermen. The great majority of former aldermen became members of the Privy Council after their term in office had expired. York's Common Council represented the town's crafts and by implication its civic community.[15]

For several centuries, Utrecht too had a local government dominated by the guilds. In 1304, while so-called guild revolutions were sweeping through the southern territories of the Netherlands, Utrecht also had its taste of revolution when the local guilds removed the patrician-dominated council and installed one whose members were selected by the guild deans. However, in 1528 Charles V, after becoming the new overlord of Utrecht and its territories, overturned the constitution, expressly forbade guild politics and created a council with the right to co-opt new members without any consultation of the guilds or citizens. This council, copied after the Holland model, would remain in power until the arrival of French revolutionaries in January 1795.[16]

In Münster, the guilds had managed to fight their way into the local structures of governance. Münster's constitution was codified in the early thirteenth century, but it continued to evolve. In collaboration with the bishop, who was also the territorial lord of Westphalia, the town managed to increase its political autonomy. Its core institution was the council, or *Rat*, whose membership was shared between twelve patricians and twelve citizens who were elected indirectly by the citizens. The patrician families were known as *Erbmänner*, a socially ambiguous group that combined noble and bourgeois characteristics. The electors also belonged to the local elite. The city lost its urban privileges after the Anabaptist takeover, in 1535, but the bishop was forced to restore them in 1541. At the time the guilds were still officially banned, because of their support of the Anabaptists, but after several petitions they too regained their former position. The seventeen guilds coordinated their policies in the *Gesamtgilde*, or Common Guild, which acted as a shadow council.[17]

In sixteenth-century Toulouse the town council (*capitoulat*) was self-selective, but it was assisted or controlled, depending on one's point of view, by no fewer than three other councils, the *Conseil Général*, the *Conseil de Bourgeoisie* and the *Conseil des Seize*. The first of these comprised about eighty men from the upper echelons of society, including former *capitouls*, but also merchants and solicitors. It met about four times a year. The *Conseil de Bourgeoisie* met more frequently and comprised a somewhat different subset of notables. The *Seize* were the previous year's *capitouls* together with the sitting *capitouls*.[18] All three councils were in the hands of the elite, but together they still provided some checks and balances.

In eighteenth-century Angers, the local government, or *corps de ville*, consisted of twelve councillors, appointed for life; four aldermen appointed for two years; a mayor and an assistant mayor, both appointed for four years with the possibility of a new appointment. They were supported by three officers: a treasurer, a *procureur* or legal advisor and a secretary, who were all appointed indefinitely. In 1732 and 1737 the merchants of Angers petitioned the French king to demand four permanent representatives on the council. The members of the *corps de ville* were, however, elected by representatives of the general assemblies of the inhabitants, organised in the sixteen parishes of the city. Each parish had the right to send two from its midst to the electoral meeting.[19]

Medieval Siena had a more complex structure because it was at one and the same time a city and a state. The combination required special efforts to coordinate the various elements of the governance structure and this coordination was entrusted to a single individual, the *podestà*, who was an outside administrator and military leader. Siena – and other Italian city-states that employed a similar official – went to great lengths to ensure that the *podestà* would not become an independent force capable of taking power into his own hands and becoming an individual ruler. Despite such safeguards, this is precisely what happened in Urbino, where the Montefeltro dynasty evolved from servants of the community into its rulers.

Siena, however, managed to avoid this sort of development. In foreign affairs the *podestà* had a double role as the commander-in-chief of the Sienese army, and the representative of the Sienese state vis-à-vis other states. As military commander his position was reinforced by the fact that upon his appointment the *podestà* would bring along a trained band of professional soldiers, who would act as the core of an army that was otherwise made up of citizen-soldiers. Domestically, he acted as chairman of the legislative Council of the Bell, and was expected to initiate new legislation. However, his role in domestic politics was constrained in various ways. First of all, his appointment was restricted to six months, later one year. After his term in office he could not be reappointed for a further year, to prevent him from creating a local following. He was, moreover, expressly ordered to remain aloof from local factional politics. The Sienese *podestà* would be recruited from Umbria and the Marche, or from Bologna, almost never from neighbouring Tuscany, which was also the most important military threat to Siena.[20]

However, the preservation of Siena's republican regime depended less on the *podestà*'s personal profile and job description than on the dense web of collective local institutions that took care of the community's affairs. Take the selection of the *podestà*. Besides the town council, this involved consultations with the merchant guild, the consuls of the nobility and twenty specially appointed representatives from each of the three districts of the city.[21] From the late thirteenth to the middle of the fourteenth century the executive consisted of nine men, known as the *Nove*, or Nine. These members were active for a mere two months, and during that period had to leave their businesses and families to live with colleagues.[22] The *Nove* initiated new legislation, but required two-thirds of the Council of the Bell to support it, before it could be written into the statute book.[23] The membership of the core institutions was always a multiple of three, reflecting the crucial importance of the three districts of Siena.[24]

The *Nove*, who had been in charge since 1271, were overthrown in 1355, after Charles IV had conquered the city. A coalition of nobles and artisans took over, but the nobles lost power within a few months. For thirteen years, the government of Siena was in the hands of the *Dodici*, the Twelve. Whereas the *Nove* had been overwhelmingly merchants, the *Dodici* were mainly entrepreneurs and artisans. In 1368 they were succeeded by what we might call a coalition government, consisting of representatives of the working classes, the artisans and the merchants. Throughout these regime changes, however, military and financial policies remained remarkably stable.[25]

Local government in all of these towns thus shared a number of common features. They were always composed of multiple institutions, providing checks and balances. Most of those institutions had a substantial membership, allowing a variety of opinions. Some offices might be for life, but many local government officials had to step down after a short period of time – one, maybe two years – preventing a monopoly of power in the hands of a single individual. For most of the time the towns we have discussed had a council that in one way or another represented either the corporate civic subcommunities, usually guilds, or the geographic subcommunities in the form of wards, neighbourhoods and so on. On paper, there was room for the participation of common citizens in civic governance, but was this also true in practice?

The Class Dimension of Urban Government

Almost everywhere, town councils recruited their members among a relatively small, usually elevated group of families.[26] Family relationships among councillors were numerous, with brothers-in-law, fathers-in-law, cousins and so on all seated simultaneously. One would, perhaps, not expect to find a cross-section of urban populations filling the seats of urban governments. For one thing, council membership usually did not carry a salary beyond a small reward for participating in the meetings, even though it could be time-consuming. As one finds repeatedly in towns across Europe, in Siena the members of the Nine were required to suspend their business commitments during their time in office.[27] Secondly, contemporaries were of the opinion that it was better to have wealthy politicians, because these would be less likely to succumb to the temptations of corruption. Whether this was true is not the point here, because social historians have concentrated on another dimension of class rule: the rise of oligarchy.

The argument in a nutshell is that most urban governments of the premodern era were subject to Robert Michels' Iron Law of Oligarchy, first formulated in 1911, which asserts that all organisations will sooner or later find themselves dominated by a small in-crowd of people who have an advantage over the average membership in terms of information and network.[28] Complaints about oligarchy, or 'family government' as contemporaries preferred to call it, were rampant in late medieval and early modern Europe, and an accurate description of the situation in many towns.

It nonetheless bears looking into, as the social background of politicians and administrators might give us a better understanding of the type of interests represented in these institutions. However, we have to keep in mind that our picture may be somewhat unbalanced because most of the collective biographies (or prosopographies) of local politicians have concentrated heavily on the core institutions at the expense of, for example, the advisory Common Councils, simply because their membership was too numerous to cover. In this section I want to establish whether oligarchy was indeed a defining feature of town councils, and if it got worse as time progressed.

For the Holland town of Leiden we have an unusually extensive series of studies tackling the social composition of the local council, beginning in the late thirteenth century and going all the way up to the end of the eighteenth.[29] Never during this period were members of the council genuine professionals, for the simple reason that such membership was only remunerated with a small attendance fee, while the paid positions, of sheriff, mayor or alderman, for example, were mainly temporary appointments for three years at most. Data concerning the earliest generations of Leiden councillors suggest that some of them originated as *ministeriales*, or servants of the Count of Holland, who maintained a court in Leiden. Noble families mixed with this group and the result was a set of families dominating local politics, often designated as a 'patriciate'. These people owned rural estates, but were at the same time active in trade and industry, especially local textiles.[30]

Their influence diminished somewhat after 1400, even though during the fifteenth century one still finds that a third of the families represented in the council had noble backgrounds. The merchants and industrialists were, however, in the ascendant.[31] By the second half of the sixteenth century, the latter had clearly won out. Nobles did not disappear altogether from the Leiden council, but they became a rarity. Instead, council members were active entrepreneurs in textiles and food production.[32]

During the seventeenth century a new type of councillor emerged who had no such ties with trade and industry; the councillor had gone to university and trained as a lawyer.[33] During the eighteenth century this trend was consolidated. University degrees had become the norm, and most councillors had no day job in addition to their administrative duties.[34]

The Leiden data suggest that the social history of urban government in premodern continental Europe can be subdivided into three eras. The first, from the eleventh century to the fourteenth, was the era of the (semi-)nobles, families whose economic power derived from urban and rural real estate. The second, which ran from the fifteenth century to the seventeenth, was the era of the merchants, in many places challenged by the artisans and their guilds. The third era, during the seventeenth and eighteenth centuries, was dominated by lawyers, people whose qualifications were academic and whose training prepared them specially for the legal dimension of government.

These three eras are not found everywhere in quite the same way. During the seventeenth and eighteenth centuries, the town council of Gloucester, England, included between 25 and 40 per cent merchants, while over time, the percentage of 'professionals' increased from 10 per cent to 25 per cent.[35] In early eighteenth-century Gdansk, more than 80 per cent of councillors were 'learned men', whereas in previous ages the merchants had predominated.[36] In French towns the displacement of the merchants by *gens du loi* had already begun in the sixteenth century.[37] In Barcelona the merchants were never a significant factor on the council.[38] Some towns did not experience any major shifts in the social composition of their councils. In Cologne, merchants were still five times more numerous than lawyers during the second half of the eighteenth century.[39] However, at a general level the Leiden pattern seems applicable to many places in Europe.[40]

This sequence of social classes might suggest a fixed separation, but this was not in fact the case. Take for example the ambiguity embodied in the Münster *Erbmänner*. In 1597 they launched a legal campaign before the High Court of the Holy Roman Empire, the *Reichskammergericht*, to obtain formal recognition as an imperial estate. The *Erbmänner* had dominated local politics in Münster for much of the Middle Ages, and over time had consolidated as a coherent social group that combined an aristocratic lifestyle with a civic legal status. They described themselves as '*adligen Patricier Bürger und Abkömmlinge der alten Geslechter*', or noble patrician citizens and descendants of the ancient lineages. In another document they presented themselves as the '*Adlige der Stadt Münster*', the nobles of the City of Münster. They had coats of arms, owned manors and refrained from 'modest occupations', i.e. trade and industry, although some of them had been active as merchants well into the sixteenth century. The court case went on for no less than eighty-eight years, and produced twelve fat volumes of legal papers before the *Erbmänner* won their case in 1685. However, their recognition as a 'genuinely ancient, noble and knightly estate' was short-lived. Already in 1709 the emperor decided to take it away from them and they were once again reduced to members of the commoners' estate.[41] As the *Erbmänner* demonstrate, membership of the council set one apart from the rest of urban society, without producing a complete separation from the other citizens.

Next to the council in charge of the daily management of urban affairs, many towns had broader councils that allowed greater participation. In fifteenth-century Berne, for example, the Inner Council (*Kleine Rat*) had twenty-seven members in 1470, but on Easter Day another 293 were elected as members of the Common Council (*Grossen Rat*). The latter came from at least 225 families, perhaps more. Members of the Common Council should be able to afford a full armament, those on the Inner Council also a horse for military purposes. Eight members of the Inner Council and seven on the Common Council were nobles, while many others tried to imitate these leading families by acquiring rural estates and patents of nobility.[42] In Marseille 771 individuals sat on the town council between 1559 and 1597, drawn from 466 different families, which at least suggests that it did not constitute a segregated class. Of these, some 20 per cent belonged to the untitled nobility (*gentilshommes* and *équyers*), a third worked in commerce and 20 per cent in industry, while only 5 per cent were professionals.[43] These figures suggest that oligarchy was not the norm everywhere.

Two conclusions seem inevitable. The first is that membership of urban councils and related offices in local government was not something the ordinary citizen could aspire to. Such jobs were time-consuming and often unreliable in terms of the income they generated. More importantly, elite families tried to make this their own preserve and installed mechanisms to ensure limited access. More often than not they succeeded. The second is that, despite the sometimes poor financial reward, elite families found the prestige and power of these urban positions, and surely also the opportunities for corruption, immensely appealing. Oligarchy was the rule. Whether or not it increased over time is less obvious, if only because it had been a feature of these institutions for as long as we can observe them. The 'democratic' origins that the citizen opposition often invoked existed on paper in the urban constitutions and in the mythology of local history, but seldom in the reality documented in the records.

Popular Politics: Elections and Common Councils

Even though throughout the Middle Ages and early modern period their membership was drawn from a restricted set of families, all municipal governments claimed to be representative in one way or another. They had two core arguments to bolster that claim. First, and perhaps most importantly, they were themselves citizens, and therefore 'mirrored' the citizen community, as Lieven de Beaufort, a Dutch municipal administrator in the eighteenth century, argued. In principle – if not in practice – every virtuous citizen could be selected to participate in local politics. Moreover, the short terms of appointment for many local offices meant that local politicians would be regularly reduced to the status of ordinary citizens. As another Dutch author claimed, this served as a reminder that they were ultimately the same as everybody else.[44] Secondly, they had sworn an oath on the occasion of their accession to office to serve the community as a whole.

Despite these arguments, the representative character of municipal government was regularly contested by the rest of the citizenry, and as a result of such protests, three additional forms of representation emerged. One was the creation of a second-level council that represented the urban community and that had to consent in important decisions, even though it was not in charge of daily operations. A second was the inclusion of citizen representatives, usually guild deans, in the core institutions of municipal government. The third consisted of elections – either direct or indirect – for municipal office. These forms of citizen participation in the political and administrative processes of medieval and early modern towns were much more common than is usually acknowledged by textbook political histories of this so-called predemocratic era. Because guilds and politics are discussed in the next section, I concentrate here on the Common Councils and on municipal elections.

London is an interesting case to start with, because not only did it become the largest city in premodern Europe, it also combined elements of all three forms of citizen participation. London freemen participated in local politics to a degree that immediately belies the idea that political life was the exclusive domain of oligarchic elites.[45] The government of the City of London consisted of the Lord Mayor, elected annually, and the Court of Aldermen, twenty-six men chosen for life as representatives of the wards of the city. In the case of a vacancy, the aldermen chose their new colleague from among candidates elected by the resident heads of households in the ward. The city's executive was assisted by a legislature of no fewer than 234 representatives of the wards, called the Common Council and elected annually. The Lord Mayor was elected from the ranks of the aldermen, by the aldermen, but nomination was limited to two names selected in Common Hall, the electoral assembly of the liverymen of the City.[46]

The liverymen constituted the upper tier of the guilds; next to the wards the guilds were, politically speaking, the most important civic institutions in London.[47] Around 1700 the City numbered an estimated 8,000 liverymen, who were 'the most zealous guardians of the historic liberties of the London citizenry', according to Gary de Krey.[48] Besides nominating the Lord Mayor, the liverymen elected (in the Common Hall) the sheriffs and other high officials of the Corporation, as well as the City's representatives in Parliament. The lower ranks of the guilds, who were all ordinary freemen of the City of London, together with the liverymen were entitled to elect the members of the Common Council during the so-called wardmotes, district meetings that took place annually on St Thomas's Day. Even the non-citizens, or mere inhabitants, of London, were included in the political process, as they had the right to participate in the selection of petty officers of their precincts and wards; they were excluded, however, from participation in the politics of the City as a whole.[49]

Paris, as a royal town, did not have any such mechanisms of participation, but Nantes, France's sixth largest city, did. In seventeenth-century Nantes the populace was involved in the political process in two ways: through annual elections and through consultations.[50] The elections concerned first and foremost the mayor and aldermen. On 30 April the electoral meeting took place in the Grande Salle of the Nantes town hall. Members of the *grand corps* were invited to these meetings, including royal officers, the former mayors and aldermen of the town, who together constituted the *Grand Bureau*, as well as the representatives of urban institutions and private citizens. Looking at their numbers, the urban community was definitely not a minority participant in these proceedings. On the contrary, in a list from 1685 there are 450 names, but '*plusieurs autres bourgeois et habitants*' (many other citizens and inhabitants) had also been present.[51] These numbers, as well as other indicators, testify to the important role of the non-office-holding part of the civic community.

In Nantes local policies were drawn up by the *corps de ville* in consultation with the local population. During the Wars of Religion the records of the municipality are full of references to *assemblées générales*, in which the officers of the civic militias were prominent participants, but where individual inhabitants of the city also attended.[52] Apart from such general *assemblées* there were also consultative meetings between the *corps de ville* and representatives of various corporative interests, especially the civic militias and the craft guilds. The main topic – discussed at almost half of the meetings – was the preservation and maintenance of local privileges. In French towns, such *assemblées* remained a common feature of civic life, even in the eighteenth century.[53]

In the medieval towns of northern Spain, although urban government had increasingly become the exclusive domain of local elites and elections were suppressed in the process, general assemblies were still held from time to time.[54] Elections were also found in Central Europe at that time. Hungarian royal towns, for example, acquired the right to elect their own town councils during the first half of the fourteenth century. Municipal councillors were often elected in general meetings open to all citizens. These were still active in the late seventeenth century.[55] In 1514 the citizens of Prague's Old and New Towns obtained the right to elect their municipal administrators through a complex system that was clearly designed to create at one and the same time a balanced outcome and to prevent corruption. Every year, three bodies would meet in common session on election day: the departing council, a council of elders and representatives of the commune. The councillors selected eight persons from the elders, the elders selected twelve persons from the commune and the commune selected four persons from the council. These twenty-four would draw lots; eight lots would have the word 'elector' written on them. These eight were then locked into a room, and had to elect the eighteen members of the next council. Their names would then be read out loud to the community by the royal chancellor.[56]

London citizens not only elected local officeholders, but also had their Common Hall, a sort of local parliament. In other towns similar institutions were known as Broad Council, or Common Council, or under some other name, but with the same political function. In Siena the Common Council consisted of the thrice 100 citizens representing the three districts of the city, plus the consuls of the merchants' and the cloth-finishers' guilds. The members, who were elected for one year, had to be residents and taxpayers of Siena during the previous ten years. The Council could meet several times per week.[57] These numbers suggest substantial civic involvement in local politics.

In York, the Common Council slowly emerged from incidental consultations of craft representatives in the late fourteenth century. These consultations were only transformed into a permanent institution in 1516–17, during a period of crisis when support from the community was especially important. Initially, the thirteen most important guilds were allowed to send two representatives to the meetings, fifteen smaller guilds only one. The original forty-one members gradually expanded to forty-eight, but this number too was more a guideline than a precise indication of the membership, which in practice could fluctuate. From 1632, York's Common Council was elected by the four wards, changing the mode of representation from an occupational to a geographical model, but retaining the underlying principle of representation of the citizen community.[58]

In the Habsburg Low Countries, Antwerp had the *Brede Raad* (Broad Council) with representatives of the twenty-four to twenty-six 'privileged' guilds. On another council, the thirteen districts each had two representatives. In Brussels, the *Wijde Raad* (literally Wide Council) consisted of former aldermen and the deans of the powerful Cloth Guild, but in the Nine Nations council, all other guild deans were represented. These councils had to be consulted on financial and other important issues.[59] In the eastern provinces of the Dutch Republic, Common Councils had similar prerogatives and also acted as electoral colleges.[60]

This discussion of individual towns demonstrates that throughout the period covered in this book various towns and cities had mechanisms that allowed citizens to participate on a regular basis in the political process. It would, however, be helpful to establish a quantitative benchmark to see how widely distributed such representation was. To gauge the relative importance of Common Councils, guild participation and elections we can employ a data set collected by Fabian Wahl, which also allows a measurement of the timing and the quantitative and geographical distribution of local representative institutions.[61] His data set covers 104 towns and cities in Austria (seven), Belgium (ten), Germany (sixty-seven), France (three), the Netherlands (thirteen) and Switzerland (four). With Germany covering two-thirds of the data, France represented by a mere three towns on the French–German border and Southern Europe and the UK completely missing, this data set cannot claim to be even remotely representative, but it is the best we have at the moment. Two observations follow from the data, one about the relative importance of each form of representation, and one about developments over time. Elections were relatively unusual, found at any time in thirty-one towns in the data set. Guild representation was more common and present in forty-nine, or almost half the towns. It was heavily concentrated in the southern half of Germany, including towns that switched between France and Germany, and in the southern Low Countries. In northern Germany and the northern Low Countries, guild representation was unusual, perhaps due to the prevalence of merchants in this region, once dominated by the Hanseatic League. Common Councils were found in forty-eight towns, all over the area covered by the Wahl data set, without an obvious geographical pattern.

I have supplemented and systematised Wahl's data by collecting similar data about the five largest cities in England, the Netherlands, Belgium, France, Germany, Switzerland and Italy, in 1500 and 1700 (Appendix 1). Three of these countries (England, France and Italy) and half of the total of thirty-five towns in my set were not represented in Wahl's data.

Our own results confirm the Wahl data set in showing that representative institutions were more numerous in 1500 than they would be in 1700. In fact, Wahl's data suggest that 1500 was the zenith of urban representative institutions, which took off in the thirteenth century, reached a peak in 1500 and then started to slowly decline (guild participation, elections in the sixteenth century) or stabilised (Common Councils, elections after 1600). From our own data, it becomes clear that in 1500 almost two-thirds (twenty-two out of thirty-five) of Europe's largest towns had formal institutions for citizen representation. In 1700 this was the case in half (seventeen out of thirty-five) of them. Despite a decline, civic participation in local governance still was a relevant factor in many towns around Europe at the beginning of the eighteenth century.

Critics have suggested that these premodern elections were superficial and ultimately futile because they tended to produce results that were socially very similar to the alternative procedures where councils selected their own successors.[62] In both cases, it is alleged, the membership of the councils consisted overwhelmingly of individuals from the wealthier parts of urban society. Such criticism implies a peculiar understanding of modern democracy. Clearly, the profile of modern-day politicians is not identical with their electorate in terms of income, education, gender or social background. If that were so, we would have had more female prime ministers and fewer academics in parliaments around the world. The point about democracy is the mandate that politicians receive from the electorate, not whether they resemble the average voter in all respects.[63]

Organisations of Popular Politics: Guilds and Neighbourhoods

Elections and representation were but two of the mechanisms allowing citizens a say in local politics. Behind these formal procedures, much more was going on. Popular politics could flourish in premodern towns because citizens were organised.[64] There is more to say on the political activities of civic militias in Chapter 5; here I concentrate on the role of guilds and neighbourhoods in local politics.

Gdansk experienced its first guild rebellion in 1378. In 1416 the guilds dismissed the city council during another rebellion, but failed to consolidate their gains. On the contrary, a new constitution gave the council extensive powers to meddle in the guilds' business. In the middle of the sixteenth century the guilds, in collaboration with local merchants, rebelled once more. In 1651–52 more protests erupted from the guilds and in 1659, when the Polish king visited Gdansk, the guilds filed a twenty-nine-point petition. Similar events occurred in 1677–78. The guilds of Gdansk failed to overthrow the local government, but maintained a vocal political presence in the town. Their demands were self-serving, but also related to general issues concerning the governance of Gdansk.[65]

In Gdansk, the local council was and remained immune to claims for guild participation. In other towns, guild participation was written into the local constitution. Particularly during the fourteenth century, such towns increased rapidly in number. The inclusion of guilds in local government happened especially in Germany and in the southern territories of the Low Countries. There are examples from other areas, but those were more isolated (London) or temporary. Already in the late thirteenth century the Florentine guilds had made their mark by creating a new office that was to become one of the most important in the city: the triumvirate called *priores artium*, or priors. One chronicler noted shortly afterwards:

> The ordinary citizens were exceedingly encouraged by the election of these three, ... ; and the frank words of those citizens who spoke of their liberty and of injuries suffered in the past so enflamed and emboldened the priors that they promulgated new ordinances and decrees, which would prove very difficult to abrogate. ... And they were called the priors of the guilds.

The priors oversaw the communal finances and ensured equal justice for all and the protection of the '*piccoli e impotenti*' against the '*grandi e potenti*'.[66] However, in the course of the fourteenth century, after swings in favour of, as well as against, their participation in politics, the Florentine guilds ultimately lost much of their influence after 1382.[67]

In Flanders, thanks to their sheer numbers but also as the major armed force in the towns, guilds rapidly gained political prominence. The importance of these two dimensions was forcefully brought home when, following a string of revolts in the previous months, the guild infantry managed to defeat a French army on horseback in the Battle of the Spurs on 11 July 1302. This resulted in a wave of guild revolutions, overturning elite-dominated councils, replacing them with guild deans and consolidating their influence by changing local constitutions. As a result, next to their primary economic functions, craft guilds became political organisations in at least seven major, as well as several middle-sized, towns in the Low Countries.[68] This was also true in many regions of the Holy Roman Empire.[69]

It has been argued that guild politics was simply elite politics in disguise. Those representing the guilds in town councils were recruited from the same elevated social backgrounds as the other councillors. This is a doubtful argument for two reasons. Even though there is plenty of evidence of elite members joining guilds to gain access to municipal office, this did not prevent ordinary guildsmen from accessing high office in many places. More importantly, to represent one's guild one usually had to be elected: candidates, in other words, had to curry favour with ordinary guildsmen in order to obtain their votes. Even if guildsmen often preferred well-to-do and well-connected representatives, they could still hold them to account.[70]

Neighbourhoods were another urban institution with representative potential. During the early modern period, the city of Ghent, with some 40,000 inhabitants, had around 200 neighbourhoods. When on 11 November 1638 Bartholomeus Dekistmaker was elected by the common inhabitants of the Burgstraat neighbourhood to be their new dean, in a meeting held in the neighbourhood chapel, he was the thirty-first to serve in that office for this particular neighbourhood since 1540. Dekistmaker was a lawyer, and by accepting his nomination he took on a series of important – and probably time-consuming – tasks. For example, neighbourhoods in Ghent were responsible for the registration of new arrivals, for the billeting of soldiers and for collecting funds to maintain the roads and pavements. They also had to organise the general oversight of their own area of the town. If anything, the job of neighbourhood dean, which seems to have been without financial compensation, became more demanding as time progressed. The reason for this was that the Ghent council, whilst trying to get a greater grip on neighbourhood issues, was simultaneously loading the neighbourhoods with an increasing number of duties. As a result, the neighbourhood dean increasingly became the intermediary between the town hall and its constituents, instead of simply the neighbourhood's representative; more and more time must have been spent on coordinating neighbourhood expectations with council regulation.[71] We see similar processes happening everywhere in seventeenth-century North-Western Europe, with neighbourhoods becoming more important and yet more regulated at the same time.[72] Nonetheless, they remained an important channel for inhabitants to raise their voices and their involvement in public affairs.

Neighbourhoods were equally important in Mediterranean Europe. In 1343 Florence was administratively reorganised and subdivided into four quarters, which were each subdivided into four districts or *gonfaloni*. The basis for the division was the organisation of the local citizen militia (*compagnie del popolo*). One of these *gonfaloni* was the Lion Rosso, or Red Lion. This particular district comprised some 530 households in 1427, and was centred on the Via Vigna Nuova. Like the other *gonfaloni*, the Lion Rosso was charged with assessing and taxing its households, as I discuss later in this chapter. At the same time it oversaw public order and the general business of the area, and to this end irregular meetings were held once or twice a year in the local parish church devoted to San Pancrazio, often on Sundays. The most important purpose of these meetings was to entrust the *gonfalone*'s administration to a group of syndics for the next six or twelve months. These syndics also had to make sure that the district's financial records were in order, to avoid problems with the town hall. From the minutes of the district meetings we know that they were usually attended by between twenty-five and thirty inhabitants, most of them representing the well-off section of the district. They would include members of the Rucellai clan, the most powerful of the Lion Rosso. For them and other patrician families, a solid power base in the *gonfalone* was an important stepping stone for their ambitions in Florentine state politics. Despite the dominance of the upper echelons of society, however, artisans were always present at the Lion Rosso meetings, and although no formal guidelines have been found, the pattern suggests a deliberate policy to include all social classes apart from the paupers, i.e. those sections of society that would be included in direct taxation.[73]

Neighbourhoods have been treated in the literature so far as mechanisms of social integration. They were, however, just as important as vehicles for popular politics as the guilds and civic militias, whose political roles historians have recognised more readily.[74] All three types of organisations shared two features. Firstly, they were often democratic to the extent that their membership came from broad sections of the middle class, and those members usually had a say in the selection of officers and the decisions those officers took. Secondly, the organisations were not only recognised by local authorities, but also employed by those same authorities, to collect information, discharge certain public functions and maintain public order. The organisations of popular politics, in other words, were an integral part of urban governance.

Instruments of Popular Politics: Consultations, Petitioning, Lobbying, Rebellion

In many premodern European towns, citizens had constitutional ways of voicing their opinions about policies and politicians. In other towns, where such means might be absent or very restricted, local authorities used a range of different instruments to exchange views about their policies with various sections of the local communities, not necessarily all of them formally organised. In this section four such instruments are discussed: consultations, usually initiated by the authorities themselves, petitions, lobbying and riots, which were almost always initiated by citizens themselves. Apart from the riot, they were considered part of normal political life in premodern towns.

In fifteenth-century Italy, especially the smaller towns held regular assemblies where all heads of households could voice their opinion. In the larger towns, assemblies were much less a routine aspect of local politics, but summoned on special occasions. In Turin, for example, such a meeting was held when the Duke of Savoy had ordered an overhaul of the local government in 1433. It is possible that this was necessitated by exceptional circumstances, but in 1447 the death of the Visconti duke brought about a revival of the Council of Nine Hundred, composed of 150 representatives of each of the city's six districts.[75]

In Angers, besides the annual elections on 1 May, regular *assemblées générales* were held where the parish representatives consulted. Between 1657 and 1789, 338 such general assemblies took place, about three each year on average. Behind the general meetings, moreover, lurked countless meetings of the inhabitants of individual parishes in Angers, where both parish and general city issues were discussed. These meetings were sometimes even attended by servants (*domestiques*), but usually dominated by merchants and artisans. The general assemblies discussed royal taxation, the preservation of local privileges, as well as day-to-day issues such as poor relief, health care, public works and so on. One of Angers' aldermen claimed there was no inhabitant whose opinion was not assessed. One need not necessarily accept that this was literally true, but neither should we overlook the important role of ordinary citizens in the political life of the town.[76]

To judge from the documents preserved in the Amsterdam archives, the most common line of communication between citizens and local authorities in that town was through petitions, many of them filed by the guilds. Hundreds of these guild petitions survive, and many more have been lost, because petitions that were turned down were immediately destroyed.[77] Many of these petitions request a change in the guilds' regulations, usually because new circumstances demand adaptation. In their petitions, significantly, the guilds tried to build a case based on the civic community that included both the authorities and themselves. In 1751, the Amsterdam carriage makers, for example, were of the opinion that 'they were paying their scot and lot, and therefore were helping to carry the burdens of the town and their guilds'. Other guilds objected that taxation in Amsterdam was substantially higher than in the countryside, or reminded the authorities of their members' contributions to the civic militias,[78] which, according to the wallpaper painters in 1786, entitled them to the 'advantages, that are due to them as inhabitants of this town, and members of their guilds, . . . with the exclusion of others, particularly aliens'.[79]

It seems that, indeed, the Amsterdam government generally looked favourably upon these guild petitions. A survey of Amsterdam local legislation – very important in the absence of any significant national legislation – has demonstrated that much of it was created on the initiative of sections of the population directly involved. More than 40 per cent of surviving petitions led to the introduction of a by-law. Even more telling, many by-laws copied the text of the petition verbatim into the Amsterdam statute book. To be sure, guilds were the single most important group of petitioners in Amsterdam; almost half the petitions preserved from the eighteenth century were signed in the name of a guild.[80]

Petitions were, of course, a common phenomenon throughout premodern Europe, and not at all limited to urban environments.[81] All social classes employed them to articulate grievances and demand redress. Local governments considered them an integral part of their governance procedures.[82] The Nine in medieval Siena, for example, were required by law to hold office hours during which citizens could submit and discuss petitions, as well as raise issues in other ways.[83] Sometimes petitions were even solicited by the authorities, as happened famously with the *cahiers de doléances* in France in 1789.[84] Frequently petitioners were individuals and their problems were practical. However, petitions could also be submitted collectively, as in Amsterdam, and address more principled issues, such as the right to gain access to the town's accounts, the regulation of the local economy and so on.[85] Clearly, petitions had the potential to turn into an instrument of popular politics.[86]

To be effective, petitions had to be backed up by lobbying, either by the petitioners themselves or by more or less professional lobbyists.[87] Petitions could also be, and at times were indeed, supported by mass mobilisation. Conversely, petitions could be used to mobilise the population for political causes, for example during the English Revolution.[88]

Possibly the most rebellious era between 1000 CE and the French Revolution was the sixteenth century, when the Reformation was a cause and catalyst of major unrest, not least in towns and cities all over Europe.[89] It has been recognised since 1962, when Bernd Moeller published a small book focusing exclusively on the imperial cities, that in Germany at least, the Reformation was to an important extent an urban phenomenon. In Wittenberg, Luther's home town, Protestantism was introduced without much popular upheaval, but in dozens of other towns, citizen committees used the religious conflict to push through religious as well as political and sometimes social reforms.[90] In the Low Countries the Reformation led to outright revolution and civil war, viz. the Dutch Revolt. In numerous towns, including major centres like Antwerp and Ghent in the south, Utrecht and, ultimately, also Amsterdam in the north, the Reformation was accompanied by major political upheavals, carried by substantial sections of the local citizenry.[91] In England, where the Reformation was first introduced by the king and his government, urbanites were both active participants and opponents of these changes.[92] In 1562, Protestants temporarily seized control of the city of Rouen, starting with a wave of iconoclastic destruction on 3 and 4 May, events for which the 'Ministers and Elders of the Reformed Church in the City of Rouen' swiftly published an apology. The city was duly sacked a second time when it was retaken by government troops, with special attention paid to the homes of the Huguenots.[93] In Paris, the civic militias and the heads of the city's sixteen districts were some of the most prominent activists among the local Catholic radicals known as the *Ligue*.[94]

Perhaps the most famous of these urban revolts of the Reformation era was the Anabaptist seizure of Münster. In 1525, while the Peasants' War was raging, the guilds of Münster had wrestled various concessions from the ruling bishop, concessions that were immediately repealed as soon as the unrest subsided. In February 1532 the Lamberti parish elected the reformed priest Bernhard Rothmann as its new vicar. As we saw earlier, the Münster guilds had a coordinating *Gesamtgilde*, and its leaders, the *Olderlute*, would emerge in the following months as the main actors of a revolutionary movement. By Christmas 1532, the clash between the urban community and the bishop had developed into an armed conflict involving civic militias as well as professional troops. During the next thirty months, Münster would become a laboratory for radical theology as well as social experiments, including the abolition of private property.[95] Those experiments were supported by foreign Anabaptists, especially from the Netherlands, but sustained throughout by a cross-section of the local population.[96] As in other Reformation upheavals, Münster's citizens were actively shaping their society.

This emphasis on the sixteenth century is not to imply that urban revolts were unknown before the Reformation.[97] Indeed, one need only to think of the Revolt of the Ciompi in Florence in the summer of 1378, a revolt against a guild regime the *Ciompi* themselves had helped to establish.[98] The Dutch Revolt had deep roots in the tradition of urban revolts from the Middle Ages, in Brabant and Flanders in particular.[99] In Münster itself, the Anabaptist revolution had been preceded by earlier revolts, which looked remarkably like that of the 1530s.[100] A recent study of late medieval urban revolts in Italy and the Low Countries concluded that in these regions 'an entire repertoire of discourses, practices, and forms of association crystalised around the conduct of conflict in ways which varied from city to city, but constituted an essential feature of political life in all of them'.[101] Likewise, the easing off of religious conflict in the first half of the seventeenth century did not bring about a let-up of urban political conflict. Another study, this time of French urban conflict, concluded that 'the French Revolution was preceded by a long tradition of urban revolts that contained many of its familiar elements and that links the seventeenth century to earlier and later popular traditions'.[102]

Urban rebellions were directed against two opponents. Locally, citizens were taking on urban elites. They were not necessarily opposed to elite rule as such, but demanded transparency and accountability, and more generally an administration that operated in the interest of the community as a whole, rather than for some sectional interest. Externally, urban citizens insisted on the autonomy of their community vis-à-vis regional and national authorities. In these struggles they often collaborated with local elites, who subscribed to the same programme of urban autonomy.[103] Such conflicts could easily intersect, creating tensions within the citizen–elite coalition.[104] However, from the citizens' point of view, both types of conflicts were essentially about the same issue: creating a political space where they, as citizens, could have an effective voice and agency. In a remarkable number of towns, they managed to achieve this.

Citizenship and the Politics of Taxation

One area where relations between authorities and citizens were at their most delicate was taxation.[105] Here again, citizens' agency was key. Taxation implies that citizens will part with some of their earnings in return for services to be delivered by the authorities. Listening to modern politicians, one might be forgiven for assuming that the majority of their constituents have no other priority than to reduce the amount of taxes they pay to the lowest amount possible. And of course most people dislike having to pay taxes, but they also tend to appreciate what they get in return for doing so: public services such as education, hospital coverage and public transportation, not to mention police protection, street lighting and so on. This paradox, that people want to enjoy the services provided by government but dislike having to pay for them, is one of the problems that governments have to overcome. In view of recent political discourse on taxation there is another paradox that we need to note: economically successful societies tend to have high levels of taxation. This is counter-intuitive in that most politicians favouring tax cuts argue that these will not only satisfy voters, but also provide a boost to the economy – a double benefit, in other words.

However, the two paradoxes are predicated on false assumptions, as is demonstrated by the modern literature on tax compliance, which suggests that wherever citizenship is organised transparently, tax morale will be high.[106] This is important because it seems that, especially in the early modern period, authorities were obsessed with finances, and would try every trick in the book to increase revenues.[107] So first of all we want to know more about how they did this. But secondly, levels of taxation and the state of public finances in general might help us to understand better the 'quality' of citizenship in various European states. I return to this topic in Part II of this book.

On 7 April 1748, commissioners in the Dutch provincial town of Zwolle were appointed to collect the Liberal Gift, a new tax introduced to cope with a French invasion that was threatening the Republic's southern border. In the eighteenth century the Dutch Republic was operating at the very limits of its fiscal possibilities, making it all the more urgent to involve citizens in the process of raising taxes.[108] In Zwolle the Common Council, representing the inhabitants of the four wards, was crucial for the introduction of new taxes, as became evident in 1748, when attempts were made to create a whole set of emergency excises on coffee and tea and on tobacco, as well as a new register for the Liberal Gift personal tax. With great patriotic fervour the provincial authorities urged their local colleagues in mid-January to supply the cash necessary to thwart any French attack. In Zwolle the 'friends of the Common Council' approved some of the proposals, but refused to accept an excise on coffee and tea, which was seen as bad for local trade, because the excise was to be levied as an import duty. Only after five rounds of negotiation with the provincial authorities did Zwolle's Common Council finally acquiesce on 11 February, when a compromise proposal was introduced. Instead of the import duty, the excise would be levied through an assessment of Zwolle's households.[109]

The commissioners charged with the assessment were appointed locally. First, eight magistrates, two for each ward or 'street', were appointed who then selected two Common Councillors from the twelve representing each 'street'. Thus a total of sixteen individuals, four for each ward, was commissioned to collect the tax.[110] The Liberal Gift relied completely on voluntary contributions. It nonetheless produced 187,333 guilders in cash and another 60,232 guilders in precious metals contributed by the local population.[111] The overall amount, raised from a population of 12,000, means that each household voluntarily contributed an average of about seventeen guilders, or the equivalent of almost one month in wages for a day labourer.

This example suggests that the Zwolle authorities were relying on several mechanisms to boost tax morale. First of all, citizen representatives were involved in the decision to introduce (or not, as the case might be) new taxes in Zwolle. Secondly, these citizen representatives were involved in the assessment of rate payers. As they lived locally, their involvement also helped guarantee a fair distribution of the tax burden. And thirdly, procedures were put in place to rectify mistakes. Together, these mechanisms provided legitimacy and a degree of transparency to the process of taxation.[112]

The mechanisms Dutch urban authorities applied were by no means unique or even new, as is demonstrated by the assessment procedures in thirteenth- and fourteenth-century Siena. In Siena, the subdivision of the town into three districts, or *terzi*, was used as a basic structure. Each *terzo* had about twenty assessors, appointed by the city council from among the inhabitants of that district. In November 1287 there were twenty-one such assessors (or *alliratori*) in Città, twenty in San Martino and nineteen in Camellia. It was their task to produce a tax register, or *lira*. They were paid a small daily allowance of two soldi for the job, which was expected to last several months. The *alliratori* were supported in their work by notaries and clerics, who acted as secretaries.

The intensity of the job was a result of the scrupulous procedure that the *alliratori* had to observe. All households were first classified on a rough-and-ready basis as either *lira maggiore*, consisting of magnates, *mediocre*, mainly merchants, or *minore*, like artisans and shopkeepers. Subsequently, each household was assessed by all twenty *alliratori*. The six highest and the six lowest assessments were ignored. The final amount of taxation due from the household was arrived at by taking the average of the remaining eight assessments. The *alliratori* were often former members of the town council, but we also find magnates, merchants and artisans appointed to the job. In other words, the authorities made sure that tax assessments could not be portrayed as an attempt by one social class to exploit another.[113] On top of this, public finances were controlled by a committee of four *Provveditori* who again represented the three districts: one from each *terzo*, and the fourth rotating between the *terzi*. Those who had served on the committee were excluded for the next eighteen months from its membership.[114]

In fifteenth-century Florence there were two alternative systems. It is not entirely clear what made the government decide in favour of one or the other, but we must assume that a cost-benefit analysis was part of it.[115] The *catasto* was a major bureaucratic operation, requiring a detailed registration and assessment of all households and their property. Under its predecessors, i.e. before 1427, extraordinary levies had been divided between the town's sixteen districts or *gonfaloni*. The *gonfaloni* were thus made responsible for the assessment of their inhabitants. As in Siena, this was done by a committee of citizens, seven or nine who would all assess every household. The results would then be handed over to the friars of the Cameldolese order, who would proceed, as in Siena, by excluding the highest and lowest assessments for each household, and calculate the average of the rest.[116] For the *catasto*, a committee of ten was selected with the help of the complex mixture of lotteries and elections that the Florentines used for other high offices as well. Eight of the ten came from the seven Major Guilds, but in terms of wealth they had the same background as the councillors. After twelve months they were replaced by a new committee of a similar social profile. As on earlier occasions, the committee began with declarations of wealth by the citizens themselves, which seem to have come in very quickly. These were then checked by the officials, and adapted where necessary.[117]

The exact procedures urban authorities utilised to raise taxes have not been studied much so far, as financial historians have concentrated on other aspects of the fiscal system. Our three examples, however, would seem to suggest that the mechanisms identified in the modern tax compliance literature were exploited to full effect by urban authorities, in order to optimise revenues. These mechanisms were designed to actively involve citizens both in the decision about the introduction of new taxes, and in the actual process of collecting them.

Conclusion

Most of the time, urban office was the preserve of local elites. Although their dominance, measured in numerical terms, fluctuated over time, as such it was a permanent feature of urban governance. In the past, historians have seen this as an indication of the exclusion of ordinary citizens from politics. Only in times of crisis, it was assumed, could the latter get a foot in the door, by turning out in large numbers, or even physically intimidating the council members. This chapter has argued that the impact of citizens on urban rulers has been systemically underestimated, because historians have overlooked, or only studied in isolation, the many channels and instruments available to citizens to influence the political process. In some towns, council members were selected through an election procedure among citizens, while in other towns designated seats on the council were in the hands of citizen representatives, often the guilds. Still other towns had a second council, with dozens or even hundreds of members recruited from outside the elite. In other words, many towns had systems of government that formally incorporated their citizens.

In addition, citizens were actively involved in the production and execution of rules and regulations. Petitions were routinely submitted to the local government and routinely converted into legislation. In times of crisis, crowds and committees pressured the council to adopt new policies. The organisation of the citizens in guilds, militias and other civic institutions created a permanent forum for political debates, and an awareness among the elites that their citizens did not take everything for granted.

Urban elites often prided themselves on their own citizen status. On numerous occasions they subscribed to the core values of urban republicanism, as we saw in the previous chapter. Among other civic processes, citizens and their organisations were made an integral part of tax collection. The purpose of that inclusion was, no doubt, to enhance the legitimacy of taxation, but at the same time it was a recognition that urban authorities were powerless without the active involvement of their citizens.

Our data suggest that formal citizen participation reached its zenith sometime around 1500. During the sixteenth century, Reformation struggles led to a reduction of formal participation, as did the consolidation of centralised rule in many countries. This, however, was not a uniform development, and in many places local constitutions continued to provide a place for citizens until the end of the Old Regime. Moreover, informal participation, resulting from civic institutions like guilds, neighbourhoods and civic militias, as well as popular politics instruments like lobbying and petitioning, not to mention rebellion, remained in force and continued to remind local ruling families of the need to keep the citizens' interests in mind – even when at the same time thinking about their own.

APPENDIX 1

Urban representative institutions in 1500 and 1700 in the largest towns and cities of seven European countries

I used De Vries 1984, appendix 1 (269–87), to establish which five[118] towns were the most populous in 1500 and 1700 in each of the countries covered by this survey. Institutional data sources are listed below for each town. The presence of a common council, guild participation or elections (or a combination of these) is indicated by 1; their absence is indicated by 0; unknowns are indicated as 'nd', no data.[119]

Belgium	1500	1700	source
Antwerp	1	1	Wahl 2015a, appendix
Bruges	1	1	Wahl 2015a, appendix
Brussels	1	1	Wahl 2015a, appendix
Ghent	1	0	Wahl 2015a, appendix
Liège	1	1	Wahl 2015a, appendix

England	1500	1700	source
London (City)	1	1	Barron 2004, 131–32; Krey 1985, 10
Bristol	0	0	Sacks 1991, 161, 167, 173
Exeter	0	1	MacCaffrey 1958, 33; Sweet 1998, 91n15
Newcastle	1	1	Fraser 2009; Wilson 1995, 292
Norwich	1	1	Pound 1974, 101–03; Evans 1979, 28, 39

France	1500	1700	source
Paris	1	0	Descimon 1994; Garrioch 2002, 130
Bordeaux	0	0	Boutruche 1966, 295
Lyon	1	1	Babeau 1884 vol. 1:86
Marseille	0	0	Kaiser 1992, 138–39; Guiral and Amargier 1983, 155
Rouen	1	1	Benedict 1981, 36; Bardet 1983, 100
Toulouse	0	0	Schneider 1989a, 62; Taillefer 2000, 61–62

Germany	1500	1700	source
Berlin	1	0	Wahl 2015a, appendix
Cologne	1	1	Wahl 2015a, appendix
Dresden	1	1	Wahl 2015a, appendix
Hamburg	0	1	Wahl 2015a, appendix
Nuremberg	1	1	Wahl 2015a, appendix

Italy	1500	1700	source
Florence	1	0	Najemy 2006, 389; Litchfield 1986, 67–68
Milan	0	0	Arcangeli 2006, 171; D'Amico 2015, 55
Naples	1	1	Sodano 2013, 112–13
Rome	0	0	Canepari 2017; Nussdorfer 1992, 81
Venice	0	0	Viggiano 2013

Netherlands	1500	1700	source
Amsterdam	0	0	Verkerk 2004, 183; Hell 2004, 247
Den Bosch	1	0	Wahl 2015a, appendix
Utrecht	1	0	Wahl 2015a, appendix
Haarlem	0	0	Ree-Scholtens 1995, 45, 148
Leiden	0	0	Brand 1996, 59; Prak 1985, 39
Rotterdam	0	0	Engelbrecht 1973, 'Inleiding'

Switzerland	1500	1700	source
Basel	1	1	Wahl 2015a, appendix
Berne	1	0	Wahl 2015a, appendix
Geneva	1	1	Wahl 2015a, appendix
Zürich	1	1	Wahl 2015a, appendix

Europe, totals	1500	1700
pop. particip.	22	17
no particip.	13	18

3 ECONOMIC CITIZENSHIP THROUGH THE GUILDS

Thomas Gent was born in Ireland, probably in 1693. He started an apprenticeship as a printer in Dublin, but ran away to England in 1710. The published version of his autobiography actually begins with Gent being seasick on the ship that took him across. Finding no printing press in Chester, his first port of call, he then travelled on to London, where he continued to learn his trade. By 1713 Gent had completed the seven years of training that were required under English law from every master artisan. During his apprenticeship he had been badly treated, he felt – 'as a servant' – but his master Midwinter assured him that this treatment was only meant to encourage his skill and ambition. And indeed, at the end of his term of apprenticeship, Midwinter offered Gent hospitality and protection: 'I do not prefer my interest to your good; and though you came [as] an almost stranger to me, God forbid that I should send you as such abroad'. He helped secure Gent some odd jobs and finally a place as a journeyman printer in York. Subsequently, Gent returned to London and his former master, where there was more work and more adventures. However:[1]

> In the year 1717 I had the great happiness of being made a freeman of the Stationers, and on 9 Oct, commenced citizen at guildhall notwithstanding the false objection raised against me in the court, by one Cornish, that I had been married in my apprenticeship;[2] but my master, Midwinter, proved him a notorious liar, and he was reprehended by the warden and others. ... Thus I became absolutely free, both in England and

> Ireland, which made me give sincere thanks to the Almighty from the inward recesses of my soul.

Gent had gone through a process that was very common in England, albeit not on the continent: by becoming a master of the Stationers' Company (or guild), he could also become a citizen of the City of London.

The guild that Gent joined was not one of London's most significant: it ranked forty-seventh during urban ceremonies in the seventeenth century, far behind the Twelve Great Livery Companies of the City.[3] In 1403, the 'text-writers' and 'limners' (illustrators) had received a privilege from the city authorities; from 1441 they called themselves the 'Company of Stationers'. The trade had benefitted enormously from Johannes Gutenberg's invention of moveable type and the subsequent expansion of book sales and other printed materials.[4] In 1557, moreover, the London Stationers received from the crown a national monopoly for the production of printed material.[5]

The Stationers' Company was in various respects an ordinary guild in a city where guilds were at the time hugely important, not merely for regulating the local economy, but also as social and political organisations – capacities in which they remain active into the twenty-first century.[6] It was at the same time unusual in its national scope. On the continent it was practically unheard of, and even in England quite rare, to find guilds with jurisdiction outside their own town and perhaps its immediate hinterland.[7] In this respect, the Stationers were an extreme example of a trait that was common to the guild system as a whole: the monopoly. In their charters, guilds would receive the right, reserved for their members, to produce and trade in specific products; in the case of the Stationers 'impressing or printing any book'. They could search premises where they suspected illicit printed works were to be found, i.e. produced by printers who were not members of the Company. The charter of 1557 gave the Stationers' Company also the right to assemble, to elect its own officials and to make its own rules.[8]

The history of the Stationers' Company and of Thomas Gent's progression to the mastership in that company, and subsequent citizenship status in the City of London, serves to highlight several themes of this chapter. What was the role of guilds in the towns of premodern Europe? And how difficult was it to join them? The case of the Stationers suggests two contrasting narratives: they held an unusually strong 'monopoly', but an 'almost stranger' found it relatively easy to join this London guild, even though he was from Ireland. And last, but not least of course, it shows how citizenship and guild membership were intimately related in premodern Europe. In many towns, candidates had to be formal citizens before they could join a guild. In some places, all citizens were required to join a guild. And in still other places, guild membership automatically conferred citizenship status.[9] To contemporaries, the connection seemed almost inalienable. Incorporated trades were also known as the 'citizens' trades'.[10] This intimate connection was articulated, for example, in many guild petitions, insisting that members were entitled to support from the council – as citizens and taxpayers.[11]

For the argument of this book, there is an additional reason to look closely at the guilds. If citizenship was to have a positive effect on society, including its economic performance, then obviously the guilds would be a channel through which this effect might be accomplished. As it is, this is precisely the topic of a fierce debate among economic historians. The argument over guilds and economy has been constructed in two distinct ways. As discussed in the Introduction, the idea of 'transaction costs' is fundamental to Douglass North's influential work. Whereas most economic theory assumes that the exchange of goods and services between two parties is free under perfect market conditions, North claims that such conditions do not exist in the real world and that there are therefore always costs; moreover, most of the time these costs are substantial. Transaction costs come in two types. One has to do with information. How do I know that the product I'm buying is the same as what is advertised? Is there an equivalent on the market that will satisfy my needs more cheaply? The other has to do with contract enforcement. If I pay for this product, will it actually be delivered? And will the producer stand by the warranty? To guarantee contract enforcement, advanced economies use a so-called third party, and for reasons of efficiency that third party is usually a public authority that can handle many conflicts over contracts in an even-handed way. At the beginning of the period covered by this book, by and large there was no such authority. As a result, the economy underperformed, simply because merchants could not trust their trading partners. According to Avner Greif, it was precisely this sort of institutional framework that the merchant guilds provided in the Middle Ages.[12]

There was also, however, another way in which the guilds could impact the economy. Since Adam Smith, in his *Wealth of Nations* in 1776, condemned guilds as 'a conspiracy against the public', generations of economists and historians have lined up to repeat the accusation. In recent years, revisionist scholars have tried to explain the emergence of guilds, and their persistence for more than half a millennium, in a more positive vein. This revisionist literature has distinguished between merchant and craft guilds, because of the different problems for which these organisations provided a solution. The problem of long-distance trade is one of information and contract enforcement. For craft guilds too, insecurity was an issue, but on top of that there were questions of technology and the training of the skilled workforce. Guilds contributed in all three areas, it has been claimed. They addressed issues of insecurity for their members by helping to create a stable economic environment, and for their customers through various instruments that helped establish quality standards; they clustered technological information, especially of the micro-invention type; and they set up an administrative system for the training of apprentices who would eventually carry on the industry in the next generation.[13]

This revisionism has not been universally accepted. Sheilagh Ogilvie has published two books and a string of articles, all arguing that merchant and craft guilds were rent-seeking organisations which sought to redistribute economic wealth to the advantage of their members and against the interest of migrants, women and other disenfranchised groups.[14] They did so through collusion with the authorities, who were receiving taxes and loans from the guilds' membership in exchange for permission to continue their rent-seeking behaviour. This is probably correct, but seems to measure their behaviour against the benchmark of perfect markets, or to elevate their impact to absolute levels.[15] The question is not whether guilds were the best solution for market failures but whether, under imperfect circumstances, they could help overcome the economic problems created by rent-seeking states, or alternatively by the absence of any state control over economic processes. One of Ogilvie's criticisms of 'institutionalists' like North and Greif is that they fail to produce empirical evidence for the beneficial effects of organisations like guilds. This is definitely a valid point. Unfortunately, it has proved equally impossible to establish the levels of rent-seeking that are the linchpin of Ogilvie's own argument.

In this area the debate must therefore remain unresolved. The point to take away from these exchanges, however, seems to be that although merchant and craft guilds were capable of supporting economic development, they did not always work their positive magic; or phrased the other way around, they were a burden on the economy, but not always and everywhere.[16] It is therefore important, in the following discussion of the citizenship aspects of these organisations, to be alert to historically variable circumstances that allowed or prevented rent-seeking.

The debate about the 'good' or 'bad' of guilds is relevant for the history of premodern citizenship in a number of ways, which mostly have to do with access to the incorporated trades, captured by the word 'monopoly'. It is usually taken for granted that guilds used their 'monopoly' power to limit access to markets to their own members, and to keep that membership as small as possible. As a result, immigrants, women, religious minorities and even the sons and daughters of local inhabitants were prevented from entering the guild, or so it is alleged. Thomas Gent's experience was remarkably different, however, as was the attitude of his master. Other issues have to do with the guilds' presumed conservatism: as rent-seekers they tried to prevent innovations that would eat away their profits. In this chapter I argue that many examples can be found to support these claims, but that as broad generalisations they are nonetheless incorrect.

The Rise and Decline of Merchant and Craft Guilds

In the nineteenth century, two rival theories were developed, particularly in Germany, about the origins of the guilds.[17] One portrayed guilds as the medieval successors of the Roman *collegia*, which originally functioned as platforms for the transmission of citizenship to urban inhabitants who did not own land. These *collegia* could be organised on an occupational basis, and they helped develop public services and public order in Roman urban society. The Codex Theodosianus (438 CE) mentions them explicitly in that role. With the collapse of the Roman Empire in the sixth century, however, the *collegia* disappeared as well, and there is no evidence of any continuity across the half millennium or so that elapsed before the guilds emerged. Likewise, the resemblance between Germanic tribal meetings and guild organisations has turned out to be nothing more than that: a similarity of form, but without any direct connection. One has to conclude that Europeans of the central Middle Ages reinvented an organisational form that had been invented in previous times by other societies, but only gradually discovered those similarities, subsequently used to dignify the guilds' pedigree.[18]

The first to emerge were merchant guilds. Merchant guilds were organisations whose members were involved in long-distance trade.[19] They were designed to overcome problems inherent in business deals where the two parties do not meet in person, but have to exchange through intermediaries and accept a time lag between delivery of the goods and their payment. These two distances, of time and space, created insecurities that were enhanced by the political fragmentation of post-Roman Europe, and again after the collapse of the Carolingian Empire. Where political institutions proved unhelpful, merchants were forced to resort to private-order solutions. The family was the most obvious of these, but by their very nature, family networks have a limited coverage in space, and are also subject to the vagaries of demographic fate. Guilds, it is argued, proved an ultimately more stable and therefore successful private-order solution, on one hand by enforcing rules among their own members, and on the other by threatening sanctions against foreign parties and their partners (e.g. other merchants from the same town as the cheater). Through the development of such collective mechanisms, Avner Greif has claimed, merchant guilds were not so much monopolising trade to limit supply and drive up the price, but on the contrary creating a secure environment that helped to expand long-distance exchange.[20]

One of the reasons why merchant guilds turned out to be a successful solution to such problems of commitment is because from the beginning merchants sought, and obtained, government sanction.[21] Merchants guilds worked in close cooperation with public authorities, and were able to pressure the authorities for more effective protection of merchant interests. No doubt the guilds' primary goal was to ensure that the benefit of their efforts accrued to their members. There is debate about whether this happened at the cost of competitors, and ultimately suppressed fresh initiatives, or whether it turned out to be also beneficial to society as a whole, because thanks to this protection merchants could invest in more daring commercial enterprises.[22] The most likely verdict is that both were true, albeit in different ways in different places.

Bruges was the most significant port in fourteenth-century Northern Europe and inevitably a focus of merchants from Germany and other regions around the Baltic, who were united in the German Hanse, or Hanseatic League. Strictly speaking, the Hanse was not a guild, but a collaboration of merchant guilds in dozens of towns.[23] Abroad, however, it acted as a single merchant organisation to protect and further the interests of its members, i.e. the towns and their merchants. In 1358 the Hanse submitted a document to the Bruges authorities, complaining about English and Spanish privateers, local tolls, deficient weighing facilities and the confiscation of German ships to fight Antwerp. In their *Claghe der Oosterlingen*, or Complaint of the Easterners, the Hanse demanded compensation for the damages suffered by its members, and when the Bruges council proved uncooperative, the Hanse moved its *Kontor* to Dordrecht, a much smaller harbour quite a distance away from Bruges. Only when Bruges offered extra privileges and a hefty 24,600 guilders was the *Kontor* moved back to Bruges in 1360. In 1392 the Hanse managed to extract an even larger compensation for losses suffered by its members due to confiscations, as well as a promise from the collective Flemish towns about future compensations. On still other occasions it obtained smaller reparations. These actions demonstrate how collective action by merchants could protect them against the insecurities of long-distance trade, at a time when local and regional authorities were routinely attempting to shortchange poorly protected merchants.[24]

The heyday of merchant guilds was the period from the eleventh century to the sixteenth. After that, several factors made international trade a more routine business. The number of transactions had increased, and instruments for payment improved. Merchants now had agents to look after their interests on their behalf. The 'feudal anarchy' of the Middle Ages had been reduced as a result of the consolidation of larger states. Gelderblom and Grafe conclude from the rise and decline of merchant guilds in Amsterdam, Antwerp, Bilbao and Bruges that in the early days of the revival of international trade merchant guilds were one of a set of institutions that supported 'thin' markets. From the mid-seventeenth century they observe a notable decline in the number of institutional instruments supporting international trade in all four commercial centres. By then state institutions were providing the sort of framework that was previously supplied by the guild.[25] This may not have been true in East-Central Europe, and it certainly was not true for the trade with non-European regions, which remained a domain of regulated trade, albeit not along the lines of the guild model because it was precisely in this trade that the first experiments with the modern company form, financed through permanent shares, were conducted.[26]

Craft guilds emerged significantly later than the merchant guilds, in the twelfth and thirteenth centuries, i.e. in the middle of a period of rapid economic expansion.[27] Clearly, craft guilds cannot have been the cause of that expansion, which predates their emergence. They may, however, have acted as a dynamic element, sustaining the growth phase of the economy. Alternatively, they may have been a sign of consolidation, and in the long run a cause of stagnation. Some examples can illustrate the point.

Clock making was already known in the Middle Ages, but with the emergence of domestic-size products, it had become a genuine industry by 1500.[28] It expanded rapidly in the following decades and by the eighteenth century observers commented on the ubiquity of watches – 70 per cent of Parisian servants owned a watch by the 1780s, and even sailors were seen carrying them.[29] This expansion was accompanied by an incorporation of the trade: clock makers' guilds were established in Paris in 1544, Geneva in 1601, Rouen in 1617, London in 1631, Lyon in 1658 and so on. In many other towns, clock makers and watchmakers joined with the blacksmiths and other metal-working trades. The most important invention in the industry, the pendulum clock, was developed by Dutch astronomer and mathematician Christiaan Huygens, but so quickly was the innovation copied by clock maker guild masters that Huygens had to drop plans to patent his invention.[30]

A similar story of guilds and innovation can be told about the silk ribbon engine loom. This invention, introduced in Leiden in 1604, permitted the production of multiple silk ribbons by a single weaver. The industry was found in many European towns, but the engine loom was adopted in only some of them. Where guilds were politically powerful, they were less inclined to accept this sort of labour-saving technology, and were able to persuade the authorities to introduce tariffs to restrain foreign competition. In other places, such as London and many Dutch towns, the authorities were more likely to take consumers' interests into account as well and force ribbon makers to adapt. However, the guilds' membership also made a difference. Where this was made up of small masters only, conservatism was more likely to prevail, while a variegated membership was more conducive to innovation.[31]

Whereas merchant guilds had already begun to decline in the sixteenth century, craft guilds actually continued until the end of the eighteenth century – and beyond. Their disappearance has often been associated with the Industrial Revolution, but in actual fact these two developments were not at all closely connected. The first industries to mechanise – coal mining, weaving and spinning – were already located in the countryside long before the invention of the steam engine. In England the guilds were never formally abolished.[32] On the continent, guilds were first abolished in countries that were actually late to industrialise, like France and the Netherlands. The chronological fit between the abolishment of the guilds and the emergence of modern industry is too poor to provide an explanation. In fact, craft guilds were abolished for political, not economic reasons.[33]

Guilds and the Economy

Critics of the guilds have concentrated their objections on what is usually called the 'monopoly' under which guilds operated. This was the article, found in the regulations of really every guild, stipulating that only members could produce or sell the products specified in those same regulations. In other words, guilds were operating a closed shop. One of the ways to find how 'closed' in fact, is to establish what percentage of households were actually involved in the corporate system.

Asking the question is unfortunately much easier than answering it. This has to do with the state of the sources available to provide an answer. Very few sources survive that allow us to count directly the number of guild masters in a city or town in a given year, and then divide that by the number of that town's inhabitants. Almost everywhere the guild records are so incomplete that an estimate of the total number of guild masters is hazardous. For Utrecht, a reconstruction of guild membership around 1650 suggests that half of all households had at least one guild member in their midst.[34] For 's-Hertogenbosch I was able, with the help of a census from 1775 and membership lists from fourteen guilds for 1750–75, to calculate that about 25 per cent of heads of households must have been members of a guild in that year.[35] Despite the uncertainty, it has nonetheless proved possible to convert similar sets of data on guild membership into reasonably reliable estimates

Table 3.1 Percentage of masters' households in selected European towns, 1550–1800

	1550–1599	1600–1649	1650–1699	1700–1749	1750–1799
London		17	21	16	9
Antwerp				23	
Ghent				43	
Utrecht	31		57		32
's-Hertogenbosch					25
Dijon	21	14			
Lyon					21–30
Rouen					28–43

Source: Minns et al. 2014

about the percentage of households headed by a guild member for a small number of towns in England, the Habsburg Netherlands and France. It makes less sense to take the whole population as a basis for estimation, because usually guild masters set up their own households; in many German towns this was even compulsory.[36] The estimates are shown in Table 3.1, and display a range from 14 per cent to 30 per cent, with outliers on both sides. Another way of saying this is that about one in four to five households was directly involved in the guild system. There is no obvious trend from the sixteenth to eighteenth century.

These figures actually underestimate the number of people indirectly connected to the corporate system, since they do not include apprentices and journeymen. Together these might add another 10 to 20 per cent of the population involved in the corporate system, albeit without the rights that mastership entailed.

Any guild career would have to start with an apprenticeship. Initially, these were unregulated, that is to say, the rules of early guilds make no mention of training. From around 1400, however, substantial legislation concerning apprenticeship began to emerge. In London the earliest regulations go back to the mid- and late thirteenth century. Two hundred years later a full set of regulations had formed. Halfway through the fourteenth century, for example, the length of an apprenticeship had been established at seven years – extraordinarily long by continental standards.[37] On the continent, guild regulations in Utrecht and 's-Hertogenbosch suggest a similar pattern.[38] The first regulation to be introduced concerned fees, beginning shortly after 1300; the next placed limits on the number of apprentices that a single master could take on, first mentioned in 1421–22. The latter rules have often been interpreted as an attempt to limit access to the craft, but as far as we know most masters only had one or two apprentices throughout their whole career, so capacity was hardly an issue. Limiting numbers could also serve the interest of the apprentice: it guaranteed attention from the master and opportunities to actually practise the craft. In the fifteenth century, registration dues were introduced. In themselves these were modest, but registration might entail other payments that were not. From then on, apprenticeship was documented by the guild and, at least implicitly, certified. With the help of these registers, craftsmen would be able to prove that they had completed their apprenticeship and could be expected to have mastered the craft. We have seen how Thomas Gent felt he was ready to terminate his apprenticeship after seven years; he was clearly aware of the rules that applied.

The variation in the length of an apprenticeship and the inconsistent pattern of examination – why tailors and not painters? – have raised suspicions that these were again instruments to make life miserable for apprentices and discourage youngsters from seeking a career in the crafts. Such suspicions are deepened by the fact that guild regulations paid very little, or no attention at all, to the contents of the training.[39] Contrary to the popular image, we now know that it was unusual for boys (or girls) to be apprenticed to their parents;[40] rather, youngsters were supposed to leave the family circle to be trained under a master, who was responsible for the contents of that training. The guilds' contribution was to provide a framework of regulation and standards, rather than the training itself; that was left to individual masters. For that reason, guild registration was often supplemented by private contracts between a master and his pupil's parents or guardians. In fact, those contracts also contained little about the contents of the training, usually stating merely that the master was to share 'all' his knowledge about the trade with his apprentice, before going on to details about room and board.[41]

The most likely reason for this silence about craft training is that much of it was (and remains) difficult to articulate in writing. Craft skills are learned on the job, in personal interactions between expert and novice.[42] During the sixteenth, seventeenth and eighteenth centuries such practical training was increasingly supplemented by classroom training, by printed manuals and by theoretical instruction.[43] However, none of that could replace the practical instructions supplied by those working in the crafts.

Despite all these caveats, the sheer numbers of apprentices coming through the guild system testify to their significance. In mid-sixteenth-century London there were an estimated 7,250 serving an apprenticeship out of a total population of about 70,000.[44] In 1700, 3,800 youngsters started an apprenticeship in London. In Bristol, a city of 20,000, between 1686 and 1696 on average 250 new apprentices were enrolled every year,[45] which would create a constant pool of about 1,500 apprentices. A survey in 1738 counted 2,089 apprentices in Ghent, in an estimated population of 40,000.[46] In Amsterdam and other towns in Holland, civic orphanages, which took the children of deceased citizens under their wings, proved very keen to place their wards with guild masters, and not just any craft practitioners.[47]

The combined effect of personal training and a migration of trained craftsmen was a circulation of technical knowledge. Again, guilds provided an important framework. In the German lands it was required of aspiring masters that they spend a considerable time on the road, working in various other towns to broaden their skills. Dietrich Meyer, a native of Zürich, where he trained as a goldsmith, started his travels in 1669. He worked in Basel, Augsburg, possibly Amsterdam and Basel again, before returning to Zürich in 1674 with a sketchbook full of designs that he had picked up along the way.[48] Technically, Meyer had completed his apprenticeship and was a journeyman; at the same time, his travels were clearly part of his education.[49] Some guilds explicitly required prospective masters to gain several years of experience before they could set up shop independently.[50] In other guilds this was the norm in practice. This was the reason why Rembrandt, for example, could contract aspiring painters who were technically no longer apprentices, but still paid him a fee to improve their skills.[51]

Formalised training and an institutionally embedded circulation of knowledge helped to improve European industrial production massively during the centuries of the guilds.[52] From the Renaissance, but especially during the seventeenth and eighteenth centuries, an increasingly wide range of consumer goods became available to a widening range of consumers. These 'populuxe' goods and the rise of fashion were two indicators that Europeans were offered more choice at competitive prices.[53] The book trade – a highly skilled craft – is just one among many examples of craft inventions with a massive direct impact on consumption, but also with unintended cultural and indeed economic side effects.[54] Apprenticeship was an important and almost universal element in the educational background of British inventors of the Industrial Revolution.[55] There is no indication that apprenticeships were becoming overall less important as time progressed, either in England or elsewhere.[56]

Craft guilds claimed to maintain quality standards through a variety of mechanisms. Many guilds required the aspiring master to demonstrate his skill by making specified products in the presence of a committee of masters. The effectiveness of this practice has been disputed, and with some reason, for it seems to have been often more of a ritual than a serious examination.[57] Tests remained the same, for example, even though the products were changing. Marking products (a trademark) to allow the identification of the producer was probably more effective, a strategy used with precious metals (especially to check the silver or gold content), in the leather industry and in stone-cutting, for example. Textile guilds also certified their products with local seals or trademarks.[58] In Amsterdam, the Silversmiths' Guild destroyed all products that were of substandard quality. In the same town, the Guild of St Luke arbitrated between members and dissatisfied customers – for example, when one Diego d'Andrade was dissatisfied with the portrait Rembrandt had made of his daughter.[59]

Guilds certainly were compatible with economic growth. During the Italian Renaissance, or during the Dutch golden age, the number of guilds increased dramatically.[60] Industrial output in England increased substantially between 1500 and 1700, two centuries during which the guilds were still influential.[61] This era witnessed dramatic growth in the population of London, where the guilds were important both economically and politically.[62] Another way of saying this is that early modern capitalism emerged in an environment where markets were supported by socio-economic organisations that allowed individuals to produce collective goods.[63]

This does not in any way prove that guilds were responsible for industrial expansion, but neither can one say that they were obviously inhibiting such developments. The same mixed picture arises from an analysis of the coincidence between the expansion of the corporate system and the increase in rates of urbanisation in Italy and the Low Countries, the two regions that provide the best quantitative data. The figures show that phases of urbanisation or economic expansion, and of de-urbanisation or stagnation and decline, were both accompanied by high guild densities.[64]

Inclusion in and Exclusion from the Guilds

In 1632 Brigitta Müller from Memmingen submitted a complaint to the local council. She was a hosier who had learned the craft of knitting from her father. Now her brother, of all people, who had received the same education, was trying to prevent her from exercising her trade. Müller argued that, because she was working in an unincorporated trade, her brother's objections were out of order. The Memmingen council agreed. Thirty years later, however, the Hosiers' Guild had been set up in Memmingen, and the male masters of that guild attempted to exclude Müller from their industry because she did not have the proper – i.e. guild-sanctioned – training. Müller responded by saying that the guild documents only spoke of male training, which did not apply to her as a female, and that anyway, as a widow, she had to care for her children. The guild dismissed her objections as 'meaningless female waffle, ... mere air and dust', and persisted in its demand to have her banned. In her case, the Memmingen council took pity and allowed her to sell her stockings from her own house, but not in the market where the guild masters had their stalls.[65]

The exclusion of Brigitta Müller from the hosiery trade seems a typical example of the way in which guilds routinely excluded competitors from their industries. It is generally assumed that restricted access to urban trades constrained the premodern economy.[66] Restricted access was part of a wider set of regulations that imposed political constraints on economic development – 'feudalism'. Guilds, of course, were established by documents that laid down the ground rules for their role in society. One constant element was the granting of the exclusive right to members of a guild, as a privilege of their membership, to produce and sell a specific range of products, to the exclusion of all non-members. This privilege is usually called the guild 'monopoly'. In recent years, questions have been raised as to the effectiveness of the monopoly: could guilds really monitor and enforce this 'monopoly', especially in large urban centres? Or were they undercut all the time by interlopers, illicit producers and others who sought to enjoy the benefits of the trade while avoiding the burdens of guild membership?

These questions are still very difficult to answer with any certainty. However, we can say something about a related issue that is closely connected to the alleged 'monopoly': how accessible actually were urban guilds to those whom we might term 'outsiders', i.e. people without a previous connection to the trade, or indeed to the urban community of which the guild claimed to be an integral part? If it can be shown that access to the 'monopoly' was open to basically anyone whose ambition it was to join, then that 'monopoly' could not so easily have led to the types of disastrous outcomes that many critics of the guilds claim they had.

Although some guilds had obtained permission to formally restrict access to their ranks and so limit the membership, this was probably exceptional.[67] Nevertheless, to acquire membership of a guild required from candidates everywhere that he – only rarely she – overcome several hurdles.

One glaring obstacle was gender; the exclusion of women is discussed separately in the next section. Two other types of hurdles in the way of the prospective guild member were skills and money. In some regions a test of morals was added as still another obstacle. As far as skills were concerned, the great majority of craft guilds imposed at least one, and often two, sorts of requirement. The first was in fact apprenticeship. A minimum number of years was almost always prescribed before a craftsman could practise as an independent master. These apprenticeship terms varied significantly by region and by craft. England had an exceptional regime: its Statute of Artificers, from 1563, created a national framework for apprenticeships, and the Statute imposed a minimum seven-year apprenticeship for all trades. On the continent, the terms of apprenticeship were set locally, and varied for each trade. In the Low Countries the standard term was two years, in France five.[68]

Besides the period of apprenticeship, some guilds also required their prospective members to first demonstrate proficiency in the trade by producing a masterpiece. In some parts of Europe, most notoriously in the Holy Roman Empire, guild membership and trade were often affected by issues of 'legitimacy' and 'honour', which could practically restrict membership and economic rights on the basis of parentage, moral behaviour or occupation.[69] Such rules were also in force in Dijon, situated quite close to German-speaking territories, and in late fifteenth- and sixteenth-century London. New masters in sixteenth-century Dijon moreover had to be 'good Catholics'.[70] In the eastern parts of the Dutch Republic rules were introduced during the seventeenth century, restricting access to local citizenship to Calvinists only. By implication, only Calvinist immigrants were admissible to the guilds. Such limitations would probably have been introduced under pressure from the guild masters who dominated local representative institutions. Similar institutions were lacking in the seaboard provinces of the Republic, where such restrictions were never introduced.[71] It is quite possible that in other places affiliation to the dominant (or state) religion was so much taken for granted that it was not even stated explicitly.

Both the apprenticeship and the acquisition of master status required the aspiring craftsman to fork out various sums of money, sometimes very substantial sums. In London, apprenticeship premiums could rise to several hundreds of pounds in the more prosperous guilds. In many craft guilds, however, masters charged far more modest premiums. In the London food, clothing, footwear, textiles, woodwork, iron and building industries average premiums were between five and ten pounds.[72]

Masterships could be cheap, but this was unusual. Moreover, many guilds distinguished between masters' sons, local residents and immigrants, with the first category paying substantially less than the second, which in turn received preferential treatment over the third. A pattern is, once again, difficult to establish. We also have to remember that membership dues were only part of the total cost of setting up one's own workshop – and for most aspiring craftsmen not the most important. Almost everywhere, the opportunity costs of training, as well as the investment necessary to start one's own business, dwarfed the obstacles created by guilds.[73]

Newly collected evidence allows us to see whether these various arrangements did indeed lead to a structural exclusion of certain social groups, and more specifically, if they created a privileged position for the relatives of the established masters of the trade. The data for masters relate to sixty-five individual guilds in eighteen different towns, plus data on a mixture of guilds for eight towns. Together, they cover more than 100,000 masters. For apprentices our sample covers a much larger number of individuals: more than 450,000. However, they come from fewer guilds and places: fourteen guilds from six towns, plus eleven towns where we can observe a mixture of various guilds. The observations cover a range of towns from Bristol to Vienna and from Gdansk (Danzig) to Madrid. Much of the data relates to England and the Low Countries, where some of the most active guild research has been concentrated, but there is sufficient evidence for France, Germany and Central Europe, and for Italy and Spain, to claim that the picture presented here is valid for Europe as a whole, rather than for a small – and possibly atypical – part of it. To overcome the dominance of the number of observations from London or Paris, the volumes have been ignored; instead, unweighted observations have been calculated. The results from tiny Wildberg (fewer than 1,500 inhabitants) therefore count for as much as those from huge London and Paris (both more than half a million), because we assume that Wildberg is potentially representative of a whole class of small towns.[74]

For both apprentices and guild masters, entry barriers did not give rise to very strong restrictions on entry based on social or geographical backgrounds. No doubt all kinds of obstacles stood in the way of those joining the guilds, but such obstacles proved surmountable for large numbers of 'outsiders'. In many places, the so-called guild monopolies were accessible to such a wide range of people that the term loses its explanatory value. This confirms earlier observations. As Shephard found in Dijon: 'During the eighteenth century the guilds of Dijon were remarkably open to non-Dijonnais'. Ehmer reached a similar conclusion for Vienna in 1997.[75] There was regional variation, but not of the sort predicted in the literature, where a distinction is often made between the 'progressive' Low Countries and England, versus the 'conservative' German lands and Mediterranean Europe. This distinction does not emerge from Table 3.2.

We nonetheless have to acknowledge that over these two centuries there were substantial differences between guilds. One reason why the picture is mixed must be that guilds themselves had conflicting interests. Exclusionary policies on the parts of guilds encouraged 'illicit' entrepreneurs to set up business outside the control of the guild, for example in the suburbs or the adjacent countryside.[76] In the eighteenth century, guilds in the Habsburg, subsequently Austrian Netherlands, at one and the same time substantially increased their fees, making it much more difficult to join their ranks, but also encouraged people to join, because this was the only way guilds could reduce their debt burden. High fees thus were not always instruments for excluding applicants, but in this case used to raise funds for the activities of the guilds at the expense of new members who were 'buying into' the services provided by the guild.[77] All of this raises questions about the freedom that guilds

Table 3.2 Openness of European guild masterships and apprenticeships to migrants and non-kin, 1600–1799, by region

	Open (> 2/3 outsiders)	Neutral (1/3 to 2/3 outsiders)	Closed (< 1/3 outsiders)	N=
Masters				
German Europe	20	35	6	61
Low Countries	13	3	5	21
England	9	21	6	36
Mediterranean Europe	11	5	0	16
Europe	53	64	17	134
Apprentices				
Europe	22	19	9	50

Note: Figures show the number of guilds (and towns) that are open, neutral or closed, based on the share of new masters who did not originate in the town and city in question, or were sons/daughters of masters in the same guild. Where both types of data are available, only the percentage of migrants was used.
Source: Prak et al. 2018, data appendix

might or might not have had to set their own admission policies. In sixteenth-century Ghent, guilds closed their ranks when the local political constellation permitted them to do so.[78] In the Wildberg district in southern Germany the authorities were willing to give the guilds what they wanted: exclusive admission policies.[79] In London, however, where guilds were always an important political force, this did not automatically lead to a closing of ranks.[80]

The authorities were equally ambivalent: they wanted strong guilds to help them impose political and social control, but they also feared the guilds as potential platforms for revolutionary activities.[81] Urban communities found it very difficult, or even impossible, to reproduce themselves demographically.[82] To maintain the size of the local population, not to mention ambitions of growth, an influx of immigrants was simply necessary. Moreover, all urban communities, but especially the larger ones, found it difficult to consistently monitor complex policies such as those selecting migrants.[83]

Overall – and this is the big point – the available data do not support the claim that guilds prevented outsiders on a large scale from joining their ranks. Their 'monopoly' was undermined by a steady influx of new members from outside the circle of the established masters. Exclusion is more visible when it comes to apprentices, but this could be explained by the tendency of parents to seek instructors in their own locality, rather than in faraway places. Guild masters, on the other hand, were socially and geographically mobile.

Gendered Guilds

If guilds were less exclusive than is often assumed when it came to migrants or non-family members, this was less obviously true for women.[84] Whereas females were described as at least potentially equal to male masters in the Middle Ages, clauses explicitly excluding women from the guilds' ranks gradually began appearing in their statutes. Changing religious attitudes may have been one of the reasons this happened, and the Reformation seems to have accelerated this development,[85] but the changes are better documented than explained. Paradoxically, women were in some ways also increasing their impact in the corporate world during the early modern period.

Many medieval guild statutes routinely assumed that a candidate-member could be of either sex. The statutes of the Tailors' Guild in The Hague, for example, stated as late as 1505 that the aspiring master had to demonstrate his skill 'as a man or woman' before the guild's examiners; the masterpiece could be either a man's or a woman's garment.[86] Two centuries earlier, in 1304, a general ordinance concerning the trades in Utrecht ordered that 'those who want to exercise an incorporated trade, be they man or woman, have to become members'.[87] Where gendered clauses are found in the regulations of medieval guilds, they tended to be inclusive. It is nevertheless difficult to assess the role of women in medieval guilds on the basis of this evidence alone. Most guild statutes remain completely silent on the subject. The fact that women were acceptable as members does not mean that they were numerous or influential within the guild.[88] It was highly unusual, for instance, for women to take up guild offices.

It does look, however, as if things were taking a turn for the worse during the sixteenth century. Thus, in 1524, the Tailors' Guild of Haarlem introduced a prohibition against women cutting new cloth, effectively barring them from the trade. The female members of the guild were allowed to continue, but 'they will die out, and no new female members shall be accepted into the guild'.[89] The same happened in London, where the Weavers' Company stipulated in 1578 that 'no manner of person or persons exercising [their trade] shall keep, teach, instruct, or bring up in the use, exercise, or knowledge of [weaving] any maid, damsel, or other woman whatsoever'.[90] Around the same time, the Nuremberg Ringmakers decided that 'from now on, no maid is to be used for any kind of work in this craft'.[91] It was a trend observed all over Europe, and it continued into later centuries.[92] The regulations of the Genevan Watchmakers' Guild, set up in 1601, had been silent on the issue of gender, but in 1690 they introduced rules that forbade women, including masters' wives and daughters, to be involved in any other aspect of the trade than the production of chains and other elements separate from the watch itself, the production of which became the sole preserve of men.[93]

The dramatic deterioration in women's positions in the corporate world has been explained in various ways.[94] Martha Howell sees the marginalisation of women as a consequence of shifts in the economy and the political role of guilds. Women's economic positions, she argues, had always been defined in the family sphere, as additional to their husbands' role, and was never seen as the mainstay of the household. As artisanal production moved away from household production into a more commercial mode, women lost their traditional foothold in the corporate world. Because they had never gained political influence within the guilds, they were now unable to counter this development by an appeal to the urban authorities.[95] Merry Wiesner has likewise argued that the guilds were a key factor in engineering these changes, but she blames the journeymen. During the sixteenth century they found it more difficult to set up shop as independent masters. Instead, journeymen were forced to live in hostels much longer, sometimes all their lives. The hostels were all-male communities, where the symbolism of male honour became much more important than it had been. These values were transferred to the guilds, as journeymen's associations clamoured for the exclusion of women from the trade, or brought their gendered identities into the guild when journeymen finally managed to win membership.[96]

According to another explanation, the guilds' negative attitude towards women was primarily defensive: threatened by shrinking markets, male masters sought to break the weaker links in the chain of the trade. Thus, in the course of the eighteenth century, when rural proto-industry was making headway in Prussia, urban guilds there tried to redefine 'real' work as a male preserve, while the sloppy products of rural industry were thrown together with women's work, as the bottom end of the trade.[97] In the process, women's roles in relation to work were recast in much more narrow ways. One telling example is the Berlin Tailors' Guild's proclamation, in 1803, that[98]

> [M]arried women must be maintained by their husbands, know housekeeping, and care for and educate their children. The unmarried may work as domestics ... or engage in other feminine occupations outside regular manufacture.

This opinion reflects a long tradition of discourse that was not necessarily new even in the sixteenth century, but much reinforced during that age.[99]

The exclusion of women did not remain a matter of guild discourse and ideology; it also translated into practice. Females were still apprenticed in large numbers in eighteenth-century England, but the great majority were trained either in husbandry, or in 'housewifery'.[100] Already in the first half of the sixteenth century, two-thirds of female apprentices in Bristol were destined for specifically female occupations, such as seamstress and, again, housewife. Even though their social backgrounds were similar to those of male apprentices, they found it increasingly difficult to establish themselves as independent producers. By 1600 it was all but impossible for women to enter Bristol's incorporated trades.[101] In Germany, commentators in the eighteenth century saw it as self-evident that girls could not be apprenticed, because 'masculine sex is one of the indispensable basic preconditions for admission to a guild'.[102]

In the eyes of the guilds, the exclusion of women from the incorporated trades may have rid them of some serious competition, but at the same time it created new problems. One was that under certain circumstances cheap female labour could also be profitable for the guild masters. According to regulations going back to the mid-sixteenth century, female silk weavers in Lyon could work in the industry alongside their husbands. During the 1730s, when more and more master silk weavers were in danger of losing their independence at the hands of the merchants, they clamoured for a right to allow their wives to go and work in another master's workshop.[103] Another problem resulted from the creation of competition from outside the guilds' own jurisdiction. This was recognised by the London Weavers' Company, which had so emphatically excluded all females, and also foreigners, from its ranks in 1578. In 1630 the guild's bailiffs, wardens and assistants pleaded with the City's aldermen to allow them to admit foreigners again into the guild, because only then would they be able to control the trade in the sprawling metropolis that was seventeenth-century London.[104] For the very same reason, if for no other, the guilds found it impossible to completely suppress female labour.

Guilds' anti-female policies did not prevent women from working in incorporated trades.[105] A survey of guild membership in Gouda showed how in 1788–89 no less than 84 per cent of the members of the large Tailors' Guild were female, while among the much smaller weavers it was still 61 per cent. Another seven guilds, including the locally important Clay-Pipemakers, had at least 10 per cent female members.[106] In some trades women actually acquired more independence after 1600. All-female guilds were not completely unknown before the seventeenth century,[107] but they acquired a new meaning after two centuries of guilds' attempts to force female labour into the framework of the artisanal family. Significantly, the new seamstresses' guilds, established almost simultaneously in Paris and in Rouen in 1675, swiftly developed a new language and social ideal that was diametrically opposed to the patriarchy of the traditional corporations. Whereas the tailors proposed a world view which emphasised family values, and women subject to male authority, the seamstresses underlined the individuality of the members. During the 1776 crisis, when Turgot abolished the guilds, the tailors depicted the future as one of total anarchy, now that both guilds and families were threatened, whereas the seamstresses pictured themselves as individuals who needed a guild of their own to protect them against undesired contacts with men.[108]

Even for women, the guild system could work in opposing directions. In most places and trades it reduced women to second-class citizens or even non-citizens, without rights to exercise their occupation of choice. It is possible, and even likely, that the guilds' negative impact on female economic citizenship became worse, especially during the sixteenth century. However, in selected guilds we see large numbers of female members, even in the eighteenth century. French seamstresses, moreover, were empowered by the establishment of their own guilds.

Governing the Guilds

When the Cloth Merchants of Dordrecht met on 14 January 1784, the day of their patron saint Pontianus, all members had to take their designated seats in the meeting room, state their name, hear the report on the previous year's finances and the board's activities 'concerning the maintenance and protection ... of our rights and privileges', approve the accounts and select the guild officials for the new year. After the meeting, a meal was served in the Militia Hall which would continue until midnight. Members were expressly instructed to behave and not 'insult their fellow members' during the festivities.[109] Such events took place routinely across premodern Europe.

Guilds received their privileges from some higher authority, usually the town council, and were also supervised by that authority, but in many respects they regulated themselves. Guilds had their own sources of income, members selected the guild officials and regular plenary meetings allowed ordinary members a say in the administration of their guild. Guilds could also have jurisdiction over trade conflicts. Because public functions, such as tax collection, local security, political representation and welfare, devolved upon guilds, participation in the guilds' affairs was almost a form of citizenship in its own right.

Although it was compulsory for anyone wanting to work independently in an incorporated trade to join the guild, contemporaries considered joining the guild as essentially a voluntary act. Joining a guild implied that one subjected oneself to the guild's jurisdiction over the trade, as well as the financial contributions demanded from the members.[110] At the same time it implied that masters had a say in the guild's affairs, and might be called upon to serve the guild in a variety of offices. The Bakers' Guild of Paris was governed by six *jurés*, who were assisted by forty members. These were selected by lot; twenty from among those who had acquired the mastership less than ten years before, and the other twenty from among the older members.[111] In Dijon too, the guilds were governed by *jurés*, while guild members met in assemblies. The *jurés*, or deans, were usually recruited from among the better-off members.[112] The same was true for the Tailors' Guild of eighteenth-century Amsterdam.

However, this was not always and everywhere the case. In 's-Hertogenbosch the wealth profile of the membership and administrators of the Tailors' and the Haberdashers' Guilds (whose memberships partially overlapped) was almost identical. The reason for this was a much greater participation of their membership in the guilds' administration. Whereas in the latter city 288 mandates were shared by ninety-seven individuals (1760–75), the Amsterdam Tailors filled 300 mandates with only thirty-five individuals (1734–94), even though the

Amsterdam guild was at least three times larger than the two combined guilds in 's-Hertogenbosch. One of the reasons for the difference was, no doubt, that in Amsterdam the board was self-selective, while in 's-Hertogenbosch the administrators were elected in a plenary meeting by the guild's membership.[113] In Ghent, the Tailors' Guild reduced the number of offices after the sixteenth century, but the number of individuals participating in the guild's administration declined even more, so that the average administrator held about four mandates across his career. The same was true in eighteenth-century Brussels, where the Tailors' Guild administrators on average held five mandates.[114] In Elizabethan London, some guilds were dominated by wealthy merchants, but others, like the Coopers or Plasterers, counted many ordinary artisans among their officials.[115]

The all-female guild of the New Drapers of Linen Clothes (*lingères en neuf*) in Rouen selected their officials in a general meeting on the Friday after Christmas. According to a (male) witness these meetings were enlivened by a 'plurality of voices [and] storms of debate'.[116] During the sixteenth century, many London companies met every quarter for a meal, at one of which they elected their officers.[117] Sometimes these elections were indirect, as for example in the Cloth-Makers' Guild of Cologne, where from 1397 twenty-nine delegates elected the deans.[118] There was a worry that such guild meetings might turn political. In many German towns, a representative of the local authorities had to be present at, or at least informed about, the meetings and the discussions that had taken place there.[119]

Guilds had their own financial resources. In the mid-eighteenth century, the Bakers and Brewers' Guild of Arnhem owned two properties that were rented out, plus claims on two public institutions and four individuals worth a substantial 1,750 guilders. It maintained one widow with a regular allowance, but also spent five times ten guilders on distributions to the general poor of Arnhem. When the accounts had been read to the assembled membership, more money was spent on food and drink.[120] In France, guild finances were not only the concern of the guilds themselves, but also mattered a great deal to the government. French public finances used corporations of all sorts, including guilds, as means of levering taxation or raising loans, or even for what amounted to financial extortion. The worst example of the latter came in 1776, when the guilds were first abolished, but then on second thought allowed to buy back their privileges against the payment of a substantial amount of money.[121] In fact, by 1776 this policy had acquired a long pedigree: the French government had for this purpose developed a strong interest in the health of guild finances. The guilds themselves in turn had to worry about their indebtedness, and were forced to introduce substantial fee increases to take care of these.[122] The same was true in many towns of the Southern Netherlands, where guilds were not merely economic, but also political organisations and felt compelled to underline their political prestige with lavish buildings. Perhaps the most famous example is Brussels, where guilds built expensive premises on the Grand Place, facing the town hall. Unfortunately, the square was destroyed in 1695 by a French bombardment – forcing the guilds into the further expense of rebuilding. In Brussels and other towns in Brabant and Flanders fees were increased substantially, both for insiders and outsiders, to help cover such costs.[123]

The guilds used a governance model that was also applied outside the world of the merchants and crafts. Actually, the word 'guild' also applied beyond the economic domain, in the worlds of charities, religious confraternities and civic militias, to name but a few. All these organisations usually had financial autonomy, elected officials and general meetings of the members. They used the vocabulary of 'brothers and sisters' when referring to the membership, thus constituting themselves as 'artificial families'.[124] Guilds were in many ways the miniature versions of the urban community; ideally, and quite often in reality, their governance model reflected the prescriptions of 'urban republicanism': open recruitment of the governors, rotation of officers, democratic influence of the membership and transparency of the organisation's finances.[125]

Guilds and the Civic Community

Members of merchant and craft guilds shared a common occupational background. Nonetheless, guilds did much more than regulate the economy or lobby for the members' economic interests. They were made responsible for fire service, tax collections or jury duties.[126] Four areas where guilds as organisations made a particularly significant contribution to the community were politics, security, religion and welfare. Perhaps with the exception of religion before the Reformation, they were not uniformly active in these areas: in some towns guilds were involved in local government, in others they were not; some guilds doubled as civic militias, others did not; only a minority of guilds provided formalised welfare schemes for their members. Still, guilds generally claimed, with some justification, that they were a mainstay of the urban community and hence of citizenship.[127] In all these areas guilds therefore provided a framework for practical citizenship. We have already discussed guilds and politics in the previous chapter, and there is more on guilds and welfare and on guilds and civic militias in the next two, so these topics can be dealt with relatively briefly here.

Guilds in Politics

The fourteenth century was such a significant turning point for the political involvement of guilds in Northern Europe that some historians have called it the era of 'guild revolutions'.[128] In Flanders, the victory of an artisan army on foot over French mounted aristocrats in the 1302 Battle of the Spurs was the overture heralding a reshuffling of town governments. In Ghent, however, it merely meant a consolidation of a privilege granted in November 1301, giving the all-important Weavers' Guild, together with the deans of fifty-three 'minor' guilds, a direct representation in the local government.[129] In France, these events inspired guilds to make similar demands – but to no avail.[130] In the German lands, guilds did achieve political influence, especially in the southern regions. In Oberschwaben, for example, guild rebellions in the middle of the century led to a 'Zunft lieplichen und freuntlichen úberein komen' in Memmingen – an agreement popular with the guilds. In Lindau, Ravensburg and Überlingen too, new constitutions gave the guilds a commanding voice in local politics.[131]

Inclusion in local constitutions had the unintended consequence of increasing government interest and interference in the guilds' internal affairs.[132] In some towns, moreover, guilds lost their political positions in subsequent centuries. On the continent, Charles V was particularly active in suppressing guild participation in politics during the first half of the sixteenth century.[133] Nevertheless, in London and Cologne, to name two major towns, guild constitutions remained in place until the end of the Old Regime. As we saw in Chapter 2, the number of towns with popular representation declined during the early modern period, but not dramatically, and as cities with guild regimes, London and Cologne were still joined by many other minor and major towns and cities.

Guilds as Defence Associations

The citizens of fourteenth-century Basel were divided into fifteen guilds or companies of very unequal size, which took care of the night watch and defence against outside attack.[134] Only the elite guilds were also required to participate in campaigns beyond the city. Participation in Basel's defence was one of three duties assumed by any Basel citizen when swearing the citizen's oath; the other two were loyalty to the magistrate and paying taxes. During wartime, immigrants willing to participate in military services could even acquire citizenship for free.[135] In Osnabrück, everyone protected by the town's defences was required to lend a hand: mere inhabitants were called up for duty alongside the members of the guilds. All guild members were, however, supposed to have their own weapon. During the sixteenth century, recruitment temporarily shifted to a neighbourhood model, but under the threat of war the more familiar guild recruitment returned. Each company marched under its own guild banner.[136]

Especially in towns where guilds were also directly involved in local governance, they became the basis of the defence organisation. This happened in many towns and cities of the Holy Roman Empire. One problem was the uneven size of guilds, ranging from a handful to sometimes hundreds of members. In Cologne it was therefore decided that only the seventeen largest guilds would constitute their own companies, while the others were assembled in five combined *Gaffel*.[137] In the sixteenth century this problem of unequal size, or perhaps simply Charles V's policy of reducing the guilds' political impact, also led to a reduction of the military role of guilds in many towns. Instead, recruitment became territorialised. This process may have been reinforced by the rise of professional soldiering, a process that accelerated precisely during the sixteenth century. In general, it would therefore seem that guilds in the early modern period lost much of their military significance.

Guilds and Religion

Invariably, guilds had patron saints. The metalworkers worshipped St Eloy; the shoemakers venerated St Crispin, while St Luke was the role model for the painters and other artists. The Haarlem Guild of St Luke had been the proud owner of a piece of the saint's skeleton which, since Protestantism was about to take over in the province of Holland, they handed over to a priest from the Southern Netherlands during the Dutch Revolt. After the religious dust had settled, the guild went to considerable lengths to repossess its relic, despite the fact that Haarlem had officially become a Protestant town, only to find that the relic had been split into tiny pieces. The guild managed to locate one bit of its former prize possession and brought it back to Haarlem, where it was safely stored together with the guild's charters and accounts and inspected annually. Haarlem's Guild of St Luke had Catholic as well as Reformed members, but it would appear that the latter were just as satisfied as the former with the return of their relic.[138] We see the same pattern in 's-Hertogenbosch, a nominally Protestant town where three-quarters of the population were nonetheless Catholic. On the patron saint's day, members of a guild would go to their own church before commencing the common celebrations.[139]

Craft organisation and religion had been closely related from the very start. In Venice, many guilds emerged out of religious brotherhoods, rather than vice versa.[140] We find the same in medieval England, France, Germany and the Low Countries.[141] In many places the brotherhood and guild would ultimately merge, but sometimes they continued to exist side by side. Whatever the case, in Catholic Europe artisans in the same trade would worship at an altar they themselves had helped to decorate, usually displaying a picture of their patron saint, and where they paid for the masses read at what they considered as their own altar.[142] The Reformation, averse as it was to saints and colourful church decorations, suppressed many of these practices, and in the Dutch Republic forced the guilds to shift their spending from religious to charitable causes. Religion nonetheless remained a feature of guild life in Protestant regions. In Catholic areas, the Counter-Reformation may even have resulted in an intensification of religious elements in guild expenditures.[143]

The Reformation forced organisations like the guilds to take sides, accommodate different views or break up. There are very few examples of the latter, but the other two alternatives are seen even within the same territory. In sixteenth-century Augsburg, the Weavers' Guild saw the Reformation as an opportunity to reinforce communal policies, which they hoped would restrain capitalist entrepreneurs from dominating the textile industry. The local butchers, on the other hand, who were doing business in a wide area beyond the town's perimeter, preferred the relaxed attitudes of the Roman Catholic authorities.[144] In Dijon Protestantism was also popular among artisans, who formed the backbone of the opposition to the Catholic town council, and inevitably the guilds were affected by the conflict. However, very few Dijon guilds committed themselves to one side or other; instead, they dealt with opposed views within their own ranks. In fact, religious affiliations seem to have been determined by personal networks that were in turn determined by a combination of work and neighbourhood solidarities.[145]

The role of religion in the corporate world changed as a result of the Reformation. However, this did not terminate the ancient connection between guilds and religion. Guilds' identities continued to be shaped by religious symbols and rites, in Protestant as well as Catholic towns.

Guilds and Welfare

When the Dutch National Assembly, the parliament created after the French invasion and parallel revolution in the Netherlands, first met in 1796, the future of the guilds was one of the important items on the agenda. Critics of the guilds berated their negative impact on the economy. Among the guilds' most prominent and vocal supporters, however, were the governors of the city of Amsterdam and they had every reason to be concerned about the consequences of the guilds' disappearance. According to a modern study, 22 per cent of Amsterdam households were covered by some sort of guild insurance, while in Utrecht and Leiden the figure was twice that.[146]

Guilds in many places maintained a range of schemes to assist members in times of adversity.[147] In sixteenth-century London, wealthy guild members left some of their estate to be distributed among the less fortunate. Robert Dowe was a successful tailor who also served as dean of his guild. Over his lifetime, Dowe donated some £3,500 for this purpose. In 1589, for example, he gave £400 to purchase some real estate in the vicinity of the Merchant Taylor's Hall. The rents of those properties were 'for the relief of the decayed state of the poor handicraft of tailory'. Six members would be provided with an annual pension of £4.[148] Such charitable activities had a long history; a survey in the late fourteenth century already established that London guilds spent substantial amounts on charitable causes.[149] In York, the Carpenters' Guild ordinance from 1482 stipulated 'that if any of the said fraternity fall to poverty, so that they may not work, ... then the foresaid brotherhood [will] give them 4d every week, as long as they live, by way of alms'.[150] In seventeenth-century Ghent the bakers, carpenters, brewers, stonemasons, skippers and mattress-cover weavers all provided weekly payments to poor members of their guilds. The Tailors in Ghent owned six houses whose rents went to six poor guild masters.[151] In Naples the Gild-Spinners' Guild set up a charitable endowment of 16,000 ducats in 1632. The local Gold-Beaters' Guild had created a similar fund in 1627 to provide assistance to members incapacitated through illness or old age. The same guild also helped to settle debts and provided marriage dowries for the eldest daughters of impoverished members.[152] In Seville, Strasbourg, Paris, Lille, Antwerp, Brussels, Mechelen (Malines), Augsburg and no doubt many more towns guilds maintained special buildings for members who were too old to work or otherwise incapacitated.[153]

The hospital of the Utrecht Metalworkers' Guild is first recorded in a document from the mid-fifteenth century: in 1450 permission was given to expand the premises. In the sixteenth century Saint Eligius (Eloy) Hospital was home to eight men and women, but by 1798 their number had shrunk to three due to budget reductions.[154] A guild hospital was highly unusual in the northern Netherlands, however. Also unusual, though slightly less so, was the possibility to be buried in a guild grave, together with one's colleagues. Eleven Utrecht guilds owned such a common grave, where the burial was free of charge. These guilds also had a special fund to help members cover the additional costs of burying the dead; both the master and his wife were covered by most of these funds. Eight more Utrecht guilds had such a fund but no grave. Of these nineteen funds, twelve were set up in the seventeenth century. Thanks to a major endowment from one of its members, the Guild of St Eloy was also able to support twenty masters with a weekly allowance of some bread and a very small amount of money, handed out after the service in the church close to the guild's hospital.[155]

The examples presented in this section – and more can be found in Chapters 4 and 5 – demonstrate how guilds were much more than professional organisations looking after their members' economic interests.

Conclusion

Membership of guilds implied, often formally but otherwise informally, membership of the wider urban community. In London and other English towns, citizenship was accessed through the guilds. In most continental towns it was the other way around: to join the guild, one first had to become a citizen. Whatever the order, guild membership implied joining a club that provided exclusive access to specific markets. In the case of Thomas Gent, whose story launched this chapter, that exclusivity was very clear: the London Stationers controlled much of the English book trade, confirming suspicions by contemporaries as well as later historians. In this chapter we have found these suspicions to be correct but incomplete. Joining this guild was not always as difficult as was often assumed. Rather than rejecting this Irish outsider, Gent's master had welcomed him into his house, 'though you came [as] an almost stranger to me', and continued to support Gent in subsequent years.[156]

Among the various aspects of premodern citizenship discussed in this book, guilds are the best documented and also the most investigated by historians. Although the guilds were abolished in much of continental Europe after the French Revolution, their legacy persists.[157] In the City of London the livery companies still are a major force; the City's town hall is still called the Guildhall. On the continent, reformers of the nineteenth and twentieth centuries had their eyes firmly on the guilds as one possible model to combat major shortcomings of modern society, and their legacy has shaped social relations in many countries.[158] The activities of employers' organisations in many modern European countries look strikingly similar to those of the guilds and even though membership is not compulsory, they often organise 90 per cent or more of the firms in their line of trade.[159] Like the guilds, these employers' organisations can be portrayed as rent-seekers, lobbying for their members' interests, but also as the producers of public goods, for example through their training programmes.

Caught between these two interpretations – pillars of society versus naked pursuit of sectional interests – what can we say about guilds from the perspective of citizenship? Philosophically, perhaps, that it would have been really surprising if organisations like guilds had not displayed these two faces. How could individuals have been persuaded in such vast numbers to join guilds, if there had been nothing in it for them? And similarly, why would the authorities have condoned such organisations on a massive scale, if they had been merely serving the private interests of their members? Advanced industrial societies all have labour unions and employers' organisations; markets with only unconstrained individual agents may exist in economics textbooks, but not in the real world. Therefore, the question must not be 'what', but 'how': how was a balance struck between these two dimensions of the guild organisations?[160]

Guilds were governed by rules that gave them legal identity and thus allowed them to act as a party in political and legal disputes. Their rules were monitored and enforced by making membership of the guild compulsory. This was the point of the 'monopoly'. It was not a monopoly at all in the way most economists define the term. Too often, the impression is given that guilds were somehow comparable to a modern firm; they were not.[161] Guilds were associations of independent producers who subjected themselves to certain rules. Sometimes those rules included the setting of prices and wages, but more often those were imposed by the authorities, as in the case of bread.[162] Most branches of trade and industry had no fixed prices or wages. The 'monopoly' could also be used, or abused, to restrict access to the trade. The discussion in the third and fourth sections of this chapter has touched on examples where this was indeed the case. Women and religious minorities were two broad categories significantly underrepresented or even absent among the membership of individual guilds. Indeed, the groups most vulnerable to guild discrimination were usually the same groups that were discriminated against in other domains of public life. Guilds were reproducing more general mechanisms of social discrimination – and in some cases making them worse.

At the same time, this chapter has presented data showing that some guilds were open to women, and more generally how in a range of cities all over Europe guilds organised a substantial percentage of urban households and were open to outsiders. Again, in the light of these data the term 'monopoly' is misleading. Indirectly, the guild system also covered many journeymen employed by the guild masters. Their agency was much restricted, because they were excluded from full membership of the guild. Journeymen nonetheless participated in many of the activities undertaken by the guild, such as religious rites or fire services. In many towns journeymen had their own organisations to protect journeymen's rights and interests and negotiate with the masters of the guild.[163]

Guilds provided a range of services, to their own members as well as to the wider urban community of which they considered themselves an integral part. It was unusual for a guild to encompass all these services; most of them combined a selection, including religious services and welfare provisions for the members, usually at their own expense. They could also include fire service, maintenance of public spaces and public order, local defence, tax collection and participation in political institutions: in other words, services which addressed both the immediate interests of the guild members and those of the community more generally.

Perhaps most importantly, guilds provided the framework for the training of the great majority of the skilled workforce. Clearly, training the next generation of artisans was primarily in the interest of the guild masters themselves. These were the people who would assist them in their workshops and ultimately take over. At the same time, vocational training benefitted society in general. The relatively low level of the European skill premium suggests that training was inclusive rather than exclusive. If we accept the argument of many economists that human capital is one of the most important stimulants of economic growth,[164] the training provided by guild masters and certified by guilds had consequences beneficial to society as a whole.

Those consequences were, however, not automatic, or even self-evident. Ogilvie would seem to be correct in her observation that in places where guilds were free to set their own conditions unopposed, they tended to create closed shops. The Wildberg district in German Württemberg, where she undertook detailed research, was clearly one such area.[165] However, the data presented here for a wide range of towns suggest that the absence of countervailing powers was exceptional, not the rule. In most towns, the local authorities prevented guilds from introducing such policies. All of this seems to confirm Epstein's claim that the 'key to the different performance by craft guilds in different European countries lies in the institutional and political frameworks in which they were embedded'.[166] Guilds themselves contributed to those frameworks, by giving ordinary craftsmen a form of economic – as well as political, social and religious – agency, which they would have found difficult to achieve single-handedly. Their collective action served the interests of the membership as well as those of the wider community. In this sense, guilds were a core feature of urban citizenship.

4 WELFARE AND THE CIVIC COMMUNITY

One of the most prominent confraternities of medieval Europe was Orsanmichele in Florence, whose first rules date from 1294. By 1325 it had some 2,000–3,000 members. Orsanmichele was one of a large number of confraternities that emerged in Florence at the time. By the middle of the fifteenth century the city boasted an impressive ninety, about half of which were purely religious; their members were flagellants who flogged themselves to atone for their sins. All confraternities had some sort of religious purpose, even the four that were mainly charitable. Orsanmichele was the largest of these four, taking its name from the Piazza Orsanmichele, the main market for grains, where a statue of the Madonna attracted one of the most important cults of late medieval Florence. In 1336 a new shrine was built for worshippers and in 1348 the confraternity inherited a considerable fortune of 350,000 gold florins. During the 1320s about 85 per cent of the confraternity's revenues, amounting to the equivalent of almost 34,000 daily wages, was spent on the poor. Some of the poor receiving support were living in the countryside controlled by Florence, but the majority were 'respectable poor' from the city itself, including members of the confraternity.[1]

Orsanmichele is a somewhat surprising variant of the thesis outlined by economic historian Peter Lindert, who claims that welfare is essentially a 'free lunch'.[2] That thesis, developed with the help of much more recent data, starts from the observation that, generally speaking, the countries with the highest per capita welfare expenditures also happen to be the richest countries. In the late eighteenth century, the most generous countries in terms of welfare expenditure were the Netherlands and Great Britain, also the two wealthiest European nations at the time. Amid constant fears of the poor taking a holiday at the expense of the taxpayer, the fact of the matter seems to be that welfare expenditure in the long run does not hamper economic growth, because its cost is offset by productivity gains.

Although Lindert's data were not available to early modern urban politicians, it is just possible that they had an intuitive understanding of these mechanisms. We catch a glimpse of this in seventeenth-century Amsterdam when it was the only town in Holland to refuse to introduce identity papers for paupers that would allow the authorities to send them back to the place from which they hailed. The Amsterdam authorities worried at times about the potential abuse of their relatively generous welfare system, but in the eyes of the Amsterdam elites the benefits of poor immigrants outweighed their cost.[3] Obviously, they justified their actions with a very different set of arguments, usually inspired by religion, or otherwise by references to the 'common good', but in 1826 they actually said in so many words that 'real harm would ... be caused' if charity were to be withheld from the local poor, or if these were deported to rural colonies for the poor, as the national government proposed at the time. A city like Amsterdam inevitably suffered from seasonal fluctuations in employment and had to look after its workers in the slack season, according to the local authorities. 'Suppose many of [the poor] left the city and settled elsewhere, what effect would this have on the city and on society?'[4]

Even if urban welfare systems underwent periods of serious tension, they proved remarkably robust over time. The reason for this has been suggested by Marco van Leeuwen.[5] He argued that social welfare is not a one-way system of the rich supporting the poor. Rather, Van Leeuwen proposed, it is part of a set of relationships in which the two classes trade favours. The propertied classes worry, for example, about public order, and welfare is one way of 'buying' the compliance of the poor. Or stated in a more positive way: poor relief helps create a sense of community.[6] Moreover, the pre-modern economy was subject to seasonal patterns and the poor were a significant part of the workforce. To encourage the poor to stay around until the following spring, when the demand for their labour would pick up again, welfare was on offer to help them through the off-season.

If only out of self-interest, urban elites were committed to helping the poor. However, this was made much easier if they could encourage the poor to help themselves, as in the Orsanmichele confraternity. And to a remarkable extent they actually succeeded. An important reason was that 'the poor' were not a separate class in society; many middle-class households had to brace themselves for hard times as well. They had a key role in the developing and sustaining of the welfare system. Social citizenship, in other words, was a key to the maintenance of welfare systems of premodern urban societies. And at the same time, welfare systems created communal bonds that reinforced civic relations.

Welfare Institutions

In the spring of 1788, the city of Hamburg, an important trading hub with some 90,000 inhabitants, introduced a general reform of its welfare institutions by creating a single organisation to look after the impoverished inhabitants. The *Allgemeine Armenanstalt*, or General Poor Relief, would be led by a council that included five members recruited from the ranks of the town council, as well as two representatives of the citizens of Hamburg. The composition of the Relief council was clearly designed to connect welfare to both the political elite and the rate-paying public. The city was divided into five *Armen Bezirke*, or welfare districts, each with two directors. The districts were subdivided into twelve quarters, each with three relief officers, giving the city a total of 180 relief officers, also recruited from among the citizens. They were given the important task to look after the 3,903 poor households registered the previous year in a comprehensive survey of poverty in Hamburg, undertaken by the officers of the civic militias.[7]

This was not the first time that the Hamburg welfare system had been overhauled. A first centralisation had been introduced in the mid-sixteenth century, and subsequently a range of new institutions had been set up during the seventeenth century. In the 1720s the city had tried to reduce the number of beggars and force the poor to accept compulsory work in the textile industry. Nor was this latest attempt at reform out of tune with the rest of the country; similar reforms were introduced all over the German lands at the time: in Berlin in 1774, Lüneburg in 1776, Bremen in 1779, Augsburg in 1782–83, Lübeck in 1784, Hanover in 1785 and, finally, Mainz in 1786. In fact, Hamburg was rather late in joining the ranks of the reformers.

What was unusual was Hamburg's General Poor Relief evaluating its own performance after a decade. In 1799 the Relief council wrote a report on what had been achieved, in which the pre-1788 situation was sketched in bleak terms. Beggars had been a plague on the streets of Hamburg, abusing the citizens' charity at the expense of the 'deserving poor'; destitute children had roamed those same streets, dirty and idle, making mischief. And most importantly no doubt: the poor lacked any incentives to go out and look for work. This the Relief had managed to change, it was claimed. Begging, but also handing out alms, had been strictly prohibited. The poor were visited by the Relief officers on a weekly basis in their own homes. The Relief had set up spinning courses to train the poor, and also several schools to educate pauper children. The number of paupers on benefits had declined by 40 per cent.

While the reform of 1788 appeared at first sight to be a success, major problems were lurking in the background. Children who should have been in school were actually absent on a massive scale. The volume of flax spun by people on benefits was too much for the local industry to handle, and moreover of a poor quality. Productivity was falling, and the wages poor people were receiving for their efforts, inevitably below market rates, were simply not enough to survive on – even if they worked from 4:00 AM till 8:00 PM, and even if the Relief subsidised their rent, clothing and fuel. Worse was to come. Shortly after the report was completed, Hamburg was hit by an unusually severe winter, the overture to several years of economic hardship; then in 1806 the city was occupied by French troops. The General Poor Relief found it impossible to cope with this series of problems.[8] All of this showed, once again, that there was no golden rule for dealing with the issue of poverty. Nevertheless, municipal governments would have to deal with it, one way or another. Many different institutional solutions were combined in the hope of at least keeping poverty manageable.

Our story must start, however, long before the Hamburg welfare reforms of the 1780s. Insofar as cities of the Roman Empire had their institutions for dealing with the various calamities that life dishes out, it is unclear how many of those survived the collapse of the Western Empire, not least because the sources are so thin on the ground.[9] There are indications of the existence of hospitals in several French towns of the sixth century: Arles, for example, where one was established by local bishop St Césaire (503–43), but also Clermont, Le Mans, Rouen,

Amiens, Reims and Metz – all episcopal sees. More hospitals were created during the Carolingian era (eighth–ninth centuries): Orléans, Nevers, Paris, but also in Rome (close to the Parthenon), in Cologne (866) and in Eichstätt (c. 900). Still more were established in German Europe during the tenth century: Augsburg, Bremen and Aix-la-Chapelle (Aachen). In Barcelona one hospital is mentioned from this same century, in England no references have been found before the Norman Conquest (1066).[10]

From the twelfth century, and accelerating during the thirteenth and fourteenth centuries, a 'revolution in charity' – the phrase was coined by André Vauchez – swept across Europe.[11] We can follow this process in detail in Toulouse, thanks to an inventory of the local hospitals dating from 1246, when the city had some 25,000–30,000 inhabitants. By the middle of the thirteenth century, Toulouse had twenty-six different hospitals, some located outside the walls. Of these, only five were mentioned for the first time in the 1246 review, and we have no idea if they were recent foundations or had earlier origins. What we do know is that of the remaining twenty-one institutions, one was already mentioned in other sources from the eleventh century; ten more can be reliably dated to the twelfth century. The remaining ten hospitals were mentioned in earlier sources from the thirteenth century.[12]

In England, the much smaller town of Cambridge had a leper hospital that was first mentioned in a document from 1169–72. A second hospital, named after St John the Evangelist, can be found in a document from October 1204. According to later testimony, the latter hospital was built on a 'very poor and empty place belonging to the community of the town of Cambridge'. This charity had been funded by donations from local citizens, but the bishop of nearby Ely was also a major sponsor and soon issues emerged over who was in charge, the town or the bishop. Around 1361 a second leper hospital was built, named after Sts Anthony and Eligius. In the second half of the fifteenth century four almshouses were opened. All these institutions had received the financial and political support of the community of Cambridge and its citizens.[13]

Toulouse and Cambridge were typical examples of the sort of bricks-and-mortar expansion of social welfare that was taking place all over medieval Europe. A data set of English hospitals and almshouses shows that at least 1,000 were active between 1350 and 1599, while another 242 are identified as active before 1350 but ceased to operate by the middle of the fourteenth century. Although these numbers include rural as well as urban establishments, the latter were overrepresented because market towns had the resources for, and an interest in, providing such public services.[14] The towns of both England and the continent became sprinkled with small – and sometimes also larger – buildings where people in need could find support and shelter. Simultaneously, two other developments were taking place. Towns instituted arrangements for the poor who continued to live in their own accommodation. Secondly, urbanites set up organisations for mutual support. Germanic Europe, including the British Isles, had a greater fondness for the first approach to poor relief, while the second proved more popular in Latin Europe.

In the medieval towns and cities of Flanders, Brabant and Holland, the most important institutions providing poor relief were the *Heilige Geesttafels*, or Tables of the Holy Spirit. These were often literally tables, situated in the back of the parish church, where bread and other forms of support would be handed out.[15] Although they were technically Church institutions, the Tables increasingly came under municipal control.[16] In 's-Hertogenbosch, as in other Brabant towns, the Table had been set up in the local cathedral – in this case in the mid-thirteenth century – to hand out food to the poor. It would continue to do so, although no longer from the church building after the Reformation, until the early nineteenth century. Almost from the beginning, the local secular authorities had an important say in the administration of the Table in 's-Hertogenbosch, and this was explicitly confirmed in a privilege from 1458.[17]

In Lyon the usual plethora of small and medium-sized institutions was supplemented, as of 1534, by an *Aumône générale*, or General Poor Relief, also called *Charité de Lyon*. This institution was the permanent successor to a temporary provision created in 1531 to deal with the acute crisis that had emerged from a confluence of famine, plague and migration from the countryside which threatened to overwhelm the city's existing charitable infrastructure. It was modelled on a similar organisation in Paris. The underlying idea was that the 'deserving poor' who would normally be able to work would be supported in their own homes, once their entitlements had been established. Orphans would be referred to the orphanages and the sick to the Hôtel-Dieu Hospital, while alien paupers were to be removed from the city altogether. It was funded through tax exemptions granted by the king, as well as the revenues from the meat excise. The main form of support was the distribution of bread. Some poor households would also receive small amounts of money to supplement the family budget.[18]

In 1614 in the city of Münster, an episcopal see with a population of 10,000–11,000, around 400 poor received a weekly distribution of bread from the municipality. During the Middle Ages poor relief in Münster had been the responsibility of the (Catholic) Church and the civic community together. However, the town council oversaw both, and almost inevitably civic charity began to overshadow that of the Church. National legislation from 1530 and 1580 laid the foundation for local poor relief, by ordering '*dass eine jede Stadt und Commun ihre Armen selbst ernehren unde unterhalten*' – 'every town and village shall feed and look after its own poor'. In 1585 this was formalised in a by-law that covered the whole range of local provisions. Initially, the regulations left the existing institutions intact, but another by-law, from 1616, promised the citizens '*guten Ordinanz*' (proper policing) of the poor, by making the system more discriminating. Hence, support would only be available to the '*waren bedürftigen Armen*', the genuine poor, while begging was to be suppressed. Still, Church and town would continue to operate side by side in the provisioning of welfare. The system would be funded through voluntary contributions, but the results were disappointing, so begging was permitted again in 1618, and in 1624 the attempt at centralisation was entirely abandoned. Instead, the council decided to create a workhouse, the first of which was set up in 1645 in the orphanage to instil a proper work ethos in the orphans. More changes were made to the organisation of local poor relief in Münster, but the next radical attempt at centralisation had to wait until the revolutionary decades around 1800.[19]

Centralisation had already been introduced in Exeter in the sixteenth century. In April 1560 an 'Order for the Poore' was entered into the Corporate Act Book. The Order consolidated earlier legislation from 1536 and 1552. 'Distributors' were appointed under the Order with the responsibility of collecting contributions from the inhabitants and distributing the revenues. The beneficiaries were registered in the Book of Distribution. A special Accounts of the Poor was to keep track of the finances. In 1565, 177 paupers received regular support; two years later their number had decreased to 130. On top of their weekly contributions, 350–500 individuals made extra donations to the poor in 1564–65.[20] A fair number of Exeter citizens were thus involved in sixteenth-century welfare, either as donors or as recipients of benefits.

During the first half of the sixteenth century a wave of initiatives to reform the organisation of charity swept across Europe. In the two decades between 1522 and 1545 alone, at least sixty towns are known to have implemented such reforms.[21] In almost all of them, attempts were made to discriminate more effectively between the 'deserving poor' and those who, by implication, were not deserving of charity. Begging was restricted everywhere. The authorities also attempted to regulate and control the activities of local charities more effectively, if possible by combining foundations into larger organisations. The timing of these reforms suggests some connection with the Reformation, but this is unlikely for two reasons: firstly, reforms were introduced in both Catholic and Protestant regions; secondly, similar reforms had already been introduced long before the Reformation.[22] In some areas, such as Northern Europe, the Reformation clearly had an impact, but it would be wrong to see it as the only reason for the reform of charity.[23] Alternative explanations refer to the rise of capitalism and the attendant emergence of a proletarian class. This was certainly a phenomenon of the late Middle Ages, but it is less clear why precisely the first half of the sixteenth century should have been the turning point in this process.[24] With reforms continuing in the second half of the century and later, two other factors seem to have been equally important. Urban authorities were all the time concerned with the potentially explosive rise in the cost of poor relief. Given the size of the problem, as well as the unpredictability of the seasons and economic fluctuations – premodern economies had no proper 'business cycle' – there was a constant need to be vigilant about the financial implications. At the same time, this was an area where local authorities could demonstrate their competence.[25] While dreading the costs of charity, local elites were also proud of their charitable achievements and built poorhouses 'like palaces'.[26] Towns were copying each other's innovations regardless of region or religion.

In several European countries the related ambitions to control the poor themselves as well as the costs of their maintenance led to a movement that has been labelled in France the '*grand renfermement*', or the great confinement.[27] In Lyon the policy was introduced in 1614, following the example of Paris. Instead of living in their own dwellings, the poor were to be moved to existing hospital buildings, later a purpose-built environment, where they would be permanently supervised by a professional staff. Municipal authorities were driving this policy, but they were encouraged by the national government and supported by national legislation.[28] The workhouse was the English equivalent of this 'great lock-up'. It was a Dutch invention from the late sixteenth century and was quickly copied around the North Sea.[29] In England the workhouse became very popular in the years around 1700 when, besides the City of London, fourteen towns received a parliamentary licence to set up such institutions which, in combination with a stricter control over parish relief, were supposed to 'win [the poor] into civility and love of their labour'.[30]

Whereas the Mediterranean countries merely expected the institutions to control the poor, the English and Dutch also hoped to make paupers' efforts profitable, or at least sufficient to cover their expenses. It was, however, an expectation that never came to fruition[31] and for precisely this reason the 'great lock up' remained quite limited in terms of the numbers of people directly affected. It was a hugely expensive form of poor relief.

Next to workhouses and transfers of money, food and clothes, mutual support constituted a third strand of poor relief in premodern European towns. As early as 852 the Synod of Reims proclaimed rules designed to curb excesses by confraternities. The implication is that such associations already existed, and in sufficient numbers to merit the precious time of the Church dignitaries present at the synod. Nonetheless, we have little detail about those early confraternities: a date, the name of their patron saint – that is about it. For Spain, some scattered references suggest that confraternities existed in the Peninsula during the Frankish period. In Catalonia one has been identified dating from 986, but a serious increase in numbers only occurred in the eleventh century. In France one of the first confraternities was set up in Poitiers in 1109, but more were found in the south than in the north of France. In the Low Countries, Brussels was probably the first town to have a confraternity, in 1186. In Germany, confraternities were much less common.[32]

We have already discussed the Florentine confraternity of Orsanmichele. Had this been a Venetian organisation, it would have been called a *scuola grande*. There were five such *scuole* in sixteenth-century Venice, and after 1552 six. Next to these, another 100-plus *scuole piccoli* were active.[33] The first *scuole grandi* originated in the thirteenth century. The poor relief they provided went primarily to their own members, who came from all walks of life. In the beginning, all members had a say in the administration of the *scuola*, but by the sixteenth century the right to vote had become increasingly restricted. The small hospitals the *scuole grandi* owned were also only accessible to members. Membership of Venetian *scuole* was initially restricted by official limits; 500–600 was reckoned to be the maximum. By 1544, however, the Scuola di S. Giovanni had already a membership of about 1,000 and by 1576 this had increased to some 1,800, most of whom obviously came from the less affluent classes in society.[34] Although members of the guilds would routinely join the *scuole grandi* and *piccoli*, some guilds had their own *scuola*, collectively known as the *scuole delle arti*. Among these were organisations of the mercers, the glass-sellers and the boatmen. Some of them had only devotional purposes, but at least the potters and the bakers explicitly looked after their impoverished members, while the tailors, painters and silk-throwsters are known to also have had their own hospital.[35]

It is generally assumed that confraternities were less common in Northern Europe and generally appeared there later. In Emden, in northern Germany, the first were set up only in the fifteenth century; by 1500 there were perhaps ten of them. These confraternities supported both their own members and the general poor. The Confraternity of Our Lady established a hospital for the poor in 1523. The Emden craft guilds did the same; technically they were also confraternities. In 1545 they were ordered to refrain from donations to the Churches and to concentrate their charitable work on poor relief. The Reformation did not cause the confraternities to disappear in Emden, at least not immediately, but the increased activities of the guilds did encourage a shift of pious donations towards the latter, limiting the scope for confraternities.[36]

Rosser's recent research on confraternities and guilds in medieval England has turned up large numbers of confraternities.[37] On the continent equally impressive numbers have been found: between 1300 and 1580 in Utrecht alone as many as 101 confraternities have been recorded, although not all were simultaneously active. Of these, sixteen also ran a hospital, while eight were connected to one of the craft guilds, which in Utrecht they dominated the town council until 1528. One dated from the twelfth century, ten from the thirteenth and thirty-four from the fifteenth. It has been estimated that every second adult male in Utrecht joined at least one, but often more, confraternities during their lifetime. Members were expected to participate once a week in a mass read in front of the confraternity altar. Indeed, the accounts of three of the Utrecht confraternities from the decades around 1500 show a predominance of religious spending, with poor relief constituting only a very small proportion of the confraternities' expenses. Nonetheless, every Sunday, after mass, the Holy Trinity Confraternity distributed alms in nine different locations, and by 1609 these distributions had become quite substantial.[38] In 1615, when the Utrecht confraternities were dissolved, forty-two were still active, some accepting both Protestants and Catholics among their members, and fifteen of these forty-two confraternities were funding general poor relief.[39] As we saw in Chapter 3, several guilds in Utrecht were also providing poor relief in various forms to their members, including common graves where members and their spouses could be buried if they could not afford a family grave of their own.

The Utrecht data suggest that, even in a city where confraternities were just as numerous as in the towns and cities of Latin Europe, their role in the provisioning of poor relief, both to their own members and to the general poor, was not as important as that of their southern counterparts. Instead, northern towns relied more on communal organisations, regulated and overseen by the municipal authorities. Hospitals were a common feature of urban life everywhere in Europe, with urban authorities and the Church both involved in welfare, but across the centuries a shift is observable from religious to public organisations.[40] Tellingly, the Parisian authorities stated in 1544 that, 'following the Edict of the King, the town must humbly accept the charge of the poor'. In fact, it had accepted that responsibility much earlier, when reforms were introduced in the second half of the fifteenth century.[41] Moreover, accepting this charge did not mean that the Church was completely absolved from the care of the poor; the shift from Church to public welfare remained partial.[42] The main point to take from our survey, however, is that premodern European urban communities always offered formalised support to their inhabitants, and that this support came in a bewildering array of institutional arrangements. Many attempts were made to reduce the complexity of the system, but these efforts were only partially successful.

Who Benefitted?

It would seem self-evident that social welfare was concerned with the 'poor', but who, exactly, were 'the poor'? Take the situation in

Berlin. By 1750 the city had 113,000 inhabitants, of whom 1,384, or one in eighty-two inhabitants, received support from local charities. In 1801 the city had grown by slightly more than 50 per cent to 173,000 inhabitants, but the number of people on benefits had increased almost tenfold, to 12,254. Now one in every fourteen Berliners was receiving benefits.[43] It is, of course, possible that Berlin was going through a stage of massive impoverishment; after all, this was the age of revolutionary warfare, even if Berlin itself would only be occupied by French troops five years later. The point is, however, that it is equally possible that the authorities in 1801 counted every individual on benefits, whereas in 1750 only the heads of households, or that in 1801 the figures included people on long-term benefits as well as those receiving only incidental support, while the latter were not included in the 1750 figures. In Venice, in the mid-seventeenth century, 1,945 people or 1.5 per cent of the population were living in the city's various hospitals for the poor. This was a massive increase over the previous half-century, because in 1593 those same hospitals had been home to only 1,290 people or 1 per cent of the city, and in 1550 the percentage had been a mere 0.5 per cent.[44] Did poverty increase so vastly, or did Venice simply lock up more of its paupers? It is also highly unlikely that this was the whole pauper population of that once prosperous city, now in decline.

These two examples serve to underline the fact that we are not currently in a position to produce consistent, comparable data for pre-modern Europe that would allow us to say that some countries had more paupers than others, or that some eras were worse than others.[45] It is quite possible that the rise of a market economy (or 'capitalism') led to a massive increase of the impoverished class in society, because an increasing share of the population became dependent on wage labour, where contracts were very insecure and wages were low.[46] Certainly, connections between labour markets and welfare reform have been demonstrated on a local level.[47] In a similar vein, the rising rate of urbanisation may well have contributed to larger numbers of poor people, but was this because the poor flocked to the towns, with their more developed welfare systems, or because towns 'made' people poorer?[48] A related explanation is the increasing inequality as it occurred across the sixteenth, seventeenth and eighteenth centuries. The trend is not very strong, and the data are so limited that we cannot draw firm conclusions, but they do suggest that, at least in the economically most dynamic regions (Italy, the Low Countries, England), inequality was rising.[49]

Whatever circumstances made people poor, the figures that we have do not seem to point to a strong increase over time, or larger numbers of poor in the centres of capitalism compared to provincial towns.[50] What we can say is that at any point in time, substantial numbers of poor people were dependent, to a greater or lesser extent, on material and financial support provided by public organisations in their home towns. Rather than concentrating on the overall numbers, however, if we want to get some sense of whom the system was actually reaching, and in what ways, we need to break down those totals into the various subcategories of the population at risk.

In 1573 the priests of Toledo were ordered to draw up lists of the local poor – 'secretly and quietly, so that negotiations and importunities do not occur'.[51] This directive already implies that the definition of poverty was negotiated by those concerned. Given the material benefits implied in inclusion on the list, this is hardly surprising. Poor people also sometimes asked to be removed from the lists, because they refused to accept the conditions imposed by the authorities. As it was, the 'poor' of Toledo in 1573 displayed a specific gender pattern. In all six parishes for which the lists survive, the majority of paupers were female. In fourteenth-century Florence, women were between two-thirds and three-quarters of the paupers supported by Orsanmichele. In the Toledo hospitals, however, the majority of inmates were male, often under twenty-five years of age. These hospitals were primarily taking care of migrants, and that might explain the specific composition of their population.[52]

In 1603 St Martins-in-the-Field, in central London, was home to 2,950 parishioners, of whom 52 were receiving permanent support, while another 123 households were helped intermittently.[53] If we count the individuals, 6 per cent of the parish could be qualified as 'poor', but if their dependants are included the percentage could easily be 20 per cent. This group was described by a contemporary as 'unable to doe anye worke towards their lyving, as old, decrepit persons, creeples and infantes'. The same commentator observed that 'the negligent poore, being otherwise sturdie and able to earne their whole lyving if they were well sett on worke', were barred from charity.[54] In Zwolle, a town of 10,000–13,000 inhabitants in one of the less dynamic regions of the Dutch Republic, on average 248 households were receiving structural benefits during the latter half of the seventeenth century. Because the average pauper household was relatively small, this amounted to 5 per cent of the population. Two-thirds of these households were headed by single women or widows. Of the adult paupers, 44 per cent were over sixty. Of 6,227 individuals found in the various welfare administrations in Zwolle between 1650 and 1700, 987, or 16 per cent, were suffering from health problems, varying from relatively short illnesses to permanent disabilities.[55] During the same period in Delft, a town about twice as large and located in the more dynamic western part of the country, the percentage of permanently supported households was significantly higher, at 10–15 per cent. In 1645 two-thirds of the adult pauper population were females.[56]

There can be little doubt that benefits were pitched in such a way that they discouraged the poor from becoming dependent on welfare, and instead encouraged them to make themselves available for work. The allowance that poor families usually received was simply insufficient to survive on. In 1819, one of Leiden's overseers of the poor acknowledged this in so many words: '[T]he support exists almost always ... as a very sober distribution of money and bread, only meant to meet their needs but hardly sufficient to sustain an animal life'.[57] This was said in a country that, reputedly, had one of the most generous welfare systems in the world at the time. Most poor families in most places therefore had no choice but to go out and find work that gave them additional income, even if they were very young, very old or otherwise disadvantaged. As far as one can tell, all the Leiden poor on benefits in 1750 had a job, the overwhelming majority in the textile industry that dominated the local economy.[58]

In Delft in 1645, the occupations of 569 men and sixty-nine women on benefits demonstrate that these poor people too were expected to work and could not rely on charity alone. At that time, more than half of the males and a full two-thirds of the females worked in industry, with the textile industry again figuring prominently. For males the army was an equally important employer, whilst the female poor in Delft were also frequently employed as domestic servants.[59] Among almost 6,000 beggars arrested in Paris in the eighteenth century we see a very similar pattern. These people may have been temporarily out of work, but the great majority of them could specify either an industrial trade – half the men and 40 per cent of the women – or other occupation as their normal source of income.[60] In Aix-en-Provence unskilled workers without fixed contracts and craftsmen were over-represented among those receiving benefits in the eighteenth century, while servants and – remarkably – soldiers were under-represented.[61] In the second half of the 1780s, almost two-thirds of the poor supported with loaves of bread in Lyon worked in the local textile industry; another 20 per cent were artisans.[62] On the basis of data from Trier, Augsburg and Antwerp spanning the late sixteenth to late eighteenth centuries, Jütte concluded that the 'distribution of occupational groups among poor relief recipients displays in almost "classic" fashion the profile of a pre-industrial urban economy'. In Cologne, he added, 70 per cent of those on relief in 1798 were suffering from illness and old age, the remainder simply from 'low wages'.[63]

These examples highlight varieties in gender, age and employment. In general it seems fair to say that women were more likely to be on benefits than men, due to the combined burden of low pay and their responsibility for taking care of children. Likewise, the very young and the very old were more likely to receive benefits than people in their twenties through to their fifties, who were more competitive on the labour market. Another substantial group of people was on incidental benefits: those for whom seasonal fluctuations and the type of their employment largely determined when they were at risk. In effect, for those in work, poor relief was a supplement to wages that were insufficient to survive on. The profile – women, elderly, physically impaired – also implies that poverty could potentially hit everyone without savings or family support – which meant a considerable part of the artisan population.

Summarising, despite complaints about welfare abuses, people on benefits were usually genuinely poor because they were, for physical or psychiatric reasons, unable to work enough to make ends meet. A second group depended on temporary benefits when they were in dire straits, whether because of the seasonal factor, an epidemic or some other misfortune. There was no separate 'pauper class'; large sections of the urban population were more or less permanently at risk of impoverishment.

Funding Welfare

Welfare was funded from a variety of sources, a mixture of compulsory and voluntary contributions. The situation in the small town of Emden, halfway through the sixteenth century, was probably fairly typical. Traditionally, the Emden population had paid a

Huusdelinge, or household rate, half of which was for the parish and half for the funding of welfare expenditures. While the surrounding county of East Frisia became Lutheran, Emden itself emerged as a northern hotbed of Calvinism. In 1557 Lutheran poor relief was separated from the municipal provisions and made voluntary. The *Becken* or bowl was administered by their own deacons. Emden's municipal administrators of the poor, however, resisted this separation. Meanwhile, Protestant refugees had been moving into Emden across the border from the Low Countries and in 1557 special deacons had to be appointed to take care of these immigrants. In 1562 a lottery was organised to raise extra funds for the local hospital, or *Gasthaus*. The deacons responsible for the refugees also introduced a 'voluntary tax' to fund their increased activities; each 'nation' – Hollanders, Brabanters and so on – was supposed to contribute according to its number.[64] Thus we see the Emden charitable institutions, under pressure of the changes brought along by Reformation and rebellion, experimenting with a range of instruments to deal with the needs that inevitably emerged in the wake of these momentous events.

Most medieval and early modern towns used a combination of public and private funding for their welfare programmes. The two were mainly distinguished by the way these contributions were collected: compulsory versus voluntary, but within those two broad categories a variety of instruments was available to local authorities.[65] In Delft, for example, whenever someone passed away, her or his best piece of clothing was supposed to go to the poor.[66] The classic case of rate-based funding, however, was England, where national legislation concerning the funding of poor relief was introduced in 1536 requiring parishes to hold weekly collections for the poor. London had already introduced such parish collections in 1533, setting an example for the rest of the country. Repeated national legislation in the following decades strongly suggests that what looked like decisive action on paper was not so easily implemented in practice. Only with the Poor Law of 1572, consolidated in 1598 and 1601, was the system set on a secure footing, with the introduction of a compulsory contribution to welfare, collected by the parish. Several towns, including Chester, York and Hull, quickly set up an administration of poor households entitled to benefit from the scheme, but in other places there was opposition to this new type of taxation. It required the crisis of the 1590s, and the threat to public order created by the misery of starving paupers, to win over the sceptics and make the poor rate generally acceptable. By the end of the seventeenth century £40,000 was raised by the poor rate in London alone, 10 per cent of the national proceeds.[67]

The introduction of a poor rate was generally unpopular. In Odense, Denmark in 1632, for example, it was as controversial as it had been in England.[68] In 's-Hertogenbosch, the citizens were therefore fortunate not to require such compulsory contributions, at least not in the seventeenth and eighteenth centuries. Here, the main institutions for poor relief, i.e. the municipal Table of the Holy Spirit and the nine district funds, mainly relied on endowments created in the late Middle Ages. By the early sixteenth century the Table of the Holy Spirit had accumulated more than forty farms, an endowment that it carefully managed and preserved over the coming centuries. The produce from the farms was made into bread in the institution's own bakery and from there passed on to the poor. When poverty increased, per capita support was ruthlessly diminished to protect the investment portfolio.[69]

Although healthy endowments were the result of wise financial management by previous generations of charity administrators, they ultimately originated from voluntary donations to the institutions in the past. The current income of many charities similarly depended on the goodwill of various social groups in local society to donate to the welfare system. Such donations may have been voluntary, but social pressures were at work to nudge people towards charity. In sixteenth-century Lyon, for example, notaries were regularly reminded by the town council of their moral duty to encourage clients to include the poor in their testaments.[70]

The modern literature on charitable giving suggests a number of mechanisms that might have encouraged them to do so. At a very general level, many people are altruistic and sympathise with the plight of others, requiring only to be made aware of need to trigger donations. At the same time, donors see benefits for themselves: charitable giving enhances one's reputation, and many people derive satisfaction from doing 'good'. Such benefaction may also be stimulated by ideological or religious encouragement. Certainly, people today give more easily when solicited for donations, but they also want to know that their gift makes a difference, and that it will be spent on the poor, rather than administration or fancy folders.[71] It is impossible to put some of these mechanisms to the test in past situations, but several of them – such as proximity, solicitation and reputation – are clearly evident in the historical record. The fact that most of this charitable giving occurred within relatively small communities, where the poor were not some anonymous group but real people whom donors met on their own doorstep, would have reinforced the power of these mechanisms.

Charitable giving came in sizes.[72] Most people gave regularly to church collections, for example, where the individual contributions were small, but the totals could add up.[73] In the Dutch town of Sneek (4,000 inhabitants during the seventeenth century) about a third of the money available for poor relief was collected every month in door-to-door collections where people donated in an open plate. The very consistent revenues suggest that the inhabitants of Sneek gave a standard sum on these occasions. In the early eighteenth century, the welfare institutions were nonetheless short of funding, so in 1715 it was decided to hold an extra annual collection, for which the members of the town council would go round in person to encourage generous contributions. Only in 1775 was a poor tax introduced in Sneek.[74] In Amsterdam the reformed deacons also made the rounds on a monthly basis; for the purpose members of the Reformed Church had a special sign of the letter L, for *lidmaat* or member, attached to the front of their house. Such collections funded more than 40 per cent of the Reformed poor relief in Amsterdam.[75]

In Italy, the membership dues for confraternities could be seen as a similar form of small voluntary contributions. Much of it was spent on the membership of the confraternity, but substantial amounts also went to the 'general' poor.[76] Between 1610 and 1630 the London parish of All Hallows Lombard Street collected annually £30–40 in poor rates, but also £17–24 from voluntary contributions. In another London parish, St Bride Fleet Street, collections and donations were regularly higher than the revenues of the poor rate, while in a third London parish, St Dunstan in the West, the rates were higher in some years but fell behind voluntary contributions in others.[77]

The London results comprise more than just collections; they also include a second type of voluntary contributions, i.e. gifts. These were given both during the donor's lifetime, and after she or he had passed away, as a result of a bequest. In late medieval York, Thomas Bracebrigg ordered 1,000 loaves of bread to be distributed among the local poor after his death, while Robert de Holme left 100 marks for cloth for the 'poor pater familias' and another 100*s* for shoes for the poor. Elena, wife of Adam Milys, in 1387 left all her clothes, while

Agnes Hustlott, a dyer's widow, left both clothing and cloth to the poor.[78]

In seventeenth-century Amsterdam at some point one administrator of the Catholic poor reported a gift 'of five hundred guilders, left at his house by a donor who wished to remain anonymous, in a brown envelope with the word "charity" inscribed on it'. Another had received 1,500 guilders – a very substantial amount – that 'had been thrown into his house one evening, without him knowing the source of the money'.[79] Much more common, however, were the gifts that people included in their testaments. In Zwolle, depending on the precise decade, 50–70 per cent of testaments included a – usually small – gift to the poor. This contrasted markedly with Leiden and Utrecht, where only 5–20 per cent of testators included the poor as their benefactors; they gave, however, on average substantially more than their Zwolle counterparts.[80] Still, the Zwolle figures were not completely out of range. In eighteenth-century Aix-en-Provence, some 70 per cent of testaments contained a donation to the poor, and some of those donations could be substantial. In 1744, for example, tailor Jean Louis Dorée left 500 livres for this purpose.[81] Finally, unknown amounts were donated by administrators who were expected to fill gaps in the day-to-day running of the charities entrusted to them. There were regular complaints about this aspect of their responsibilities.[82]

Most voluntary contributions were supplied by ordinary citizens, rather than the elites.[83] Two precious sources from Zwolle demonstrate this. In the mid-1660s the inhabitants of Zwolle were asked to donate to the building of a new orphanage. All households were listed in a large register, and their future donations were subsequently pencilled in. A donation was recorded for 82 per cent of households and for those who declined the invitation a proper excuse was usually provided: they were too poor, or had passed away in the meantime. The Zwolle City Poor Chamber kept meticulous records, not just of the amounts of monthly donations to the citywide collections, but also of the type of coins people donated. It can therefore be established that on average 1.5 coin was donated per household, 61 per cent in pennies, the smallest possible amount, strongly suggesting that these were handed in by the working-class inhabitants. Data from Delft in 1749 demonstrate that the rich districts of that town donated substantially more to charitable causes than the poor – but that the poor districts were donating as well.[84]

This contribution by the poor is easily overlooked, perhaps because the elites did make the most visible contributions – specifically in the form of private foundations, the third and most substantial form of voluntary charity. Late medieval York had about twenty almshouses, set up by individuals during their lifetime. Robert de Holme, prior of York, had one erected in the Monkgate area during the 1350s.[85] Almost every premodern town had several, sometimes dozens, of small hospitals, poorhouses or chambers, created by an individual benefactor, or a couple. Most Dutch towns had their *hofjes*, literally courtyards, and other types of almshouses, named after their generous donors. It would cost 20,000–30,000 guilders to create such an institution. Very often they were set up by people expecting to die without any children to whom they might otherwise have bequeathed their fortune.[86] Their name would instead be preserved for future generations through the foundation they had helped to create. The importance of this personal identification of benefactors was also visible in places where they could not impose their own name on the institution as a whole. The Ospedale di Carità in Turin accepted busts and memorial tablets of its most prominent benefactors, to be displayed in the corridors, refectories, dormitories and courtyards. Not only the poor were reminded of their generosity, but so were the benefactors' peers whenever they visited the hospital.[87]

Supporting the poor gave rise to much soul-searching on the part of the donors. Two principles – still very much underpinning the policies of modern welfare states – underlay all forms of support, but were particularly pronounced where money and goods changed hands. On one hand it was felt that the poor were entitled to alms from their wealthier fellow citizens because they were poor through no fault of their own. Illness, handicaps, the early death of the head of the household, numerous offspring, let alone poor harvests or harsh winters – none of these could be directly blamed on their victims. Poverty, from this point of view, was a question of bad luck. These were the 'deserving' poor. At the same time, donating money, food, clothes and so on might well create the wrong incentives. Lazy profiteers were bound to prefer benefits over work. Were all the poor really in need? In the sixteenth century several popular tracts, most famously one published in Bruges by the Spanish scholar Juan Luis Vives in 1526 under the title *De subventione pauperum*, suggested that generous handouts had created a class of people who preferred to live as beggars. Vives wanted to restrict access to charity to the 'deserving' poor. That in itself was not a novel idea; after all, did anyone propose to give charity to people who did not need it? What Vives really had in mind was what we would now call 'welfare dependence', that is a class of people so accustomed to charity that they were unable to fit into a work rhythm. The importance of his work was not so much in the analysis, but in the remedy he proposed. Vives called upon welfare institutions to exert greater control over their charges. He wanted the civic authorities to investigate and register the poor and establish who among them might be able to work, and who was genuinely incapable. Vives is often charged with promoting the centralisation of poor relief, and given the numerous institutions providing poor relief in any single town of premodern Europe, this might have been a remedy against 'charity shopping'; but in fact he merely proposed that the local government would make sure that the institutions worked properly, that is gave help to those who needed it and helped the others to find jobs.[88]

Still, we have to realise that the 'poor' were, to an important extent, also taking care of themselves. Guild and confraternity charity were funded by, but also for the benefit of, the membership. In Zamora, Spain, with its population of c. 8,600 in the mid-sixteenth century, 150 confraternities of usually thirty to forty members acted as mutual aid groups. Most of them were mixed in social terms.[89] The members in many Italian medieval confraternities were primarily artisans. Figures concerning Perugia and Assisi in the sixteenth century suggest that between a quarter and a third of the adult population may have joined at least one confraternity.[90] As we saw in the previous chapter, around 1800 one in five Amsterdam households was covered by guild insurance, while in Utrecht and Leiden the percentage was perhaps twice as high.[91] In Amsterdam, Utrecht and Leiden, moreover, the journeymen, who were normally excluded from guild welfare, had their own mutual assistance. In Utrecht these were especially numerous: ten are known to have existed at some point during the seventeenth and eighteenth centuries, of which five were still operating in 1812, when together they had 1,500 members.[92]

It has been suggested that voluntary giving was 'crowded out' by compulsory rates, and as a result declined over time. In England this development may have taken place during the seventeenth century, a period of strong increases in welfare spending. The decline was therefore more relative than absolute, as voluntary donations remained significant.[93] However, it is quite possible that the figures capture only a part of the total sums donated, and omit substantial parts.[94] The decrease in voluntary contributions in the Dutch Republic during the eighteenth century may have been due more to the changed fortunes of the Dutch Republic after its golden age came to an end, than to 'crowding out'.[95]

Bas van Bavel and Auke Rijpma have attempted to estimate the overall levels of welfare spending in premodern European societies in relation to the total size of their economies.[96] Their figures are inevitably approximations because the evidence is fragmented. Nonetheless, their figures do suggest some interesting features of welfare spending before the welfare state. First and foremost, no European society spent even 5 per cent of its total wealth on poor relief, a percentage that should be compared with modern levels of 20 per cent and more in the affluent societies of the post-war world. However, we should keep in mind that most Western countries did not do much better in the first half of the twentieth century than the best performers – the Low Countries and England – managed before 1800.[97] After those strong performers, the next group, which included Italy and France, spent between 0.5 and 2 per cent of GDP on poor relief. Central European countries may have done worse, but we have no way of knowing. There are no indications that poor relief in German towns was substantially lower than in Italian or Dutch towns.

Their figures also allow us to make very rough calculations on the contribution of welfare to the total budget of an average poor household in premodern Europe. If we assume that, taken together, the poorest 20 per cent of the population earned 5 per cent of GDP, then it looks as if welfare added half of that percentage to their total earnings in the most generous regions, and perhaps a quarter in the less well-endowed countries. In total, welfare may thus have added between a fifth and a third to the total budget of the poor. This percentage would have been higher for those on permanent relief, and lower for individuals and households who received only temporary benefits.

The scattered data that we have on the funding and spending of poor relief institutions demonstrate that at least the most generous societies spent at levels which remained normal throughout the nineteenth century and even in the run-up to World War II. Much of the money raised for the support of people unable to earn their own livelihood through the labour market came from voluntary donations. Like modern welfare states, premodern authorities were constantly trying to make the system more efficient.[98] For the towns in the Low Countries, three major waves of reforms have been identified: one in the early sixteenth century, discussed earlier; a second in the decades around 1600, when the Dutch Republic emerged as a separate country and the Reformation was introduced, and a third at the end of the eighteenth century, during the revolutionary era.[99] None of these produced a stable result. Expedients like forced labour were repeatedly reintroduced, to be abandoned again after a few years. Forced labour was recommended by Vives in the Habsburg Netherlands in the early sixteenth century and still tried in Hamburg in the late eighteenth. Hamburg, however, was not the only town to discover that forced labour was so inefficient that it very quickly proved unsustainable. There was no simple solution to the problem of poverty, and as long as starving the poor to death was not an acceptable option, communities and their authorities had to set aside money to cope with their destitute fellow creatures.

Conclusions

From the point of view of citizenship, several features stand out in the history of welfare in premodern Europe. Even though, with very few exceptions, nobody had a legal entitlement to poor relief, all urban communities in Europe provided elaborate welfare arrangements on which the poor in those communities could exercise at least a moral claim. There are strong indications that elites were aware of the fact that they themselves had a real stake in providing poor relief: public order, health and labour market concerns were all given as reasons to help the poor. The poor, from their side, could expect some help, if they behaved properly, and if they were willing to work when work was available.[100]

Premodern European towns used a wide range of institutional arrangements to deliver poor relief. We find those institutions existing side by side in most communities. Over the centuries many attempts were made to increase the efficiency of the system, in terms of control over the poor and financial sustainability, through centralisation, and the merging of smaller institutions into larger. It is, however, not at all evident that one solution was markedly better than the rest. As a result, various set-ups continued to exist, with little convergence towards an 'optimal' model.[101]

The middle and upper classes reacted to the plight of the poor by devoting both time and money to poor relief. Under various sorts of pressure, a remarkable amount of the funds for poor relief was raised through voluntary contributions. While the poor were not legally entitled to support, the non-poor could not be legally compelled to contribute. 'Proximity' to the poor, in terms of religious, occupational, neighbourhood or urban community, nonetheless encouraged large numbers of urbanites to donate small, but sometimes also very substantial, sums of money for their relief. Poor relief thus contributed, imperfectly but nonetheless significantly, to the creation of an urban community.

5 CITIZENS, SOLDIERS AND CIVIC MILITIAS

One of the world's best-known works of art from the early modern period depicts a group of Amsterdam citizens – in a very specific role. The subject matter of Rembrandt's *Night Watch*, painted between 1640 and 1642, is the civic militia: the figures in the *Night Watch* are performing a whole range of military activities, even though it is quite clear that they are citizens, not professional soldiers. In the painting we see the officers of an Amsterdam civic militia company on their round, depicted against the dark shape of a town gate.[1] In seventeenth-century Amsterdam, civic militias patrolled the city at night; one of their duties was to shut the gates and take the keys to the home of the presiding burgomaster. In the centre of the picture is the company's commanding officer, Frans Banningh Cocq, who, as the son of a German immigrant, was understandably proud of the status he had achieved in his home town. He and his fellow officers paid Rembrandt 100 guilders each to have their portraits included. The painting was to be displayed in the *doelen*, or militia hall, where it could be viewed by the members of their own and other militia companies, as well as ordinary passers-by.[2] A hundred guilders, i.e. the equivalent of six months of a labourer's wages, for a portrait that would not become private property, was a substantial amount of money, suggesting how much importance was attached to the public presentation of one's person in a militia context.

In between the officer portraits, Rembrandt painted imaginary figures busy loading their weapons. These underlined the military role of the militias, as a civic defence force. Somewhat surprisingly, two little girls are also included in the picture, one actually caught in a spotlight and therefore quite visible. She is the company's mascot, but her presence has also been interpreted as symbolising the connection between the militias and the chambers of rhetoric, the amateur literary societies for the urban upper middle classes.[3] In this interpretation, the girl invokes a social and cultural context for the militia company, and immediately puts the military activities of those portrayed into a civic perspective. To fully appreciate that context, it is important also to realise that in the towns of the provinces of Holland and Zeeland alone, 135 such larger-than-life canvases have been preserved from the sixteenth and seventeenth centuries.[4] Having one's portrait painted and displayed in a militia environment was obviously no mean thing. But then, of course, neither was the tradition that Rembrandt invoked in the *Night Watch* merely imaginary.

'War made the state, and the state made war', American sociologist Charles Tilly famously wrote.[5] The volume of essays he published in 1975 argued that European state formation was the result of military competition and that European states had developed their institutions in response to the challenges of this military competition. Taxation, and the bureaucracies necessary to collect those taxes, were portrayed by various authors in the book as the pivotal instruments in state-making.[6] This analysis of the process of state formation dovetailed nicely with another Big Idea about early modern Europe: the Military Revolution.[7] Launched by Michael Roberts in a lecture in 1955, the Military Revolution thesis captured a number of major changes in European warfare and its financing. The basic idea, which only caught on in the 1970s, was that in the early modern period, European armies, which had previously been composed overwhelmingly of temporary citizen-soldiers, became permanent professional forces, and therefore more effective, but also hugely more expensive. As a result, states were forced to increase taxes and raise loans. This in turn caused states to expand their scale and scope.[8]

Together, these two master narratives of the early modern history of Europe have pushed citizens as military actors into the side wings. One implication of the fiscal-military state thesis is that after the late Middle Ages citizens were no longer directly involved in the business of violence. Through the tax mechanism they presumably left this to the professional soldiers in full-time employment – often misleadingly labelled 'mercenaries' – and only with the *levée en masse*, in the wake of the French Revolution, was the idea of the citizen-soldier revived.[9] In this chapter I argue that this chronology is wrong. The popularity of the Military Revolution thesis among historians and historical sociologists has led to an emphasis on standing armies and a neglect of the mutation of the role of the militias. Contrary to this currently dominant version of early modern history, this chapter seeks to demonstrate that both the idea and practice of the citizen-soldier remained a vital ingredient of the sociopolitical structures of society.[10] Influential political theorists in the 'republican' tradition worried in their writings about the military dimension of citizenship, a dimension that remains significant even today in some Western countries, most notably the United States.[11] This chapter discusses three key texts from the European tradition of republican political theory, before turning to the practices of citizen-soldiering. These are analysed in two sections: one dealing with the Middle Ages, i.e. the era before the Military Revolution, and another addressing the role of civic militias after professional soldiering became the dominant form of interstate violence. I argue that although civic militias became less important as military forces, they remained significant as political forces throughout the early modern period. Citizen-soldiers, in other words, were not so much made redundant by the Military Revolution, but forced to shift from one foot to the other.

Debates about Citizens as Soldiers

Armed citizenship and civic militias have an impressive pedigree in Europe. They go back to the Middle Ages and the Renaissance, and before that to Greek and Roman antiquity. But as far as the civic militias are concerned as a political issue, the story really starts with Niccolò Machiavelli (1469–1527). Machiavelli was, in his works and active life, very much concerned with the militias.[12] *The Prince*, composed in the 1510s, includes a diatribe against professional troops, which had come to dominate Italian battlefields (pp. 42–44).[13] Machiavelli portrays mercenaries, and their *condottieri* leaders, as unreliable forces, unreliable because they were only in it for the money. Their military effectiveness, according to Machiavelli's persuasive logic, was mainly limited to peacetime. For the mercenaries military service was, after all, a way of making a living. Moreover, because their interests were exclusively financial, the enemy could easily buy them off, leaving one's own state denuded of protection. To avoid such painful experiences, Machiavelli strongly recommended the use of civic militias, i.e. troops consisting of citizens, people with a real stake in the fighting. Citizens were protecting their own homes, families and property. In Greek and Roman antiquity such citizen militias had worked well; Machiavelli cited several examples of their military effectiveness.

At the same time, Machiavelli was of the opinion that civic militias were good for the polity: 'It is impossible to have good laws if good arms are lacking, and if there are good arms there must also be good laws' (pp. 42–43). The reader is left in no doubt that 'good arms' means an army composed of citizens (p. 51).[14] What is more, a prince who conquers certain lands and finds his new subjects unarmed should start arming them: 'For when you arm them, these weapons become your own' (p. 72). On the other hand, 'if you disarm your subjects, you begin to offend them, for you show that you do not trust them, either because you are weak and cowardly or because you are too suspicious. And both these reasons cause you to become hated' (pp. 72–73). A wise prince, in other words, creates loyalty in his subjects by demonstrating his trust in them, and the best way to achieve this is by giving them arms.

Italian ideas were revived and reshaped during the English Civil War. It was in particular James Harrington's *Oceana*, first published in 1655, which created this 'Machiavellian moment'.[15] Harrington found his inspiration among the Classics (as Machiavelli had), as well as among the Florentines. For Harrington, however, the citizens were not so much urbanites as rural folk. In Harrington's ideal state, citizens were defined by their ownership of property, i.e. land. His citizenship, as with almost all republican authors, was gendered in the sense that females did not come into consideration. And all citizens were supposed to contribute to the defence of the realm. States that relied on 'servants' for their defence could only afford to do so if they lay outside the reach of their enemies, like Venice, and would anyway never be great.[16]

Harrington's opinions should be read, obviously, against the background of England's recent political history. The Parliamentarians in the Civil War were convinced that Charles I had abused the army to eradicate all opposition against his policies. Unfortunately, the New Model Army that Parliament had employed to prevent Charles from executing his designs had subsequently evolved into an oppressive force in its own right. All of this could demonstrate only one point: professional soldiers were dangerous and better avoided altogether. Hence the debate over 'standing armies', which continued for decades in the British Isles.[17] Scottish author Andrew Fletcher (1653–1716) was a late entrant into this debate. His *Discourse of Government with Relation to Militias* was first published in 1697, and again in revised form in 1698.[18] Fletcher was familiar with Machiavelli's work, even though he does not quote Machiavelli in his *Discourse*.[19] He was a firm believer in the feudal system, for 'this constitution of government put the sword into the hand of the subject' (p. 3). The feudal barons' way of life had been altered fundamentally by the Discoveries, as these bred a demand for new luxuries among the upper classes. Because their estates did not produce the cash to buy those luxuries, they converted the military service of their tenants into monetary rents. The government then used the money to hire soldiers. Thus the barons lost their monopoly of the sword. To make matters worse, the rise of gunpowder caused a major shift in the ways wars were fought. Soldiering became an occupation, and professional soldiers were in the pay of the sovereign. Thus, 'the power of the sword was transferred from the subject to the king' (p. 7). And as the barons were now serving in the king's standing army as officers – and earning good money in the process – they became the monarch's most loyal supporters (p. 7).

Fletcher was convinced that standing armies were completely unnecessary for the British Isles, protected as they were by the sea. He argued that they were an innovation, a break, in other words, with a long militia tradition (p. 12). But what good would it do, he asked, to prevent the risk of foreign conquest, when 'standing armies will enslave us' (p. 19)? Whilst mercenaries were a pest and a threat, militiamen 'would always preserve the publick liberty' (p. 21). To have a militia was not merely beneficial from a military point of view, but could also create the best possible society. The Swiss were proof of that, according to Fletcher, as they were 'the freest and happiest' people of Europe (p. 22).

In the 1780s the debate on the relative merits of standing armies and civic militias also emerged in the Dutch Republic. Fletcher's *Discourse* was published in a Dutch translation in 1774.[20] As we will see in what follows, the Dutch had a long and significant militia tradition, and it was precisely this tradition that was invoked, in proper Machiavellian fashion, to demonstrate the desirability of citizens in arms. A 'call to arms' was included in an anonymous treatise that was distributed in the night of 25 September 1781 in towns throughout the Dutch Republic. *To the People of the Netherlands* read the provocative title of the seventy-page pamphlet.[21] Its author was later discovered to be Joan Derk Baron Van der Capellen tot den Poll (1741–84), who also happened to be the translator of Fletcher's *Discourse*. He claimed that the original inhabitants of the Netherlands, the Batavians, had been a free people who took decisions in general assemblies, 'where the whole people met in arms and every Batavian was equally important' (p. 3).[22] By the time of the Dutch Revolt such general assemblies had disappeared, mainly for practical reasons. However, the citizens' representatives in the guilds, civic militias or common councils still made sure their voice was heard in the council chambers of the towns throughout the Republic.

Unfortunately, Prince William of Orange, leader of the Revolt, had already managed to suppress such popular consultations in the province of Holland in 1581, and under his descendants things had gone from bad to worse. The Orange stadholder were not merely the most important nobles in the country, as well as its most powerful politicians, but also commanders-in-chief of the Republic's army and navy. They had abused their position by steadily replacing Dutch officers with foreigners, who would be loyal only to them (pp. 16, 41). Through a constant repositioning of the garrison regiments, Van der Capellen argued, the Oranges had prevented the soldiers from taking root in the towns where they were billeted (p. 57). As a result, the army had developed from an instrument to fight foreign foes into one of domestic oppression.

To the People of the Netherlands also referred to other nations that had fared badly under princes who were not accountable to any representative institution. It was therefore an obvious conclusion that 'a people that wants to behave sensibly and prudently, should make sure to be the strongest at all times' (p. 19). Van der Capellen conceded that professional soldiers are necessary to fight proper wars, also because citizens have other things on their minds. But in order not to be suppressed by those same troops, citizens must have a rifle at home and make sure they are trained to use it. Preferably they should exercise every Sunday, under the command of officers elected by the companies. This might look far-fetched, but in fact it was not, as the Americans and also the Swiss did exactly the same, according to Van der Capellen. It was not even an innovation, as the Union of Utrecht, the Dutch Republic's informal constitution from 1579, had already announced the creation of such a civic militia (pp. 19–20).[23] Therefore, *To the People of the Netherlands* concludes, arming the citizens and training them to use their arms would help restore civic freedom and thus the prosperity of the country as a whole.

The foregoing discussion has sampled three items from a rich literature in three different political contexts and from three different centuries, but it should already have demonstrated a number of things. First of all, throughout the early modern period, civic militias played a central role in some of the significant contributions to the debate about the best possible forms of government. The three authors discussed here agreed that militias were a vital ingredient of any healthy constitution. Whereas professional armies were likely to become instruments of oppression in the hands of the government, civic militias would allow citizens a 'voice' in the business of the realm.[24] This agreement of opinions is no coincidence, of course. The writings by Machiavelli, Fletcher and Van der Capellen were all part of the same tradition of republican theory and discourse.[25] At the same time, our authors differed over who should be armed. Machiavelli seemed to want to limit this to the propertied classes, but Fletcher and Van der Capellen were less restrictive; in their system all males could, and indeed should, serve as militiamen. Machiavelli and Fletcher were also convinced that militia forces were in fact superior from a military point of view to professional standing armies. Fletcher seemed to take into account the extraordinary situation of Great Britain as an island state. Only Van der Capellen acknowledged, albeit in passing, that amateur soldiers were probably no match for professional opponents. A third aspect all three authors agreed on was the low cost of militia forces and the impact this could have on levels of taxation. Replacing professionals with militias would strike a blow against this second weapon in the hands of central government: its cash reserves. Note how, in this respect as well as in relation to the preservation of the constitution, the debate on militias was much more a debate concerning domestic rather than international politics.

In one aspect, however, the authors connected the militia issue in very different ways to the structure of society as a whole. For Machiavelli and Van der Capellen militias were typically urban institutions. They were both at ease with commercial society. Van der Capellen, in *To the People of the Netherlands*, actually compared Dutch society to the East India Company, and portrayed the people of the Netherlands as 'shareholders' in their society (p. 21). Fletcher, on the other hand, was deeply suspicious of commerce. In his argument militia service would bring back the sobriety of feudal society.

Amateur Soldiers in the Middle Ages

During the Middle Ages there was very little debate about militia forces, for the simple reason that they were ubiquitous. Every state relied primarily on temporary units composed of amateur soldiers. Urbanites were expected to serve just as much as rural folk. For medieval princes, towns provided three resources for their military advantage. They were strongholds that could ward off enemies, they were a financial source to be tapped for military as well as other purposes and they were a source of manpower.[26] Urban populations, or at least the male part of it, had to organise their own defence, as well as follow their sovereign into battle. How did they do this?

All medieval European towns had some form of compulsory military service for able-bodied men. The precise conditions varied from place to place, but men could expect to be called upon to perform their military duty. On one hand, citizens were expected to defend their own town, by manning the gates and ramparts when the town was under siege or otherwise threatened. On the other hand, citizen units were supposed to perform police duties, usually in the form of a night watch.[27] On top of this, and more contentiously, citizen-soldiers were asked to follow their lord, or their local government, on offensive campaigns beyond the perimeter of the town and its direct hinterland.

Early references to urban militias date from the twelfth century, even though they must have existed earlier.[28] For the towns of Brabant, Boffa has proposed the following chronology. From the twelfth to the mid-thirteenth century a *levée-en-masse* forced all able-bodied men to rally to the town's defence whenever there was an emergency. The well-off would appear on horseback; the rest acted as foot soldiers. From the mid-thirteenth to the early fifteenth century, the guilds in Brabant's towns took over as the framework for recruitment. Citizens marched under the banner of their guilds; the guilds raised their admission fees to cover the costs of equipment. The first half of the fifteenth century saw the introduction of a new phase with the creation of militia guilds, elite units whose members trained regularly and held shooting competitions. And finally, in the second half of the fifteenth century the new Burgundian lords of Brabant introduced the possibility of transforming personal service into a monetary contribution used to pay permanent, professional soldiers to do the job.[29]

This chronology is not necessarily applicable everywhere else in Europe, but it helps highlight a number of important elements of the civic militias of the late Middle Ages. Firstly, there is the context of recruitment. Two models seem to have dominated: a geographical model and a corporate model. In the geographical model, the town would be divided into a number of militia precincts and men would march under the banner of their precinct.[30] This model was applied in Paris, for example, where in the seventeenth century militia precincts would be closed off with the help of heavy chains hung across the entry routes, to mark their boundaries.[31] In Utrecht the eight militia precincts, introduced after 1528, had remarkably romantic names: Turkey, Popish Standard, Fortune, Blood Pit, Black Journeymen, Orange Trunk, Tar Pitches, Arbalest. They each had a strong identity to match these names, much like the urban districts in Siena that were similarly used for the recruitment of the militiamen – and still compete in the *Palio* horse race in the twenty-first century.[32]

The alternative model used the guild system to bring men together for military service. In Utrecht until 1528, when Charles V took over the city and broke their power, twenty-two craft guilds had not only dominated the political life of the town, but also its military organisation. They were responsible for raising local troops, as well as for the maintenance of the ramparts; each guild had been assigned a specific part of the physical defences.[33] There does not seem to have been a consistent pattern in the application of either the geographical or guild model, other perhaps than that the guild model was more likely to be preferred in those towns where the guilds were also politically influential. It was no coincidence that they became the foundation of recruitment in Flanders and Brabant exactly during the time of what has been termed the 'guild revolutions' of 1302 and subsequent years.[34] The absence of a consistent pattern was reinforced by the fact that some towns switched between systems. In many German towns, for example, the geographical system was transformed into the corporate.[35] In Cologne, however, the corporate system was abandoned again in 1583 in favour of the geographical.[36]

A second issue is training. How were all these butchers, bakers and blacksmiths to make a useful contribution on the battlefield? We have to remember that they were not considered absolutely vital. During much of the Middle Ages battles were dominated by cavalry. Insofar as cavalrymen were not recruited from the nobility, they came from the circles with more leisure time and hence more opportunity to develop their riding skills.[37] Civilian infantry forces would travel with their precinct's wagon, the *carroccio*, that not only carried the supplies, but also served as a rallying point on the battlefield. Equally important for sustaining cohesion in such amateur units was their occupational or neighbourhood solidarity.[38] These factors actually allowed urban infantry troops to win some notable battles against the regulars employed by princes. For example, those of Milan, together with militias from Lodi, Verona, Vercelli, Piacenza and the Marche towns, were victorious in 1176 against Frederic Barbarossa.[39] In 1302, Flemish urban militias won a similarly remarkable victory against the French king. This latter victory also marked the emergence of the infantry as a more permanently significant military force.[40]

These changes were partly the result of the superior organisation of citizens, for example in craft guilds, and partly due to technological changes such as the emergence of a new type of bow. This gave infantry troops superior fire power – and caused wars to become much bloodier in the process.[41] It also required citizen-soldiers to become better trained. Such training was already provided by town governments in the early fifteenth century, but it was set on a regular footing by the creation of shooting guilds (*schuttersgilden*).[42] In Northern Europe the first of these shooting guilds emerged in Flanders and Brabant in the late thirteenth century.[43] They quickly spread to adjacent regions, first in the Low Countries and France. Around 1400 shooting guilds were already being established in the Rhineland, and from there they spread further, to the Hansa towns in the Baltic area, as well as the eastern and southern parts of the Holy Roman Empire. By the end of the fifteenth century they had reached the Austrian lands and in that same century they appeared in Burgundy, through its contacts with the Low Countries. In the sixteenth century English towns finally adopted the same institutions; in 1537–38 the Guild of St George in London was patented by Henry VIII.[44]

Shooting guilds were created with a military purpose in mind, but they were not, in themselves, military entities.[45] Their objective was to train civilians in the use of arms, to prepare them for military service. Particularly the rise of the arbalest contributed to the dissemination of the shooting guild, because the foot bow was difficult to handle unless one was properly trained in its use. Shooting guilds provided training grounds – those of the London Guild of St George were located at

St Martin-in-the-Fields – and once a year there was an opportunity for the members to demonstrate their skill in a competition, by shooting at a wooden bird, normally a parrot, raised on a large vertical pole. The man who managed to hit the parrot would be the guild's 'king' for the next year. In the Tyrol such competitions are recorded in the fifteenth century.[46]

Women were not by definition excluded from shooting guilds, but they did not, as far as we know, participate in competitions. Female heads of households were expected to contribute to militia service – but only financially.[47] It is therefore no coincidence that the only female in Rembrandt's *Night Watch* is very much an outsider to the action taking place around her. Civic militias created a male world, built around arms and drink, and underlined by specific rituals and gestures. The toasts to 'friendship' that were a regular feature of militia meals had a gendered implication, as did the references of loyalty, which concerned the urban community as a whole, but especially the male confraternity of the militia. In the Dutch militia paintings we see males shaking hands and pledging loyalty with their hands on their hearts. Equally in evidence are numerous 'Renaissance elbows' pointing towards the viewer, a popular reference to male boldness and control.[48]

For males, the shooting guilds exercised exclusivity; as in the craft guilds, only those with full rights of citizenship were accepted as members.[49] This immediately suggests a potential for shooting guilds to position themselves as representatives of the citizen community. Shooting guilds had around two dozen members, perhaps 150 at most. This was small compared to the number of militiamen that major towns could field at times. Florence raised 1,400 cavalry and circa 4,000 foot soldiers in 1260 from among its citizens.[50] Bruges supplied 1,254 men for a military campaign in 1303.[51] Basel could raise around 1,900 militiamen in 1421.[52] These were all significant proportions of the male population in such towns. The members of the shooting guilds would constitute but a fraction of these forces.

However, citizen troops would almost never fight alone; they would be accompanied by regulars.[53] One of the other things that the Military Revolution debate has obscured is that professional soldiers were already a feature of the Middle Ages. Italian towns used professional units from the earliest recorded instances. Alongside the Milanese citizens in 1260 fought 200 mounted mercenaries.[54] They are recorded in Venice in the tenth century, while in the north the Duke of Anjou employed professionals in 991, as did the German emperor Frederick Barbarossa during his Italian campaigns of the 1160s.[55] What happened over the course of time – relatively early in Italy, later in the rest of Europe – was that these professional troops became an increasingly prominent part of a sovereign's armed forces.[56] As a result, the role of civic militias as an offensive weapon declined.

Citizen-Soldiers after the Military Revolution

Paradoxically, we are much better informed about various aspects of civic militias of the early modern period, even though it is usually assumed that by then they had been marginalised as a result of the rise of professional soldiering. Most great powers of the early modern period maintained a reserve army, to be called up in times of war. Louis XIV's defence minister Louvois created a royal militia of 25,000 men. In the 1740s as many as 80,000 French militiamen served in the War of the Austrian Succession. Brandenburg-Prussia reformed its militias in 1693, and Spain revived its militias in the eighteenth century.[57] But only in seventeenth-century Britain and Switzerland were the militias still the backbone of the military establishment – even though the British also had a professional army. It is perhaps no coincidence that both countries were favoured by natural circumstances, which provided them with borders that were relatively easy to protect. In both countries the militias' role was that of a home guard; it was not assumed that they would act as offensive forces.

The English militias were a feudal force, reformed under Elizabeth I in 1558. These reforms were inaugurated by the double threat emanating from enemies within (Mary Tudor's supporters) and from outside (Philip II's Spain). Their feudal origins are clearly visible in the conception, in 1558, of the militias as temporary forces, springing to life in times of military crisis. They recruited on a compulsory basis. It was soon evident, however, that amateur forces would be useful only if properly exercised. Hence in 1573 so-called trained bands were set up, special militia units that received additional training and were rewarded for their trouble with a small allowance.[58] Militia service could be fulfilled by a replacement and the upper classes seem to have been eager to let their inferiors do the dirty work for them.

German towns, at least the imperial cities, were in the unique position that they were more or less independent states in their own right. As result, their civic militias were and remained more military in nature than those of other continental countries.[59] Augsburg, for example, employed its own professional soldiers for the defence of the city, but citizens were expected to make a contribution as well. The Augsburg civic militias performed police duties and paraded on official occasions. Citizens were required to supply their own arms, but these were kept in the city's arsenal, the *Zeughaus*. Later, a payment to the *Zeugamt* made the private ownership of firearms superfluous.[60] Militia service itself could be fulfilled by a replacement, which led increasingly to the proletarianisation of the militias' membership.[61] Besides companies of foot soldiers, the civic militias of Augsburg also consisted of artillery and cavalry companies.[62]

In 1610 the civic militias of Utrecht received new statutes, which give a fair idea of what their role in society was supposed to be. Article 5 defined it as: 'to protect the city of Utrecht, and all its citizens and inhabitants, against all violence, disturbance and violation from within and without, everything for the security, quiet and peace of everyone, as will be commanded by the Colonel, under orders of the sovereign and the local magistrate'.[63] An elucidation of these statutes from 1619 indicated that there would be eight companies, of 150 men each.[64] In the eight militia districts the officers were involved in much more than just the night watch, or military defence organisation. From private notes kept by David Jan Martens as commanding officer of Utrecht's Turkey Company during the 1780s, we learn that no collections, including tax collections, could be held in the district without him announcing these to the inhabitants. Martens was asked to give his opinion on all citizenship applications from his district. The Turkey district was subdivided into twenty smaller neighbourhood units, each with its own neighbourhood sheriff. These sheriffs were required to register newcomers and to check the taverns, as well as the fire pumps, fire ladders and sewers in their area. They should also warn the neighbours to clear their part of the sidewalk of snow during the winter. The sheriffs were responsible for ensuring a sufficient number of neighbourhood participants in any funerals from their district.[65] The neighbourhood sheriffs executed these (unpaid) chores under the supervision of militia officers like Martens.[66] These were not mere formalities. In February 1752, for example, the commanders of all eight districts advised Utrecht's burgomasters to continue refusing the right of citizenship to Catholic newcomers, unless the applicant proved vital to the community.[67]

The militias in Nantes were called out during riots. Especially in times of food scarcity, the militias were notified to be vigilant and in case of disturbances called upon to restore public order. In 1630, with local elites divided about political issues, taxes rising and epidemics playing havoc on the population, the militia was called out to protect the meetings of the town council, while all other inhabitants were expressly forbidden to carry arms inside the town's perimeter. In 1675 taxes were again rising sharply, due to the war against the Dutch Republic begun in 1672 (the so-called *guerre d'Hollande*), and in April of that year the militias had to quell a popular uprising, which at one point saw the bishop of Nantes taken hostage by disaffected crowds.[68]

The British equivalent of the urban militias found in Dutch and French towns was the so-called watch. Watchmen could be called up in times of military crisis, but they also paraded on festive occasions and performed the night watch, as their name suggests.[69] They were, in other words, police forces. In Hooker's *History of Exeter* (late sixteenth century), for instance, the task of the 'watchemen and wardesmen' is described as: 'to serve by night and the other by Daye'.[70] They operated from the town hall and were to make sure that the town gates were properly shut at night, and generally to supervise their respective districts 'that their [*sic*] be no misrule kept'.[71] In Bristol, the watchmen paraded the streets of the city during a civic ceremony in 1571; London's 'marching watch' would do the same on similar occasions.[72] The city of Edinburgh had its town guards, with an identical role to play.[73]

As military forces the militias' qualities were not very impressive. This was true even in Britain, where the militias retained more of their military character than in most continental countries. Lack of training cannot have been the only cause of this underperforming. In London, the Guild of St George acted as one of those shooting guilds that were also found on the continent.[74] It was an institution mainly for militia officers in the London companies. Other towns followed London's example and set up similar guilds. All captains of the London trained bands were enrolled as members in 1614. The Guild, by then known, after its training grounds, as the Society of the Artillery Garden, was quick to adopt the Dutch methods of drill and other innovations pioneered by Maurice of Orange.[75] The English militias' theatre of operations was England itself, and civil conflict hardly ever amounted to a pitched battle. This was true even during the Civil War. The London-trained bands were said to have performed honourably in the face of professional opponents, and at Turnham Green even sustained casualties, but they never really had to demonstrate that they were fireproof.[76]

Civic militias in the Dutch Republic received only limited drill practice.[77] After 1600 Utrecht was safe from Spanish attacks, but in the spring of 1672 the French overran substantial parts of the country. The Utrecht militias' performance was disappointing, to say the least. The Dutch troops under William III were refused shelter in the city, while just a few days later Utrecht was handed to the French without a shot fired! In other Dutch towns the militias proved equally hopeless as military forces.[78] In Paris, a commentator had already observed in 1595: 'They are just like dogs that only bark and bite on their own doorstep'.[79] In Utrecht even that would prove too optimistic a description.

All of this underscores the point: civic militias of the early modern period were first and foremost police forces. They did, at the same time, retain elements of their former role as military units. They were called upon to help defend their own towns, and sometimes even required to venture outside their own turf. This sustained a self-image that was supported by military paraphernalia and historical tales of past bravery, just enough to maintain the credibility of republican arguments about citizens-in-arms.

Although technically every able-bodied male was required to serve in the militia, the Utrecht regulations of 1702 limited participation to those who could afford to bring their own weapon.[80] Moreover, in practice it was households rather than individuals that were the units of recruitment: every household was supposed to supply one militiaman.[81] In actual fact, the number of men was much smaller than the number of households. According to a survey in July 1786, the Turkey district of Utrecht had 539 households, but its militia company came to only 174 in June 1784. In other words, a mere 32 per cent of all households were involved in the militia. This figure is slightly higher than the percentage for the city as a whole, which came to 29 per cent; as a percentage of the total population, the strength of the eight Utrecht militias, 1,793 men in total, amounted to 7.3 per cent.[82] The Nantes militia had a membership of approximately 2,000, i.e. 10 per cent of the population. In the eighteenth century, when the population increased, the militias remained at the same strength, reducing the percentage to about 5 per cent.[83] In the diocese of Albi around 1,800 were on active service in 1694, 2 per cent from a population of 90,000, but that comprised a substantial rural area as well.[84] In 1703, fourteen Augsburg militia companies numbered a total of 2,800 men. That was about 10 per cent of the urban population at the time. However, 1703 was a year of high military alert, due to the War of the Spanish Succession. In September 1673 a mere 900 men had been drafted into four militia companies.[85]

In terms of social background, the Utrecht militiamen, at least at the end of the eighteenth century, belonged overwhelmingly to the solid middle classes. D. J. Martens' Turkey Company in 1785 had several journeymen in its ranks, but most of the members were independent artisans, practising such trades as bookbinder, sculptor (two), wigmaker, tailor (five), pharmacist, merchant, hat maker, shoemaker (four), carpenter (four) and shopkeeper (five).[86] Evidence from 's-Hertogenbosch suggests the same pattern.[87]

Social equality was reinforced by rituals and sociability. The Utrecht regulations of 1619 already stipulated that only those who actually consumed drink during the night watch would be required to pay for the company's alcohol consumption.[88] Drinking and eating were important aspects of militia life.[89] After Martens gained his command in May 1781, he immediately invited his fellow officers to his home, where toasts were raised 'with the use of the Company's goblet'.[90] Many Dutch militia companies owned highly elaborate (and quite expensive) silver drinking vessels, which were passed round the table on solemn occasions for all the officers to share, symbolising the bond of company membership.[91] After the annual muster, Martens received his fellow officers for the 'captain's meal'.[92] On such occasions 'harmony' and 'friendship' were key words in the speeches and compulsory toasts, underlining the unity of the community that the militia represented and was bound to maintain.[93] The Haarlem portrait painter Frans Hals set his famous militia pieces around a table.[94] Another expression of the same intention was the presence of militiamen at the funeral of their colleagues.[95]

English militias were organised on a regional basis. Individual counties, or a combination, were required to raise the number of militiamen assigned to them and make sure that these troops were properly trained. The counties were also financially responsible for their own units. Because those called up could send a replacement, a proletarianisation of the militia units was almost inevitable.[96] Data from eighteenth-century Exeter demonstrate this. A town of 11,000 inhabitants in the late seventeenth century, and 16,000 at the end of the eighteenth, Exeter was a county in its own right.[97] The Borough Militia was recruited from four precincts within the city, with their prosaic names East Within, West Within and so on, as well as four precincts *extra muros*, with the equally predictable names East Without, West Without etcetera. Each precinct was supposed to muster ten men. The roll of 1770 was, however, a depressing fifty-two names short of full strength.[98] The majority of the twenty-eight men actually serving were indeed substitutes, like Thomas Gall, whose name already appears on the list as substitute for Thomas Wilson, but two years later took the place of Matthew Cosseraty the Younger. Most of the Exeter substitutes were unable to sign their name.[99]

With many working-class substitutes serving in the English militias, the urban middle classes had reason to be suspicious of their loyalty. This may have been why Exeter's city council, the Chamber, chose to rely on the city watch, rather than the local militia, during the troubled times of the Civil War. On 23 January 1642 the Chamber made the first moves to prepare the city for whatever was to come. It was decided that forty inhabitants, 'men to be confided in', would be added to the officers and volunteers who would take turns at the watch. 'Disaffected persons', on the other hand, were to be disarmed, while a muster of men and arms, as well as 'trayners', i.e. members of trained bands, and volunteers would be undertaken.[100] In August it was decided that 'there shall be 32 persons charged to warde everie day and 32 persons to watch everie night'.[101] As these watches turned out to be on almost permanent duty, the watchmen were temporarily taken into the pay of the community.[102]

Civic militias thus continued to recruit substantial numbers of men throughout the early modern period. At any one time, around 7.5 per cent of the urban population – and by implication a much higher percentage of the adult males – participated in the militias. Their social composition varied, without any clear pattern emerging from the available information. Many towns had a preference for middle-class militiamen. These acted as the propertied forces keeping the working classes in check.[103] There were, however, other places where replacements were acceptable and that led to an influx of lower-class recruits. This served the interests of middle-class men reluctant to spend a night out patrolling the town, but it also created political anxiety in those same circles about the loyalty of the force. Such anxieties were entirely justified.

Militia Politics

As organisations composed of citizens, of whatever social background, the civic militias were almost inevitably caught up in local politics. Machiavelli thought this was one of the main purposes of having civic militias. It is therefore not surprising to find militiamen using their organisations as a platform to voice political claims, and reinforcing those claims by the fact that they were armed. Shooting guilds were, for example, consulted by Dutch urban governments in times of crisis, as happened in Amsterdam in 1542.[104] Their great opportunity came with the Dutch Revolt in the second half of the sixteenth century. Local authorities were desperate to establish legitimacy for their decisions, which one way or another were bound to be controversial. In Leiden this happened on the very first day of the Revolt, when the support of the militia was required to restore order after a wave of iconoclastic rioting. Whereas normally the militia would be ordered out by the burgomasters, it was now considered better to consult first, not only the officers but also the regular members. In Haarlem in September 1566, during a technically illegal meeting, militiamen volunteered their advice on how the most important posts in the city should be filled. In Delft it was the council who summoned the militiamen to a meeting on 6 October, referring to them as 'members of the town'.[105] In Amsterdam, where the city council had taken the side of the Habsburg government up to 1578, it was a coup by the local militias that finally forced the Catholic council to make way for a Protestant successor, which was elected by representatives of the militia. One of its first acts was to organise a huge dinner for the revolutionary militiamen, 'to plant and let grow once more the love and unity among the citizens'.[106]

During the 1580s, the civic militias in the rebel territories were completely overhauled. Instead of the former guild structure and voluntary participation, William of Orange introduced compulsory service for all able-bodied men between the ages of eighteen and sixty, recruited by district. The former 'shooting guilds' became 'burgher companies', but in practice they retained their colloquial name of *schutterij*.[107] They thus inherited the shooting guilds' position of spokesmen for the community.[108] In the 1780s there were complaints about the decline of the Dutch civic militias.[109] These complaints concerning the militias' military capabilities – or rather the lack of them – should be read in conjunction with Van der Capellen's appeal to revive the militias as military units, capable of substituting for, or at least providing a counterweight against, the professional troops commanded by the Orange stadholder. As Van der Capellen had recommended, military exercise societies were set up to drill militiamen several times a week. The participation in these exercise societies was voluntary, and a demonstration of one's adherence to the anti-Orange camp. Utrecht was one of the towns where the militia companies set up such exercise societies. Those of the Turkey Company were looking for training grounds in early 1783.[110] During the following four years the militias, and more particularly the exercise society *Pro Patria et Libertate*, recruited from the ranks of the militias, were the backbone of the revolutionary Patriot movement in Utrecht.[111] Once again they claimed to be the spokesmen of the civic community. In a Draft Constitution, published in 1784, the militias were even put in charge of organising local elections.[112]

In Paris, during the summer of 1648, militias barricaded their districts with the help of the chains provided to defend these districts.[113] Apart from their police duties and contribution to local defence, the Parisian *milices bourgeoises* were generally seen as institutions representing the community as a whole.[114] The militias of Paris had been reorganised in 1562, exchanging an essentially corporative for a territorial model. The reorganisation did not, however, fundamentally alter the militias' social composition, which remained middle class, and more specifically dominated by craftsmen – at least insofar as the rank and file were concerned.[115] As in other towns, in France and elsewhere, the militias of Paris were inspired by egalitarian ideals so dear to early modern citizens. (These ideals notwithstanding, the Parisian militias as elsewhere were of course exclusively male institutions.) The citizens, however, found militia service more attractive to support in theory than to sustain in practice, and as a result there were innumerable conflicts over absenteeism, and a permanent pressure to permit replacement by social inferiors who would be financially rewarded for their trouble.[116]

In mid-seventeenth century London, trained bands played a decisive role in swinging the support of the City to the Parliamentary side. In January 1642 they mobilised spontaneously, against the express wishes of the Lord Mayor, who was their formal commander. The Committee of Safety, also known as the Militia Committee, dominated City politics during the early stages of the crisis. The Militia Committee expanded the trained bands from 6,000 to 8,000 men, on a voluntary basis. Significantly, apprentices who signed up were promised the freedom, i.e. citizenship, of the City after their tour of duty.[117]

All these examples show not only how the militias could be a significant political force in their communities, but also in many places served as the main vehicle for citizen agency. In that sense, Machiavelli was right: arming citizens almost automatically implied that local authorities had to listen to those same citizens, and pay attention to their concerns.

Conclusions

The evidence presented here therefore suggests a number of broader conclusions. First, and perhaps most importantly: the monopoly of violence in the hands of early modern national governments remained very incomplete, even after the Military Revolution. On the contrary, national governments were keen to encourage their citizens to bear arms and contribute supplementary military services, at low cost to the public treasury. Secondly, with the rise of professional soldiering, civic militias became increasingly irrelevant as military forces. Only the Swiss Confederacy and England, favoured by natural conditions, could continue to rely on militias for military purposes. Thirdly, even though their military role became less significant, civic militias continued to play an important role in early modern town life. Scattered figures from the Dutch Republic and France suggest that between 5 and 10 per cent of the population, that is as much as a quarter of all households, was involved in the militias at any one time, and that by implication a much larger segment of the population must have been involved in them during their life cycle. Fourthly, through the discourse of classical republicanism, as first articulated in Renaissance Italy but subsequently developed and adapted in other parts of Europe, civic militias provided a significant dimension to conceptions of citizenship. As such, they not only felt compelled to defend their community against military enemies but also acted as the defenders of the political integrity of that community. They were simultaneously forces of public order and disorder. Therefore, fifthly and finally, as institutions encompassing significant sections of the urban community, militias shaped the ritual and political lives of medieval and early modern towns, providing at one and the same time identity and voice to that community.

The militiamen in Rembrandt's *Night Watch* may have been unique in the way they were captured on canvas, but their ambition to be portrayed while serving with their fellow citizens would have appealed to men in similar positions everywhere in premodern Europe. Through its inclusion in the American constitution it continues to do so today.[118]

Part II

CITIES AND STATES, OR THE VARIETIES OF EUROPEAN CITIZENSHIP

The chapters in Part I have outlined how urban communities emerged across Europe and how those urban communities involved their citizens in local governance, in the regulation of their economies, in the funding and organisation of local welfare and in the provisioning of military security and public order. We have seen how civic involvement could fluctuate across time and space, but by and large, I have argued, when viewed from the local perspective, civic arrangements as they were established in the central Middle Ages endured down to the end of the Old Regime. The chapters demonstrated that citizen involvement was substantial in terms of numbers, and significant in terms of its impact on the way urban societies were organised.

In Part II I want to shift our focus away from the purely local. In the following chapters, therefore, there is inevitably a shift away from the actor-centred discussion in Part I to a more institutional emphasis. Even though these chapters provide plenty more examples of civic participation in urban affairs, my purpose is now to try and connect these local arrangements to the state and the way states were organised. More specifically, I investigate to what extent state structures were open to civic involvement, through the representation of urban interests. As we see in

Chapter 9, this was actually not the case in the majority of European states at the time. Chapter 9 investigates why this was so, by analysing state–city relations in Germany, France, Spain and East Central Europe. In Chapters 6–8, however, I look in greater detail at three cases that were, each in its own way, exceptions to this general rule: the Italian city-states of the Renaissance, the Dutch Republic of the seventeenth century and England in the eighteenth century. We will see that citizen involvement in state affairs could be direct, especially where city and state more or less overlapped, but also indirect, through the representation of towns in regional or national parliaments.

The choice of these three exceptions is, of course, not entirely random. Precisely these three regions were also among the most successful of the period in terms of their economic performance. I argue that this was no coincidence, but that their economic success was built on a foundation of citizen involvement, whose impact in these three regions was not only felt at the local level, but also in national state policies.

6 ITALIAN CITY-STATES AND THEIR CITIZENS

In March 1432, three ambassadors from Sigismund of Luxemburg arrived in Siena to announce that their master would be visiting the city. Sigismund had been the German king since 1411, and the king of Italy since 1431. Now he would be travelling to Rome, where the pope was to crown him Holy Roman Emperor. A second embassy visited Siena in May, when the city agreed to receive the king, but with a number of conditions. Siena wanted to be acknowledged as a '*Vicario dell'Impero*' in perpetuity, and to have its statutes and form of government recognised by the king and future emperor. In other words, while accepting Sigismund as the king of Italy with an implied authority, Siena at the same time wanted to make sure he confirmed its autonomy as a city-state. The emperor and his huge retinue arrived on 12 July, to be welcomed in the city centre by the local dignitaries, as well as crowds of citizens. He was handed the keys of the city, which he kissed before returning them, saying, 'You be the protectors of your own city of Siena'.[1] The demands by the local government, and the emperor's reaction, reveal the somewhat ambiguous status of Italian city-states in this period. Technically, they were still subject to the authority of the king of Italy and the Holy Roman Emperor, two titles that had been combined in the same person for centuries. Practically, city-states were independent, pursuing their own policies and setting their own rules.

By 1432, Siena was past its prime. It had taken a direct hit from the plague, in the middle of the previous century, when its population of about 40,000 was decimated to perhaps a third of that figure. Siena never really recovered. Until the arrival of the Black Death, however,

Siena had been one of those rapidly growing Italian towns whose cultural achievements still dazzle us today. Its economy benefitted from the town's location on the pilgrim route to Rome, but also from the international banking activities of several major commercial firms.[2] By 1262 Siena had a written constitution, but elements for such a constitution already dated from around 1180.[3] As we saw in Chapter 2, Siena's government was a mixture of elite and popular elements, of military and economic interests. As well as a variety of representative councils, the city had a *podestà*, who acted as the highest civil servant and was recruited from outside. The *podestà* was in charge of the Sienese army and brought along his own staff. Because of permanent anxieties about the potential power in the hands of a single person, his appointment was limited to a single year, and he had to leave Siena within a week of the end of his term. In 1252, a countervailing office was created in the Captain of the People, representing the citizens.[4] The republican ideology of this government was visually captured in the famous Lorenzetti murals adorning the walls of the Sala dei Nove in the Palazzo Pubblico, the council chamber where the Nine, Siena's government at the time, held its meetings. The fresco cycle, conceived between 1337 and 1339, reminds spectators of the dangers of bad government, equated with tyranny, and the benefits of republican self-government that brings peace and prosperity to the urban community – and its *contado*. Lorenzetti's works, in other words, conceive of Siena as a state.[5]

The construction of the Palazzo Pubblico began in 1297, when Siena was going through a period of rapid expansion.[6] The Black Death reversed that trajectory, but it was by no means the only reason Siena was struggling after the mid-fourteenth century. It still suffered from internal divisions, which had been the cause of numerous regime changes.[7] These changes, however, had also occurred during the years of expansion, so instability as such was not the problem. What had changed was the degree and nature of outside pressures that the community had to deal with.

Mercenaries were regularly raiding the city.[8] Other powers were increasingly interfering with local politics. In 1452 the city was threatened by Neapolitan troops. In 1456 a conspiracy was uncovered that aimed to hand the city to King Alfonso of Naples. Pope Pius II, who was elected in 1458, came from a local family and used his new position to insist on the readmission of several magnate families who had been banned from the city and its offices.[9] The list of adversities goes on and on.[10] As a result, public finances became increasingly tight, requiring extraordinary measures.

In 1487 the popular regime, seemingly unable to address the problems adequately, was overthrown. The next year, the citizens of Siena were disarmed and in 1495 a French guard was stationed in Siena. Pandolfo Petrucci, a banker maintaining good relations with the French soldiers who accompanied him as bodyguards, became the *signore*, or leader of the local government, with the citizens increasingly pushed to the margins.[11] In 1526 the Republic of Siena was overwhelmed by Habsburg troops. The citizens threw them out in 1552, but were forced to allow them back in after an eighteen-month siege. Siena was subsequently handed over to the Duchy of Tuscany, ally of the Habsburgs and long-time enemy of the Sienese.

Siena, of course, was not unique in its spectacular flowering or its subsequent stagnation and decline; its history formed part of what is known as the Italian Renaissance. Because of the Italian city-states' impressive economic and cultural efflorescence, their historiography has been enlisted in various larger narratives, perhaps most famously Jacob Burckhardt's 'rise of the individual', launched in 1860. In this chapter, however, the emphasis is on the emergence of collective arrangements, which allowed citizens to act in the public domain. Burckhardt's thesis was part of a modernisation framework that saw the Italian city-states as the birthplace of the modern world, including the capitalist economy and democratic rule.[12] Unfortunately, or so it was argued, the Italians allowed these promising beginnings to wither, as the example of Siena so strongly suggests. The how and what of this remarkable trajectory is the topic of this chapter, still focusing on citizenship, but now framing its development in the context of state formation.[13]

Medieval Italy

The Italian late Middle Ages and Renaissance is one of the highlights of world history and culture. No country has more UNESCO World Heritage Sites than Italy, and many of these – including the city centre of Siena – have the Renaissance to thank for their inclusion. The Renaissance produced such household names as brilliantly innovative painters Fra Angelico, Leonardo da Vinci and Michelangelo Buonarroti; Filippo Brunelleschi's spectacular dome for the *Duomo* in

Florence; Dante's *Divina Comedia* and Boccaccio's *Decameron*, as well as major works of political theory by the likes of Leonardo Bruni and Niccolò Machiavelli. It was, however, much more than a cultural phenomenon. Or perhaps we should say: this cultural efflorescence was riding on a massive wave of societal change and economic prosperity.[14]

This societal change was directly connected to a huge increase in levels of urbanisation in medieval Italy. While urbanisation was only slowly increasing in much of Europe between 1000 and 1300, Italian figures probably doubled during this period, to reach around 15 per cent of the population as a whole. After the losses of the Black Death in the middle of the fourteenth century, resulting in a decline in urbanisation, Italian cities managed to recover. Apart from the Low Countries Italy remained ahead of the rest of Europe.[15] Urbanisation was in turn intimately related to the economic upsurge of the peninsula, where merchants pioneered new methods of accounting and established new commercial networks with the Middle East from whence they supplied the rest of Europe with Asian luxury goods. Italian industries, meanwhile, developed their own export markets, most notably in textiles. There can be no doubt that in 1300 Italy was the wealthiest region in Europe, and still was in 1500, albeit now together with the western provinces of the Low Countries.[16] These successes of the Italian city-states have been related to the patronage of powerful individuals, like the Medici in Florence, but also to the 'civic culture' that embraced large sections of the population.[17]

The Italian city-states' successes may have been spectacular, but they were also relatively short-lived. From roughly the middle of the sixteenth century – the point in time was not the same everywhere – they lost some of their vitality. Urbanisation rates flattened, and so did the economy. Clearly, these city-states were subject to a dynamic that prevented them in the long run from consolidating the magic formula – if there ever was one. The Italian city-states were to an important extent also unique. Other regions had their fair share of autonomous cities, but in terms of numbers and in the level of their autonomy, Italian city-states had no equivalent anywhere else in Europe. As the name suggests, they were essentially cities that displayed the trappings of a state. They had the sovereign power to select their own rulers, to legislate and to wage war and conclude treaties. Most city-states ruled over a substantial hinterland, the *contado*.[18] Italian urban elites were often landowners whose income came from rural investments.[19] Several of these city-states developed into territorial states, absorbing other independent cities in the process. Famously, Pisa lost its independence in 1406 when it became part of the Florentine state. By implication, Pisa was still a commune, but no longer a city-state. All of this had an impact on the involvement of citizens in the ruling of their polities. City-states potentially gave urban citizens a direct say in the governance of the state; in territorial states that direct connection was lost.

The Communes

In the eleventh and early twelfth centuries, independent urban communities emerged as novel institutions. There was no blueprint or larger plan behind this development.[20] The commune emerged out of a series of partly localised conflicts between urban groups, and between those groups and the bishops, who at the time were in charge of the majority of Italian towns.[21] Because it was a major force in this development and has been exceptionally well studied, we should start tracing the emergence of the communes in Milan.

The first documents referring to consuls representing the commune of Milan, and actually referring to individual consuls, date from 1117 and 1130. From 1138 onwards consular judgements in legal disputes are documented more regularly. Twenty documents relating to the consular office survive from the 1150s, while by 1200 the number exceeds 200 per decade. These documents testify to the fact that in the twelfth century the commune of Milan had become formalised. This, obviously, was the outcome of a long and arduous process. In the 1040s a group of *cives* had mounted a rebellion against the reigning archbishop, Ariberto. Almost certainly, these 'citizens' were not ordinary people, but rather a section of the upper stratum of merchants, rentiers and officials.[22] In 1045 the affair was settled with an agreement that gave them a say in the election of the local archbishop. The agreement was confirmed by various oaths sworn by the stakeholders. In that same year, an 'assembly of all the citizens' was indeed consulted during the selection of the new archbishop, Guido de Velate, and a similar involvement is recorded for later elections.[23]

The population of Milan – and this time probably a much wider section – became further involved in politics with the Pataria movement, between 1057 and 1075. This movement was on the face of it concerned about purely ecclesiastical issues, such as the sale of church offices (simony) and the negative impact of married clergy on the validity of the sacraments. When, however, the Pataria attacked Bishop Guido's election as simoniac because the emperor had ignored the preferences of the Milanese, it entered the realm of politics. The Pataria movement led to regular meetings of citizens, involving a broad section of the urban community.[24] Pataria leader Erlembaldo actually governed the city for two years when neither of two rival successors of Guido as archbishop managed to establish himself in the city. Erlembaldo was then killed in another uprising, this time by the elites.

There is no need to follow all the intricate details of local politics, but it is worth noting that a document from Cremona in 1097 mentions the way a dispute was settled in Milan *in consulate civium*, 'in the consulate of the citizens'. It would be another twenty years before another document appeared with the word 'consul', but clearly some sort of civic organisation was being created that was no longer temporarily connected to an emergency, but had a fixed character and personnel. Moreover, this organisation was representing a wider group of people, i.e. the urban community, or at least a relevant part of that community. And thus the *comune* was born.[25]

Some earlier developments were already working in this direction. Merchants and artisans were forming organisations, known as *ministeria*, with their own elected officials. In the tenth century, bishops were consolidating their role in local government by separating the town as a jurisdiction from the countryside. These urban jurisdictions were placed immediately under the authority of the emperors, but in actual fact were governed by bishops.[26] This created the potential for the collective inhabitants to become a juridical person. The canon law reform, gradually introduced from the mid-eleventh century but usually identified with Pope Gregory VII (r. 1073–85), would achieve precisely this, by creating the 'corporation'.[27] This explains why the events that were to have such momentous effects in Italy also affected other areas in Europe.[28] As far as the Church was concerned, from the early twelfth century towns could consider themselves as organisations acknowledged by the law.

What was happening in Milan had its parallels in other urban communities, sometimes even before the Milanese events.[29] In Genoa, a *compagna* was formed shortly before the city was to participate in the First Crusade that started in 1099. An instruction for the local consuls from 1143 regulated the membership of the *compagna*, jurisdiction over its members and their commercial activities, and allowed the consuls to settle trade agreements with other cities. In 1186 the consuls created three permanent markets in the city. More than most Italian towns, with the obvious exception of Venice, Genoa's was a commercial economy and its commune therefore more concerned with trade issues. Still, even Genoese merchants were also substantial landowners.[30]

Like Genoa's, Pisa's commune was one of the earliest to emerge from the confusing events of the eleventh century. Perhaps this was because Pisa seemed to be doing well while so many other towns were in dire straits. Also like Genoa, it was a commercial town; in August 1113 some 300 ships left its port to raid the Balearic Islands. The building of its cathedral from the 1060s, both innovative and eye-catching in its design, testifies to the civic pride of its inhabitants. It was adorned with various texts exalting the works of the Pisans. One of those, referencing the expedition against the Arabs in Palermo from 1064, explicitly mentions the participation of local '*omnes maiores medii pariterque minores*' ('all the grandees, the middling and minor people').[31] The Pisans were caught up in the struggles between the pope and the emperor, but with both sides trying to woo them, this gave the community various privileges. In 1081 Emperor Henry IV promised Pisans a say in the election of the future marquises of Tuscany, as well as significant trade privileges. The diploma with which these were established refers to a *communis consensus* of the *cives*, suggesting institutional mechanisms of consensus-building among the citizens. A Sardinian document from the same year mentions *consoles* of Pisa, although these are possibly just the city elite rather than designated officials. Other documents, from a few years later, refer to a *commune colloquium civitate*, or 'common assembly of the city'. Consuls began to be referenced around this time, and before the century was out seem to have consolidated into proper communal officers. As such they appear for the first time in 1109, representing the city in the purchase of two castles.[32]

The events that we have outlined here for Milan, Genoa and Pisa were repeated all over northern and central Italy. The common pattern was that they led to the emergence of autonomous city governments. The communes established assemblies of citizens. Attached to these, offices for the day-to-day management of the commune also emerged, with their selection procedures and fixed terms. New legal institutions were created as well. These developments happened in response to increased insecurity as a result of the diminished influence of the emperor, and his clash with the Catholic Church.[33] They were probably also a response to a greater demand for the protection of the expanding regional and international trade.[34] By the late twelfth century, communal governments were sufficiently confident to start building town halls where municipal services were concentrated.[35]

With such developments occurring more or less simultaneously in various places, clearly more than just local issues were shaping events. Urban growth and economic expansion were an important backdrop, but in the foreground political issues were occupying centre stage. In the first half of the eleventh century a series of urban revolts had shifted authority away from the Holy Roman Emperor, who had been incapable of suppressing them. In Italy, bishops had become more powerful as a result, because they had both the prestige and the administrative capabilities to fill the gap.[36] At the same time, however, the struggle between pope and emperor over ecclesiastical appointments, known as the Investiture Contest, weakened the bishops' position vis-à-vis urban elites and their supporters.[37] This created an opportunity structure for civic collective action, and the subsequent consolidation of the organisations that emerged in the process.

From Communes to City-States

A succession of Lombard Leagues, between 1167 and 1250, marked the development from communes to city-states. These leagues too emerged out of the contest for control over Italy. There had been predecessors, of course. In 1093, for example, Milan, Cremona, Lodi and Piacenza joined forces against Emperor Henry IV. What distinguished the 1167 league was its size and longevity. In the spring of 1167 Bergamo, Brescia, Cremona, Mantua, Milan and possibly Ferrara, all situated in the Po valley of Lombardy, rose against Emperor Frederick Barbarossa. This league followed on the heels of another anti-imperial alliance between Verona and the towns in its hinterland. Both leagues were an expression of the great concerns in the newly formed communes about the emperor's attempts to regain control over Italy. Apart from a military campaign launched in 1166, this also included the sending of governors and other imperial officials into the towns. Many of these were, rightly or wrongly, soon accused of corruption.

The handful of original league members managed to quickly round up more support, in the case of Lodi after a siege, but others joined voluntarily. Paradoxically, the league had also been made possible by the emperor's destruction of Milan during a previous campaign, in 1162. While the other towns had grown weary of Milan's attempts to dominate the region, this was now no longer an issue as the emperor came to be perceived as a direct threat to their own very existence. By December 1167 the membership had grown to sixteen cities. There was no single treaty uniting the rebel towns; rather, they were allied through a series of bilateral and multilateral agreements. Significantly, those treaties were confirmed by popular assemblies in the participating cities.[38]

The united cities were soon indicated in the sources as *Societas Lombardie*, or the Lombard League, and rightly so, because it quickly developed coordinating institutions. The most important of these was the *colloquium* or *parlamentum*, the assembly that was held regularly. Like the *diet* of the Holy Roman Empire itself, the assembly had no fixed location, but would meet close to the river Po to allow easy access for participants. The Lombard League had three purposes that together indicate precisely the coordination challenges faced by individual communes. The first was common defence. All cities had to underwrite the rule that war and peace would be declared and concluded by the membership in unison. The League also coordinated military campaigns, even though relatively few of those were actually held. The second purpose was dispute settlement between cities. At the 1173 assembly, for example, a territorial conflict between Pavia and Piacenza was adjudicated. Thirdly, the League tried to promote trade between its members by removing barriers. Already in 1168 it was decided that all tolls discriminating against members as had been erected in the previous thirty years would be abolished. The Lombard League developed into a corpus, and found an identity in the common fight against what was perceived as the constant oppression of Lombardy by outside forces.[39]

The Lombard League emerged at a time when warfare in Italy was developing from a contest between purely part-time soldiers to one involving professionals as well. As early as 1176 the combined mercenary and citizen forces of the Lombard League claimed an important victory against Frederick Barbarossa's army.[40] In Florence, the first foreign mercenaries make an appearance in the city accounts in 1208, and by 1260 the city employed 200 mercenary cavalry, thousands of infantrymen, archers and sappers. At the same time, militiamen could also be called up to serve side by side with the professionals.[41] It was precisely their possession of more or less permanent military forces that distinguished Italy's fifty-odd city-states from ordinary cities.[42]

Heyday of the City-States

The death of Frederick II in 1250 marked the end of the wars between the Holy Roman Emperor and the city-states that remained, nominally, his subjects. For two and a half centuries there might be foreign invasions, but the struggle for dominance was now mostly an Italian affair. City-states were, most of the time, fighting each other.[43] As Machiavelli famously argued, popular government was a source of military strength, if only because citizens were serving alongside professional companies in their militia units.[44] From very early on, however, city-states had difficulties in coordinating military action and the administrative processes that supported the armed forces. As a result, special offices were introduced in the decades around 1200 to overcome this deficit, notably the *podestà*. This outsider, usually appointed for a year, brought in his own staff to administer the city. He was therefore simultaneously an administrative and a military coordinator. By the middle of the thirteenth century several cities accepted – or were forced to accept – leaders of local parties as strongmen, no longer appointed on specified terms but indefinitely, as *signori* – or, in the eyes of their opponents, despots. The rise to power of the Viscontis, completed in 1395 with Giangaleazzo Visconti's investiture as Duke of Milan, is one among numerous examples.[45] The cities of the Po valley were the first to experiment with these innovations, but the same process also took place in Florence, albeit somewhat later.

Like other cities, Florence had moved through the stages of setting up a commune.[46] Consuls were first recorded in 1138; in 1192–93 the first *podestà* was appointed. The earliest *podestà* were recruited locally, from the landed families who dominated the city politically, socially and, above all, militarily. Members of these families made up the cavalry of the Florentine army. However, the commercial and industrial classes of the city were busy organising in guilds, and in 1250, significantly on the heels of a military defeat of the Ghibelline elite party that had dominated Florentine politics, the *popolo* took over the reins of the city – and immediately ordered a reorganisation of the militia districts. In the following decade, the city government would be supported, and held in check, by a broad council of men selected through the guilds and militia districts. The magnates, on the other hand, were formally excluded from office. In 1255–56 the various councils of Florence numbered 661 individuals; one of these councils had doctors and notaries as members, but also a tailor and two shoemakers.

The commercial character of the popular regime was underlined when it was decided, in 1252, to issue gold coins with the image of the city's patron, John the Baptist. Genoa took the same step in the same year. Since the Carolingians had produced gold coins in conscious emulation of the Roman Empire more than 400 years prior, no European state had taken this step before Emperor Frederick II reintroduced them in 1231. Now Florence and Genoa were staking this manifest claim to economic sovereignty. Soon, however, the new regime that had the Guelf–Ghibelline rivalry to thank for its establishment became itself embroiled in the civil wars that were constantly erupting. The imperial army was also an active participant. In 1260 Florence was forced to maintain an army of 16,000, recruited from the city and the *contado*, which was quite apart from the militias, charged with domestic security. The Florentine army was badly beaten on 4 September by a Sienese–Ghibelline army, taking down the popular government with it and leading to widespread destruction of Guelf properties in the city.[47]

By the middle of the thirteenth century, the formation and balance of power in the Florentine state was thus intimately linked with its expanding economy on one hand, and with the conflicts between cities and the overall struggle for domination of the Italian peninsula on the other. In these struggles, the support of broader sections of the population was vital. Thus, in 1266 the guilds became involved in Florence's government once again. At the same time, Charles of Anjou, younger brother of the French king, called in by the pope as a counterweight to German claimants, was made *podestà* for ten years. During the 1270s the so-called priorate of the guilds was consolidated, giving first six, later twelve major guilds the right to act as electors for several councils. This second popular regime also introduced a complete overhaul of Florence's Ordinances of Justice, published in January 1293, creating a formal federation of the guilds, while at the same time introducing crippling penalties for elite violence. The popular government expressed its opposition to the magnates by building its own public fortress in the Palazzo Vecchio, started in 1298.[48]

In the next century, elite struggles for power were punctuated by popular revolts and periods of popular government. When the elites were in charge, they still had to worry about the potential for protest inherent in Florence's thick weave of corporatist institutions, such as confraternities, neighbourhoods, guilds and militia companies.[49] Despite this political volatility, Florence's population tripled over the thirteenth century, perhaps even quadrupled to 120,000. Following the plague in 1348, however, the city struggled to reach half that number by the end of the fourteenth century. A quarter of Florentine households depended on the textile industry, which was the mainstay of the local economy. The population increase and public projects also caused the building industry to flourish. Moreover, between the mid-thirteenth century and the arrival of the Black Death, international trade and finance made Florence one of the focal points of a rapidly developing European network. Simultaneously, the city emerged as one of the most innovative centres of artistic creativity in European history.[50]

On a smaller scale, the same happened in many other cities. Pisa, some forty miles downstream from Florence, went through an equally spectacular period of growth in the thirteenth century. The total income of its citizens in 1288 was an estimated eight times larger than it had been just half a century earlier. The population had tripled since 1164, so a substantial amount of this was real income growth per capita. Luxury industries were doing well, especially the cloth trade introduced from Lombardy. As a port, Pisa also benefitted from the expanding trade in grain and wine that it conducted mainly with North Africa and Sardinia. During these years of growth and prosperity, Pisa too experienced a popular revolution. As in many other cities, it happened in the wake of Frederick II's death. In 1254, a Captain of the People is first mentioned, and in 1259 a popular constitution, the *Breve pisani populi*, was established. It was the first of a series of revolutions and regime changes, which came to a temporary halt with the establishment of another popular regime in 1295.[51]

Such changes were characteristic of the period, but one city-state managed to avoid them: Venice in this period seems like a model of stability. What made Venice exceptional? And how exceptional was it, in fact? In some areas there can be little doubt that it was indeed different. Firstly, it might be argued that Venice was the only genuine city-state in Italy. As an erstwhile colony of Byzantium it was no longer subject to its former master, nor to the authority of the Holy Roman

Emperor. Venice, in other words, was a truly sovereign city and the political conflicts between pope and emperor were marginal to Venetian politics.[52] Secondly, it was ruled by a patriciate with aristocratic features, the most obvious of which was its legal limitation to a specific set of families who passed on their patrician status by inheritance. Thirdly, as stated, Venice experienced little of the violent political conflicts and none of the regime changes characteristic of other Renaissance city-states. Historical scholarship that has chipped away at all kinds of the self-congratulatory myths of which Venetian stability is such a wonderful example has so far been unable to topple this one.[53] So, why was the population of Venice prepared to put up with this state of affairs, even while it was no doubt aware of the revolutions in other city-states?[54]

The historiography has looked overwhelmingly at the elites, and remarkably little at the rest of Venice's large and growing population. And it is true that in the formal institutions the popular voice was weak. The *doge*, formerly the duke, was assisted by six ducal councillors, a Senate of forty and the Great Council. From 1297 the latter was accessible to every individual whose family was registered as aristocratic.[55] In 1414, a ledger seeking to establish which families were entitled to seats in the Great Council identified 164 as extant and active.[56] The Venetian nobility is estimated to have made up between 4 and 8 per cent of the population.[57] In purely numerical terms, the Venetian elite was obviously small, but possibly larger, in fact, than elites in other European towns of the time.[58]

As in other Italian cities, the citizens were organised in guilds and confraternities. Several of the most important trades in Venice were not incorporated; the merchants, for example, or the mariners. In the 1260s there probably was some guild unrest, and this was immediately followed by legislation against guild political activities.[59] Nevertheless, in the thirteenth century there were at least fifty guilds, by no means an exceptionally low number. Moreover, the number increased over time.[60] The confraternities of Venice were as active as any. The Venetian *Scuole Grandi*, moreover, were only accessible to *cittadini*, and excluded the patricians.[61] Neighbourhoods, on the other hand, were not the power base for the 'great' families that they were in other Italian city-states.[62] Neither was citizenship more inaccessible in Venice than elsewhere.[63] From a comparative perspective, the *popolani* of Venice were not less organised, nor did they have fewer reasons to complain, than those of other Italian city-states.[64]

There thus comes a point when the spotlight has to be turned towards the elites. Elite conflict was an important source of political instability elsewhere, and this the Venetians tried hard to prevent. Their ranks were legally closed from 1297, although in practice it was still possible to join. Especially in the decades immediately after this so-called *Serrata*, or closing, the membership of the Great Council increased quite dramatically, from 582 in 1298, to double that number in 1314; in 1350 the Great Council still had a membership of almost 900. Around 1380, during the War of Chiogga, more new families were admitted.[65] In the first half of the fifteenth century, new legislation sought to limit the size of the patriciate, but numbers of active nobles remained high.[66] In the mid-seventeenth century, when the Venetian state was in financial dire straits, about 100 families managed to buy a noble title.[67] Directly beneath the patriciate, a second elite of 'citizens' (*cittadini*) provided a second pillar for the regime.[68] They were, for example, the most prominent members in six *Scuole Grandi*, the most important charitable confraternities.[69] The constitution of the Venetian elite as an urban nobility possibly distinguished its mode of behaviour from less clearly defined oligarchies elsewhere. Its code of honour disapproved of civic (as opposed to military) violence, and the patriciate set great store by class unity. It would seem that, by and large, it managed to uphold those self-imposed standards.[70]

Although in all Italian city-states expansion was first and foremost propelled by overseas commerce and industry, they also became increasingly interested in the *contado*. One reason was straightforward: growing urban populations were in need of more and more food. The *contado* was the first supplier, and as such also an object of profitable urban investments. Simultaneously, it delivered much of the manpower for urban industries and provided a military buffer. Since many elite families held extensive rural properties anyway, urban policies primarily served to intensify relations with the *contado*.[71] Even Venice, with its mercantile elite, was expanding its mainland territories, called Terraferma, and increasing its grip, to create military buffers and increase revenues, although the Venetians themselves would argue that the mainland cities had voluntarily subjected themselves to their dominance.[72] From very early on, territorialisation was part and parcel of the formation of city-states. In the next centuries, this process would gradually shift the emphasis of the city-state away from the city and towards the state.

City-States Become Regional States

With the exception of Venice, city-states had notoriously volatile politics.[73] The fire that devastated a substantial part of Florence in 1304 as a result of deliberate actions by rival elite factions was just an extreme example of the often violent clashes, not only among elite families themselves, but also between elites and the 'common people'. The problem was not conflict as such, but the inability to deal with it in a regulated fashion. One important reason for this failure was that many males were armed – and the authorities expected them to be armed. The elite families served as the communities' cavalry, while ordinary citizens could expect to be called up for militia infantry duties. Weapons were supplied by the men themselves, not by the community. Violent regime changes were the order of the day in the thirteenth, fourteenth and fifteenth centuries. They were often accompanied by forced expulsion of families from the city, often for many years. In Lucca, a plot was discovered in 1370 to overthrow the government. In May 1392 another political conflict in Lucca came to a boil, with several fatalities and banishments of those considered responsible, i.e. the losers.[74] In Bologna, attempts to overthrow the local government were recorded twice in 1376, in 1386, in 1389, twice again in 1399 and once more in 1401.[75] These examples could be extended to every Italian city and city-state. Only Venice, as we have seen, seemed by and large immune from such clashes.

In the fourteenth and fifteenth centuries, domestic violence was exacerbated by new developments in interstate violence. Mercenaries, both foreign and domestic, made their first appearance on the Italian battlefields in the thirteenth century. They fought side by side with local amateur troops. As the numbers of professionals rose, however, they increasingly became a problem. City-states hired mercenary units on a temporary contract, and because they were expensive, cities were keen to get rid of the 'free companies', as they were called, as soon as possible. However, if no alternative employment emerged, these troops, far away from home, were left with little choice but to raid and plunder as they moved from one place to another like termites. To make things worse, opposing factions in various city-states would invite them with the offer of plunder rather than regular pay. Between 1342 and 1399 Siena suffered their unwelcome attentions on no fewer than thirty-seven occasions, i.e. once every eighteen months. Raids could cause human and material devastation, but could sometimes be avoided by paying a ransom. One way or another, however, the free companies were a huge burden on local finances.[76]

During the second half of the fifteenth century, the technology of warfare changed spectacularly. With the development of gunpowder artillery, town walls became obsolete, and had to be replaced by more complex and more expensive defence works. These were known as *trace italienne*, after the area where they were first developed. Handguns also appeared on the battlefield, requiring troops to devote more time to drill and exercise because of the difficulty of handling the new tools of destruction. These innovations received their baptism of fire during the Italian wars of the late fifteenth and early sixteenth centuries.[77]

Such developments increased pressure on state governments in two ways. First and foremost, the new technology was more destructive: after decades of incessant warfare, many towns and regions were laid to waste.[78] Secondly, the financial stakes were raised. Because of the early use of professional soldiers, Italian city-states had been forced relatively early to develop instruments for raising extra revenue, i.e. a public debt. Initially, city-states resorted to forced loans, but these were gradually replaced by voluntary subscriptions, giving citizens an opportunity to signal their approval of their government's performance. Declining interest rates suggest they were doing well, probably because the governors were also leaders of the local business community.[79] Still, military expenditures increased during the fifteenth century to unprecedented levels. In Florence a war against neighbouring Lucca that also attracted Milanese involvement forced the state during most of the 1420s to spend sums that had been required only exceptionally in earlier centuries. During the preceding two decades, Florence had fought wars against Milan, Pisa and Naples, all drawn out over several years. The debts accumulated during these conflicts made the Florentine Republic increasingly dependent on local banking families.[80]

The pressures of warfare exposed – as contemporaries were well aware – a flaw of popular governments: they had always found it difficult to coordinate military efforts. Francesco Guicciardini's *Dialogo del Reggimento di Firenze*, written in the 1520s, lists a string of shortcomings, including the impossibility of articulating a long-term strategy, how to negotiate with other powers, the lack of resolution and, indeed, the impossibility for a collective government to provide leadership to the troops. As Guicciardini has one of his characters sum up the situation: 'Government of the many is lacking in quite a number of important things: secrecy, speed and, what is worse, resolution'.[81] In most city-states, these pressures would ultimately lead to single-handed, hereditary government by a member of the local elite. No longer the *podestà*, who had been an outsider rotated every year, or even the *signore* of the fourteenth century, these new leaders, as yet without a name, held a permanent position, came from the local community and were surrounded by their own relatives, as well as other elite families. An early example was Castruccio Castracani, who emerged as captain-general of Lucca in the aftermath of its comprehensive defeat by Pisan troops in August 1314. Castracani was a local merchant who had been appointed with all due constitutional limitations. His financial clout made him popular with the troops as well as with his fellow merchants, who preferred the leadership of one of their own over power-sharing with the wider community. In 1320 Castracani was made *signore* for life. He built strong diplomatic relations with Emperor Ludwig of Bavaria, who made him a duke in 1327.[82] It was a sign of things to come.

In Lucca's case, Castracani's single-headed leadership looked like no more than a stay of execution, because after his death in the following year, it was first forced to accept the patronage of the emperor, subsequently of the lord of Verona, Mastino della Scala.[83] In 1342 Lucca still felt so threatened by Florence that it placed itself under the rule of Pisa, effectively giving up its independence. In 1369 it was 'liberated' again by the emperor, but subsequently sold to various magnates and ultimately to Florence. Lucca managed to survive as an independent republic only because it was so small that it bothered none of its neighbours.[84] In Milan, the Viscontis, who had been *signori* there since the late thirteenth century, became dukes in 1395. However, the most famous instance of this development was, of course, once again provided by Florence.

In the beginning, the Medici regime looked like many of its contemporaries. Cosimo de Medici's return from a brief exile in 1434 and his subsequent leadership over Florentine politics was not fundamentally different from similar developments in other city-states. However, by the time he died in 1464 two things had changed. The government decreed that his tomb would be adorned with a special inscription: 'Pater Patriae', a concept seemingly at odds with the republican idea of collective rule. This was underlined by the succession of his son Piero, another break with the republican tradition that privileged competence over inheritance. Both Piero and his successor, Lorenzo, claimed to be ordinary citizens, but the latter's nickname – 'il Magnifico' – belied that conceit.[85] It is true that the Medici regime faltered after Lorenzo's death in 1492 and the family was out of office and in exile again for two decades. That, however, proved but an interlude. In 1512, after another international conflict on Italian soil, the Medicis returned to power in Florence. And then, with the help of Charles V's conquest of Tuscany in 1530, another Cosimo de Medici was made Duke of Tuscany in 1537.[86]

The appointment came on the heels of an intense debate about the political future of the city and its state. Machiavelli, in a discourse from 1520, proposed a system of governance that would satisfy the needs of the '*primi*' and '*mezzani*', i.e. the elite and upper citizen strata, as well as the '*universalità dei cittadini*'. The first group would delegate sixty-five men to staff the Signoria, the second would be represented by a council of 200, the third by Florence's traditional Great Council, with 1,000 members. The first two, moreover, would be allowed to meet only in the presence of the sixteen 'standard bearers' (*gonfalonieri*) who were in charge of the civic militia companies of Florence's sixteen districts.[87] But it was not to be. The fact that the Holy Roman Emperor changed the constitution of one of Italy's principal republics in itself signalled the consolidation of a new era. The nature of the change spoke volumes and by then Machiavelli himself had already been forced into exile by the Medici regime shortly after their return. The era of the city-states was definitely over. Instead, the major city-states developed into regional states, where the city was also a state capital and local elites were heavily involved in the governance of the state.[88]

Conclusion

Medieval Italy constituted a unique environment, not least from the perspective of citizenship. Four elements help explain its precocious development.[89] First of all, in this heartland of the former Roman Empire, a network of towns had long been established, and managed to survive during the post-Roman era. Secondly, the Roman Catholic Church, with its headquarters located in Rome, had an even greater influence in Italy than in the rest of medieval Europe. Thirdly, feudal landowners in Italy were also urban residents and forged an unusually strong connection between town and countryside. Fourth and finally, the ultimate source of authority, in the case of Italy the Holy Roman Emperor, was unusually far removed from the peninsula. These four features each contributed an element to the emergence of city-states in Italy. The survival of towns implied a survival of urban populations with the potential to develop into a cohesive political actor. The prominent position of bishops increased the likelihood that developments affecting the Church would spill over into the urban public domain. Coalitions of landowners and merchants ideally allied military with economic power, while the physical distance of the emperor created a potential for independent action by towns and cities. In the eleventh century these four elements came together to create 'communes', some of which subsequently developed into city-states. City-states were urban communes adorned with the trappings of statehood. They raised their own armies and the taxes to pay for the soldiers, and this enabled them to execute their own foreign policy. Many Italian city-states gave their citizens a substantial role in local governance.

Initially, Italian city-states were politically and economically very successful: even in 1500 the region boasted levels of urbanisation and wealth well above the rest of Europe (apart, perhaps, from the Low Countries). In earlier centuries the difference had been even more significant.[90] However, the situation that created the Italian city-states in the long run also proved the cause of their undoing. The city-states' success created intense rivalry and attracted the attention of outsiders. The result was an endless series of armed conflicts between city-states, exacerbated by interventions from non-Italian powers. To pay for these wars, the cities were forced to increasingly exploit their rural hinterland. Simultaneously, internal conflicts, some about the spoils of this exploitation, many others about the distribution of the costs, weakened communal political cohesion, which increasingly led to authoritarian forms of rule. All these factors caused the Italian city-states to enter a long phase of economic and demographic stagnation and in the process to transform themselves into regional states.

To what extent were these developments shaped by citizens, through their participation in popular governments? And did their contribution have a positive or negative impact on the outcome? Several attempts have been made, with the help of quantitative methods, to establish a relationship between prosperity, expressed as urban growth, and political regime. These attempts are plagued by three problems: data points are half or even whole centuries apart; the distinction between oligarchy and popular regimes is far from clear-cut; and the quality of population figures, necessary to establish 'success' or 'failure', is often questionable. As a result, conclusions have been reached that do not always sit easily together. De Long and Shleifer concluded, for premodern Europe as a whole, that authoritarian – they called it absolutist – rule was bad for urban growth.[91] Bosker and colleagues confirmed this conclusion for Italy specifically: a change from constrained to authoritarian rule had a negative impact on growth.[92] Percoco showed how the presence of medieval local constitutions positively influenced local economic development in Italy in the very long run.[93] Stasavage concluded, on the basis of another European survey, that autonomous cities indeed grew relatively fast during their first 100–200 years of autonomy, but found their growth rates matched or even overtaken by non-autonomous (i.e. princely) cities after these one or two centuries. According to Stasavage, autonomous cities developed oligarchies, as well as merchant and craft guilds, which stifled new initiatives, whereas princes might encourage innovation.[94]

On the basis of the discussion in this chapter, we can, I think, conclude with three generalisations that are commensurate with most of the findings of these quantitative exercises. First, by and large the period of economic efflorescence in medieval Italy built upon the establishment of independent communes, and subsequent city-states. Secondly, the Early Renaissance, with its economic prosperity and cultural innovation, broadly coincided with the high point of popular government, i.e. with the greatest influence of citizens in local rule, even if many of the famous artists were working for the courts. Third and finally, the following period of stagnation broadly coincided with more authoritarian types of rule in many Italian states, i.e. with very restricted roles for citizens. How regions with high levels of 'civicness' during the Renaissance managed to revitalise this institutional capital during the nineteenth and twentieth centuries has not yet been fully explained, but we should be sceptical about the straightforward continuity thesis as postulated by Putnam.[95]

7 THE DUTCH REPUBLIC
The Federalisation of Citizenship

On Sunday, 21 January 1610, at 6:00 AM (!), the presiding burgomaster of Utrecht was roused by a messenger sent by the commanding officers of the town's eight civic militia companies, demanding an interview with the city council.[1] Their eight companies had in the meantime been called up, and were gathered in the square in front of the town hall. By 9:00 AM the council was ready to hear the complaints. On behalf of the citizens of Utrecht, the commanding officers, or *burgerhopmans*, demanded in effect a reintroduction of the local constitution of 1304, as had been in force until 1528. This implied that henceforth the council would be elected, not by co-option as had been the practice since 1528, but through the citizens' representative institutions. However, in places where the former constitution had given a key role to the deans of the guilds, it should now read *hopmans*, and the franchise would be given, not to the guild members, but to the militiamen in their eight companies. The proposal also stated that the commanding officers should henceforth be elected by the members of their companies, instead of being appointed by the council.[2] Further demands requested changes in the provincial government, better to protect the interests of the city, and a general maintenance of the city's ancient privileges and particularly those of the guilds, and insisted that 'the prosperity of the city of Utrecht and its community will be the ultimate law and privilege'.[3]

The 1610 rebellion was one more episode in a long series of urban revolts in Utrecht that had begun with the local guilds' successful claim to power in 1304. Their rule came to an end when Charles

V managed to include the bishopric of Utrecht in his Low Countries domains in 1528. Charles not only built a fortress to ensure the city's loyalty – with heavy irony it was called Vredenborch, or Peace Keep – but he also reformed the local constitution with the express design of excluding the guilds.[4] During the early stages of the Dutch Revolt, in the winter of 1576–77, the Utrecht militias laid siege to Vredenborch Castle, helping to oust the Habsburg garrison. The castle itself was destroyed in the aftermath. After putting down a mutiny by German mercenaries in April 1577, the militias had effectively replaced the guilds as spokesmen for the civic community. It was in this latter capacity that they successfully lobbied the provincial States to accept William of Orange as stadholder, thus bringing both the city and the province of Utrecht into the rebel camp.[5]

In 1610 the Utrecht council, having lost its previous means of protection, immediately stood down, declaring that no one would want to rule against the express wishes of the citizens, and proceeded to organise elections according to the militias' proposals. A subsequent investigation of the citizens' complaints by the provincial States of Utrecht created more controversy. In early March there was another call to arms of the militias, following a deliberately planted rumour that a 500-men-strong garrison was about to enter Utrecht. For a full week the militias were in charge of the city, seeking satisfaction for their demands. On 31 March professional troops did actually arrive, and after nine days of negotiation, and after commander-in-chief Maurice of Nassau threatened that if necessary he would take the city by force, these were finally admitted into Utrecht. On 16 April, the States of Utrecht felt it was safe to return to their headquarters in the city.[6]

This episode from Utrecht's local history is one of many demonstrating how in the Low Countries local politics had national reverberations. During the Dutch Revolt (1568–1648), urban citizens changed the fate of the nation – indeed helped create a completely new country. Why this happened, and how citizens continued to be involved in the governance of that country, is the topic of this chapter.[7]

Towns of the Low Countries and the World Economy

On the world stage, the Netherlands is a small country – and always has been. Still, there was a time when its name was on everybody's lips. During much of the seventeenth century the Dutch dominated European and, indeed, world trade. In that same period, the Dutch army and navy were also a prominent presence on the European battlefields. Scholars working in the Dutch Republic, like Descartes and Spinoza, were among the avant-garde of the Scientific Revolution. Dutch artists from the period, including Rembrandt and Vermeer, are household names even today. The history of the Dutch Republic, at least during its golden age, is therefore a story of far more than local importance. It affected much of the rest of Europe, as well as many non-European regions.[8]

Two aspects of the Dutch golden age stand out in particular: the levels of economic growth and per capita income, and the development of the Dutch state. Both these phenomena were quite extraordinary from a comparative point of view. Estimates for GDP/capita in various European countries between 1500 and 1800 suggest that the normal situation was one of stagnation. The Southern Netherlands (present Belgium) experienced some modest growth; Spain and Italy endured, if anything, decline. The Dutch economy, on the other hand, went through a spectacular phase of growth: between circa 1580 and 1650 national income per capita increased by about 50 per cent.[9] In Holland the economy expanded by more than 1 per cent per annum. All sectors contributed to these growth figures, albeit some more than others.[10] Simultaneously, the Dutch state went through a similarly spectacular growth phase. According to the most recent estimates the Dutch army in the 1630s and 1640s was about 60,000 strong. These figures take on their real meaning when we translate them into per capita numbers. In the Dutch Republic every thirty inhabitants were supporting one soldier. France, with a population roughly ten times larger, at the time had an army 80,000 men strong.[11] It was no wonder that the Dutch were by far the most heavily taxed nation in Europe. Per capita taxation in Holland during the seventeenth century was three to five times as high as in England and France.[12]

The Dutch golden age had been preceded by an equally spectacular, two-stage growth phase in the southern Low Countries. During the late Middle Ages, first Flanders and subsequently Brabant had evolved into the staples of interregional trade for all of Northern Europe.[13] Bruges in the fourteenth and fifteenth centuries, and Antwerp during the sixteenth, connected trade routes from the north and the south, and increasingly also with the non-European world. From 1498 Portuguese spices, imported from Asia, landed in Antwerp, not Lisbon. Both Bruges and Antwerp maintained very close trade relations with England, the source of imported wool, with French markets (a source of grain), and with the German hinterland. Although technically not a member, Bruges acted as the western outpost of the German Hanse network, and was also the northernmost destination for many Italian merchants. Both Bruges and Antwerp were teeming with foreigners and had special facilities to house them.[14] In many respects, they were the northern equivalents of the Italian Renaissance cities. However, both were part of a larger territory, where they had to reckon with princes who did not come from an urban or mercantile background. Being embedded in a larger territorial framework clearly had advantages: for example, Antwerp might not have been the recipient of the Portuguese spice trade without the Habsburg dynastic connections between the two regions. At the same time, the towns of the Low Countries were regularly at loggerheads with those same princes – about autonomy, but also about citizen involvement. The new constitution Charles V imposed on Utrecht in 1528 was just one example of this long-running conflict. The agency of urban elites and citizens, I argue in this chapter, played a vital part in the success of the Low Countries on the world stage.

Urban Revolutions from the Battle of the Spurs (1302) to the Dutch Revolt (1568–1585)

Although the artisans' victory over the French mounted aristocracy in the Battle of the Spurs in 1302 struck contemporaries like a bolt of lightning, it was in fact the most spectacular event in a struggle that had already been under way for at least a half century.[15] After 1302, artisans managed to stake a claim in government in many of the important towns throughout the Low Countries.[16] In Bruges a new constitution handed the community nine out of thirteen seats on the local magistrate bench, while the lord (the count of Flanders) retained four.[17] Ghent had already received a new constitution in 1301 according to which the count of Flanders and the urban community, represented by the outgoing magistrates, each appointed four electors, who would then elect the twenty-six new aldermen for the next year. After 1302, the guilds were able to gain substantial influence in these elections, mainly at the expense of the count.[18]

Similar developments were taking place in the Duchy of Brabant. In Louvain, during the years 1303–05, artisan representatives ruled the town until the duke of Brabant helped the patricians to regain power.[19] In Brussels the revolution took place in 1303, but was equally short-lived.[20] 's-Hertogenbosch had its guild revolution in the winter of 1305–06; a reconciliation with the elites occurred shortly afterwards. The latter revolt nonetheless gave citizens some control over the imposition of new taxes in the town.[21] Malines, a separate enclave within the Duchy, was also swept up by the political tsunami and in 1305 won the right to appoint its own magistrate. This once again included representatives of the artisan organisations.[22] Antwerp, Brabant's other main town, merely experienced a mild revolution; its 1306 constitution confirmed a complete return to patrician rule. However, Antwerp was the exception and smaller towns in Brabant, like Tienen and Zoutleeuw, gained new constitutions with guilds winning a direct influence in local government.[23]

In the northern territories of the Low Countries, the impact of the guild revolutions was limited. The main exception was Utrecht, where the guilds had already forced their way into the local government at least once before. They managed to repeat this in 1304, when they imposed a new constitution on the city, in the guild ordinance of 1304. This ordinance, promulgated by the common elders of the Utrecht guilds, determined that henceforth the twenty-four members of the Utrecht town council would be selected and sworn in by the elders of the guilds.[24]

In Utrecht this revolutionary constitution proved durable; in other towns the citizens lost much ground, which they attempted to regain in a second wave of urban rebellions, triggered by the death of their sovereign, Charles the Bold, on the battlefield in January 1477. Since 1302 political alignments had fundamentally changed in the Low Countries. Over the course of the fourteenth and fifteenth centuries, through a string of strategic marriages the dukes of Burgundy had acquired a dozen territories, including the economically most vibrant, i.e. Flanders and Brabant. They had also initiated a process of political convergence, including a new overarching institution, the States-General, where representatives of the individual territories could discuss taxation and other issues with the sovereign.[25]

In the dukes of Burgundy, the towns of the Low Countries had acquired formidable opponents, as the city of Liège experienced in 1468. Liège had had the temerity to rebel twice in two years. The first rebellion had left the city bereft of its urban privileges; the attempt to regain them led to its almost complete destruction. The same happened in Dinant, where the duke wanted to set an example for other towns in the region. And when spared the fate of physical destruction, the Burgundians still had a repertoire of symbolic humiliation. In December 1440, representatives of Bruges were forced to demonstrate their loyalty to Duke Philip the Good by appearing before their lord barefoot and in white penitential garb, after Philip had defeated a local rebellion that had seen his local governor murdered by the insurgents. Following a Ghent rebellion – the latest in a series of rebellions in 1401, 1404, 1406, 1411, 1414, 1423, 1437 and 1440 – which was defeated in 1452–53, the leaders of the community were similarly forced to beg for mercy and to hand over the guild banners. This could count as a lucky escape, because the duke had actually been advised 'that the said town of Ghent should be demolished and razed to the ground ... never to be repopulated'.[26]

When Charles the Bold perished in 1477 without male issue, the States-General forced his heir, Mary of Burgundy, to sign up to a Great Privilege that restored much of the towns' and provinces' former autonomy. Mary, however, immediately married Maximilian of Habsburg and together they attempted to undo the concessions of 1477. To achieve this, they would have had to deal with the elites as well as with the guilds in especially Bruges and Ghent, who had used this window of opportunity to demand a restoration of their political rights. They were up in arms in 1477 and 1479, respectively.[27] More unrest followed after Mary herself passed away in 1482; Ghent and Bruges once again rebelled against their sovereign to demand greater autonomy. Maximilian was actually taken hostage in Bruges in 1488, and only released when, after three months of captivity, he had made various concessions – which he promptly reneged on after his release. It took until late 1492 before all urban resistance in Flanders had been subdued.[28]

The third wave of rebellion was the result of failed attempts by the Habsburgs – first Charles V, then Philip II – to root out Protestantism in the Low Countries.[29] Some people might have felt sympathetically towards the Protestants, but many more were upset by the ways in which the government was ignoring traditional checks and balances in its persecution of heretics. That balance had been shifting away from local and regional governance anyway, as a result of the reinforcement of central government institutions in Brussels in previous decades. Ghent, for example, had been forced by Charles V in 1540 to accept a new constitution that very much reduced the political power of the guild deans.[30] At the same time, the recent inclusion of the northern territories of Friesland and Groningen (1524), Utrecht and Overijssel (1528), and finally Guelders (1543) had strengthened the camp of the opponents of centralisation. So when Philip in 1568 sent a Spanish army to the Low Countries in reaction to a wave of Protestant iconoclasm, a clash was inevitable.

Although it might be argued that the Dutch Revolt was launched as an aristocratic rebellion, the towns were active and indeed vital participants from the outset. In the southern territories, the Revolt created an opportunity for the instauration of more or less autonomous Calvinist republics in Antwerp, Brussels, Ghent and Malines.[31] In the north, the tide turned in favour of the rebels when towns – first Brill, then Flushing – started to admit rebel troops from the spring of 1572. By the end of the year, most of Holland and Zeeland, i.e. the most urbanised parts of the Northern Netherlands, were in rebel hands. Citizens and their organisations were instrumental in this change. In Gouda, for example, despite it being considered by the government in Brussels as a '*bonne ville*', the citizens turned against a new tax introduced to pay for the suppression of Protestantism. Gouda's civic militia officers declared in March 1572 that their men would not protect tax farmers and might even prevent the collection of the new taxes, perceived as illegitimate because they had not been approved by the provincial states assemblies. When rumours suggested a Spanish garrison might be stationed in the town, Gouda openly declared in favour of the rebels.[32] Spanish troops, instruments of a deliberate policy of terror, who were moreover inclined to plunder because of arrears in pay, were perhaps the single strongest motivators of the rebel towns. Once towns crossed the divide to the rebel side, there was no turning back, as was underlined by the sack of Antwerp in November 1576. Widely publicised as the Spanish Fury, it was said (though this may have been an exaggeration) to have cost the lives of 8,000 inhabitants, close to 10 per cent of the population.[33]

In early 1579, the rebel towns and provinces, which at the time included Antwerp, Ghent and Bruges, signed a treaty to coordinate their efforts, including the creation of a common army and a uniform system of taxation to pay for these troops.[34] The Union of Utrecht would become the foundational document for the Dutch Republic as it was slowly emerging. The southern provinces were brought back under

Habsburg rule when Spanish troops managed to overwhelm Antwerp in 1585, causing an outflow of some 100,000 refugees from Brabant and Flanders, mostly to the rebel territories in the north. The result was a welcome boost to the economy of the newly established Dutch Republic.

Urban Citizenship in the Dutch Republic

The politicians of the Dutch Republic pretended that, despite the Revolt, it was business as usual, and most pre-Revolt privileges remained in force. Nonetheless, the Revolt and the ensuing creation of the Dutch Republic had created a novel political constellation insofar as the sovereignty to which they had been subject before had devolved into the hands of the towns themselves. Due to the combined effects of pretended continuity and actual revolution, the constitution of the Republic was a bit of a mess. First of all, once the rebel provinces had declared their independence in 1581, nobody quite knew which institution had inherited the sovereign powers from Philip II. Some claimed it had to be the States-General, but others argued that it was the provincial states assemblies.[35] Grand Pensionary Johan de Witt, in effect Holland's prime minister, wrote as late as 1652:[36]

> These provinces do not constitute *una respublica*, but each province *alone* is a *souveraine respublica*, and as such these United Provinces should not bear the name of *respublica* (in the singular), but rather the name of *respublicae foederatae* or *unitae*, in the plural.

If this argument was accepted – and many politicians believed it to be true and acted accordingly – then the towns were subject to a sovereign provincial states assembly in which they themselves held key positions. In Holland, the most populous and wealthiest province, contributing almost 60 per cent of the Republic's budget and shouldering most of its debts, the towns cast eighteen out of nineteen votes in the states assembly. In Friesland the towns counted for a mere quarter of the votes cast in the provincial states, whereas in all other provinces it was at least 50 per cent. Urban interests dominated the national politics of the Republic. Urban citizenship therefore mattered in the Dutch Republic well beyond the confines of the cities themselves.[37]

As in the rest of Europe, citizenship in the Dutch Republic was a purely local institution, conferred by birth or acquired by purchase. Although exact figures are lacking, it can be safely assumed that about half the urban population had formal citizenship rights.[38] Only citizens could serve the community in major offices. Therefore, all the local councillors were citizens. More generally, the local constitutions suggested that councils represented the citizen community. It thus seemed only fair that citizens should be entitled to a say in local affairs. And because in the Dutch Republic local affairs tended to be also provincial affairs, which in turn had an important impact on national affairs, such claims went a long way politically. In some parts of the country, notably the eastern provinces, the civic community was formally represented by a Common Council that had to be consulted before important decisions affecting the whole community could be taken. As a result, Zwolle's Common Council gave its solemn approval to the peace treaties the Dutch Republic concluded with Spain in 1648, with England in 1654 and again in 1667, with France in 1697, the alliance with the emperor and England in 1702, the Treaty of Utrecht in 1714 and so on.[39]

In the west, citizens were clamouring for similar rights, when they were not already available. Because there was no formal representation of the citizen community in the towns of Holland – their councils were recruited through co-option – the middle classes used the civic militias as their main vehicle for political mobilisation. Under normal circumstances, however, urban politics in Holland was dominated by the merchants, whose political programme was clear-cut. The Amsterdam burgomaster, Cornelis Hooft, who was also active as a grain merchant in the Baltic trade, summed up the gist of their policy: 'Our power and interest consist of the *Imperium maris* and international trade'.[40] Johan de Witt, who did not have a personal interest in trade, was nonetheless of the same opinion.[41] Such attitudes are typical of the whole so-called regent class in charge of Holland's politics during the seventeenth and eighteenth centuries. These people might feel the state belonged to them, but as a result of the small scale of their domains (apart from Amsterdam, all Holland's towns had fewer than 70,000 inhabitants) and in the absence of a substantial police force, urban elites were vulnerable to political pressure, especially from the well-organised middle classes, whose guild petitions and militia revolts ensured that citizen priorities were not forgotten. Hooft, well aware of the role ordinary citizens had played in the Dutch Revolt, argued that their opinions had to be taken seriously; 'they are our strongest asset', he insisted.[42] Such arguments faded as the Revolt passed from lived experience into a distant and stylised memory, but the regents were regularly reminded of the political claims of their citizens during waves of civic rebellion that occurred in the 1610s, in 1672, after William III's death in 1702, in 1748 and finally during the Patriot Revolution of the 1780s.[43] Each time, these events coincided with international tensions reaching fever pitch: in the 1610s when the question was whether and how to continue the war against Spain, and again in 1672 when the country was under attack from England, France and the prince-bishops of Münster and Cologne. In 1702 the War of the Spanish Succession was erupting; in 1747 another French invasion threatened the country's independence. The Patriot Revolution was the direct outcome of the government's embarrassment during the Fourth Anglo–Dutch War. International crisis and citizen mobilisation were thus directly linked, underlining the connection between local citizenship and national politics.[44]

The Towns and the Dutch State

The Dutch Revolt produced a durable coalition of cities and provinces after 1572.[45] This coalition was – at least during the seventeenth century – large enough to compete with the territorial states of Western Europe. However, to do so successfully, the founding fathers of the Dutch Republic had to solve the problem of stable coordination at two levels: the provincial (between individual cities within each province) and the state (between the provinces). Since Holland and Zeeland constituted the centre of the state, it makes sense to focus on the genesis of their political institutions first.

During the central Middle Ages, Holland and Zeeland had been underdeveloped regions of Western Europe, with relatively low levels of urban development compared with neighbouring Flanders and Brabant. In this period the territorial state, governed by the count of Holland (who also acted as count of Zeeland), provided the framework in which the emerging cities slowly acquired political influence. For example, already at an early stage (in the late thirteenth century) they lent large amounts of money to the count in return for extensions of their privileges. To channel this process, the States of Holland evolved out of ad hoc institutions of consultation between the count and his subjects, in particular representatives of the nobility and the cities. In 1428, when

Holland became part of the emerging Burgundian state, the States of Holland were formalised as an institution, in which the cities occupied almost all seats; only one was reserved for the nobility, which was also representing the countryside. Gradually, the states assembly became the main platform for policy formation and consultation, and the place where the representatives of the cities monitored each other's actions.[46] During the middle decades of the sixteenth century, cooperation between the cities of Holland intensified, in particular as a result of the pressure to raise taxes and increase the borrowing power of Holland. Within the framework of the States of Holland they developed a strong mutual understanding and created the foundations for a collective organisation of the public finances of the province.[47]

The Revolt of 1568 further intensified these processes, because the towns formed the backbone of the resistance against the Spanish forces – with the important initial exception of Amsterdam, which until 1578 took the side of Philip II.[48] Urban privileges were very much at stake in this conflict, with the towns insisting on maintaining and expanding their own autonomy. On the other hand, William of Orange, the leader of the revolt and (former) stadholder (governor) on behalf of Philip II, was the most important force for coherence during the initial stages of the Revolt. The tension between these two main agents of Holland politics – the coordinating role of the stadholders versus the particularistic ambitions of the cities – was to remain a crucial feature of Dutch politics through the seventeenth and eighteenth centuries.[49]

Within the Republic, the province of Holland provided leadership and took on most of the public debt. In fact, this was the source of the Republic's stability: the fact that none of the towns could dominate the States of Holland, let alone the country as a whole.[50] From abroad it might seem as if Amsterdam was in control, but in the Republic people knew better, and not least in Amsterdam; 'it is a republic of persuasion', the deputies of Amsterdam remarked realistically in 1731.[51] In the States of Holland, each of the eighteen enfranchised towns commanded a single vote, tiny Brill with fewer than 5,000 inhabitants as well as mighty Amsterdam with its 200,000. Amsterdam's influence was balanced by coalitions of smaller towns. Just as an informal league of such small towns operated successfully in the 1720s and 1730s, so during the seventeenth century had shifting coalitions similarly succeeded in making their voices heard.[52]

Despite inequalities, the Dutch urban system was far less polarised than those of France or Britain, both dominated by a capital city that dwarfed all the other cities. Amsterdam, late in joining the Revolt, became the economic centre of the county, but failed to become its political leader. Moreover, the towns of Holland, although divided by their niche trades and industries, were at the same time united in a single economic and urban system. Physical integration was created between 1636 and 1647, and then extended from 1656 to 1665, by the building of a dense network of towboat canals which provided a system of public transport with regular services against a modest price.[53]

The towns of Holland benefitted from shared institutions, and from a long tradition of collaboration. There was no real equivalent at the 'national' level of the newly formed Dutch Republic. A significant step towards the establishment of the new state in the north was the Union of Utrecht, concluded in January 1579. Essentially a defensive alliance between rebel regions and towns, the document came to be seen in later years as the equivalent of the Republic's constitution. In the scope of just twenty-six clauses, the Union managed to lay down the ambitions of the rebels for their collaboration, as well as the potential difficulties they faced in realising those ambitions. The dilemma of the new state was formulated in the very first clause, stating (in a single sentence) that on one hand the united provinces would behave 'as if they constituted only a single province', but at the same time that all regional and urban 'special and particular privileges, franchises, exemptions, rights, statutes, laudable and long-practiced customs' and so on would be carefully maintained and protected by each individual member of the union.[54]

One hundred years later, in 1673, William Temple, former English ambassador in The Hague and astute observer of Dutch political life, could still write about the Dutch state[55]

> that It cannot properly be stiled a Commonwealth, but is rather a Confederacy of Seven Soveraign Provinces united together for their common and mutual defence, without any dependance upon the other. But to discover the nature of their Government from the first springs and motions, It must be taken yet into smaller pieces, by which it will appear, that each of these provinces is likewise composed of many little states or Cities, which have several marks of Soveraign Power within themselves, and are not subject to the Soveraignty of their province.

Making a similar point, Montesquieu, who toured the country in 1729, argued that the Dutch Republic was a federation of 'about fifty republics, all very different the one from the other'.[56]

To counterbalance the ever-present tendencies of 'particularism', the Dutch relied on two institutions. The first were the States-General, which existed before 1572 as the representative body of all provinces of the Habsburg state, and was re-established in 1579 as the coordinating body for the rebel provinces only. The States-General were preoccupied almost exclusively with foreign policy. Each of the seven provinces had one vote, and for important decisions unanimity was required. The provinces took weekly turns at presiding over the meetings. As time went on, they found it increasingly difficult to reach decisions during meetings and more and more issues were referred to special committees, where a handful of insiders worked out a compromise deal.[57]

Another factor in the integration of the Dutch political system was the stadholders, even though their position too was riddled with contradictions.[58] Before the Revolt, the stadholder had been the representative of the sovereign in the various provinces. William of Orange had thus been governor of Holland, Zeeland and Utrecht, first under Charles V, later under Philip II. As he became the leader of the Revolt, which he moreover supported with substantial amounts of his personal fortune, it was considered impossible to do away with his office after the abjuration of the king, even though that would have been the obvious consequence. Attempts to make William himself the new sovereign met with fierce resistance. Amsterdam burgomaster Hooft, when informed about these plans, fumed 'that many prominent citizens will rather leave, than stay with us under those conditions'. He claimed that many towns would not have joined the Revolt, had they known that it would come to this.[59] When in 1674 the possibility was floated to make William's great-grandson duke of Guelders, and thus the sovereign in one of the seven provinces, Amsterdam strongly opposed the proposal, which was abandoned as a result.

Nonetheless, the stadholders could act as policy coordinators. Apart from the fact that the stadholderate of several provinces was combined in the hands of a single individual, he could also rally support for his policies from the six provinces that feared Holland's overbearing influence. He had a special interest in his coordinating role because the stadholder's office was usually combined with the position of supreme commander of the army and the navy, potentially the most important victims of local and regional particularism. Even in Holland the urban elites, who liked to oppose their own republicanism with the court's aristocratic policies and culture, were not convinced that the country could afford to go without an 'eminent head'. Two experiments to do so nonetheless, both ended in humiliating military defeats, in 1672 and 1747, and a fall from grace of the republican regimes dominated by those in favour of unlimited local autonomy.[60]

Perhaps it was not so much the leadership of the Orange dynasty, the distribution of institutionalised power, or even their common economic interests that pushed the towns and provinces together, but the fact that they were engaged, first in a struggle for survival, then in a series of other wars. Before 1648 the urgency of war forced through decisions that would otherwise have been very hard to sell in every single province. After 1648, when external pressures abated, free-rider problems increasingly rose to the surface. This became abundantly clear in the early eighteenth century. In 1702 William III died without male issue, initiating a second so-called stadholder-less period. Unfortunately, this happened at the tail end of a long series of very expensive land wars that the Republic had been forced to fight with France. These wars, which started in 1672, culminated in the War of the Spanish Succession (1703–13), which left the Dutch Republic financially broken. In 1715 the treasury had to stop interest payments on the national debt, signalling in effect a state bankruptcy. The Republic's politicians, whose personal fortunes were closely tied to the national debt, knew they could not afford another war and opted for a position of neutrality. At the same time, everyone agreed, a restructuring of the public debt was of the greatest importance. This, however, proved extremely hard to realise now that the external pressure was off. The other provinces saw the debt as essentially Holland's problem. Within Holland, the cities were trying to shove the burden onto their neighbours.[61] Discord became so bad that in the 1730s one leading politician (and successor to De Witt in the grand pensionary's office) exclaimed to the French ambassador that 'he wished the Republic did not suppose that peace abroad was assured'.[62]

From the beginning, the Dutch state took a keen interest in the mercantile activities of its citizens.[63] In some ways, the two were even completely integrated. Before the middle of the seventeenth century, the Dutch navy, like navies everywhere, relied mainly on merchant vessels to execute its duties – and vice versa naval operations were privatised through privateering, which was a lucrative business, especially in the province of Zeeland. The famous Dutch admiral Michiel de Ruyter began his career as a pirate, before he was recruited to lead naval operations. The close connection between state and trade was underlined by a cash nexus: the navy was financed through import and export duties.[64]

This connection was equally visible in the non-European trade. The Dutch East India Company (VOC) was initiated by Holland's grand pensionary, Johan van Oldenbarnevelt, who expected the company to open a new front against the Spaniards in Asia. Similarly, the West India Company (WIC) was as much a military as a commercial operation. Its most notable accomplishment was the capture of the Spanish silver fleet off the Cuban coast in 1628. Both the VOC and the WIC were tightly controlled by urban elites. The two companies operated under monopoly licences, provided by the States-General in 1602 and 1621, respectively.[65]

With the state deeply immersed in commerce, it comes as no surprise to find towns taking a similarly keen interest in state affairs, as is demonstrated by the positions taken up by the Holland towns during the roughly two decades of negotiations in the run-up to the Treaty of Münster that ended the Dutch Revolt after eighty years of fighting. These positions were very much determined by economic interests. Towns with a large international trade network, notably Amsterdam, Rotterdam and Dordrecht, favoured peace, whereas towns that relied on industry, set up by immigrants from the Southern Netherlands and protected by high tariffs and other obstacles, feared competition from southern producers and favoured a continuation of the war.[66]

From the second half of the seventeenth century, the States-General, in consultation with both commercial and industrial urban interests, became increasingly proactive in economic policy. In 1725, for example, a new tariff policy was introduced that sought to balance various interests and support the Dutch economy in the struggle with its mercantilist neighbours.[67] In the Dutch Republic, the towns and the state were hand in glove when it came to economic policies.

Citizens and Public Finances

One area where we can observe civic involvement in policy making at close quarters was the introduction of new taxes. As was argued in Chapter 2, public finances have an important citizenship component. The capacity of states to raise taxes is a prime indicator of the support they enjoy among their citizens. Comparing per capita tax revenues for Holland, England and France, two features stand out.[68] First of all, the spectacular rise of per capita taxation during the early decades of the Republic: although a revolution was under way and the political structures were in turmoil, Dutch authorities were clearly able to increase their income, a strong indicator that the Dutch Revolt was enjoying strong popular support. The second feature is the high level of per capita taxation in Holland, compared to England and France. England's levels of taxation began to increase massively in the second half of the seventeenth century, a topic that I return to in the next chapter. France, in the meantime, was performing sluggishly compared to its two military rivals, for reasons explained in Chapter 9.

The Dutch Republic had no national system of public finance as we understand it today. Instead, its public finances were organised regionally, or even locally. During the seventeenth century less than 20 per cent of the money employed by the central institutions was raised directly by the States-General; the rest was provided by the provinces.[69] The Union of Utrecht had intended to introduce uniform taxes throughout the country, but these never materialised. Their absence created serious coordination problems, for which solutions had to be found. In 1583, to prevent endless rounds of negotiations over the distribution of the tax burden, the Dutch authorities introduced a system of fixed quotas for each region's contribution to the central treasury. This system was adopted from the tax policies under the former Habsburg rulers. The quota distribution was operational from 1585 – even if it took until 1616 before the system had more or less taken its final form. This was only substantially revised at the very end of the eighteenth century.[70] The system underscored Holland's supremacy in the Republic: Holland paid a mighty 58 per cent of all contributions to the national treasury. Only Friesland, set at 11.7 per cent, came anywhere near this amount. The other provinces were set below (Zeeland, at 9 per cent), or far below (Overijssel, at 3.6 per cent) a tenth of the total tax burden. At the end of the eighteenth century, Holland's share actually exceeded 60 per cent.

The success of Dutch public finance in the seventeenth and eighteenth centuries was, therefore, first and foremost Holland's success. The total income of the States of Holland increased from less than 1 million guilders in the 1570s to about 10 million in the early 1620s, and nearly 18 million in the run-up to the Treaty of Münster (1648), while the population had not even doubled during that period.[71] There was something distinctly ironic about this enormous increase in taxation in Holland during the Dutch Revolt, since resistance to 'oppressive' taxation had been one of its original causes.[72] This oppression, however, had less to do with the rates of taxation than with their imposition without proper consent from the States-General and the provinces. The taxes levied by the rebels after 1572 raised the cost of living considerably, but this was acceptable because they had popular support.[73]

The sharp increase in taxation and the persistence of high levels of taxation throughout the seventeenth and eighteenth centuries indicate that tax morale in Holland was high. Although tax riots did occur, they were rare. A survey of public disturbances in Holland revealed a mere twenty-four tax riots between 1600 and 1795; of these twenty-two were of a purely local character.[74] In 1748 a wave of protest, originating in the northern provinces of Groningen and Friesland, caused the authorities to abolish tax farming and introduce a system of publicly organised tax collection. Even in 1748, objections were directed more against the method, and hence the legitimacy, than against the levels of taxation.[75]

The capacity of the Dutch state to raise these substantial revenues astounded contemporaries like Temple; he reported that the price of a simple meal of fish and sauce in Amsterdam included as many as thirty different taxes. This capacity was predicated on a delicate system of negotiations between and within local communities, as is demonstrated in Leiden during the 1740s. At the time, Leiden had about 33,000 inhabitants. Holland's coffers had been depleted by the long series of wars with France, fought between 1672 and 1713. In 1740, the Republic was nonetheless dragged into the War of the Austrian Succession and another new tax became necessary, the *Personele Quotisatie*, or Personal Levy of 1742. The Personal Levy was based on a combination of assessed income and so-called outward appearances of wealth, such as the number of servants employed by each household, the rental value of the house they inhabited, the presence of coaches and so on.[76]

The Leiden municipal archives contain extensive documentation that allows us to understand how the directives of the States of Holland were put into effect, the crucial aspect being the assessment procedure itself. In Leiden this delicate task was placed in the hands of the *bonmeesters*, or ward officials. The *bonmeesters* were primarily responsible for firefighting, but they were also in charge of collecting contributions for the maintenance of the town's rampart, and were more generally employed by the town hall for all kinds of chores.[77] The *bonmeesters* were appointed by the town council. Already in the seventeenth century, and possibly earlier, these *bonmeesters* had been asked to assess their fellow citizens for tax purposes.[78] The *bonmeesters* of 1742 were solid middle-class men, working as butchers, drapers, merchants and surgeons. Only a handful of them might be called upper-class in terms of their wealth. None of them sat on the municipal council, however, nor did any appear to be related to council members.[79] Their roots in the wards provided them with intimate knowledge of their inhabitants. The *bonmeesters* were expected to go from door to door in their districts and fill out a small printed form for each household, a task which took close to two weeks per ward to complete.[80]

In January 1743, a special committee from the States of Holland came to Leiden to check the tax registers compiled by the *bonmeesters*. The States' committee set out to compare the registers for the Personal Levy with other tax registers.[81] Another committee, this time with local councillors as members, was set up by the States of Holland to oversee revisions.[82] The revisions, however, had to be finalised by the States itself. Individual complaints were treated very seriously, despite the significant numbers involved; in November 1745 the commission discussed no fewer than 232 separate files.[83]

In 1748 the political situation was much more volatile than it had been in 1742. Like many other places, Leiden was swept up in a tidal wave of riots, initially directed against tax farmers, but soon spilling over into the political arena. Tax farmers' homes were plundered and town councillors were attacked for their corruption and ineffectiveness.[84] The States of Holland reacted to these disorders by abolishing its cherished excises in favour of what amounted to an income tax, similar to the *Personele Quotisatie* of 1742. Despite the general political crisis, the assessment of the population was organised in 1749 in a manner that was very similar to that of 1742, with the *bonmeesters* once again shouldering most of the work. In twenty-three out of a total of twenty-seven districts at least one of the assessors had already done the same job six years earlier. This degree of continuity signalled to the population that the assessment process would be as fair as it had been, even though its character was to be slightly different. At the same time, the States of

Holland had made the job easier by simply assessing the new tax owed by Leiden at the same amount that it had formerly contributed in the abolished excises.

In August 1748 the *bonmeesters* were once more sent from door to door to fill out printed tax forms. Afterwards, their work was checked by a committee, consisting of members of the town council and 'commissioners from the citizens'.[85] The latter were clearly included to add legitimacy to the procedures. There was also a printed form available for those who wanted to lodge a complaint. Several of these carried a declaration from the lord of the neighbourhood, confirming that the complaint was justified.[86] The committee of the States of Holland that had come to Leiden to check the assessment in 1743 was conspicuously absent, perhaps to avoid inflaming a still volatile situation. In 1749, however, there was no real need for such supervision, as it was the local authorities' responsibility to work out how to collect the assigned sum of money.

We have discussed these procedures in detail in order to demonstrate how the Dutch state's operations penetrated the capillaries of Dutch civil society, and to show how it was seeking legitimacy in procedures that involved ordinary citizens, while at the same time ensuring that local agency would not lead to shirking. The Leiden procedures of 1742 and 1749 suggest that taxation was made palatable in Holland through a coherent set of procedures. Firstly, assessment was placed in the hands of local institutions. The assessors were supposed to be familiar with the inhabitants of their district, whilst the inhabitants were informed about who was going to assess them. There was, in other words, familiarity on both sides. Secondly, assessment was essentially left to the citizens themselves. The Leiden *bonmeesters* were sufficiently removed from the ruling – and in 1749 discredited – regent regime to enable them to be accepted by the inhabitants as 'one of us', instead of 'one of them'. Thirdly, free-riding in the community as a whole, through a collusion of citizens and regents, was avoided through either a detailed investigation of the assessment registers (in 1743) by the States of Holland, or a fixed target set by the States that the town had to meet in whatever way it fancied (in 1749).

The Dutch state did not always choose the 'soft' or 'inclusive' approach. One problem that plagued the Dutch Republic throughout the two centuries of its existence was the contribution of the other six provinces, which at times resorted to free-riding in the knowledge that

Holland was always going to act as lender of last resort. In the 1620s and 1630s the province of Friesland, for example, built up substantial arrears in its contribution to the States-General budget. After many warnings and protracted negotiations, Holland persuaded the other provinces to send in the army. Friesland was effectively occupied in 1632, in 1634 and again in 1637, and forced to pay up – or as one Holland deputy in the States-General preferred to call it, to 'tame Frisians with troops'.[87]

Conclusion

The Dutch model was much admired – but very difficult to imitate, because it combined two unusual ingredients: the presence of a high level of urbanisation and the absence of a dominant centre. Under such conditions coordination was complex. In more or less similar environments – northern and central Italy come to mind – coordination proved impossible, and city-states became embroiled in quasi-permanent warfare among themselves. The Swiss Republic is another comparable case, albeit with much lower levels of urbanisation. The Swiss, protected by their mountains, decided that only a minimal amount of coordination would suffice; yet despite this they went through several civil wars. Southern Germany, a third region with similar features, would be mired by the weak coordination offered by the Holy Roman Empire, as is discussed in Chapter 9. By the end of the sixteenth century, with European merchants expanding their activities across the globe, this was not the way to dominate world trade, as the Dutch aspired – and for some time actually managed – to do. In the seventeenth century, the Dutch Republic with all its global interests could not stand aloof. Its struggle for independence and its commercial interests both required a strong army and navy, and therefore close collaboration among provinces that otherwise preferred to be left alone. So why did it work?

At the end of the eighteenth century an influential political programme, published in 1785 during a period of revolution that would ultimately lead to the end of the Republic, explained to its readers the 'genius' of the Dutch constitution. It might seem complicated at first sight, said the anonymous authors, but in fact it served its main purposes remarkably well: protection and enhancement of shipping, commerce and manufacturing, as well as the maintenance of the Union and the provincial forms of government. When looked at from this angle, the constitution could not be denied 'a certain degree of soundness, of perfectness, yes even clarity'. It was argued that three elements were responsible for that enviable situation. In the first place, the Dutch republican constitution was firmly founded upon the sovereignty of the people; second, each part of the general society had its own government, and could look after its own interests; third, because the constituencies were small, they provided the best guarantee for maintaining liberty.[88]

This was a pretty accurate analysis of the Republic's constitution and its practical application. Local elites played a pivotal role in this system of divided authority. In all provinces this included urban elites; in Holland they were completely in charge. These urban elites were subject to the same tendencies of oligarchy that were active everywhere in Europe, but at the same time they were under constant pressure from their own citizens: ideologically, because they subscribed to the idea that, by being citizens themselves, they represented the civic community and that their rule was at least implicitly subject to the approval of those same citizens; practically, because citizens were organised in neighbourhoods, in guilds and, most significantly, in their civic militias. Time and again the latter demonstrated their capacity to mobilise political opposition. All civic organisations were routinely involved in shaping local policies, through elections, participation in decisions, petitions and formal and informal meetings with local officials.

Via the provincial states assemblies, local politicians had a direct say in national politics. These were discussed in great detail in urban council chambers all over the country. The negotiations preceding the Treaty of Westphalia demonstrate very clearly how local interests impacted decisions of national importance. They also demonstrate how those local interests could potentially bring the system to a halt. Stalemate, however, was not the default position during much of the seventeenth century. Coordination and leadership were provided by the Orange stadholders, commanders of the armed forces, and by Holland's leading politicians, such as Johan van Oldenbarnevelt and Johan de Witt, both commoners who emerged from urban politics. Significantly, both the stadholders and the grand pensionaries had to provide this leadership informally; there was no formal platform for them to work from. They managed, but it was a fragile construction.

In that sense, it cannot come as a surprise that in the long run this system proved difficult to sustain. The 'Dutch century', also known as Holland's golden age, indeed petered out in the decades around 1700. De Vries and Van der Woude have argued that economies go through some sort of natural life cycle of about 100 years, and the Dutch golden age was simply subject to that general rule. Innovations were certainly diminishing by 1700. However, the more obvious problem was the growth of public debt at a time when coordination became even more of a problem. In 1702 William III died without a successor. In England, where he was king, his wife continued the reign, assisted by a cabinet. In the Netherlands most provinces, including the crucial province of Holland, decided to defer the appointment of a successor to a later date. In the event, that would turn out to be 1747, almost half a century later. In the meantime, the Dutch, alongside the English, were fighting the War of Spanish Succession against Louis XIV (1702–13). By the end of the war, Holland's debt service was consuming more than half of its regular revenues. For the first time, Holland was incapable as well as unwilling to continue this kind of expenditure. In 1715 the States-General had to restructure its debts. Holland too reduced its interest rates on existing loans. There was talk of new taxation, but this time it proved impossible to overcome discord. The Republic was forced to adopt a neutral position, but in the absence of war, or the threat of war, compromise between the various parties proved even more elusive. The Dutch Republic in the eighteenth century was struggling with failures of coordination: bottom-up rule, which had been key to the success of the seventeenth century, was powerless in the absence of individuals or institutions that could tie the various interests into a coherent policy.

Whereas citizenship had underpinned Holland's golden age, it thus contributed to its problems in the eighteenth century. To be effective, citizenship alone was not enough. Urban communities had to be tied into a system of national coordination. This had been relatively straightforward in Italian city-states, but in the Dutch Republic such coordination proved much more challenging. England, the topic of our next chapter, had the advantage of an early set of national institutions. These, however, had to become more receptive to urban civic interests before they could become as effective as those of the Dutch.

8 CITIZENSHIP IN ENGLAND
From the Reformation to the Glorious Revolution

In the autumn of 1484 a 'grete riot [was] commyted within the Citie of Yorke and the franchisez thereof', as it was expressed in a letter from the earl of Northumberland that was read out in the meeting of the town council on 8 October. The earl of Northumberland was York's political patron, and he wanted more details. The next week, no fewer than two letters from the king himself were read out, this time in a meeting of the Common Council, with 'the substance of the hole body of the said Citie' in attendance. It was made very clear that the king was unhappy – 'displeased', the letter stated in so many words – about the fact that the citizens had not used the proper channels to raise their concerns, and that the local government had been unable to maintain public order.[1]

Nine years later, in 1493, the abbot of St Mary and King's Receiver Richard Chomley were charged by the king with the adjudication in a dispute between the weavers and cordwainers that the local authorities had failed to settle. The York government retorted that this was a purely municipal issue and that it would not accept such interference. Only after the abbot had declared that he had no intention whatsoever of trespassing on local privileges and that the committee merely wanted to talk to the parties involved in the dispute and suggest ways forward did the local authorities accept this outside involvement. In the event, they confirmed the solution that the abbot and Chomley proposed.[2]

In 1504 the Crown took a stronger position when the York Commons submitted a list of demands to the Council and threatened that they 'wold not proceede to any eleccion unto tyme the Maier and [Council] graunted theym all theyr askyngs and desyrez'. The king demanded in a letter that the ringleaders be transferred to London, and this indeed happened. The searchers of the various guilds were also forced to swear an oath of loyalty to the king, as the latter had insisted.[3]

During the Middle Ages, political interactions of the Crown with the community of York were thus a mixture of admonition, reprimand and correction. This, however, was to change gradually but fundamentally over the following two centuries. In 1621, while the 'instructions for the citizens in Parliament' representing York as a borough insisted on collaborating with representatives from other towns to protect their interests against London wholesalers, the York MPs themselves reminded their fellow citizens that they were 'tending to the public and the good of the commonwealth'.[4] By 1640 York was to side with Parliament in its conflict with the Crown. The citizens themselves had become more self-confident, but also more aware of an antagonism between the organs of state and Church on one hand, and their own municipal institutions on the other.[5]

In England, the position of towns and cities was very different from the situation in either Italy or the Low Countries. In fact, it could be argued that the relations between towns and the Crown fitted the pattern found throughout much of premodern Europe, where monarchs had to deal with urban interests, but there was one major difference from the rest of Europe and that was, of course, Parliament. Whereas many European states had representative assemblies, few of these had the combination of permanence and effectiveness that the English Parliament managed to display across the Middle Ages and the early modern period.[6] However, the effects of this only became manifest during the series of crises that erupted in the seventeenth century. As is well known, those crises ultimately created a situation, through the 1689 Bill of Rights, in which Parliament gained the upper hand, precisely when monarchs seemed to be winning out in the rest of Europe. It is a textbook truth that the Glorious Revolution changed the nature of the political game in the British Isles. In the economic history literature the focus has been very much on its impact on English property rights.[7] However, this chapter concentrates on the role of towns in the political system, and by implication the role of urban citizens. I argue that not only were towns significant actors in the seventeenth-century conflicts between Crown and Parliament, but also that these conflicts, and the way in which they were ultimately resolved by the Bill of Rights, allowed urban interests to be increasingly articulated at the state level.

England's Urban Renaissance

In the sixteenth century, England cut a poor figure in the European league table of urbanisation, ranking seventh in 1500 and without advance by 1600.[8] During the seventeenth century, however, it began a steady climb, taking it to fourth place in 1700 and second place – after the Dutch Republic – by 1800. This remarkable rise was entirely due to England's strong performance; while other countries were increasing their urban populations, England was doing the same, but at a much faster pace.[9] Change was in the air everywhere. The number of small market towns went up from fewer than 600 in the late sixteenth century to more than 700 in the late seventeenth.[10] By that time twenty-seven of those towns had populations of more than 5,000.[11] London's expansion was especially spectacular, moving up from 80,000 in 1550, to 400,000 inhabitants in 1650. In the seventeenth century London was already the largest city in Europe, but equally significantly English provincial towns were now also making an impact. England, in other words, was becoming urbanised at a faster rate than any other European country.[12]

Economic growth likewise happened in England at a pace that outstripped all its rivals. During the late Middle Ages England's economic performance had been sluggish, but in the second half of the fifteenth century a corner was turned. Initially, much of that growth was eaten up by simultaneous population growth, but during the second half of the seventeenth century, despite the political turmoil of the period, with the English Civil War, Restoration and Glorious Revolution, GDP per capita began to increase more consistently and from the middle of the eighteenth century at increasingly substantial rates.[13] By that time, the Industrial Revolution was also under way.

Invisible in these numbers, but in the long run perhaps equally important, was the changing position of towns in the country's political and cultural make-up. Following the Reformation, in the 1540s, increasing numbers of towns gained greater autonomy through incorporation. Moreover, urban culture now featured more significantly in the way the English conceived their own society.[14] How all these developments were connected has been debated by many generations of historians; debates that cannot be settled here, of course; but what is nonetheless striking about the development of urbanisation, economic growth and institutional change is their chronology. The creation of new boroughs, and the granting of extended privileges to existing boroughs, preceded the rise in the rate of urbanisation. Urbanisation, in its turn, preceded the Industrial Revolution. The data are too imprecise to read too much into them, but they still seem firm enough to reject any idea that institutional reform was predicated on economic growth and urban expansion. If anything, it was the other way around.

Towns and Crown in the Middle Ages

Urban institutions had emerged before the Normans conquered England in 1066. At the time, the City of London must have had its aldermen and wardmotes, while Cambridge, York, Stamford, Lincoln and Chester had their own law courts. Such institutions were setting these places apart from the countryside. By the late eleventh century a burgess could be identified as someone 'who paid his share in borough dues'. In the twelfth century urban privileges were extended, usually at the behest of the urban communities themselves. A lot of it was copied from other towns. Initially, these urban privileges were established in a hotchpotch of documents, and it would take quite some time for them to consolidate into a more systematic set of regulations. Protection against 'extortion, oppression and disorder' was the first priority of urban communities. During that same era merchant guilds were set up, sometimes prior to the acquisition of privileges for the whole community, whilst the inhabitants were also made collectively responsible for the payment of royal taxes.[15]

In many English towns, citizenship seems to have emerged out of these privileges, but more specifically out of the requirement to pay 'scot and lot', i.e. contribute to royal taxes. In twelfth-century Norwich, for example, charters provide an inclusive definition of the burgesses, to create the widest possible tax base.[16] In some towns, however, it was the merchant guild that helped define citizenship. This was the case in York, where the Guild Merchant was already recorded in 1080, and guild aldermen are mentioned in a document from circa 1100. Later in the twelfth century the king imposed a fine because some inhabitants had attempted to make the guild into a 'commune'. A larger sum of money then made the inhabitants exempt from certain royal levies, and in 1191 there is reference to the 'citizens of York' (*cives Eboracenses*). However, the first register of new citizens starts only a century later.[17]

In Wells, a cathedral city of circa 2,000 inhabitants in the late fourteenth century, about half the adult male population had formal citizen rights. The citizens were united in one large guild that encompassed all different occupations. The guild's membership and that of the borough community were really one and the same. Civic participation was high. Of those registered as citizens in the century after 1377, no fewer than three-quarters held some sort of public office at some point in their lives. Around 1300, the citizens of Wells tried to convert their 'civic' guild into a merchant guild, on the assumption that it would allow them greater freedom vis-à-vis the bishop. In 1329 they managed to strike a deal with the incoming bishop and in 1341 the Crown allowed them further privileges, after the citizens of Wells had offered the king a substantial sum of money. They now received permission to elect their own mayor and aldermen. The bishop, however, fought back in the courts and the next year some of the privileges were annulled, leading to riots in 1343, and the creation of a 'sworn community'. Even though the *communitas* was never formally recognised, it continued to function as the local government and to negotiate with the bishops, who did not object to its existence as long as the Wells citizens were prepared to fulfil their financial obligations towards the Church. From the 1370s, the borough community also selected a Member of Parliament.[18] A 'broad range of participation' was the norm in many English towns at the time.[19]

During this period the formal position of towns remained fluid. That position was being slowly defined through a range of charters, each primarily addressing a specific issue, and not yet amounting to a coherent programme of urban autonomy.[20] English towns were not fully autonomous anyway. As subordinates of the Crown they tried as far as possible to stay clear of national controversies like the Wars of the Roses. Towns might throw in their weight with other interested parties, but were not in a position to change policies by themselves.[21] In the second half of the fourteenth century, however, their bargaining position improved somewhat as the Crown turned increasingly to urban communities for financial support, rather than relying on individual merchants or merchant consortia. The unintended consequence of this change in policy was also to empower the local representative institutions that were asked to agree to such loans to the Crown. In return they would ask for new commercial privileges, or for additional elements to their borough charter.[22] Both the towns and the Crown were figuring out in the process where they stood in relation to each other. As was demonstrated by the events in York related at the beginning of this chapter, this was a situation of shifting balances.

London was, of course, always going to be a special case. Both its size – already 30,000–40,000 by the mid-fifteenth century – and its political position as capital and seat of government, would ensure that the Crown paid close attention to the political mood on its doorstep. Both the City and the Crown were very much aware of their interdependence: the City needed help from the government to protect its commercial interests, while the Crown needed the City – not only because of the revenue it generated, but also to provide loans when cash was urgently needed. However, precisely because they were condemned to each other, neither party wanted to allow the other to dominate its politics. For example, in 1392 Richard II revoked London's charter, and the City spent £30,000 to get it restored. Throughout this period there was constant wrangling between the two.[23]

But it would be wrong to see such conflicts as signs of a structural opposition between the Crown and the towns in the late Middle Ages. In general, the two were complementary elements in the constitution of the country, elements that could both live with this 'division of labour'.[24] The Crown would insist on the fact that it was the sovereign and therefore ultimately the highest authority in the land. The towns would insist on the autonomy that their charters and other privileges gave them. Both were seeking to expand their positions, but usually without much aggression. Most of the time, the Crown and the towns lived peacefully side by side.

The Reformation and the Towns

Between 1540 and 1640 the urban institutional landscape in England was radically transformed. Whereas in 1500 there had been thirty-eight incorporated boroughs, and forty-four in 1540, this number then started to increase at a rate of almost fourteen per decade over the next 100 years. By 1560 the number had already almost doubled, by 1600 it had tripled and by 1640 there were four and a half times as many incorporated boroughs as there had been in 1500. The total now stood at 181.[25]

The timing shows that the new incorporations were first and foremost a by-product of the more general institutional rearrangements that followed in the wake of the Reformation, set in motion with the creation of the Church of England in 1534. The Reformation caused the government to involve itself much more, and in much more detailed ways, with the business of local government.[26] First of all, because it had to ensure the introduction of the new rites and all that came with it; but secondly because the Reformation had massive implications for church properties, many of which were located in urban environments. Precisely because the Reformation created greater interference in their local business than had been customary, towns were keen to defend their autonomy against these outside authorities. The national government also had its own reason to strengthen local institutions, since it needed local authorities to push through its massive reform programme.[27] Towns that had been under the authority of the Church were thus able to benefit directly from the changed balance of power. In Beverley, Yorkshire, for example, the bishop lost his grip on the town in 1542. It took some thirty years for the local elites to consolidate their independence, but in 1573 they managed to obtain a charter that incorporated Beverley as a borough. As happened elsewhere, the initiative had come from the citizens of Beverley themselves.[28] With a similar programme in mind the urban authorities of Worcester spent huge sums of money on legal advice when the town was seeking incorporation in the 1550s; they clearly thought it was worth their while.[29] Exeter had been elevated to county status in 1535, but solicited another charter in 1550.[30]

The increase in incorporation in turn led to much stronger representation of urban interests in Parliament, where the number of seats controlled by incorporated boroughs rose to about 250 in 1641.[31] If we follow Michael Braddick in his portrayal of the English state as a 'coordinating centre', presiding over a network of local authorities, the increased representation of the urban localities in the centre must be rated as a very significant development.[32] In many towns MPs were selected by either the burgesses directly, or by their representatives sitting on the town councils. In other words, these MPs, irrespective of their own social background, were representing an urban 'interest'.[33] The selection process was bewilderingly varied, but always consisted of several steps. In Barnstaple, in Devon, one of the seats was owned by the Chichester family, the other controlled by the earls of Bath, who held the office of town recorder. In York, on the other hand, the council nominated four candidates – almost always local people – who were then presented to the burgesses. They would choose two, who would be presented for selection a couple of days later. In many towns, a committee system would mediate between the constituency it was supposed to represent, and the elites' ambition to control the outcome.[34]

A lot has been made of the 'oligarchies' that came to dominate the towns during this period. It is quite possible that a smaller number of families were increasing their grip on urban offices,[35] but it would be wrong to infer from this observation that urban government was previously open to all and sundry. That was never the case, especially since high offices in towns were usually poorly remunerated and incurred serious expense.[36] Accepting office also implied that one was in a position to spend time, often a great deal of time, serving the public. In Great Yarmouth very substantial fines were introduced in the seventeenth century to compel councillors to commit to their public duties. The size of the council in the same town was reduced by a quarter in 1703, when it proved impossible to find enough members who were able and willing to devote time to public office.[37] Urban office might be as much a burden as a source of profit.

Many urban offices, moreover, remained elective, and this suggests that the electorate found oligarchy less objectionable than inexperience, or the temptations of corruption that were supposed to be stronger for the less well off.[38] And where oligarchy was a dominant feature of urban political life – which was the case in most incorporated boroughs – it did not necessarily mean that these people were merely lining their own pockets, even if they did not ignore the interests of their families and relatives. There is ample evidence that they took the interests of the community as a whole to heart, if only because they had to be re-elected.[39] More importantly, the emphasis on oligarchy has obscured the conflicts that emerged and persisted among local elites, as well as the levels of civic participation that were also characteristic of urban political life.[40]

It would be equally wrong to portray these towns as 'independent' or 'autonomous' in any radical way.[41] Even when they were trying to increase their political room for manoeuvre, they were very conscious of their position within the larger framework of the English state. Many continued to ally themselves with powerful aristocratic patrons, whose utility was increasing as they became more integrated in the power structures of the state. Towns cultivated these relationships by presenting their patrons with elaborate gifts, and otherwise paying homage, but also by accepting them as officers in the urban political structures. At least fifty-two towns created an office of High Steward in the decades around 1600, and presented this office to a political patron. The patrons in return founded hospitals and other charities, or would sponsor lectureships and schools. Even for towns that had their own parliamentary representative, the influence of a powerful patron might prove more effective in furthering local interests. Places that wanted to obtain charters of incorporation would be well advised to engage such a patron.[42]

The period did, however, witness a strong upsurge in what I earlier called 'urban republicanism'.[43] Richard Butcher (1586/7–1664), town clerk of Stamford, in Lincolnshire, described 'cities or towns corporate as ... small County Palatinates within themselves', which would be best served by 'magistrates of their own members ... to make laws, constitutions and ordinances, to bind themselves and every member within their jurisdiction'. The citizens, Butcher explained, had 'a power within themselves in their Common Hall assembled, to make laws as peculiar and proper rules for their better government, the said assembly being a little court of Parliament'.[44] Such ideas would persist beyond the Civil War, for example in John Locke's works in the late seventeenth century and into the eighteenth.[45] However, in Butcher's lifetime the old balance between Crown and towns was still in place, not least, perhaps, because urban authorities were keen to avoid conflict and doing their utmost to prevent disunity. To that end, elections were preferably depoliticised.[46]

Therefore, when Henry Ireton claimed during the Putney debates in October 1647 that 'the freemen of corporations were looked upon by the former constitution to comprehend the permanent interest of the kingdom', although he might have been corrected a century earlier for overstating the importance of urban constituencies, by the middle of the seventeenth century he was making a statement of fact.[47]

Urban Divisions during Civil War and Restoration

The Civil War put the relationship between towns and Crown on a whole new footing. Differences of opinion that in previous decades could have been papered over now came to a head in unprecedented ways. Towns were more or less forced to take sides, even though most urban elites desperately tried to avoid exactly that, anticipating that it would spell trouble either way. The corporation of York was above all keen to preserve its autonomy. Even after York was occupied by Royalist forces, its civic leaders were still prepared to defy the king on issues of urban autonomy. When the Parliamentarians took charge after the Battle of Marston Moor in July 1644, the civic authorities likewise attempted to prevent government interference. The new members of the municipal institutions were as determined on this point as their predecessors had been.[48]

It was for precisely this sort of reasons that the Bristol Corporation actively supported calls on both parties in the conflict to settle their dispute. The Corporation argued that civil strife, let alone civil war, would damage the nation's trading interests, a great deal of which was concentrated in Bristol. It also professed a profound dislike for conflict as a means of resolving disputes in general and pleaded for a return to the type of politics that looked for compromise solutions, necessary to maintain political and social unity. Its analysis was most prescient, because when 'accommodation' failed, local divisions became increasingly linked with national debates. In Bristol those divisions were specifically related to access to trade. On one side, the overseas merchants, united in the Society of Merchant Venturers, dominated the Corporation, with three-quarters of the membership of the Common Council coming from this section of society. On the other side, artisans and shopkeepers opposed the Corporation's policies and allied themselves with the parliamentary cause. Religious issues added another edge to the political clashes in Bristol.[49] In Oxford, military occupation – first by the Royalists, then by the Parliamentarians – similarly created a much stronger connection between local and national political alliances.[50]

London's extraordinary size and the geographical proximity of the court to the City, but especially the mutual dependence of mercantile and royal interests, ensured that relations between Crown and City continued to be of prime importance.[51] By the middle of the seventeenth century this mutual dependence was firmly institutionalised along three lines. The first were the chartered companies, most notably the Merchant Adventurers (1407), more recently the Turkey (1581) later Levant (1605), and the East India (1600) Companies and then the Virginia, Massachusetts Bay and Providence Island Companies, as well as several others. The chartered trading companies were the backbone of England's overseas trade, but at the same time fiercely resented – and undercut – by those merchants who found themselves excluded by these privileges. Moreover, the various chartered trades were competing among each other for control of the City's political machinery. In the years leading up to the Civil War, the colonial interests in the New World in particular were claiming their place under the political sun, at the expense of established mercantile interest groups, while the latter saw their position as intimately related to the fate of the Crown.[52]

The second strand in the relationship between Crown and City was financial. The collection of various customs duties had been farmed out since Elizabeth's reign, and were then united in 1604 in a single Great Farm, which only the very richest merchants were in a position to operate. These people simultaneously acted as major private lenders to the monarch.[53] In case of an emergency, usually of a military nature, the Crown would turn to London's merchant community for financial assistance. It was the only place in the country where sufficient resources could be mobilised at short notice.

Apart from individual contributions, the Crown had also been relying on institutional financial support, the third strand. In 1617, for example, the City as such underwrote a £100,000 loan to the Crown, only to discover that James I did not honour his debts, with interest payments forthcoming only at irregular intervals. The same happened with a £60,000 loan that the City had guaranteed in 1625, immediately after Charles I ascended to the throne. As a result of such bad debts, the Corporation was unable to raise further capital after 1628. It failed to produce a £100,000 loan requested in June 1639, and only after Parliament met again in October was the City prepared to raise £50,000 from the livery companies as a loan to the Crown.[54] All this suggests a relationship that was at one and the same time close yet strained.

Charles' 'personal rule' made the problems much worse after 1629. In the absence of parliamentary support, the king's dependence on the City bankers to finance his expenses and help him collect revenue could only increase. For that reason, he was willing to expand the City's jurisdiction over the suburbs, where most of the population growth was taking place. However, the City was reluctant to do so because it feared that this would ultimately weaken its authority. As a result, a proposal to this effect from the Privy Council in 1632 was turned down. The

Crown, desperately looking for new sources of revenue, then began incorporating the suburbs and creating institutions there that competed with those of the City. When in 1642 Charles made a last-ditch attempt to woo the City's rulers, he offered to dismantle these incorporations and hand over the suburbs to the City after all. By then, however, other forces had taken over.[55]

Starting in September 1640 radical supporters of Parliament had staged a series of events and campaigns of mass petition in London to assert their religious and political claims. The first such petition, in September 1640, attracted in the order of 10,000 signatures; a second, delivered to the House of Commons in December, was signed by some 15,000 inhabitants, 10–20 per cent of all adult male inhabitants of the capital, and a year later a similar number signed still another petition. Radical activists were recruited from among the merchants and craftsmen of the city, while apprentices and women were also actively involved in many of the radical initiatives. Through the wardmotes, the grass-roots units of London's corporate politics, the Common Council elected by those wardmotes and the Common Hall, where the mayor and aldermen were elected by representatives of the London companies (guilds), radicals were able to bring London firmly into the Parliamentarian camp. Conservative merchants who supported the king were sidelined by citizen politics.[56] This radical support for a greater role for representative institutions coincided with clashes about accountability within the companies.[57] In other words, radical reforms were demanded at all levels of England's institutional structures.

The restoration of the monarchy in 1660 seems to have been met with no general dissatisfaction among urban governors. In Norwich there was widespread celebration.[58] Perhaps local elites were anxious about their job prospects, but perhaps they also expected a more stable government than the Protectorate had been able to deliver. The Crown, however, did not exactly reciprocate with gestures of reconciliation. On the contrary, the Corporations Act of 1661 created a two-year period in which towns were subjected to extensive purges of their governing bodies. Not all of this was initiated by the Crown. Quite a few towns delivered themselves, as it were, on a plate by asking for renewal of their charters and for the removal of controversial aldermen and councillors. Mostly these purges were spillovers from the Civil War era, when opposing groups of local politicians had used their hold on power to apply the law against their opponents. In many cases, on the other hand, the king explicitly requested the removal of people who opposed his reign, or had been implicated in the regime that killed his father. In all, 468 individuals in thirty-six towns lost their posts, i.e. one third of all urban officeholders.[59] In a town like Great Yarmouth, which was hit particularly hard by the purges of 1662–63 (and would be again in 1688), the exclusion of many experienced administrators forced the community to recruit less suitable replacements.[60] Another innovation of the 1661 Act was the introduction of standard clauses in urban charters that reduced their uniqueness and created a more uniform urban regime.[61]

The 1660s also saw the introduction of another innovation in the Crown's policies vis-à-vis the towns: the use of *quo warranto* procedures. Under *quo warranto* the King's Bench could revoke a town's charter when it was found that the town had acted against the law. Proof of that was never difficult to find. There is no evidence of a deliberate policy to apply this instrument, but it became very effective nonetheless in the campaign to reduce urban autonomy. In most cases, the initiative came from within the towns themselves – for example, from disaffected former officeholders who had lost their post in one or another purge. Appealing to the King's Bench, they tried to invoke the *quo warranto*, but with the unintended consequence that towns were threatened with the loss of their charter and being placed directly under the control of the Crown. Faced with this threat, towns were often prepared to hand over their charter and accept a new one, even if this was less favourable; a bad charter was still better than no charter at all. In the process, the king usually obtained the right to confirm local appointments – or reject those he did not like.[62]

In the 1680s there would be another radical change in the relationship between Crown and towns. During the previous two decades, eighty-five borough charters had been issued or reissued, and in the five years from early 1682, another 134 were refashioned. Technically, the majority of these towns were asking for a new charter themselves. Often, such requests were the outcome of more local conflict. In Nottingham, for instance, the council was tied on the issue in July 1682, and the request for a new charter was only submitted because the mayor supported the move. It led to demonstrations, with hundreds of citizens chanting, 'no new charter'. (The new charter fortuitously arrived at 11:00 AM on election day of that year.) One of the innovations of the 1680s was the introduction of uniform articles in all new charters, permitting the king to remove corporation members at will.[63]

Not all towns felt compelled to hand over their charter. The City of London in particular resisted the policy, and was therefore targeted by the Crown. In 1682 the King's Bench launched a *quo warranto* procedure against the City. The City claimed that its charter was 'immortal' and could only be revoked by Parliament; the Crown argued that it had been issued by the king and could therefore be revoked by him. The courts agreed with the sovereign's argument. In June 1683 a compromise of sorts was arrived at: the charter would remain in place, but in return the king was allowed control over all important appointments. For the next five years, a royal commission was to oversee the City's political life. Only livery companies loyal to the king and his policies were permitted to vote in the Common Hall, while companies branded as disloyal were served with *quo warrantos* themselves and threatened with the loss of their privileges. Even supporters of the king agreed that the policy was designed to reduce the City to the 'status of a small village'. The signal to the rest of the country was loud and clear: hand over your charter voluntarily, or else.[64]

These policies were intended to control urban politics as such, but also had the ulterior aim of influencing Parliament.[65] It was with the latter objective in mind that James II completely reversed the policy in late 1688. This happened, however, after he himself had initiated another round of charter issues in 1687 and 1688, this time to undermine the position of the Church of England in the boroughs, in favour of Catholicism. As a result of the changes, thousands of local officeholders, most of them otherwise loyal supporters of the Crown and its policies, lost their posts. Local administration was slowly grinding to a halt, while support for some sort of radical intervention was growing. Sensing that the tide was turning, James then performed his dramatic U-turn in October 1688. All new charters were revoked and the previous ones reinstated.[66] In London the livery companies' charters were similarly restored, as was the City's own charter.[67] But it was all too late. Those who might have hailed the move were out of office, and the people whose posts were now under threat were completely baffled.[68]

Urban Interests and National Politics after the Glorious Revolution

In 1689, the number of boroughs (i.e. towns) represented by MPs in Parliament was around 200, controlling more than three-quarters of all seats, just as in 1640. Around half of these MPs were returned by urban freemen, constituting the largest bloc of votes in Parliament.[69] Many of the actual members still had a gentry background, but the share of overseas merchants in Parliament doubled from 3.7 to 7.6 per cent of the members. After 1690, about one in ten MPs had a direct interest in commerce; the overwhelming majority of these were representing urban constituencies. The number of petitions to Parliament with a commercial topic meanwhile rose more than fivefold.[70] This is not to say that urban interests dominated Parliament, or exclusively set the political agenda for the English – and later British – state. It does, however, tell us that the urban communities were a political force to reckon with, and that aligning these urban interests with those of the state was one of the main challenges for the government. Building on developments that had begun under Cromwell's republican government and been taken over by Charles II, that alignment was consolidated in the political procedures of the Bill of Rights and its aftermath.[71]

North and Weingast, in a paper published in 1989, have famously argued that the Bill of Rights created a new property rights regime. Now that Parliament exercised ultimate control, the Crown could no longer encroach on its subjects' properties. This, according to North and Weingast, helps explain why investors were all of a sudden willing to buy government bonds on an unprecedented scale, and the state could run up a huge debt against ever-lower interest rates. Gregory Clark has, however, convincingly demonstrated that property rights had been secure in England since well before 1689, and that very little changed in this respect with the Glorious Revolution.[72] If anything, 1689 increased instability, rather than decreasing it. Nonetheless, tax revenues went up dramatically in the following decades, as did parliamentary scrutiny of how they were spent. At the same time, interest rates declined from 10 per cent in 1693 to the Dutch levels of 2.5–3 per cent in the 1720s.[73] Whereas during the Restoration era only 45 per cent of financial legislation had been successfully concluded, and 50 per cent under William and Mary, this increased to 80 per cent during the first half of the eighteenth century, and even further during the second half.[74] These data suggest a strong correlation between successful parliamentary procedures and public trust in the government.

Changes occurred on two levels, first and foremost nationally. After 1689 English governments were reluctant to interfere directly in urban politics. They strenuously tried to avoid the impression that they wanted to repeat the mistakes made by James II. Only fourteen borough charters were issued under William and Mary, the lowest number of any reign since the thirteenth century.[75] The King's Bench was no longer available to settle partisan scores in the boroughs. Instead of trying to suppress political conflict, judicial procedures were now used to hammer out compromise solutions, without excluding one party or the other. Moreover, these procedures were terminated more quickly than they had been in the past. To dissuade parties from employing judicial procedures in order to upset their opponents, the price of launching a case before the King's Bench was raised. It took some three decades for the dust to settle, but eventually all of this helped corporations to resume the business that had been paralysed by the instability of the decades preceding the Glorious Revolution.[76] In other words, a new balance between towns and national government had finally been achieved.

This, secondly, also helped to transform local politics. Urban life itself was changing as urban populations multiplied.[77] The 'English urban renaissance' consisted of a massive increase in public life in all its aspects.[78] At the same time that communal investments and activities were reaching unprecedented levels, paradoxically, partisanship also became accepted as a fact of life, much as it had become nationally. During the 'age of oligarchy' – a serious misnomer as far as urban politics is concerned – parliamentary elections were in most cases contested.[79] Even if those selected in the process were not exactly socially representative of the population as a whole, the emphasis on oligarchy is to miss the point that they were elected for their views, not their class background, and by a relatively wide franchise. In Newcastle upon Tyne, for example, 35–40 per cent of all adult males were freemen, and therefore entitled to vote. Urban politics as such was becoming ever livelier during the eighteenth century. Newcastle saw the publication of no fewer than seven newspapers already before 1760, including the *Newcastle Courant* from 1711 and the *Newcastle Journal* from 1739, while in 1769 the *Newcastle Chronicle* was launched. The same was happening elsewhere. In 1735 there were twenty-five regional newspapers, all published in towns; by 1782 the number had doubled, while the number of printed copies of each title increased perhaps as much as fivefold.[80]

At the same time, the number of clubs, associations and societies was increasing possibly even more spectacularly. Voluntary associations had already emerged – perhaps we should say re-emerged – in the late sixteenth century, but had made little impact.[81] Modest increases followed throughout the seventeenth century, but in 1688 the national number was still a couple dozen at best. The late seventeenth century provided a turning point, with numbers rising to above 200 for England alone by the 1730s, and about double for the British Isles as a whole. From the 1760s, another acceleration took place, taking the number to well above 1,000 by the end of the eighteenth century. The first Masonic lodge, for example, was set up in London in 1717; by 1740 there were more than 180 Masonic lodges throughout the country. These and similar associations were mostly apolitical, and perhaps that was even their point: to establish a 'neutral arena' away from party-political conflict. However, they did create new forms of civic sociability, not only in the cultural domain (music, the arts, science), but also campaigning for moral reform, a cause that became quite popular in the first half of the eighteenth century.[82] This surge in associations was accompanied by a flood of texts reflecting on phenomena like 'company' and 'society'. By the late seventeenth century, one in every fifty newly published books carried one or other of these words in its title, demonstrating that the interest in sociability had reached almost obsessive levels.[83]

In the meantime, yet another shift had occurred. While contested elections had previously been seen as a sign of the failure to manage the process, they now became the norm.[84] The Triennial Act of 1694 required Parliament to be dissolved at least every three years. During the reign of Queen Anne (1702–14) five general elections were held and many seats were contested.[85] Urban parliamentary elections were a serious business. In 1754 in Bristol, for instance, the Whig candidate spent a formidable £30,000 to persuade the electorate to support him. That Bristol electorate increased in size from circa 3,600 in 1713 to 5,900 in 1781, an increase partly the result of political conflict itself. Local parties in power would enfranchise up to hundreds of individuals during election times, in return for their votes.[86] The net effect of such attempts to prejudice election results was nonetheless a substantial growth of the 'political nation'.

Even if some of these people had acquired formal citizenship in return for a tied vote, the communities of freemen were as a whole not so easily cajoled into political submission. Parliamentary patrons, mostly aristocrats, still had to 'earn' their control, by consulting with their constituencies, courting the electorate and promoting their concerns, by seeing local bills through Parliament and by protecting them from economic legislation that would have a negative impact on their businesses.[87]

In Great Yarmouth, for example, seventy-five were made freemen of the town in the run-up to the parliamentary election of 1721, yet Horace 1st Viscount Townshend, the town's patron, found it necessary also to woo the local elites in an attempt to win one of the parliamentary seats for his son and, on top of that, to spend £820 on his campaign.[88] What might look like a manipulated election result was not taken for granted by the candidate. Towns started to send their representatives detailed Instructions about bills they had to support or introduce on behalf of the borough. The popular press discussed these Instructions and portrayed them as a self-evident element of the mechanism of representation: Instructions articulated the electorate's opinions.[89]

Some of the new urban centres that emerged in the course of the eighteenth century, such as Birmingham, Manchester and Sheffield, were not represented in Parliament because they had no borough status. It has been argued over and over again that this demonstrates that the economic and political worlds were quite separate, and that these new places thrived precisely because they were not handicapped by the institutional old regime. That argument is difficult to settle,[90] but it is also perhaps beside the point. The economic dynamic of eighteenth-century Great Britain was not just coming from those new industrial centres. The established towns, London in particular, but also Bristol and Norwich, were growing at an almost equally impressive pace.[91] Even though London itself was only represented by ten MPs, the Whig faction in Parliament usually included twenty-seven to thirty-five 'monied men' from the City.[92]

London's interest was, however, about much more than *haute finance*, as the Whigs were constantly reminded by their opponents. Tory radicals dominated especially the outer wards of the City. They were supported by the manufacturers and crafts, while the Whigs found their supporters especially among the international merchants and bankers. At the same time, both parties commanded broad support from all classes in society. The government in Westminster closely monitored City politics, having learned the lesson of the Civil War that London had the potential to upset the whole system. In 1725, in an attempt to shackle opposition politics in the capital, the City Elections Act managed to limit the city franchise after similar attempts had failed in 1715 and 1723. It could, nonetheless, be argued that this act was also a failure, as Pitt the Elder was able to rattle the political establishment mainly with the help of a large popular following in the London wards.[93]

In no other town did the government attempt to interfere so blatantly in local politics, testimony to London's continued importance as a force in national politics.[94] London, however, was not the exception but the rule when it came to the involvement of citizens in the political process, an involvement that was no longer restricted to local issues but now encompassed national politics as well. Across a range of issues, the two had become closely intertwined. The Glorious Revolution had thus achieved what most political theorists and political practitioners had dreaded for centuries: it had created a political system based on conflict.[95] Yet it was precisely by bringing larger numbers of people into the political realm, and by allowing them to disagree openly about issues, that there was no longer the need for radical interventions and revolutions. A new set of rules for the political domain had been hammered out, after the previous rules had proved unworkable. England had not become a democracy, even by the middle of the eighteenth century, but it had made serious progress in that direction, precisely through the discovery by its political elites that conflict and civic participation could produce stability – when channelled in the proper ways.

Conclusions

During the Middle Ages, the relations in England between town and Crown very much resembled those on the continent. It was the time of what French historian Bernard Chevalier has termed '*leur accord parfait*' – their perfect understanding.[96] The towns took care of local business and executed royal policies. In return, the Crown provided them with the instruments to do so and otherwise left them alone. Tensions between the two parties were ironed out by aristocratic brokers who acted as classic patrons, i.e. providing access at court for urban concerns in return for favours from the towns in the shape of offices, presents and so on.

This normally harmonious relationship became increasingly strained in the second half of the sixteenth century, for three reasons. The discoveries of new sea routes were creating new business opportunities and urban merchant communities were anxious to capitalise on them, which increased competition between towns. The Dutch Revolt and other international conflicts involved the English state to a greater extent in the business of the continent than it had been since the end of the Hundred Years' War in the mid-fifteenth century. The Military Revolution had, moreover, significantly increased the costs of that involvement, which forced the Crown to increase revenues. Finally, the Reformation created new religious divisions that proved very persistent, also in the political domain.

Initially these issues were dealt with in the tried and trusted manner of incorporation: the Crown allowed increasing numbers of communities to set themselves up as independent units within the feudal constitution. In the long run, that strategy was bound to backfire, however, because it created an ever-larger number of stakeholders, making it ever more complicated for the Crown to please each and every one of them. In the course of the seventeenth century divisions intensified, culminating in the three-stage revolution of the Civil War, the Restoration and, finally, the Glorious Revolution. Although this half-century had its years of stability, the overall picture was one of great instability, both nationally and locally. In the process, national and urban politics, and their alignment, were fundamentally reshaped in two distinct ways. First and foremost, conflict rather than unity became the norm of national as well as urban politics. These conflicts, which would ultimately crystallise in the division between two political parties, connected the local to the national, and vice versa. Secondly, a feature that had all along set English state formation apart from its continental counterparts suddenly became fundamentally important: the representation of local interests in Parliament. First Charles II and subsequently James II sought to reform urban constitutions to allow greater control of urban politics by the Crown, and also to produce greater control of Parliament as a result. These attempts, in the early 1660s, the early 1680s and the late 1680s, ultimately had exactly the opposite effect: towns became increasingly confused and frustrated by their relationship with the Crown.

The Glorious Revolution did not create a *tabula rasa*, but it changed and in the long run helped to clarify the rules of the game. First and foremost, of course, it confirmed Parliament as the proper forum for national political conflict and the ultimate source of authority.[97] From an urban perspective this was helpful, perhaps because property rights were better secured, but especially because this was a forum where towns actually had a say. Political conflict, in the meantime, continued unabated, but procedures to settle those conflicts were worked out in the decades following 1689 in ways that allowed urban business to proceed more predictably than had been the case under the later Stuarts. The 'stability' that various historians have detected as setting in around 1715 was not so much an end to political conflict, since urban parliamentary seats in particular continued to be heavily contested.[98] What had changed was that political conflict no longer created political stalemate, nor led inevitably to the political destruction of one of the opposing sides. Instead of overturning the decisions of a previous government, English – and from now on indeed British – politicians designed procedures that allowed a variety of interests to come to terms with their differences.[99] The success rate of legislative initiatives in Parliament increased dramatically from 1689.[100]

Urban economic interests were among those that stood to gain from these new procedures, as has been demonstrated for investments in infrastructure. Similarly, the financial sector expanded, not only during the 1690s but much more clearly from the 1710s onward.[101] New estimates of the British growth figures, however, show no immediate impact of the Glorious Revolution. What they do show is that, in the latter half of the seventeenth century, the English, and later British, economy was taking a quantum leap forward.[102] The English state had been strongly involved in the promotion of commercial and industrial interests well before 1689, and for obvious reasons London had been pivotal to this connection between Crown and trade.[103] From this perspective, the Glorious Revolution was just another step along a path that had begun a century or so earlier with the establishment of a string of chartered companies in the 1580s.[104]

Of course, this chapter does not argue that the steam engine was the result of citizenship arrangements; there were much more specific circumstances leading up to the creation of that particular product of human ingenuity.[105] However, insofar as the invention of the steam engine was part – a quite spectacular part – of a much broader set of changes, institutions in general and urban citizenship in particular do seem to have been significant factors behind the Industrial Revolution; the chronological coincidence is too striking to overlook. This chapter has moreover demonstrated that institutionally, much more was happening than the ascendance of Parliament and the rise of party politics. Rather, several of the economic changes can be related to the more effective representations of urban interests, and therefore of local citizenship, at a national level. The way in which the English state was embedded in its citizen community was one of the reasons it could become so remarkably successful during the eighteenth and nineteenth centuries.

9 CITIES AND STATES IN CONTINENTAL EUROPE

In 1512 several towns participating in the Imperial Diet (*Reichstag*) meeting in Trier complained about nobles and ecclesiastics who abused their position as out-burghers to claim tax exemptions. This was an issue with a history. In the late Middle Ages towns all over Europe were trying to extend their influence beyond their walls. They had all kinds of motives, including the suppression of rural competition, securing food supplies for their own citizens and enlarging the tax base supporting the town's armed forces. One of the instruments to do this was the institution of the out-burgher. Basically, it created urban citizenship in the countryside. This situation was fraught with contradictions, especially when it came to aristocratic out-burghers, who hoped to benefit from civic privileges but refused to assume the accompanying duties. The council of Ulm, for example, informed its counterpart in Freiburg-im-Breisgau that in 1476 it had accepted five nobles as out-burghers in return for a substantial amount of money, but only after they had agreed to stay away from Ulm. Freiburg itself had a long series of conflicts with its noble out-burghers.[1]

In 1512 the German towns objected that nobles and ecclesiastics, 'under their pretended freedoms', tried to avoid paying taxes and nonetheless claimed to have the same rights as urban citizens. In the face of this opposition from the towns, Emperor Maximilian resisted any change to the situation. Nevertheless, Strasbourg and other Alsatian towns did manage to have a decision postponed to the next Diet. It would seem that the emperor accepted Strasbourg's claims, including the prediction that the citizens of that town might revolt if they were frustrated in this matter. In 1521 the issue returned at the Diet in Worms, more famous for its hearing of the 'Luther affair'. This time the nobles submitted a document defending their position. Strasbourg was eager to respond, but could not persuade the other imperial cities to support its opposition to the nobles. Strasbourg nonetheless submitted an extensive treatise, arguing against the continuation of this unacceptable situation. The issue returned on the agenda of the Urban Diet (*Städtetag*), the following year in Esslingen, but subsequently petered out.[2]

The out-burgher issue once again underlines the complexities of citizenship in early modern states. Much of the trouble came from the historical trajectories those states were going through. None had political structures that one might call straightforward, but in the Holy Roman Empire the situation was extraordinarily confusing. The Empire was a conglomerate of substantial territories ruled by princes, sometimes by prince-bishops, as in Westphalia under the bishop of Münster; of autonomous towns, both large and small; of ecclesiastical institutions like monasteries; and of individual nobles in charge of mini-territories. These territories, towns, monasteries and individuals were all to an important extent sovereigns in their own right, and most of them employed soldiers. Technically, all were subject to the ultimate authority of the Emperor, but in practice the princes of the larger territories were serious rivals to the Holy Roman Emperor.

The position of the Emperor himself was also riddled with issues. First and foremost, that position was not hereditary, but at the disposal of seven so-called electors: four princes and three prince-bishops, who elected a successor when the Emperor passed away. Even though members from the House of Habsburg were continually elected to fill the position between 1438 and 1806, they had to negotiate each time with and bribe the electors in order to achieve this. Charles V famously was challenged by French King Francis I, who put himself forward as a rival candidate. Many of Charles' predecessors and successors did not become Emperor immediately upon their election. Charles himself was first made King of the Romans, in June 1519, and only promoted to Emperor in 1530. Technically, the position of King of the Romans became vacant at this promotion, and Charles, unusually, used the opportunity to have his brother Ferdinand elected King in 1531, allowing Charles himself to pay more time and attention to his Spanish realm. All this implies that the title of Holy Roman Emperor looked impressive, but in actual fact its authority had to be established by each individual Emperor, and was continually challenged – often successfully – by the princes in particular.[3] The Holy Roman Emperor had only a limited capability to force the member states, and instead had to rely on building consensus and on symbolic power.[4]

In no medieval or early modern European country were cities and states completely at peace all of the time. Periods of amicable relations alternated with periods of tension, or even outright warfare. Much of these tensions were the result of financial dire straits that states found themselves in, as a result of the arms race that characterised much of the period. Some countries managed to align urban and national state interests, at least for a considerable time, as we saw in the three previous chapters. In Italy, the Low Countries and England, the towns had gained a constitutional role that allowed them and their citizens a structural participation in the process of policy development. In other countries such a constellation did not emerge, if their elites were at all interested in such an '*entente cordiale*'. In Germany, for example, the position of the towns in the imperial structure was always poorly defined, and towns became increasingly marginalised during the early modern period. As a result, it proved very difficult, often impossible, to coordinate urban interests in Germany, as was the case in much of Europe. However, the reasons for this lack of urban coordination, and hence the impossibility for urban citizens to help shape state policies, were different in each country. In this chapter I discuss the Holy Roman Empire and France in detail, before turning briefly to Spain and East Central Europe.

Germany: Urban Leagues and Diets

In the Holy Roman Empire, urban coordination primarily worked through urban leagues.[5] The first urban league on German territory was the *Rheinische Bund*, established on the initiative of Mainz, Worms and Oppenheim in April 1254.[6] Mainz and Worms, both bishoprics, had been working together for much longer, but were now formalising those collaborations, and covering a much larger space. In July Cologne, Speyer, Strasbourg, Basel and many other towns joined; according to one source '*plus quam LX*', or more than sixty towns participated in the league.[7] Three developments created the preconditions for this league. Urbanisation in various German regions had reached a level that made it worthwhile and possible to coordinate urban interests. In the previous century, moreover, the establishment of urban councils had created an institutional foundation for towns to act in unison. Finally, the collapse of the authority of the Hohenstaufen imperial dynasty, extinct in 1250, created a dangerous power vacuum within the Holy Roman Empire that also made it imperative for the towns to establish closer collaboration.[8] The aim of the *Rheinische Bund* was to secure a safe and peaceful environment, facilitating interurban traffic and trade. It was recognised by the pope, and also by the Holy Roman King, at the time Count William of Holland. William, however, died in January 1256 and the struggle over his succession may well have precipitated the dissolution of the league. Members still met in March (Mainz) and August (Würzburg) 1256, where it was decided to raise a uniform poor tax, and rules were established for the handling of stolen goods. However, in May 1257 the league disintegrated as a result of internal conflict and military adversity.

The *Rheinische Bund* was not an exclusively urban league, even if the majority of its members were towns. This was equally true for subsequent urban leagues. Up to the middle of the fifteenth century, and in some regions of the Holy Roman Empire well into the sixteenth, urban leagues came and went. They usually had their own council (*Rat*) with the authority to declare war or peace. Towns sent delegates with instructions. Until the middle of the fourteenth century, treaties insisted on unanimity, but later leagues accepted majority voting, even if sometimes a two-thirds majority was required for a binding decision. Usually a small number of major towns dominated the league. A common treasury for military expenditures was seldom established. In most of the founding treaties, both the council and the citizens of the participating towns were explicitly mentioned as parties.[9]

The main purpose of the urban leagues was to ensure '*pax et iustitia*', or peace and adjudication, typically two mechanism that require careful coordination. The law had to be maintained not only among the members, who might have different legal systems, but also against rapacious nobles and princes. In the volatile circumstances of the late Middle Ages, when especially in the German lands authority was not localised, the creation of some sort of public order was urgent. Without it, the long-distance trade that constituted the economic backbone of most towns would be seriously jeopardised. At the same time, the ruling elites of the member towns saw urban leagues as a bulwark against local rebellious movements, and were willing to help their colleagues when these found themselves beleaguered by their own citizens.[10]

Although urban leagues were found all over the Holy Roman Empire, southern Germany was their prime territory. This was due to the presence of a specific type of town in the region, the *Reichsstadt*, or imperial city. Constitutional historians Karl Bader and Gerhard Dilcher distinguish no fewer than six types of urban communities in late medieval Germany. The bishops' sees were the oldest and most prestigious. They included Mainz, Worms, Speyer, later also Strasbourg, Basel, Regensburg, and later still Cologne. Sometimes Augsburg and Konstanz are also included in this group. Next in line were the imperial cities, discussed in greater detail later. Whereas the first two types had much autonomy, the third type, comprising territorial towns, were subject to a lord, the *Stadtherr*, in many cases a prince. If the territorial town was the prince's capital, it was called *Residenzstadt*, or residency. Next in line was what Bader and Dilcher called the '*grundherrliche Stadt*', basically a smaller version of the territorial town. And finally there were some exceptional variants that need not bother us here.[11]

The imperial cities were a unique feature of the Holy Roman Empire, precisely the result of its multilayered structure.[12] The great majority of German towns – between 3,000 and 4,000 in all, many of them small – answered to the princes. Imperial cities, however, were directly subject to the Emperor. Their number was in dispute and varied. At the end of the thirteenth century there were more than 100. An official list from 1521 names eighty-five, but in fact only sixty-eight were recognised as imperial cities at the time. Some, like Basel and Mulhouse, had by then joined the Swiss Confederacy, while others, including Metz, Toul and Verdun (1552), later also Colmar and Hagenau (1648), and finally Strasbourg (1681), were to be annexed by France. By 1800 there were only fifty-one imperial cities left, half the medieval number.[13] However, it was said that in the mid-eighteenth century another 139 German towns claimed, or aspired to, status as an imperial city, and behaved as if they were.[14] In size they too varied from substantial to tiny. In the sixteenth century, Augsburg and Nuremberg had 30,000–45,000 inhabitants and were major commercial and industrial centres. Most imperial cities were much smaller, 2,000–10,000 inhabitants, and some, like Zell am Hamersbach and Bopfingen, were hardly larger than a village.[15]

Several sees were known also as 'free towns', after the citizens had managed to liberate themselves from the bishop's authority. This happened during the Middle Ages in Cologne, Mainz, Speyer, Worms, Strasbourg and Basel. These free towns were among the most active in urban leagues and other coordination efforts of the urban communities. The distinction between the 'free' and 'imperial' towns gradually evaporated and in the early modern period the whole group came to be known as the *freie Reichsstädte*, or free imperial cities.[16]

Augsburg was one such imperial city, and at the end of the eighteenth century its citizenship ideals and practices were in full bloom.[17] Every year the citizens of Augsburg would renew their citizen's oath – and there were many of them; in 1730 5,614 households, covering 87.5 per cent of the city's population, were headed by a citizen. The majority were artisans. Most citizen households were headed by a male, but a substantial 828 were widows and another 143 were single women. Being a citizen of Augsburg brought various rights, but also duties. There was pressure on citizens to marry, and every new citizen had to present himself in his militia uniform to demonstrate that he was able to participate in the local defence. This service was required for between twenty and thirty years and entailed participation in guard duties. Next to the militiamen, whose services went unpaid, Augsburg also employed 250 professional soldiers, giving the city its own, albeit small, military force.[18] Militarily, Augsburg was a small state.

The imperial cities saw the Empire in many ways as a nuisance. In Bader's oft-quoted phrase, they had a '*negatives Reichsbewusstsein*', a negative attitude towards the Empire.[19] Ideally, the Emperor protected them against powerful neighbours (read: princes), but as the latter might be more powerful than the Emperor, this help was often worthless. For this reason, the imperial and other towns regularly entered into alliances. In southern Germany these tended to be formalised in treaties that constituted the foundation of an urban league; the northern Hanse, on the other hand, developed more organically.[20] Most of the leagues were regional, but sometimes they covered large territories. The *Rheinische Bund* was an example, and later the Swabian League, actually a series of leagues in southern Germany. The Swabian League had twenty-seven members in 1377, and forty in 1385. Like similar leagues, it also had noble and even princely members. The leadership of the League was in the combined hands of a noble and an urban *Hauptmann*. The Swabian League had a *Bundestag* (parliament), where members met to discuss policies and sometimes even military action.[21] Its military role was, however, terminated with the South-German Towns' War (also known as the *Erste Markgrafenkrieg*) of 1449–50.[22]

One issue that the urban leagues were particularly concerned about was the Emperor's policy of using his towns as pawns. In return for a loan, he would pledge his town, which might as a result become subject to a 'private' lord. The first documented cases date from the 1170s, and in the thirteenth century the policy continued apace. During the consecutive reigns of Louis the Bavarian and Charles IV (1314–78) a total of 117 pawns were created on imperial cities, almost two a year. Only a handful of imperial cities were never pawned. There was always the possibility of lifting the pledge, but usually at great expense to the community.[23]

Like the southern leagues, the Hanse in northern Germany was concerned with urban autonomy and tried to support its members against pressures from the princes and other rival authorities, such as the Teutonic Order in Poland. However, in some areas the Hanse was different, and not merely because it had non-German members. First of all, it had not been established at a specific moment, but had expanded gradually. Secondly, at least in its early stages, the Hanse was an organisation of merchant guilds rather than urban governments. The alliance evolved only gradually into a league of towns, and this had an impact on the third distinctive aspect: for the Hanse commerce was always more important than politics. Whereas the Urban Diets were connected to the agenda of the *Reichstag*, the Hanse concentrated on trade issues. Finally, the Hanse held general assemblies, but its decisions were difficult to enforce; there was no common army or financial mechanism to finance concerted action.[24]

In the south, the Swiss Confederacy constituted another special case. Its origins were rural rather than urban, starting with the union of the mountainous regions of Uri, Schwyz and Unterwalden in the late thirteenth century. During the course of the fourteenth century, three urban members acceded; first Lucerne in 1332, and then Zürich and Berne in 1351–53. In 1481 and 1501 another four urban members were added: Fribourg, Solothurn, Basel and Schaffhausen. Of the ultimately thirteen full members of the Swiss Confederacy, the *Dreizehn Orte* or Thirteen Cantons, seven were therefore considered urban, with Zug seen as semi-urban. Four of the urban members were ruled by patrician elites, three others by guild regimes. Geneva joined as an associate member in 1526. Many of these urban partners were not simply towns, but ruled over large territories. In terms of surface area, Berne was, in fact, Europe's second largest 'city-state', after Venice.[25]

The members of the Swiss Confederacy were connected through multiple treaties, but lacked a constitution that had been signed by all. Technically, the Swiss remained within the Holy Roman Empire until at least the mid-seventeenth century, but already in the sixteenth century it was acknowledged that they were independent.[26] The Swiss Confederacy was first and foremost a mutual defence league. It did not have central institutions or a single army. In times of crisis temporary arrangements were put in place which dissolved when the crisis was over.[27] The Swiss thus had a state by default, which survived under the protection of a favourable natural environment, as well as the increasing dependence of other nations on the soldiers produced by the mountain areas. Whenever differences between the cantons seemed insurmountable, as happened repeatedly, it was usually the French who mediated.[28] The growth of army sizes in other countries also worked to the advantage of the Swiss, whose private entrepreneurs and public institutions benefitted from renting out regiments. As a consequence, the Confederacy was possibly the only state in early modern Europe with a positive financial balance. Mounting debt was one of the powerful propellers of state centralisation elsewhere, but it did not apply in the Swiss cantons.[29] In the absence of an institution for domestic political coordination, the impact of urban citizenship remained confined to the regions.

German towns and their ruling elites were also sceptical about the Empire because the Emperor became embroiled in expensive wars – and their financial fall-out was felt by the towns. The Emperor was not alone to blame. The rise of the Ottomans and the threat they posed to the Empire's south-eastern borders clearly was an exogenous factor. But from the fifteenth century the Emperor was also a major player in the successive bids for dominance over continental Europe, incurring huge expenses as a consequence.[30] These contributions were decided by the Imperial Diet, where the towns' position was precarious. Here too, therefore, coordination was imperative, if the towns wanted to protect their interests.

The Imperial Diet only became institutionalised in the second half of fifteenth century; it was known earlier as *Hoftag*, in effect an advisory council.[31] Even after 1500 the Diet had no fixed place to meet, no fixed meeting schedule and no fixed composition. As for its location: many Diets took place in south German imperial cities. Nuremberg, Regensburg, Speyer and Worms all regularly hosted the meetings, which could take place at several years' intervals.[32] Who would be invited was not fixed either. For example, in 1471 about eighty towns received an invitation, in 1585 none. The invitations often arrived too late to put together a proper delegation. Smaller towns were anyway reluctant to send delegates, because of the substantial expenses involved in participating. Nor was it very clear if their presence would make much of a difference, because the *Reichstag* had no proper voting procedures. As a result, many towns decided to abstain. In 1489, even though all sixty plus imperial cities had been invited to participate, only nineteen actually turned up.[33]

To defend their interests more effectively, the towns decided, in 1471, to set up a parallel structure. These *Städtetage*, or Urban Diets, were distinct from urban leagues because they had no council or treaty, but could play similar roles. Their specific purpose, however, was to coordinate urban inputs to the Imperial Diets and imperial politics more generally. Urban Diets had their precursors in smaller meetings that had taken place in 1438 in Ulm and in 1440 in Strasbourg, but now they became much more serious. Between 1471 and 1474, the Urban Diet met no fewer than nine times, in 1480–82 seven times, in 1486–89 another eight times. After 1489 its frequency declined, but off and on, usually in connection with Imperial Diet meetings, the towns sat together to work out a common position. These meetings were normally held in one of the southern towns, and these were also the most frequent participants. Of a potential sixty-nine attendants, fifty-eight showed up at least once, but only twenty-two attended more than half the meetings between 1495 and 1545. The ten imperial cities from the Alsace, which had their own organisation, were on most occasions represented by Colmar and Hagenau. Frankfurt, Augsburg, Ulm and Nuremberg, on the other hand, missed very few meetings. These four towns, together with Strasbourg, also acted as regional coordinators. Many of the meetings were hosted by Speyer and Esslingen, both located in the southern heartland of the imperial cities.[34]

The Urban Diet's *raison d'être* was the increasing financial demands imposed by the imperial institutions. After yet another such decision by the 1486 Imperial Diet, to which the towns had not even been invited, an obviously frustrated Strasbourg council complained:[35]

> It is unfair to oppose a Holy Roman Emperor or King, . . . but it is equally unfair and unheard of that an Emperor or King, together with the princes, can arbitrarily impose new burdens and distribute these according to the favour they have of this or that town.

Nonetheless, during Maximilian's reign (1486–1519) the towns and the King (subsequently Emperor) hammered out a *modus operandi* that suited everybody's purposes. Confronted with a choice between princely tyranny and Habsburg patronage, the towns preferred the latter. What united the two parties was a common enemy: the great princely houses of Wittelsbach and Hohenzollern in particular. These 'overmighty subjects' were a threat to both the Emperor and the towns.[36] To be sure, Maximilian could enter such an alliance with some confidence, because his father had managed to cut short the urban bid for power during the South-German Towns' War of 1449–50. Although that war formally ended in a draw, it effectively spelled the end of the towns as a military factor in German politics. As the Augsburg chronicler Burkard Zink observed of the imperial cities after the war: 'They are now divided and separated from one another . . . and are as helpless as sheep without a shepherd'.[37]

The Swabian League, launched in 1488 as an alliance of towns and lesser nobles, was encouraged and patronised by Maximilian. At its zenith it was almost an alternative government in southern Germany, seeking to stabilise public order in the region, while at the same time securing the autonomy of its members and support for the Emperor. The towns wanted security from the Emperor, while the Emperor was hoping to get access to their purses. To this end, he actively courted the towns, spending a quarter of his reign visiting one or another imperial city.[38]

One of the other purposes of the Urban Diet was to provide mutual protection. Here it overlapped with urban leagues. When Count Ulrich of Württemberg wanted to punish the town of Reutlingen in 1519 after one of his servants was killed there, an army of the assembled towns forced him not only to lift the siege, but also to abandon his position as ruler of Württemberg. Only fifteen years later did he manage to return to his capital Stuttgart. This, however, was an unusual success.

When the same Count Ulrich threatened Esslingen in 1542, the Urban Diet was too divided to put up a fight. Indeed, the Urban Diet suffered from structural weaknesses. It was not a parliament and it did not have a formal position within the Empire's constitution. It therefore lacked the means to force participants into a unified position. The larger towns tended to dominate the discussions, but when serious opposition emerged, issues would be referred to smaller committees to sort out a compromise. Another sign of the Diet's informal character was the absence of a serious budget. Some funds were available to organise meetings, but none for the military action that might back up its decisions, or even threaten such actions. The Reutlingen campaign in 1519 was the result of an extraordinary unanimity, soon to be fundamentally undermined.[39]

During the first years of Charles V's reign the towns hoped to continue the collaboration that had been established under his grandfather Maximilian. In fact, they had embraced Charles' election campaign. Charles, however, was as much in the debt of the princely electors. He promised them, for instance, that he would leave them in possession of whatever imperial pawns they held, which might include towns.[40] Moreover, he was not German himself and spent much of his time in the Low Countries or in Spain. Whereas Maximilian had been close at hand for much of the time, simply gaining access to Charles proved much more difficult for the towns' delegates. He was also deeply suspicious of the religious situation in many towns – and with good reasons.[41]

Luther's actions for religious reform were to have a devastating impact on every aspect of the German political system, including the towns' capacities to collaborate and on their relationship with the Emperor. Simmering tensions boiled over once they became infused with religious divisions. The Urban Diet in Ulm in July 1525, when the Peasants' War was at its most intense, was poorly attended. Religious affiliations were becoming more important than political solidarities. In 1531 the Schmalkaldic League was launched, an alliance of Catholic towns and princes. Ulm was one of the founding members, while Augsburg joined in 1536. The Swabian League was dissolved in 1534. In the mid-1520s the imperial cities of Augsburg, Nuremberg and Ulm had already started talks about closer cooperation and in May 1533 they formalised their collaboration in the Three Cities' League. The large towns no longer wanted to look after the small, which they had to support against powerful neighbours, while the small towns were useless when the large towns found themselves beleaguered. Instead, Augsburg, Nuremberg and Ulm promised each other troops and money in case of a military emergency.[42] New lines were drawn which divided the towns structurally rather than coincidentally.[43]

Charles V himself, moreover, proved no friend of the towns. Possibly as a result of his upbringing in the Low Countries, where powerful towns tried to dictate policies and were a hotbed of rebellion and Protestantism, Charles was aware of their potential as a source of money, but otherwise there was little love lost between this Emperor and his towns.[44] After Charles' abdication, in 1555, the towns decided to accept the status quo, which implied that they could be involved in the *Reichstag*'s policy-making, but without a legal ground for this involvement, and that therefore ultimately they were dependent on the goodwill of the other Estates. It took another century for their participation to be formally acknowledged in the Treaty of Westphalia of 1648, when the towns were granted a *votum decisivum* beside the electors and the princes. However, the precise implication of this vote remained poorly defined.[45] In 1671 the council of Nuremberg complained in a letter to Frankfurt that 'in the Imperial Diet the honour and position of the imperial cities is held in contempt'. No fewer than thirty-seven, i.e. more than half, had failed to show up at the Diet of that year, and the urban representatives often allowed the emperor's officials to dictate their policies.[46] Moreover, Imperial officials increasingly interfered in urban conflicts, between citizens and their local councils, inserting themselves into the heart of urban politics.[47]

The changed position of the towns was exemplified by the situation in Württemberg. In the early sixteenth century the collective towns had driven the duke of Württemberg into exile, after his attempt to subjugate Reutlingen. In the early eighteenth century his successor used every opportunity to rub in the marginality of the representatives of the town of Stuttgart, his capital. Its council had kindled the displeasure of Duke Eberhard Ludwig (reigned 1692–1733) by condemning his cohabitation with a mistress. In revenge, the duke had the Stuttgart councillors placed in the lowliest seats at official dinners, insisted that the council refrain from any discussion of ducal decrees and tried to force his own men on to the council. In 1710, he suppressed on his own authority several official posts in the Stuttgart administration, and reduced the salary of several others, issues that were clearly the remit of the council, which was nonetheless completely ignored.[48]

Urban Diets continued to be organised throughout the eighteenth century – until August 1802, when the last one assembled in Ulm. In the wake of Napoleon's success and his defeat of Imperial and other armies, even the host itself was sceptical of the prospects for maintaining the autonomy that imperial cities had enjoyed for about half a millennium.[49] These developments were underscored by population figures. In 1500, the largest towns were commercial centres, and usually imperial cities as well: Cologne, Nuremberg, Dantzig (Gdansk), Augsburg, Prague and Lübeck. By 1800, Cologne had dropped to ninth place, Nuremberg to eighteenth. Instead, capitals like Vienna and Berlin were now dominating the urban rankings. Cologne and Hamburg were the only imperial cities still figuring among the top ten.[50]

During the Middle Ages, towns and cities in the Holy Roman Empire, especially the imperial cities, had achieved high levels of autonomy. As discussed in Chapter 2, in many of these towns citizens were closely involved in local governance, through various institutional mechanisms, but from the mid-fifteenth century this autonomy came under pressure. Initially, the rising costs of warfare required the Emperor to demand larger financial contributions from 'his' towns. The Reformation added more pressure, because the loyalty of towns was now also at stake. In the territories, centralisation made the towns weaker while the princes became stronger. In the Empire as a whole, the towns had not achieved a well-defined position before 1500, and these new pressures only made the problem worse. As a state, the Holy Roman Empire was further weakened by the Thirty Years' War. Compared to Italy, the Low Countries and England, the German towns had a double problem: they were part of a comparatively weak state, and within that state they were forced to play second fiddle. As a result, urban citizenship had little impact on national policies and therefore remained relatively ineffective outside the local context.

The French Towns and 'Absolutism'

In France, as in so many other countries, the towns and the Crown had worked out a stable relationship during the later Middle Ages. As in those other countries, this relationship was fundamentally altered as a result of the Reformation, and in the case of France the subsequent Wars of Religion. It had, of course, not always been peaceful between the French king and his towns. During the Hundred Years' War (1337–1453), many towns had rebelled against financial impositions, lack of security and what seemed like a total absence of responsibility on the part of the magnates. In 1358 the population of Paris rose in arms. In 1379–82 a wave of insurrections flooded the country: first in the south, where Le Puy, Montpellier, Nîmes and other towns revolted, followed in the north by Rouen, Paris again and then towns across Normandy and Picardy. In 1417 many towns sided with the duke of Burgundy in his conflict with King Charles VI. However, after two terrible decades of warfare, famine, plague and economic catastrophe, they decided their safest bet was to side with Charles VII (reigned 1422–61) who promised peace and stability – and delivered.[51]

The alliance with the king inaugurated a century of close collaboration between the sovereign and his *bonnes villes*. Louis XI, even more than his father, tried to establish an open relationship, writing regularly to explain his policies. The representatives of Amiens, after one meeting with the king, reported how they had been received '*aimablement*', and that the king had invited them for a conversation, saying, 'I want to talk to my good friends from Amiens, not as ambassadors, but as friends'. Louis allowed more towns their own set of communal privileges, and gave urban elite families noble titles. He also intervened in urban elections, sometimes forcefully, but as the monarchy grew more confident, there was less necessity to do so. The king was interested in the towns' financial potential, granting tax privileges to those towns that maintained their own defences. He also borrowed increasingly from wealthy *bourgeois*. Under pressure from rising military expenditures, his successor was forced to demand parts or all of the towns' own revenues, in 1517 and 1518, again in 1532–33 and in 1541. The towns were forced to pay for the king's infantry. Economic adversity and Protestantism were fanning the flames of discontent that began to emerge once again.[52]

The Wars of Religion (1562–98) further upset the delicate balance between sovereign and towns, for the same reasons as the Reformation had done in the Holy Roman Empire: domestic and international warfare increased the pressure on the financial dimension of the political system, while at the same time religious struggles raised questions about political loyalty to unprecedented levels of importance. Sovereigns simply could not afford to ignore what was happening in towns around their realm. This was especially so in France, where a large number of towns had been very active in the Catholic League, while others had emerged as hotbeds of Protestantism. Both camps had enlisted arguments from 'urban republicanism' to bolster their ideological positions, mixing religion into issues concerning the city-state nexus.[53] When Henri IV succeeded to the throne in 1589, he did not have a programme aimed at subjecting the towns, let alone to establish anything like 'absolutism'.[54] His priority was to re-establish public order and stability and in that context he dealt with opposition wherever that proved necessary, in Catholic as well as in Protestant towns. The latter, however, were generally loyal to somebody they considered their own king, even after he had converted to Catholicism. Their loyalty was rewarded with the Edict of Nantes (April 1598), which gave the Protestants freedom of conscience throughout the realm and freedom of worship in more than 200 designated towns. The Catholics were free to worship everywhere, i.e. in Protestant as well as in Catholic towns.

Despite the relatively favourable situation for the Catholics, the Catholic towns were the more difficult problem for Henri. In Paris, which did not have a formal urban charter, he gently inserted candidates of his own preference, without overtly breaking with the customs of urban appointment procedures.[55] In several other towns, League plots were uncovered. In Amiens, one of the towns where the League remained active, Henri pushed through the appointment of aldermen loyal to his government, against a citizen community that insisted on the maintenance of its voting rights. In Nantes, where he proposed a candidate for mayor and was refused, he insisted in a personal letter to the council:

> I am writing this letter to you in my own hand so that sieur de la Bouchelière will be elected. He has no fault and I will be obeyed. If not, I will find ways to make myself obeyed.

He was obeyed. For a long time historians saw these confrontations as part of bigger plan called 'absolutism', but on second sight it looks more like a string of separate incidents. Still, there was an underlying pattern: no alternative sources of authority were tolerated that could rival with the king's.[56] This pattern carried over into the seventeenth century.

Franche-Comté had long been an independent territory, ruled by the dukes of Burgundy and then by their successors from the

Habsburg dynasty. Besançon, its largest city, had been an imperial city since 1184. Its council was annually renewed through a combination of co-option and election. The region was first ravaged by the Thirty Years' War, then by a temporary occupation by the French. In 1674 the French were back, this time for good. The terms of surrender looked very promising and suggested an equality between the region and Louis XIV that, of course, could never exist. Within a year Besançon and the royal officials were at loggerheads, first about expenditures on the ramparts, then about military contributions and the elections of local officials. The controller general of finances, one of the royal officials, spoke scathingly of the town's privileges. The town, despite being almost bankrupt, offered a substantial sum to have them confirmed, the crown demanded double the amount. When the council refused to provide 50,000 livres (circa 3,000 pounds) at short notice in 1676, the citizens' rights to elect their officials was curtailed. In September Besançon's constitution was reformed, turning it into a provincial town with little autonomy. The council tried to put up a fight, but the response was to be threatened with military occupation.[57]

Besançon's fate was perhaps an extreme case, but in its general outline still fairly typical of how French royal policies impacted urban autonomy and the agency of its citizens during the seventeenth century.[58] Other towns had similar experiences. La Rochelle, a Protestant stronghold, was a 'republic' according to a local pamphlet in 1621. After a fourteen-month blockade, when its population was said to have been reduced by three-quarters, the town was subjugated by the king in October 1628. Subsequently, the town's privileges and institutions were all abolished. Many new officials were brought in from outside, and in 1655 Colbert bought the sheriff's office for himself.[59]

Colbert was also the architect of Louis XIV's urban policy. As in Germany, that policy was dictated by financial considerations, even though the conditions were very different. Whereas the Emperor had problems extracting revenue from his autonomous towns, France's system of public finance was underpinned by the systematic exploitation of public offices and privileges, including urban ones.[60] Offices were sold to raise money (*rachat des offices*), privileges were abolished only to be revived after their former owners had offered a substantial payment to the Crown. Towns were also forced to hand over 'voluntary gifts' (*dons gratuit*). Between 1694 and 1709 Auxerre, a town of around 8,000 inhabitants in Burgundy, spent an estimated 730,000 livres, or

45,000 pounds, to buy back offices and privileges once securely held by the municipality. An edict from 1683, designed by Colbert and in force (except between 1764 and 1771) until the French Revolution, transferred control of local finances from the towns to the Crown. The annual budget was determined by the Crown's representative, the *intendant*. Extra expenditures were only permitted after obtaining permission from the same *intendant*. If additional means were required, the government's permission was again necessary before supplementary *octrois* could be introduced. This policy was designed to limit local spending in order to create room for financial claims from Paris.[61]

Such policies could be justified with reference to the towns' republican tendencies, i.e. their continuing insistence on an autonomy constructed in opposition to the authority of the King. Take for example the *Ormée* movement in Bordeaux, which erupted in the spring of 1649 and created a situation that amounted to civil war in the area for the next four years. The *Ormée* proper began as a series of meetings in 1651, where hundreds of Bordeaux citizens met in the open air and produced a political programme for their movement that smacked of the urban republicanism discussed in Chapter 1.[62] The anonymously published *Manifeste des Bourdelois* claimed that the rebels had 'raised the standard of liberty' and proclaimed Bordeaux to be a 'republic'. It stated as the movement's main objectives the right to meet, debate and assist at the determination of the city's public affairs, the recruitment of a civic militia and the exclusion from the city of anyone suspected of siding with the royal governor.[63] In their 'Articles of the Union of the *Ormée*' the leadership pledged to fight for the city's privileges and franchises, and if necessary give their lives for the purpose. They also claimed, as 'titled bourgeois', to have a voice in local politics.[64] The civic militias were the movement's organisational strongholds but, threatened by a royal army intent on taking the city by force, they surrendered Bordeaux in July 1653.

A similar string of events played out in the Burgundian capital of Dijon, where internal conflicts during the Fronde (1648–53) had given the provincial governor increased scope for meddling in local politics. Already in the first half of the century the Crown had tried to get more control over the selection of local officials. Now the governor nominated candidates for the post of mayor, and in 1668 the *intendant* simply appointed the mayor of his choice, whereas in the not so distant past this had been the privilege of the local citizens. In the 1670s almost all important posts were filled by people selected by the *intendant* and by the end of the century they were up for sale, forcing the town to spend substantial sums to repossess them.[65] In Toulouse, capital of the Languedoc, the same sort of process unfolded during the second half of the seventeenth century. In the wake of the Fronde, the first president of the *Parlement*, who had himself been appointed by the Crown, began to systematically undermine the authority and independence of the municipal authorities, the *capitouls*. From 1683, an *intendant* took over and under the edict of that year took control of both the local finances and the appointment of *capitouls*. Here too the by now familiar game of abolishing offices and privileges, and then offering them for resale to the town, was used with devastating effect on urban autonomy and citizen agency.[66]

Louis XIV 'exploited the towns whenever he could', and his successors followed this example. Obviously, there was another side to these policies. To maintain the flow of money, the Crown also had to pay attention to the towns' needs. In fact, Dijon and Toulouse, together with towns like Rouen, Amiens and Lyon, were doing well during Louis' long reign, and so were Bordeaux and Nantes – even Marseille, which had a reputation for being treated particularly badly. Paris did not come into the equation, because it had never been an autonomous city in the first place, and royal interference was simply the continuation of a long tradition.[67] Yet having said that, the French state of the eighteenth century was not particularly responsive to the needs of the towns – or their citizens. There were two main reasons for that. The first was an absence of national representational institutions. Since the Estates General had been summoned for the last time in 1614, there was no national assembly where urban interests could be collectively articulated. Only in 1788–89 were the towns once more in a position to influence national politics.[68] The second reason was financial. The French state ascertained its credit, not through institutions but through a small group of individuals, *financiers*. If these were bourgeois – most of them were nobles, or became ennobled as a result of their activities – they were definitely not connected to urban institutions. Rather, they were royal officials.[69]

Underpinning the French financial system were corporative institutions, but these were instrumentalised in ways reminiscent of the town pawnings that had so upset the imperial cities of the medieval Holy Roman Empire. The selling of municipal offices by the Crown was another way of filling the royal coffers while undermining urban agency. These also created inheritable offices, and thus entrenched privilege, which in the long run benefitted neither party. In 1789 the whole edifice came crashing down.[70] On the other side of the equation, urban citizenship and civic organisations were possibly less coherently institutionalised in France than in many other countries. French towns made no clear distinctions between formal citizens and mere inhabitants.[71] Citizenship was not a prerequisite for guild membership and in most French towns neither guilds nor militias had any political role.

During the late Middle Ages and early modern period, other countries were equally struggling to strike the right balance between towns and national government. In Spain the towns seemed poised to play the lead. In the Castilian Cortes only towns were represented, even if their number gradually declined from circa 100 to 18 by the end of the fifteenth century, subsequently followed by only a modest increase.[72] In the second half of the fifteenth century, close cooperation with the monarch had also allowed the towns to extend their autonomy, but by around 1500 the aristocratic families were once more in the ascendance.[73] The towns hoped to reinforce their position with the Comunero Revolt that erupted in March 1520, shortly after Charles V succeeded to the Castilian throne. They were, however, militarily defeated by Charles at Tordesillas in December, although it took another two years to completely subdue the rebels.[74] Despite his comprehensive military victory, Charles still had to strike a political deal with the towns, since they were the only actors in the Cortes. So Charles and his successors pursued a policy of reducing the status of towns, and to great effect.

In Spain urban privileges were traditionally given to communities that elsewhere would be considered villages. Starting with Charles V, this policy would be driven to new extremes. Urban rights were offered for sale, beginning with the villages situated next to the proper towns. By 1700, almost three-quarters of settlements in Castile had acquired urban privileges; in all of Spain almost 15,000 communities held urban privileges.[75] These towns were able to limit royal interference. Sales of offices, for example, were provisional and not permanent as in France, and usually to individuals acceptable to, or even selected by the council, with possibly inputs from the civic community that could make its voice heard in 'open councils' (*concejo abierto*). But after 1664 the Castilian Cortes was no longer summoned, so that urban lobbying now had to be channelled through a fiscal office, the *Sala de Millones*. Towns were successful in keeping the state at arm's length most of the time, but paid the price of poor coordination at all levels. In the absence of institutional instruments to reconcile conflict and avoid rent-seeking, urban agency actually weakened the Spanish state, rather than strengthening it.[76]

Compared to Western Europe, the towns of East Central Europe were always in a structurally weaker position, because of the limited urbanisation in the region. During the Middle Ages this did not prevent them from attaining levels of autonomy comparable to those of the West. In the fourteenth century, urban leagues emerged in Poland.[77] In 1485, five Hungarian towns created an urban league to coordinate their inputs in the national parliament. However, as pressures of international warfare and religious conflict mounted, the balance shifted towards the princes. In Poland, legislation from 1454, confirmed in the constitution of 1505, undermined the political influence of towns. Between 1508 and 1534, no fewer than thirty-eight major urban rebellions broke out in the region.[78] Religious conflict also weakened the political resolve of urban governments when confronted with a citizen opposition.

While some Polish towns held a status equivalent to that of the German imperial cities, many were 'private' towns subject to a feudal lord. Resident nobles were more generally a prominent feature of Polish towns. After the period of urban rebellions, civic organisations were curtailed; in 1538 and 1552 the Polish government tried to abolish the guilds. Only Cracow, Poznan, Lublin (from 1569) and Lwow (from 1658) had a seat in the Polish parliament *Sejm*, and from 1565 they could only participate in deliberations directly relevant to themselves, but not discuss general issues of state.[79] There was little reason for the Polish king to seek the support of towns that were too few in numbers and lacked political clout.[80]

In Prussia, step by step the towns were subjected to government control: they were excluded from regional assemblies, had to accept the expansion of fortresses and billeting of ever larger garrisons, deal with fiscal constraints, and legislation aimed at creating a uniform administrative framework, designed to undermine urban autonomy.[81] After Prussia invaded and took over Silesia, the same policy was imposed on Wroclaw (Breslau); the formerly 'semi-independent city-state' was from now on run by Prussian state officials.[82] In Russia, the legal status of towns had always been ill-defined and therefore uncertain. Many were fortresses, where military officers and royal administrators dominated local governance. Urban autonomy counted for little and, if anything changed, it became even more restricted during the course of the early modern period.[83]

Conclusion

At heart, citizenship is a mechanism for coordinating actions between individuals and the authorities in charge of a local or national community. Part I of this book explored the workings of this mechanism in local contexts across four different dimensions. Part II investigated how these local mechanisms could be integrated into the working of the state, adding temporal and geographical variation to the blanket treatment of Part I. The first three chapters of Part II discussed three models for achieving such coordination. In Italian city-states, the city and the state overlapped to a large extent. In the Low Countries, cities dominated the federal institutions that determined national policies. In post-Reformation England, later Great Britain, a national Parliament included an increasing number of urban representatives.

This chapter discussed countries where effective coordination between urban interests and the state did not emerge.[84] It is important that we keep reminding ourselves that in premodern Europe this was in fact the default situation. Italy, the Low Countries and England were the exceptions, while Germany, France, Spain, Poland and Prussia displayed the normal state of affairs. It therefore makes more sense to explain the good fortune of the exceptions than the presumed shortcomings of the majority, as so often happens in historical surveys of the period. Italy and the Low Countries benefitted from early high levels of urbanisation, which made it relatively easy for urban institutions to dominate nascent coordinating institutions. England was perhaps a singular case: it was unusually accessible for foreign trade because of the peculiarities of its geography, and because it had inherited from the Norman Conquest an unusual type of parliament which could serve as a platform for the articulation of urban interest.

In Germany, the Holy Roman Empire created a situation that was inherently more complex due to its size and the fact that state formation took place on the level of the individual princely states, rather than the empire as a whole. In that situation, the special status of imperial cities helped protect their autonomy, but at the same time made it more difficult to achieve coordination. Urban leagues were usually short-lived, and when they were not – as in the case of the northern Hanse – they had to forsake political aspirations. France was the only major country where the Crown managed to increase its grip on municipal appointments and politics. Combined with the absence of a national assembly, this situation seriously curtailed the scope for urban agency at state level. In East Central Europe, towns were in a structurally weaker position because of their relatively low share of the population. With pressures rising, they were bound to lose out against the sovereigns and lords. Finally, in Spain urban interests were weakened through the creation of an abundance of towns. There was probably no country in Europe where urban citizenship was more widespread than Spain; as a result, a sort of proto-national citizenship emerged in Spain already well before 1800.[85] However, precisely this generalisation of citizenship without national representative mechanisms made it more difficult for towns to create the kind of political impact necessary for positive action. As in much of the rest of Europe, Spanish town governments felt compelled to take a negative stance vis-à-vis the national government and its institutions: preventing it from interfering in local affairs remained their ultimate political objective. Whereas the basic features of urban citizenship were pretty uniform across Europe, their effects were not, and the different ways in which local political arenas connected to national institutions would seem to go a long way towards explaining the temporal and geographical variations.

Part III

CITIZENSHIP OUTSIDE EUROPE

In this third part I widen the canvas of my investigation, by bringing in two world regions beyond Europe: Asia and the Americas.[1] In doing so, I return to the four practical dimensions of citizenship defined in Part I of this book. This is especially important because, as we see in what follows, Asian cities had no formal citizenship. Therefore, the only feasible comparison with Europe must concentrate on citizenship practices. In the Americas, on the other hand, we do find citizenship as a formal status, as it was imported from Europe by the colonists. In these two chapters I also raise questions about the relationship between cities and states, as discussed in Part II, but this is not be my focus, because it is my primary objective to establish whether urban citizenship-as-practice can be found in these two regions – and, if so, what its 'quality' might have been. We need that assessment in order to test Weber's claim that European citizenship was somehow superior to Asian forms of governance, but also to see how citizenship fared in a colonial context.

Obviously, comparisons with the European developments that have been described and analysed in the first two parts of this book are very different for Asia, on one hand, and the Americas on the other. Asia had its indigenous institutions and historical trajectories and these were only superficially, if at all, affected by Europeans. As in Europe we should be sensitive to Asia's internal variations. Chapter 10 concentrates on two of the major empires in Asia, the Chinese and Ottoman empires, because they provide the sort of urban history literature that is necessary for this type of analysis.

In the Americas, indigenous citizenship is very poorly documented, but whatever was present was completely overhauled by European colonisers. I concentrate in Chapter 11 on the Spaniards and the English. In the Americas, it makes more sense to make citizenship comparisons, not between the colony and the mother country, but between colonists and indigenous people, as well as the Africans brought over as slaves and their descendants. Moreover, there is an influential literature that compares colonial institutions in the Spanish and British-American territories. Strong claims have been made for the superiority of British colonial institutions. My comparative history of urban citizenship also provides an opportunity to test such claims.

To sum up, the two following chapters return to the agenda set out in Part I, and to a somewhat lesser extent of Part II, but they do so against the background of the issues relevant to Asia and the Americas, respectively. In this part of this book, I should add, the limitations of the author's linguistic skills have an even more obvious impact on the material that could have been included than in the European chapters. I must apologise to scholars who have reported their results in Arabic, Chinese, Spanish, Turkish or another relevant language for having used only those bits that have filtered through in languages that I can read with some degree of confidence. It is the inevitable handicap of global comparisons.

10 ORIGINAL CITIZENSHIP IN CHINA AND THE MIDDLE EAST

In 1609, the inhabitants of the Chinese city of Nanjing did something remarkable: they voluntarily compiled tax registers and handed these to the local authorities, demanding that these registers be used for a reform of the tax system. Until 1421 Nanjing had been the primary capital of the Ming Empire, and even after having lost that status it remained a very substantial city with an estimated population at the time of 100,000–150,000. For several decades Nanjing's inhabitants had been clamouring for reform and demanding that corvée labour be converted into monetary contributions, i.e. taxes. Even more remarkable was the reaction of the authorities. Rather than send in the military, as one might expect from such a presumably authoritarian regime as the Ming, a local official named Ding Bin interviewed rich and poor people about their views on taxation. He called a meeting of the five heads of the city's wards, summoned central officials to another meeting, and finally had his staff visit private homes in especially the poorer neighbourhoods to establish the living conditions of their inhabitants. After collecting all these data and views, a system was set up in which each household received a ticket, stating the amount it owed in taxes. On the first of May the residents were called out to deposit their taxes into boxes at a designated station in their neighbourhood. In Ding's own account, the enthusiasm with which people came to make their deposits was specifically noted.[2] As the events in 1609 suggest, the absence of formal citizenship did not prevent the inhabitants of Nanjing participating in various kinds of practices that were central to citizenship in

Europe, immediately questioning Weber's idea that there was no such thing as citizenship in China.[3]

Trying to identify traces of citizenship in these two Asian empires fits a broader historiographical trend.[4] In the not so distant past, the Chinese, Mamluk and Ottoman empires were portrayed as the standard examples of oppressive regimes. Their emperors were seen as premodern dictators who did not tolerate opposition and therefore eliminated all potential threats to their position. Such threats might emanate from political institutions outside the court, or elites such as the aristocracy or merchants. Today, however, the consensus view among historians is very different. Emperors are no longer cast as the powerful villains; their problem was the lack of resources at their disposal.[5] Historians have come to realise that if the kings of England, France and Spain were having massive problems controlling the outer regions of their domains because of the logistical problems they faced in an era of slow communications, the Chinese, Mamluks and Ottomans faced even greater challenges in overcoming the handicap of distance.[6] They were therefore limiting their ambitions, and like their European counterparts, they were forced to allow regional and local authorities substantial freedom of action, provided these observed the basic elements of the deal with the political centre.[7] Those elements included loyalty to the imperial system and resistance to any attempts at devolution, maintenance of public order and the procurement of revenue to support the central military and bureaucratic apparatus.

In setting up a comparison between Europe and Asia we need to steer clear of such formal definitions of citizenship as the documented membership of an urban commune, the definition used by Weber himself. There can be no doubt that such a form of citizenship was not available in Asia. (If this were the benchmark, the present chapter would be superfluous.) However, as Bin Wong pointed out in 1997, such comparisons inevitably lead to conclusions of European superiority, because they employ culturally embedded concepts from the European experience as if they were generally applicable.[8] For precisely this reason I have utilised in this book a more open definition of citizenship as a set of political, economic, social and military practices. This definition has allowed us so far to include in our discussions a wider range of social classes than merely those people who held formal citizen status, and it now allows us to analyse in similar fashion the ways in which relations between public authorities and the urban populations within their domain of authority were organised in Asia.

The absence of formal urban citizenship was the consequence of the absence of urban privileges in Asia. This situation also impacted the preservation of historical records. Especially in China, the sources for our topic are much more limited than in Europe. Moreover, because records from the imperial administration are more abundant, their perspective has dominated Asia's premodern historiography. As a result, we sometimes need to question established wisdoms on the basis of very limited sources. To broaden the source material for this chapter, I have accepted evidence from the nineteenth century for the history of premodern citizenship in these areas. Obviously, one should not assume that China or the Middle East remained static, and one must also be alert to the possibility that nineteenth-century observations were the outcome of recent changes. It seems to me that this inclusion is nonetheless acceptable because – with the exception of Egypt – the areas discussed in this chapter were not immediately affected by the French Revolution. Whereas 1789 marked a clear break in the political history of continental Europe, with major implications for the development of its citizenship regimes, no such rupture happened in the regions discussed in the following pages.[9]

China

The single most striking aspect of China's institutional history is undoubtedly the longevity of its system of rule. There may have been interruptions, there were changes in ruling dynasties, the borders changed and were at times overrun by invaders, but when all is said and done, China's imperial structure survived in its basic form from 220 BCE to the overthrow of the last Qing emperor in 1911, i.e. for more than 2,000 years. No European polity comes even close to that. China's emperors were themselves convinced that this was the result of their benevolent attitude towards their subjects, an opinion recently given a new lease of life by Jean-Laurent Rosenthal and Bin Wong. In their analyses of the different developmental trajectories of Europe and China, Rosenthal and Wong have contrasted the light and usually peaceful touch of China's system of governance with Europe's high levels of military spending and related heavy tax burden. They see this, paradoxically, as a major reason the Industrial Revolution was more likely to take off in Europe.[10] However, most historians, including those whose work Weber studied so carefully 100 years ago, saw China's emperors as brutal oppressors, determined to nip the emergence of any potential rivals in the bud. As a result, according to these authors, China remained an agrarian and bureaucratic empire, the fate of which was very much determined by policies developed in the capital and the imperial court.

One area where the picture has changed is the socio-economic character of the Chinese empire. There is no doubt that China was still overwhelmingly rural in the late eighteenth century. However, it is easy to overlook the fact that Europe was in the same position. In 1800, less than 10 per cent of Europeans lived in an urban community of 10,000 or more inhabitants. In some countries, notably England, the Low Countries and Italy, that percentage was substantially higher, but many other parts of Europe were distinctly less urbanised. For late nineteenth-century China, an urban percentage of 5–6 per cent has been proposed.[11] Clearly, this is lower than the European average, but not completely out of range. Some regions, most notably the lower Yangzi delta, may have come close to 10 per cent, a figure comparable to Germany's in the mid-nineteenth century.[12] It was, moreover, probably significantly higher in earlier times. The most recent figures suggest an urban percentage for China as a whole in the order of 12 per cent in 1630, and as high as 18 per cent in the lower Yangzi region.[13] These estimates include, however, communities from 2,000 and up, while the European figures only cover towns of 10,000 and more. To make them comparable, we should probably multiply the European percentages by 1.5.[14] Even then, the Chinese figures for 1630 give it an urbanisation rate of the same order as the European average, and set China's most urbanised regions not quite in the same range as Italy and the Low Countries, but well above England, France or Germany.[15] We should, moreover, never forget that during the premodern era perhaps as much as half of the world's urban population lived in Chinese towns and cities.[16]

Urban Governance

Chinese towns did not have the same type of formal status as that created by urban privileges in Europe. They were and remained formally part of a hierarchical structure of public administration.

As a result, the highest authority in towns was exercised by officials appointed by the emperor and his government. In practice, however, this small group of outsiders depended heavily on the cooperation of, and self-organisation by, local inhabitants. In the nineteenth century many, perhaps even most, urban services were provided by non-governmental corporate groups and financed either through assessments and dues levied by these groups, or through the income from corporate property. Urban leadership developed out of the local gentry and merchants, who used these organisations as a power base, but were also constrained by the membership's aspirations and expectations, and the organisations' *modus operandi*.[17] Three distinct but at the same time overlapping forms of self-organisation were especially important in the towns and cities of Ming and Qing China: the guilds and the benevolent societies, to be discussed in subsequent sections of this chapter, and the neighbourhood organisations that are the focus of the next few pages.

In nineteenth-century Hankou neighbourhoods could be sealed off by special gates or doors, creating a domain of communal safety. The identity of the neighbourhood was reinforced by the common worship at the neighbourhood temple. Already in the eighteenth century, neighbourhood officials (*baojia*) had been introduced in Hankou to register the inhabitants and distribute communal tasks among them. The head of the ward (*baozheng*) was made responsible for public order, and for assessing inhabitants for tax purposes. The same official was also involved in the provisioning of social welfare and other public services. Officially, the appointment was for one year only, probably to prevent abuses, but already in the eighteenth century a limited number of families seem to have cornered most of the appointments, suggesting that the position was one of real influence.[18]

The ward officials were in a delicate position as intermediaries between the local authorities and their neighbourhood constituents, as is demonstrated by the protests in seventeenth-century Nanjing. In 1609, as we have seen, petitions were submitted against labour services, including the night watch, enforced by neighbourhood captains. Protesters were also unhappy that gentry families were not included in this type of duty. As well as demanding a conversion into monetary contributions, they also insisted on the introduction of financial budgets that would be open to public scrutiny. Such petitions were a customary channel of communication between citizens and authorities at the time.

Flyers, folk songs and theatre performances were also used to mobilise public opinion in seventeenth-century Chinese towns. Citizens' opinions were sought, for example about the introduction of new local taxes.[19]

Although historians of premodern China tend to insist on the absence of much public unrest compared to the rebelliousness of European towns,[20] protest did occur in China. As in Nanjing, the citizens of Hangzhou were dissatisfied with the labour services they were supposed to provide and wanted them converted into monetary payments. A large-scale uprising, mobilising more than 2,000 people in 1582, had to be put down with military force.[21] In seventeenth-century Suzhou, merchants tried to prevent an expansion of the city walls because it would entail tearing down their properties. Inhabitants of Gaochun organised five petition campaigns in protest against the building of new walls. Such campaigns were well-organised, by people who were aware of the relevant legislation and tried to use that to their advantage.[22]

The existence of urban civic organisations has given rise to an intense debate about the existence of a 'public sphere' in premodern China, similar to what Jürgen Habermas saw as the foundation of democracy in Europe. The problem is the slipperiness of the concept itself: even with respect to Europe there have been widely divergent interpretations, and by implication different dates have been proposed for its emergence, contesting Habermas' own claim that a 'public sphere' only emerged in the second half of the eighteenth century.[23] The essence of Habermas' idea was that at some point the conditions for a genuine public debate about public policies had arisen which the authorities could not ignore, and which thus helped to shape those policies. Did such a thing exist in China? There is, of course, no straightforward 'yes or no' answer.[24] The answer should be 'no' because some elements of the concept were clearly missing in China, such as a (national) press that could address issues of national concern, the natural rights that many eighteenth-century reformers in Europe invoked to make their case or the social contract between citizens and their rulers that had been so dear to reformers of an earlier era.[25] Other features, however, were present in China, including very significant 'social associations not dominated by the state' that could act as intermediaries between the government and its citizens.[26] Ultimately, we have to decide what are the most significant elements, while reminding ourselves that the 'public sphere' in most countries of nineteenth-century Europe was confined to a quite narrow group of people.

Guilds

One such type of social association was the guild. Guilds were a prominent feature of Chinese towns in the late imperial period. Information about their nineteenth-century incarnations suggests a significant role in urban life. Their number increased rapidly in China precisely at the time when they were being abolished in many European countries. This could well have been the result of the new economic opportunities arising from trade expansion and the simultaneous political and military insecurities of the late Qing period. A survey drawn up after the fall of the last emperor in 1911, but professing to start in 1655, might lead us to the conclusion that Chinese guilds were mainly a phenomenon of the nineteenth century, albeit with roots in the sixteenth.[27] This early twentieth-century survey includes almost forty guilds for all of China between 1644 and 1720, which would make China a very late developer compared to Europe. However, in the new town of Hankou, no fewer than fifteen guild were established during that same period.[28] Beijing, which of course was very much older as a city, already had seventy guilds before the end of the Ming (1644). Subsequently, the number increased to 220 by the end of the eighteenth century.[29] Early references to Chinese guilds go back as far as the eleventh and thirteenth centuries, when the first guilds were also established in Europe, but a major upsurge took place only in the sixteenth century. It therefore looks as if the 1911 survey underestimated the number of premodern guilds in China, even if they emerged later than in Europe.[30]

In the beginning, guilds in China were temple associations.[31] The parallel with European guilds' origins in religious brotherhoods is striking. Temples would provide meeting space, and common worship acted as a focus for activities and solidarity. The basis for the organisation of guild foundations, especially in their early stages, was almost always the common origin of the membership from a particular region, possibly combined with a shared occupation. In Hankou, of twenty-eight guilds created before 1796, six were purely occupational, the others either based in shared origins (thirteen), or a combination of origin and occupation (nine). In the second half of the nineteenth century purely occupational organisations became predominant.[32] The significance of a common-origin basis for guilds is thought to lie in the importance the Chinese attached to burial with their relatives. The organisations have therefore also been called 'native place lodges'.[33] This led Weber to conclude that Chinese guilds reinforced what he saw as a primitive attachment to lineage.[34] Indeed, returning the corpses of deceased members to their native places was and remained an important feature of these guilds, but it would seem to be an unacceptable reduction of their function to focus on merely this one aspect.

Besides the maintenance of ties with the region of origin, the most important purpose of guilds was to create stability for their trade. Chinese guilds regulated weights and measures, set prices (usually in conjunction with the local authorities), maintained codes of occupational conduct and lobbied local government to promote the interests of the membership. For those familiar with European guilds, the most notable difference is the absence of 'monopolies'. There is no hint of an exclusive access to particular trades for the members of this or that guild; membership was available to everyone who originated from the region, or was active in the occupation covered by the guild.[35] Chinese guilds did not have apprenticeship arrangements,[36] but they did offer social assistance.

Guilds in China would hold meetings where members could discuss issues of common concern – again as in Europe. Inevitably, some families would become prominent as guild officers and occupy more than what was perhaps their fair share of guild offices. Recorded examples of ordinary members exposing abuses in their guild to the local authorities imply that the dominance of such prominent members was constrained by an outside authority. Common worship of patron deities helped reinforce the bonds of solidarity within the guild community, as did the extensive building programmes that many guilds undertook. Beginning usually with a temple *cum* meeting place, Chinese guilds would ultimately own huge compounds that included hostels for itinerant merchants and artisans, and a stage for the performance of plays and operas. The *Hui-chan* guild of Hankou, for example, owned a small temple complex in the suburbs, when in 1694 twenty-four of the most prominent members decided to raise money for a new and more conspicuous set of buildings located within the town walls. In 1717 a new west hall was added, and in 1721 another lecture hall. The compound would ultimately consist of around 100 different rooms, occupying a substantial part of a new street, Hsin-an Street, maintained by the guild, and leading to a pier in the river that was also built and maintained by the guild. When floods destroyed the pier in 1796, members could donate funds for its reconstruction in exchange for bonds.[37]

Chinese guild organisations were initiated by the members themselves, and could expect to be sanctioned by the government, either formally in writing, or otherwise in practice.[38] Surveying the evidence, it seems fair to say that Chinese guilds were first and foremost civic organisations that sought to integrate their mobile membership into the framework of the urban community, while at the same time allowing the urban authorities access to the worlds of migrants, businessmen and the crafts.

Poor Relief

China had a rudimentary system of social welfare that swung into action especially in times of food scarcity, but also during other catastrophes. This granary system was maintained by the government throughout the empire.[39] On top of that, the authorities tried to control prices, to provide ordinary people with access to food at all times. However, as in other premodern societies, price controls were only partially effective, and there was considerable demand for routine welfare, not least in China's large urban centres.[40] This type of welfare was left almost completely to private initiative, albeit with the active support of the local authorities.

In Chinese cities the guilds were also important providers of welfare. Their compounds would often include hostels providing shelter to mobile workers and merchants.[41] More importantly, they paid for funerals, sometimes in the guild burial grounds, but also for the return of members' corpses to their native region to be buried together with their forebears.[42] Besides the guilds, so-called benevolent societies (*shantang*) emerged in the late sixteenth century. The first two that we are aware of were set up in 1590 in Yucheng, in the lower Yangzi delta, and the model then quickly spread to other cities. The benevolent societies had limited membership, with each member pledging to contribute a certain amount of money and time to the cause. They were almost exclusively urban organisations. The division of labour with the guilds remained unclear. In some instances the benevolent society seems to have been a subdivision of the guild: sometimes it was a parallel organisation, in other cases they were completely separate from the guild. Benevolent societies did, however, employ the guild model for their own organisation. They also owned property and kept written records of their financial transactions. Besides food, they also provided medical assistance as a means of preventing outbreaks of epidemic diseases.[43] To be eligible for charity, poor people had to be recommended. Familiarity with benefactors, and therefore patronage, was an important element of the system. Paupers who were caught drinking or gambling could expect to be excluded.[44]

There were strong incentives for civic charity in premodern China. Promoting the welfare of society as a whole was recommended by Confucianism as a goal worth pursuing, and the rich were encouraged to shoulder this type of responsibility. Benefactors advertised their charitable acts in pamphlets, in the expectation that it would enhance their social status. It was more or less expected that members of benevolent societies would hand over as much as 10 per cent of their income. Obviously, charity was also perceived as a prop of the existing social hierarchy, a vital element in the maintenance of public order, as well as a means to gain influence – or at least popularity with local authorities. During times of crisis, the authorities actively supported the work of benevolent societies, as happened for example in 1641 in the towns of the Yangzi delta.[45] In the nineteenth century such support became more regular, and sometimes even took the form of specific taxes being designated for supporting the work of the benevolent societies.[46] Besides poor relief, guilds and benevolent societies assumed the responsibility for provisioning other public services, including firefighting, the maintenance of streets and, in the nineteenth century, also street lighting, bridges and public parks, as well as ferries, all of them accessible to the general public.[47]

Charitable trusts had no legal status and in this sense they differed from their European equivalents. In practice, however, guilds and benevolent societies owned property, were self-governing and worked in close cooperation with the civic administration.[48] As in Europe, they provided a range of services to people in need who could make a moral but not a legal claim for assistance. For its beneficiaries, this dimension of citizenship was therefore precarious.

Urban Defence

Although China experienced long periods of domestic peace, Chinese towns were heavily fortified. In fact, the Chinese character *cheng* can mean 'wall' as well as 'city'. In modern Chinese the word for town is *chengshi*, a combination of 'wall' and 'market'. It is therefore fair to say that urban defences were an integral part of the whole urban concept. Although precise figures are lacking, the number of walled towns in premodern China is reckoned to have run to several thousand. Especially during the Ming period, town walls were constructed and reconstructed on a scale unprecedented in world history.[49] This was not always popular; Nanjing citizens whose houses had to be destroyed to make way for the new ramparts protested vehemently.[50]

These towns were guarded by permanent garrisons; I found no traces of any parallel organisation of civic militias recruited from the ranks of the inhabitants. During Qing times, when China was effectively occupied by foreign (Manchu) forces, this would in any case have been most unlikely. However, in 1799 during the White Lotus rebellion, and again in 1853 during the Taiping, the guilds of Hankou helped organise local defence.[51] The same happened in other towns during the Taiping, for example in Shanghai, where 500 'braves' were recruited in 1860.[52]

It would seem that medieval Chinese towns did have a system of watches (*huofu*), manned by towns' inhabitants, whose duty was to patrol the walled cities and their suburbs at night. During the sixteenth century participation in the night watch was converted into a cash payment, and thus became part of the fiscal system instead of the system of labour services. In Hangzhou citizens protested at this and other forced labour contributions.[53] In 1641 it was suggested in Taicang that the members of the local benevolent society would take up archery practice, but nothing came of it.[54] In seventeenth-century Nanjing there are hints of a (controversial) night watch recruited among the inhabitants, but it is impossible to claim with any certainty that this was an equivalent of the European militia system.[55]

This absence of civic militias might be related to the claim that China was a relatively peaceful society. China was nonetheless plagued, at intervals, by large-scale and destructive domestic conflict, for example during the Ming–Qing transition of the seventeenth century, the White Lotus rebellion of the late eighteenth century, and the Taiping rebellion of the nineteenth. The elaborate fortification of Chinese towns also contradicts the idea that peace was the default situation in China. It was certainly not taken for granted by Chinese towns themselves. Nevertheless, it does seem that China's pattern of domestic violence was distinct from that of Europe: instead of frequent, relatively small incidents, China suffered from a pattern of rare, but extraordinarily intense domestic conflict that possibly made a militia system less effective.

China's Premodern Citizenship Regime

In a recent survey of China's long-term development, Brandt, Ma and Rawski have argued that Europe's advance over China should be explained as the result of principal-agent flaws in the Chinese state – in other words as a problem of citizenship. Our survey of Chinese citizenship practices lends ammunition to that argument. Rather than the oppressive nature emphasised by previous generations of scholars, Brandt, Ma and Rawski see the weakness of the central government as its main problem. Yes, it was remarkably stable compared to its European counterparts, and also managed to make do with low levels of taxation; but as a consequence local governments had hardly any money to spend. The result therefore was that they had to raise revenue informally, creating a system riddled by corruption and dependent on the cooperation of local elites.[56] My investigation strongly suggests that civic organisations also became part of this arrangement. To sustain an urban society in the context of a 'thin' state, substantial local autonomy, a robust civil society, significant levels of citizen organisation with active craft and merchant guilds, as well as social welfare provisions cutting across lineage solidarities, were almost inevitable. One finds, however, few traces of military forms of citizenship. In that regard, the Chinese state effectively guarded its monopoly of violence. In other areas of urban governance Chinese citizens combined to initiate public services, as in the case of the Hankou guild taking care of infrastructure, or volunteered to pay extra taxes, as in Nanjing.

Middle East

Although it has taken a different shape, not least because of an important French strand, the historiography of the Middle East has undergone a trajectory not unlike the Chinese.[57] Weber's picture of the region's social make-up as clan-based dominated historians' portrayals of its past for much of the twentieth century.[58] In this version of their history, the indigenous peoples were oppressed by an empire whose elites were pastoralists with a strong military outlook. Urban interests were merely tolerated, and only encouraged for fiscal reasons. The central government took little notice, and urban pressure groups were no match for bureaucrats. The region's economic underdevelopment was an almost inevitable result of this fixated sociopolitical structure.

Two things have changed in recent decades. Scholars have stopped taking at face value the self-portrait provided by documents from the central archives. The Ottoman Empire in particular is now portrayed in a more optimistic light; in Şevket Pamuk's words, '[t]he Ottomans were flexible and pragmatic from the start'.[59] While the picture of the top of the pyramid was changing, new perspectives also emerged on its foundations with scholars calling into question the idea of a powerless society.[60] A range of arguments were put forward questioning Weber's portrayal. It was, for example, pointed out that the cities of the Middle East had been among the most populous and most advanced of Eurasia during the ninth to eleventh centuries, while Europeans were still trying to come to terms with the traumas of the collapse of the Roman Empire.[61] During the Ottoman period (early sixteenth to early twentieth centuries), after a period of decay, the major cities of the region grew to sizes comparable to Europe's metropoles.[62] The most recent estimates show that in terms of urbanisation the Middle East was actually ahead of Europe until the eighteenth century. That gap had been slowly narrowing since 1000 CE, when the Middle East had been three times more urbanised than Europe. Clearly, the pace of urbanisation in the Middle East was well below that of Europe as a whole. In terms of population impact, however, the Middle East ranked above Europe for almost the entire period covered here.[63] Perhaps more importantly still, in the context of this chapter, scholars have begun to uncover a rich communal life in these cities that seemed to contradict the claim that society was constrained by family and clan structures.[64]

These shifts have rejuvenated the debate about 'the Islamic city'. The whole concept, which also went back to Weber, is now very much in doubt, even in the revised version launched by Ira Lapidus in his famous *Muslim Cities in the Later Middle Ages* from 1967. In this book Lapidus questioned Weber's portrait of the Middle East, and sought to replace it by a superior model, informed by a deep knowledge of the available sources in Arabic that had been inaccessible to Weber himself. Lapidus demonstrated persuasively that the cities he concentrated on, Aleppo in Syria and Cairo in Egypt, had communal structures, more specifically neighbourhoods, religious communities and brotherhoods and youth associations, all of which shaped the lives of urbanites. He insisted, however, that none of these had the kind of independence granted to European corporations: urban governance remained the province of bureaucrats appointed by the central government.[65]

More recent voices in this debate on 'the Islamic City' object that the whole concept implies that religion was somehow the defining characteristic of these societies, that many of the generalisations were using one or two examples to characterise a huge area stretching from Morocco to the Iranian border and beyond, and that the whole idea of using the European experience as a template made it impossible to think about the Middle East on its own terms.[66]

In what follows I want to trace the details of local organisation in the towns and the cities of the Middle East, without assuming beforehand that they were inferior to those of the West, or that they were completely dominated by the central government institutions. For reasons that are explained in due course, the military and economic dimensions of citizenship (militias and guilds) are discussed together, rather than separately in this section.

Urban Governance

Under Ottoman rule, cities had no independent statute. The highest local authority was the governor, or *pasha*, and he would always be appointed by the central government. The same applied to other high offices. This was most obviously so in the capital Istanbul, where the imperial and local governments were almost indistinguishable, but it applied equally in major towns such as Aleppo, Cairo or Damascus.[67] When looking at systems of local governance from a formal point of view, we have to say that it was a mere branch of the central executive. Yet in day-to-day practice the situation was not quite so black and white, as we can see from local politics in eighteenth-century Aleppo.

Aleppo at the time had circa 100,000 inhabitants.[68] Due to its long-distance commerce, Aleppo was a city with an ethnically as well as religiously mixed population. Such mixtures were a characteristic feature of all major cities in the Ottoman Empire. As everywhere else, the highest official was the *pasha*, who was appointed for one year only, and then moved on to a similar posting elsewhere in the empire. The first was appointed in 1520, shortly after the arrival of the Ottomans. Their invasion had been welcomed by Aleppo's inhabitants, who had suffered from many abuses under the preceding Mamluk regime.[69] The governor was primarily responsible for the military security of the city and its hinterland, and had to ensure the transfer of tax revenues to Istanbul. He was in charge of the janissary garrison, but also had his own forces which were mainly used for controlling the countryside and ensuring the regular flow of revenue.

The governor was theoretically in complete charge of Aleppo; in practice he enlisted the help of many others. For one, he was advised by a council, or *divan*, composed of local officials and notables. The *divan* was 'the most important formal setting for local participation in policymaking'. Its membership included the *qadi*, who was the highest judicial official and like the *pasha* appointed by Istanbul; a variable number of *a'yans*, or local notables; the leading *ulama* (religious leader); the head of the *ashraf*, who were families claiming direct descent from the Prophet, and finally the commanding officer of the janissary corps. This council met regularly, but no minutes were taken.[70] The *a'yan* have been characterised as 'local gentry'. They owned landed properties in the region. In the seventeenth and eighteenth centuries these families were in the ascendant, when they also gradually gained hereditary control over tax farms. Their dominance was, however, checked by other groups in the city.

On one hand there were the *ashraf*, an especially coherent subset of the Muslim community. Muslims made up about 80 per cent of Aleppo's population, Christians another 15 per cent, while most of the remaining 5 per cent were Jewish.[71] The other countervailing force were the janissaries, the garrison of professional soldiers who became increasingly integrated into the local artisan and working-class community. The janissaries, who in Aleppo were 5,000–10,000 strong, were a particularly active political force. They fought pitched battles with the governor's own *dali* troops – for example, in 1775 when the janissaries refused to accompany the governor on a military campaign and managed to oust him from the city. On this occasion they were supported in their protests by a large file of complaints, collected by the *qadi* from various sections of the local population. In 1784 the janissaries again removed a *pasha* from office and from the city itself, and in the early years of the nineteenth century they were effectively masters of the city.[72] The janissaries relied on support from the guilds and neighbourhoods, as well as on their own weapons.

Neighbourhoods and guilds were equally important in Cairo. Like Aleppo, the Egyptian capital was governed by a *pasha* and *qadi*, both appointed by the central government. At the same time, the city showed 'a high level of popular dissent'.[73] It was subdivided into fifty-three neighbourhoods, each headed by a neighbourhood leader, or *shaykh al-hārah*,[74] whose responsibilities were to maintain public order and help collect local taxes.[75] Next to the neighbourhoods, a large number of guilds organised the local population on an occupational basis. Janissaries were active participants in Cairo's local politics, much as they were in Aleppo. In other words, the city had a plethora of community organisations, endorsed by the government but not completely controlled by it.[76] This was true of Ottoman cities more generally.[77] The balance might vary from one town to another, but local community organisations were found everywhere as active participants in urban governance.[78] In times of crisis, they provided the contexts for articulating grievances and mobilising the forces of opposition.[79]

Unfortunately, the centuries before the arrival of the Ottomans are poorly documented. Jerusalem, Safad and Tripoli had vibrant neighbourhoods during the Mamluk period (thirteenth–fifteenth centuries), when there were public hearings and the *ulama* acted as local leaders.[80] In Cairo, the Ottomans reportedly preserved much of the institutional structure as they found it when they conquered the city in 1517.[81] The level of public services in medieval Cairo was, moreover, unheard of in Western Europe with its presumably superior urban institutions. Cairo had street lighting in the Mamluk period, whereas Amsterdam was the first Western European city to introduce it – in the late seventeenth century. Cairo's Great Hospital, built in the late thirteenth century, provided patients with their own beds and bedclothes, as well as private chamber pots, notwithstanding its capacity of 6,000.[82] Were these fruits of superior centralised power, the results of a deep commitment to the local community, or both? It is very difficult to say at this point, but I cannot rule out the second interpretation.

Economic and Military Organisation

Craft and merchant guilds were a common phenomenon in Ottoman towns and cities. Those of Istanbul, Aleppo, Jerusalem and Cairo especially (apart from Jerusalem all among the larger cities of the empire, and Istanbul and Cairo indeed of the premodern world more generally) have been studied in such detail that we can discuss them with confidence. One thing that the modern scholarship on Ottoman guilds has achieved is to dispel the idea that these were mere instruments in the hands of the authorities to oversee and control the mass of the population.[83] Instead, a much richer picture has emerged.[84] As in Europe, the organisational form of the guild was not clearly distinguished from other community organisations, but for purposes of comparison we are focusing here on occupational guilds, whose membership consisted of craftsmen, shopkeepers and merchants, or others working in the service sector. This would therefore include the water-bearers, for instance, whose Cairo guild numbered more than 3,000 members in the eighteenth century.[85]

Guilds were numerous as well as popular, in the sense that they organised a very substantial part of urban populations in the Ottoman Empire.[86] Istanbul had seventy-six guilds in the beginning of the seventeenth century and possibly twice that number by the end of the century.[87] Eighteenth-century Cairo numbered 200–250 guilds, of which thirty-nine had a membership of more than 1,000.[88] It is not at all clear how and especially when they originated. There can be no doubt that guilds existed in Byzantium as late as the twelfth century, if not necessarily in the provinces. Some of these guilds were initiated by the state, others by craftsmen themselves.[89] Perhaps they disappeared afterwards and were only revived by the Ottoman authorities.[90] Cairo, however, had occupational organisations before the arrival of the Ottomans.[91] The fact of the matter is that we only have reliable information about the guilds of the seventeenth and eighteenth centuries.

It is possible that some of these guilds were created on the authorities' initiative, but it is unlikely that this always happened.[92] It is better to think of Ottoman guilds as an interface between the members and the authorities. The election of guild officials is a case in point. The headmen, usually known as *shaykh*, were officially appointed by a judge, or *qadi*, but their names were put forward by the members themselves. Moreover, a delegation of the members had to confirm before the *qadi* that they were willing to accept the *shaykh*. And even if they did, we find quite a few instances of guilds subsequently asking the court to dismiss their *shaykh* when they had apparently lost faith in him – and of the courts acting on such a request. Guilds in Cairo had this degree of control over their own governors, and in Istanbul, notwithstanding the close control that the government imposed on its capital city, the situation was similar.[93] Another indication of the guilds' relative autonomy is the membership meetings, where issues relating to the trade would be discussed.[94] There is no clear indication, however, that these guilds had their own sources of income.

Ottoman guilds regulated trade, in the sense that they might set quality controls and prices for both raw materials and final products. All of this would happen in consultation with the authorities, but not necessarily on the initiative of those authorities. Guilds regularly made their wishes known by petitioning the authorities, and their proposals were usually accepted and absorbed into the body of regulatory documents. The *shaykh* was the arbiter in trade disputes. Ottoman guilds also had an important role in the collection of taxes – possibly more significant than their European counterparts. Like European craftsmen and shopkeepers, guilds in the Ottoman Empire were infused with an ideology of equality.[95]

The Ottoman guilds provided only limited social assistance. They did not set aside funds for that purpose, let alone maintain separate institutions to take care of members in their old age, or for members falling ill. However, they did organise festivities that could reinforce ties of solidarity within the guild community, as well as communal meals. Istanbul guilds were known to organise days out in the countryside, complete with picnic baskets to refresh the participants during the trip.[96] Those in Cairo would participate in public parades with their own float, drawn by two asses.[97]

In Europe the guilds, insofar as they had military functions, seem to have lost them in the early modern period, whereas in the Ottoman Empire the opposite happened. During the seventeenth and eighteenth centuries, members of the janissary infantry troops increasingly joined the guilds. They did so for economic reasons. These troops would be stationed as permanent garrisons in particular towns, with little else to occupy them apart from the occasional watch. Janissary pay scales were correspondingly low, forcing many of them into civilian side jobs. Because the janissaries held various privileges with regard to taxation and otherwise, there was simultaneously a reverse movement: individual craftsmen and traders would join a corps to enjoy the privileges and also the protection that such an armed organisation was offering. Clearly, there was a price to be paid, usually 5–10 per cent of one's capital at death. But many considered it a price worth paying.[98]

As a result of this double movement, the world of the guilds and the world of the military became intertwined. Guilds did not usually involve themselves in local politics, outside the realm of their occupations.[99] This in itself may have contributed to the impression that they were somehow different and less effective than European guilds, but perhaps, historians have simply been looking in the wrong places. Even when the guilds were mainly quiescent, their janissary members were politically very active indeed. In Aleppo they became the single most important political force during the second half of the eighteenth century.[100]

Welfare

Provisioning for the poor (*zakat*) is one of the Five Pillars of Islam.[101] Together with the voluntary alms (*sadaqa*) it is mentioned explicitly in the Quran as a way of pleasing God. Biographies of important figures would never fail to mention their contribution to such pious charity.[102] Islamic welfare was, at the same time, handicapped by the absence of a formal organisation like the Church that could coordinate charity.[103] Having said that, the towns and cities of the Middle East had their fair share of charities, including pensioners' homes, hospitals, caravanserais, funds for the release of prisoners of war, as well as the poor relief provided by religious organisations.[104] As in Europe it is difficult to detect a system in the variety of charities. Nonetheless, two types of welfare seem to have been especially common in the region.

The first of these was neighbourhood welfare. In eighteenth-century Aleppo, the headman of the neighbourhood collected funds for a range of public services including the maintenance of public spaces and the removal of waste, as well as welfare for resident paupers.[105] The second system consisted of the well-known *waqfs*. These were usually urban institutions.[106] Technically, a *waqf* was 'an object which was endowed for a specific purpose in perpetuity'.[107] They were usually set up by well-off donors, and these could include the sultan himself. Ottoman sultans created important institutions with a *waqf* governance structure in all important cities of their empire. These *waqf* foundations included mosques, madrasas (i.e. religious schools) and welfare institutions. Other *waqfs* were set up by local elites, and might acquire additional funding in the course of time.

The *waqfs* have been criticised as one of the institutions that held back the economic development of premodern Islamic societies. They compared unfavourably with European corporations because they were family rather than community based, and because their governance structure was set in stone by the founders; Islamic law did not permit changes.[108] For the early modern era the comparison is perhaps less unfavourable to the *waqf*. In Europe, where their nearest counterparts were foundations rather than corporations,[109] these foundations were very common in the realm of welfare. They often retained strong links with the family of the patron and could be just as long-lasting and inflexible as a *waqf*.[110]

Cities, Citizenship and the State in the Ottoman Empire

The whole issue of urban citizenship in the Ottoman Empire hinges on one's evaluation of the power of the Ottoman state. Many scholars have argued that it was a strong state, because it managed to control local – and more specifically urban – authorities. Others have pointed out that Islam itself did not acknowledge the state as such, and that the Ottomans were subject to the same technological constraints on communication that limited the effectiveness of other imperial governments seeking to dominate large territories.[111] The position of the *pashas* is a case in point. Their rotation, annual in theory but sometimes two or three years in practice, prevented the development of local roots and 'going native', forcing them to nurture their relationship with the central government. At the same time, it made them more dependent on the information from, and collaboration with, local elites, who were thus able to manipulate the government agents and promote their own agendas.[112] The stability of the Ottoman Empire has been ascribed to precisely this delicate balance between central control and local participation. There is general agreement that the central government was more in control in the sixteenth and early seventeenth centuries than later, and that particularly in the course of the eighteenth century it embarked on a course of decentralisation. Due to a dearth of local studies it is currently difficult to gauge how much local agency the early stages of Ottoman rule allowed for, not to mention the centuries preceding the arrival of the Ottomans.

With these caveats we can still say that within urban communities the Middle East displayed various types of organisations that encompassed the inhabitants not only in passive, but also in all kinds of active ways.[113] Neighbourhoods, religious organisations, *waqfs* and guilds were very much in evidence in urban communities, and even if their role became more prominent over the course of time, they already existed in the earlier period. Much has been made of their dependence on official permission and regulation. There is, however, a strong tendency in the literature to put European corporations on a pedestal of complete autonomy, and find similar institutions elsewhere falling short of that ideal. The truth of the matter is that complete autonomy was rare in Europe itself. European corporations received their privileges from a superior authority and those privileges could be revoked. European authorities regularly interfered in the 'domestic' arrangements of corporations, and insisted on a say in their governance. If they did not directly appoint the directors of such corporations, they usually wanted at least to confirm the members' choice. In the Middle East, neighbourhoods, guilds and *waqfs* were held collectively responsible for their actions. Even if organisations had no legal identity, they were routinely treated by the authorities as if they had.[114] They thus provided urban citizens with a variety of instruments to act in the public domain and to interact with the authorities.[115]

Conclusion

As was to be expected, this comparative history of citizenship-as-practice in late medieval and early modern Asia points up similarities as well as differences. Three major points do stand out, however. The first is that there was a lot going on in China and the Middle East that could be defined as 'citizenship', i.e. established mutual claims and expectations between inhabitants and authorities. These claims and expectations were institutionalised in a variety of organisational forms. Even if technically the authorities were ultimately in charge, it was almost impossible to determine who, under routine circumstances, had the final say: the members of various local organisations or the imperial authorities and their delegates. These civic organisations created a mix of public and club goods, helping to lubricate social and economic processes. No doubt such arrangements were beneficial to the membership of these organisations, for otherwise they would have been extremely difficult to sustain. However, in both Asian empires there seems to have been a general understanding that such benefits could also have a positive impact beyond the membership and worked simultaneously for the 'common good'. In Asia, as much as in Europe, three types of organisations especially created agency for citizens: occupational guilds, neighbourhoods and religious fraternities. European towns, however, had their civic militias, not found in a similar form in either China or the Middle East.

A second important point of comparison relates to the position of urban government. It is quite clear that urban government as a separate institution became established in Europe but was unknown in the Middle East and China.[116] In the two Asian empires, local governance was part of the national administrative structure, whereas in Europe it had its own position, which was, moreover, articulated in a series of documents that were highly valued by European urban communities: literally, in fact, because they were willing to spend substantial amounts of money on obtaining – and later preserving – such 'privileges'. As is well known, these urban privileges emerged out of the feudal system in Europe, whereas other parts of Eurasia did not experience a similar prolonged period in which central authority was so weak that it had to parcel out its sovereign powers. Urban constitutions in Europe created a platform for a specific political ideology that we might call 'urban republicanism'.[117] Nothing similar seems to have emerged in the Asian regions examined here. Although it is tempting to see this urban republicanism as in some way connected to the emergence of capitalism, it has been pointed out that in actual fact it was quite opposed to capitalist practices, for example in its insistence on social egalitarianism. Urban republicanism was the ideology of the craftsman and shopkeeper, not of the merchant-entrepreneur.[118] While Confucianism and Islam presumably held back their respective societies, Europe's urban ideology was very different, but it is not immediately obvious why it should contribute to a trajectory of social development and economic growth.

The third element might provide a solution to the conundrum. This is the position of towns and urban interests in the national domain. Because local government was subservient to the imperial government, towns in China or the Middle East had no direct representation in national institutions. They could petition the national government, as Istanbul's guilds used to do in the seventeenth century,[119] or send delegations to the capital, as the inhabitants of Aleppo did in 1784 after ousting the governor from their city,[120] but they had no platform from which to articulate their particular demands and interests on a routine basis. In several European countries such institutions were available to towns, in the form of regional and national parliaments. Having said that, an important caveat is in order. It is generally agreed among historians of the period that the zenith of urban autonomy in Europe was in the late Middle Ages. As we saw in the previous chapter, from the sixteenth century, 'voracious states' – I'm borrowing Wim Blockmans' felicitous phrase – were clamping down on urban 'freedoms', not only in much of Northern and Central Europe, but also in France, under Louis XIV in the seventeenth century.[121] This is significant for two reasons. The first is that precisely in this respect there was no common pattern that applied throughout Europe. By 1700, French or Polish towns were not obviously more autonomous than those of China or the Middle East. This restriction of urban freedoms and independence, its citizenship if you will, was being imposed in Europe precisely during the period when it was making its economic leap forward. With the increase in central state authority, the situation in Scandinavia, East Central Europe and France increasingly came to resemble citizenship patterns in China and the Middle East. In some regions of Europe, however, citizenship was more developed, 'stronger', than it was, or had been, anywhere in China or the Middle East.

11 RECREATING EUROPEAN CITIZENSHIP IN THE AMERICAS

When Benjamin Franklin moved from Boston to Philadelphia, arriving in October 1723, he was exchanging one of the most democratic towns in British America for a place that, in terms of citizenship, could well be called underdeveloped.[1] Previous decades of wrangling between the Penn family, who were the colony's private owners, and the community dominated by the Quakers, the colony's first settlers, had created uncertainty as to the inhabitants' rights and duties, while Philadelphia's civic life, such as it was, had been dominated by the Quakers' Society of Friends. Franklin, the quintessential organiser, would change that. By mobilising the civic energies of numerous Philadelphians almost single-handedly, from 1727 he helped to launch in quick succession the Junto debating clubs, a watch, a voluntary fire service, the first public library in the New World and a hospital; he started petitions and an initiative to pave the streets of central Philadelphia, not to mention his many ideas for public improvement expressed in the pages of the local newspaper that he published.[2]

Philadelphia was also a town without proper militias. This was the situation in all of Pennsylvania, the result of Quaker pacifism and its peculiarity as a private property type of colony. By the middle of the eighteenth century, however, voluntary equivalents began to emerge. It was once again Franklin who helped set up the first of these organisations in 1747, and a second in 1755. They were social and political clubs under the cloak of militia exercises. The membership, who called themselves 'Associators', were primarily artisans. In the 1770s they became increasingly active, demanding greater accountability from the local government, and in 1774 they managed to get some from their own ranks elected to the city council.[3]

On 25 April 1775 another voluntary organisation was created in Philadelphia 'for the purpose of defending with arms their property, liberty, and lives', at a meeting reportedly attended by 8,000 people. Within days the first companies were recruited in the city's wards and in June about 2,000 Philadelphians were already exercising. In September a Committee of Privates was formed to speak for the rank and file. This Committee of Privates self-consciously modelled itself on the Agitators in the English New Model Army from the seventeenth century, and would soon prove to be the most radical of the middle-class organisations. The Committee's fourteen members included two schoolmasters, a shopkeeper, a merchant, a master shoemaker and a master carpenter. Two were members of local guilds. They opposed the stationing of regular troops, but also demanded regulation of food prices and extension of the franchise, i.e. the type of claims one would also find in European guild petitions. In 1776 Philadelphia militiamen were indeed given the vote. During the American Revolution of the same year, the Philadelphia Associators imprinted their views on the constitution for the state of Pennsylvania, drafted by a committee chaired by the inevitable Franklin.[4]

The story of Benjamin Franklin's efforts to introduce civic organisations demonstrates two issues explored further in the following pages. The first is that citizens in the New World did not automatically benefit from the sort of civic organisations once available to them in the Old World. The second is that there was a demand for such organisations. Franklin's successes were no doubt the product of his extraordinary personality, but they also tapped into a genuine interest, as we shall see.

When Europeans had begun to explore and then subsequently to colonise the New World, from around 1500 onwards, citizenship was one of the import products they brought with them. Creating citizenship was not, of course, necessarily uppermost in the minds of the explorers and conquerors. Nonetheless, it entered the picture at a remarkably early point.[5] Santo Domingo, nowadays the capital of the Dominican Republic, was probably the first community with Spanish urban privileges in the New World, and it got them as early as 1511. And when Hernán Cortés arrived in June 1519 in mainland Central America, one of the first things he did was create a town: Villa Rica de Vera Cruz, now Veracruz in Mexico.[6] Because they received urban charters, the inhabitants of such towns would inevitably gain formal citizenship rights with the privileges set out in the charter. Thus began the transfer of one European institution to another part of the world. The diverse origins of colonial citizenship, in Spanish, Portuguese, Dutch, French and English contexts, help explain some of the features of the citizenship regimes that emerged in the Americas. Local circumstances, and even Native traditions, likewise helped to shape citizenship as it evolved in these parts. An important theme in this chapter is this interplay between native institutional traditions and colonial transformation.

Our investigation of citizenship also lands us squarely in the middle of an ongoing debate about the role of institutions in the divergent developments of North and South America. In their analysis of the fate of the town of Nogales, preciously situated on the border of Mexico and the United States, Daron Acemoglu and James Robinson claim that only the differential institutional make-up of the two countries can explain why the American half of Nogales is doing so much better, economically and otherwise, than its Mexican counterpart. Acemoglu and Robinson make, however, an additional claim. They state, in so many words, that the way in which the two societies 'formed during the early colonial period' is to blame for this state of affairs.[7] James Mahoney similarly blames the 'power configurations that were originally put in place during colonialism' for the different fates of the formerly Spanish and British regions of the Americas.[8]

This ostensibly plausible interpretation, however, ignores rather different types of argument about what went wrong during the colonial period. Some historians blame the given circumstances facing the colonisers in the two regions. According to Stanley Engerman and Kenneth Sokoloff, natural endowments and the size of Native populations created stark contrasts between North and South America. The latter was rich in mineral resources, precious metals in particular, and had soils suitable for plantation economies. The initially successful exploitation of these resources, crucially with the help of forced labour, became a handicap when modern economic growth demanded different types of economic organisation. The North American colonies, in contrast, relied on small-farm agriculture and craft industry. They, moreover, had a more or less homogeneous population of European immigrants which made it easier to introduce democratic institutions, while Central and South American institutions had to come to terms with ethnically mixed populations.[9]

Douglass North, William Summerhill and Barry Weingast, on the other hand, see poor institutional set-ups as the outcome of a combination of factors: the differences between metropoles – England compared favourably with Spain – as well as distinctly different relationships between the metropolis and its colonies. While the British maintained liberal policies towards their colonial populations in the New World, the Spanish Crown sought to extract large revenues to bolster its public debt. The silver fleets, sailing annually from the Caribbean to Seville, and the absence of a British equivalent, symbolised this difference – or so they claim.[10] A variation of this type of argument sees the religious contrast as significant: in the long run Protestants were more effective capitalists and colonisers than Catholics.[11]

This chapter contributes to the debate by providing a new perspective. Instead of concentrating on states and their 'national' institutions, I am concerned with local institutions, i.e. looking upwards from the bottom of society, rather than down from the top. The evidence on citizenship presented in this chapter has to take on board the factors suggested by the historians discussed earlier, i.e. we have to pay attention to the citizenship arrangements as they were introduced from Europe and the level of autonomy open to the coloniser communities. And perhaps most importantly, we have to establish how ethnicity impacted on citizenship, in both its formal and practical aspects. Finally, we will have to return to the vexed issue of timing: was the institutional difference between the British and Spanish colonies a given from the time of their establishment, or did it perhaps only emerge during the revolutionary era, i.e. in the decades around 1800, when the European mother countries were in turmoil and the New World colonies acquired independence?

New Circumstances, Old Institutions

Spanish and English colonisers brought their own ideas and experiences of citizenship with them across the Atlantic. These were then introduced into two vastly different environments.[12] Whereas Central and South America had traditions of urban life and centralised states, the Indians of North America were either nomads or at most lived in small rural communities. Their tribes were much less organised than the Mexican (Aztec) and Inca empires had been. And whereas, for this and other reasons, the Spaniards could take over substantial parts of the societies they encountered upon arrival, the English rejected the natives' style of life and their institutions as basically uncivilised and therefore useless.

From the point of view of urban life, English settlers had to start from scratch, while Spanish settlers could take over urban communities, even if they radically reshaped them.[13] Tenochtitlan, the Mexican stronghold (now Mexico City), stunned Cortes and his men when they first saw it in November 1519; with its estimated 150,000–200,000 inhabitants it was significantly larger than any Spanish city at the time.[14] It has been argued that the inhabitants of Tenochtitlan enjoyed something resembling citizenship status. What's more, Mexican urban citizenship arrangements were accessible to both men and women.[15] The presence of such urban communities and institutions can only have reinforced the Spaniards' predilection for creating urban communities in newly conquered territories, because this is exactly how Spain itself had been created in the face of Muslim opposition in the Iberian Peninsula.[16] The Spanish colonisers continued to display a strong preference for urban concentration, even after European diseases had wiped out the great majority of the indigenous population. Around 1600 a systematic attempt was made to concentrate inhabitants of numerous hamlets in New Spain into larger settlements.[17]

The combined effect of Indian traditions and colonial policies was still clearly evident by the middle of the eighteenth century, when an estimated 13 per cent of the population in Spanish America lived in towns of 20,000 and more, whilst in the British colonies of North America a mere 8 per cent lived in communities of more than 2,500 inhabitants. The same startling contrast emerges from figures relating to individual towns. In 1742 the largest urban community in British America was Boston, with 16,000 inhabitants. Only Philadelphia and New York City also had populations of more than 10,000. At the same time the populations of no fewer than nine towns in the Spanish viceroyalties of the New World exceeded the 10,000 threshold, six of them exceeded 25,000, whilst the two largest, Lima and Mexico City, reached 52,000 and 112,000, respectively.[18] Clearly, the urban impact in the two regions was very different. By European standards, Spanish America was an urbanised region, with a level of urbanisation above that of the Scandinavian countries and those of East Central Europe.[19]

These different levels of urbanisation had a distinct impact on the formal status of citizens in North and South America. In both regions the status of urban citizen as such was a creation of the colonial administration, imported from the metropolis. In South America, as in Spain itself, there was very little difference between urban and rural communities from a legal and political point of view; even villagers held citizenship. By contrast, in North America the subjection of the colony to the authority of the metropolis reduced to a minimum the number of urban communities with the full range of formal citizenship and thus made urban citizenship a public good that was in short supply.

In New York City citizenship as a formal status had been introduced when the town was still called New Amsterdam. The citizens' status was continued after the English took over in 1664. In 1675 New York was incorporated under English law, and English rules of citizenship were introduced.[20] Between 1657 and 1661, 260 men had acquired citizen status, but in 1675 all free adult males were automatically granted citizen status. Between 1695 and 1735, another 1,700 men were made citizens.[21] New York's citizenship regulations were modelled on those of London: citizenship could be acquired by local birth, apprenticeship, redemption, i.e. purchase, and as a gift from the mayor or an alderman.[22] Only those who were formal citizens were allowed to exercise a trade or open a shop. Citizens were also privileged to vote in local elections. In 1811 the citizen's oath was still sworn by applicants, and in 1815 new rules were introduced regulating citizen status. However, by that time new names were no longer being registered, suggesting that it was rapidly becoming redundant.[23]

Access through apprenticeship required free-born birth. This meant that no bondmen's sons could become apprentices and hence citizens, but it very obviously also excluded slaves.[24] Still, in 1741 an estimated one in five inhabitants of New York City was of African descent. In 1791 the city had more than 3,000 African-American inhabitants, most of them slaves, and even those who were no longer slaves were still barred from citizen status.[25]

In South America, the establishment of communities implied the establishment of formal citizenship. Who was a *vecino* (citizen) was initially registered meticulously by the Spanish colonial authorities.[26] Access was easy, but regulated. Individuals who petitioned for *vecino* status normally argued that they were willing to become and remain members of the local community, which they would demonstrate by acquiring real estate. *Vecino* status was open to people of Spanish, Indian and mestizo descent. In the course of the seventeenth century, petitions for *vecino* status petered out. Instead of a legal category, the term *vecino* came to mean social status, equivalent to 'Spanish-origin'. In places of mixed racial composition, the *vecinos* as a result had become an exclusive social group by the beginning of the eighteenth century. In places with an exclusively non-Spanish population, the formal status of citizen would remain accessible to the Indian, mestizo and black inhabitants. Formal citizenship in Latin America was thus subject to a double transformation: it became increasingly racially segregated and at the same time it became less important for everyday purposes.

Formal citizenship was a feature of all colonial societies in the New World. It was probably more generally accessible in the Spanish-ruled territories, and might include inhabitants who were not of Spanish descent. In that sense it was more inclusive than the all-white citizenship regime of North America. At the same time, and perhaps even for this very same reason, formal citizenship made less of an impact in the Spanish colonies than in the British. These observations should be understood against the backdrop of the quite different balance between white and non-white populations in North America, where four in five were of European extraction in 1825, and in South America, where it was the exact opposite and whites formed a relatively small minority.[27]

Whereas the formation of formal citizenship was shaped by the interaction between European traditions and local circumstances, the formation of urban government was constrained by the relationship between colony and metropolis. The English government saw its American colonies as a source of raw materials and a market for industrial products, while the Spanish government was more interested in the aggrandisement of its empire and prepared, if necessary, to forego revenues in order to achieve that. The Spanish Crown was also willing to grant a significant degree of autonomy to local units of government.[28] Urban jurisdictions were large, encompassing a substantial hinterland.[29] Quito, for example, covered an area of 200 by 80 miles. Towns always had a *foro*, or charter, outlining their privileges. Their governments were presided over by two *alcaldes*, who combined the functions of sheriff and burgomaster. They were assisted by at least twelve *regidores* (aldermen) and a *cabildo* (town council). The *alcaldes* were elected by the *regidores* from amongst the *vecinos* (citizens). The members of the councils were elected in general assemblies of the citizens, sometimes even by secret ballot.[30] This system might exclude significant proportions of the population. In towns with racially mixed populations, Indians, blacks and mestizos usually did not have the vote. In the newly created towns with exclusively Native populations, all the political positions would be occupied by Indians, and their town councils functioned as a 'corporate body'. So-called free coloured towns, located in frontier areas, provided their Afro-American inhabitants with similar political opportunities.[31]

Culhuacán, in the Valley of Mexico, had been inhabited for approximately 3,000 years before the Spaniards arrived. In the second half of the sixteenth century it had some 3,600 Native inhabitants, and the presence of the Spanish colonial authorities was mostly limited to the appointment of the *corregidor* (governor). Like other towns in the area, Culhuacán had long been used to a significant degree of autonomy, which was largely continued under Spanish rule, even though its political structures were reformed to match the Spanish model. The town council was responsible for public order, taxation and, more generally, the protection of local interests. The *alcaldo* and *regidores* together 'regulated local life'. An important instrument in that regulation were the Culhuacán town wards. Every inhabitant was a member of a ward. Ward elders registered real estate transfers and handed out poor relief. They also collected some of the taxes. Remarkably, women could be elected as ward elders, perhaps another continuation of precolonial traditions.[32] In Cuernavaca, a much smaller Indian town located south of Mexico City, many older elements of governance were preserved, but the Spaniards did require the introduction of elections for the recruitment of local officials. Disputed elections were a common feature of many urban communities in colonial Mexico in the seventeenth and eighteenth centuries.[33]

The Valley of Mexico had a tradition of urban republicanism that long predated the Spanish presence, but was continued into the colonial era. In 1731, the inhabitants of Chihuahua, located 1,000 miles to the north-west of Mexico City, referred to their town as a 'republic' in a petition demanding the removal of their *corregidor*. The population was indeed divided into 'republicans' and 'plebe', i.e. citizens and non-citizens. The citizens made up the majority of militiamen, and their opinions were often sought by the local authorities through *cabildos abiertos* and *juntas*. The latter were unofficial guilds, of merchants and vintners for example. The collective understanding of the republican character of their community was almost entirely secular.[34]

The *cabildo abierto*, or open council, was a feature of urban governance throughout Spanish America. It was not approved by the Crown, but nor was it expressly forbidden. From the viceroyalty of Peru examples have been recorded in Quito, Santiago de Chile and Buenos Aires. In Quito at least six were held between 1534 and 1600, not exactly frequently but still enough to suggest that it was seen as a possible instrument to help create legitimacy. That this was indeed the purpose is suggested by the fact that they always dealt with principled issues, for example taxation, or property rights. The fifteen held in seventeenth-century Buenos Aires almost all dealt with financial issues, such as requests from the Crown for extra contributions.[35]

As early as 1553 the first offices in Spanish America were put up for sale. The number of venal offices was expanded in 1591, and in 1606 a huge list of such posts was officially published. These '*officios vendibles y renuciables*' thus became the property of those who could fork out the requisite amounts of money. As a result, the metropolis started to lose control over such offices. Even though the *alcalde* office was not for sale, the number of Latin American, as opposed to Spanish-born, incumbents increased rapidly. In the second half of the sixteenth century thirteen out of seventy *alcaldes* appointed in Peru had been born locally; in the seventeenth century this had increased to 71 per cent, and in the eighteenth to four out of five.[36] Local authorities therefore became even more independent from the Crown.

In North America, the European tradition of urban autonomy was probably strongest in New York City. This was the result of two circumstances: its early development, and its Dutch ancestry. While most English settlements in North America were still villages, New Amsterdam already had 5,000 European inhabitants by the mid-seventeenth century. Moreover, the Dutch authorities had given New Amsterdam urban privileges in 1657, and when the English took over in 1664 they continued that status. Under English law this was somewhat anomalous but, nevertheless, with the Dutch urban charter came formal rights of citizenship for those who might claim access to the local privileges. Access had also been granted to all English inhabitants on the occasion of the acquisition of New Amsterdam.

Urban autonomy, and, by implication, 'freedom', were at the same time precarious, because the New York colony was a private possession of the king's younger brother James, the Duke of York. In his place, a governor was put in charge of the colony. On his arrival in the New World in 1683, the new governor, Thomas Dongan, created an Assembly to assist him in governing New York. This concession was his response to various protests against the way in which James had exercised his authority, including the tax regime imposed on the local population in his name. The Assembly immediately asked for a proper charter of incorporation – a request which may have been inspired by the numerous charters of incorporation issued in England itself during the 1680s.[37] Come October the Assembly had drafted a 'Charter of Libertyes and Priviledges', which Dongan signed and sent to London for confirmation by the Crown.[38] By the time the Duke of York was ready to return the document with his signature, he had, however, succeeded his brother as king of England and had second thoughts about the wisdom of such a privilege in the context of national colonial policies. As a result, the Charter was never properly registered.[39]

In New York the Charter nonetheless gained force of law, and formed the constitutional basis for the city's local government, which was settled in the local Common Council.[40] It did not, however, completely satisfy the ambitions of the local freemen, as became clear during the Glorious Revolution. The introduction of the Charter had been followed by the imposition, by the governor, of 'patents', making the smaller settlements subject to 'trustees' representing the government. This led to 'much unhappiness', reinforced by the imposition of yet more taxes.[41] When in April 1689 news of the dramatic events in England reached the shores of North America, this immediately led to disturbances in Boston, where colonial offices and officers were attacked by angry inhabitants. Within weeks the unrest migrated to New York, where the militia had been mobilised to deal with threatening Indian activities. On 22 May, the New York City militia demanded improvements to the town's defences. Words between the commander of the fortress and some militia officers then led to a mobilisation of the militia without prior authorisation, and within days the city was taken over by the militias, led by one of their officers, Jacob Leisler, a merchant of German extraction. He took command of the city for the best of the next two years – and paid for it with his life after the arrival of English officials sent over by the new monarchs.[42] Still, Leisler's Rebellion did help to get another Charter accepted in 1691 which gave more rights to the citizens.

During the early eighteenth century Boston and Philadelphia grew vigorously and by mid-century had achieved population numbers well above 10,000. The governance of the towns of New England was remarkably 'bottom-up': town meetings allowed all adult males to participate in discussions, although only freemen, i.e. formal citizens, had the vote.[43] Bostonians held 'town meetings' from 1634 onwards; in 1635 eight such meetings took place, in 1698 the male inhabitants met six times.[44] The Boston town meetings elected six 'selectmen' as the local governing body. In 1760, Boston's conservative elite attempted to eliminate the 'town meeting', but this had the opposite effect of strengthening the popular party.[45]

In Philadelphia, the owner of the proprietary territory of Pennsylvania, William Penn, directly appointed the local officeholders. However, here too the artisan middle class, under the inspired leadership of Benjamin Franklin, began to organise, forming crafts and militia organisations around the middle of the eighteenth century, organisations that would develop into the mainstay of the local revolutionary forces during the 1770s.[46] In Charleston, passing the 10,000 mark around the middle of the eighteenth century, attempts by locals to have the local government incorporated were vigorously opposed by the governor of South Carolina. As soon as British occupying forces left in 1783, the incorporation was swiftly enacted.[47]

Metropolitan systems of local governance thus provided models for those in the colonies. At the same time, the imperatives of distance, as well as the specific social features of colonial rule, forced the colonies to diverge from the metropolitan model. In North America, outside New York City, the traditions of corporatism were weak, partly due to an absence of any native tradition of urbanism, and partly due to the dominance of private interests in colonial governance. Even New York City was part of the 'private' colony of the Duke of York. However, the corporate institutions created by the Dutch provided a platform for civic politics that culminated in Leisler's Rebellion. In Philadelphia they had to be invented from scratch.[48] In Spanish America, Castilian forms of rule were introduced, giving urban citizens a substantial role in local government. At the same time, these Spanish institutions were capable of incorporating indigenous traditions of urban rule. Moreover, Indian and Afro-American communities were allowed self-government on terms more or less identical to those of the white settlers. Such institutional liberties were not available to the non-whites of North America. Formal citizenship and citizens' participation were both more institutionalised in the Spanish territories.

Civic Organisations in the New World

Our discussion of urban governance and formal citizenship has already pointed up significant differences between the English and Spanish territories in the New World. To what extent were these patterns confirmed, or mitigated, by civic organisations that allowed wider groups, with or without formal citizenship, to participate in the public life of their communities?

Guilds

Guilds in Latin America, modelled on European examples, were established from early on. In Mexico City guilds were set up during the 1540s and 1550s. In Lima the carpenters and bricklayers elected their first overseers and set up an exam system and the council of Mexico City forced the local hat-makers to create a guild after complaints had been filed about shoddy work. The silk weavers, chain-makers, cord-makers, gilders, painters and shoemakers had preceded them – all during the sixteenth century.[49] These guilds were primarily occupational organisations, but also provided welfare, worshipped their patron saint and initiated the next generation into the 'mystery' of the craft.

Apprentices included natives and mestizos, as well as Spanish descendants. This was not self-evident, because like other social organisations, Latin American guilds had to take up a position vis-à-vis the issue of race. Africans were more or less universally excluded, mestizos as well, at least initially, but Indians had been made welcome from early on. In fact, the purpose of guild organisations was also to regulate competition from native artisans. In due course, the other excluded groups managed to gain access too. The reason was simple: in the face of continuous demand for labour, it proved very difficult to exclude them. In 1788 even female silk-winders in Mexico managed to get their own guild.[50]

As a result, Spanish America had numerous craft guilds and a substantial membership, especially in the larger towns. In 1788 the guilds of Mexico City are reckoned to have had a total of 18,642 members.[51] That might be as much as 15 per cent of the population, or more than half of all adult males, on a par with European standards. Smaller places like Bogotá or Buenos Aires had no guilds, or a mere handful. However, in 1780 all industries in Buenos Aires were ordered to set up a guild.[52] This goes to show that the authorities were not opposed to guild organisations, and indeed welcomed them, as a means of regulating urban industries as well as the urban middle classes. The guilds of Spanish America thus helped broad sections of the population to obtain economic rights, irrespective of the colour of their skin.[53]

As in Spain, guilds in Spanish America had no formal political rights. It could be that economic growth in the eighteenth century undermined the impact of guilds on the economy, but this is difficult to prove. Although the authorities in Madrid were keen to continue the guild system, their concerns may well have been only indirectly related to the core business of the guilds. For example, some guilds also formed the basis of urban militia units that the authorities could ill afford to lose, but would if they allowed the guild system to unravel.[54]

In North America, on the other hand, the colonial authorities were reluctant to create special interest organisations for industrial producers.[55] These were seen as potential competition for rural interests, but more importantly as a possible source of protectionism against imports from the metropolis, whose interests were considered paramount.[56] Guilds, insofar as they existed at all, were seldom chartered by the authorities and hence not in a position to enforce regulations.[57] Local authorities imposed rules on apprenticeship. In England, as we have seen, the 1563 Statute of Artificers prescribed the unusually long period of seven years for a proper apprenticeship. Due to the urgent demand for labour, this rule had been relaxed in the colonies, where only four years were required before a craftsman qualified for master status. It was soon discovered, however, that this had a negative impact on product quality.[58] In Boston concerns were raised in 1660, and in New York City it was decided in 1711, to return to the seven years of the statute book, because after four years apprentices 'were seldom masters of their trades'. Apprentices who completed their seven-year term would automatically acquire the freedom of the city, as was standard practice in England.[59] Formal status as a citizen was also a requirement for artisans and shopkeepers in Philadelphia to work independently, even though this rule does not seem to have been very strictly enforced.[60] However, the generally negative attitude towards guilds deprived North American citizens of the possibility of organising and representing their economic interests.

It is not surprising, therefore, that craftsmen themselves tried to launch a variety of private organisations that would help them promote those interests. In the absence of official recognition, many of these organisations found it difficult to sustain themselves over the years, but their recurrence testifies to a genuine demand. In Philadelphia a Carpenters' Company was created in 1724. The Cordwainers' Fire Company, set up in the same town in 1760, was a thinly veiled attempt to create an occupational organisation, whilst the Taylors' Company of 1771 had the same objective. The silversmiths of Philadelphia had been clamouring for quality regulation in the 1760s.[61] The Cordwainers' Fire Company required an apprenticeship from aspiring members, and other craft organisations too were concerned with quality control, fearing the competition from British manufacturers. The problem was that, in the absence of a legal framework, none of the organisations could really enforce its rules and regulations.[62]

Artisan politics became more urgent in British America as the eighteenth century progressed. Calls for greater economic independence from the metropolis and the growth of urban industries weakened the colonial opposition to artisan organisations.[63] Forms of 'artisan republicanism' were already gaining credibility before the Revolution broke out.[64] In New York City the Sons of Liberty, or Liberty Boys, dominated by merchants, was challenged from 1774 by a General Committee of Mechanics that was more democratic than the Liberty Boys and also demanded more accountability from the authorities. The members of the Committee were prominent campaigners for independence, and when it arrived they demanded a referendum on the draft constitution. In 1785 they reformed themselves into a General Society of Mechanics and Tradesmen which, among other things, provided credit to its members.[65]

For various reasons, craft guilds in the colonies had more restricted roles than those available to European guilds. In both North and South America the most important cause of this restriction was precisely the colonial relationship. In North America, the colonial authorities were unwilling to grant occupational organisations corporate status to prevent them competing with metropolitan producers. In Central and South America guilds as such were permitted, but they remained instruments of economic control, rather than of artisans' self-organisation. Guilds were also undermined by the peculiarities of the labour market in the colonies. Slavery and race created subdivisions that were absent in Europe, and the very strong demand for labour made it even more difficult to control labour markets than it had been in Europe.

For all of these reasons, guilds in the American colonies failed to become more than poor replicas of their European counterparts.

Civic Welfare

In 1699 the governor of New York, Richard Coote, Earl of Bellomont, turned down an order from London to set up a workhouse, stating that 'there is no such thing as a beggar in this town or country'.[66] Although this was not true, it is easy to see how he might have come to this assumption. The Americas were land-abundant and, after the decimation of the native populations, they were also labour-scarce societies. Given those conditions, anyone capable of working should be able to find some sort of livelihood without recourse to welfare benefits. Moreover, the inhabitants of European origin had come over voluntarily, and should presumably have included the risk of poverty in the cost-benefit analysis of their migration. New England towns had a 'warning out' system that allowed them to remove inhabitants who had been reduced to poverty.[67] As it was, Coote, like so many contemporaries, was overlooking some basic facts about welfare. In Europe itself, as was discussed in Chapter 4, the majority of individuals on poor relief were incapable of working, either because they were too old or disabled, or as single parents had to take care of their offspring, or simply because, due to adverse weather or other circumstances, jobs were temporarily unavailable. These circumstances applied in the New World as much as in the Old.[68]

Coote's objections were ignored, and the very next year a property was purchased by the municipal authorities for a workhouse that opened its doors in 1701. The creation of the workhouse may have been simply the result of the gradual introduction of English institutions into the formerly Dutch colony. In these years, enthusiasm for the workhouse reached an apogee in the British Isles, where many hoped that, by forcing them to work, the poor would pay for their own maintenance.[69] In New York it never reached that position, perhaps because of the continuing role of the original arrangements as they had been introduced by the Dutch settlers, whereby the Church – in this case the Dutch Reformed Church – took care of all the poor, both Calvinists and others.[70] Poor relief was therefore technically provided by the Church but in practice was a public service available to every inhabitant, irrespective of faith.

Poor relief in New York City remained, however, primarily funded through civic charity. Much of it was supplied by the wards, where voluntary donations were collected to fund the activities of the overseers of the poor.[71] This system of voluntary contributions was another feature borrowed from the Dutch.[72] An additional source of private charity was the common-origin organisations, like the French Benevolent Society that provided support for French immigrants who found themselves impoverished.[73] The Dutch Reformed Church likewise continued to support Dutch immigrant families and their descendants.[74] As in Europe, the supply of public welfare had shifted away from the Churches to the municipal authorities. In eighteenth-century Philadelphia, the overseers of the poor were in charge of distributing alms to pauper families, and collecting the poor rate that financed their work. In Philadelphia too a workhouse was set up in the 1760s, but was soon beset by the usual problems: it was much more expensive to assume the entire responsibility for pauper families than to supplement their income but allow them to stay in their own homes.[75]

The same over-optimistic expectations were evident in eighteenth-century Latin America. In 1774 Viceroy Bucarelli ordered the opening of a workhouse in Mexico City, to stem the tide of beggars and other vagrants. This workhouse was part of a much wider programme of reform and modernisation undertaken by the Bourbon monarchy, both in the colonies and in Spain itself. The Mexico City poorhouse was financed by the Catholic Church, by private donations and by the state, and it held 650 inmates in 1780.[76] In Quito, a city of 25,000 in the late eighteenth century, a similar workhouse was launched in 1785. It became home to a mixed population of Spanish descendants and Indians, reflecting the composition of the municipal population as a whole.[77] The citizens of both Mexico City and Quito were encouraged to sponsor the funding of the workhouse; in Mexico City they contributed around 30 per cent of the original outlay.[78]

The New World may have been 'the land of the free and the home of the brave' for many migrants, but for some of them at least its realities turned out to be less wonderful. Indeed, some causes of poverty have very little to do with circumstances and a great deal to do with the human condition. Colonial communities therefore had to address the problem of pauperism from the very start. In both the English and Spanish Americas, role models and legislation borrowed from the metropolis made a significant impact on the design of institutional frameworks. Both were also forced to redesign and reinforce their welfare arrangements in the late seventeenth and eighteenth centuries, as their colonies became more populous and as a result more complex societies. As in Europe, public authorities and religious organisations were and remained key to the provision of charity, but they needed citizens to help fund and administer welfare.

Civic Militias

The first European settlers arrived in the New World under the umbrella of private initiative, even if states were lurking in the background.[79] As colonialism took shape, states began to station troops in the newly conquered territories. However, given the size of these territories and the limited resources, the state could only provide minimal protection so that the colonists also needed to fend for themselves. As a result, military citizenship became especially prominent in the Americas, as is still visible in the famous – or infamous, depending on one's evaluation of private gun ownership – Second Amendment of the American Constitution.

In Spanish America the army acted as the default body for defence purposes. Civic militias were perceived as supplementary troops. The professionals made no attempt to hide their disdain for the amateurism of the militiamen. Their critical opinions were based on close observation, as professionals were much involved in the daily operations of the militias. Given the space they were supposed to secure, the number of professional soldiers stationed in the colonies was relatively minute. In 1760 Veracruz had a garrison of 1,000, Mexico City 1,700, but the rest of the viceroyalty of New Spain was served by a mere 1,700 armed men.[80] As a result, militias were a necessary evil. The first militias were set up by a decree of 7 October 1540. As was also standard practice in many European towns, militiamen were required to bring their own arms. Militias were created in all Spanish American towns, but their greatest significance was in border areas and along the coast. Officers were appointed by the town's government, sometimes after an election by the men. Professional officers acted as advisors, also to optimise coordination between regular and amateur forces.[81]

Necessity also gave rise to a remarkable feature of the Spanish American militia system: racially mixed companies, and even 'free-coloured' companies. These latter were originally non-white companies, which emerged as early as the mid-sixteenth century, but would eventually become dominated by former African slaves. In the first half of the eighteenth century the viceroyalty of New Galicia had thirty-seven companies of Spanish, i.e. white, men, twenty-three that were composed of 'pardos, mulatos, negros and coyotes', and another sixteen that were 'racially mixed, indio and mestizo' units. In total almost 4,000 men were bearing arms in these militia units. In Mexico City the men in the free-coloured units were overwhelmingly artisans: in other words, the poor were excluded.[82] This mirrors the social composition of similar organisations in Europe and was no doubt inspired by the same considerations: the authorities liked the idea of cheap armed forces, but were anxious about the revolutionary potential of arming their citizens. The frequent involvement of militias in political upheavals, not to mention their prominent role in the American Revolution, provided confirmation in plenty for such anxieties.[83] From the same point of view, however, arming the non-white inhabitants in the Spanish colonies amounted to the granting of a major element of citizenship status to these sections of the population.

The British colonies went through a very different military and social experience, which the militias, moreover, helped shape to a much greater extent than in their southerly equivalents. The earliest English colonists were not so keen to copy the English militia system that they had left behind in the British Isles. Instead, they were protected by a motley crew of veterans from the Eighty Years' War in the Low Countries. These men, however, were less than ideal members of the religious communities that the Puritans hoped to create, and they were also expensive to maintain. Against their original intentions, the colonists were compelled to set up the trained bands that they had hoped to avoid in the New World. The larger towns of Massachusetts all set up such trained bands in the 1630s, voluntary units of men over the age of sixteen, open to freemen and non-freemen alike and with the ranks allowed to elect their own officers. The Charlestown militiamen opined that these free elections 'hath rendered us the most happy people that wee know of in the world'.[84]

One remarkable aspect of these early trained bands was that they recruited indiscriminately. Only the officers were supposed to be freemen. Otherwise, all classes and races were accepted. In 1652 it was ordained in Massachusetts, in so many words, that 'all Scotsmen, Negers, & Indians inhabiting with or servants to the English shalbe listed & are hereby enjoyned to attend traynings'. Note, however, that these individuals were all subject to the authority of an Englishman. In 1668, as part of a wider rollback of popular participation in civic affairs, elections were abandoned.[85] In Virginia, on the other hand, blacks and slightly later also indentured servants, were already excluded from militia service quite early. In South Carolina the turning point came in 1739, when a large slave revolt was put down only with considerable effort. From then on, its militias became exclusively white organisations. By the middle of the eighteenth century this applied everywhere in the British colonies: Indians, free blacks, mulattos, white servants and apprentices, as well as men without a fixed abode, were all excluded from the militias.[86] Exclusion was clearly motivated by considerations of class and race.

The system had undergone another subtle but significant change. The original militias were confined to police and representational duties, 'hallmarks of respectability' and a public demonstration of 'full citizenship in the community'. When it came to the real fighting, against Indians, or French and Spanish colonial competitors, another type of militia unit was employed. These consisted of lower-class volunteers, who expected to be paid for their efforts.[87] The latter units resembled the British trained bands, largely consisting of replacements paid by the people for whom they substituted.

The original militia, however, consisting of citizens, maintained the powerful dream of the citizen army. We have seen how Benjamin Franklin managed to make this the centrepiece of his political activities. Philadelphia's Committee of Privates, which he helped to launch, was not alone in its opposition to standing armies. Two factors reinforced the suspicion of professional soldiers among the British colonists. The first was the debate, probably more lively in the British Isles than anywhere else in Europe, about the dangers of a standing army in the seventeenth century. Because England had been relatively late in absorbing the innovations of the Military Revolution, the creation of a professional military force coincided with the attempts of the Stuart monarchy to exercise tighter control over its citizens. There were thus good grounds for the suspicion that this standing army would serve primarily a domestic purpose, rather than improve England's capacity to defend itself against foreign foes. This debate made a deep impression on the American colonists.[88] And in the course of the eighteenth century they too had increasingly good reasons for seeing the army as a force of domestic oppression rather than defence. More troops were stationed in the colonies to help their expansion into French and Spanish territories. However, as tensions rose between the colony and the metropolis, military reinforcements became less concerned with those foreign powers, and directed more at policing the interior of the British colonies.

During the initial stages of the American Revolution and its war of independence, urban and rural militiamen were heavily involved in the fighting. They soon lost their taste for the soldier's life, and increasingly handed over to white and black working-class volunteers who were paid for their contribution. Rhetorically, however, the militiamen stayed on the battlefield.[89] They would be rewarded in the Second Amendment to the Constitution, established as part of the Bill of Rights in 1791, which read: 'A well regulated Militia, being necessary to the security of a free State, the right of the people to keep and bear Arms, shall not be infringed'.[90] Despite heated debates about slavery and its (un)acceptability in a 'free state', the right to bear arms was, and for the foreseeable future remained, the exclusive prerogative of white Americans. Because Indian tribes had sided with the French against the British, that added another reason to exclude them.[91] The revolutionaries could not afford to split their own ranks over the abolition of slavery, so Afro-Americans were likewise excluded from carrying arms outside the context of military service. It would take another seven decades, and then four years of bloody civil war, not only to bring slavery to an end, but also to give African Americans full citizenship in the Fourteenth Amendment of 1868. Native Americans would have to wait until 1924 to receive full citizenship rights in their own country.

Conclusion

This chapter cannot pretend to cover all aspects of the institutional history of the New World. I have deliberately focused on one institution, and ignored the significant role of the Church as well as the rural communities that housed the majority of the population and where slavery was much more in evidence. What the foregoing pages have attempted to do is establish a precise comparison in one institution: urban citizenship. I have analysed citizenship with three questions in mind: how did the colonial situation transform citizenship arrangements imported from the metropolis, how did issues of ethnicity impact on citizenship and was it true that this particular institution was somehow worse designed and implemented in the Spanish colonies than in the British? It is now time to draw up the balance sheet. Even if we can see numerous local differences between the citizenship arrangements in Spanish and British colonies, some consistent patterns emerge that can help us answer our three questions.

As to the first, we have seen how the models of urban citizenship in the metropolis exerted a powerful influence on the sort of citizenship arrangements implemented in the colonies. In addition, we find a consistent contrast between the attitudes of Spanish and British governments towards their colonies: whereas the Spanish authorities supported the establishment of local citizenship in their colonies, the English, later British authorities were more reluctant to do so in theirs. Particularly in the eighteenth century, urban citizenship was fiercely contested in places like New York and Philadelphia. We find little of this in Latin America – possibly because it has not been investigated by historians, but more likely because there was no need for it. The kinds of civic institution that Benjamin Franklin and his contemporaries were fighting for were already available in the South.

As to the second question, another significant pattern emerges from the comparison: ethnicity was handled very differently in North and South America.[92] In both parts of the New World, settlers of European origin or descent held many privileges over the Native population or over former slaves of African origin, not to mention those who were still enslaved and therefore denied citizenship altogether. In North America there were some possibilities for free blacks to participate in citizenship practices during the seventeenth century, but those openings disappeared completely during the eighteenth. By the start of the American Revolution, citizenship was a whites-only institution in the United States. The implications of this development remain visible in the twenty-first century.[93] In contrast, citizenship in Spanish America was open from its sixteenth-century beginnings, and remained open down to the end of the Old Regime, to various ethnic communities. This was partly due to Native traditions that predated the colonial era, but it was also the result of the sort of citizenship that the Spaniards had developed in their own country during the Reconquista.[94]

Putting these two conclusions together leads us to a more or less straightforward answer to our final question. This comparative investigation of citizenship practices in Spanish and British America does not confirm the idea of 'bad' institutions in South America and 'good' ones in North America. On the contrary, if we were to set them side by side on the eve of the American Revolution, Spanish urban citizenship would seem to be the better established, wider-ranging and more inclusive of the two. This result supports revisionist histories of Spain's colonial policies which emphasise the problems faced by European governments to control developments in the Americas.[95] It would also seem to corroborate the work of those economic historians who argue that the distinct trajectories of North and South America originated in the decades around 1800 when the colonies achieved independence.[96] An institutional gap was opened by the revolutionary episodes. The independence of the United States had to be established against the powerful forces of the British Empire, which required the mobilisation of significant sections of the population, and resulted in the inclusion of civic militias in the American constitution. The Latin American revolutionaries, on the other hand, were familiar with the outcome of the French Revolution. They were facing a weakened Spanish Empire. Their revolutions were mostly internal struggles for power, settled to the disadvantage of citizens. The institutional difference between North and South America thus seems to have been less the result of long-term trends and structures, but rather of the intervening process of decolonisation in the two regions, and the institutions that emerged out of the revolutionary episodes around 1800.[97]

CONCLUSIONS
Citizenship before and beyond the French Revolution

Citizenship regulates the relation between the governors and the governed. From the point of view of the governors, its purpose is to allow them to govern. From the point of view of the governed, its purpose is to be governed well. In the long run, to be governed well is in the interest of both the governed and the governors. What it means to be governed well was and is, of course, a contentious issue. Citizenship thus defined is a feature of any polity, but it comes in different shapes. Citizenship therefore has a history, and this history matters for the way we experience citizenship today and how we conceive of its future.

Before the French Revolution

This book has charted the development of this relation between governors and governed in urban environments over almost a millennium before the modern period, i.e. before national citizenship was invented and formalised in the aftermath of the French Revolution. It has been shown how, in an era of political anarchy and economic growth, European towns began to experiment with new forms of governance from circa 1000 CE onwards. From this bottom-up movement emerged communes with a formal membership which became known as citizenship, but also a set of organisations and practices that included wider groups of urban society than merely those who held formal citizenship.

These practices related first of all to the governance of the urban community as such. Even though urban governors were usually recruited from the upper strata of local society, the wider community often participated in their selection, and even where this did not happen, other channels allowed ordinary citizens to influence political decision-making that affected them. These channels ranged from the presence of a representative council, to consultations of citizens, to petitions and to citizen participation in a broad range of administrative processes. In the absence of any significant professional police force and knowing that their citizens were armed, even the threat of rebellion could have an impact. Rebellions were frequent and when they were not around the corner, local elites were still aware of the potential. Even though many town councils were subject to oligarchic tendencies, local authorities could not ignore the opinions of their citizens.

This was also because European urban communities encompassed numerous civic organisations. An average town in the Middle Ages or early modern period had dozens of craft and merchant guilds, possibly even more religious confraternities that often doubled as social welfare institutions and, through their civic militias, empowered citizens almost literally. Many of these organisations followed more or less democratic procedures, in the sense that there were general meetings where important issues were discussed, and the board of the organisation would be elected, or at least confirmed, by the membership. Because they raised their own funds, these organisations were financially independent from the local authorities, even if these checked the accounts and provided other forms of oversight.

Citizenship arrangements before 1789 varied from country to country, and in their details also from town to town. Although there was no obvious geographical or temporal pattern to this variation – in terms of open versus restricted access, or limited versus extensive rights – citizenship was much more widespread than is often assumed, even as a formal institution. Cities where formal citizen status was limited to an elite, like Berne and Venice, were exceptional. It was quite usual to find at least a third, but often half, and sometimes even two-thirds of all (urban) households headed by a citizen. Local citizenship was predominantly a male institution. Women had difficulty obtaining formal citizen status, and when they did, found their rights of citizenship seriously curtailed. By no means did all households, let alone all individuals, have formal citizen status. Working-class households, for instance, were less likely to have formal citizen status than households in the middle and upper strata of society. Nonetheless, a significant number of households did and formal citizenship reached deep into the social hierarchy. Citizenship practices included still wider strata of society.

In some aspects the organisational landscape of European towns changed during the roughly 800 years covered by this book. Most civic organisations, and indeed the town itself as a corporate institution, did not exist in 1000 CE, but by 1300 the whole gamut of organisations was there. After that point in time, names would change, and numbers might go up or down. Within the guild system, for example, guilds of long-distance commerce became less important, while craft guilds became more important. Civic militias lost much of their military role after circa 1500, and by implication their civic and police duties became more significant. South of the Alps, poor relief was probably more the preserve of confraternities, whereas in the north local authorities took charity more into their own hands. However, everywhere voluntary contributions from citizens were and remained a pivotal element of the system. Despite regional and temporal variations, with regard to all of these aspects, it is possible to speak of a single model of premodern urban citizenship. This model was built around the tens of thousands of civic organisations that enabled their numerous, mostly urban, members to act in the public domain.

The implication of our results is that the contrast between premodern and post-revolutionary citizenship, as we find it in European textbook narratives, is first and foremost the result of a change in perspective. Before the French Revolution citizenship was overwhelmingly a local institution, whose significance has been largely overshadowed by the introduction of national citizenship after 1789. This book has emphasised the value of liberating the concept of citizenship from its legal and national shackles, and the value of the local reorientation pioneered by Isin and Sassen.

While local models of citizenship were broadly similar across time and space, the way they were embedded in state contexts was not. On the contrary, in this respect variations were significant and consequential. In all European countries, the Middle Ages and early modern period constituted an age of rapid – and some would argue revolutionary – state formation. Almost everywhere, this state formation created fundamental oppositions between local communities and state institutions. The proper relations between the two were debated and fought over again and again by contemporaries. Nonetheless, for a time at least, three regions were able to establish some sort of balance that aligned the interests of citizens and states.

Italy, the Low Countries and England were, by common consent, the most economically advanced in successive stages of European history between roughly 1000 and 1800 CE. The three regions shared two features that set them apart from the rest of Europe. The first was that urbanites made up a relatively large share of the population: rates of urbanisation were high in Italy and the Low Countries from early on, while in England they started to increase later, but very rapidly carried England to the top of the urbanisation league table. Secondly, urban interests became represented directly at state level. The ways in which these regions achieved coordination between urban political institutions and the state differed, and in each case they succumbed to problems of sclerosis and overstretch in the long run. Whether this was due to inherent flaws in their particular political systems, or part of a broader historical pattern, should be the topic of another book.[1] But for 100–200 years this alignment of the interests of citizens and states gave states more taxes, and hence greater capacity, whilst giving citizens better economic policies, and ultimately greater welfare.

Why would this be so? The literature on state formation suggests two reasons, and this investigation of citizenship regimes supports the importance of both: competition and coordination.[2] Due to the competition between thousands of cities and dozens of states, Europe offered its populations a wealth of institutional menus to choose from. The migration of merchant communities, first from Bruges to Antwerp, and later on to Amsterdam, shows how appreciative contemporaries were of such choice, and how they used that choice to their advantage. At the same time, best practices could, at least potentially, move rapidly from one place to another.[3] In other words, competition encouraged a movement around the continent of both institutions and people. At roughly the same time, a small number of regions managed to become zones of high-intensity growth.[4] These regions, mostly situated in an area that has been described as Europe's 'dorsal spine', or the 'blue banana', combined high levels of urbanisation with low levels of state integration.[5] Whereas initially states organised around urban institutions – i.e. city-states – produced the most effective form of coordination, in the long run larger units were required to remain competitive in the economic and military struggle for survival.

If we accept the proposition that institutions helped determine the quality of societies, we are now in a better position to specify some of the claims in the recent social science literature. Whilst our European data provide support for Putnam's emphasis on the contribution of civic institutions to prosperity, his construct of a straight line from the Middle Ages to the present has to be questioned. The mechanisms that determined the regional variations that he uncovered in Italy remain unclear. In Besley's model the electoral mechanisms of modern democracy are held responsible for a positive outcome, but in the urban communities of the premodern era, because of their small size, personal interactions between officeholders and citizens could act as a brake on elite misbehaviour. We have found confirmation for Acemoglu and Robinson's thesis that economic development was predicated on political transformations, but we have also shown that their emphasis on the Glorious Revolution exaggerated the importance of property rights, under-rated the role of citizens through the representation of urban interests and overlooked the half millennium leading up to 1689 as a formative period of both European citizenship and capitalism. North, Wallis and Weingast are too optimistic about the nineteenth century, and too pessimistic about the preceding centuries, as we see in the following section, where we look at the impact of the French Revolution. None of these theories provides an adequate explanation for the emergence of successful citizenship regimes in precisely Italy, the Low Countries and England. Historical contingency still seems the best answer.

Our definition of citizenship as a set of practices rather than a formal institution has enabled us to revisit the contrast between Europe and the rest of the world. Thus, the opposition between Asia and Europe which rests on the absence of an Asian idea of citizenship is in fact found to be less fundamental once citizenship practices in Asia resembling those found in Europe are taken into account. In the cases of the Ottoman and Chinese Empires, historians have generally been too optimistic about the capabilities of governments in far-away capitals to steer and control the business of urban communities in often remote parts of their empires.

From a local perspective, empires actually had much in common with the European states with which they are routinely contrasted. The proper comparison is not with Italian city-states, the Low

Countries or England, but rather with the Holy Roman Empire, Spain or Poland. In such a comparison, what we find in Asia does not seem so fundamentally distinct from the patterns of European citizenship. The one truly distinctive element of European urban citizenship is that it had an ideological component with the potential to develop into the kind of inclusive arrangements promised – but not initially delivered – by the French Revolution. The similarities are especially striking in the economic (guilds) and social (welfare) domains. Civic militias and local representative councils, on the other hand, were less developed in Asia than in most European towns. Local political institutions, however, lost substantial powers in East Central Europe, and also in France. Absolutism made European urban citizenship more akin to the equivalent situation in Asian towns.

The contrasting developments in the Spanish and English colonies in the New World also provide an opportunity to gauge the results of a natural experiment on the medium and long-term impact of premodern citizenship arrangements. From the very beginning of their settlement, the Spanish colonisers transferred European institutions to their colonies, with urban institutions modelled on the situation in Spain itself. Citizenship in Spanish colonies was more egalitarian and inclusive than citizenship in English colonies, and although Spanish colonial institutions discriminated against native Americans and former slaves of African descent, they were nonetheless accessible to them. Our positive assessment of urban citizenship in the Spanish colonies chimes with the more positive assessment of their economic performance as was recently proposed.[6]

The English colonial authorities, on the other hand, were reluctant to grant North Americans the right to set up the kinds of institution that existed in the mother country. In New England civic institutions were nonetheless quite common, but in New York and Philadelphia they were limited. Demands for greater citizen participation in local governance, or even the right to set up guilds, were repeatedly rejected there. In the struggles over local governance, native Americans and former slaves of African descent were generally excluded from civic initiatives. During the American Revolution, citizen participation became much more widespread and important, helping to unleash the country's great potential for economic growth and prosperity. However, the American Revolution delivered an inclusive and encompassing citizenship for whites only. The prosperity that it helped to create was racially skewed;

not only did it lead to a bloody civil war in the mid-nineteenth century, it continues to plague American society in the twenty-first century.

Local coordination through civic organisations was a feature of towns and cities in Asia and the New World as well as in Europe. Citizenship varied across all continents, but those variations were confined to a relatively small spectrum. From a global perspective, European citizenship had some unique features, most notably its conceptualisation in political theory and in a civic ideology, but it was not as fundamentally different from citizenship arrangements elsewhere as Max Weber proposed early in the twentieth century. The effects that he ascribed to European citizenship in general, actually only materialised in very few European regions. These regions managed to connect the integrating capacities of urban citizenship, and the coordinating capacities of urban environments, with the capacity of the state to provide military protection for schemes of economic expansion.[7]

Beyond the French Revolution

The negative verdict on premodern citizenship was shaped by the events in late eighteenth-century France. The revolutionaries themselves were very sceptical about what they saw as the feudal heritage of the Old Regime and on 4 August 1789, they abolished it in one gigantic sweep. In 1791, the *Loi Le Chapelier* forbade guilds and journeymen organisations and more generally 'combinations'. All sorts of civic organisations could now be declared illegal. These revolutionary changes happened, perhaps predictably, in a country where urban citizenship had always been comparatively underdeveloped, and had been further weakened by a century and a half of royal policies. In fact, the French state had already attempted to abolish the guilds in 1776.[8]

After 1791, other parts of Europe followed suit, either when they were incorporated into the French Empire, or otherwise of their own volition: Belgium in 1795, the Netherlands and Switzerland in 1798, the Italian states in 1806, Westphalia in 1808, northern Germany in 1810.[9] The limited evidence stemming from the Netherlands that is currently available shows that it became easier to access urban trades after the abolition of the guilds.[10] Gradually, however, complaints emerged about the decline of skills, and more importantly of political agency. Early labour unions that sought to empower the workers – very often artisans – were seldom direct continuations of guilds, but they borrowed heavily from the guild vocabulary and discourse.[11]

The abolition of the guilds was part of an encompassing programme of creating – to use Pierre Rosanvallon's expression – 'generality'. In France in particular, the Revolution sought to clear away all 'corporatist' vestiges. As one contemporary wrote in 1793: 'The constitution recognises only one corporation, that consisting of all the French; it concerns itself with only one interest, that of the nation, which comprises the combined interests of all citizens'.[12] The same logic was at work in the newly formed United States of America. The first draft of the American Constitution opened with the phrase 'We the people of the States of New Hampshire, Massachusetts, Rhode-Island and Providence Plantations, Connecticut', and so on, but in the final draft this became 'We, the people of the United States'.[13] In practice, this lofty ideal of a single people was full of contradictions. All citizens were supposed to be equal, but in actual fact they were anything but, as women were soon to find out.[14] French citizens received the right of free assembly, but from 1791 they were not permitted to associate. The Haitian Revolution of 1791 laid bare the limitations of the 'equality' discourse.[15] In the newly formed United States of America former slaves might be free, but they were not citizens; between 1783 and 1820 their position solidified as mere 'denizens'.[16]

From the point of view of citizenship, Europe in the nineteenth century was a different place than it had been. It would be helpful if we could make direct quantitative comparisons between citizenship rates in pre-industrial Europe and similar measures in the nineteenth century, but for various reasons this is impossible. The package of rights on offer to citizens varied widely around Europe, within and between both the premodern and post-1789 worlds. The rights of citizens differed between England and German-speaking cities in 1700, but also between Hamburg in 1710 and Hamburg in 1800 or 1848. We can nonetheless try to get some sense of what it meant to be a citizen in nineteenth-century Europe, by comparing some key figures. For a start, democracy had given citizens the right to participate in national elections. For a long time, however, access to this right remained very restricted, judging from the small percentages of enfranchised citizens throughout most of the nineteenth century in most European countries.[17]

Compared to the absence of any national voting rights outside the British Isles before 1800, this looks like progress; yet if one sets these data against the long tradition of citizens' participation in public

Table 12.1 Enfranchised population as percentage of the adult population, 1820–1899

	1820s	1830s	1840s	1850s	1860s	1870s	1880s	1890s
Austria						10.6	13.0	35.7
Belgium		1.9	3.1	3.3	3.6	3.7	3.9	37.3
Denmark			25.7	25.8	25.8	26.7	28.3	30.0
France	0.5	0.9	36.3	42.0	42.0	43.7	41.6	42.0
Germany						37.4	37.3	37.8
Italy					3.4	3.8	14.1	16.6
Netherlands				4.6		5.0	11.8	20.9
Norway	11.1	10.0	9.7	9.3	8.8	8.5	11.8	16.6
United Kingdom		6.0	6.8		14.5	14.9	29.3	29.3

Notes: Highest recorded values per decade are included in the table. Adults consist of those aged twenty and above.
Source: Flora et al. 1983, ch. 3

administration in many towns, and recognizes that, after the French Revolution, municipalities in many parts of Europe had to sing to the tune of central state institutions, the picture looks decidedly less favourable. Denmark and France were early democracies; in the rest of Europe democracy was perhaps an ideal, but definitely not a practice. Only from the 1870s do we see enfranchisement rise above 10 per cent in a significant number of countries.

Similarly, the figures currently available for social spending suggest that, apart from a spike during the Napoleonic Wars, per capita expenditures on social security decreased markedly in northern and central Italy, in the western provinces of the Netherlands and in England between the middle of the eighteenth century and the first half of the nineteenth, or even the 1880s. Data on France and Belgium show the same pattern. From the United States, a series for the city of Philadelphia shows stability between 1770 and 1850, but no progress.[18] This trend again suggests that urban populations probably did not experience greater access to the social rights associated with citizenship until well into the second half of the nineteenth century.[19]

Numbers mean less when we look at the military dimension of citizenship; still, the trend was unmistakably the same. The French Revolution, through the *levée en masse* and conscription, created a genuine citizen army.[20] At the same time, the decades of revolutionary warfare forced states to centralise their armed forces; the restoration after 1815 required them to depoliticise those same forces. In the Netherlands, where civic militias had been the mainstay of the revolutionary Patriot movement during the 1780s, the local militias were, between 1798 and 1811, merged step by step into the national military structures and deprived of political agency.[21] In Prussia, the role of the popular *Landwehr* was curtailed in 1813 in favour of the regular army, precisely because of fears it might become a platform for liberal agitation. In France, the army was purged in 1815–16, reformed in 1818, and purged again in 1830 to clip its political wings.[22]

All in all, we see little movement towards more agency for citizens during most of the nineteenth century in any of the four dimensions of citizenship charted in this book. In many European countries, the French Revolution had swept away urban citizenship and its institutions, and replaced it with the principles of national citizenship, but preciously little of its practices. Modern citizenship was only properly established in the later nineteenth century and the early decades of the twentieth, with the creation of labour unions, employers' organisations and political parties capable of articulating citizens' demands and helping to transform these into real policies. Significantly, many of these organisations were first established, and their policies first implemented, in towns and cities before being extended to cover the nation as a whole.[23] Seen from this perspective, national, or 'modern', citizenship is not necessarily the culmination of a historical arc that was destined to make landfall on the shores of a modern paradise. Rather, it is a phase of a historical process that is bound to continue as long as citizenship and its implications remain contested – as they are likely to be for the foreseeable future.[24]

Revising our ideas about citizenship in the past has implications for our visions of the future. In Europe, national citizenship as it was established by the French Revolution is going through particularly stressful times. Its problems are partly caused by the European Union, which is busy creating a supranational EU form of citizenship. Globalisation and migration are fanning the flames. Those flames, however, have been created by national citizenship itself. In the nineteenth and twentieth centuries, national states promised political voice and socio-economic security to those holding national citizenship. Nationalism also gave citizens a cultural identity, with a shared language and history. In the twenty-first century none of this looks secure any longer, and national governments find it increasingly difficult to satisfy their citizens, not to mention the migrants who are also raising their voices.

If we are willing to accept this book's argument that urban citizenship was not as bad as it was portrayed by the revolutionaries who sought to overthrow it, and that national citizenship was not as perfect as they claimed, it is perhaps time to reconsider its abolition. That is not a plea for the dismantling of the national state, because in this new constellation urban citizenship would offer an additional citizenship arrangement that is multidimensional, rather than exclusively local.[25] The reintroduction of urban citizenship would indeed imply devolving some of national governments' prerogatives to local authorities, but this process is long overdue and already under way.[26] Local citizen initiatives are blossoming, and local authorities could support these more effectively if they were embedded in some form of local citizenship. This could be acquired as a form of *ius domicile*, as Rainer Bauböck has proposed.[27] A 'nested' or 'multilevel' form of citizenship would have the potential to combine the strength of local citizenship in engagement and commitment with the strength of national citizenship in equality and freedom.[28] If the objective of citizenship is ultimately to create agency for the individual members of society, then surely it would be better to utilise several, rather than one, institutional resource for that purpose. In Europe especially, but in fact worldwide, urban citizenship has a pedigree that is not only worth revisiting; it could indeed be a source of political and social inspiration.

NOTES

Acknowledgements

1. Under the European Union's Seventh Framework Programme for research, technological development and demonstration, grant agreement no 320294.
2. Isin 2012a.

Introduction

1. Soliday 1974, 40–53; Koch 1983, 76–81; Roth 1996, 65–75.
2. Soliday 1974, chs 5–6; Koch 1983, 8–28.
3. Koch 1983, 29–34, 40–45, 47 (quote), 54–55, 70, 331–38. For other German towns and cities, see the fourteen titles in the *Stadt und Bürgertum* series, edited by Lothar Gall; cf. Gall 1991.
4. Compare Prak 1999, 253–59 and chs 12–16; also Ramos 2007, 176–79.
5. Isin 2002; Sassen 2006; Gordon and Stack 2007.
6. For details, see pp. 15-16 below.
7. In this book, as in much of the historiography, 'premodern' mainly covers the medieval and early modern eras, in this case more specifically between roughly 1000 and 1800 CE.
8. R. Smith 2002, 105–06; see also Heater 1999.
9. Isin 2012b, 109.
10. Marshall 1950, ch. 1. Although the two are obviously closely related, especially in the works of Thomas Paine (2000 [1791/92]), this book does not discuss the issue of human rights; see Hunt 2007, ch. 1.
11. Bottomore 1992; Bulmer and Rees 1996; Turner 1997.
12. Sassen 2002, and 2006, ch. 6; also Crowley 1998.
13. J. Shaw 2007; Dougan, Shuibhne and Spaventa 2012.
14. *EU Citizenship Report 2013*, http://ec.europa.eu/commission_2010–2014/reding/factsheets/citizenship-report/.
15. See e.g. Heater 1990, ch. 1; the historical chapters (part 2) in Isin and Turner 2002; as well as Lefebvre 2003, 16; Hindess 2004, 314; Isin and Turner 2007, 6.
16. Fahrmeir 2007, 9, 27.

17. Cf. Isin 1999, 2002, 2007 and 2008a; also Somers 1993, 589; Bauböck 2003; and Staeheli 2003, as well as a German historiography as exemplified in Riedel 1972, and Dilcher 1988 and 1996a. A local history using this approach is Roney 2014.
18. Isin and Nielsen 2008. On the practices approach, see the pioneering work by Bourdieu 1980, as well as Reckwitz 2002; this approach has been dignified as 'praxiography', e.g. in Bueger 2014. The focus on practices implies that I have largely ignored a substantial historiography of the idea of citizenship, as summarised in Costa 1999.
19. Isin and Turner 2002, 2; Isin and Nielsen 2008; Andrijasevic 2013.
20. Tilly 1995, 8.
21. I changed the word 'state' into 'polity' to allow for urban citizenship.
22. Cf. Herzog 2003, 20.
23. Bellamy 2008, 3, 6.
24. Tilly 2004, 117; Tilly here also portrays citizenship as a post-1789 phenomenon.
25. North, Wallis and Weingast 2009.
26. A different chronology is proposed by Bavel, Ansink and Besouw 2017, 123–28.
27. The subtitle of Acemoglu and Robinson 2012, ch. 13.
28. Acemoglu and Robinson 2012, 202, 208.
29. Putnam 1993 and 2000.
30. Putnam 1993, 85 and ch. 5.
31. Brucker 1999; Muir 1999; C.F. Black 2009; Eckstein and Terpstra 2009.
32. Van Dijck, De Munck and Terpstra 2017.
33. Sen 1999, 10 (quote), 18, 157, 190–92, 294.
34. Besley 2006.
35. De Moor 2008, and 2015, ch. 1.
36. Bowles and Gintis 2011; see also Axelrod 1984; M. Taylor 1987; E. Ostrom 1990.
37. Olson 1971 [1965], 38; Ogilvie 2011, 420–21.
38. On economic coordination, Seabright 2010.
39. Cf. S. R. Epstein 2000a, 8.
40. E.g. Tilly 1993; Te Brake 1998.
41. Streeck and Schmitter 1985, 124–36 (quotes at 125); also Holbach 2016.
42. The technical term is gross domestic (or: national) product per inhabitant, abbreviated as GDP/capita, which is used throughout this book.
43. Zanden 2001, 71–73, and 2009, 38; Acemoglu, Johnson and Robinson 2002, 1232; Bertinelli and Black 2004. For surveys of European and global urbanisation, see de Vries 1984; Hohenberg and Lees 1985; Clark 2009 and 2013; Bosker, Buringh and Van Zanden 2013; Yi, Van Leeuwen and Van Zanden 2015.
44. De Vries 1974; Hoffman 1996.
45. Bosker, Buringh and Van Zanden 2013, 1433.
46. Maddison 2001, 2003 and 2007.
47. R.C. Allen 2001; Broadberry and Gupta 2006; Allen, Ma, Bassino, Moll-Murata and Van Zanden 2011; Malanima 2011; Zanden and Van Leeuwen 2012; Broadberry, Campbell, Klein, Overton and Van Leeuwen 2015.
48. I do this in the spirit outlined in Kenneth Pomeranz, 'The data we have vs. the data we need: A comment on the state of the "Divergence" debate (Part I)', https://nephist.wordpress.com/2017/06/06/the-data-we-have-vs-the-data-we-need-a-comment-on-the-state-of-the-divergence-debate-part-i/.
49. Skocpol 1984; D. Smith 1991.
50. B. Moore 1966; Wallerstein 1974; Skocpol 1979; Swaan 1988; Tilly 1990 and 1993; Ertman 1997; North, Wallis and Weingast 2009.
51. The best example is Ragin 1987.

52. For a variety of approaches in comparative history, see Mahoney and Rueschemeyer 2003.
53. Tilly 1984, chs 6 and 7.
54. Weber 1968 [1922], 1240.
55. Weber 1968 [1922], 1226.
56. Weber 1968 [1922], 1226–33; see also Isin 2003, 316–20.
57. Nippel 2000, 25–26.
58. Weber 1968 [1922], 1241, 1248–49.
59. Weber 1968 [1922], 1281–82.
60. Nippel 1991, 27–28.
61. Isin 2005.
62. Nippel 1991, 20.
63. Pomeranz 2000; see also Frank 1998.
64. The best introduction to the 'great divergence' debate currently available is Vries 2013.
65. Zanden 2009.
66. Rosenthal and Wong 2011, ch. 6; for a similar argument Hoffman 2015.
67. E.g. Clark 2013, 3, 221, 231, 386, 421, 452, 584.
68. B. Moore 1966, 174; Acemoglu, Johnson and Robinson 2002, 1240; Le Galès 2002, 21, 34–37; Sassen 2006, 55–57, 67–71. To be sure, Pirenne himself published more sophisticated versions of the story: Pirenne 1939.
69. T. Scott 2012, 130–35, 149, 158, 164–92, 218–21.
70. Blickle, Fuhrmann and Würgler 1998; Blickle 2000.
71. De Vries 1984, 39; Zanden 2009, 40.

1 Formal Citizenship

1. Bowsky 1967, 208–10.
2. Kirshner 1973, 694–95.
3. Anderson 1983.
4. Bowsky 1967, 197–203, 210, 215, 226–30.
5. Bader and Dilcher 1999, 447.
6. Möller 1998, 22–23; Hafner 2001, 63, 261.
7. Deeters 1987, 32–33.
8. Oexle 1985; Bader and Dilcher 1999, 263, 271–74, 278, 280–82; Wickham 2014.
9. N. Heuvel 1946, 306 ('s-Hertogenbosch); Rappaport 1989, 29, 35 (London); Isenmann 2012, 223, 237 (Cologne).
10. Berman 1983, ch. 12; Isenmann 2012, 195–207.
11. More about this in Part II.
12. Friedrichs 2000, 13–17; also chapter 2.
13. Müller-Herrenschwand 2002, 482.
14. Walker 1971, 140; Berkenvelder 2005, 123.
15. Zeller 2015, 68.
16. Bonin 2005, 111; also Mottu-Weber 1996, 33–34; Isenmann 2012, 147.
17. McCants 1997, chs 3 and 4; Kuijpers and Prak 2002, 128.
18. Isenmann 2002, 225–27, and 2012, 146–47; Berkenvelder 2005, 125–27; Pult Quaglia 2006, 108; Junot 2009, ch. 2.
19. Barry 2000, 189.
20. Cf. Isenmann 2002, 229–30.
21. Soliday 1974, 41; Friedrichs 1979, 39n8.
22. This paragraph is based on Nader 1990, 27–45, and Herzog 2003, ch. 2.

23. Herzog 2003, 31.
24. Tingle 2000, 101; Bonin 2005, 51–53; Zeller 2015, 93, 96.
25. Di Corcia 1978.
26. Wells 1995, 31, and 1999, 441; also Sahlins 2004, 66–68.
27. Sahlins 2004, 141, 159; also Bayard 1990, 310; Cerutti 2007.
28. Kivelson 2002, 474–75, 486–87; also Kamenskii 2015.
29. Dilcher 1996c, 142–43; also Carter 1994, 65.
30. Kuijpers and Prak 2002, 119.
31. Obradors-Suazo 2017.
32. Kint 1996, 161; Prak 1999, 35.
33. Bellavitis 2001, 65, and 2015; on Venetian citizenship also Pullan 1971, 99–111.
34. Rappaport 1989, 23–24; Minns and Wallis 2012, 570.
35. Kuijpers and Prak 2002, 123.
36. Niggemann 2013, 47–50; De Meester 2014; Linden 2015, 46, 48.
37. Lindemann 1990, 61.
38. E.g. Kuijpers and Prak 2002, 123; Berkenvelder 2005, 196.
39. Roth 1996, 71n91.
40. Studer 2002, 170; compare also Müller-Herrenschwand 2002, 484.
41. Wiesner 1986, esp. 13–35, and 1998; Roper 1987; Howell 1988.
42. Berkenvelder 2005, 383–91.
43. Kuijpers 2005, 127.
44. Sharlin 1978; also de Vries 1984, 179–98.
45. De Vries 1984, ch. 10; Moch 2003, ch. 2; Clark 2009, 59–62, 160–64.
46. Gerber 2002, 263.
47. Gerber 2002, 255–56; Schwinges 2002.
48. Fuks-Mansfeld 1989, 39.
49. Kuijpers and Prak 2002, 123–24; also Cavallar and Kirshner 2011.
50. Prak 2002, *passim* (quote on 163).
51. Gilomen 2002, 126–54; Isenmann 2012, 153–58.
52. Israel 1998, 54–55.
53. Soliday 1974, 15, 180–81, ch. 7; also Hsia 2006.
54. Nader 1990, 30.
55. Merrick 1987, 52, 59 (quote), 66; Bonin 2005, 60; Zeller 2015, ch. 2.
56. Wallis et al. 2015, table 4.
57. Prak 1995, 336–37; Kuijpers 2005, 130–34.
58. Wallis et al. 2015, table 4.
59. Most of the groundwork for this section was done in a paper, 'The scale and scope of citizenship in early modern Europe: Preliminary estimates', produced for the bEUcitizen project by Chris Minns (lead author), Clare Crowston, Raoul De Kerf, Bert De Munck, Marcel Hoogenboom, Patrick Wallis and myself; the paper is cited as Minns et al. 2014. This part of the research was funded by the EU under the FP7 framework.
60. Kuijpers and Prak 2002, 124–25; also Schultheiss 1972, 190; Boone and Stabel 2002, 319; Müller-Herrenschwand 2002, 497.
61. Mettele 1998, 33; Minns et al. 2014.
62. Schultheiss 1972, 188.
63. Minns et al. 2014, 34–35, table 3; this calculation ignores the exclusively English data on the nineteenth century.
64. Deeters 1987, 77–78; Lindemann 1990, 67; Hahn 1991, 16; Möller 1998, 27.
65. All numbers in this paragraph are from Minns et al. 2014.

66. On Nördlingen: Friedrichs 1979, ch. 2.
67. Minns et al. 2014, table 3.
68. This paragraph relies entirely on Haemers 2012, 151–55; quotes on 153 and 155, respectively.
69. Prak 2000b, 77.
70. Liddy and Haemers 2013, 790–91 (quote on 791).
71. Liddy and Haemers 2013, 793–800 (quotes at 793 and 794); also Haemers 2009, 268, and for a later age Withington 2001.
72. Holmes 1973; Najemy 1979, and 1982, 9, 14, 242–43.
73. Najemy 1979, 61.
74. Najemy 1982, 228.
75. Najemy 1979, 66.
76. Najemy 1982, 268, 304; compare also Brucker 1977.
77. Prak 1999, 210–11; also Prak 1997.
78. Hafner 2001, ch. 5 (quote on 150).
79. These developments are discussed in the Conclusion of this book.
80. For its visual expression, see Gamboni and Germann 1991.
81. Schilling 1992a, 6–30; I have adapted the order of Schilling's features to suit the purposes of my own argument. See also Mager 1988, 73–74; Lindemann 2015, 78–86.
82. Najemy 1982; Blickle 1988 and 2000, ch. 8, but also Friedeburg 1994.
83. Prak 1991a, 379.
84. Bierschwale and Van Leeuwen 2005, 60–67.
85. Prak 1994, 61.
86. A. Black 1996, 111, disagrees. For classical republicanism, see Gelderen and Skinner 2002.
87. Pocock 1975, ch. 3 esp. 74; Nauert 1995, 13, 33–34, 70–71; but see also Maissen 2006.
88. Two important early contributions are Pocock 1975, and Haitsma Mulier 1980.
89. Lengen 1995.
90. Althusius [1965], 28.
91. Costa 1999, 89–90.
92. Costa 1999, 44.
93. See also Hüglin 1997; A. Black 2003, ch. 11; Carney, Schilling and Wyduckel 2004.
94. Schwerdhoff 1994, 96.
95. National Library of the Netherlands: Knuttel 14844; see also Pethegem 1988; Dixhoorn 1999; Hafner 2001, 166–67.
96. Woltjer 1975.
97. Dumolyn 2008; also Schwerdhoff 1994, 109; Boone 1997; Wells 1999, 444; Dutour 2012, 195.
98. See the essays collected in Lecuppre-Desjardin and Van Bruaene 2010; also Rubinstein 1958, 183–86; Rublack 1984, 27; Q. Skinner 1986, 9–14, 43, and 1999, 9–14; Isenmann 1997, 190, 213; Corteguera 2002; Meier 2002; Dumolyn 2008, 13–17; Haemers 2009, 263–69.
99. Isenmann 2003, 414; also Isenmann 2010.
100. Bierschwale and Van Leeuwen 2005, 68–69 (quote at 69) and *passim*; also Oostrom 2013, 150–75.
101. Suter 2000, 34 (quote); Lerner 2012, 34.
102. Lantschner 2015, 29–39.
103. Prak 1991a, 379; also Wallace 1994, 931–32.
104. Barry 2000, 194–95; also Filmer 2000; Rosser 2015.

2 Urban Governance

1. Würgler 1995, 78–81.
2. Parts of this chapter have been published earlier in Prak 2012.
3. The classic work is Namier 1929. On prosopography, see the almost equally classic Stone 1971 and the more recent Keats-Rohan 2007. Modern examples of this type of work include Diefendorf 1983; Clark 1984; Maillard 1984; Jong 1985; Kooijmans 1985; Prak 1985; Cowan 1986; Litchfield 1986; R. Schneider 1989b; Schuttelaars 1998; Junot 2009; see also Friedrichs 2000, ch. 2.
4. Underdown 1985; classics include Rudé 1964; Hobsbawm and Rudé 1969.
5. For a European survey, see Te Brake 1998; earlier surveys include Zagorin 1982 and Bercé 1987.
6. Some of the more influential surveys were written in the 1990s, among them Tilly 1990; Downing 1992; Ertman 1997. They all share this fixation on national politics.
7. Beik 1985; also Cosandey and Descimon 2002, and Collins 2009, preface to the second edition.
8. Data in S. R. Epstein 2000a, 20–23; Epstein's interpretation is somewhat different from the one presented here. See also Zanden and Prak 2006 and Stasavage 2011, 39.
9. I'm following here in the footsteps of Friedrichs 2000, ch. 2.
10. On the early Italian developments: Wickham 2015, and Chapter 6.
11. Clark 2009, 21; also Verhulst 1999.
12. Bensch 1995, 48–52, 63, 68–70, 81–82, 172–78, 181 (quote), 206–20; also Dutour 2012.
13. Mundy 1954, 5, 14–16, 30–33, 46.
14. Mundy 1954, chs 11–12.
15. Palliser 1979, 60–69; see also Liddy 2017, ch. 6.
16. Prak 2000b, 77.
17. Hsia 1984, 16–30; Kirchhoff 1988; Hanschmidt 1994, 268–78.
18. R. Schneider 1989a, 198.
19. Maillard 1984, 33–35, 75–76.
20. Bowsky 1981, 23–24, 28; Waley 1991, 42, claims they usually came from Lombardy and Emilia Romagna.
21. Waley 1991, 42.
22. Waley 1991, 48; Ascheri 2001.
23. Bowsky 1981, 85–86; Waley 1991, 49, 52.
24. Waley 1991, 46.
25. Caferro 1998, 21–24, 184–85.
26. Cowan 1986, chs 5–6; also Jong 1985; Kooijmans 1985; Prak 1985; Amelang 1986; Verkerk 1992; Adams 2005; Junot 2009, ch. 6; Marraud 2009.
27. Waley 1991, 48; also Bowsky 1981, 306–09.
28. Leach 2005; also Blockmans 2010a, 324.
29. Lamet 1979; Prak 1985; Kan 1988; Noordam 1994; Brand 1996.
30. Kan 1988, chs 2 and 3.
31. Brand 1996, 256–57.
32. Lamet 1979, 185–89.
33. Noordam 1994, 80, 83–85.
34. Prak 1985, 125–26, 209, 211.
35. Clark 1984, 315, 318.
36. Lindberg 2009, 621.

37. Irvine 1989, 125; Descimon 2003.
38. Amelang 1986, 27.
39. Nicolini 1979, 250 (table 31); also Herborn 1985, 344; Looz-Corswarem 1985, 431–32.
40. Schilling 1992b; Friedrichs 2000, ch. 2.
41. Oer 1998, 1, 4 (quote), 18–19 (quotes); see also Weikert 1990.
42. Schmid 1995, 81, 88–91; for Cologne, see Militzer 1980.
43. Kaiser 1992, 143–45; for Paris, see Diefendorf 1983, 34–49.
44. Prak 1994b, 61; Velema 2007, 59; also Bader and Dilcher 1999, 553–54.
45. I am not convinced by Archer's argument that the freemen's options were unduly constrained because many of the candidates in local elections were proposed by those holding office, or because their wealth did not reflect that of the average London household: I. Archer 1991, 19–20, 64, 68–69; see the final paragraph of this section.
46. Krey 1985, 10.
47. On London guilds, see Gadd and Wallis 2002a.
48. Krey 1985, 40.
49. Krey 1985, 40–41; also Latham 2012 and Liddy 2017, ch. 4.
50. The following is a summary of Saupin 1996, chs 3 and 4.
51. Saupin 1996, 86–87.
52. Saupin 1996, 110 (quote); for other Breton towns, Saupin 1991.
53. Babeau 1884 vol. 1, 55–68; Bordes 1972, ch. 9; Holt 1991, 98–101, 105, 109; Gal 2000, 82–85.
54. Naegle and Solórzano 2014, 588–93, 595; Solórzano 2014, 184–86.
55. Németh 2009.
56. Hrdlička 2009, 102–07.
57. Bowsky 1981, 85–98; Waley 1991, 49–52.
58. Palliser 1979, 61–62, 67–68.
59. Van Honacker 1994, 93–95.
60. Prak 1994b, 64–70.
61. Wahl 2015a, 2015b and 2016.
62. Friedrichs 2000, 17–18.
63. Cf. Holt 1991, 99–100; Prak 1994b.
64. Tilly 1978.
65. Cieslak and Biernat 1995, 54, 69–72, 85–92, 221–28; compare Solórzano 2014, 188–203.
66. Najemy 1982, 27.
67. Najemy 1982, *passim*, and 2006, ch. 6; also Nussdorfer 1992, ch. 8.
68. Dumolyn 2014, 22–23, 26, 29–34.
69. Schulz 1994 and 2010, ch. II.4; see also Soly 2008.
70. Cf. Dumolyn 2014, 46–47.
71. Deceulaer and Jacobs 2002; also Deceulaer 2009, esp. 196–97.
72. Lis and Soly 1993, 6; see also Dorren 1998 and 2001, ch. 3; Walter 1971, 13.
73. Kent and Kent 1982, 13, 75–86, 107–16, and *passim*; also Eckstein 1995; Nubola 2009, 41; and, for a later age, Rosenthal 2015.
74. See Chapters 3 and 5.
75. C. Shaw 2006, 172–74.
76. Maillard 1984, 86; also Robbins 1997, 218–19.
77. These petitions can be found in Gemeentearchief (Municipal Archive) Amsterdam, archive 5061 (Judicial archives), n°s 684–725: petitions to the Aldermen; and 5028

(Burgomasters), 515–19: petitions filed by the guilds. For the analysis of their contents, see Prak 1996.

78. Gemeentearchief Amsterdam, 5061: 697, n° 1 (1751).
79. Gemeentearchief Amsterdam, 5061: 723, n° 23 (1786). Compare 5061: 694, n° 46 (1747-'48); 5061: 702, n° 9 (1756); 5061: 713, n° 1 (1770); 5061: 720, n° 6 (1778).
80. Nierop 1997, 286–87; also Kümin and Würgler 1997, 46–58.
81. Zaret 1996, 1509–13; Heerma van Voss 2001; Cerutti 2010 and 2012, ch. 3.
82. Nubola 2001, 47.
83. Bowsky 1981, 57; compare Haemers 2014 and 2016.
84. Shapiro and Markoff 2001.
85. Solórzano 2014, 189–91, 199.
86. Würgler 2001; Vermeesch 2012, 99–103.
87. Vermeesch 2012.
88. Zaret 1996.
89. Cunningham and Grell 2000.
90. Moeller 1962; also Greyerz 1985; H. Schmidt 1986; Hsia 1987; Cameron 1991, ch. 15; Hamm 1995 and 1996; Te Brake 1998, ch. 2; Close 2009, chs 4–5.
91. B. Kaplan 1995, ch. 3; Marnef 1996; Nierop 2000; Dambruyne 2002, 644–77.
92. Tittler 1998, chs 7–10; also Collinson and Craig 1998.
93. Benedict 1981, ch. 4 (quote on 98).
94. Descimon 1983; Diefendorf 1991, ch. 10.
95. Klötzer 1992, 22, 25, 32, 34, 36 and *passim*.
96. Kirchhoff 1973, 36–37 (table 5), 40 (table 5a), 48, 87; also Schilling 1975.
97. Compare Dumolyn, Haemers, Herrer and Chalet 2014; Lantschner 2015.
98. Najemy 1982, 243.
99. Boone and Prak 1995, 101–13; Boone 2007 and 2010a, ch. 2; Arnade 2008, ch. 4 and *passim*.
100. Kirchhoff 1980, 161, 231, and *passim*; also Kannowski 2001.
101. Lantschner 2015, 207.
102. Beik 1997, 264; also Hildebrandt 1974; Friedrichs 1978.
103. Blockmans 1988; Boone and Prak 1995, 100; Te Brake 1998, 15–16; Friedrichs 2000, 22–24.
104. Te Brake 1989.
105. Most of this section was first published in Prak and Van Zanden 2009, 143–44, 154–55.
106. Feld and Frey 2002; also Andreoni, Erard and Feinstein 1998; Frey 2003; Torgler and Schneider 2005; Frey and Torgler 2007; Luttmer and Singhal 2014; and, finally, Levi 1988.
107. Rosenthal 1998.
108. Aalbers 1980, 3–23; Liesker 1985.
109. Historisch Centrum Overijssel (HCO), Oud Archief Zwolle (OAZ), 217: Resolution of council and common council, pp. 217–32; see also 8 April 1748 (pp. 246–47).
110. HCO, OAZ, 4516, no. 1: Commissioners for the Liberal Gift, 7 April 1748.
111. HCO, OAZ, 4516, no. 15: Revenue of the Liberal Gift.
112. For an example of what would happen in their absence: Diefendorf 2016, 205.
113. Bowsky 1970, 71–76, 82–85, 305–08.
114. Bowsky 1970, 2–6.
115. Kent and Kent 1982, 24.
116. Herlihy and Klapisch-Zuber 1978, 26; Kent and Kent 1982, 25–26.
117. Herlihy and Klapisch-Zuber 1978, 78–85, 95–99, 630; also McLean 2005.

118. But six in France and the Dutch Republic, and four in the Swiss Confederacy.
119. In collecting the data I have received help from Andrea Gamberini, Christian Liddy, Laurie Nussdorfer, Andreas Rehberg and Giulio Sodano.

3 Economic Citizenship through the Guilds

1. Gent 1832, 11–12 (first quote), 66–67 (second quote). I owe this reference to Patrick Wallis.
2. Apprenticeship contracts usually contained a provision forbidding the apprentice to marry: J. Lane 1996, 195.
3. Gadd 2004, 40; see also Gadd and Wallis 2002a.
4. Pettegree 2010.
5. Blayney 2014, ch. 11; Gadd 2016.
6. Ward 1997; Gadd and Wallis 2002b, 1; Melling 2003; Berlin 2008.
7. Gadd and Wallis 2008.
8. Blayney 2014, 1024–25 (quote).
9. Schmid 1996; Lourens and Lucassen 2000; Dambruyne 2002, 184; Kluge 2007, 128–32; Sonkajärvi 2008, 50.
10. Wallis 2008, 234.
11. Prak 1996.
12. Greif 2006, ch. 4.
13. See the papers collected in Epstein and Prak 2008a, and especially the editors' 'Introduction' (2008b); also Davids and De Munck 2014; Wallis and Prak 2019.
14. Ogilvie 1997, 2007 and 2011 are the key works.
15. E.g. in Ogilvie and Carus 2013, 419.
16. Cf. Horn 2015, 38.
17. Rosser 2015, 8–9, 19–28.
18. Oexle 1981, 333–37, and 1985; S. A. Epstein 1991, ch. 1; Kluge 2007, 35–42; Schulz 2010, 40.
19. This definition excludes the companies created for non-European trade that emerged around 1600, because these had no members, but rather employed merchants, whose efforts led to one balance sheet total, whereas in guilds members worked for their own profit (or loss). It also excludes the Hanse, or Hansa, which was a league of towns rather than merchants. Lumping all of these together, as in Ogilvie's 2011 survey of the subject, ultimately creates unnecessary confusion.
20. Greif 2006, 121.
21. Dilcher 1996b, 11–14, 26.
22. Greif 2006 versus Ogilvie 2011.
23. Schmidt-Wiegand 1999, 8.
24. Gelderblom 2013, 172–73.
25. Gelderblom and Grafe 2010; also Gelderblom 2013.
26. Lindberg 2009; Gelderblom, de Jong and Jonker 2013; Petram 2014.
27. For terminology Schmidt-Wiegand 1999; Heusinger 2010, 39; Dumolyn 2014, 17–18; Rosser 2015, 3–6.
28. Landes 1983.
29. De Vries 2008, 1–3.
30. Turner 2008, 267, 269–70; for shipbuilding: Unger 1978, chs 2, 5 and 6.
31. Pfister 2008a; but critical remarks in Davids and De Munck 2014, 8.
32. Berlin 2008.
33. Haupt 2002; for France also Bossenga 1991 and S. Kaplan 2001.

34. Rommes 1998, 143; Slokker 2010, 55.
35. Prak 1999, 91.
36. Walker 1971, 85; Farr 1988, 22; Roper 1989, 137.
37. Hovland 2006, 151–52, 168, 172.
38. The following was compiled from the documents collected in Overvoorde and Joosting 1896–97 and N. Heuvel 1946; see also Dijkman, Moll-Murata and Prak 2014.
39. Davids 2007, 67–68.
40. Cerutti 1990, 167; De Munck 2007, 165; Humphries 2010, 273; Heusinger 2016, 168, 170; Prak et al. 2018.
41. S. Kaplan 1993, 439–40.
42. Epstein and Prak 2008b, 5–7.
43. Thunder 2004; Davids 2007, 75–77; De Munck and Soly 2007, 6–8; P. Smith 2010.
44. Rappaport 1989, 232; also Humphries 2003, 79, and Wallis 2008, 832.
45. Minns and Wallis 2012, 559.
46. Dambruyne 2002, 756.
47. McCants 1997, 82; Davids 2007, 72–75; Nederveen Meerkerk 2007, 261–72; Schalk 2014, 10.
48. Lanz 1995, 41.
49. Kluge 2007, 174–98; Reith 2008.
50. Wesoly 1985, 263–71, 405–06.
51. Bruyn 1991; also Goosens 2001, 79–81, 85–86; De Kerf 2013, 23–49.
52. S. R. Epstein 2004.
53. Fairchilds 1993; Jardine 1996; de Vries 2008.
54. Baten and Van Zanden 2008.
55. R. C. Allen 2009, ch. 10; also Humphries 2010, ch. 9.
56. Humphries 2010, ch. 9.
57. De Munck 2007, 74–81.
58. De Munck 2008, 216–17; Caracausi 2017, 405–12, disagrees.
59. Hesselink 1999, 143; Prak 2008, 164.
60. Mocarelli 2008, 165 (table 2); De Munck, Lourens and Lucassen 2006, 39 (table 2.2), 65; also Unger and Van Waarden 1999, 446–60, for the theoretical argument.
61. Broadberry et al. 2015, 139 (table 4.03).
62. Wrigley 1967; Berlin 1997, 77; Gadd and Wallis 2008, 314.
63. Cf. Persson 1988, 51–53, and Gelderblom 2013, 199.
64. Laborda-Peman 2017, ch. 2.
65. Wiesner 1996, 98–99.
66. This section contains the edited text of a paper that I wrote together with Clare Crowston (Illinois), Christopher Kissane (LSE), Chris Minns (LSE) and Patrick Wallis (LSE), and their contributions, as well as permission to use those, are gratefully acknowledged. The research was funded by the EU under the FP7 programme, under grant 320294.
67. Kluge 2007, 230, 233.
68. Wallis et al. 2015, table 2; also De Munck 2011, 230–32.
69. Stuart 2006; also Walker 1971, 73–77, 85, 89–91, 102–06; Roper 1989, 38, 136–39.
70. Farr 1988, 22–23.
71. Prak 2002.
72. Minns and Wallis 2013, 342.
73. Wallis et al. 2015.

74. For a fuller discussion, see Prak et al. 2018.
75. Shephard 1986, 177; Ehmer 1997, 172, 187.
76. S. Kaplan 1988; Hoffmann 2007.
77. De Munck and Davids 2014.
78. Dambruyne 1998.
79. Ogilvie 1997.
80. Krey 1985, 40–41; Rappaport 1998, 184–201.
81. Reynolds 2002, 68, 75; Soly 2008.
82. De Vries 1984, 179–97.
83. D. W. Allen 2012, ch. 2.
84. This section contains a modified version of Prak 2004, 189–93.
85. The process was, however, already under way before Luther: Herlihy 1990, ch. 7; see also Hafter 2007, 37–41.
86. Panhuysen 2000, 206.
87. Quast 1980, 30.
88. E.g. Bennett 1996, 63–64.
89. Panhuysen 2000, 206.
90. Ward 1997, 128.
91. Wiesner 1986, 126.
92. Howell 1986a, 88–89; Honeyman and Goodman 1991, 610–12; Wiesner 1993, 103.
93. Monter 1980, 203.
94. General discussion in Honeyman and Goodman 1991 and Crowston 2008.
95. Howell 1986a, 89–90, 133, 137; also Howell 1986b.
96. Wiesner 1989.
97. Quataert 1985.
98. Quataert 1985, 1133.
99. Roper 1989, 31.
100. Snell 1985, 279–82.
101. Krausman Ben-Amos 1991, 229–30, 234; 1994, 135.
102. Ogilvie 2003, 97.
103. Hafter 1995, 48–57.
104. Ward 1997, 131, 142.
105. Vanja 1992, 463; Musgrave 1997; Werkstetter 2001, 466–71; Crowston 2008, 28–30; Fridrich 2013, 146–47; González Athenas 2013, 153, 165, and 2016; Ojala 2016; Rivière 2016, 106–08; for the opposite view D. Heuvel 2013, and Heuvel and Ogilvie 2013.
106. A. Schmidt 2009, 179.
107. Wensky 1982; Coffin 1994, 774.
108. Crowston 2000, and 2001, ch. 4; see also Coffin 1994; Truant 1995; Musgrave 1997; Hafter 2007; and Horn 2015, 225–26.
109. Gemeentearchief Dordrecht, Archive 16, 14.5, Resoluties Lakenkopersgilde, 14 January 1784.
110. Oexle 1981, 298, 301–02.
111. S. Kaplan 1996, 162.
112. Farr 1988, 18, 30.
113. Panhuysen 2000, 52–60.
114. Deceulaer 2001, 353; also Dambruyne 1998, 54–62.
115. I. Archer 1991, 104–07.
116. Hafter 2007, 96.
117. I. Archer 1991, 116; Woodward 1995, 33; Rosser 2015, 122–24.
118. Kluge 2007, 354.

119. Broadhead 1996, 582–83; Kluge 2007, 342–43.
120. Gemeentearchief Arnhem, Oud-archief Arnhem, gedeponeerde archieven, Resoluties bakkers- en brouwersgilde 1478, fol. 63r and various dates; 1517, various dates.
121. S. Kaplan 2001, 112; also S. Kaplan 1986, and Hafter 2007, 31–35.
122. S. Kaplan 1996, 177.
123. Dambruyne 2006, 203; De Munck and Davids 2014, 198.
124. A. Black 2003, 4 (quote); also Dilcher 1985, 102–07; Schmidt-Wiegand 1985, 43; Rosser 1997 and 2015, 58–60; S. R. Epstein 2006, 243–44; Najemy 2006, 41–42.
125. Schreiner 1996.
126. Kluge 2007, 306–07.
127. Such claims are discussed in Prak 1996; also Corteguera 2002, 34–38.
128. Wyffels 1951, 23–32, 143; Isenmann 2012, 252–63; More on this in Chapter 2.
129. Boone 1994, 35; also Prak 2006, 76–77, and Boone 2010a, 67–73.
130. Coornaert 1968, 87–88.
131. Eitel 1970, 18–22 (quote p. 20); also Oelze 2009.
132. Steensel 2016, 50–54.
133. Naujoks 1985.
134. More on this topic in Chapter 6.
135. Bernouli 1918, 120–22, 125.
136. Blömker 1931, 48, 52–53, 78–81.
137. Kraus 1980, 109.
138. Taverne 1972, 58–59.
139. Vos 2007, 170–81.
140. Mackenney 1987, ch. 2.
141. Farr 2000, 228–35; Thijs 2006, 158–59; Kluge 2007, 313–15; Rosser 2015.
142. Taverne 1972, 59–62; Goudriaan 1996; Kluge 2007, 315–16; Rosser 2015, 131–33.
143. Thijs 2006, 165–70.
144. Broadhead 1996.
145. Farr 1985, 203–14.
146. M. Leeuwen 2012b, 63, and 2016, 82.
147. National surveys in Fröhlich 1976 (Germany) and Bos 1998 (Netherlands).
148. Rappaport 1989, 195; see also City of London Livery Companies Commission, *City of London Livery Companies Commission. Report: Volume 4* (London, 1884), British History Online, www.british-history.ac.uk/livery-companies-commission/vol 4 (accessed 14 October 2016).
149. I. Archer 2002b, 18
150. Woodward 1995, 82.
151. Deceulaer 2001, 364–65.
152. Assante 1998, 428.
153. Farr 2000, 230–31; Masure 2017, 117.
154. Rommes and Van der Spek 2004, 27–28, 97.
155. Slokker 2010, 172, 174–75; also Bos 1998, ch. 4, and 2006.
156. Gent 1832, 12.
157. E.g. in France: Sewell 1980, but also Hunt and Sheridan 1986; for England and Germany: Lenger 1991, Hoogenboom et al. 2018.
158. Crouch 1993, ch. 10; Hoogenboom et al. 2017.
159. Waarden 1992.
160. Cf. Pierson 2004, 175–76.
161. Pfister 2008b, 27, 50, argues they might be considered a 'functional substitute'.
162. S. Kaplan 1996, chs 18–19; de Vries 2009.
163. Lis and Soly 1994; Truant 1994, esp. ch. 4.

164. Mokyr 2017, 123.
165. Ogilvie 1997, 2003 and 2007.
166. S. R. Epstein 1998, 698.

4 Welfare and the Civic Community

1. Henderson 1994, 42, 196, 198–99, 202–09, 254, 260; on Italian confraternities: Terpstra 2000.
2. Lindert 2004, ch. 10.
3. Davids 1985, 150; Kuijpers 2005, 131–38, 293–309; Lucassen 2012, 224–29.
4. M. Leeuwen 2000, 74.
5. M. Leeuwen 1994.
6. Lynch 2003, chs 3–5, and 2010.
7. Lindemann 1990, 52, 122, 140.
8. Lindemann 1990, 17, 22, 83–84, 111, 137–42, 148, 158–60, 165–68, 177–80; also Lindemann 2010.
9. There was, perhaps, more continuity in the ideas about charity: Mollat 1978, 31.
10. Brodman 1998, 50–52.
11. Mollat 1978, 165; possibly only in the fourteenth or even the fifteenth century in South-East Europe: Miljan and Škreblin 2017, 104.
12. Mundy 1966.
13. Rubin 1987, 99–101, 111–13, 119–20, 127–28; quote at 107.
14. McIntosh 2011, 69–71.
15. Blockmans and Prevenier 1978, 44–52.
16. Rijpma 2012, 42.
17. Prak 1994a, 150–51.
18. Gutton 1970, 266–79; Tingle 2006, 535–36, 539–40.
19. Hanschmidt 2000, 226, 232–37, 240, and 2002, 28 (quote), 73, 87; also Küster 1995, 23–28.
20. Brodie 2012, 110, 114–15, 126–27.
21. Lis and Soly 1979, 87–89; Mitchison 1991, ch. 1; Junot 2000.
22. Pullan 1988, 180; Flynn 1989, 91–92; Jütte 1994, 104, 108; Terpstra 1994, 119; Cavallo 1995, 25, 32; Fehler 1999, 71–72; Klein 2001, 356–57.
23. Grell and Cunningham 1997.
24. Lis and Soly 1979 versus de Vries 1981. On proletarianisation, also Bavel 2007.
25. Cavallo 1995, 21.
26. Cavallo 1995, 127–40; also Spierenburg 1991, 87–88; Kevorkian 2000, 168.
27. See also Foucault 1975, ch. II.1.
28. Gutton 1970, 295–303, 326ff.
29. Spierenburg 1991, ch. 3.
30. Slack 1988, 195–200 (quote at 196); Lees 1998, 61–64.
31. Spierenburg 1991, ch. 3.
32. Brodman 1998, 188–201.
33. Mackenney 1987, 244–52.
34. Pullan 1971, 33–34, 64, 84–86, 88; Mackenney 1987, ch. 2; d'Andrea 2013.
35. Mackenney 1987, 61–64; for Bologna: Terpstra 1995, 3, 93, 96–97, 101, 116, 123; for Milan and Paris: Garrioch 2017.
36. Fehler 1999, 32, 37–38, 41–43, 90, 93–94, 97, 101–07, 273.
37. Rosser 2015, 50.
38. Bogaers 2008, 431–32, 435, 481.
39. B. Kaplan 2000, 102, 104, 105.

40. Cunningham 2005, 3–4; but see also the discussion in King 2011, 49–53.
41. Broomhall 2012, 137–39, 145 (quote).
42. For France: Hickey 1997, 102, 107, 109; Goudot 2015, 489; Diefendorf 2016, 206.
43. Dross 2002, 74.
44. Pullan 1971, 375.
45. Lees 1998, 44–46.
46. This is the thesis of Lis and Soly 1979.
47. Patriquin 2007; Teeuwen 2010, 56–57; Allegra 2015, 169–72.
48. Kuijpers 2005, ch. 6, esp. 278–83.
49. Milanovic, Lindert and Williamson 2011, 266; Soltow and Van Zanden 1998, 52–54, 105, 193; Alfani 2015; Ryckbosch 2016; Alfani and Ryckbosch 2016.
50. Jütte 1994, 54 (table 6).
51. Martz 1983, 202.
52. Martz 1983, 204, 208, 211, 214; for Florence, Henderson 1994, 260.
53. I. Archer 1991, 153.
54. I. Archer 1991, 183.
55. Wijngaarden 2000, 40, 86, 88, 93, 155, 158.
56. Vlis 2001, 64, 76, 188.
57. Pot 1994, 204.
58. Pot 1994, 256, 258; compare Prak 1993b, 31.
59. Vlis 2001, 188 (table 11).
60. Roche 1987, 205.
61. Fairchilds 1976, 75–78.
62. Gutton 1970, 44.
63. Jütte 1994, 41–42.
64. Fehler 1999, 81, 122, 126, 129, 134, 144, 172, 177, 182, 186.
65. Lindemann 2010; Lynch 2010.
66. Vlis 2001, 326–40.
67. Slack 1988, 118, 122–26, 149–56, 170–71.
68. Ladewig Petersen 1997, 156.
69. Prak 1994a.
70. Gutton 1970, 276.
71. Bekkers and Wiepking 2011, 930–42.
72. Heerma van Voss and Van Leeuwen 2012, 182.
73. Teeuwen 2012.
74. Spaans 1996, 387–90.
75. M. Leeuwen 1996, 140–41; more on Dutch collections in Teeuwen 2012, and in Nederveen Meerkerk 2012, 250.
76. Pullan 1971, 84–85; Henderson 1994, 198–201, 256–60.
77. Krausman Ben-Amos 2008, 85–89; also Tomkins 2006, ch. 3.
78. Cullum and Goldberg 1993, 28–29.
79. M. Leeuwen 1996, 140.
80. Nederveen Meerkerk 2012, 252.
81. Fairchilds 1976, 56.
82. Fairchilds 1976, 42; Nederveen Meerkerk 2012, 260.
83. M. Leeuwen 2000, 96.
84. Teeuwen 2012, 282–85.
85. Cullum and Goldberg 1993, 30, 32.
86. Looijesteijn 2012, 207–10.
87. Cavallo 1995, 134–39.
88. Vives 2002, 94–109 (book ii, ii–iii); also Michielse 1990, 6–10.

89. Flynn 1989, 16–17, 25, 33.
90. C. F. Black 1989, 39.
91. M. Leeuwen 2012b, 63.
92. Bos 1998, 172.
93. Hadwin 1978, 117; Slack 1988, 170–72.
94. I. Archer 2002a, 238–43.
95. Teeuwen 2015, 158.
96. Bavel and Rijpma 2016.
97. Lindert 2004, 12–13 (table 1.2).
98. Compare Lindert 2004, ch. 12.
99. Nederveen Meerkerk and Vermeesch 2009, 138–43; also Prak 1998.
100. Cf. Lees 1998, 73–81.
101. King 2011, 60–62.

5 Citizens, Soldiers and Civic Militias

* This chapter was published as 'Citizens, soldiers and civic militias in late medieval and early modern Europe', *Past & Present* 288 (2015), 93–123. Thanks are due to the editors of *P&P* for their comments.

1. Haverkamp-Begemann 1982.
2. On these so-called militia pieces Carasso-Kok and Levy-Van Halm 1988.
3. Haverkamp-Begemann 1982, 93–101. See also Dixhoorn 2009; Dixhoorn and Speakman Sutch 2008.
4. Carasso-Kok and Levy-Van Halm 1988, 390–95.
5. Bean 1973; Tilly 1975b, 42.
6. Tilly 1975a, 1985 and 1990; other works using this perspective include Downing 1992, 239; Ertman 1997, 317; Jer. Black 1999, 209; Gunn 1999, 115; Glete 2002, 214–15; Pettegree 2002, 315; Greengrass, 2006, 78–81.
7. Tallett and Trim 2010. Core works include G. Parker 1988; Jer. Black 1991 and 2002; Tallett 1992; Rogers 1995a; Hammer 2007.
8. M. Roberts 1956.
9. On the reforms introduced in the wake of the French Revolution: Hippler 2008.
10. For the related but nonetheless different issue of interactions between citizens and (professional) soldiers, see Withington 2008 and 2011; also Vermeesch 2006; Hart 2014, ch. 4.
11. Skocpol 1995 argues that the American welfare state was designed to compensate citizen-soldiers for their contributions in fighting World War II; also Chapter 11 in this book.
12. Bayley 1961 240–67; Mallett 1990, 173–80.
13. Quotes come from Machiavelli 1988. Machiavelli's *The Art of War* (transl. and ed. by Christopher Lynch, Chicago, IL: University of Chicago Press, 2003), at first sight perhaps more appropriate as a source, is really a book about strategy and tactics, rather than about the politics of citizen-soldiers. See also Caferro 1998; Maire Vigueur 2003; Grillo 2008.
14. Machiavelli 1988, xiii.
15. Pocock 1975, esp. ch. xii.
16. Harrington 1992, esp. 75–76.
17. Schwoerer 1974; Malcolm 1994.
18. Fletcher 1997. The main secondary source is Robertson 1985.
19. Fletcher 1997, 88, 111n38, 113.
20. Klein 1995, 78.

21. Capellen 1987; all quotes have been translated from this Dutch edition.
22. On the role of the Batavians in the Dutch Republic, Schöffer 1975.
23. Also Spits 1979.
24. Hirschman 1970.
25. Gelderen and Skinner 2002.
26. Boffa 2004, 133.
27. E.g. Blömker 1931, 78–79; Bowsky 1969, 11–12; Sauerbrey 1989, 55.
28. Waley 1968, 71–72; Ruiz 1977, 7–9; Verbruggen 1977, 128–29.
29. Boffa 2004, 139–46.
30. E.g. Powers 1988, 101.
31. Descimon 1990; for a hint of similar chains in London, see D. Allen 1972, 297.
32. Bowsky 1981, 127; B. Kaplan 1995, 125–32.
33. *Gilden van Utrecht* 1896, vol. 1, cciv, ccxvi–ccxvii.
34. Wyffels 1951, ch. IV; also Bernouli 1918, 120, 122.
35. Sauerbrey 1989, 41.
36. Heinzen 1939, 95.
37. The best study is Maire Vigueur 2003.
38. Verbruggen 1977, 125–26.
39. Verbruggen 1977, 126.
40. Rogers 1995b, 57–58.
41. Rogers 1995b, 59–63.
42. Gunn 2010.
43. Reintges 1963, 58–60.
44. Reintges 1963, 50–74.
45. Tlusty 2011, 189.
46. Stolz 1918, 158.
47. For Utrecht, see *Gilden van Utrecht* 1896, vol. 1, ccvii–ccviii, ccxi.
48. Roodenburg 1991; Spicer 1991; Tlusty 2011, ch. 5.
49. Reintges 1963, 299.
50. Waley 1968, 76.
51. Verbruggen 1977, 143.
52. Bernouli 1918, 129.
53. DeVries 2008.
54. Waley 1968, 76; Caferro 1998, ch. 1.
55. Verbruggen 1977, 117–19.
56. Gunn, Grummitt and Cools 2007, 20–23; Buylaert, Van Camp and Verwerft 2011, 150.
57. Corvisier 1979, 53–59; for Spain also MacKay 1999, and Ruiz Ibáñez 2009, part I; France and Italy are also included in Brunet and Ruiz Ibáñez 2015.
58. Beckett 1991, 20, 23.
59. On German civic militias, see Tlusty 2011.
60. Kraus 1980, 76–88.
61. Kraus 1980, 77–78.
62. Kraus 1980, ch. 5.
63. Water 1729, 589: Ordonnantie ... voor de schutterij van de stad Utrecht, 1 June 1611.
64. Water 1729, 591.
65. On these small neighbourhoods Bogaers 1997.
66. Het Utrechts Archief (HUA), Stadsarchief (SA) II, 2078: Private notes by D. J. Martens as commanding officer of the Turkey district. See also HUA, SA II, 2064: 21–29 April 1747, 24 November 1747, 27 July 1751, 2 April 1753.

67. HUA, SA II, 2064: 28 February 1752; on refusing citizenship to Catholics, see also Prak 2002, 162–63.
68. Saupin 1996, ch. 5, 127–51, and 2006.
69. Beckett 1991,15.
70. Vowell 1919, 819.
71. Vowell 1919, 820.
72. Beckett 1991, 15.
73. Houston 1993, 42.
74. K. Roberts 1996, 95.
75. K. Roberts 1996, 96–97.
76. K. Roberts 1996, 106.
77. Knevel 1994, 253.
78. On the Holland towns, Knevel 1994; also Prak 1999, ch. 4.
79. Descimon 1987, 601; for George Washington's similar verdict, Bashir and Gray 2015, 317–18.
80. Water 1729, 597 (art. 14).
81. HUA, SA II, 2064: 17 April 1748.
82. Inhabitants per district are recorded on a separate sheet of paper, dated 10 July 1786, in a bound volume of correspondence of the Turkey Company: HUA. SA II: 2076; the number of men and non-commissioned officers, 1,597 and 96, respectively, in the records of the Turkey Company: HUA, SA II, 2075, 18 June 1784.
83. More numbers in Babeau 1884, 22, some of which look suspiciously high, however.
84. Bonin 2005, 250, 251n1.
85. Kraus 1980, 21, 124–26.
86. The names of the militiamen serving in May 1785 in the Turkey Company, under the command of D. J. Martens, were recorded in the accounts of the company: HUA, SA II, 2077. These were combined with a tax assessment from 1793, in HUA, SA II, 2051. I am grateful to Joost van der Spek for helping me collect these data.
87. Prak 1993a, 919–20.
88. Water 1729, 597 (art. 45).
89. See also Knevel 1994, 297–304.
90. HUA, SA II, 2077: Accounts of the Turkey Company, 14 May 1781.
91. Bergh-Hoogterp 1988.
92. HUA, SA II, 2075: 4 August 1784; see also 2064: 10 March 1788.
93. HUA, SA II, 2075: 15 October 1783, 3 February 1784.
94. Köhler and Levy-Van Halm 1990.
95. Water 1729, 589 (art. 16); HUA, SA II, 2075: 18 January 1784.
96. Western 1965, 256. For similar developments in eighteenth-century Geneva: Cicchini 2014.
97. MacCaffrey 1958; Stoyle 1996.
98. Devon Record Office, Exeter City Archives, Miscellaneous papers, box 3: 'Militiamen now serving . . . 28 February 1770'.
99. Devon Record Office, Exeter City Archives, Miscellaneous papers, box 3, 'A roll of the persons . . . 31 March 1768'.
100. 'Documentary Evidence for the Civil War Defences of Exeter, 1642-43', ed. by Mark Stoyle, Exeter Museums Archaeological Field Unit, Report No. 92.10, 1–2.
101. Stoyle 1996, 174.
102. 'Documentary Evidence', 4–8.
103. Hamon 2012, 281.
104. *Resoluties* 1986, 58.

105. Grayson 1980, 35–63, esp. 41, 45, 47 (quote).
106. As quoted in Lievense-Pelser 1979, 49; see also Junot 2015, 43–44.
107. On these reforms, see Knevel 1994, ch. 3.
108. For Amsterdam this process is discussed in detail in Prak 1995, 347–52.
109. HUA, SA II, 2075, fol. 1 (1783).
110. HUA, SA II, 2075, fol. 2 (February 1783).
111. Sas 1987, 21, 27, 34–36.
112. *Concept-Reglement op de Regeerings Bestelling van de Provintie Utrecht* (Utrecht, 1784), 29 (art X.I).
113. Descimon 1989.
114. Beik 1997, 79–84; Coste 2008, 184–85; Carpi 2015, 30.
115. Descimon 1993.
116. Descimon 1987, 604, and 1993, 901–04.
117. Nagel 1996, 71, 75, 79; Lindley 1997.
118. See Chapter 11.

6 Italian City-States and Their Citizens

1. Nevola 2007, 33–37.
2. Waley 1991, 26–35; Ascheri 2003, 14–18.
3. Hook 1979, 8; Ascheri 1992, 113–14.
4. Bowsky 1981, 23–24, 34–38.
5. Q. Skinner 1999; also Rubinstein 1958; Q. Skinner 1986; Nevola 2007, 5–10.
6. Bowsky 1981, 285–86; Waley 1991; Nevola 2007.
7. Bowsky 1981; Ascheri 2001.
8. Caferro 1998, ch. 2.
9. C. Shaw 2006, ch. 2, 39–55; see also Robertson 2002, chs 3–4.
10. Caferro 1998; also Fochesato 2013.
11. C. Shaw 2006, 94, 111, 121–25, 138, 140.
12. Wickham 2015, 4–5; helpful historiographical surveys in Coleman 1999, and Wickham 2015, 8–20.
13. As the topic of this chapter is city-states, the Papal State and southern Italy are ignored here. For urban relations with the state in Sicily: Titone 2009. For the development of the commune in Rome, Wickham 2015, ch. 4. The argument in this chapter has been inspired especially by S. R. Epstein 2000b.
14. Useful introductions to the culture of Renaissance Italy in Goldthwaite 1993; Nauert 1995; Welch 1997.
15. Zanden 2009, 40 (table 1); also Lachmann 2000, 50–51 (tables 3.1 and 3.2).
16. Malanima 2005,101–04, and 2011, 189; Pezzolo 2014; Broadberry et al. 2015, 375 (table 10.02).
17. For this latter point of view, see Putnam 1993, and the criticisms in Brucker 1999; Muir 1999; Eckstein and Terpstra 2009.
18. T. Scott 2012 discusses relations between cities and *contados* at length. See also Chittolini 1979a and 1994.
19. Chittolini 1979a; Wickham 1981, 80, 86–88; Dean 1988; Maire Vigueur 2003; Malanima 2005, 101.
20. This is the thesis of Wickham 2015; see also Dartmann 2012.
21. An astonishing number of dioceses dotted the Italian landscape; around 250 on the peninsula mainland alone. Almost every medium-sized Italian town had its own bishop who, moreover, was also politically in charge of the community where his see was located: Hay 1977, 10.

22. Keller 1976, 184, 190–94; Dartmann 2012, 63–76.
23. Wickham 2015, 23.
24. Dartmann 2008, 98–100.
25. This paragraph follows the story as related in Wickham 2015, ch. 2 (quotes on 23 and 26); see also Dartmann 2012, ch. 2.
26. Dilcher 1967, 48–50, 54, 69–70.
27. Berman 1983, 19, 215–21, ch. 12.
28. Reynolds 1997, 162–63, 173–80; also Keller 1988.
29. Communes were not exclusively urban, but because our interest is in urban citizenship and city-states I restrict the discussion to the urban commune nonetheless: Coleman 1999, 375.
30. S. A. Epstein 1996, 24–25, 33–37, 47–48, 61, 86; Wickham 2014, 40–44.
31. Campopiano 2014, 230.
32. Dilcher 1967, 129; Wickham 2015, ch. 3, and 2014, 36–40.
33. Wickham 1981, 172, 174, 181, 191; Tabacco 1989, 171–75.
34. Wickham 2015, 5; also Jones 1997, 103–51; S. R. Epstein 2000b, 280–83.
35. Maire Vigueur 2008, 209–12.
36. Coleman 2004, 29–31.
37. T. Scott 2012, 22–23; see also Hartmann 1993.
38. Raccagni 2010, 19–20, 25–26, 28, 35, 37, 41, 56, 57, 60.
39. Raccagni 2010, 55, 58, 81–82, 103, 105, 111, 119–21, 126, 129.
40. Verbruggen 1977, 126.
41. Waley 1968, 73, 76, 96–97; also Caferro 1998, xiii, 3.
42. S. R. Epstein 2000b, 277; Maire Vigueur 2003, 246; Scott 2012, 55, has a map showing the city-states that had formed by the thirteenth century.
43. Covini 2000, 10–11, 33.
44. Waley 1968, 74.
45. Martines 1983, ch. 7; Jones 1997, ch. 4, and 2010; Dean 2004; Jane Black 2010; Meek 2010.
46. Najemy 2006 is the best survey currently available; see also Lachmann 2000, ch. 3.
47. Waley 1968, 76; Najemy 2006, 63–71.
48. Najemy 2006, 72–87.
49. Najemy 1982, and 2006, chs 5–6.
50. Najemy 2006, 97–105, 112–17, 225, ch. 11; also Goldthwaite 1980 and 2009.
51. Herlihy 1958, ix, 36, 56–60, 154, 164.
52. F. Lane 1973, 97, 109.
53. Much attention has been paid to the creation of the myth of 'stability' by Renaissance elites, but it has not been rejected as false: Martin and Romano 2000, 2–7; Ferraro 2012, ch. 6; Knapton 2012, 139–41; Viggiano 2013, 69. Queller 1986 is an attack on the patriciate's reputation for righteousness, not on the stability thesis as such.
54. Cf. Mackenney 1987, 2.
55. F. Lane 1973, 95–98.
56. Chojnacki 1994, 345.
57. Ruggiero 1980, 64; Crouzet-Pavan 2002, 217; Pult Quaglia 2006, 109.
58. Burke 1994, 17.
59. Lane 1973, 106–07; Mackenney 1987, 3.
60. Romano 1987, 165n38 and ch. 4; Mackenney 1987, 10 and ch. 2.
61. Pullan 1971, 99.
62. Romano 1987, 123.
63. Bellavitis 2001, 65, and 2015; also Pullan 1971, 99–111.

64. Vivo 2007, ch. 3.
65. Rösch 2000, 77, 80; also Chojnacki 1973, and Ruggiero 1980, 56–58.
66. Chojnacki 1994.
67. Burke 1994, 12.
68. Pullan 1971, 99–107; Bellavitis 2001, chs 1–3.
69. Finlay 1980, 45–47; Grubb 2000; Bellavitis 2001, ch. 3.
70. F. Lane 1973, ch. 18; Finlay 1980, 58; Ruggiero 1980, ch. 5; Crouzet-Pavan 2002, ch. 5; Ferraro 2012, ch. 3; Queller 1986, however, disagrees.
71. Chittolini 1979a, introduction; T. Scott 2012, 24–28, 32, 43.
72. Law 1992, 161–66; Chittolini 1994, 35–36; Isaacs 1997, 299–304.
73. Chittolini 1979a, 7–11; S. R. Epstein 2000b, 284; T. Scott 2012, 31–32; also Bowsky 1972, 229–32; Martines 1972; Tabacco 1989, 222–36, 267. Contemporaries worried about this aspect: Pocock 1975, 111, 185, 194, 265, 301.
74. Meek 1978, 183–84, 267–72.
75. Lantschner 2015, 96.
76. Caferro 1998, 3, 15, 19–20, 135–36, 156–57; also Somaini 2012, 246–47.
77. See Chapter 5; also Mallett 2006, and Mallett and Shaw 2012.
78. Caferro 1998; Mallett and Shaw 2012, 290–96.
79. Frantianni and Spinelli 2006; also Tracy 2003, 20–22; Chilosi 2014.
80. Hale 1977, 20; also Molho 1995, Connell and Zorzi 2000 and Najemy 2006, 255–56, 262, 266.
81. Guicciardini 1994, 63; C. Shaw 2006, 249; also Pocock 1975, ch. 8.
82. Green 1986, 53–56, 62, 69, 78, 80–88, 118, 201.
83. Green 1995, chs 1–3.
84. Meek 1978 and 1980; Bratchel 1995; T. Scott 2012, 108–11.
85. Hale 1977, 42–43, 73.
86. Najemy 2006, 434–44, and ch. 15; also Stephens 1983; Tanzini 2012.
87. Najemy 2006, 238–39.
88. For early discussions, Fasano Guarini 1978; Chittolini 1979a and 1979b; see also Litchfield 1986; Fasano 2013.
89. Jones 1997, 51–67, 79–92; also Chittolini 1994, 30–31.
90. Malanima 2011, 188–89.
91. De Long and Shleifer 1993, 695–96.
92. Bosker et al. 2008, 122.
93. Percoco 2014, 71–72.
94. Stasavage 2014, 338–39. The author claims that the cut-off was after 100 years, but with the next data point another 100 years away it would seem more correct to say 100–200 years.
95. Putnam 1993, ch. 5; also Sodano 2013, 123–26; Percoco 2014.

7 The Dutch Republic

1. Felix 1919.
2. Document summarising the citizens' demands, reprinted in Felix 1919, iv.
3. Felix 1919, ix.
4. B. Kaplan 1995, 119.
5. B. Kaplan 1995, 135.
6. For similar militia rebellions, see Knevel 1988.
7. This chapter contains materials previously published in Boone and Prak 1995, in Prak 2000a, 2006, in Zanden and Prak 2006 and in Prak and Van Zanden 2009.
8. For a survey: Prak 2005.

9. Zanden and Van Leeuwen 2012; Broadberry et al. 2015, 375; also de Vries and Van der Woude 1997.
10. Zanden and Van Leeuwen 2012, 136.
11. Nimwegen 2006, 54.
12. See later in this chapter.
13. Surveys in Nicholas 1992; Blockmans and Prevenier 1999; Blockmans 2010b; Van Bruaene, Blondé and Boone 2016.
14. Gelderblom 2013, ch. 2.
15. Trio, Heirbaut and Van den Auweele 2002; Dumolyn and Haemers 2005, 374–75; also Boone 2010a, ch. 2.
16. Wyffels 1951, 24–31.
17. Dumolyn 1997, 105–07.
18. Boone 1990, 35, 47 and *passim*, and 1994.
19. Van Uytven 1980, 219.
20. Wyffels 1951, 29; Favresse 1961, 150–52.
21. N. Heuvel 1946, 21–22.
22. Marnef 1987, 51.
23. Wyffels 1951, 30–31.
24. Overvoorde and Joosting 1896–97, vol. I, n° 109 (1304), and n° 111 (1341); Vijlbrief 1950, 27.
25. Blockmans and Prevenier 1999, ch. 5.
26. Boone 1996, 19; also Dumolyn 1997; Haemers 2004; Arnade 2008, 14–16, 27, 34, and 2013; Blockmans 2010b, 480–95.
27. Haemers 2009, 12–14, and ch. 3.
28. Dumolyn and Haemers 2005, 381; Blockmans 2010b, 520–30.
29. For the continuities with earlier waves of rebellion: Boone and Prak 1995, 111–13; Boone 2007 and 2010b.
30. Dambruyne 2002, 137–38.
31. Marnef 1987 and 2001; Dambruyne 2002, 644–77; Weis 2010.
32. Hibben 1983, ch. 2.
33. G. Parker 1979, 141–42, 178; also G. Parker 2004, ch. 8; Arnade 2008, ch. 6.
34. Groenveld and Leeuwenberg 1979.
35. Bruin 1979; Tracy 2008, 289–95.
36. Quoted from Bruin 1991, 129.
37. Prak 2005, ch. 11.
38. Prak 1993a, 923–27, and 1997, 404–09; Rommes 1998, 44; Kuijpers and Prak 2002, 124–30; Minns et al. 2014.
39. Streng 1997, 112n106.
40. Hooft 1871–1925, I-216.
41. Rowen 1978, 188.
42. Hooft 1871–1925, II-8.
43. Prak 1991b, 78, with further references.
44. Skocpol 1979, 24, 110, 285.
45. The ideas inspiring the rebels are discussed in Gelderen 1992.
46. Tracy 1990, ch. 1; Kokken 1991, ch. 1.
47. Tracy 1985 and 1990; Zuijderduijn 2009.
48. Koopmans 1990.
49. Price 1994.
50. Hart 1994.
51. Aalbers 1980, 117.
52. Aalbers 1980, 66–81; Groenveld 1990.

53. de Vries 1978, ch. 2; Hart 1994 and 1995.
54. Rowen 1972, 70; the original text of the Union of Utrecht has been published in Groenveld and Leeuwenberg 1979.
55. W. Temple 1972 [1673], 52.
56. Montesquieu 1951 [1748], 370; also Masterson 1975.
57. Grever 1981 and 1982; Bruin 1991, chs 8–9.
58. Mörke 1997, 37–42.
59. Hooft 1925, 7.
60. Prak 1989; Mörke 1997.
61. Aalbers 1980; Hovy 1980.
62. Aalbers, 1977, 92.
63. Israel 1989, 410–13 and *passim*; Adams 2005; Hart 1993a and 2014; see also numerous case studies in Lesger and Noordegraaf 1999.
64. Bruijn 1993, chs 6–7; Hart 2014, ch. 6.
65. Prak 2005, ch. 7.
66. Israel 1979.
67. Hovy 1966, ch. 2 and *passim.*
68. Zanden and Prak 2006, 130.
69. Hart 1993b, 86. For a brief introduction, see Hart 1997.
70. Zwitser 1991, ch. 4; Israel 1995, 286–87.
71. Fritschy 2003.
72. Janssens 1974.
73. Fritschy 2003, 63, 83; Tracy 2008, 44, 249.
74. Dekker 1982, 28–29.
75. Geyl 1936; Jongste 1984, chs 5–6; Prak 1991a.
76. Official resolution by the States of Holland on 17 March 1742: *Groot-Placaetboeck, Vervattende de Placaten, Ordonnantien ende Edicten van de Hoogh Mogende Herren Staten Generael der Verenighde Nederlanden ende Van de Ed, Groot mog. Heeren Staten van Hollandt ende West-Vrieslandt; midtsgaders van de Ed. Mog. Heeren Staten van Zeelandt* vol. 7 (1770), pp. 1131–35.
77. Official resolution by the States of Holland on 17 March 1742: *Groot-Placaetboeck, Vervattende de Placaten, Ordonnantien ende Edicten van de Hoogh Mogende Herren Staten Generael der Verenighde Nederlanden ende Van de Ed, Groot mog. Heeren Staten van Hollandt ende West-Vrieslandt; midtsgaders van de Ed. Mog. Heeren Staten van Zeelandt* vol. 7 (1770), pp. 1131–35.
78. Maanen 1978, 8.
79. Their 'middling' station is described in Pot 1988.
80. Gemeentearchief Leiden (GALeiden), Stadsarchief II (SA II), 4038: Introduction Personal Levy 1742: report 15 January 1743.
81. Gemeentearchief Leiden (GALeiden), Stadsarchief II (SA II), 4038: Introduction Personal Levy 1742: advice from the pensionary to the mayors, 9 June 1745.
82. GALeiden, SA II, 4070: Records of the commission.
83. GALeiden, SA II, 4072–73: Copies of letters sent by the commission.
84. Prak 1991a.
85. GALeiden, SA II, 4088: Records of the taxation commission; the quoted phrase was used on 12 February 1749. The fruits of their labour have been analysed in Diederiks, Noordam and Tjalsma 1985.
86. GALeiden, SA II, 4151: Complaints; see files of the widow of Anthony Sival, Marijtje Maas and Japick Ziera.
87. Spanninga 2012, 182 (quote), 201, 287.

88. For the source of the quote and a further analysis of this document, Prak 1991b, 90–91, and Prak 1999, 193–95.

8 Citizenship in England

1. *York Civic Records*, vol. 1: 103–05.
2. *York Civic Records*, vol. 2: 97–99.
3. *York Civic Records*, vol. 2: 191–93 (quote on p. 191); vol. 3: 1–2.
4. Withington 2005, 65.
5. Withington 2001, 133, 149.
6. Zanden, Buringh and Bosker 2012, 841–42; see also Cohn 2013, part II and 320–21.
7. North and Weingast 1989.
8. The title for this section was borrowed from Borsay 1989.
9. De Vries 1984, 39 (table 3.7), 64 (table 4.9); also Clark 2000a.
10. Dyer 2000, 433–34.
11. Langton 2000, 463.
12. Wrigley 1985.
13. Broadberry et al. 2015, 208 (table 5.07), 375–76 (table 10.02).
14. Harris 2013, 43; Withington 2017.
15. Reynolds 1977, 94–99, 102–03.
16. Reynolds 1977, 123–24; see also Liddy 2017, ch. 2.
17. Palliser 1997, 88–92; another example in Gauci 1996, 21.
18. D. G. Shaw 1993, 44, 109–35, 142, 157, 164–65.
19. Rosser 1989, 235–37 (quote on p. 235).
20. Palliser 1997, 89–90.
21. Rigby and Ewan 2000, 293.
22. Liddy 2005, 38–41.
23. Barron 1981 and 2004, chs 1–2.
24. Zagorin 1969, 120.
25. Withington 2005, 19.
26. Part of what was once known as the 'Tudor revolution in government': Coleman and Starkey 1986. See also Hindle 2000, 4–13.
27. Eastwood 1997, 12.
28. Tittler 1998, 148, 151, 155, 161–63.
29. Dyer 1973, 192–93.
30. MacCaffrey 1958, 27.
31. Withington 2005, 38–39.
32. Braddick 2000, 19 (quote), also 90: 'The state was a coordinated network of agencies exercising political power'.
33. Wilson 1995, ch. 7.
34. Kishlansky 1986, 31–37.
35. Evans 1974, 46–49, and 67, with further references; Tittler 1998, 182, ch. 10.
36. Brittnell 1986, 118–19, 127, 218–21, 227.
37. Gauci 1996, 27–33.
38. Jack 1996, 77–78.
39. Clark 1984, 336–37; Gauci 1996, 32–40.
40. Barry 1994; Withington 2005, 52–53.
41. Sacks 1991, 7.

42. Patterson 1999, 17–24, 32, 43, 59, 75–76, 164–79. For Exeter and the earls of Bedford: MacCaffrey 1958, 205–10. Worcester did not seek aristocratic patronage and was an exception in this: Dyer 1973, 213–15.
43. Withington 2001, 129, uses the term 'civic republicanism'.
44. Barry 2000; Withington 2005, 58, and ch. 3.
45. Sweet 1998, 92–95; Withington 2007, 1032.
46. Gauci 1996, 24–26.
47. Barry 2000, 181 (quote), 184.
48. D. Scott 1992, 49–50, 53, 58.
49. Sacks 1992, 108–13, 117.
50. Roy 1992, 138, 158.
51. Pearl 1961, 69–70.
52. Brenner 1993, 668–69.
53. Zagorin 1969, 132–34.
54. Zagorin 1969, 137–40.
55. Pearl 1961, 13–22, 43–44; Ashton 1979, 165–66, 209.
56. Lindley 1997, 10, 15, 102, 104, 139–42, 166–67, 169–72, 182–85, 201–02.
57. Carlin 1994.
58. Evans 1979, 227–28.
59. Halliday 1998, 58–80, 91, 95.
60. Gauci 1996, 63.
61. Evans 1979, 239.
62. Halliday 1998, 26, 150–62.
63. Halliday 1998, 192, 212, 224–26, 234–36.
64. Levin 1969, 2 (quote), 29, 50–57, 89–90, and *passim*.
65. Pincus 2009, 157–60.
66. Halliday 1998, 238–39, 244–49. Levin 1969, Appendix A, offers a complete list of all new charters issued in 1680–88.
67. Levin 1969, 93.
68. Knights 1997, 1169.
69. Barry 2000, 184; Withington 2005, 38–39; Borsay 2009, 129.
70. Gauci 2001, 199, 203, 212, 215; Beckett 2014, 40–41.
71. On the pre-1689 foundations: Brewer 1989, ch. 1; O'Brien 2014, 362–66.
72. North and Weingast 1989; Clark 1998; also Beckett 2014, 37–39, 47–55.
73. Stasavage 2003, 74, 78.
74. Hoppit 2002, 269, 279.
75. Sweet 1999, 64–67.
76. Gauci 1996, 262; Halliday 1998, 301–03, 306, 321.
77. Eastwood 1997, ch. 3.
78. Borsay 1989.
79. Rodgers 1989, 230; Wilson 1995, 9.
80. Wilson 1995, 32, 37, 297.
81. For the earlier period Rosser 2015, 50.
82. Clark 2000a, 26, 58, 60, 64, 76, 128.
83. Withington 2010, 110–11.
84. Kishlansky 1986, ch. 8, 226.
85. Carruthers 1996, 41, 46.
86. Rodgers 1989, 288, 298; Sweet 1999, 121.
87. Gauci 1996, 193–94; Sweet 1999, 60.
88. Gauci 1996, 250–52.
89. Rodgers 1989, 240–41; Beckett 2014, 42.

90. Sweet 1999, 39.
91. Broadberry et al. 2015, 406–13.
92. Stasavage 2003, 111.
93. Rodgers 1989, 29, 35, 127–28, 142–46.
94. Hoppit 2000, 410.
95. Knights 2005, ch. 7. Plumb 1973 saw one-party rule as a source of stability; S. Taylor 2013, 277, identifies this as a major weakness in Plumb's argument.
96. Chevalier 1988.
97. Parliament sat for twenty weeks during 1680–88, and for 53.5 months from 1689 to 1697: Beckett 2014, 39; Zanden, Buringh and Bosker 2012, 844.
98. Pincus and Robinson 2010, 16–18.
99. Bogart 2011.
100. Hoppit 1996, 121 (table 5).
101. Stasavage 2003, chs 4–5; Gauci 2011.
102. Broadberry et al. 2015, 204–05 (tables 5.05 and 5.06).
103. Zahedieh 2010, 35–54.
104. Brenner 1993, chs 2–3 and *passim*; Ormrod 2003, ch. 10; Gauci 2001, ch. 5.
105. R. C. Allen 2009; Mokyr 2009; see also Beckett 2014.

9 Cities and States in Continental Europe

1. T. Scott 2012, 156, 158, 162 and *passim*.
2. G. Schmidt 1984, 200–04 (quote at 200).
3. Blockmans 2008, 49; for Charles' politics, see also Soly 1999 and Tracy 2002.
4. Stollberg-Rilinger 2008, 305 and *passim*.
5. For a comparison with the Lombard League in Italy: Maurer 1987.
6. Buschmann 1987; Bönnen 2006; Distler 2006, 8–9, 105–06; Schilp 2009; Schulz 2009.
7. Distler 2006, 105.
8. Schildhauer 1975, 151; Dilcher 1987, 242.
9. Distler 2006, 117, 130, 135–38, 157; also Engel 1975.
10. Distler 2006, 181–201, 208.
11. Bader and Dilcher 1999, 411–26; also Isenmann 2012, ch. 3.
12. For an intimate and memorable view of life in early modern small-town Germany: Walker 1971, chs 1–4.
13. The numbers come from Johanek 2000, 296, and Hafner 2001, 15.
14. Walker 1971, 20.
15. Brady 1985, 11; Johanek 2000, 299; Close 2009, 23; also Forsén 2002.
16. Johanek 2000, 296–97.
17. For other south German imperial cities, Hafner 2001.
18. Kraus 1980, 99, 183; Roeck 1989, 210–15; Möller 1998, 22–28; also Rogge 1996 for the late Middle Ages.
19. Quoted in Isenmann 1979, 9; also G. Schmidt 1984, 264.
20. Schildhauer 1975, 156; also Distler 2006, 38–45; Hammel-Kiesow 2015, 63.
21. Laufs 1971, ch. 2; Isenmann 2012, 319–25.
22. Isenmann 1979, 14; Brady 1985, 16.
23. Landwehr 1967, 7, 21–24, 27–29, 90.
24. Schildhauer 1975, 160–62; Moraw 1994, 119–22; Distler 2006, 53–68; Puhle 2006, 38–42; North 2015; Sarnowsky 2015, 93–99.
25. Stercken 2000, 326; Würgler 2008, 29–31; also Church and Head, 2013, chs 1–2 for a primer of Swiss medieval and early modern history.

26. Peyer 1978, 75–79; Maissen 2006 and 2008.
27. Peyer 1978, 94–97.
28. Würgler 2008, 35–43.
29. Körner 1999.
30. Isenmann 1979, 66–68, 83; Heinig 1988, 97–102; Moraw 1994, 112. On Charles V's role: Soly 1999; Tracy 2002; and Blockmans 2008.
31. G. Schmidt 1984, 248.
32. Brady 1985, 10.
33. Isenmann 1979, 91, 94, 108–11, 132.
34. G. Schmidt 1984, 38–39, 47–49, 94; Brady 1985, 231–32; Close 2009, 26–29.
35. Isenmann 1979, 127.
36. The expression comes from Hexter 1961, 19–22.
37. Brady 1985, 16, 18 (quote).
38. Brady 1985, 53–54, 72, 81–84; Close 2009, 29–32.
39. G. Schmidt 1984, 105–10, 210–11, 222.
40. Landwehr 1967, 94–95; Tracy 2002, 99.
41. G. Schmidt 1984, 173–74; Brady 1985, 134–42.
42. Brady 1985, 185–88, 193–200; Close 2009, 61–73.
43. Buchstab 1976, 44–48.
44. For the relationship between Charles and his native Ghent: Dambruyne 2002, 613–34; also Prevenier and Boone 1989; Te Brake 2003. Possibly his most traumatic experience with towns was in Spain: Espinosa 2009.
45. Isenmann 1979, 172–75.
46. Schroeder 1991, 103 (quote), 106, 108; also Iländer 2000, 30.
47. Hildebrandt 1974, 239–40; Schilling 1993, 86–87.
48. Vann 1984, 203–04.
49. Schroeder 1991, 74–75.
50. François 1978, 590.
51. Chevalier 1982, 93–100; also Petit-Dutaillis 1970, pts 1 and 2.
52. Chevalier 1982, 101–08 (quote at 101); also Benedict 1989, 8–9.
53. Descimon 1983, 50–65; Holt 1995, ch. 5; Finley-Croswhite 1999, 11–12; Konnert 2006.
54. Fundamental critiques of the concept of 'absolutism' in Cosandey and Descimon 2002, and Collins 2009, esp. the preface to the second edition.
55. Descimon 1988.
56. Finley-Croswhite 1999, 4, 23–37, 67–72 (quote at 67), 77, 81–86, 90, 104–06, 182–85; also Descimon 1988, 122–26.
57. Dee 2009, 16–24, 33–37, 40–41, 45–46, 51–57.
58. Esp. N. Temple 1975.
59. D. Parker 1980, 21, 52–54, 155 (quote); Robbins 1997, 35, 62.
60. Bien 1987.
61. N. Temple 1975, 71–80; also Bossenga 1987, 120; Wallace 1994, 919; Bayard 1997, 63–64.
62. Beik 1997, ch. 10.
63. Ranum 1993, 251–52 (quote at 251); also Westrich 1972, 51–59; Beik 1997, 242–49.
64. Beik 1997, 239–40.
65. Breen 2007, 72, 92, 97–99, 102, 113–17, 123–27, 137.
66. R. Schneider 1989a, 206–12; also Maillard 1984, 106–09; Collins 2009, 218, 231.
67. Beik 1994, *passim* (quote at 71); Saupin 1996, 98–104, 118–24.
68. Hunt 1976.

69. Dessert 1984, esp. chs 4–5.
70. Collins 2009, 208–27, 308–22; also Bordes 1968; Bossenga 1987; Saupin 2002, 231–32.
71. Bonin 2005, 51–53; Tingle 2000, 101; Zeller 2015, 93, 96.
72. Thompson 1993, chs 6 and 8; MacKay 1999, 42; Ruiz 2007, 124–25.
73. Haliczer 1981, 115–27; also Ferrero Micó 2009, 41–42.
74. Haliczer 1981, 137, 166; Pelizaeus 2007, 41–42, 57–63; Espinosa 2009, 71–82.
75. Nader 1990, 2–3, 7, 27, 105, 119, and 1996; Espinosa 2009, 106–08; Grafe 2012, 180.
76. Grafe 2012, ch.6; Irigoin and Grafe 2008, 178–79 and 2013, 217–23; also Thompson 1993, ch. 7; Mackay 1999, 59; Herzog 2003, ch. 4.
77. Biskup 1980, 165.
78. Miller 2008, 124–27, 130, 169, 172; also Kubinyi 1980, 236–45, and Friedrich 1999, 52–54.
79. Bogucka 1982, 141–47.
80. Wyrobisz 1989, 152; also Rădvan 2015, 180–82. This view is challenged in Tóth, Czoch and Németh 2017, 191.
81. Heinrich 1981, 158, 163.
82. Davies and Moorhouse 2003, 252.
83. Davies 2006; C. Shaw 2006, 579, 586.
84. For the broader context, Elliott 1992.
85. Herzog 2007.

10 Original Citizenship in China and the Middle East

1. Regrettably, Africa had to be excluded, because its historical record for the centuries covered by this book is limited to archaeological data and foreign testimonies, insufficient to deal adequately with citizenship. Cf. Connah 1987, 2; Freund 2007, ch. 2.
2. Fei 2009, 2, 29, 52–55; see also Brook 2010, 118–19.
3. Weber 1968 [1922], 1227, 1229.
4. There is a tradition that opposes states and empires as two distinct polities; in this chapter empire is treated as a subset of states, distinguished by their size and multiethnic populations: Burbank and Cooper 2010, 8–11; Marcocci 2016.
5. Burbank and Cooper 2010, 133, 139–40, 205, 208–09, 218; also Karaman and Pamuk 2010, 624–25; Brandt, Ma and Rawski 2014, 66–73, 79.
6. G. Skinner 1977a, 19–21; Brook 2010, 31–32.
7. Rowe 2009, 48–49, 52; Rosenthal and Wong 2011, 212.
8. Wong 1997, 4–7; on citizenship specifically, Wong 1999.
9. Rowe 2017, 127.
10. Rosenthal and Wong 2011.
11. Rozman 1973, 279–85.
12. De Vries 1984, 45.
13. Yi, Van Leeuwen and Van Zanden 2015, 16 (table 10).
14. De Vries 1984, 63–67.
15. European figures from de Vries 1984, 39 (table 3.7), multiplied by 1.5.
16. Rozman 1973, 6; see also G. Skinner 1977d, 345; Cartier 2002.
17. G. Skinner 1977e, 548–49.
18. Rowe 1989, 81–82, 297, 301–03, 313.
19. Fei 2009, 29–62, 95.
20. E.g. Rowe 1989, 207–15.

21. Fuma 1993, 65–70.
22. Fei 2009, 94, 101, 112.
23. Calhoun 1992, chs 8–13.
24. The most important contributions, by Huang, Rankin, Rowe and Wakeman, were published in a special issue of *Modern China* 19 (1993) and later published as a separate volume, edited by Brook and Frolic 1997; also Wong 1997, 124–26.
25. Rowe 1993, 149, 153, and 2002, 543.
26. Rankin 1993, 159 (quote); Huang 1993.
27. Moll-Murata 2008, 247.
28. Rowe 1984, 277.
29. Belsky 2005, 41–42.
30. Moll-Murata 2008, 218; Tan 2013, 239.
31. Goodman 1995, 91–92.
32. Rowe 1984, 277; Goodman 1995, 119–21, 137–38.
33. Belsky 2005, 6.
34. Weber 1968 [1922], 1241, 1260; due to high adoption rates, Chinese 'lineages' were not necessarily biological lines of descent: Faure 1997; Lee and Feng 1999, 49.
35. Rowe 1984, 294–97.
36. Dijkman, Moll-Murata and Prak 2014.
37. Rowe 1984, 303–06.
38. Fewsmith 1983, 622.
39. Will and Wong 1991; Shiue 2004.
40. Rowe 1989, 94, 99.
41. Rowe 1984, 317, and 2002, 546–50; L. C. Johnson 1995, 132; Belsky 2005, 138.
42. Goodman 1995, 90; L. C. Johnson 1995, 136; Belsky 2005, 121.
43. Rowe 1989, 105–07, 112; J. Smith 2009, 36, 46, 48, 50, 56, 98, 120, 220–21.
44. J. Smith 2009, 84, 143–47.
45. J. Smith 2009, 5, 60, 114, 121, 234, 248–78; also Rowe 1989, 92; Goodman 1995, 110.
46. L. C. Johnson 1995, 108.
47. Rowe 1984, 318–19, and 1989, 139–41,169; L. C. Johnson 1995, 144.
48. Rowe 1989, 123–24.
49. Farmer 2000, 463, 467–68, 486.
50. Goodman 1995, 77–83.
51. Rowe 1984, 319–20.
52. Goodman 1995, 126.
53. Fuma 1993, 48–49.
54. J. Smith 2009, 141.
55. Fei 2009, 29.
56. Brandt, Ma and Rawski 2013, 72–76; also Zelin 1985.
57. I have disregarded the North African regions of the Mamluk and Ottoman Empires, apart from Egypt.
58. Behar 2003, 7–8; compare Weber 1968 [1922], 1233, 1244.
59. Pamuk 2004, 228. See also Eldem, Goffman and Masters 1999, 11; Barkey 2008, 12; Tezcan 2010, 8, 233; Yilmaz 2015.
60. E.g. Faroqhi 1986; Raymond 1995 and 2002; Adanir 2006, 158.
61. Abu-Lughod 1989, 357; Bosker, Buringh and Van Zanden 2013, 1424.
62. Raymond 1984, 5–8.
63. Bosker, Buringh and Van Zanden 2013, 1424.
64. This is discussed in detail later.
65. Lapidus 1967; and for a summary Lapidus 1969.

66. Abu-Lughod 1987, 155–56, 159, 162; Eldem, Goffman and Masters 1999, 1–16; Feldbauer 2002, 81–83; Isin 2005, 39, 45–46; Luz 2014, 11–18, 228–30.
67. Mantran 1962, 124–25; Khoury 2008, 78.
68. Abdel-Nour 1982, 69 and other works cited in the following footnotes.
69. Masters 1999, 21–22.
70. Marcus 1989, 82; also Bodman 1963, 34; McGowan 1994, 661; Tezcan 2010, 197; Yilmaz 2015, 253–54.
71. Marcus 1989, 40.
72. Bodman 1963, 55–69; Marcus 1989, 73, 83–92; Raymond 2002, 67–74; also Tezcan 2010, 213–24.
73. Zubaida 2008, 230.
74. Abu-Lughod 1971, 71.
75. Raymond 1995, 38–39.
76. Raymond 1995 and 2002.
77. Compare Barbir 1980, 89–90; Schatkowski Schilcher 1983, 107–10; Khoury 1997, 2; Behar 2003, ch. 2.
78. Raymond 1984, 5–19; Adanir 2006, 161.
79. Raymond 2002; Faroqhi 2009, ch. 8; Elbendary 2015, 125–36; Lantschner 2014, 565–68.
80. Luz 2014, chs 4 and 8.
81. Raymond 2000, 195; also Raymond 1984, 19, and 1985, 130.
82. Raymond 2000, 121, 244.
83. This was the position Gabriel Baer defended in various articles that opened up the topic: see Baer 1970 and part III, 'The Turkish Guilds', in Baer 1982.
84. Faroqhi 2009. The modern historiography of Ottoman guilds, like that of their European counterparts, emphasises their 'flexibility': Yi 2004, 112; Faroqhi 2005, 18; Yildirim 2008, 80.
85. Raymond 1973–74, 514.
86. Baer 1970, 18–20.
87. Yi 2004, 42, 128.
88. Raymond 1973–4, 508–14; Faroqhi 2009, 129–30.
89. Maniatis 2001, 341–42; Yildirim 2008, 77.
90. Baer 1970; Maniatis 2001, 351–57.
91. Winter 1992, 248.
92. Masters 1988, 201.
93. Raymond 1973–4, 552–57; Masters 1988, 201–03; Ghazaleh 1999, 36, 43–44, 47–48; Yi 2004, 72–74.
94. Raymond 1973–74, 559–60; Hanna 1984, 8–9, 59; Yi 2004, 60.
95. Hanna 1984, 10; Faroqhi 2009, 214; Wilkins 2010, ch. 4.
96. Yi 2004, 85.
97. Raymond 1973–74, 568–74; Faroqhi 2009, 145–47.
98. Raymond 1973–74, 692–93; McGowan 1994, 659; Faroqhi 2009, ch. 7; Tezcan 2010, 199–212.
99. Faroqhi 2009, ch. 8; for guild riots in Istanbul, however, Yi 2004, 213–32.
100. Bodman 1963, 106–25; Masters 1988, 73, 83–93; Raymond 2002, 67–74.
101. Singer 2008.
102. Lev 2005, 4, 21, 28.
103. Marcus 1989, 212; Lev 2005, 157.
104. Lev 2005, ch. 6.
105. Marcus 1989, 214–15, 297–98.
106. Lev 2005, 68; Gerber 2010, 75.

107. R. Leeuwen 1999, 11.
108. Kuran 2011, 110–14.
109. Auke Rijpma pointed this out to me; see also Isin 2008a, 39.
110. Cf. R. Leeuwen 1999, 65; for a European example, Cavallo 1995.
111. Gerber 2010, 68.
112. Khoury 2008; Karaman and Pamuk 2010, 607, 617–18.
113. Cf. Arjomand 2004.
114. Cohen 1984, 46.
115. Cf. Wilkins 2010, 289.
116. Cf. Friedrichs 2009 and 2010.
117. Schilling 1992.
118. Friedrichs 1975; Blickle 1981; DuPlessis and Howell 1982.
119. Yi 2004, 197–211.
120. Bodman 1963, 115.
121. Blockmans 1994.

11 Recreating European Citizenship in the Americas

1. I have benefitted from many helpful references by Simon Middleton on British America, and Caroline Pennock on the military in Spanish America.
2. Roney 2014, ch. 3 and *passim*; see also Franklin 2005, 80, 82–83, 87–88, 96–99.
3. Ryerson 1974, 577, 581, 586; Schultz 1993, 28, 33; Roney 2014, ch. 7.
4. Rosswurm 1987, 49, 56, 67–70, 100; Ryerson 1978, 117–18; Nash 2005, 269–72; Roney 2014, ch. 7.
5. Herzog 2003, 43.
6. Elliott 2006, 4.
7. Acemoglu and Robinson 2012, 9.
8. Mahoney 2010, 227; also Adelman 1999; Lange, Mahoney and vom Hau 2006.
9. Engerman and Sokoloff 1997, 2002, 2008 and 2012; also Allen, Murphy and Schneider 2012; Bértola and Ocampo 2012, 50–52.
10. North, Summerhill and Weingast 2000.
11. Landes 1998, ch. 12.
12. Elliott 2006.
13. Compare Richter 2011, 21.
14. Bray 1972, 167.
15. Pennock 2011, 528, 529, 536.
16. Herzog 2003, 17.
17. Cline 1949.
18. Elliott 2006, 262.
19. Compare data in de Vries 1984, 39, 56–57, 59; also Kinsbruner 2005, 132; Burkholder and Johnson 2008, 183–91. By focusing on these areas – the north-east of the present United States, the Valley of Mexico and the Andes – this chapter disregards the Atlantic littoral of South America, as well as the southern regions of North America and the islands in the Caribbean, and thus by implication the plantation economies that in so many ways dominate our picture of the New World.
20. McAnear 1940, 418; Middleton 2006, 38–40.
21. Hodges 1988, 229; Seybolt 1918, 19.
22. Seybolt 1918, 4–5; Hodges 1988, 228.
23. Seybolt 1918, 34–35.
24. Seybolt 1918, 11; Hodges 1988, 228.
25. Davis 1985, ix; White 1991, 4.

26. The following is based on Herzog 2003, ch. 3; see also Conway 2014.
27. Engerman and Sokoloff 2002, 53.
28. Grafe and Irigoin 2012, 612; also Elliott 2006, 134; Espinosa 2009, 263.
29. Urban communities were distinguished between capital (*municipalidad*), *ciudad* with at least 4,000 inhabitants and smaller communities called *pueblos*. Kinsbruner 2005, 5, 33.
30. J. Moore 1954, 79–82; Kinsbruner 2005, 33–35; Espinosa 2009, 264.
31. Kinsbruner 2005, 36, 42 (quote), 46.
32. Cline 1986, 36–41 (quote), 53–58; Pennock 2011.
33. Haskett 1991, 2742.
34. Martin 1996, 82–84.
35. J. Moore 1954, ch. 8.
36. Burkholder 1986, 82–83; also Burkholder and Chandler 1972.
37. Withington 2005, 19.
38. Lovejoy 1964.
39. Ritchie 1977, 48–50, 169, 171–72, 176–77; Hulsebosch 2005, 46–53.
40. Ritchie 1977, 182.
41. Ritchie 1977, 183–86.
42. Merwick 1990, ch. 5; also Reich 1953; Middleton 2006, 93–95; Richter 2011, 303–13.
43. Zuckerman 1970; Zimmerman 1999, ch. 2; Janiskee 2010, ch. 1. Syrett 1964, 360, however, claims that all propertied inhabitants could vote and that 'property qualifications did not disenfranchise very many people during the late colonial and Revolutionary periods'; also Brown 1955, 91.
44. Zimmerman 1999, 19; on Boston as a 'city-state', Peterson 2006.
45. Nash 1979, 30–31, 273–82.
46. Nash 1979, 54–75, 16, 199, 231–32, 282–90; also Zuckerman 1970, ch. 4.
47. Hart 2017, 200, 203.
48. This explains the unusual position of New York as highlighted in Shorto 2004.
49. Ly. Johnson 1986, 230–31.
50. Kinsbruner 2005, 91–95; also Lockhart and Schwartz 1983, 146; Johnson 1986, 243.
51. C. Archer 1977, 147.
52. Ly. Johnson 1986, 233, 246.
53. Ly. Johnson 1986, 237–39, 243.
54. Ly. Johnson 1986, 232, 244–46.
55. They are conspicuously missing in Tomlins 1999.
56. Olton 1975, 19–20.
57. Middleton 2006, 114–15.
58. Bridenbaugh 1950, 138.
59. Seybolt 1918, 12 (quote), 13.
60. Bridenbaugh 1950, 143–44; Olton 1975, 8.
61. Bridenbaugh 1950, 144–46; Olton 1975, 15–16; Roney 2014, 71, 74–78.
62. Olton 1975, 16–17.
63. Bridenbaugh 1950, 97–105.
64. Bridenbaugh 1950, 173–80; Wilentz 1984, 61–66.
65. Lynd 1967, 88–89, 93, 95–96, 104–05.
66. Ross 1988, 138; Middleton 2006, 122.
67. Zuckerman 1970, 112–13.
68. Cf. Mohl 1971, 14–15, 33; Alexander 1980, 15–21.
69. Slack 1999, 133–42.

70. D. Schneider 1938, 9–10, 13–14; Carras 2004. For Holland, compare C. Parker 1998, ch. 6.
71. D. Schneider 1938, 65–66; also Cray 1988.
72. M. Leeuwen 2012a; Teeuwen 2012.
73. Mohl 1971, 20, 28.
74. D. Schneider 1938, 38–39.
75. Nash 1976; Alexander 1980, 86–91, 98.
76. Arrom 2000, 11, 14, 18, 51–53, 81.
77. Milton 2007, 29, 153, 161.
78. Arrom 2000, 50–53; Milton 2007.
79. Lockhart 1972, chs 2 and 6; Restall 2003, ch. 2; Mawson 2016.
80. Campbell 1976; Grafe and Irigoin 2012, 634.
81. C. Archer 1977, 137–39; Vinson 2002, 10–12.
82. Vinson 2002, 25, 105–07.
83. See Chapter 5.
84. Breen 1972, 81–83 (quote at 83).
85. Breen 1972, 84–86, 92, 96 (quote at 84).
86. Shy 1963, 177, 181–82.
87. Shy 1963, 182–83 (quote at 182).
88. Malcolm 1994.
89. Nash 2005, 216–22, 272–76; also Raphael 2013, 125–26, 131.
90. Malcolm 1994, ch. 8; Cornell 2006.
91. Nash 2005, 115–24, 152–66, 210–16, 323–39, 345–46; Richter 2011, ch. 16.
92. Cf. also Richter 2011, 212.
93. Baldwin 2009, 216.
94. Cf. Herzog 2003, 17, 61; Kinsbruner 2005, 86.
95. Grafe 2006; Grafe and Irigoin 2012.
96. Coatsworth 1998, 2005, 2008; Prados de la Escosura 2006; also Arroyo Abad, Davies and Van Zanden 2012, 160; Arroyo Abad and Van Zanden 2016, 1202–03.
97. Cf. Przeworski and Curvale 2008; also Bulmer-Thomas 2003, 29.

Conclusions

1. As Wallerstein (1980, 38) wrote of the Dutch Republic's golden age: 'To be at the summit is to be certain that the future will not be yours, however much the present is; but it is sweet nonetheless'. Also Kennedy 1987 and Bavel 2016.
2. This paragraph is based on a paper I wrote with Regina Grafe. See also Irigoin and Grafe 2013, 217–23.
3. Cf. Gelderblom and Grafe 2010, and Gelderblom 2013.
4. De Vries 2001.
5. Wallerstein 1980, 75; Davids and Lucassen 1995, 11–19; Isaacs and Prak 1996, 208–10.
6. Grafe and Irigoin 2012, 637; Arroyo Abad and Van Zanden 2016.
7. This is a restatement of what I think is the core argument of Stasavage 2011 and O'Brien 2014.
8. S. Kaplan 2001, chs 3–4; Fitzsimmons 2010, ch. 1.
9. Kluge 2007, 428–29; see also the essays in Haupt 2002.
10. Heuvel and Ogilvie 2013, 83; Schalk 2015, 71–74.
11. Sewell 1980; Hunt and Sheridan 1986; Prak 2014, 294–96.
12. Rosanvallon 2007, 4, 30 (quote), 45.
13. Bradburn 2009, 97–98.

14. Hufton 1992.
15. Koekkoek 2016, chs 2–3; compare Hunt 2007, chs 4–5.
16. Bradburn 2009, 262 and ch. 7.
17. Tilly 2004, 213–15.
18. Lindert 2004, 46, 59; Bavel and Rijpma 2016, 180.
19. Lindert 2004, 20–21, chs 4 and 7.
20. Hippler 2008; also Somers 1998, 122–31.
21. Prak 1999, 272–76.
22. Best 1982, 208–09, 216–19.
23. Clark 2009, 337–44.
24. To keep in touch with the latest developments, read the works of Engin Isin and the journal *Citizenship Studies* that he co-edits.
25. Isin and Nyers 2014, esp. the contributions by Hartley Dean, Teresa Pullano and Katherine E. Tonkiss; also Isin 2008b, and Wood 2014.
26. Frug 2008; also V. Ostrom 1994.
27. Bauböck 2003, 150.
28. Faist 2001; Hooghe and Marks 2003.

BIBLIOGRAPHY

Aalbers, Johan (1977), 'Holland's financial problems (1713–1733) and the wars against Louis XIV', in: A. C. Duke and A. A. Tamse (eds.), *Britain and the Netherlands*, vol. 6: *War and Society* (The Hague: Martinus Nijhoff), 79–93.

(1980), *De Republiek en de vrede van Europa: De buitenlandse politiek van de Republiek der Verenigde Nederlanden na de Vrede van Utrecht (1713), voornamelijk gedurende de jaren 1720–1733* (Groningen: Wolters-Noordhoff).

Abdel-Nour, Antoine (1982), *Introduction à l'histoire urbaine de la Syrie ottomane (XVI–XVIIIe siècle)* (Beirut: Librairie Orientale).

Abu-Lughod, Janet (1971), *Cairo: 1001 Years of the City Victorious* (Princeton, NJ: Princeton University Press).

(1987), 'The Islamic city: Historic myth, Islamic essence, and contemporary relevance', *International Journal of Middle East Studies* 19: 155–76.

(1989), *Before European Hegemony: The Modern World-System A.D. 1250–1350* (Oxford: Oxford University Press).

Acemoglu, Daron, Simon Johnson and James Robinson (2002), 'Reversal of fortune: Geography and institutions in the making of the modern world income distribution', *Quarterly Journal of Economics* 117: 1231–94.

Acemoglu, Daron, and James Robinson (2012), *Why Nations Fail: The Origins of Power, Prosperity and Poverty* (London: Profile Books).

Adams, Julia (2005), *The Familial State: Ruling Families and Merchant Capitalism in Early Modern Europe* (Ithaca, NY: Cornell University Press).

Adanir, Fikret (2006), 'Semi-autonomous provincial forces in the Balkans and Anatolia', in: Suraiya Faroqhi (ed.), *Cambridge History of Turkey*, vol. 3: *The Later Ottoman Empire, 1603–1839* (Cambridge: Cambridge University Press), 157–85.

Adelman, Jeremy (1999), 'Introduction: The problem of persistence in Latin American history', in: Jeremy Adelman (ed.), *Colonial Legacies: The Problem of Persistence in Latin American History* (New York, NY: Routledge), 1–13.

Alexander, John K. (1980), *Render Them Submissive: Responses to Poverty in Philadelphia, 1760–1800* (Amherst, MA: University of Massachusetts Press).

Alfani, Guido (2015), 'Economic inequality in north-western Italy: A long-term view (fourteenth to eighteenth centuries)', *Journal of Economic History* 75: 1058–96.

Alfani, Guido, and Wouter Ryckbosch (2016), 'Growing apart in early modern Europe? A comparison of inequality trends in Italy and the Low Countries, 1500–1800', *Explorations in Economic History* 61: 143–53.

Allegra, Luciano (2015), 'Becoming poor in eighteenth-century Turin', *Journal of Interdisciplinary History* 46: 153–83.

Allen, David (1972), 'The role of the London trained bands in the Exclusion Crisis, 1678–1681', *English Historical Review* 87: 287–303.

Allen, Douglas W. (2012), *The Institutional Revolution: Measurement and the Economic Emergence of the Modern World* (Chicago, IL: University of Chicago Press).

Allen, Robert C. (2001), 'The great divergence in European wages and prices from the Middle Ages to the First World War', *Explorations in Economic History* 38: 411–47.

(2009), *The British Industrial Revolution in Global Perspective* (Cambridge: Cambridge University Press).

Allen, Robert C., Debin Ma, Jean-Pierre Bassino, Christine Moll-Murata and Jan Luiten van Zanden (2011), 'Wages, prices, and living standards in China, 1738–1925: In comparison with Europe, Japan, and India', *Economic History Review* 64: 8–38.

Allen, Robert C., Tommy E. Murphy and Eric B. Schneider (2012), 'The colonial origins of the divergence in the Americas: A labour market approach', *Journal of Economic History* 72: 863–94.

Alm, James, Roy Bahl and Matthew N. Murray (1990), 'Tax structure and tax compliance', *Review of Economics and Statistics* 72: 603–13.

Althusius, Johannes [1965], *The Politics,* an abridged translation of the 3rd edition of *Politica methodice digesta atque exemplis sacris et profanes illustra*, transl. Frederick S. Carney (London: Eyre and Spottiswoode; orig. 1603–12).

Amelang, James (1986), *Honored Citizens of Barcelona: Patrician Culture and Class Relations, 1490–1714* (Princeton, NJ: Princeton University Press).

Anderson, Benedict (1983), *Imagined Communities: Reflections on the Origin and Spread of Nationalism* (London: Verso).

d'Andrea, David (2013), 'Charity and confraternities', in: Eric Dursteler (ed.), *A Companion to Venetian History 1400–1797* (Leiden: Brill), 421–47.

Andreoni, James, Brian Erard and Jonathan Feinstein (1998), 'Tax compliance', *Journal of Economic Literature* 36: 818–60.

Andrijasevic, Rutvica (2013), 'Acts of citizenship as methodology', in: Engin Isin and Michael Saward (eds.), *Enacting European Citizenship* (Cambridge: Cambridge University Press), 47–65.

Arcangeli, Letizia (2006), 'Milan during the Italian Wars (1499–1529): Experiments in representation and definitions of citizenship', in: Christine Shaw (ed.), *Italy and the European Powers: The Impact of War, 1500–1530* (Leiden: Brill), 159–85.

Archer, Ian (1991), *The Pursuit of Stability: Social Relations in Elizabethan London* (Cambridge: Cambridge University Press).

(2002a), 'The charity of early modern Londoners', *Transactions of the Royal Historical Society* 12: 223–44.

(2002b), 'The livery companies and charity, 1500–1700', in: Ian Gadd and Patrick Wallis (eds.), *Guilds, Society, and Economy in London, 1450–1800* (London: Centre for Metropolitan History), 15–28.

Archer, Christon I. (1977), *The Army in Bourbon Mexico, 1760–1810* (Albuquerque, NM: University of New Mexico Press).

Arjomand, Saïd Amir (2004), 'Coffeehouses, guilds and oriental despotism: Government and civil society in late 17th and early 18th century Istanbul, Isfahan, and as seen from Paris and London', *European Journal of Sociology* 45: 23–42.

Arnade, Peter (2008), *Beggars, Iconoclasts and Civic Patriots: The Political Culture of the Dutch Revolt* (Ithaca, NY: Cornell University Press).

(2013), 'Carthage or Jerusalem? Princely violence and the spatial transformation of the medieval into the early modern city', *Journal of Social History* 39: 726–48.

Arrom, Silvia M. (2000), *Containing the Poor: The Mexico City Poor House, 1774–1871* (Durham, NC: Duke University Press).

Arroyo Abad, Leticia, Elwyn Davies and Jan Luiten van Zanden (2012), 'Between conquest and independence: Real wages and demographic change in Spanish America, 1530–1820', *Explorations in Economic History* 49: 149–66.

Arroyo Abad, Leticia, and Jan Luiten van Zanden (2016), 'Growth under extractive institutions? Latin American per capita GDP in colonial times', *Journal of Economic History* 76: 1182–1215.

Ascheri, Mario (1992), 'Statuten, Gesetzgebung und Souveränität: Der Fall Siena', in: Giorgio Chittolini and Dietmar Willoweit (eds.), *Statuten, Städte und Territorien zwischen Mittelalter und Neuzeit in Italien und Deutschland*. Schriften des Italienisch-Deutschen Historischen Instituts in Trient, vol. 3 (Berlin: Duncker & Humblot), 113–55.

(2001), 'La Siena del "buon governo" (1287–1355)', in: Simonetta Adorni Braccesi and Mario Ascheri (eds.), *Politica e cultura nelle republicche italiane dal medioevo all'età moderna: Firenze – Genova – Lucca – Siena – Venezia* (Rome: Istituto Storico Italiano per l'Età Moderna et Contemporanea), 81–107.

(2003), *Siena e la città-stato del medioevo italiano* (Siena: Betti).

Ashton, Robert (1979), *The City and the Court, 1603–1643* (Cambridge: Cambridge University Press).

Assante, Franca (1998), 'The prophets of welfare: The *monti* and *conservatori* in Neapolitan guilds in the early modern age', in: Alberto Guenzi, Paola Massa and Fausto Piola Caselli (eds.), *Guilds, Markets and Work Regulations in Italy, 16th–19th centuries* (Aldershot: Ashgate), 423–35.

Axelrod, Robert (1984), *The Evolution of Cooperation* (s.l.: Basic Books).

Babeau, Albert (1884), *La ville sous l'Ancien Régime*. 2nd edn. 2 vols. (Paris: Didier).

Bader, Karl S., and Gerhard Dilcher (1999), *Deutsche Rechtsgeschichte: Land und Stadt, Bürger und Bauer im Alten Europa*. Enzyklopädie der Rechts- und Staatswissenschaft (Berlin: Springer).

Baer, Gabriel (1970), 'Guilds in Middle Eastern history', in: Michael A. Cook (ed.), *Studies in the Economic History of the Middle East from the Rise of Islam to the Present* (London: Oxford University Press), 11–30.

(1982), *Fellah and Townsman in the Middle East: Studies in Social History* (London: Frank Cass).

Baldwin, Peter (2009), *The Narcissism of Minor Differences: How America and Europe Are Alike: An Essay in Numbers* (New York, NY: Oxford University Press).

Barbir, Karl (1980), *Ottoman Rule in Damascus, 1708–1758* (Princeton, NJ: Princeton University Press).

Bardet, Jean-Pierre (1983), *Rouen aux XVIIe et XVIIIe siècles: Les mutations d'un espace social*, vol. 1 (Paris: Société d'édition d'enseignement supérieur).

Barkey, Karen (2008), *Empire of Difference: The Ottomans in Comparative Perspective* (Cambridge: Cambridge University Press).

Barron, Caroline M. (1981), 'London and the Crown, 1451–61', in: J. R. L. Highfield and Robin Jeffs (eds.), *The Crown and the Local Communities in England and France in the Fifteenth Century* (Gloucester: Sutton), 88–109.
(2004), *London in the Later Middle Ages: Government and People 1200–1500* (Oxford: Oxford University Press).
Barry, Jonathan (1994), 'Bourgeois collectivism? Urban association and the middling sort', in: Jonathan Barry and Christopher Brooks (eds.), *The Middling Sort of People: Culture, Society and Politics in England, 1550–1800* (Basingstoke: Macmillan), 84–112.
(2000), 'Civility and civic culture in early modern England: The meanings of urban freedom', in: Peter Burke, Paul Harrison and Paul Slack (eds.), *Civil Histories: Essays Presented to Sir Keith Thomas* (Oxford: Oxford University Press), 181–96.
Bashir, Hassan, and Phillip W. Gray (2015), 'Arms of the republic: Republicanism and militia reforms during the UC Constitutional Convention and the first Federal Congress 1787–1791', *History of Political Thought* 36: 310–30.
Baten, Joerg, and Jan Luiten van Zanden (2008), 'Book production and the onset of modern economic growth', *Journal of Economic Growth* 13: 217–35.
Bates, Robert H., John H. Coatsworth and Jeffrey G. Williamson (2007), 'Lost decades: Postindependence performance in Latin America and Africa', *Journal of Economic History* 67: 917–43.
Bauböck, Rainer (2003), 'Reinventing urban citizenship', *Citizenship Studies* 7: 139–60.
Bavel, B. J. P. van (2007), 'The transition in the Low Countries: Wage labour as an indicator of the rise of capitalism in the countryside, 1300–1700', *Past & Present*, 195 (supplement 2): 286–303.
(2016), *The Invisible Hand? How Market Economies Have Emerged and Declined since AD 500* (Oxford: Oxford University Press).
Bavel, B. J. P. van, Erik Ansink and Bram van Besouw (2017), 'Understanding the economics of limited access orders: Incentives, organizations and the chronology of developments', *Journal of Institutional Economics* 13: 109–31.
Bavel, B. J. P. van, and Auke Rijpma (2016), 'How important were formalized charity and social spending before the rise of the welfare state? A long-run analysis of selected Western European cases, 1400–1850', *Economic History Review* 69: 159–87.
Bayard, Françoise (1990), 'Naturalization in Lyon during the *Ancien Régime*', *French History* 4: 277–316.
(1997), *Vivre à Lyon sous l'Ancien Régime* (Paris: Perrin).
Bayley, C. C. (1961), *War and Society in Renaissance Florence: The De Militia of Leonardo Bruni* (Toronto: University of Toronto Press).
Bean, Richard (1973), 'War and the birth of the national state', *Journal of Economic History* 33: 203–21.
Beckett, Ian F. W. (1991), *The Amateur Military Tradition, 1558–1945* (Manchester: Manchester University Press).
Beckett, John (2014), 'The Glorious Revolution, Parliament, and the making of the first industrial nation', *Parliamentary History* 33: 36–53.
Behar, Cem (2003), *A Neighbourhood in Ottoman Istanbul: Fruit Vendors and Civil Servants in the Kasap Ilyas Mahalle* (Albany, NY: State University of New York Press).
Beik, William (1985), *Absolutism and Society in Seventeenth-Century France: State Power and Provincial Aristocracy in Languedoc* (Cambridge: Cambridge University Press).

(1994), 'Louis XIV and the cities', in: James L. McClain, John M. Merriman and Ugawa Kaoru (eds.), *Edo and Paris: The State, Political Power and Urban Life in Two Early Modern Societies* (Ithaca, NY: Cornell University Press), 68–85.

(1997), *Urban Protest in Seventeenth-Century France: The Culture of Retribution* (Cambridge: Cambridge University Press).

Bekkers, René, and Pamela Wiepking (2011), 'A literature review of empirical studies of philanthropy: Eight mechanisms that drive charitable giving', *Nonprofit and Voluntary Sector Quarterly* 40: 924–73.

Bellamy, Richard (2008), *Citizenship: A Very Short Introduction* (Oxford: Oxford University Press).

Bellavitis, Anna (2001), *Citoyennes et citoyens à Venise au XVIe siècle: Identité, mariage, mobilité sociale*. Collection de l'École de Rome, vol. 282 (Rome: École Française de Rome).

(2015), 'Gender and Citizenship in Early Modern Venetian Guilds'. Paper presented at the 17th World Economic History Congress in Kyoto.

Belsky, Richard (2005), *Localities at the Center: Native Place, Space, and Power in Late Imperial China* (Cambridge, MA: Harvard University Asia Center).

Benedict, Philip (1981), *Rouen during the Wars of Religion* (Cambridge: Cambridge University Press).

(1989), 'French cities from the sixteenth century to the Revolution: An overview', in: Philip Benedict (ed.), *Cities and Social Change in Early Modern France* (London: Routledge), 7–68.

Bennett, Judith M. (1996), *Ale, Beer, and Brewsters in England: Women's Work in a Changing World, 1300–1600* (New York, NY: Oxford University Press).

Bensch, Stephen P. (1995), *Barcelona and Its Rulers, 1096–1291* (Cambridge: Cambridge University Press).

Bercé, Yves-Marie (1987), *Revolt and Revolution in Early Modern Europe: An Essay on the History of Political Violence* (Manchester: Manchester University Press).

Bergh-Hoogterp, Louise E. van den (1988), 'Der Schutters Schat: Het Zilverbezit van de Schutterijen in de Noordelijke Nederlanden', in: M. Carasso-Kok and J. Levy-Van Halm (eds.), *Schutters in Holland: Kracht en zenuwen van de stad* (Zwolle/Haarlem: Waanders), 141–63.

Berkenvelder, F. C. (2005), *Stedelijk burgerrecht en burgerschap: Een verkennende inventarisatie in Deventer, Kampen en Zwolle (1302–1811)* (Zwolle: Waanders).

Berlin, Mike (1997), '"Broken all in pieces": Artisans and the regulation of workmanship in early modern London', in: Geoffrey Crossick (ed.), *The Artisan and the European Town, 1500–1900* (Aldershot: Scolar Press), 75–91.

(2008) 'Guilds in decline? London livery companies and the rise of a liberal economy, 1600–1800', in: S. R. Epstein and Maarten Prak (eds.), *Guilds, Innovation and the European Economy, 1400–1800* (Cambridge: Cambridge University Press), 316–42.

Berman, Harold J. (1983), *Law and Revolution: The Formation of the Western Legal Tradition* (Cambridge, MA: Harvard University Press).

Bernard, Leon (1970), *The Emerging City: Paris in the Age of Louis XIV* (Durham, NC: Duke University Press).

Bernouli, August (1918), 'Die Organisation von Basels Kriegswesen im Mittelalter', *Basler Zeitschrift für Geschichte und Altertumskunde* 17: 120–61.

Bertinelli, Luisito, and Duncan Black (2004), 'Urbanization and growth', *Journal of Urban Economics* 56: 80–96.

Bértola, L., and J. A. Ocampo (2012), *The Economic Development of Latin America since Independence* (Oxford: Oxford University Press).

Besley, Timothy (2006), *Principled Agents? The Political Economy of Good Government* (Oxford: Oxford University Press).
Best, Geoffrey (1982), *War and Society in Revolutionary Europe, 1770–1870* (Bungay: Fontana).
Bien, David (1987), 'Offices, corps, and a system of state credit: The uses of privilege under the Ancien Regime', in: Keith Michael Baker (ed.), *The French Revolution and the Creation of Modern Political Culture* (Oxford: Oxford University Press), 89–114.
Bierschwale, Heike, and Jacqueline van Leeuwen (2005), *Wie man eine Stadt regieren soll: Deutsche und niederländische Stadtregimentslehren des Mittelalters*. Medieval to Early Modern Culture, vol. 8 (Frankfurt/Main: Peter Lang).
Biskup, Marian (1980), 'Die Rolle der Städte in der Ständevertretung des Königreiches Polen, einschliesslich des Ordenstaates Preussen im 14./15. Jahrhundert', in: Bernhard Töpfer (ed.), *Städte und Ständestaat: Zur Rolle der Städte bei der Entwicklung der Ständeverfassung in europäischen Staaten vom 13. bis zum 15. Jahrhundert* (Berlin: Akademie Verlag), 163–93.
Black, Antony (1996), 'The commune in political theory in the Late Middle Ages', in: Peter Blickle (ed.), *Theorien kommunaler Ordnung in Europa*. Schriften des Historischen Kollegs, Kolloquien, vol. 36 (Munich: Oldenbourg), 99–112.
(2003), *Guild and State: European Political Thought from the Twelfth Century to the Present* (New Brunswick, NJ: Transaction).
Black, Christopher F. (1989), *Italian Confraternities in the Sixteenth Century* (Cambridge: Cambridge University Press).
(2009), 'The Putnam thesis and problems of the early modern transition period', in: Nicholas A. Eckstein and Nicholas Terpstra (eds.), *Sociability and Its Discontents: Civil Society, Social Capital, and Their Alternatives in Late Medieval and Early Modern Europe* (Turnhout: Brepols), 227–45.
Black, Jane (2010), 'Giangaleazzo Visconti and the ducal title', in: John E. Law and Bernadette Paton (eds.), *Communes and Despots in Medieval and Renaissance Italy* (Farnham: Ashgate), 119–30.
Black, Jeremy (1991), *A Military Revolution? Military Change and European Society, 1550–1800* (London: Macmillan).
(1999), 'Warfare, crisis, and absolutism', in: Euan Cameron (ed.), *Early Modern Europe: An Oxford History* (Oxford: Oxford University Press), 206–30.
(2002), *European Warfare, 1494–1660* (London: Routledge).
Blayney, Peter (2014), *The Stationers' Company and the Printers of London 1501–1557*. 2 vols. (Cambridge: Cambridge University Press).
Blickle, Peter (1981), *Deutsche Untertanen: Ein Widerspruch* (Munich: Beck).
(1988), 'Kommunalismus und Republikanismus in Oberdeutschland', in: Helmut Koenigsberger (ed.), *Republiken und Republikanismus im Europa der Frühen Neuzeit*. Schriften des Historischen Kollegs, Kolloquien, vol. 11 (Munich: Oldenbourg), 57–75.
(2000), *Kommunalismus: Skizzen einer gesellschaftlichen Organisationsform*. 2 vols. (Munich: Oldenbourg).
Blickle, Peter, Rosi Fuhrmann and Andreas Würgler (eds.) (1998), *Gemeinde und Staat im alten Europa,* special issue of the *Historische Zeitschrift* 25.
Blockmans, Wim (1988), 'Alternatives to monarchical centralisation: The great tradition of revolt in Flanders and Brabant', in: Helmut G. Koenigsberger (ed.), *Republiken und Republikanismus im Europa der frühen Neuzeit*. Schriften des Historischen Kollegs, Kolloquien, vol. 11 (Munich: Oldenbourg), 145–54.

(1994), 'Voracious states and obstructing cities: An aspect of state formation in preindustrial Europe', in: Charles Tilly and Wim Blockmans (eds.), *Cities and the Rise of States in Europe, A.D. 1000–1800* (Boulder, CO: Westview Press).
(2008), *Karel V, keizer van een wereldrijk 1500–1558* (Kampen: Omniboek).
(2010a), 'Inclusiveness and exclusion: Trust networks at the origins of European cities', *Theory and Society* 39: 315–26.
(2010b), *Metropolen aan de Noordzee: De geschiedenis van Nederland 1100–1560* (Amsterdam: Prometheus).
Blockmans, Wim, and Walter Prevenier (1978), 'Poverty in Flanders and Brabant from the fourteenth to the mid-sixteenth century: Sources and problems', *Acta Historiae Neerlandicae* 10: 20–57.
(1999), *The Promised Lands: The Low Countries under Burgundian Rule, 1369–1530* (Philadelphia, PA: University of Pennsylvania Press).
Blömker, Heinrich (1931), *Die Wehrverfassung der Stadt Osnabrück bis zum Westfälischen Frieden*. PhD dissertation, Westfälische Wilhelms Universität Münster.
Bodman, Herbert (1963), *Political Factions in Aleppo* (Chapel Hill, NC: University of North Carolina Press).
Boele, Anita (2013), *Leden van één lichaam: Denkbeelden over armen, armenzorg en liefdadigheid in de Noordelijke Nederlanden 1300–1650*. Middeleeuwse Studies en Bronnen, vol. 143 (Hilversum: Verloren).
Boffa, Sergio (2004), *Warfare in Medieval Brabant, 1356–1406* (Woodbridge: Boydell).
Bogaers, Llwellyn (1997), 'Geleund over de onderdeur: Doorkijkjes in het Utrechtse buurtleven van de Vroege Middeleeuwen tot in de zeventiende eeuw', *Bijdragen en Mededelingen betreffende de Geschiedenis der Nederlanden* 112: 336–63.
(2008), *Aards, betrokken en zelfbewust: De verwevenheid van cultuur en religie in katholiek Utrecht, 1300–1600* (Utrecht: Levend Verleden Utrecht).
Bogart, Dan (2011), 'Did the Glorious Revolution contribute to the transport revolution? Evidence from investment in roads and rivers', *Economic History Review* 64: 1073–1112.
Bogucka, Maria (1982), 'Polish towns between the sixteenth and the eighteenth centuries', in: H. Fedorowicz, M. Bogucka and H. Samsonowicz (eds.), *A Republic of Nobles: Studies in Polish History to 1864* (Cambridge: Cambridge University Press), 135–52.
Bonin, Pierre (2005), *Bourgeois, bourgeoisie et habitanage dans les villes du Languedoc sous l'Ancien Régime* (Aix-en-Provence/Marseille: Presses Universitaires d'Aix-Marseille).
Bönnen, Gerald (2006), 'Der Rheinische Bund von 1254/56: Voraussetzungen, Wirkungsweise, Nachleben', in: Franz J. Felten (ed.), *Städtebünde: Städtetage im Wandel der Geschichte* (Stuttgart: Franz Steiner), 13–35.
Boone, Marc (1990), *Gent en de bourgondische hertogen ca. 1384–ca. 1453: Een sociaal-politieke studie van een staatsvormingsproces*. Verhandelingen van de Koninklijke Academie van Wetenschappen, Letteren en Schone Kunsten van België, Klasse der Letteren, vol. 133 (Brussels: Koninklijke Academie van Wetenschappen, Letteren en Schone Kunsten).
(1994), 'Städtische Verwaltungsorgane vom 14. bis 16. Jahrhundert: Verfassungsnorm und Verfassungswirklichkeit im spätmittelalterlichen flämischen Raum am Beispiel Gent', in: Wilfried Ehbrecht (ed.), *Verwaltung und Politik in Städten Mitteleuropas: Beiträge zu Verfassungsnorm und Verfassungswirklichkeit in altständischer Zeit*. Städteforschung, vol. A/34 (Cologne: Böhlau), 21–46.

(1996), 'Destroying and reconstructing the city: The inculcation and arrogation of princely power in the Burgundian-Habsburg Netherlands (14th–16th centuries)', in: Martin Gosman, Arjo Vanderjagt and Jan Veenstra (eds.), *The Propagation of Power in the Medieval West* (Groningen: Egbert Forsten), 1–33.

(1997) 'La construction d'un républicanisme urbain: Enjeux de la politique municipale dans les villes flamandes au bas moyen âge', in: Denis Menjot and Jean-Luc Pinol (eds.), *Enjeux et expressions de la politique municipale (XIIe–XXe siècles)* (Paris: l'Harmattan), 41–60.

(2007), 'The Dutch Revolt and the medieval tradition of urban dissent', *Journal of Early Modern History* 11: 351–75.

(2010a), *A la recherché d'une modernité civique: La société urbaine des anciens Pays-Bas au bas Moyen Age* (Brussels: Éditions de l'Université de Bruxelles).

(2010b), 'Les républiques calvinistes et la tradition médiévale des révoltes urbaines dans les Pays-Bas', in: Monique Weis (ed.), *Des villes en révolte: Les Républiques urbaines aux Pays-Bas et en France pendant la deuxième moitié du XVIé siècle.* Studies in European Urban History (1100–1800), vol. 23 (Turnhout: Brepols), 7–23.

Boone, Marc, and Maarten Prak (1995), 'Rulers, patricians and burghers: The great and little traditions of urban revolt in the Low Countries', in: C. A. Davids and J. Lucassen (eds.), *A Miracle Mirrored: The Dutch Republic in European Perspective* (Cambridge: Cambridge University Press), 99–134.

Boone, Marc, and Peter Stabel (2002), 'New burghers in the late medieval towns of Flanders and Brabant: Conditions of entry, rules and reality', in: Rainer Christoph Schwinges (ed.), *Neubürger im Späten Mittelalter: Migration und Austausch in der Städtelandschaft des alten Reiches (1250–1550).* Beiheft Zeitschrift für Historische Forschung, vol. 30 (Berlin: Duncker & Humblot), 317–32.

Bordes, Maurice (1968), *La réforme municipale du controleur général Laverdy et son application (1764–1771)* (Toulouse: Association des publications de la Faculté des lettres et sciences humaines de Toulouse).

(1972), *L'administration provincial et municipal en France au XVIIIe siècle* (Paris: Société d'édition d'enseignement supérieur).

Borsay, Peter (1989), *The English Urban Renaissance: Culture and Society in the Provincial Town, 1660–1770* (Oxford: Clarendon Press).

(2009), 'Geoffrey Holmes and the urban world of Augustan England', *Parliamentary History* 28 (2009): 126–36.

Bos, Sandra (1998), *"Uyt liefde tot malcander". Onderlinge hulpverlening binnen de Noord-Nederlandse gilden in internationaal perspectief (1570–1820)* (Amsterdam: IISG).

(2006), 'A tradition of giving and receiving: Mutual aid within the guild system', in: Maarten Prak, Catharina Lis, Jan Lucassen and Hugo Soly (eds.), *Craft Guilds in the Early Modern Low Countries: Work, Power and Representation* (Aldershot: Ashgate), 174–93.

Bosker, Maarten, Steven Brakman, Harry Garretsen, Herman de Jong and Marc Schramm (2008), 'Ports, plagues and politics: Explaining Italian city growth 1300–1861', *European Review of Economic History* 12: 97–131.

Bosker, Maarten, Eltjo Buringh and Jan Luiten van Zanden (2013), 'From Baghdad to London: Unravelling urban development in Europe, the Middle East, and North Africa, 800–1800', *The Review of Economics and Statistics* 95: 1418–37.

Bossenga, Gail (1987), 'City and state: An urban perspective on the origins of the French Revolution', in: Keith Michael Baker (ed.), *The French Revolution and the*

Creation of Modern Political Culture, vol. 1: *The Political Culture of the Old Regime* (Oxford: Pergamon Press), 115–40.

(1991), *The Politics of Privilege: Old Regime and Revolution in Lille* (Cambridge: Cambridge University Press).

Bottomore, Tom (1992), 'Citizenship and social class: Forty years on', in: T. H. Marshall and T. Bottomore (eds.), *Citizenship and Social Class* (London: Pluto), 55–93.

Bourdieu, Pierre (1980), *Le sens pratique* (Paris: Minuit; translated as *Practical Reason: On the Theory of Action*, 1998).

Boutruche, Robert (ed.) (1966), *Bordeaux de 1453 à 1715. Histoire de Bordeaux*, vol. 4 (Bordeaux: Fédération historique du Sud-Ouest).

Bowles, Samuel, and Herbert Gintis (2011), *A Cooperative Species: Human Reciprocity and Its Evolution* (Princeton, NJ: Princeton University Press).

Bowsky, William M. (1967), 'Medieval citizenship: The individual and the state in the Commune of Siena, 1287–1355', *Studies in Medieval and Renaissance History* 4: 195–243.

(1969), 'The medieval commune and internal violence: Police power and public safety in Siena, 1287–1355', *The American Historical Review*, 73: 1–17.

(1970), *The Finance of the Commune of Siena, 1287–1355* (Oxford: Clarendon Press).

(1972), 'The anatomy of rebellion in fourteenth-century Siena: From commune to signory?', in: Lauro Martines (ed.), *Violence and Civil Disorder in Italian Cities, 1200–1500* (Berkeley, CA: University of California Press), 229–72.

(1981), *A Medieval Italian Commune: Siena under the Nine, 1287–1355* (Berkeley, CA: University of California Press).

Bradburn, Douglas (2009), *The Citizenship Revolution: Politics and the Creation of the American Union, 1774–1804* (Charlottesville, VA: University of Virginia Press).

Braddick, Michael (2000), *State Formation in Early Modern England, c. 1550–1700* (Cambridge: Cambridge University Press).

Brady, Thomas A. (1985), *Turning Swiss: Cities and Empire, 1450–1550* (Cambridge: Cambridge University Press).

Brand, Hanno (1996), *Over macht en overwicht: Stedelijke elites in Leiden (1420–1510)* (Leuven-Apeldoorn: Garant).

Brandt, Loren, Debin Ma and Thomas G. Rawski (2014), 'From divergence to convergence: Reevaluating the history behind China's economic boom', *Journal of Economic Literature*, 52: 45–123.

Bratchel, Michael E. (1995), *Lucca 1430–1494: The Reconstruction of an Italian City-State* (Oxford: Clarendon Press).

Bray, Warwick (1972), 'The city state in central Mexico at the time of the Spanish conquest', *Journal of Latin American Studies* 4: 161–85.

Breen, Michael P. (2007), *Law, City and King: Legal Culture, Municipal Politics, and State Formation in Early Modern Dijon* (Rochester, NY: University of Rochester Press).

Breen, T. H. (1972), 'English origins and New World development: The case of the covenanted militias in seventeenth-century Massachusetts', *Past & Present* 57 (1972): 74–96.

Brenner, Robert (1993), *Merchants and Revolution: Commercial Change, Political Conflict, and London's Overseas Traders, 1550–1653* (Cambridge: Cambridge University Press).

Brewer, John (1989), *The Sinews of Power: War, Money and the English State, 1688–1783* (London: Unwin Hyman).

Bridenbaugh, Carl (1950), *The Colonial Craftsman* (New York, NY: New York University Press).

Brittnell, R. H. (1986), *Growth and Decline in Colchester, 1300–1525* (Cambridge: Cambridge University Press).

Broadberry, Stephen, and Bishnupriya Gupta (2006), 'The early modern great divergence: Wages, prices and economic development in Europe and Asia, 1500–1800', *Economic History Review* 59: 2–31.

Broadberry, Stephen, Bruce Campbell, Alexander Klein, Mark Overton and Bas van Leeuwen (2015), *British Economic Growth, 1270–1870* (Cambridge: Cambridge University Press).

Broadhead, P. J. (1996), 'Guildsmen, religious reform and the search for the common good: The role of the guilds in the early Reformation in Augsburg', *The Historical Journal* 39: 577–97.

Brodman, James William (1998), *Charity and Welfare: Hospitals and the Poor in Medieval Catalonia* (Philadelphia, PA: University of Pennsylvania Press).

Brook, Timothy (2010), *The Troubled Empire: China in the Yuan and Ming Dynasties* (Harvard, MA: Harvard University Press).

Brook, Timothy, and B. Michael Frolic (eds.) (1997), *Civil Society in China* (Boulder, CO: Westview Press).

Broomhall, Susan (2009), *Charity and Religion in Medieval Europe* (Washington, DC: Catholic Press of America).

(2012), 'The politics of charitable men: Governing poverty in sixteenth-century Paris', in: Anne M. Scott (ed.), *Experiences of Poverty in Late Medieval and Early Modern England and France* (Farnham: Ashgate), 133–57.

Brown, Robert E. (1955), *Middle-Class Democracy and the Revolution in Massachusetts, 1691–1780* (Ithaca, NY: Cornell University Press).

Brucker, Gene (1977), *The Civic World of Early Renaissance Florence* (Princeton, NJ: Princeton University Press).

(1999), 'Civic traditions in pre-modern Italy', *Journal of Interdisciplinary History* 29: 357–77.

Bruijn, Jaap R. (1993), *The Dutch Navy of the Seventeenth and Eighteenth Centuries* (Columbia, SC: University of South Carolina Press).

Bruin, Guido de (1979), 'De soevereiniteit in de Republiek: Een machtsprobleem', *Bijdragen en Mededelingen betreffende de Geschiedenis der Nederlanden* 94: 27–40.

(1991), *Geheimhouding en verraad: De geheimhouding van staatszaken ten tijde van de Republiek (1600–1750)* (The Hague: Sdu).

Brunet, Serge, and José Javier Ruiz Ibáñez (eds.) (2015), *Les milices dans la première modernité* (Rennes: Presses universitaires de Rennes).

Bruyn, Josua (1991), 'Rembrandt's workshop: Function and production', in: Christopher Brown, Jan Kelch and Pieter van Thiel (eds.), *Rembrandt: The Master and His Workshop*, vol. 1: *Paintings* (Berlin: Altes Museum), 68–89.

Buchstab, Günter (1976), *Reichsstädte, Städtekurie und Westfälische Friedenskongress: Zusammenhänge von Sozialstruktur, Rechtsstatus and Wirtschaftskraft* (Münster: Aschendorff).

Bueger, Christian (2014), 'Pathways to practice: Praxiography and international politics', *European Political Science Review* 6: 383–406.

Bulmer, Martin, and Anthony M. Rees (eds.) (1996), *Citizenship Today: The Contemporary Relevance of T. H. Marshall* (London: UCL Press).

Bulmer-Thomas, Victor (2003), *The Economic History of Latin America since Independence*. Cambridge Latin American Studies, vol. 77 (Cambridge: Cambridge University Press).

Burbank, Jan, and Frederick Cooper (2010), *Empires in World History: Power and the Politics of Difference* (Princeton, NJ: Princeton University Press).

Burke, Peter (1994), *Venice and Amsterdam: A Study of Seventeenth-Century Élites*. 2nd edn. (Cambridge: Polity).

Burkholder, Mark A. (1986), 'Bureaucrats', in: L. S. Hoberman and S. M. Scolow (eds.), *Cities and Society in Colonial Latin America* (Albuquerque, NM: University of New Mexico Press), 77–103.

Burkholder, Mark A., and D. S. Chandler (1972), 'Creole appointments and the sale of audiencia positions in the Spanish empire under the early Bourbons, 1701–1750', *Journal of Latin American Studies* 4: 187–206.

Burkholder, Mark A., and Lyman L. Johnson (2008), *Colonial Latin America*. 6th edn. (New York, NY: Oxford University Press).

Buschmann, Arno (1987), 'Der Rheinische Bund von 1254–1257: Landfriede, Städte, Fürsten und Reichsverfassung im 13. Jahrhundert', in: Helmut Maurer (ed.), *Kommunale Bündnisse Oberitaliens und Oberdeutschlands im Vergleich* (Sigmaringen: Thorbecke), 167–212.

Buylaert, Frederik, Jan Van Camp and Bert Verwerft (2011), 'Urban militias, nobles and mercenaries: The organization of the Antwerp army in the Flemish-Brabantine Revolt of the 1480s', *Journal of Medieval Military History* 9: 146–66.

Caferro, William (1998), *Mercenary Companies and the Decline of Siena* (Baltimore, MD: Johns Hopkins University Press).

Cahen, Claude (1959), *Mouvements populaires et autonomisme urbain dans l'Asie musulmane du Moyen Age* (Leiden: Brill).

Calhoun, Craig J. (ed.) (1992), *Habermas and the Public Sphere* (Cambridge, MA: MIT Press).

Cameron, Euan (1991), *The European Reformation* (Oxford: Clarendon Press).

Campbell, Leon G. (1976), 'The army of Peru and the Túpac Amaru Revolt, 1780–1783', *The Hispanic American Historical Review* 56: 31–57.

Campopiano, Michele (2014), 'The problem of origins in early communal historiography: Pisa, Genoa and Milan compared', in: Marco Mostert and Anna Adamska (eds.), *Uses of the Written Word in Medieval Towns*. Medieval Urban Literacy, vol. 2 (Turnhout: Brepols), 227–50.

Canepari, Eleonora (2017), *La Construction du Pouvoir Local: Élites Municipal, Liens Sociaux et Transactions Économiques Dans l'Espace Urbain: Rome 1550–1650* (Rome: École française de Rome).

Capellen, Joan Derk van der (1987), *Aan het volk van Nederland: Het Patriottisch program uit 1781*, ed. by H. L. Zwitser (Amsterdam: Bataafsche Leeuw).

Caracausi, Andrea (2017), 'Information asymmetries and craft guilds in pre-modern markets: Evidence from Italian proto-industry', *Economic History Review* 70: 397–422.

Carasso-Kok, M., and J. Levy-Van Halm (eds.) (1988), *Schutters in Holland: Kracht en zenuwen van de stad* (Zwolle/Haarlem: Waanders).

Carlin, Norah (1994), 'Liberty and fraternities in the English Revolution: The politics of London artisans' protests, 1635–1659', *International Review of Social History* 39 (1994): 223–54.

Carney, Frederick S., Heinz Schilling and Dieter Wyduckel (eds.) (2004), *Jurisprudenz, politische Theorie und politische Theologie*. Beiträge zur politische Wissenschaft, vol. 131 (Berlin: Duncker & Humblot).

Carpi, Olivia (2015), 'La milice bourgeoise comme instrument de reconstruction identitaire de la communauté citadine à Amiens, dans le premier tiers du XVIIe siècle', in: Serge Brunet and José Javier Ruiz Ibáñez (eds.), *Les milices dans la première modernité* (Rennes: Presses universitaires de Rennes), 21–34.

Carras, Irmgard (2004), '*Who cared? The poor in 17th-century New Amsterdam, 1628–1664*', *New York History* 85: 247–63.

Carruthers, Bruce G. (1996), *City of Capital: Politics and Markets in the English Financial Revolution* (Princeton, NJ: Princeton University Press).

Carter, F. W. (1994), *Trade and Urban Development in Poland: An Economic Geography of Cracow, from Its Origin to 1795* (Cambridge: Cambridge University Press).

Cartier, Carolyn (2002), 'Origins and evolution of a geographical idea', *Modern China* 28: 79–143.

Cavallar, Osavaldo, and Julius Kirshner (2011), 'Jews as citizens in late medieval and Renaissance Italy: The case of Isacco da Pisa', *Jewish History* 25: 269–318.

Cavallo, Sandra (1995), *Charity and Power in Early Modern Italy: Benefactors and Their Motives in Turin, 1541–1789* (Cambridge: Cambridge University Press).

Cerutti, Simona (1990), *La ville et les métiers. Naissance d'un langage corporatif (Turin 17e–18e siècles)* (Paris: Éditions de l'EHESS).

(2007), 'À qui appartiennent les biens qui n'appartiennent à personne? Citoyenneté et droit d'aubaine à l'époque moderne', *Annales HSS* 62: 355–83.

(2010), 'Travail, mobilité et légitimité: Suppliques au roi dans une société d'Ancien Régime (Turin, XVIIIe siècle)', *Annales HSS* 65: 571–611.

(2012), *Étrangers: Étude d'une condition d'incertitude dans une société d'Ancien Régime* (Montrouge: Bayard).

Chevalier, Bernard (1982), *Les bonnes villes de France du XIVe au XVIe siècle* (Paris: Aubier Montaigne).

(1988), 'L'état et les bonnes villes en France au temps de leur accord parfait (1450–1550)', in: Neithard Bulst and Jean-Pilippe Genet (eds.), *La ville, la bourgeoisie et la genêse de l'état moderne (xiie–xviiie siècles)* (Paris: Editions du CNRS), 71–85.

Chilosi, David (2014), 'Risky institutions: Political regimes and the cost of public borrowing in early modern Italy', *Journal of Economic History* 74: 887–915.

Chittolini, Giorgio (1979a), *La formazione dello stato regionale e le istituzioni del contado: Secoli XIV e XV* (Turin: Einaudi).

(1979b), 'Introducione', in: Giorgio Chittolini (ed.), *La crisi degli ordinamenti comunali e le origini dello stato del Rinascimento* (Bologna: Il Mulino), 7–50.

(1994), 'Cities, "city-states", and regional states in North-Central Italy', in: Charles Tilly and Wim P. Blockmans (eds.), *Cities and the Rise of States in Europe, A.D. 1000 to 1800* (Boulder, CO: Westview Press), 28–43.

Chojnacki, Stanley (1973), 'In search of the Venetian patriciate: Families and factions in the fourteenth century', in: J. R. Hale (ed.), *Renaissance Venice* (London: Faber and Faber), 47–90.

(1994), 'Social identity in Renaissance Venice: The second *Serrata*', *Renaissance Studies* 8: 341–58.

(2000), 'Identity and ideology in Renaissance Venice: The third *Serrata*', in: John Martin and Dennis Romano (eds.), *Venice Reconsidered: The History and Civilization of an Italian City-State, 1297–1797* (Baltimore, MD: Johns Hopkins University Press), 263–94.

Church, Clive H., and Randolph C. Head (2013), *A Concise History of Switzerland* (Cambridge: Cambridge University Press).

Cicchini, Marco (2014), 'Milices bourgeoises et garde soldée à Genève au XVIII siècle', *Revue d'histoire moderne et contemporaine* 61: 120–49.

Cieslak, Edmond, and Czesław Biernat (1995), *History of Gdansk* (Gdansk: Wydawn).

Clark, Gregory (1998), 'Commons sense: Common property rights, efficiency and institutional change', *Journal of Economic History* 58: 73–102.
Clark, Peter (1984), 'The civic leaders of Gloucester 1580–1800', in Peter Clark (ed.), *The Transformation of English Provincial Towns, 1600–1800* (London: Hutchinson), 311–45.
(2000a), *British Clubs and Societies 1580–1800: The Origins of an Associational World* (Oxford: Oxford University Press).
(2000b), 'Introduction', in Peter Clark (ed.), *The Cambridge Urban History of Britain,* vol. 2: *1540–1840* (Cambridge: Cambridge University Press), 1–30.
(2009), *European Cities and Towns 400–2000* (Oxford: Oxford University Press).
(ed.) (2013), *The Oxford Handbook of Cities in World History* (Oxford: Oxford University Press).
Cline, Howard F. (1949), 'Civil congregations of the Indians in New Spain, 1598–1606', *Hispanic American Historical Review* 29: 346–69.
Cline, S. L. (1986), *Colonial Culhuacan, 1580–1600: A Social History of an Aztec Town* (Albuquerque, NM: University of New Mexico Press).
Close, Christopher W. (2009), *The Negotiated Reformation: Imperial Cities and the Politics of Urban Reform, 1525–1550* (Cambridge: Cambridge University Press).
Coatsworth, John H. (1998), 'Economic and institutional trajectories in nineteenth-century Latin America', in: John H. Coatsworth and Alan M. Taylor (eds.), *Latin America and the World Economy since 1800* (Cambridge, MA: Harvard University Rockefeller Center for Latin American Studies), 23–54.
(2005), 'Structures, endowments, and institutions in the economic history of Latin America', *Latin American Research Review* 40: 126–44.
(2008), 'Inequality, institutions and economic growth in Latin America', *Journal of Latin American Studies* 40: 545–69.
Coffin, Judith G. (1994), 'Gender and the guild order: The garment trades in eighteenth-century Paris', *Journal of Economic History* 54: 768–93.
Cohen, Amnon (1984), *Jewish Life under Islam: Jerusalem in the Sixteenth Century* (Cambridge, MA: Harvard University Press).
(2001), *The Guilds of Ottoman Jerusalem* (Leiden: Brill).
Cohn, Samuel K., Jr. (2013), *Popular Protest in Late Medieval English Towns* (Cambridge: Cambridge University Press).
Coleman, C., and D. Starkey (eds.) (1986), *Revolution Reassessed: Revisions in the History of Tudor Government and Administration* (Oxford: Clarendon Press).
Coleman, Edward (1999), 'The Italian communes: Recent work and current trends', *Journal of Medieval History* 25: 373–97.
(2004) 'Cities and communes', in: David Abulafia (ed.), *Italy in the Central Middle Ages, 1000–1300* (Oxford: Oxford University Press), 27–57.
Collins, James B. (2009), *The State in Early Modern France.* 2nd edn. (Cambridge: Cambridge University Press).
Collinson, Patrick, and John Craig (eds.) (1998), *The Reformation in English Towns, 1500–1640* (Basingstoke: Macmillan).
Connah, Graham (1987), *African Civilizations: Precolonial Cities and States in Tropical Africa: An Archaeological Perspective* (Cambridge: Cambridge University Press).
Connell, William J., and Andrea Zorzi (eds.) (2000), *Florentine Tuscany: Structures and Practices of Power* (Cambridge: Cambridge University Press).
Conway, Richard (2014), 'Spaniards in the Nahua city of Xochimilco: Colonial society and cultural change in central Mexico, 1650–1725', *The Americas* 71: 9–35.
Coornaert, Émile (1968), *Les corporations en France avant 1789* (Paris: Les Éditions Ouvrières).

Cornell, Saul (2006), *A Well-Regulated Militia: The Founding Fathers and the Origins of Gun Control in America* (New York, NY: Oxford University Press).
Corteguera, Luis R. (2002), *For the Common Good: Popular Politics in Barcelona, 1580–1640* (Ithaca, NY: Cornell University Press).
Corvisier, André (1979), *Armies and Societies in Europe 1494–1789* (Bloomington, IN: Indiana University Press).
Cosandey, Fanny, and Robert Descimon (2002), *L'absolutisme en France: Histoire et historiographie* (Paris: Seuil).
Costa, Pietro (1999), *Civitas: Storia della cittadinanza in Europa*, vol. 1: *Dalla civiltà comunale al settecento* (Gius: Laterza).
Coste, Laurent (2008), 'Les milices bourgeoises en France', in: Jean-Pierre Poussou (ed.), *Les sociétés urbaines au XVIIe Siècle: Angleterre, France, Espagne* (Paris: Presse de l'université Paris-Sorbonne), 175–88.
(2015), 'Entre autonomie et tutelle: Le renouvellement des édilles dans la France d'Ancien Régime (du milieu du XVIe siècle au déclenchement de la Révolution)', in: Michel Pauly and Alexander Lee (eds.), *Urban Liberties and Citizenship from the Middle Ages up to Now / Libertés et citoyenneté urbaines du moyen âge à nos jours / Städtische Freiheiten und bürgerliche Partizipation vom Mittelalter bis heute. Actes du Colloque 2009 de la Commission internationale pour l'Histoire des villes.* Beiträge zur Landes- und Kulturgeschichte, vol. 9 (Trier: Porta Alba), 185–99.
Covini, Maria Nadia (2000), 'Political and military bonds in the Italian state system, thirteenth to sixteenth centuries', in: Philippe Contamine (ed.), *War and Competition between States: The Origins of the Modern State in Europe* (Oxford: Clarendon), 9–36.
Cowan, Alexander F. (1986), *The Urban Patriciate: Lübeck and Venice, 1580–1700.* Quellen und Darstellungen zur hansischen Geschichte N. F., vol. 30 (Cologne: Böhlau).
Cray, Robert E., Jr. (1988), *Paupers and Poor Relief in New York City and Its Rural Environs 1700–1830* (Philadelphia, PA: Temple University Press).
Crouch, Colin (1993), *Industrial Relations and European State Traditions* (Oxford: Clarendon Press).
Crouzet-Pavan, Elisabeth (2002), *Venice Triumphant: The Horizons of a Myth* (Baltimore, MD: Johns Hopkins University Press).
Crowley, John (1998), 'The national dimension of citizenship in T. H. Marshall', *Citizenship Studies* 2: 165–78.
Crowston, Clare (2000), 'Engendering the guilds: Seamstresses, tailors, and the clash of corporate identities in Old Regime France', *French Historical Studies* 23: 339–71.
(2001), *Fabricating Women: The Seamstresses of Old Regime France, 1675–1791* (Durham, NC: Duke University Press).
(2008), 'Women, gender and guilds in early modern Europe: An overview of recent research', in: Jan Lucassen, Tine De Moor and Jan Luiten van Zanden (eds.), *The Return of the Guilds*, supplement 16 of the *International Review of Social History* 53 (Cambridge: Cambridge University Press), 19–44.
Cullum, P. H., and P. J. P. Goldberg (1993), 'Charitable provision in late medieval York: "To the praise of God and the use of the poor"', *Northern History* 29: 24–39.
Cunningham, Andrew (2005), 'Some closing and opening remarks', in: Ole Peter Grell, Andrew Cunningham and Bernd Roeck (eds.), *Health Care and Poor Relief in 18th- and 19th-Century Southern Europe* (Farnham: Ashgate), 1–9.

Cunningham, Andrew, and Ole Peter Grell (2000), *The Four Horsemen of the Apocalypse: Religion, War, Famine and Death in Reformation Europe* (Cambridge: Cambridge University Press).

D'Amico, Stefano (2015) 'Spanish Milan, 1535–1706', in: Andrea Gamberini (ed.), *A Companion to Late Medieval and Early Modern Milan: The Distinctive Features of an Italian State* (Leiden: Brill), 46–68.

Dambruyne, Johan (1998), 'Guilds, social mobility and status in sixteenth-century Ghent', *International Review of Social History* 43: 31–78.

(2002), *Corporatieve middengroepen: Aspiraties, relaties en transformaties in de 16de-eeuwse Gentse ambachtswereld.* Verhandelingen van de Maatschappij voor Geschiedenis en Oudheidkunde te Gent, vol. 28 (Ghent: Academia Press).

(2006), 'Corporative capital and social representation in the Southern and Northern Netherlands, 1500–1800', in: Maarten Prak, Catharina Lis, Jan Lucassen and Hugo Soly (eds.), *Craft Guilds in the Early Modern Low Countries: Work, Power and Representation* (Aldershot: Ashgate), 194–223.

Dartmann, Christoph (2008), 'Die Repräsentation der Stadtgemeinde in der Bürgerversammlung der italienischen Kommune', in: Jörg Oberste (ed.), *Repräsentationen der mittelalterlichen Stadt.* Forum Mittelalter Studien, vol. 4 (Regensburg: Schnell & Steiner), 95–108.

(2012), *Politische Interaktion in der italienischen Stadtkommune (11.–14. Jahrhundert).* Mittelalter-Forschungen, vol. 36 (Ostfildern: Thorbecke).

Davids, C. A. (1985), 'De migratiebeweging in Leiden in de achttiende eeuw', in: H. A. Diederiks, D. J. Noordam and H. D. Tjalsma (eds.), *Armoede en sociale spanning: Sociaal-historische studies over Leiden in de achttiende eeuw* (Hilversum: Verloren), 137–56.

(2007), 'Apprenticeship and guild control in the Netherlands, c.1450–1800', in: Bert De Munck, Steven L. Kaplan and Hugo Soly (eds.), *Learning on the Shop Floor: Historical Perspectives on Apprenticeship* (Oxford: Berg), 65–84.

Davids, C. A., and Bert De Munck (2014), 'Innovation and creativity in late medieval and early modern European cities: An introduction', in: Karel Davids and Bert De Munck (eds.), *Innovation and Creativity in Late Medieval and Early Modern European Cities* (Farnham: Ashgate), 1–33.

Davids, Karel, and Jan Lucassen (1995), 'Introduction', in: Karel Davids and Jan Lucassen (eds.), *A Miracle Mirrored: The Dutch Republic in European Perspective* (Cambridge: Cambridge University Press), 1–25.

Davies, Brian (2006), 'Local government and administration', in: Maureen Perrie (ed.), *The Cambridge History of Russia,* vol. 1: *From Early Rus' to 1689* (Cambridge: Cambridge University Press), 464–85.

Davies, Norman, and Roger Moorhouse (2003), *Microcosm: Portrait of a Central European City* (London: Pimlico).

Davis, John A. (2005), 'Health care and poor relief in Southern Europe in the 18th and 19th centuries', in: Ole Peter Grell, Andrew Cunningham and Bernd Roeck (eds.), *Health Care and Poor Relief in 18th- and 19th-Century Southern Europe* (Farnham: Ashgate), 10–33.

De Kerf, Raoul (2013), *De circulatie van technische kennis in het vroegmoderne Antwerpse ambachtswezen, 1500–1800 (casus kuipers en edelsmeden)*, PhD thesis, Universiteit Antwerpen.

De Long, J. Bradford, and Andrei Shleifer (1993), 'Princes and merchants: European city growth before the Industrial Revolution', *Journal of Law and Economics* 36: 671–702.

De Meester, Jan (2014), 'To kill two birds with one stone: Keeping immigrants in by granting free burghership in early modern Antwerp', in: Karel Davids and Bert De Munck (eds.), *Innovation and Creativity in Late Medieval and Early Modern European Cities* (Farnham: Ashgate), 95–113.
De Moor, Tine (2008), 'The silent revolution: A new perspective on the emergence of commons, guilds and other forms of corporative collective action in Western Europe', in: Jan Lucassen, Tine De Moor and Jan Luiten van Zanden (eds.), *The Return of the Guilds,* supplement 16 of the *International Review of Social History* 53 (Cambridge: Cambridge University Press), 179–212.
(2015), *The Dilemma of the Commoners: Understanding the Use of Common Pool Resources in Long-Term Perspective* (Cambridge: Cambridge University Press).
De Munck, Bert (2007), *Technologies of Learning: Apprenticeship in Antwerp Guilds from the Sixteenth Century to the End of the Ancien Régime.* Studies in European Urban History (1100–1800), vol. 11 (Turnhout: Brepols).
(2011), 'Gilding golden ages: Perspectives from early modern Antwerp on the guild debate, *c.* 1450–*c.* 1650', *European Review of Economic History* 15: 221–53.
(2012), 'Skills, trust and changing consumer preferences: The decline of Antwerp's craft guilds from the perspective of the product market, c.1500–c.1800', *International Review of Social History* 53: 197–233.
De Munck, Bert, and Karel Davids, with the help of Ellen Burm (2014), 'Beyond exclusivism: Entrance fees for guilds in the early modern Low Countries, c. 1450–1800', in: Karel Davids and Bert De Munck (eds.), *Innovation and Creativity in Late Medieval and Early Modern European Cities* (Aldershot: Ashgate), 189–224.
De Munck, Bert, Piet Lourens and Jan Lucassen (2006), 'The establishment and distribution of craft guilds in the Low Countries, 1000–1800', in: Maarten Prak, Catharina Lis, Jan Lucassen and Hugo Soly (eds.), *Craft Guilds in the Early Modern Low Countries: Work, Power and Representation* (Aldershot: Ashgate), 32–73.
De Munck, Bert, and Hugo Soly (2007), '"Learning on the shop floor" in historical perspective', in: Bert De Munck, Steven L. Kaplan and Hugo Soly (eds.), *Learning on the Shop Floor: Historical Perspectives on Apprenticeship* (New York, NY: Berghahn), 3–32.
de Vries, Jan (1974), *The Dutch Rural Economy in the Golden Age, 1500–1700* (New Haven, CT: Yale University Press).
(1978), *Barges and Capitalism: Passenger Transportation in the Dutch Economy, 1632–1839 A.A.G.-Bijdragen,* vol. 21 (Wageningen: Afd. Agrarische Geschiedenis).
(1981), 'Armoede en kapitalisme in pre-industrieel Europa: Een bespreking', *Tijdschrift voor Sociale Geschiedenis,* 7: 48–57.
(1984), *European Urbanization, 1500–1800* (London: Methuen).
(2001), 'Economic growth before and after the Industrial Revolution', in: Maarten Prak (ed.), *Early Modern Capitalism: Economic and Social Change in Europe, 1400–1800* (London: Routledge), 177–94.
(2008), *The Industrious Revolution: Consumer Behavior and the Household Economy, 1650 to the Present* (Cambridge: Cambridge University Press).
(2009), 'The political economy of bread in the Dutch Republic', in: Oscar Gelderblom (ed.), *The Political Economy of the Dutch Republic* (Farnham: Ashgate), 85–114.
de Vries, Jan, and Ad van der Woude (1997), *The First Modern Economy: Success, Failure, and Perseverance of the Dutch Economy, 1500–1815* (Cambridge: Cambridge University Press).

Dean, Trevor (1988), *Land and Power in Late Medieval Ferrara* (Cambridge: Cambridge University Press).

(2004), 'The rise of the *signori*', in: David Abulafia (ed.), *Italy in the Central Middle Ages, 1000–1300* (Oxford: Oxford University Press), 104–24.

Deceulaer, Harald (1998), *Pluriforme patronen en een verschillende snit: Sociaal-economische, institutionele en culturele transformaties in de kledingsector in Antwerpen, Brussel en Gent, 1585–1800*. PhD dissertation, Vrije Universiteit Brussel.

(2001), *Pluriforme patronen en een verschillende snit: Sociaal-economische, institutionele en culturele transformaties in de kledingsector in Antwerpen, Brussel en Gent, 1585–1800* (Amsterdam: IISG).

(2009), 'Implications of the street: Entitlements, duties and conflicts in neighbourhoods in Ghent (17th–18th centuries)', in: Manon van der Heijden, Elise van Nederveen Meerkerk, Griet Vermeesch and Martijn van der Burg (eds.), *Serving the Community: The Rise of Public Facilities in the Low Countries* (Amsterdam: Aksant), 194–216.

Deceulaer, Harald, and Marc Jacobs (2002), 'Les implications de la rue: Droits, devoirs et conflits dans les quartiers de Gand (XVIIe–XVIIIe siècles)', *Revue d'Histoire Moderne et Contemporaine* 49: 26–53.

Deceulaer, Harald, and Bibi Panhuysen (2006), 'Dressed to work: A gendered comparison of the tailoring trades in the northern and southern Netherlands, 16th to 18th centuries', in: Maarten Prak, Catharina Lis, Jan Lucassen and Hugo Soly (eds.), *Craft Guilds in the Early Modern Low Countries: Work, Power and Representation* (Aldershot: Ashgate), 133–56.

Dee, Darryl (2009), *Expansion and Crisis in Louis XIV's France: Franche-Comté and Absolute Monarchy, 1674–1715* (Rochester, NY: University of Rochester Press).

Deeters, Joachim (1987), 'Das Bürgerrecht der Reichsstadt Köln seit 1396', *Zeitschrift der Savigny-Stiftung für Rechtsgeschichte, Germanistische Abteilung* 104: 1–83.

Dekker, Rudolf (1982), *Holland in beroering: Oproeren in de 17de en 18de eeuw* (Baarn: Ambo).

Descimon, Robert (1983), *Qui étaient les Seize? Mythes et réalités de la Ligue parisienne (1585–1594)*. Mémoires publiés par la fédération des sociétés historiques et archéologiques de Paris et de l'Île-de-France, vol. 34 (Paris: Librairie Klincksieck).

(1987), 'Solidarité communautaire et sociabilité armée: Les compagnies de la milice bourgeoise à Paris (XVIe–XVIIe siècles)', in: F. Thélamon (ed.), *Sociabilité, pouvoirs et société: Actes du colloque de Rouen*. Publications de l'Université de Rouen, no. 110 (Rouen: Publications de l'Université de Rouen), 599–610.

(1988), 'L'échevinage Parisien sous Henri IV (1594–1609): Autonomie urbaine, conflits politiques et exclusives sociales', in: Neithard Bulst and J.-Ph. Genet (eds.), *La ville, la bourgeoisie et la genèse de l'état moderne (XIIe–XVIIIe siècles)* (Paris: Éditions du CNRS), 113–50.

(1989), 'Les barricades Frondeuses (26–28 Âout 1648)', in: Roger Duchêne and Pierre Ronzeaud (eds.), *La Fronde en questions: Actes du 18ème colloque du Centre Méridional de Rencontres sur le XVIIIème siècle* (s.l.), 245–62.

(1990), 'Les barricades de la Fronde parisiènne: Une lecture sociologique', *Annales ESC* 45: 397–422.

(1993), 'Milice bourgeoise et identité citadine à Paris au temps de la Ligue', *Annales ESC* 48: 885–906.

(1994), 'Le corps de ville et les élections échevinales à Paris aux XVIe et XVIIe siècles', *Histoire, Économie et Société* 13: 507–30.

(2003), 'The "bourgeoisie seconde": Social differentiation in the Parisian municipal oligarchy in the sixteenth century', *French History* 17: 388–424.
Dessert, Daniel (1984), *Argent, pouvoir et société au Grand Siècle* (Paris: Fayard).
Dessi, Roberta, and Salvatore Piccolo (2016), 'Merchant guilds, taxation and social capital', *European Economic Review* 83: 90–110.
DeVries, Kelly (2008), 'Medieval mercenaries: Methodology, definitions, and problems', in: John France (ed.), *Mercenaries and Paid Men: The Mercenary Identity in the Middle Ages* (Leiden: Brill), 43–60.
Di Corcia, Joseph (1978), '*Bourg, bourgeois, bourgeois de Paris* from the eleventh to the eighteenth century', *Journal of Modern History* 50: 207–33.
Diederiks, H. A., D. J. Noordam and H. D. Tjalsma (eds.) (1985), *Armoede en sociale spanning: Sociaal-historische studies over Leiden in de achttiende eeuw*. Hollandse Studiën, vol. 17 (Hilversum: Verloren).
Diefendorf, Barbara B. (1983), *Paris City Councillors in the Sixteenth Century: The Politics of Patrimony* (Princeton, NJ: Princeton University Press).
(1991), *Beneath the Cross: Catholics and Huguenots in Sixteenth-Century Paris* (New York, NY: Oxford University Press).
(2016), 'Civic engagement and public assistance in sixteenth-century Paris', in: Barbara B. Diefendorf (ed.), *Social Relations, Politics, and Power in Early Modern France: Robert Descimon and the Historian's Craft* (Kirksville, MO: Truman State University Press), 184–211.
Dijkman, Jessica, Christine Moll-Murata and Maarten Prak (2014), 'How to become a master craftsman? Guild regulation of vocational training and qualification in the East and the West (late Middle Ages and early modern period)', unpublished paper.
Dilcher, Gerhard (1967), *Die Entstehung der lombardischen Stadtkommune: Eine rechtsgeschichtliche Untersuchung*. Untersuchungen zur Deutschen Staats- und Rechtsgeschichte NF, vol. 7 (Aalen: Scientia).
(1985), 'Die genossenschaftliche Struktur von Gilden und Zünften: Kaufmännische und gewerbliche Genossenschaften im frühen und hohen Mittelater', in: Berent Schwineköper (ed.), *Gilden und Zünfte: Kaufmännische und gewerbliche Genossenschaften im frühen und hohen Mittelalter* (Sigmaringen: Jan Thorbecke), 183–242.
(1987), 'Reich, Kommunen, Bünde und die Wahrung von Recht und Friede: Eine Zusammenfassung', in: Helmut Maurer (ed.), *Kommunale Bündnisse Oberitaliens und Oberdeutschlands im Vergleich* (Sigmaringen: Thorbecke), 231–47.
(ed.) (1988), 'Res publica: Bürgerschaft in Stadt und Staat', special issue of *Der Staat*.
(ed.) (1996a), *Bürgerrecht und Stadtverfassung im Europäischen Mittelalter* (Cologne: Böhlau).
(1996b), 'Marktrecht und Kaufmannsrecht im Frühmittelalter', in: Gerhard Dilcher (ed.), *Bürgerrecht und Stadtverfassung im europäischen Mittelalter* (Cologne: Böhlau), 1–40.
(1996c), 'Zum Bürgerbegriff im späteren Mittelalter: Versuch einer Typologie am Beispiel von Frankfurt am Main', in: Gerhard Dilcher (ed.), *Bügerrecht und Stadtverfassung im europäischen Mittelalter* (Cologne: Böhlau), 115–82.
Distler, Eva-Marie (2006), *Städtebünde im deutschen Spätmittelalter: Eine rechtshistorische Untersuchung zu Begriff, Verfassung und Funktion*. Studien zur europäische Rechtsgeschichte, vol. 207 (Frankfurt am Main: Vittorio Klostermann).

Dixhoorn, Arjan van (1999), '"Voorstanden van de vrije wetten": Burgerbewegingen in Arnhem en de Republiek tussen 1702 en 1707', *Tijdschrift voor sociale geschiedenis* 25: 25–54.

(2009), *Lustige geesten: Rederijkers in de Noordelijke Nederlanden, 1480–1650* (Amsterdam: Amsterdam University Press).

Dixhoorn, Arjan van, and Susie Speakman Sutch (eds.) (2008), *The Reach of the Republic of Letters: Literary and Learned Societies in Late Medieval and Early Modern Europe*. 2 vols. (Leiden: Brill).

Dolan, Claire (1989), 'The artisans of Aix-en-Provence in the sixteenth century: A micro-analysis of social relationships', in: Philip Benedict (ed.), *Cities and Social Change in Early Modern France* (London: Unwin Hyman), 174–94.

Dorren, Gabriëlle (1998), 'Communities within the community: Aspects of neighbourhood in seventeenth-century Haarlem', *Urban History* 25: 173–88.

(2001), *Eenheid en verscheidenheid: De burgers van Haarlem in de Gouden Eeuw* (Amsterdam: Bert Bakker).

Dougan, Michael, Niamh Nic Shuibhne and Eleanor Spaventa (eds.) (2012), *Empowerment and Disempowerment of the European Citizen* (Oxford: Hart).

Downing, Brian M. (1992), *The Military Revolution and Political Change: Origins of Democracy and Autocracy in Early Modern Europe* (Princeton, NJ: Princeton University Press).

Dross, Fritz (2002), 'Health care provision and poor relief in Enlightenment Prussia', in: Ole Peter Grell, Andrew Cunningham and Robert Jütte (eds.), *Health Care and Poor Relief in 18th- and 19th-Century Northern Europe* (Aldershot: Ashgate), 69–111.

Dumolyn, Jan (1997), *De Brugse opstand van 1436–1438*. Standen en landen, vol. 101 (Kortrijk-Heule: UGA).

(2008), 'Privileges and novelties: The political discourse of the Flemish cities and rural districts in their negotiations with the dukes of Burgundy (1384–1506)', *Urban History* 35: 5–23.

(2014), 'Guild politics and political guilds in fourteenth-century Flanders', in: Jan Dumolyn, Jelle Haemers, Hipólito Rafael Oliva Herrer and Vincent Challet (eds.), *The Voices of the People in Late Medieval Europe: Communication and Popular Politics*. Studies in European Urban History (1100–1800), vol. 33 (Turnhout: Brepols), 15–48.

Dumolyn, Jan, and Jelle Haemers (2005), 'Patterns of urban rebellion in medieval Flanders', *Journal of Medieval History* 31: 369–93.

Dumolyn, Jan, Jelle Haemers, Hipólito Rafael Oliva Herrer and Vincent Challet (eds.) (2014), *The Voices of the People in Late Medieval Europe: Communication and Popular Politics*. Studies in European Urban History (1100–1800), vol. 33 (Turnhout: Brepols).

Duplessis, Robert, and Martha Howell (1982), 'Reconsidering the early modern urban economy: The cases of Leiden and Lille', *Past & Present* 94: 49–84.

Dutour, Thierry (2012), 'Le consensus des bonnes gens: La participation des habitants aux affaires communes dans quelques villes de la langue d'oïl (XIIIe–XVe siècle)', in: Philippe Hamon and Catherine Laurent (eds.), *Le pouvoir municipal de la fin du Moyen Âge à 1789* (Rennes: Presses Universitaires de Rennes),187–208.

Dyer, Alan D. (1973), *The City of Worcester in the Sixteenth Century* (Worcester: Continuum).

(2000), 'Small market towns 1540–1700', in: Peter Clark (ed.), *The Cambridge Urban History of Britain*, vol. 2: *1540–1840* (Cambridge: Cambridge University Press), 425–50.

Eastwood, David (1997), *Government and Community in the English Provinces, 1700–1870* (Basingstoke: Macmillan).
Eckstein, Nicholas A. (1995), *The District of the Green Dragon: Neighbourhood Life and Social Change in Renaissance Florence* (Florence: Olschki).
Eckstein, Nicholas A., and Nicholas Terpstra (eds.) (2009), *Sociability and Its Discontents: Civil Society, Social Capital, and Their Alternatives in Late Medieval and Early Modern Europe* (Turnhout: Brepols).
Ehmer, Josef (1997), 'Worlds of mobility: Migration patterns of Viennese artisans in the eighteenth century', in: Geoffrey Crossick (ed.), *The Artisan and the European Town, 1500–1900* (Aldershot: Scolar Press), 172–99.
Eitel, Peter (1970), *Die oberschwäbischen Reichsstädte im Zeitalter der Zunftherrschaft: Untersuchungen zu ihrer politischen und sozialen Struktur unter besonderer Berücksichtigung der Städte Lindau, Memmingen, Ravensburg und Überlingen* (Stuttgart: Müller & Gräff).
Elbendary, Amina (2015), *Crowds and Sultans: Urban Protest in Late Medieval Egypt and Syria* (Cairo: American University of Cairo Press).
Eldem, Edhem, Daniel Goffman and Bruce Masters (1999), *The Ottoman City between East and West* (Cambridge: Cambridge University Press).
Elliott, John H. (1992), 'A Europe of composite monarchies?', *Past & Present* 137: 48–71.
(2006), *Empires of the Atlantic World: Britain and Spain in America* (New Haven, CT: Yale University Press).
Engel, Evamaria (1975), 'Städtebünde im Reich von 1226 bis 1314 – eine vergleichende Betrachtung', in: Konrad Fritze, Eckhard Müller and Johannes Schildhauer (eds.), *Bürgertum – Handelskapital – Städtebünde.* Hansische Studien, vol.3 (Weimar: Verlag Hermann Böhlau's Nachfolger), 177–209.
Engelbrecht, E. A. (1973), *De vroedschap van Rotterdam 1572–1795.* Bronnen tot de geschiedenis van Rotterdam, vol. 5 (Rotterdam: Gemeentelijke Archiefdienst).
Engerman, Stanley L., and Kenneth L. Sokoloff (1997), 'Factor endowments, institutions, and differential paths of growth among New World economies: A view from economic historians of the United States', in: S. Haber (ed.), *How Latin America Fell Behind* (Stanford, CA: Stanford University Press), 260–304.
(2003), 'Factor endowments, inequality, and paths of development among New World economies', *Economia* 3: 41–88.
(2008), 'Debating the role of institutions in political and economic development: Theory, history, and findings', *Annual Review of Political Science* 11: 119–35.
(2012), *Economic Development in the Americas since 1500: Endowments and Institutions* (New York, NY: Cambridge University Press).
Epstein, Stephan R. (1998), 'Craft guilds, apprenticeship and technological change in pre-industrial Europe', *Journal of Economic History* 53: 684–713.
(2000a), *Freedom and Growth: The Rise of States and Markets in Europe, 1300–1750* (London: Routledge).
(2000b), 'The rise and fall of Italian city-states', in: Mogens Herman Hansen (ed.), *A Comparative Study of Thirty City-State Cultures* (Copenhagen: Royal Danish Academy of Sciences and Letters), 277–93.
(2004), 'Labour mobility, journeyman organisations and markets in skilled labour Europe, 14th–18th centuries', in: L. Hilaire-Pérez and A. Garçon (eds.), *Les chemins de la nouveauté: Innover, inventer au regard de l'histoire.* Collection CTHS Histoire, vol. 9 (Paris: CTHS), 411–30.

(2006), 'The rise of the West', in: John A. Hall, and Ralph Schroeder (eds.), *An Anatomy of Power: The Social Theory of Michael Mann* (Cambridge: Cambridge University Press), 233–62.

Epstein, Stephan R., and Maarten Prak (eds.) (2008a), *Guilds, Innovation and the European Economy, 1400–1800* (Cambridge: Cambridge University Press).

(2008b), 'Introduction: Guilds, innovation and the European economy, 1400–1800', in: Stephan R. Epstein and Maarten Prak (eds.), *Guilds, Innovation and the European Economy, 1400–1800* (Cambridge: Cambridge University Press), 1–24.

Epstein, Steven A. (1991), *Wage Labor and Guilds in Medieval Europe* (Chapel Hill, NC: University of North Carolina Press).

(1996), *Genoa and the Genoese 958–1528* (Chapel Hill, NC: University of North Carolina Press).

Ertman, Thomas (1997), *The Birth of the Leviathan: Building States and Regimes in Medieval and Early Modern Europe* (Cambridge: Cambridge University Press).

Espinosa, Aurelio (2009), *The Empire of the Cities: Emperor Charles V, the* Comunero *Revolt, and the Transformation of the Spanish System.* Studies in Medieval and Reformation Traditions, vol. 137 (Leiden: Brill).

Evans, J. T. (1974), 'The decline of oligarchy in seventeenth-century Norwich', *Journal of British Studies* 14: 46–76.

(1979), *Seventeenth-Century Norwich: Politics, Religion and Government, 1620–1690* (Oxford: Clarendon Press).

Fahrmeir, Andreas (2007), *Citizenship: The Rise and Fall of a Modern Concept* (New Haven, CT: Yale University Press).

Fairchilds, Cissie (1976), *Poverty and Charity in Aix-en-Provence, 1640–1789* (Baltimore, MD: Johns Hopkins University Press).

(1993), 'The production and marketing of populuxe goods in eighteenth-century Paris', in: John Brewer and Roy Porter (eds.), *Consumption and the World of Goods* (London: Routledge), 228–48.

Faist, Thomas (2001), 'Social citizenship in the European Union: Nested membership', *Journal of Common Market Studies* 39: 37–58.

Farmer, Edward L. (2000), 'The hierarchy of Ming city walls', in: James D. Tracy (ed.), *City Walls: The Urban Enceinte in Global Perspective* (Cambridge: Cambridge University Press), 461–87.

Faroqhi, Suraiya (1986), 'Political initiatives "from the bottom up" in the sixteenth- and seventeenth-century Ottoman Empire: Some evidence for their existence', in: Hans-Georg Majer (ed.), *Osmanistische Studien zur Wirtschafts- und Sozialgeschichte* (Wiesbaden: Otto Harrasowitz), 24–33.

(2005), 'Understanding Ottoman guilds', in: Suraiya Faroqhi and Randi Deguilhem (eds.), *Crafts and Craftsmen of the Middle East: Fashioning the Individual in the Eastern Mediterranean* (London: I. B. Taurus), 3–40.

(2009), *Artisans of Empire: Crafts and Craftspeople under the Ottomans* (London: I. B. Taurus).

Farr, James R. (1985), 'Popular religious solidarity in sixteenth-century Dijon', *French Historical Studies* 14: 192–214.

(1988), *Hands of Honor: Artisans and Their World in Dijon, 1550–1650* (Ithaca, NY: Cornell University Press).

(1997), '"On the shop floor": Guilds, artisans, and the European market economy, 1350–1750', *Journal of Early Modern History* 1: 24–54.

(2000), *Artisans in Europe, 1300–1914* (Cambridge: Cambridge University Press).

Fasano, Giulio (2013), 'Governing the city', in: Tommaso Astarita (ed.), *A Companion to Early Modern Naples* (Leiden: Brill), 109–29.

Fasano Guarini, Elena (1978), 'Introduzione', in: Elena Fasano Guarini (ed.), *Potere e società negli stati regionali italiani del '500 e '600* (Bologna: Il Mulino), 7–47.
Faure, David (1996), 'The lineage as business company: Patronage versus law in the development of Chinese business', in: R. A. Brown (ed.), *Chinese Business Enterprise: Critical Perspectives on Business and Management*, vol. 1 (London: Routledge), 82–106.
Favresse, L. (1961), *Études sur les métiers bruxellois au Moyen Âge* (Brussels: Centre d'histoire économique et sociale).
Fehler, Timothy G. (1999), *Poor Relief and Protestantism: The Evolution of Social Welfare in Sixteenth-Century Emden* (Aldershot: Ashgate).
Fei, Si-yen (2009), *Negotiating Urban Space: Urbanization and Late Ming Nanjing* (Cambridge, MA: Harvard University Asia Center).
Feld, Lars B., and Bruno S. Frey (2002), 'Trust breeds trust: How taxpayers are treated', *Economics of Governance* 3: 87–99.
Feldbauer, Peter (2002), 'Die Islamitische Stadt im "Mittelalter"', in: Peter Feldbauer, Michael Mitterauer and Wolfgang Schwentker (eds.), *Die vormoderne Stadt: Asien und Europa im Vergleich* (Vienna: Oldenbourg), 79–106.
Felix, D. A. (1919), *Het oproer te Utrecht in 1610* (Utrecht: Oosthoek).
Ferraro, Joanne (2012), *Venice: History of the Floating City* (Cambridge: Cambridge University Press).
Ferrero Micó, Remedion (2009), 'The financial autonomy of the municipalities and the Valencian parliament', *Parliaments, Estates and Representation* 29: 36–52.
Fewsmith, Joseph (1983), 'From guild to interest group: The transformation of public and private in late Qing China', *Comparative Studies in Society and History* 25: 617–40.
Filmer, Paul (2000), 'Embodying citizenship: Corporeality and civility in early modernity', *European Review of History* 7: 109–21.
Finlay, R. (1980), *Politics in Renaissance Venice* (London: Ernest Benn).
Finley-Croswhite, S. Annette (1999), *Henry IV and the Towns: The Pursuit of Legitimacy in French Urban Society, 1589–1610* (Cambridge: Cambridge University Press).
Fitzsimmons, Michael P. (2010), *From Artisan to Worker: Guilds, the French State, and the Organization of Labor, 1776–1821* (New York, NY: Cambridge University Press).
Fletcher, Andrew (1997), *Political Works*, ed. by John Robertson. Cambridge Texts in the History of Political Thought (Cambridge: Cambridge University Press).
Flora, Peter J., Alber R. Eichenberg, J. Kohl, F. Kraus, W. Pfenning and K. Seebolm (1983). *State, Economy, and Society in Western Europe, 1815–1975: A Data Handbook*, vol. 1: *The Growth of Mass Democracies and Welfare States* (Frankfurt: Campus Verlag).
Flynn, Maureen (1989), *Sacred Charity: Confraternities and Social Welfare in Spain, 1400–1700* (London: MacMillan).
Fochesato, Mattia (2013), 'Did oligarchies really work better? Public finance in late medieval Siena' (mimeo).
Forsén, Björn (2002), 'Was there a south-west German city-state culture?', in: Mogens Herman Hansen (ed.), *A Comparative Study of Six City-State Cultures* (Copenhagen: Royal Danish Academy of Sciences and Letters), 91–105.
Foucault, Michel (1975), *Surveiller et punir: Naissance de la prison* (Paris: Gallimard).
François, Etienne (1978), 'Des républiques marchandes aux capitales politiques: Remarques sur la hiérarchie urbaine du Saint-Empire à l'époque moderne', *Revue d'histoire moderne et contemporaine* 25: 587–603.

Frank, Andre Gunder (1998), *ReOrient: Global Economy in the Asian Age* (Berkeley, CA: University of California Press).

Franklin, Benjamin (2005), *The Autobiography of Benjamin Franklin: Penn Reading Project Edition*, ed. by Peter Conn (Philadelphia, PA: University of Pennsylvania Press).

Frantianni, Michele, and Franco Spinelli (2006), 'Italian city-states and financial evolution', *European Review of Economic History* 10: 257–78.

Fraser, Constance M. (2009), 'The economic growth of Newcastle-upon-Tyne, 1150–1536', in: Diana Newton and A. J. Pollard (eds.), *Newcastle and Gateshead before 1700* (Chichester: Phillimore), 41–64.

Freund, Bill (2007), *The African City: A History* (Cambridge: Cambridge University Press).

Frey, Bruno S. (2003), 'Deterrence and tax morale in the European Union', *European Review* 11: 385–406.

Frey, Bruno S., and Benno Torgler (2007), 'Tax morale and conditional cooperation', *Journal of Comparative Economics* 35: 136–59.

Fridrich, Anna C. (2013), 'Women working in guild crafts: Female strategies in early modern urban economies', in: Deborah Simonton and Anne Montenach (eds.), *Female Agency in the Urban Economy: Gender in European Towns, 1640–1830* (New York: Routledge), 134–50.

Friedeburg, Robert von (1994), '"Kommunalismus" und "Republikanismus" in der Frühen Neuzeit? Überlegungen zur politischen Mobilisierung sozial differenzierter ländlicher Gemeinden unter Agrar- und Sozialhistorischem Blickwinckel', *Zeitschrift für Historische Forschung*, 21: 65–91.

Friedrich, Karin (1999), *Other Prussia: Royal Prussia, Poland and Liberty, 1659–1772* (Cambridge: Cambridge University Press).

Friedrichs, Christopher (1975), 'Capitalism, mobility and class formation in the early modern German city', *Past & Present* 69: 24–49.

(1978), 'Citizens or subjects? Urban conflict in early modern Germany', in: Miriam U. Chrisman and Otto Gründler (eds.), *Social Groups and Religious Ideas in the Sixteenth Century* (Kalamazoo, MI: American Society for Reformation Research), 46–58.

(1979), *Urban Society in an Age of War: Nördlingen, 1580–1720* (Princeton, NJ: Princeton University Press).

(2000), *Urban Politics in Early Modern Europe* (London: Routledge).

(2009), 'Urban elections and decision-making in early modern Europe and Asia: Contrasts and comparisons', in: Rudolf Schlögl (ed.), *Urban Elections and Decision-Making in Early Modern Europe, 1500–1800* (Newcastle upon Tyne: Cambridge Scholars Publishing), 300–21.

(2010), 'What made the Eurasian city work? Urban political cultures in early modern Europe and Asia', in: Glenn Clark, Judith Owens and Greg T. Smith (eds.), *City Limits: Perspectives on the Historical European City* (Montreal and Kingston: McGill-Queen's University Press), 29–64.

Fritschy, Wantje (2003), 'A "financial revolution" reconsidered: Public finance in Holland during the Dutch Revolt, 1568–1648', *Economic History Review* 56: 57–89.

Fröhlich, Sigrid (1976), *Die Soziale Sicherung bei Zünften und Gesellenverbänden.* Sozialpolitische Schriften, vol.38 (Berlin: Duncker & Humblot).

Frug, Gerald E. (2008), *City Bound: How States Stifle Urban Innovation* (Ithaca, NY: Cornell University Press).

Fuks-Mansfeld, R. G. (1989), *De Sefardim in Amsterdam tot 1795: Aspecten van een joodse minderheid in een Hollandse stad* Hollandse Studiën, vol. 23 (Hilversum: Verloren).
Fuma, Susumu (1993), 'Late Ming urban reform and the popular uprising in Hangzhou', in: Linda Cooke Johnson (ed.), *Cities of Jiangnan in Late Imperial China* (Albany, NY: State University of New York Press), 47–80.
Gadd, Ian Anders (2004), 'Were books different? The Stationers' Company in Civil War London, 1640–1645', in: Anne Goldgar and Robert I. Frost (eds.), *Institutional Culture in Early Modern Society* (Leiden: Brill), 35–58.
(2016), 'The Stationers' Company in England before 1710', in: I. Alexander and H. T. Gómez-Arostegui (eds.), *Research Handbook on the History of Copyright Law*. Research Handbooks in Intellectual Property (Cheltenham: Elgar), 81–95.
Gadd, Ian Anders, and Patrick Wallis (eds.) (2002a), *Guilds, Society and Economy in London 1450–1800* (London: Centre for Metropolitan History).
(2002b), 'Introduction', in: Ian Anders Gadd and Patrick Wallis (eds.), *Guilds, Society and Economy in London 1450–1800* (London: Centre for Metropolitan History), 1–14.
(2008), 'Reaching beyond the city wall: London guilds and national regulation, 1500–1700', in: S. R. Epstein and Maarten Prak (eds.), *Guilds, Innovation and the European Economy, 1400–1800* (Cambridge: Cambridge University Press), 288–315.
Gal, Stéphane (2000), *Grenoble au temps de la Ligue: Étude politique, sociale et religieuse d'une cité en crise (vers 1562–vers 1598)* (Grenoble: Presses Universitaires de Grenoble).
Gall, Lothar (ed.) (1991), *Vom alten zum neuen Bürgertum: Die mitteleuropäische Stadt im Umbruch 1780–1820*. Stadt und Bürgertum, vol. 3 (Munich: Oldenbourg).
Gamboni, Dario, and Georg Germann, with François de Capitani (eds.) (1991), *Zeichen der Freiheit: Das Bild der Republik in der Kunst des 16. bis 20. Jahrhunderts Ausstellung Bernisches Historisches Museum* (Bern: Stämpfli & Cie).
Garrioch, David (2002), *The Making of Revolutionary Paris* (Berkeley, CA: University of California Press).
(2017), '"Man is born for society": Confraternities and civil society in eighteenth-century Paris and Milan', *Social Science History* 41: 103–19.
Gauci, Perry (1996), *Politics and Society in Great Yarmouth, 1660–1772* (Oxford: Clarendon).
(2001), *The Politics of Trade: The Overseas Merchants in State and Society, 1660–1720* (Oxford: Oxford University Press).
(ed.) (2011), *Regulating the British Economy, 1660–1850* (Farnham: Ashgate).
Gelderblom, Oscar (2013), *Cities of Commerce: The Institutional Foundations of International Trade in the Low Countries, 1250–1650* (Princeton, NJ: Princeton University Press).
Gelderblom, Oscar, A. de Jong and J. P. B. Jonker (2013), 'The formative years of the modern corporation: The Dutch East India Company VOC, 1602–1623', *Journal of Economic History*, 73: 1050–76.
Gelderblom, Oscar, and Regina Grafe (2010), 'The rise and fall of the merchant guilds: Re-thinking the comparative study of commercial institutions in premodern Europe', *Journal of Interdisciplinary History* 40: 477–511.
Gelderen, Martin van (1992), *The Political Thought of the Dutch Revolt 1550–1590* (Cambridge: Cambridge University Press).
Gelderen, Martin van, and Quentin Skinner (eds.) (2002), *Republicanism: A Shared European Heritage*. 2 vols. (Cambridge: Cambridge University Press).

Gent, Thomas (1832), *The Life of Mr. Thomas Gent, Printer of York* (London: Thomas Thorpe).
Gerber, Haim (2010), 'The public sphere and civil society in the Ottoman Empire', in: Haim Gerber (ed.), *State and Society in the Ottoman Empire* (Farnham: Ashgate Variorum), 65–82.
Gerber, Roland (2002), 'Die Einbürgerungsfrequenzen spätmittelalterlicher Städte im regionalen Vergleich', in: Rainer Christoph Schwinges (ed.), *Neubürger im Späten Mittelalter: Migration und Austausch in der Städtelandschaft des alten Reiches (1250–1550)*. Beiheft Zeitschrift für Historische Forschung, vol. 30 (Berlin: Duncker & Humblot), 251–88.
Geyl, Pieter (1936), *Revolutiedagen te Amsterdam (Augustus–September 1748): Prins Willem IV en de Doelistenbeweging* (The Hague: Nijhoff).
Ghazaleh, Pascale (1999), *Masters of the Trade: Crafts and Craftspeople in Cairo, 1750–1850* (Cairo: American University in Cairo Press).
Gilden van Utrecht tot 1528: Verzameling van rechtsbronnen, De (1896), 2 vols, ed. by J. C. Overvoorde and J. G. Ch. Joosting (Utrecht: Nijhoff).
Gilomen, Hans-Jörg (2002), 'Städtische Sondergruppen im Bürgerrecht', in: Rainer Christoph Schwinges (ed.), *Neubürger im Späten Mittelalter: Neubürger im Späten Mittelalter: Migration und Austausch in der Städtelandschaft des alten Reiches (1250–1550)*. Beiheft Zeitschrift für Historische Forschung, vol. 30 (Berlin: Duncker & Humblot), 125–67.
Glete, Jan (2002), *War and the State in Early Modern Europe: Spain, the Dutch Republic and Sweden as Fiscal-Military states, 1500–1660* (London: Routledge).
Gmür, Rudolf (1984), 'Die Städte in der schweizerischen Verfassungsgeschichte von 1798 bis 1848', in: Hellmut Naunin (ed.), *Städteordnungen des 19. Jahrhunderts: Beiträge zur Kommunalgeschichte Mittel- und Westeuropas* Städteforschung, vol. A19 (Cologne: Böhlau), 44–102.
Goldthwaite, Richard A. (1980), *The Building of Renaissance Florence: An Economic and Social History* (Baltimore, MD: Johns Hopkins University Press).
(1993), *Wealth and the Demand for Art in Italy, 1300–1600* (Baltimore, MD: Johns Hopkins University Press).
(2009), *The Economy of Renaissance Florence* (Baltimore, MD: Johns Hopkins University Press).
González Athenas, Muriel (2013), 'Legal regulation in eighteenth-century Cologne: The agency of female artisans', in: Deborah Simonton and Anne Montenach (eds.), *Female Agency in the Urban Economy: Gender in European Towns, 1640–1830* (New York, NY: Routledge), 151–68.
(2016), 'Handlungsspielräume von Kölner Zunfthandwerkerinnen in der Frühen Neuzeit', in: Eva Jullien and Michel Pauly (eds.), *Craftsmen and Guilds in the Medieval and Early Modern Periods*. VSWG Beiheft 234 (Stuttgart: Franz Steiner), 125–40.
Goodman, Bryna (1995), *Native Place, City, and Nation: Regional Networks and Identities in Shanghai, 1853–1937* (Berkeley, CA: University of California Press).
Goosens, Marion E. W. (2001), *Schilders en de markt: Haarlem 1605–1635*. PhD dissertation, Universiteit Leiden.
Gordon, Andrew, and Trevor Stack (eds.) (2007), 'Citizenship beyond the state', special issue of *Citizenship Studies* 11: 117–228.
Goudot, Gregory (2015), 'Between town and church: Public assistance and charity in the sixteenth and seventeenth centuries', *French History* 29: 469–90.
Goudriaan, Koen (1996), 'Gilden en broederschappen', in: Koen Goudriaan et al., *De gilden in Gouda* (Zwolle: Waanders), 19–63.

Grafe, Regina (2012), *Distant Tyranny: Markets, Power, and Backwardness in Spain, 1650–1800* (Princeton, NJ: Princeton University Press).

Grafe, Regina, and Alejandra Irigoin (2006), 'The Spanish empire and its legacy: Fiscal re-distribution and political conflict in colonial and post-colonial Spanish America', *Journal of Global History* 1: 241–67.

(2012), 'A stakeholder empire: The political economy of Spanish imperial rule in America', *Economic History Review* 65: 609–51.

Grayson, J. C. (1980), 'The civic militia in the County of Holland, 1560–81: Politics and public order in the Dutch Revolt', *Bijdragen en Mededelingen betreffende de Geschiedenis der Nederlanden* 95: 35–63.

Green, Louis (1986), *Castruccio Castracani: A Study on the Origins and Character of a Fourteenth-Century Italian Despotism* (Oxford: Clarendon Press).

(1995), *Lucca under Many Masters: A Fourteenth-Century Italian Commune in Crisis (1328–1342)* (Florence: Olschki).

Greengrass, Mark (2006), 'Politics and warfare', in: Euan Cameron (ed.), *The Sixteenth Century* (Oxford: Oxford University Press), 58–88.

Greif, Avner (2006), *Institutions and the Path to the Modern Economy: Lessons from Medieval Trade* (Cambridge: Cambridge University Press).

Grell, Ole Peter, and Andrew Cunningham (eds.) (1997), *Health Care and Poor Relief in Protestant Europe 1500–1700* (London: Routledge).

Grever, John H. (1981), 'Committees and deputations in the assemblies of the Dutch Republic 1660–1668', *Parliaments, Estates and Representation* 1: 13–33.

(1982), 'The structure of decision-making in the States-General of the Dutch Republic 1660–1668', *Parliaments, Estates and Representation* 2: 125–53.

Greyerz, Kapar von (1985), 'Forschungsbericht: Stadt und Reformation: Stand und Aufgaben der Forschung', *Archiv für Reformationsgeschichte* 76: 6–63.

Grillo, Paolo (2008), *Cavalieri e popoli in armi: Le istituzioni militari nell'Italia medievale* (Bari: Laterza).

Groenveld, S. (1990), *Evidente factiën in den staet: Sociaal-politieke verhoudingen in de 17e-eeuwse Republiek der Verenigde Nederlanden.* Zeven Provinciën Reeks, vol. 1 (Hilversum: Verloren).

Groenveld, S., and H. Leeuwenberg (eds.) (1979), *De Unie van Utrecht: Wording en werking van een verbond en een verbondsacte.* Geschiedenis in veelvoud, vol. 6 (The Hague: Martinus Nijhoff).

Grubb, James S. (2000), 'Elite citizens', in: John Martin and Dennis Romano (eds.), *Venice Reconsidered: The History and Civilization of an Italian City-State, 1297–1797* (Baltimore, MD: Johns Hopkins University Press), 339–64.

Guicciardini, Francesco (1994), *Dialogue on the Government of Florence*, ed. and transl. by Alison Brown (Cambridge: Cambridge University Press).

Guignet, Philippe (1990), *Le pouvoir dans la ville au XVIIIe siècle: Pratiques politiques, notabilité et éthique sociale de part et d'autre de la frontière franco-belge* (Paris: EHESS).

Guiral, Pierre, and Paul Amargier (1983), *Histoire de Marseille* (Paris: Mazarine).

Gunn, Steven (1999), 'War, religion, and the state', in: Euan Cameron (ed.), *Early Modern Europe: An Oxford History* (Oxford: Oxford University Press), 50–73.

(2010), 'Archery practice in early Tudor England', *Past & Present* 209: 53–81.

Gunn, Steven, David Grummitt and Hans Cools (2007), *War, State, and Society in England and the Netherlands, 1477–1559* (Oxford: Oxford University Press).

Gutton, Jean-Pierre (1970), *La société et les pauvres: L'exemple de la généralité de Lyon, 1534–1789* (Paris: Les Belles Lettres).

Hadwin, J. F. (1978), 'Deflating philanthropy', *Economic History Review* 31: 105–17.

Haemers, Jelle (2004), *De Gentse opstand 1449–1453: De strijd tussen rivaliserende netwerken om het stedelijk kapitaal* Standen en landen, vol. 105 (Kortrijk-Heule: UGA).

(2009), *For the Common Good: State Power and Urban Revolts in the Reign of Mary of Burgundy (1477–1482)*. Studies in European Urban History, vol. 17 (Turnhout: Brepols).

(2012), 'Bloed en inkt: Een nieuwe blik op opstand en geweld te Leuven, 1360–1383', *Stadsgeschiedenis* 7: 141–64.

(2014), '*Ad petitionem burgensium*: Petitions and peaceful resistance of craftsmen in Flanders and Mechelen (13th–16th centuries)', in: Jesús Ángel Solórzano Telechea, Beatriz Arízaga Bolumburu and Jelle Haemers (eds.), *Los grupos populares en la ciudad medieval Europea* (Logroño: Instituto de Estudios Riojanos), 371–94.

(2016), 'Révolte et requête: Les gens de métiers et les conflits sociaux dans les villes de Flandre (XIIe–XVe siècles)', *Revue historique* no. 677: 27–56.

Hafner, Urs (2001), *Republik im Konflikt: Schwäbische Reichsstädte und bürgerliche Politik in der frühen Neuzeit* Oberschwaben: Geschichte und Kultur, vol. 8 (Tübingen: Biblioteca academica).

Hafter, Daryl (1995), 'Women who wove in the eighteenth-century silk-industry of Lyon', in: Daryl Hafter (ed.), *European Women and Preindustrial Craft* (Bloomington, IN: Indiana University Press), 42–64.

(2007), *Women at Work in Pre-Industrial France* (University Park, PA: Pennsylvania State University Press).

Hahn, Hans-Werner (1991), *Altständisches Bürgertum zwischen Beharrung und Wandel: Wetzlar 1689–1870*. Stadt und Bürgertum, vol. 2 (Munich: Oldenbourg).

Haitsma Mulier, E. O. G. (1980), *The Myth of Venice and Dutch Republican Thought in the Seventeenth Century* (Assen: Van Gorcum).

Hale, J. R. (1977), *Florence and the Medici: The Pattern of Control* (London: Thames & Hudson).

Haliczer, Stephen (1981), *The Comuneros of Castile: The Forging of a Revolution, 1475–1521* (Madison, WI: University of Wisconsin Press).

Halliday, Paul D. (1998), *Dismembering the Body Politic: Partisan Politics in England's Towns, 1650–1730* (Cambridge: Cambridge University Press).

Hamm, Berndt (1995), 'The urban Reformation in the Holy Roman Empire', in: Thomas A. Brady, Heiko A. Obermann and James D. Tracy (eds.), *Handbook of European History: Late Middle Ages, Renaissance and Reformation*, vol. 2: *Visions, Programs and Outcomes* (Leiden: Brill), 193–227.

(1996), *Bürgertum und Glaube: Konturen der städtischen Reformation* (Göttingen: Vandenhoeck & Ruprecht).

Hammel-Kiesow, Rolf (2015), 'The early Hanses', in: Donald J. Harreld (ed.), *A Companion to the Hanseatic League* (Leiden: Brill), 15–63.

Hammer, Paul E. J. (ed.) (2007), *Warfare in Early Modern Europe 1450–1660* (Aldershot: Ashgate).

Hamon, Philippe (2012), 'Rennes au temps de la Ligue: Pouvoir municipal et pouvoirs dans la ville', in: Philippe Hamon and Catherine Laurent (eds.), *Le pouvoir municipal de la fin du Moyen Âge à 1789* (Rennes: Presses Universitaires de Rennes), 271–84.

Hanna, Nelly (1984), *Construction Work in Ottoman Cairo (1517–1798)*. Supplément aux Annales Islamologiques, Cahier 4 (Cairo: Institut Français d'Archéologie Orientale).

Hanschmidt, Alwin (1994), 'Zwischen bürgerlichen Stadtautonomie und fürstlicher Stadtherrschaft', in: Franz-Josef Jakobi (ed.), *Geschichte der Stadt Münster*, vol. 1 (Münster: Aschendorff), 249–99.

(2000), 'Zur Armenpolizei und Armenversorgung in der Stadt Münster im 17. Jahrhundert', in: Peter Johanek (ed.), *Städtisches Gesundheits- und Fürsorgewesen vor 1800*. Städteforschung, vol. A50 (Cologne: Böhlau), 225–41.

(2002), 'Armut und Bettelei: Armenpolizei und Armenfürsorge in der Stadt Münster im 17. Jahrhundert', in: F. Jakobi et al. (eds.), *Strukturwandel der Armenfürsorge* (Münster: Aschendorff), 27–92.

Harrington, James (1992), 'The commonwealth of Oceana and a system of politics', in: J. G. A. Pocock (ed.), *Cambridge Texts in the History of Political Thought* (Cambridge: Cambridge University Press).

Harris, Ron (2013), 'Could the crown credibly commit to respect its charters? England, 1558–1640', in: D'Maris Coffman, Adrian Leonard and Larry Neal (eds.), *Questioning Credible Commitment: Perspectives on the Rise of Financial Capitalism* (Cambridge: Cambridge University Press), 21–47.

Hart, Emma (2017), 'City government and the state in eighteenth-century South Carolina', *Eighteenth-Century Studies* 50: 195–211.

't Hart, Marjolein (1993a), 'Freedom and restrictions: State and economy in the Dutch Republic, 1570–1670', in: Karel Davids and Leo Noordegraaf (eds.), *The Dutch Economy in the Golden Age: Nine Studies* (Amsterdam: NEHA), 105–30.

(1993b), *The Making of a Bourgeois State: War, Politics and Finance during the Dutch Revolt* (Manchester: Manchester University Press).

(1994), 'Intercity rivalries and the making of the Dutch state', in: Charles Tilly and Wim P. Blockmans (eds.), *Cities and the Rise of States in Europe, A.D. 1000 to 1800* (Boulder, CO: Westview Press), 196–217.

(1995), 'The Dutch Republic: The urban impact upon politics', in: C. A. Davids and J. Lucassen (eds.), *A Miracle Mirrored: The Dutch Republic in European Perspective* (Cambridge: Cambridge University Press), 57–98.

(1997), 'The merits of a financial revolution: Public finance, 1550–1700', in: Marjolein 't Hart, Joost Jonker and Jan Luiten van Zanden (eds.), *A Financial History of the Netherlands* (Cambridge: Cambridge University Press), 11–36.

(2014), *The Dutch Wars of Independence: Warfare and Commerce in the Netherlands, 1570–1680* (London: Routledge).

Hartmann, Wilfried (1993), *Der Investiturstreit*. Enzyklopädie Deutscher Geschichte, vol. 21 (Munich: Oldenbourg).

Haskett, Robert (1991), *Indigenous Rulers: An Ethnohistory of Town Government in Colonial Cuernavaca* (Albuquerque, NM: University of New Mexico Press).

Haupt, Heinz-Gerhard (ed.) (2002), *Das Ende der Zünfte: Ein europäischer Vergleich*. Kritische Studien zur Geschichtswissenschaft, vol. 151 (Göttingen: Vandenhoeck & Ruprecht).

Haverkamp-Begemann, E. (1982), *Rembrandt: The Nightwatch* (Princeton, NJ: Princeton University Press).

Hay, D. (1977), *The Church in Italy in the Fifteenth Century* (Cambridge: Cambridge University Press).

Heater, Derek (1990), *Citizenship: The Civic Ideal in World History, Politics, and Education* (Manchester: Manchester University Press).

(1999), *What Is Citizenship?* (Cambridge: Polity Press).

Heerma van Voss, Lex (2001), 'Introduction', in: Lex Heerma van Voss (ed.), *Petitions in Social History* (*International Review of Social History* 46, Supplement 9) (Cambridge: Cambridge University Press), 1–10.

Heerma van Voss, Lex, and Marco H. D. van Leeuwen (2012), 'Charity in the Dutch Republic: An introduction', *Continuity and Change* 27: 175–97.

Heijden, Manon van der, Elise van Nederveen Meerkerk, Griet Vermeesch and Martijn van der Burg (eds.) (2009), *Serving the Community: The Rise of Public Facilities in the Low Countries* (Amsterdam: Aksant).

Heinig, Paul-Joachim (1988), 'Städte und Königtum im Zeitalter der Reichsverdichting', in: Neithard Bulst and J.-Ph. Genet (eds.), *La ville, la bourgeoisie et la genèse de l'état moderne (XIIe–XVIIIe siècles)* (Paris: Éditions du CNRS), 87–111.

Heinrich, Gerd (1981), 'Staatsaufsicht und Stadtfreiheit in Brandenburg-Preussen unter dem Absolutismus (1660–1806)', in: Wilhelm Rausch (ed.), *Die Städte Mitteleuropas im 17. und 18. Jahrhundert* (Linz/Donau: s.n.), 155–72.

Heinzen, Toni (1939), *Zunftkämpfe, Zunftherrschaft und Wehrverfassung in Köln: Ein Beitrag zum Thema 'Zünfte und Wehrverfassung'*. PhD dissertation, Universität zu Köln.

Hell, Maarten (2004), 'De Oude Geuzen en de Opstand: Politiek en lokaal bestuur in tijd van oorlog en expansie, 1578–1650', in: Willem Frijhoff and Maarten Prak (eds.), *Geschiedenis van Amsterdam*, vol. 2A: *Centrum van de wereld, 1578–1650* (Amsterdam: SUN), 241–97.

Henderson, John (1994), *Piety and Charity in Late Medieval Florence* (Oxford: Clarendon).

Herborn, Wolfgang (1985), 'Der graduierte Ratsherr: Zur Entwicklung einer neuen Elite im Kölner Rat der frühen Neuzeit', in: Heinz Schilling and Herman Diederiks (eds.), *Bürgerliche Eliten in den Niederlanden und in Nordwestdeutschland: Studien zur Sozialgeschichte des europäischen Bürgertums im Mittelalter und in der Neuzeit*. Städteforschung, vol. A/23 (Cologne: Böhlau), 337–400.

Herlihy, David (1958), *Pisa in the Early Renaissance* (New Haven, CT: Yale University Press).

(1990), *Opera muliebria: Women and Work in Medieval Europe* (New York, NY: McGraw-Hill).

Herlihy, David, and Christiane Klapisch-Zuber (1978), *Les Toscans et leur familles: Une étude du catasto florentin de 1427* (Paris: Presses de la Fondation Nationale des Sciences Politiques).

Herzog, Tamar (2003), *Defining Nations: Immigrants and Citizens in Early Modern Spain and Spanish America* (New Haven, CT: Yale University Press).

(2007), 'Communities becoming a nation: Spain and Spanish America in the wake of modernity (and thereafter)', *Citizenship Studies* 11: 151–72.

Hesselink, Lidewij (1999), 'Goud- en zilversmeden en hun gilde in Amsterdam in de 17de en 18de eeuw', *Holland* 31: 127–47.

Heusinger, Sabine von (2010), 'Von "Antwerk" bis "Zunft": Methodische Überlegungen zu den Zünften im Mittelalter', *Zeitschrift für historische Forschung* 37: 37–71.

(2016), 'Vater, Mutter, Kind: Die Zunftfamilie als Wirtschaftseinheit', in: Eva Jullien and Michel Pauly (eds.), *Craftsmen and Guilds in the Medieval and Early Modern Periods*. VSWG Beiheft 234 (Stuttgart: Franz Steiner), 157–73.

Heuvel, Daniëlle van den (2013), 'Guilds, gender policies and economic opportunities for women in early modern Dutch towns', in: Deborah Simonton and Anne Montenach (eds.), *Female Agency in the Urban Economy: Gender in European Towns, 1640–1830* (New York, NY: Routledge), 116–33.

Heuvel, Daniëlle van den, and Sheilagh Ogilvie (2013), 'Retail development in the consumer revolution: The Netherlands, c.1670–c.1815', *Explorations in Economic History* 50: 69–87.

Heuvel, N. H. L. van den (ed.) (1946), *De ambachtsgilden van 's-Hertogenbosch vóór 1629: Rechtsbronnen van het bedrijfsleven en het gildewezen.* Werken der Vereeniging tot uitgaaf der bronnen van het oud-vaderlandsch recht, series 3 no. 13 (Utrecht: Kemink).

Hexter, J. H. (1961), *Reappraisals in History: New Views on History and Society in Early Modern Europe* (New York, NY: Harper & Row).

(1979), *On Historians: Reappraisals of Some of the Masters of Modern History* (Cambridge, MA: Harvard University Press).

Hibben, C. C. (1983), *Gouda in Revolt: Particularism and Pacifism in the Revolt of the Netherlands 1572–1588* (Utrecht: Hes).

Hickey, Daniel (1997), *Local Hospitals in Ancien Régime France: Rationalization, Resistance, Renewal, 1530–1789* (Montreal: McGill-Queen's University Press).

Hicks, John (1969), *A Theory of Economic History* (Oxford: Clarendon Press).

Hildebrandt, Reinhard (1974), 'Rat contra Bürgerschaft: Die Verfassungskonflikte in den Reichsstädten des 17. und 18. Jahrhunderts', *Zeitschrift für Stadtgeschichte, Stadtsoziologie, und Denkmalpflege* 1: 221–41.

Hindess, Barry (2004), 'Citizenship for all', *Citizenship Studies* 8: 305–15.

Hindle, Steve (2000), *The State and Social Change in Early Modern England, c. 1550–1640* (Houndmills: Macmillan).

Hippler, Thomas (2008), *Citizens, Soldiers and National Armies: Military Service in France and Germany, 1789–1830* (London: Routledge).

Hirschman, Albert O. (1970), *Exit, Voice and Loyalty: Responses to Decline in Firms, Organizations, and States* (Cambridge, MA: Harvard University Press).

Hobsbawm, E. J., and George Rudé (1969), *Captain Swing* (Harmondsworth: Allen Lane).

Hodges, Graham R. (1988), 'Legal bonds of attachment: The freemanship law of New York City, 1648–1801', in: W. Pencak and C. E. Wright (eds.), *Authority and Resistance in Early New York* (New York, NY: New York Historical Society), 226–44.

Hoffman, Philip T. (1996), *Growth in a Traditional Society: The French Countryside, 1450–1715* (Princeton, NJ: Princeton University Press).

(2015), *Why Did Europe Conquer the World?* (Princeton, NJ: Princeton University Press).

Hoffmann, Philip R. (2007), 'In defence of corporate liberties: Early modern guilds and the problem of illicit artisan work', *Urban History* 34: 76–88.

Hohenberg, Paul, and Lynn Hollen Lees (1985), *The Making of Urban Europe 1000–1950* (Cambridge MA: Harvard University Press).

Holbach, Rudolf (2016), 'Mittelalterliche Zünfte und Handwerker im Lichte wirtschafts-, sozial- und kulturwissenschaftlicher Theorien', in: Eva Jullien and Michel Pauly (eds.), *Craftsmen and Guilds in the Medieval and Early Modern Periods.* VSWG Beiheft 234 (Stuttgart: Franz Steiner), 15–36.

Holmes, George (1973), 'The emergence of an urban ideology at Florence *c.* 1250–1450', *Transactions of the Royal Historical Society* 23: 111–34.

Holt, Mack P. (1991), 'Popular political culture and mayoral elections in sixteenth-century Dijon', in: Mack P. Holt (ed.), *Society and Institutions in Early Modern France* (Athens, GA: University of Georgia Press), 98–116.

(1995), *The French Wars of Religion, 1562–1629* (Cambridge: Cambridge University Press).

Honeyman, K., and J. Goodman (1991), 'Women's work, gender conflict, and labour markets in Europe, 1500–1900', *Economic History Review* 2nd series 44: 608–28.

Hooft, Pieter Corneliszoon (1871–1925), *Memoriën en Adviezen.* 2 vols. Ed. by H. A. Enno van Gelder (Utrecht: Kemink).
Hoogenboom, Marcel, Christopher Kissane, Maarten Prak, Patrick Wallis and Chris Minns (2018), 'Guild traditions, economic development and the formation of national political economies in Germany, the United Kingdom and the Netherlands in the 19th and early 20th centuries' *Theory and Society* 47.
Hooghe, Liesbet, and Gary Marks (2003), 'Unraveling the central state, but how? Types of multi-level governance', *American Political Science Review* 97: 233–43.
Hook, Judith (1979), *Siena: A City and Its History* (London: Hamilton).
Hoppenbrouwers, Peter (2013), 'An Italian city-state geared for war: Urban knights and the *cavallate* of Todi', *Journal of Medieval History* 39: 240–53.
Hoppit, Julian (1996), 'Patterns of parliamentary legislation, 1660–1800', *The Historical Journal* 39: 109–31.
(2000), *A Land of Liberty? England 1689–1727* (Oxford: Clarendon Press).
(2002), 'Checking the Leviathan, 1688–1832', in: Donald Winch and Patrick K. O'Brien (eds.), *The Political Economy of British Historical Experience, 1688–1914* (Oxford: Oxford University Press), 267–94.
Horn, Jeff (2015), *Economic Development in Early Modern France: The Privilege of Liberty, 1650–1820* (Cambridge: Cambridge University Press).
Houston, R. A. (1993), 'The military and Edinburgh society', *War & Society* 11: 41–56.
Hovland, Stephanie R. (2006), *Apprenticeship in Later Medieval London (c.1300–c.1530)*, PhD thesis, University of London (Royal Holloway).
Hovy, J. (1966), *Het voorstel van 1751 tot instelling van een beperkt vrijhavenstelsel in de Republiek* (Groningen: Wolters).
(1980), 'Institutioneel onvermogen in de 18de eeuw', in: D. P. Blok et al. (eds.), *Algemene geschiedenis der Nederlanden*, vol. 9 (Haarlem: Fibula-Van Dishoeck), 126–38.
Howell, Martha (1986a), *Women, Production, and Patriarchy in Late Medieval Cities* (Chicago, IL: University of Chicago Press).
(1986b), 'Women, the family economy and the structures of market production in cities of Northern Europe during the Middle Ages', in: Barbara Hanawalt (ed.), *Women and Work in Pre-Industrial Europe* (Bloomington, IN: Indiana University Press), 198–222.
(1988), 'Citizenship and gender: Women's political status in northern medieval cities', in: Mary Erler and Maryanne Kowaleski (eds.), *Women and Power in the Middle Ages* (Athens, GA: University of Georgia Press), 37–61.
Hrdlička, Josef (2009), 'Symbols of consent: The rituals of the election and renovation of the city council in early modern Czech cities, 1550–1700', in: R. Schlögl (ed.), *Urban Elections and Decision-Making in Early Modern Europe, 1500–1800* (Newcastle upon Tyne: Cambridge Scholars), 94–115.
Hsia, Ronnie Po-chia (1984), *Society and Religion in Münster, 1535–1618* (New Haven, CT: Yale University Press).
(1987), 'The myth of the commune: Recent historiography on city and Reformation in Germany', *Central European History* 20: 203–15.
(2006), 'Jews before the law: Corporate statutes and judicial practices for a minority in cities of the Holy Roman Empire, 16th–17th centuries', in: Marc Boone and Maarten Prak (eds.), *Statuts individuels, statuts corporatifs et statuts judiciares dans les villes européennes (moyen âge et temps modernes) / Individual, Corporate, and Judicial Status in European Cities (Late Middle Ages and Early Modern Period)* (Louvain/Apeldoorn: Garant), 225–36.

Huang, Philip C. C. (1993), '"Public sphere" / "civil society" in China? The third realm between state and society', *Modern China* 19: 216–40.

Hufton, Olwen H. (1992), *Women and the Limits of the French Revolution* (Toronto: University of Toronto Press).

Hügin, Thomas O. (1997), 'Have we studied the wrong authors? On the relevance of Althusius as a political theorist', in: Giuseppe Duso, Werner Krawietz and Dieter Wydunckel (eds.), *Konsens und Konsoziation in der politische Theorie des frühen Föderalismus*. Rechtstheorie, Beiheft 16 (Berlin: Duncker & Humboldt), 219–40.

Hulsebosch, Daniel J. (2005), *Constituting Empire: New York and the Transformation of Constitutionalism in the Atlantic World, 1664–1830* (Chapel Hill, NC: University of North Carolina Press).

Humphries, Jane (2003), 'English apprenticeship: A neglected factor in the first Industrial Revolution', in: Paul A. David and Mark Thomas (eds.), *The Economic Future in Historical Perspective* (Oxford: Oxford University Press), 73–103.

(2010), *Childhood and Child Labour in the British Industrial Revolution* (Cambridge: Cambridge University Press).

Hunt, Lynn (1976), 'Committees and communes: Local politics and national revolution in 1789', *Comparative Studies in Society and History* 18: 321–46.

(2007), *Inventing Human Rights: A History* (New York, NY: W. W. Norton).

Hunt, Lynn, and George Sheridan (1986), 'Corporatism, association, and the language of labor in France, 1750–1850', *Journal of Modern History* 58: 813–44.

Iländer, Beate (2000), 'Verfassung und Verwaltung der Reichsstadt Hall vom Ende des Dreissigjährigen Krieges bis zum Ende der Reichsstadtzeit (1648–1806)'. PhD dissertation, Eberhard-Karls Universität Tübingen.

Irigoin, Alejandra, and Regina Grafe (2008), 'Bargaining for absolutism: A Spanish path to nation-state and empire building', *Hispanic American Historical Review* 88: 173–209.

(2013), 'Bounded Leviathan: Fiscal constraints and financial development in the early modern Hispanic world', in: D'Maris Coffman, Adrian Leonard and Larry Neal (eds.), *Questioning Credible Commitment: Perspectives on the Rise of Financial Capitalism* (Cambridge: Cambridge University Press), 199–227.

Irvine, Frederick M. (1989), 'From Renaissance city to Ancien Régime capital: Montpellier *c.*1500–*c.*1600', in: Philip Benedict (ed.), *Cities and Social Change in Early Modern France* (London: Routledge), 105–33.

Isaacs, Ann Katherine (1997), 'States in Tuscany and Veneto, 1200–1500', in: Peter Blickle (ed.), *Resistance, Representation, and Community* (Oxford: Clarendon Press), 291–304.

Isaacs, Ann Katherine, and Maarten Prak (1996), 'Cities, bourgeoisies, and states', in: Wolfgang Reinhard (ed.), *Power Elites and State Building* (Oxford: Oxford University Press), 207–34.

Isenmann, Eberhard (1997), 'Norms and values in the European city, 1300–1800', in: Peter Blickle (ed.), *Resistance, Representation, and Community* (Oxford: Clarendon Press), 185–215.

(2002), 'Bürgerrecht und Bürgeraufnahme in der spätmittelalterlichen und frühneuzeitlichen Stadt', in: Rainer Christoph Schwinges (ed.), *Neubürger im Späten Mittelalter: Migration und Austausch in der Städtelandschaft des alten Reiches (1250–1550)*. Beiheft Zeitschrift für Historische Forschung, vol. 30 (Berlin: Duncker & Humblot), 203–49.

(2003), 'Ratsliteratur und städtische Ratsordnungen des späten Mittelalters und der frühen Neuzeit: Soziologie des Rats – Amt und Willensbildung – politische Kultur', in: Pierre Monnet and Otto Gerhard Oexle (eds.), *Stadt und Recht im*

Mittelalter / La ville et le droit au Moyen Âge. Veröffentlichungen des Max-Planck-Instituts für Geschichte, vol. 174 (Göttingen: Vandenhoeck & Ruprecht), 215–479.

(2010), 'The notion of the common good, the concept of politics, and practical policies in late medieval and early modern German cities', in: Élodie Lecuppre-Desjardin and Anne-Laure Van Bruaene (eds.), *De Bono Communi: The Discourse and Practice of the Common Good in the European City (13th–16th c.)*. Studies in European Urban History, vol. 22 (Turnhout: Brepols), 107–48.

(2012), *Die Deutsche Stadt im Mittelalter, 1150–1550: Stadtgestalt, Recht, Verfassung, Stadtregiment, Kirche, Gesellschaft, Wirtschaft* (Vienna: Böhlau).

Isin, Engin (ed.) (1999), 'Cities and citizenship in a global age', special issue of *Citizenship Studies* 3: 165–283.

(2002), 'City, democracy and citizenship: Historical images, contemporary practices', in: Engin F. Isin and Bryan S. Turner (eds.), *Handbook of Citizenship Studies* (London: Sage), 305–16.

(2003), 'Historical sociology of the city', in: Gerard Delanty and Engin F. Isin (eds.), *Handbook of Historical Sociology* (London: Sage), 312–25.

(2005), 'Citizenship after orientalism', in: F. Keyman and A. Icduygu (eds.), *Citizenship in a Global World: European Questions and Turkish Experiences*. Routledge Studies in Governance and Change in the Global Era (London: Routledge), 31–51.

(2007), 'City.state: Critique of scalar thought', *Citizenship Studies* 11: 211–28.

(2008a), 'Beneficence and difference: Ottoman Awqaf and "other" subjects', in: S. Mayaram (ed.), *The Other Global City* (London: Routledge), 35–53.

(2008b), 'The city as the site of the social', in: Engin F. Isin (ed.), *Recasting the Social in Citizenship* (Toronto: Toronto University Press), 261–80.

(2012a), 'Citizens without nations', *Environment and Planning D: Society and Space* 30: 450–67.

(2012b), *Citizens without Frontiers* (London: Bloomsbury).

Isin, Engin, and Greg M. Nielsen (eds.) (2008), *Acts of Citizenship* (London: Palgrave).

Isin, Engin, and Peter Nyers (eds.) (2014), *Routledge Handbook of Citizenship Studies* (London: Routledge).

Isin, Engin, and Bryan S. Turner (2002a), 'Citizenship studies: An introduction', in: Engin F. Isin and Bryan S. Turner (eds.), *Handbook of Citizenship Studies* (London: Sage), 1–10.

(eds.) (2002b), *Handbook of Citizenship Studies* (London: Sage).

(2007), 'Investigating citizenship: An agenda for citizenship studies', *Citizenship Studies* 11: 5–17.

Israel, Jonathan I. (1979), 'The Holland towns and the Dutch–Spanish conflict, 1621–1648', *Bijdragen en Mededelingen betreffende de Geschiedenis der Nederlanden* 94: 41–69.

(1989), *Dutch Primacy in World Trade 1585–1740* (Oxford: Clarendon Press).

(1995), *The Dutch Republic: Its Rise, Greatness, and Fall 1477–1806* (Oxford: Oxford University Press).

(1998), *European Jewry in the Age of Mercantilism, 1550–1750* (London: Littman Library of Jewish Civilization).

Jack, Sybil M. (1996), *Towns in Tudor and Stuart Britain* (Basingstoke: Macmillan).

Janiskee, Brian P. (2010), *Local Government in Early America: The Colonial Experience and Lessons from the Founders* (Lanham, MD: Rowman & Littlefield).

Janssens, G. (1974), 'Brabant in verzet tegen Alva's tiende en twintigste penning', *Bijdragen en Mededelingen betreffende de Geschiedenis der Nederlanden* 89: 16–31.

Jardine, Lisa (1996), *Worldly Goods: A New History of the Renaissance* (New York, NY: Norton).

Johanek, Peter (2000), 'Imperial and free towns of the Holy Roman Empire: City-states in pre-modern Germany?', in: Mogens Herman Hansen (ed.), *A Comparative Study of Thirty City-State Cultures* (Copenhagen: Royal Danish Academy of Sciences and Letters), 295–319.

Johnson, Linda Cooke (1995), *Shanghai: From Market Town to Treaty Port, 1074–1858* (Stanford, CA: Stanford University Press).

Johnson, Lyman (1986), 'Artisans', in: L. S. Hoberman and S. M. Socolow (eds.), *Cities and Society in Colonial Latin America* (Albuquerque, NM: University of New Mexico Press), 227–50.

Jones, Philip J. (1997), *The Italian City-State: From Commune to Signoria* (Oxford: Clarendon).

(2010, orig. 1965), 'Communes and despots: The city state in late-Medieval Italy', in: John E. Law and Bernadette Paton (eds.), *Communes and Despots in Medieval and Renaissance Italy* (Farnham: Ashgate), 3–24.

de Jong, J. J. (1985), *Met goed fatsoen: De elite in een Hollandse stad, Gouda 1700–1780*. Hollandse Historische Reeks, vol. 4 (Amsterdam/Dieren: De Bataafsche Leeuw).

de Jongste, J. A. F. (1984), *Onrust aan het Spaarne: Haarlem in de jaren 1747–1751*. Hollandse Historische Reeks, vol. 2 (s.l.: De Bataafsche Leeuw).

Junot, Yves (2000), 'L'Aumône Générale de Valenciennes (1531–1566): Ordre public, richesse et pauvreté jusqu'à la veille de la Révolte des Pays-Bas', *Revue du Nord* 82 (no. 334): 53–72.

(2009), *Les bourgeois de Valenciennes: Anatomie d'une élite dans la ville (1500–1630)* (Villeneuve d'Asq: Presses Universitaires de Septentrion).

(2015), 'Les milices bourgeoises au temps des guerres civiles: Force de déstabilisation ou instrument de pacification de la société urbaine? (Valenciennes, anciens Pays-Bas espagnols, 1560–1600)', in: Serge Brunet and José Javier Ruiz Ibáñez (eds.), *Les milices dans la première modernité* (Rennes: Presses universitaires de Rennes), 35–46.

Jütte, Robert (1994), *Poverty and Deviance in Early Modern Europe* (Cambridge: Cambridge University Press).

Kaiser, Wolfgang (1992), *Marseille au temps des Troubles: Morphologie sociale et luttes de factions, 1559–1596* (Paris: Éditions de l'EHESS).

Kamenskii, Alexander (2015), 'Citizenship in eighteenth-century Russian towns', in: Michel Pauly and Alexander Lee (eds.), *Urban Liberties and Citizenship from the Middle Ages up to Now / Libertés et citoyenneté urbaines du moyen âge à nos jours / Städtische Freiheiten und bürgerliche Partizipation vom Mittelalter bis heute. Actes du Colloque 2009 de la Commission internationale pour l'Histoire des villes Beiträge zur Landes- und Kulturgeschichte*, vol. 9 (Trier: Porta Alba), 201–09.

Kan, F. J. W. van (1988), *Sleutels tot de macht: De ontwikkeling van het Leidse patriciaat tot 1420* (Hilversum: Verloren).

Kannowski, Bernd (2001), *Bürgerkämpfe und Friedebriefe: Rechtliche Streitbeilegungen in spätmittelalterlichen Städten*. Forschungen zur deutschen Rechtsgeschichte, vol. 19 (Cologne: Böhlau).

Kaplan, Benjamin (1995), *Calvinists and Libertines: Confession and Community in Utrecht, 1578–1620* (Oxford: Clarendon Press).

(2000), 'A clash of values: The survival of Utrecht's confraternities after the Reformation and the debate about their dissolution', *De Zeventiende Eeuw* 16: 100–17.

Kaplan, S. L. (1986), 'Social classification and representation in the corporate world of eighteenth-century France: Turgot's "carnival"', in: Steven L. Kaplan and Cynthia Koepp (eds.), *Work in France: Representations, Meaning, Organizations, and Practice* (Ithaca, NY: Cornell University Press), 176–228.

(1988), 'Les corporations, les "faux ouvriers" et le faubourg Saint-Antoine au XVIIIe siècle', *Annales HSS* 43: 353–78.

(1993), 'L'apprentisage au XVIIIe siècle: Le cas de Paris', *Revue d'histoire moderne et contemporaine* 40: 436–79.

(1996), *The Bakers of Paris and the Bread Question, 1700–1775* (Durham, NC: Duke University Press).

(2001), *La fin des corporations* (Paris: Fayard).

Karaman, K. Kinvanç, and Şevket Pamuk (2001), 'Ottoman finances in European perspective, 1500–1914', *Journal of Economic History* 70: 593–629.

Keats-Rohan, Katherine S. B. (ed.) (2007) *Prosopography: Approaches and Applications: A Handbook* (Oxford: Occasional Publications UPR, parts available at http://prosopography.modhist.ox.ac.uk/course_syllabuses.htm).

Keller, Hagen (1976), 'Die Entstehung der italienischen Stadtkommune als Problem der Sozialgeschichte', *Frühmittelalterliche Studien* 10: 169–211.

(1988), '"Kommune": Städtische Selbstregierung und mittelalterliche "Volksherrschaft" im Spiegel italienischer Wahlverfahren des 12.-14. Jahrhunderts', in: Gerd Althoff, Dieter Gerhard Geuenich, Otto Gerhard Oexle and Joachim Wallasch (eds.), *Person und Gemeinschaft im Mittelalter: Karl Schmid zum fünfundsechzigsten Geburtstag* (Sigmaringen: Thorbecke), 573–616.

Kennedy, Paul (1987), *The Rise and Fall of the Great Powers: Economic Change and Military Conflict from 1500–2000* (New York, NY: Vintage Books).

Kent, D. V., and F. W. Kent (1982), *Neighbours and Neighbourhood in Renaissance Florence: The District of the Red Lion in the Fifteenth Century* (Locust Valley, NJ: J. J. Augustin).

Kevorkian, Tanya (2000), 'The rise of the poor, weak, and wicked: Poor care, punishment, religion, and patriarchy in Leipzig, 1700–1730', *Journal of Social History* 34: 163–81.

Khoury, Dina Rizk (1997), *State and Provincial Society in the Ottoman Empire: Mosul, 1540–1834* (Cambridge: Cambridge University Press).

(2008), 'Political relations between city and state in the Middle East, 1700–1850', in: Peter Sluglett (ed.), *The Urban Social History of the Middle East, 1750–1950* (Syracuse, NY: Syracuse University Press), 67–103.

King, Steven (2011), 'Welfare regimes and welfare regions in Britain and Europe, c.1750 to 1860s', *Journal of Modern European History* 9: 42–65.

Kinsbruner, Jay (1987), *Petty Capitalism in Spanish America: The Pulperos of Puebla, Mexico City, Caracas, and Buenos Aires* (Boulder, CO: Westview Press).

(2005), *The Colonial Spanish-American City: Urban Life in the Age of Atlantic Capitalism* (Austin, TX: University of Texas Press).

Kint, An (1996), 'Becoming civic community: Citizenship in sixteenth-century Antwerp', in: M. Boone and M. Prak (eds.), *Statuts individuels, statuts corporatifs et statuts judiciares dans les villes européennes (moyen âge et temps modernes) / Individual,*

Corporate, and Judicial Status in European Cities (Late Middle Ages and Early Modern Period) (Louvain/Apeldoorn: Garant), 157–69.
Kirchhoff, Karl-Heinz (1973), *Die Täufer in Münster 1534/35*. Veröffentlichungen der Historischen Kommission Westfalens, vol. 22 (Münster: Aschendorff).
(1980), 'Die Unruhen in Münster/W. 1450–1457: Ein Beitrag zur Topographie und Prosopographie einer städtischen Protestbewegung; mit einem Exkurs: Rat, Gilde und Gemeinheit in Münster 1354–1458', in: Wilfried Ehbrecht (ed.), *Städtische Führungsgruppen und Gemeinde in der werdende Neuzeit Städteforschung*, vol. A9 (Cologne: Böhlau), 153–312.
(1988), 'Gesamtgilde und Gemeinheit in Münster (Westf.) 1410 bis 1661: Zur Entwicklung einer bürgerschaftlichen Vertretung innerhalb der Ratsverfassung', in: Karl-Heinz Kirchhoff, *Forschungen zur Geschichte von Stadt und Stift Münster: Ausgewählte Aufsätze und Schriftenverzeichnis*, ed. by Franz Petri, Peter Schöller, Heinz Stoob and Peter Johanek (Warendorf: Fahlbusch), 235–79.
Kirshner, Julius (1973), 'Civitas sibi faciat civem: Bartolus of Sassoferrato on the making of a citizen', *Speculum* 48: 694–713.
Kishlansky, Mark (1986), *Parliamentary Selection: Social and Political Choice in Early Modern England* (Cambridge: Cambridge University Press).
Kivelson, Valerie (2002), 'Muscovite "citizenship": Rights without freedom', *Journal of Modern History* 74: 465–89.
Klein, Alexander (2001), '"Den armen Notdürftigen ... gepuerliche Handraichung ton": Das Freiburger Armenwesen in der frühen Neuzeit', in: Heiko Haumann and Hans Schadek (eds.), *Geschichte der Stadt Freiburg-im-Breisgau*, vol. 2 (Stuttgart: Theiss), 354–67.
Klein, S. R. E. (1995), *Patriots republikanisme: Politieke cultuur in Nederland (1766–1787)* (Amsterdam: Amsterdam University Press).
Klötzer, Ralf (1992), *Die Täuferherrschaft von Münster: Stadtreformation und Welterneuerung*. Reformationsgeschichtliche Studien und Texte, vol. 131 (Münster: Aschendorff).
(1997), *Kleiden, Speisen, Beherbergen: Armenfürsorge und soziale Stiftungen in Münster im 16. Jahrhundert (1535–1588)*. Studien zur Geschichte der Armenfürsorge und der Sozialpolitik in Münster, vol. 3 (Münster: Aschendorff).
Kluge, Arnd (2007), *Die Zünfte* (Stuttgart: Franz Steiner).
Knapton, Michael (2012), 'Venice and the Terraferma', in: Andrea Gamberini and Isabella Lazzarini (eds.), *The Italian Renaissance State* (Cambridge: Cambridge University Press), 132–55.
Knevel, Paul (1988), 'Onrust onder Schutters: De Politieke Invloed van de Hollandse Schutterijen in de Eerste Helft van de Zeventiende Eeuw', *Holland: Regionaal-Historisch Tijdschrift* 20: 158–74.
(1994), *Burgers in het geweer: De schutterijen in Holland, 1550–1700*. Hollandse Studiën, vol. 32 (Hilversum: Verloren).
Knights, Mark (1997), 'A city revolution: The remodelling of the London Livery Companies in the 1680s', *English Historical Review* 112: 1141–78.
(2005), *Representation and Misrepresentations in Later Stuart Britain: Partisanship and Political Culture* (Oxford: Oxford University Press).
Koch, Rainer (1983), *Grundlagen bürgerlicher Herrschaft: Verfassungs- und sozialgeschichtliche Studien zur bürgerlichen Gesellschaft in Frankfurt am Main (1612–1866)*. Frankfurter Historische Abhandlungen, vol. 27 (Wiesbaden: Steiner).

Koekkoek, René (2016), *The Citizenship Experiment: Contesting the Limits of Civic Equality and Participation in the Age of Revolution*, PhD thesis, Universiteit Utrecht.
Köhler, Neeltje, and Koos Levy-Van Halm (1990), *Frans Hals: Militia Pieces* (Zwolle: Waanders).
Kokken, H. (1991), *Steden en staten: Dagvaarten van steden en Staten van Holland onder Maria van Bourgondië en het eerste regentschap van Maximiliaan van Oostenrijk (1477–1494)*. Hollandse Historische Reeks, vol. 16 (The Hague: Stichting Hollandse Historische Reeks).
Konnert, Mark W. (2006), *Local Politics in the French Wars of Religion: The Towns of Champagne, the Duc de Guise, and the Catholic League, 1560–95* (Aldershot: Ashgate).
Kooijmans, Luuc (1985), *Onder regenten: De elite in een Hollandse stad, Hoorn 1700–1780*. Hollandse Historische Reeks, vol. 4 (Amsterdam/Dieren: De Bataafsche Leeuw).
Koopmans, J. W. (1990), *De Hollandse Steden en de Opstand: De Ontwikkeling van hun Functies en Organisatie in de Periode 1544–1588*. Hollandse Historische Reeks vol. 13 (The Hague: Stichting Hollandse Historische Reeks).
Körner, Martin (1999), 'The Swiss Confederation', in: Richard Bonney (ed.), *The Rise of the Fiscal State in Europe, c.1200–1815* (Oxford: Oxford University Press), 328–57.
Kraus, Jürgen (1980), *Das Militärwesen der Reichsstadt Augsburg 1548 bis 1806: Vergleichende Untersuchungen über städtische Militäreinrichtungen in Deutschland vom 16.-18. Jahrhundert*. Abhandlungen zur Geschichte der Stadt Augsburg, vol. 26 (Augsburg: Mühlberger).
Krausman Ben-Amos, Ilana (1991), 'Women apprentices in the trades and crafts of early modern Bristol', *Continuity and Change* 6: 227–52.
(1994), *Adolescence and Youth in Early Modern England* (New Haven, CT: Yale University Press).
(2008), *The Culture of Giving: Informal Support and Gift Exchange in Early Modern England* (Cambridge: Cambridge University Press).
de Krey, Gary Stuart (1985), *A Fractured Society: The Politics of London in the First Age of Party 1688–1715* (Oxford: Clarendon).
Kubinyi, András (1980), 'Zur Frage der Vertretung der Städte im Ungarischen Reichstag bis 1526', in: Bernhard Töpfer (ed.), *Städte und Ständestaat: Zur Rolle der Städte bei der Entwicklung der Ständeverfassung in europäischen Staaten vom 13. bis zum 15. Jahrhundert* (Berlin: Akademie Verlag), 215–46.
Kuijpers, Erika (2005), *Migrantenstad: Immigratie en sociale verhoudingen in zeventiende-eeuws Amsterdam* (Hilversum: Verloren).
Kuijpers, Erika, and Maarten Prak (2002), 'Burger, ingezetene, vreemdeling: burgerschap in Amsterdam in de 17e en 18e eeuw', in: J. Kloek and K. Tilmans (eds.), *Burger: Een geschiedenis van het begrip 'burger' in de Nederlanden van de Middeleeuwen tot de 21ste eeuw* (Amsterdam: Amsterdam University Press), 113–32.
Kümin, Beat, and Andreas Würgler (1997), 'Petitions, *gravamina* and the early modern state: Local influence on central legislation in England and Germany (Hesse)', *Parliaments, Estates and Representation* 17: 39–60.
Kuran, Timur (2011), *The Long Divergence: How Islamic Law Held Back the Middle East* (Princeton, NJ: Princeton University Press).

Küster, Thomas (1995), *Alte Armut und neues Bürgertum: Öffentliche und private Fürsorge in Münster von der Ära Fürstenberg bis zum Ersten Weltkrieg (1756–1914)* (Münster: Aschendorff).

Laborda-Peman, Miguel (2017), *Beyond Markets and Hierarchies in Pre-Industrial Europe: The Evolution of Institutions for Collective Action in Historical Perspective*. PhD dissertation, Universiteit Utrecht.

Lachmann, Richard (2000), *Capitalists in Spite of Themselves: Elite Conflict and Economic Transitions in Early Modern Europe* (Oxford: Oxford University Press).

Ladewig Petersen, E. (1997), 'The wrath of God: Christian IV and the poor in the wake of the Danish intervention in the Thirty Years' War', in: Ole Peter Grell and Andrew Cunningham (eds.), *Health Care and Poor Relief in Protestant Europe 1500–1700* (London: Routledge), 147–66.

Lamet, Sterling A. (1979), *Men Government: The Patriciate of Leyden, 1550–1600*. PhD dissertation, University of Massachusetts, Amherst.

Landes, David (1983), *Revolution in Time: Clocks and the Making of the Modern World* (Cambridge, MA: Belknap Press).

(1998), *The Wealth and Poverty of Nations: Why Some Are so Rich and Some so Poor* (New York, NY: W. W. Norton).

Landwehr, Götz (1967), *Die Verpfändung der deutschen Reichsstädte im Mittelalter. Forschungen zur deutschen Rechtsgeschichte*, vol. 5 (Cologne: s.n.).

Lane, Frederic C. (1973), *Venice: A Maritime Republic* (Baltimore, MD: Johns Hopkins University Press).

Lane, Joan (1996), *Apprenticeship in England, 1600–1914* (London: UCL Press).

Lange, Matthew, James Mahoney and Matthew vom Hau (2006), 'Colonialism and development: Comparative analysis of Spanish and British colonies', *American Journal of Sociology* 111: 1412–62.

Langton, John (2000), 'Urban growth and economic change: From the late seventeenth century to 1841', in: Peter Clark (ed.), *The Cambridge Urban History of Britain*, vol. 2: *1540–1840* (Cambridge: Cambridge University Press), 453–90.

Lantschner, Patrick (2014), 'Fragmented cities in the later Middle Ages: Italy and the Near East compared', *English Historical Review* 130 (544): 546–82.

(2015), *The Logic of Political Conflict in Medieval Cities: Italy and the Southern Low Countries, 1370–1440* (Oxford: Oxford University Press).

Lanz, H. (1995), 'Training and workshop practice in Zurich in the seventeenth century', in: D. Mitchell (ed.), *Goldsmiths, Silversmiths and Bankers: Innovation and the Transfer of Skill, 1550 to 1750*. Centre for Metropolitan History Working Papers Series, no. 2 (London: Allan Sutton), 32–42.

Lapidus, Ira M. (1967), *Muslim Cities in the Later Middle Ages* (Cambridge, MA: Harvard University Press).

(1969), 'Muslim cities and Islamic societies', in: Ira M. Lapidus (ed.), *Middle Eastern Cities: A Symposium on Ancient, Islamic, and Contemporary Middle Eastern Cities* (Berkeley, CA: University of California Press), 47–79.

Latham, Mark (2012), 'From oligarchy to a rate payer's democracy: The evolution of the Corporation of London, 1680s–1750s', *Urban History* 39: 225–45.

Laufs, Adolf (1971), *Der Schwäbische Kreis: Studien über Einungswesen und Reichsverfassung im deutschen Südwesten zu Beginn der Neuzeit*. Untersuchungen zur deutschen Staats- und Rechtsgeschichte, vol. 16 (Aalen: Scientia).

Law, John E. (1992), 'The Venetian mainland state in the fifteenth century', *Transactions of the Royal Historical Society* 2: 153–74.

Le Galès, Patrick (2002), *European Cities: Social Conflicts and Governance* (Oxford: Oxford University Press).
Leach, Darcy K. (2005), 'The Iron Law of *what* again? Conceptualizing oligarchy across organizational forms', *Sociological Theory* 23: 312–37.
Lecuppre-Desjardin, Élodie, and Anne-Laure Van Bruaene (eds.) (2010), *De bono communi: The Discourse and Practice of the Common Good in the European City (13th–16th c.)*. Studies in European Urban History, vol. 22 (Turnhout: Brepols).
Lee, James, and Wang Feng (1999), 'Malthusian models and Chinese realities: The Chinese demographic system 1700–2000', *Population and Development Review* 25: 33–65.
Lees, Lynn Hollen (1998), *The Solidarities of Strangers: The English Poor Laws and the People, 1700–1948* (Cambridge: Cambridge University Press).
Leeuwen, Marco H. D. van (1994), 'Logic of charity: Poor relief in preindustrial Europe', *Journal of Interdisciplinary History* 24: 589–613.
(1996), 'Amsterdam en de armenzorg tijdens de Republiek', *NEHA-Jaarboek* 59: 132–61.
(2000), *The Logic of Charity: Amsterdam, 1800–1850* (London: MacMillan).
(2012a), 'Giving in early modern history: Philanthropy in Amsterdam in the golden age', *Continuity and Change* 27: 301–43.
(2012b), 'Guilds and middle-class welfare, 1550–1800: Provisions for burial, sickness, old age, and widowhood', *Economic History Review* 65: 61–90.
(2016), *Mutual Insurance 1550–2015: From Guild Welfare and Friendly Societies to Micro-Insurers*. Palgrave Studies in the History of Finance (London: Palgrave).
Leeuwen, Richard van (1999), *Waqfs and Urban Structures: The Case of Ottoman Damascus* (Leiden: Brill).
Lefebvre, Edwige Liliane (2003), 'Republicanism and universalism: Factors of inclusion and exclusion in the French concept of citizenship', *Citizenship Studies* 7: 15–36.
Lengen, Hajo von (1995), *Die 'Emder Revolution' von 1595: Kolloquium der Ostfriesland-Stiftung am 17. März 1995 zu Emden* (Aurich: Ostfriesische Landschaft).
Lenger, Friedrich (1991), 'Beyond exceptionalism: Notes on the artisanal phase of the labour movement in France, England, Germany and the United States', *International Review of Social History* 36: 1–23.
Lerner, Marc (2012), *A Laboratory of Liberty: The Transformation of Political Culture in Republican Switzerland, 1750–1848* (Leiden: Brill).
Lesger, Clé, and Leo Noordegraaf (eds.) (1999), *Ondernemers en bestuurders: Economie en politiek in de Noordelijke Nederlanden in de late Middeleeuwen en vroegmoderne tijd* (Amsterdam: NEHA).
Leunig, Tim, Chris Minns and Patrick Wallis (2011), 'Networks in the pre-modern economy: The market for London apprenticeships, 1600–1749', *Journal of Economic History* 71: 413–43.
Lev, Yaacov (2005), *Charity, Endowments, and Charitable Institutions in Medieval Islam* (Gainesville, FL: University Press of Florida).
Levi, Margaret (1988), *Of Rule and Revenue* (Berkeley, CA: University of California Press).
Levin, J. (1969), *The Charter Controversy in the City of London, 1660–1688, and Its Consequences* (London: Athlone).
Liddy, Christian D. (2005), *War, Politics and Finance in Late Medieval English Towns: Bristol, York and the Crown, 1350–1400* (London: Boydell).
(2017), *Contesting the City: The Politics of Citizenship in English Towns, 1250–1530* (Oxford: Oxford University Press).

Liddy, Christian D., and Jelle Haemers (2013), 'Popular politics in the late Medieval city: York and Bruges', *English Historical Review* 128: 771–805.

Liesker, R. (1985), 'Tot zinkens toe bezwaard: De schuldenlast van het Zuiderkwartier van Holland, 1672–1794', in: S. Groenveld, M. E. H. N. Mout and I. Schöffer (eds.), *Bestuurders en geleerden* (Amsterdam/Dieren: De Bataafsche Leeuw), 151–60.

Lievense-Pelser, E. (1979), 'De Alteratie en de financiële toestand', *Jaarboek Amstelodamum* 71: 38–54.

Lindberg, Erik (2009), 'Club goods and inefficient institutions: Why Danzig and Lübeck failed in the early modern period', *Economic History Review* 62: 604–28.

Lindemann, Mary (1990), *Patriots and Paupers: Hamburg, 1712–1830* (New York, NY: Oxford University Press).

(2010), 'Voluntarism in social welfare and urban government: The case of Hamburg, 1700–1799', *Journal of Urban History* 36: 316–31.

(2015), *The Merchant Republics: Amsterdam, Antwerp, and Hamburg, 1648–1790* (Cambridge: Cambridge University Press).

Linden, David van der (2015), *Experiencing Exile: Huguenot Refugees in the Dutch Republic, 1680–1700* (Farnham: Ashgate).

Lindert, Peter H. (2004), *Growing Public: Social Spending and Economic Growth since the Eighteenth Century*, vol. 1: *The Story* (Cambridge: Cambridge University Press).

Lindley, Keith (1997), *Popular Politics and Religion in Civil War London* (Aldershot: Scholar Press).

Lis, Catharina, and Hugo Soly (1979), *Poverty and Capitalism in Pre-Industrial Europe* (Atlantic Highlands, NJ: Humanities Press).

(1993), 'Neighbourhood social change in West-European cities: Sixteenth to nineteenth centuries', *International Review of Social History* 38: 1–30.

(1994), 'An "irresistible phalanx": Journeymen associations in Western Europe, 1300–1800', in: Catharina Lis, Jan Lucassen and Hugo Soly (eds.), *Before the Unions: Wage Earners and Collective Action in Europe, 1300–1800* (Cambridge: Cambridge University Press), 11–52.

Litchfield, R. Burr (1986), *Emergence of a Bureaucracy: The Florentine Patricians 1530–1790* (Princeton, NJ: Princeton University Press).

Lockhart, James (1972), *The Men of Cajamarca: A Social and Biographical Study of the First Conquerors of Peru* (Austin, TX: University of Texas Press).

Lockhart, James, and Stuart B. Schwartz (1983), *Early Latin America: A History of Colonial Spanish America and Brazil* (Cambridge: Cambridge University Press).

Looijesteijn, Henk (2012), 'Funding and founding private charities: Leiden almshouses and their founders', *Continuity and Change* 27: 199–239.

Looz-Corswarem, Clemens von (1985), 'Die politische Elite Kölns im Übergang vom 18. zum 19. Jahrhundert', in: Heinz Schilling and Herman Diederiks (eds.), *Bürgerliche Eliten in den Niederlanden und in Nordwestdeutschland: Studien zur Sozialgeschichte des europäischen Bürgertums im Mittelalter und in der Neuzeit.* Städteforschung, vol. A/23 (Cologne: Böhlau), 421–44.

Lourens, Piet, and Jan Lucassen (2000), '"Zunftlandschaften" in den Niederlanden und im benachbarten Deutschland', in: W. Reininghaus (ed.), *Zunftlandschaften in Deutschland und den Niederlanden im Vergleich.* Schriften der historischen Kommission für Westfalen, vol. 17 (Münster: Aschendorff), 11–43.

Lovejoy, David S. (1964), 'Equality and empire: The New York Charter of Libertyes, 1683', *William and Mary Quarterly* 21: 493–515.

Lucassen, Leo (2012), 'Cities, states and migration control in Western Europe: Comparing then and now', in: Bert De Munck and Anne Winter (eds.), *Gated Communities? Regulating Migration in Early Modern Cities* (Aldershot: Ashgate), 217–40.

Luttmer, Erzo F. P., and Monica Singhal (2014), 'Tax morale', *Journal of Economic Perspectives* 28: 149–68.

Luz, Nimrod (2014), *The Mamluk City in the Middle East: History, Culture, and the Urban Landscape* (New York, NY: Cambridge University Press).

Lynch, Katherine A. (2003), *Individuals, Families, and Communities in Europe, 1200–1800: The Urban Foundations of Western Society* (Cambridge: Cambridge University Press).

(2010), 'Social provisions and the life of civil society in Europe: Rethinking public and private', *Journal of Urban History* 36: 285–99.

Lynd, Staughton (1967), *Class Conflict, Slavery and the United States Constitution* (New York, NY: Bobbs-Merrill).

Maanen, R. J. C. van (1978), 'De vermogensopbouw van de Leidse bevolking in het laatste kwart van de zestiende eeuw', *Bijdragen en Mededelingen betreffende de Geschiedenis der Nederlanden* 93: 1–42.

MacCaffrey, Wallace T. (1958), *Exeter 1540–1640: The Growth of an English County Town* (Cambridge, MA: Harvard University Press).

Machiavelli, Niccolò (1988), *The Prince*, ed. by Quentin Skinner and Russell Price. Cambridge Texts in the History of Political Thought (Cambridge: Cambridge University Press).

MacKay, Ruth (1999), *The Limits of Royal Authority: Resistance and Obedience in Seventeenth-Century Castile* (Cambridge: Cambridge University Press).

Mackenney, Richard (1987), *Tradesmen and Traders: The World of the Guilds in Venice and Europe, c.1250–c.1650* (London: Croom Helm).

Maddison, Angus (2001), *The World Economy: A Millennial Perspective* (Paris: OECD Development Centre).

(2003), *The World Economy: Historical Statistics* (Paris: OECD Development Centre).

(2007), *Contours of the World Economy, 1–2030 AD* (Oxford: Oxford University Press).

Mager, Wolfgang (1988), 'Respublica und Bürger: Überlegungen zur Begründung frühneuzeitlicher Verfassungsordnungen', in: Gerhard Dilcher (ed.), *Res publica: Bürgerschaft in Stadt und Staat* (Berlin: Duncker & Humblot), 67–94.

Mahoney, James (2010), *Colonialism and Post-Colonial Development: Spanish America in Comparative Perspective* (New York, NY: Cambridge University Press).

Mahoney, James, and Charles Rueschemeyer (eds.) (2003), *Comparative Historical Analysis in the Social Sciences* (Cambridge: Cambridge University Press).

Maillard, Jacques (1984), *Le pouvoir municipal à Angers de 1657 à 1789* (Angers: Presses de l'Université d'Angers).

Maire Vigueur, Jean-Claude (2003), *Cavaliers et citoyens: Guerre, conflits, et société dans l'Italie communale, XII et XIIIe siècles* (Paris: EHESS).

(2008), 'Les inscriptions du pouvoir dans la ville: Le cas de l'Italie communale (XIe–XIVe siècle)', in: Élisabeth Crouzet-Pavan and Élodie Lecuppre-Desjardin (eds.), *Villes de Flandre et d'Italie (XIIIe–XVIe siècle)*. Studies in European Urban History, vol. 12 (Turnhout: Brepols), 207–33.

Maissen, Thomas (2006), *Die Geburt der Republic: Staatsverständnis und Representation in der frühneuzeitlichen Eidgenossenschaft* (Göttingen: Vandenhoeck & Ruprecht).

(2008), 'Inventing the sovereign republic: Imperial structures, French challenges, Dutch models and the early modern Swiss Confederation', in: André Holenstein, Thomas Maissen and Maarten Prak (eds.), *The Republican Alternative: The Netherlands and Switzerland Compared* (Amsterdam: Amsterdam University Press), 125–50.

Maitte, Corine (2002), 'Le réformisme éclairé et les corporations: l'Abolition des Arts en Toscane', *Revue d'Histoire Moderne et Contemporaine* 49: 56–88.

Malanima, Paolo (2005), 'Urbanisation and the Italian economy during the last millennium', *European Review of Economic History* 9: 97–122.

(2011), 'The long decline of a leading economy: GDP in central and northern Italy, 1300–1913', *European Review of Economic History* 15: 169–219.

Malcolm, Joyce Lee (1994), *To Keep and Bear Arms: The Origins of an Anglo–American Debate* (Cambridge, MA: Harvard University Press).

Mallett, Michael (1990), 'The theory and practice of warfare in Machiavelli's republic', in: Gisela Bock, Quentin Skinner and Maurizio Viroli (eds.), *Machiavelli and Republicanism* (Cambridge: Cambridge University Press), 173–80.

(2006), 'The transformation of war, 1494–1530', in: Christine Shaw (ed.), *Italy and the European Powers: The Impact of War, 1500–1530* (Leiden: Brill), 3–21.

Mallett, Michael, and Christine Shaw (2012), *The Italian Wars 1494–1559: War, State and Society in Early Modern Europe* (Harlow: Pearson).

Maniatis, George C. (2001), 'The domain of private guilds in the Byzantine economy, tenth to fifteenth centuries', *Dumbarton Oaks Papers* 55 (www.doaks.org/etexts.html): 339–69.

Mantran, Robert (1962), *Istanbul dans la seconde moitié du xviie siècle* (Paris: Maisonneuve).

Marcocci, Giuseppe (2016), 'Too much to rule: States and empires across the early modern world', *Journal of Early Modern History* 20: 511–25.

Marcus, Abraham (1989), *The Middle East on the Eve of Modernity: Aleppo in the Eighteenth Century* (New York, NY: Columbia University Press).

Marnef, Guido (1987), *Het calvinistisch bewind te Mechelen 1580–1585*, Standen en Landen, vol. 87 (Kortrijk-Heule: UGA).

(1996), *Antwerp in the Age of Reformation: Underground Protestantism in a Commercial Metropolis, 1550–1577* (Baltimore, MD: Johns Hopkins University Press).

(2001), 'The towns and the Revolt', in: Graham Darby (ed.), *The Origins and the Development of the Dutch Revolt* (London: Routledge), 84–106.

Marraud, Mathieu (2009), *De la ville à l'état: La bourgeoisie parisienne XVIIe–XVIIIe siècle* (Paris: Albin Michel).

Marshall, Thomas Humphrey (1950), *Citizenship and Social Class and Other Essays* (Cambridge: Cambridge University Press).

Martin, Cheryl E. (1996), *Governance and Society in Colonial Mexico: Chihuahua in the Eighteenth Century* (Stanford, CA: Stanford University Press).

Martin, John, and Dennis Romano (2000), 'Reconsidering Venice', in: John Martin and Dennis Romano (eds.), *Venice Reconsidered: The History and Civilization of an Italian City-State, 1297–1797* (Baltimore, MD: Johns Hopkins University Press), 1–35.

Martines, Lauro (ed.) (1972), *Violence and Civil Disorder in Italian Cities, 1200–1500* (Berkeley, CA: University of California Press).

(1983), *Power and Imagination: City-States in Renaissance Italy* (Harmondsworth: Allen Lane).

Martz, Linda (1983), *Poverty and Welfare in Habsburg Spain* (Cambridge: Cambridge University Press).
Masters, Bruce (1988), *The Origins of Western Economic Dominance in the Middle East: Mercantilism and the Islamic Economy in Aleppo, 1600–1750* (New York, NY: New York University Press).
(1999), 'Aleppo: The Ottoman Empire's caravan city', in: Edhem Eldem, Daniel Goffman and Bruce Masters (eds.), *The Ottoman City between East and West* (Cambridge: Cambridge University Press), 17–78.
Masterson, M. P. (1975), 'Holland's fifty republics: François Michel Janiçon and Montesquieu's federal theory', *French Studies* 29: 27–41.
Masure, Hadewijch (2017), 'Poor boxes, guild ethic and urban community building in Brabant, c. 1250–1600', in: Justin Colson and Arie van Steensel (eds.), *Cities and Solidarities: Urban Communities in Pre-Modern Europe* (London: Routledge), 115–31.
Maurer, Helmut (ed.) (1987), *Kommunale Bündnisse Oberitaliens und Oberdeutschlands im Vergleich* (Sigmaringen: Thorbecke).
Mawson, Stephanie J. (2016), 'Convicts or *conquistadores*? Spanish soldiers in the seventeenth-century Pacific', *Past & Present* 232: 87–125.
McAnear, Beverly (1940), 'The place of the freeman in old New York', *New York History* 21: 418–30.
McCants, Anne E. C. (1997), *Civic Charity in a Golden Age: Orphan Care in Early Modern Amsterdam* (Urbana, IL: University of Illinois Press).
McGowan, Bruce (1994), 'The age of the *ayans*, 1699–1812', in: Halil İnalçik and Donald Quataert (eds.), *An Economic and Social History of the Ottoman Empire 1300–1914* (Cambridge: Cambridge University Press), 637–758.
McIntosh, Marjorie K. (2011), *Poor Relief in England, 1350–1600* (Cambridge: Cambridge University Press).
(2014), 'Poor relief in Elizabethan English communities: An analysis of collectors' accounts', *Economic History Review* 67: 331–57.
McLean, Paul D. (2005), 'Patronage, citizenship, and the stalled emergence of the modern state in Renaissance Florence', *Comparative Studies in Society and History* 47: 638–64.
Meek, Christine (1978), *Lucca 1369–1400: Politics and Society in an Early Renaissance City-State* (Oxford: Oxford University Press).
(1980), *The Commune of Lucca under Pisan Rule, 1342–1369* (Cambridge, MA: The Medieval Academy of America).
(2010), '"Whatever's best administered is best": Paolo Guinigi *signore* of Lucca, 1400–1430', in: John E. Law and Bernadette Paton (eds.), *Communes and Despots in Medieval and Renaissance Italy* (Farnham: Ashgate), 131–43.
Meier, Ulrich (2002), 'Gemeinnutz und Vaterlandsliebe: Kontroversen über die normativen Grundlagen des Bürgerbegriffs im späten Mittelalter', in: Rainer Christoph Schwinges (ed.), *Neubürger im Späten Mittelalter: Migration und Austausch in der Städtelandschaft des alten Reiches (1250–1550)*. Beiheft Zeitschrift für Historische Forschung, vol. 30 (Berlin: Duncker & Humblot), 53–81.
Melling, John Kennedy (2003), *Discovering London's Guilds and Liveries* (Princes Risborough: Shire).
Merrick, Jeffrey (1987), 'Conscience and citizenship in eighteenth-century France', *Eighteenth-Century Studies* 21: 48–70.
Merwick, Donna (1990), *Possessing Albany, 1630–1710: The Dutch and English Experiences* (Cambridge: Cambridge University Press).

Mettele, Gisela (1998), *Bürgertum in Köln 1775–1870: Gemeinsinn und freie Association*. Stadt und Bürgertum, vol. 10 (Munich: Oldenbourg).
Michielse, H. C. M. (1990), 'Policing the poor: J. L. Vives and the sixteenth-century origins of modern social administration', *Social Service Review* 64: 1–21.
Middleton, Simon (2006), *From Privileges to Rights: Work and Politics in Colonial New York City* (Philadelphia, PA: University of Pennsylvania Press).
Milani, Giuliano (2005), *I comuni italiani* (Gius: Laterza).
Milanovic, Branko, Peter H. Lindert and Jeffrey G. Williamson (2011), 'Pre-industrial inequality', *The Economic Journal* 121 (551): 255–72.
Militzer, Klaus (1980), 'Führungsschicht und Gemeinde in Köln im 14. Jahrhundert', in: Wilfried Ehbrecht (ed.), *Städtische Führungsgruppen und Gemeinde in der werdende Neuzeit*. Städteforschung, vol. A9 (Cologne: Böhlau), 1–24.
Miljan, Suzana, and Bruno Škreblin (2017), 'The poor of medieval Zagreb between solidarity, marginalisation and integration', in: Justin Colson and Arie van Steensel (eds.), *Cities and Solidarities: Urban Communities in Pre-Modern Europe* (London: Routledge), 98–114.
Miller, Jaroslav (2008), *Urban Societies in East-Central Europe, 1500–1700* (Aldershot: Ashgate).
Milton, Cynthia E. (2007), *The Many Meanings of Poverty: Colonialism, Social Compacts, and Assistance in Eighteenth-Century Ecuador* (Stanford, CA: Stanford University Press).
Minns, Chris, Clare Crowston, Raoul De Kerf, Bert De Munck, Marcel Hoogenboom, Maarten Prak and Patrick Wallis (2014), 'The scale and scope of citizenship in early modern Europe: Preliminary estimates', unpublished paper, bEUcitizen project, work package 3.
Minns, Chris, and Patrick Wallis (2012), 'Rules and reality: Quantifying the practice of apprenticeship in early modern England', *Economic History Review* 65: 556–79.
(2013), 'The price of human capital in a pre-industrial economy: Premiums and apprenticeship contracts in 18th-century England', *Explorations in Economic History* 50: 335–50.
Mitchison, R. (1991), *Coping with Destitution: Poverty and Relief in Western Europe* (Toronto: University of Toronto Press).
Mocarelli, Luca (2008), 'Guilds reappraised: Italy in the early modern period', in: Jan Lucassen, Tine De Moor and Jan Luiten van Zanden (eds.), *The Return of the Guilds,* supplement 16 of the *International Review of Social History* 53 (Cambridge: Cambridge University Press), 159–78.
Moch, Leslie Page (2003), *Moving Europeans: Migration in Western Europe since 1650*. 2nd edn. (Bloomington, IN: Indiana University Press).
Moeller, Bernd (1962), *Reichsstadt und Reformation*. Schriften des Vereins für Reformationsgeschichte, vol. 180 (Gütersloh: Gerd Mohn).
Mohl, Raymond A. (1971), *Poverty in New York, 1783–1825* (New York, NY: Oxford University Press).
Mokyr, Joel (2009), *The Enlightened Economy: An Economic History of Britain, 1700–1850* (New Haven, CT: Yale University Press).
(2017), *A Culture of Growth: The Origins of the Modern Economy* (Princeton, NJ: Princeton University Press).
Molho, Anthony (1995), 'The state and public finance: A hypothesis based on the history of late medieval Florence', in: Julius Kirshner (ed.), *The Origins of the State in Italy 1300–1600* (Chicago, IL: University of Chicago Press, orig. a special issue of the *Journal of Modern History*), 97–135.
Mollat, Michel (1978), *Les pauvres au Moyen Âge: Étude sociale* (Paris: Hachette).

Möller, Frank (1998), *Bürgerliche Herrschaft in Augsburg, 1790–1880* Stadt und Bürgertum, vol. 9 (Munich: Oldenbourg).

Moll-Murata, Christine (2008), 'Chinese guilds from the seventeenth to the twentieth century: An overview', in: Jan Lucassen, Tine De Moor and Jan Luiten van Zanden (eds.), *The Return of the Guilds*. International Review of Social History, Supplement 16 (Cambridge: Cambridge University Press), 213–47.

Monter, E. William (1980), 'Women in Calvinist Geneva (1550–1800)', *Journal of Women in Culture and Society* 6: 189–209.

Montesquieu, Charles, baron de (1951), *De l'esprit des lois*, in *Œuvres Complètes*, vol. 86, ed. by Roger Caillois (Paris: Gallimard; orig. 1748).

Moore, Barrington, Jr. (1966), *Social Origins of Dictatorship and Democracy: Lord and Peasant in the Making of the Modern World* (Boston, MA: Beacon Press).

Moore, John P. (1954), *The Cabildo in Peru under the Hapsburgs: A Study in the Origins and Powers of the Town Council in the Viceroyalty of Peru, 1530–1700* (Durham, NC: Duke University Press).

Moraw, Peter (1994), 'Cities and citizenry as factors of state formation in the Roman-German empire of the late Middle Ages', in: Charles Tilly and Wim P. Blockmans (eds.), *Cities and the Rise of States in Europe, A.D. 1000 to 1800* (Boulder, CO: Westview Press), 100–27.

Moritz, Werner (1981), *Die bürgerlichen Fürsorgeanstalten der Reichsstadt Frankfurt a. M. im späten Mittelalter* (Frankfurt am Main: Kramer).

Mörke, Olaf (1997), *'Stadholder' oder 'Staetholder'? Die Funktion des Hauses Oranien und seines Hofes in der politischen Kultur der Republik der Vereinigten Niederlande im 17. Jahrhundert*. Niederlande Studien, vol. 11 (Münster: Lit).

Mottu-Weber, Liliane (1996), 'Le statut des étrangers et de leurs descendants à Genève (XVIe–XVIIIe siècles)', in: Denis Menjot and Jean-Luc Pinol (eds.), *Les immigrants et la ville: Insertion, intégration, discrimination (XII–XXe siècles)* (Paris: L'Harmattan), 27–42.

Muir, Edward (1999), 'The sources of civil society in Italy', *Journal of Interdisciplinary History* 29: 379–406.

Müller-Herrenschwand, Katharina (2002), 'Brugges Bevölkerung und Wirtschaft zwischen 1282 und 1492 im Spiegel der Einbürgerungsquellen', in: Rainer Christoph Schwinges (ed.), *Neubürger im Späten Mittelalter: Migration und Austausch in der Städtelandschaft des alten Reiches (1250–1550)*. Beiheft Zeitschrift für Historische Forschung, vol. 30 (Berlin: Duncker & Humblot), 479–505.

Mundy, John H. (1954), *Liberty and Political Power in Toulouse, 1050–1230* (New York, NY: John Hine).

(1966), 'Charity and social work in Toulouse, 1100–1250', *Tradition* 22: 203–87.

Musgrave, Elizabeth (1993), 'Women in the male world of work: The building industries of eighteenth-century Brittany', *French History* 7: 30–52.

(1997), 'Women and the craft guilds in eighteenth-century Nantes', in: Geoffrey Crossick (ed.), *The Artisan and the European Town, 1500–1900* (Aldershot: Scolar Press), 151–71.

Nader, Helen (1990), *Liberty in Absolutist Spain: The Habsburg Sale of Towns, 1516–1750* (Baltimore, MD: Johns Hopkins University Press).

(1996), '"The more communes, the greater the king": Hidden communes in absolutist theory', in: Peter Blickle (ed.), *Theorien kommunaler Ordnung in Europa*. Schriften des Historischen Kollegs, Kolloquien, vol. 36 (Munich: Oldenbourg), 215–23.

Naegle, Gisela, and Jesús Ángel Solórzano Telechea (2014), '*Gechlechter* und *Zünfte, Prinçipales* und *Común*: Städtische Konflikte in Kastilien und dem spätmittelalterlichen Reich', *Zeitschrift für historische Forschung* 41: 561–618.
Nagel, Lawson (1996), '"A great bouncing at every man's door": The struggle for London's militia in 1642', in: Stephen Porter (ed.), *London and the Civil War* (London: Macmillan), 65–88.
Najemy, John M. (1979), 'Guild republicanism in Trecento Florence: The successes and ultimate failure of corporate politics', *American Historical Review* 84 (1979): 53–71.
(1982), *Corporatism and Consensus in Florentine Electoral Politics, 1280–1400* (Chapel Hill, NC: University of North Carolina Press).
(2006), *A History of Florence 1200–1575* (Oxford: Blackwell).
Namier, Lewis (1929), *The Structure of Politics at the Accession of George III* (London: Macmillan).
Nash, Gary B. (1976), 'Poverty and poor relief in pre-Revolutionary Philadelphia', *The William and Mary Quarterly* 33: 3–30.
(1979), *The Urban Crucible: Social Change, Urban Consciousness and the Origins of the American Revolution* (Cambridge, MA: Harvard University Press).
(2005), *The Unknown American Revolution: The Unruly Birth of Democracy and the Struggle to Create America* (New York, NY: Viking).
Nauert, Charles (1995), *Humanism and the Culture of Renaissance Europe* (Cambridge: Cambridge University Press).
Naujoks, Eberhard (1985), *Kaiser Karl V. und die Zunftverfassung: Ausgewählte Aktenstücke zu den Verfassungsänderungen in den oberdeutschen Reichsstädten (1547–1556)* (Stuttgart: Kohlhammer).
Nederveen Meerkerk, Elise van (2007), *De draad in eigen handen: Vrouwen en loonarbeid in de Nederlandse textielnijverheid, 1581–1810* (Amsterdam: Aksant).
(2012), 'The will to give: Charitable bequests, *inter vivos* gifts and community building in the Dutch Republic, c. 1600–1800', *Continuity and Change* 27: 241–70.
Nederveen Meerkerk, Elise van and Griet Vermeesch (2009), 'Reforming outdoor relief: Changes in urban provisions for the poor in the northern and southern Low Countries (c.1500–1800)', in: Manon van der Heijden, Elise van Nederveen Meerkerk, Griet Vermeesch and Martijn van der Burg (eds.), *Serving the Community: The Rise of Public Facilities in the Low Countries* (Amsterdam: Aksant), 135–54.
Németh, István (2009), 'Pre-modern state-urban policy at a turning point in the kingdom of Hungary', in: Rudolf Schlögl (ed.), *Urban Elections and Decision-Making in Early Modern Europe, 1500–1800* (Newcastle upon Tyne: Cambridge Scholars), 276–99.
Nevola, F. (2007), *Constructing the Renaissance City* (New Haven, CT: Yale University Press).
Nicholas, David (1992), *Medieval Flanders* (London: Longman).
Nicolini, Ingrid (1979), *Die politische Führungsschicht der Stadt Köln gegen Ende der reichsstädtischen Zeit* (Cologne: Böhlau).
Nierop, H. F. K. van (1997), 'Popular participation in politics in the Dutch Republic', in: Peter Blickle (ed.), *Resistance, Representation, and Community* (Cambridge: Cambridge University Press), 272–90.
(2000), *Het foute Amsterdam* (inaugural address) (Amsterdam: Vossius Pers).

Niggemann, Ulrich (2013), 'Craft guilds and immigration: Huguenots in German and English cities', in: Bert De Munck and Anne Winter (eds.) *Gated Communities? Regulating Migration in Early Modern Cities* (Farnham: Ashgate), 45–60.
Nimwegen, Olaf van (2006), *'Deser landen crijchsvolck': Het Staatse leger en de militaire revoluties 1588–1688* (Amsterdam: Bert Bakker).
Nippel, Wilfried (1991), 'Introductory remarks: Max Weber's "The City" revisited', in: Althony Molho, Kurt Raaflaub and Julia Emlen (eds.), *City States in Classical Antiquity and Medieval Italy* (Stuttgart: Franz Steiner Verlag), 19–30.
(2000), 'Webers "Stadt": Entstehung – Struktur der Argumentation – Rezeption', in: H. Bruhns and W. Nippel (eds.), *Max Weber und die Stadt im Kulturvergleich* (Göttingen: Vandenhoeck & Ruprecht), 11–38.
Noordam, Dirk Jaap (1994), *Geringde Buffels en Heren van Stand: Het Patriciaat van Leiden, 1574–1700* (Hilversum: Verloren).
Norberg, Kathryn (1985), *Rich and Poor in Grenoble, 1600–1814* (Berkeley, CA: University of California Press).
North, Douglass C., and Barry R. Weingast (1989), 'Constitutions and commitment: The evolution of institutions governing public choice in seventeenth century England', *Journal of Economic History* 49: 803–32.
North, Douglass C., and Robert Paul Thomas (1973), *The Rise of the Western World: A New Economic History* (Cambridge: Cambridge University Press).
North, Douglass C., John Joseph Wallis and Barry R. Weingast (2009), *Violence and Social Orders: A Conceptual Framework for Interpreting Recorded Human History* (Cambridge: Cambridge University Press).
North, Douglass, William Summerhill and Barry R. Weingast (2000), 'Order, disorder and economic change: Latin America versus North America', in B. Bueno de Mesquita and H. L. Root (eds.), *Governing for Prosperity* (New Haven, CT: Yale University Press), 17–58.
North, Michael (2015), 'The Hanseatic League in the early modern period', in: Donald J. Harreld (ed.), *A Companion to the Hanseatic League* (Leiden: Brill), 101–24.
Nubola, Cecilia (2001), 'Supplications between politics and justice: The northern and central Italian states in the early modern age', in: Lex Heerma van Voss (ed.), *Petitions in Social History* (International Review of Social History 46, Supplement 9 (Cambridge: Cambridge University Press), 35–56.
(2009), 'Elections and decision-making on the outskirts of the empire: The case of Trento', in: Rudolf Schlögl (ed.), *Urban Elections and Decision-Making in Early Modern Europe* (Newcastle upon Tyne: Cambridge Scholars), 34–51.
Nussdorfer, Laurie (1992), *Civic Politics in the Rome of Urban VIII* (Princeton, NJ: Princeton University Press).
O'Brien, Patrick Karl (2014), 'The formation of states and transitions to modern economies: England, Europe, and Asia compared', in: Larry Neal and Jeffrey G. Williamson (eds.), *The Cambridge History of Capitalism*, vol. I: *The Rise of Capitalism, from Ancient Origins to 1848* (Cambridge: Cambridge University Press), 357–402.
Obradors-Suazo, Carolina (2017), 'Making the citizen, building the citizenry: Family and citizenship in fifteenth-century Barcelona', in: Justin Colson and Arie van Steensel (eds.), *Cities and Solidarities: Urban Communities in Pre-Modern Europe* (London: Routledge), 25–42.
Oelze, Patrick (2009), 'Decision-making and civic participation in the Imperial City (fifteenth and sixteenth century): Guild conventions and open councils in Constance', in: Rudolf Schlögl (ed.), *Urban Elections and Decision-Making in Early Modern Europe* (Newcastle upon Tyne: Cambridge Scholars), 147–78.

Oer, Rudolfine freiin von (1998), *Der münsterische 'Erbmännerstreit': Zur Problematik von Revisionen Reichkammergerichtliche Urteile.* Quellen und Forschungen zur höchsten Gerichtsbarkeit im Alten Reich, vol. 32 (Cologne: Böhlau).

Oexle, Otto Gerhard (1981), 'Gilden als soziale Gruppen in der Karolingerzeit', in: Herbert Jankuhn, Walter Janssen, Ruth Schmidt-Wiegand and Heinrich Tiefenbach (eds.), *Das Handwerk in vor- und frühgeschichtlicher Zeit* (Göttingen: Vandenhoeck & Ruprecht), 284–354.

(1985), 'Conjuratio und Gilde im frühen Mittelalter: Ein Beitrag zum Problem der sozialgeschichtlichen Kontinuität zwischen Antike und Mittelater', in: Berent Schwineköper (ed.), *Gilden und Zünfte: Kaufmännische und gewerb-liche Genossenschaften im frühen und hohen Mittelalter.* Konstanzer Arbeitskreis für mittelalterliche Geschichte, Vorträge und Forschungen, vol. 29 (Sigmaringen: Jan Thorbecke Verlag), 151–214.

Ogilvie, Sheilagh (1997), *State Corporatism and Proto-Industry: The Württemberg Black Forest, 1580–1797* (Cambridge: Cambridge University Press).

(2003), *A Bitter Living: Women, Markets, and Social Capital in Early Modern Germany* (Oxford: Oxford University Press).

(2004), 'Guilds, efficiency, and social capital: Evidence from German proto-industry', *Economic History Review* 57: 286–333.

(2007), '"Whatever is right, is right?" Economic institutions in pre-industrial Europe', *Economic History Review* 60: 649–84.

(2011), *Institutions and European Trade: Merchant Guilds, 1000–1800* (Cambridge: Cambridge University Press).

(2014), 'The economics of guilds', *Journal of Economic Perspectives* 28/4: 175–92.

Ogilvie, Sheilagh, and A. W. Carus (2013), 'Institutions and economic growth in historical perspective', in: Phillippe Aghion and Steven N. Durlauf (eds.), *Handbook of Economic Growth*, vol. 2A (Burlington, VT: Elsevier Science), 403–513.

Ojala, Maija (2016), 'Sex matters? Artisan widows and the urban labour market in Northern Europe', in: Eva Jullien and Michel Pauly (eds.), *Craftsmen and Guilds in the Medieval and Early Modern Periods.* VSWG Beiheft 234 (Stuttgart: Franz Steiner), 141–55.

Olson, Mancur (1971, orig. 1965), *The Logic of Collective Action: Public Goods and the Theory of Groups* (Cambridge, MA: Harvard University Press).

Olton, Charles S. (1975), *Artisans for Independence: Philadelphia Mechanics and the American Revolution* (Syracuse, NY: Syracuse University Press).

Oostrom, Frits van (2013), *Wereld in woorden: Geschiedenis van de Nederlandse literatuur, 1300–1400* (Amsterdam: Bert Bakker).

Ormrod, David (2003), *The Rise of Commercial Empires: England and the Netherlands in the Age of Mercantilism, 1650–1770* (Cambridge: Cambridge University Press).

Ostrom, Elinor (1990), *Governing the Commons: The Evolution of Institutions for Collective Action* (Cambridge: Cambridge University Press).

Ostrom, Vincent (1994), *The Meaning of American Federalism: Constituting a Self-Governing Society* (San Francisco, CA: ICS Press).

Overvoorde, J. C., and J. G. C. Joosting (eds.) (1896–97), *De gilden van Utrecht tot 1528: Verzameling van rechtsbronnen.* Werken der Vereeniging tot uitgave der bronnen van het oude vaderlandsche recht, series 1 no. 19 (The Hague: Nijhoff).

Paine, Thomas (2000, orig. 1791/92), *The Rights of Man (Parts I and II)*, in: Bruce Kuklick (ed.), *Thomas Paine, Political Writings* (Cambridge: Cambridge University Press).

Palliser, David M. (1979), *Tudor York* (Oxford: Oxford University Press).

(1997), 'The birth of York's civic liberties, c. 1200–1354', in: Sarah Rees-Jones (ed.), *The Government of Medieval York: Essays in Commemoration of the 1396 Royal Charter* (York: Borthwick Institute), 88–107.

Pamuk, Şevket (2004), 'Institutional change and the longevity of the Ottoman Empire, 1500–1800', *Journal of Interdisciplinary History* 35: 7–32.

Panhuysen, Bibi (2000), *Maatwerk: Kleermakers, naaisters, oudkleerkopers en de gilden (1500–1800)* (Amsterdam: IISG).

Parker, Charles H. (1998), *The Reformation of Community: Social Welfare and Calvinist Charity in Holland, 1572–1620* (Cambridge: Cambridge University Press).

Parker, David (1980), *La Rochelle and the French Monarchy: Conflict and Order in Seventeenth-Century France* (Leiden: Brill).

Parker, Geoffrey (1979), *The Dutch Revolt* (Harmondsworth: Penguin).

(1988; 2nd edn. 1996), *The Military Revolution, 1500–1800: Military Innovation and the Rise of the West* (Cambridge: Cambridge University Press).

(2004), *The Army of Flanders and the Spanish Road, 1567–1659: The Logistics of Spanish Victory and Defeat in the Low Countries' Wars*. 2nd edn. (Cambridge: Cambridge University Press).

Patriquin, Larry (2007), *Agrarian Capitalism and Poor Relief in England, 1500–1860: Rethinking the Origins of the Welfare State* (Houndmills: Palgrave).

Patterson, C. F. (1999), *Urban Patronage in Early Modern England: Corporate Boroughs, the Landed Elite, and the Crown, 1580–1640* (Stanford, CA: Stanford University Press).

Pauly, Michel, and Alexander Lee (eds.) (2015), *Urban Liberties and Citizenship from the Middle Ages up to Now*. Beiträge zur Landes- und Kulturgeschichte, vol. 9 (Trier: Porta Alba Verlag).

Pearl, Valerie (1961), *London and the Outbreak of the Puritan Revolution: City Government and National Politics, 1625–43* (London: Oxford University Press).

Pelizaeus, Ludolf (2007), *Dynamik der Macht: Städtischer Widerstand und Konfliktbewältigung im Reich Karls V.* (Münster: Aschendorff).

Pennock, Caroline Dodds (2011), '"A remarkably patterned life": Domestic and public in the Aztec household city', *Gender and History*, 23: 528–46.

Percoco, Marco (2014), 'Path dependence, institutions and the density of economic activities: Evidence from Italian cities', *Papers in Regional Science* 93: 53–76.

Pérez, Liliane (2008), 'Inventing in a world of guilds: Silk fabrics in eighteenth-century Lyon', in: S. R. Epstein and Maarten Prak (eds.), *Guilds, Innovation and the European Economy, 1400–1800* (Cambridge: Cambridge University Press), 232–63.

Persson, Karl Gunnar (1988), *Pre-Industrial Economic Growth: Social Organization and Technological Progress in Europe* (Oxford: Blackwell).

Peterson, Mark (2006), 'Boston pays tribute: Autonomy and empire in the Atlantic world, 1630–1714', in: Allan I. Macinnes and Arthur H. Williamson (eds.), *Shaping the Stuart World, 1603–1714* (Leiden: Brill), 311–35.

Pethegem, P. (1988), 'La notion de ville impériale aux Pays Bas: Quelques réflections sur Deventer en tant que "ville impériale"', in: P. L. Nève and O. Moorman van Kappen (eds.), *Conservare Jura* (Deventer: Kluwer), 115–37.

Petit-Dutaillis, Charles (1970), *Les communes françaises: Caractères et évolution des origines au XVIIIe siècle* (Paris: Albin Michel; orig. 1947).

Petram, Lodewijk (2014), *The World's First Stock Exchange* (New York, NY: Columbia University Press).

Pettegree, Andrew (2002), *Europe in the Sixteenth Century* (Oxford: Blackwell).

(2010), *The Book in the Renaissance* (New Haven, CT: Yale University Press).
Peyer, Hans Conrad (1978), *Verfassungsgeschichte der alten Schweiz* (Zürich: Schulthess).
Pezzolo, Luciano (2014), 'The via italiana to capitalism', in: Larry Neal and Jeffrey Williamson (eds.), *The Cambridge History of Capitalism*, vol. 1: *The Rise of Capitalism from Ancient Origins to 1848* (Cambridge: Cambridge University Press), 267–313.
Pfister, Ulrich (2008a), 'Craft guilds and technological change: The engine loom in the European silk ribbon industry in the seventeenth and eighteenth centuries', in: S. R. Epstein and Maarten Prak (eds.), *Guilds, Innovation and the European Economy, 1400–1800* (Cambridge: Cambridge University Press), 172–98.
(2008b), 'Craft guilds, the theory of the firm, and early modern proto-industry', in: S. R. Epstein and Maarten Prak (eds.), *Guilds, Innovation and the European Economy, 1400–1800* (Cambridge: Cambridge University Press), 25–51.
Pierson, Paul (2004), *Politics in Time: History, Institutions and Social Analysis* (Princeton, NJ: Princeton University Press).
Pincus, Steve (2009), *1688: The First Modern Revolution* (New Haven, CT: Yale University Press).
Pincus, Steve, and James A. Robinson (2010), 'What really happened during the Glorious Revolution?', unpublished paper, available at http://scholar.harvard.edu/jrobinson/publications/what-really-happened-during-glorious-revolution.
Pirenne, Henri (1939), *Les villes et les institutions urbaines*. 2 vols. (Paris: Alcan).
Plumb, J. H. (1973), *The Growth of Political Stability in England, 1675–1725* (Harmondsworth: Penguin; orig. 1967).
Pocock, J. G. A (1975), *The Machiavellian Moment. Florentine Political Thought and the Atlantic Republican Tradition* (Princeton, NJ: Princeton University Press).
Pomeranz, Kenneth (2000), *The Great Divergence: China, Europe, and the Making of the Modern World Economy* (Princeton, NJ: Princeton University Press).
Pot, Peter (1988), 'Tussen medelijden en spaarzaamheid: De regenten van het Leidse Huiszittenhuis 1700–1795', *Holland* 20: 65–85.
(1994), *Arm Leiden: Levensstandaard, bedeling en bedeelden, 1750–1854*. Hollandse Studiën, vol. 31 (Hilversum: Verloren).
Pound, John F. (1974), *Government and Society in Tudor and Stuart Norwich, 1525–1675*, PhD thesis, University of Leicester.
Powers, James F. (1988), *A Society Organized for War: The Iberian Municipal Militias in the Central Middle Ages, 1000–1284* (Berkeley, CA: University of California Press).
Prados de la Escosura, Leandro (2006), 'The economic consequences of independence in Latin America', in: Victor Bulmer-Thomas, John H. Coatsworth and Roberto Cortés Conde (eds.), *The Cambridge Economic History of Latin America* (Cambridge: Cambridge University Press), 463–504.
Prak, Maarten (1985), *Gezeten burgers: De elite in een Hollandse stad, Leiden 1700–1780*. Hollandse Historische Reeks, vol. 6 (Amsterdam/Dieren: De Bataafsche Leeuw).
(1989), 'Republiek en vorst: De stadhouders en het staatsvormingsproces in de Noordelijke Nederlanden, 16e–18e eeuw', *Amsterdams Sociologisch Tijdschrift* 16: 28–52.
(1991a), 'Burgers in beweging: Ideaal en werkelijkheid van de onlusten te Leiden in 1748', *Bijdragen en Mededelingen betreffende de Geschiedenis der Nederlanden* 106: 365–93.

(1991b), 'Citizen radicalism and democracy in the Dutch Republic: The Patriot movement of the 1780s', *Theory and Society* 20: 73–102.

(1993a), 'Identité urbaine, identités sociales: Les bourgeois de Bois-le-Duc au XVIIIe siècle', *Annales ESC* 48: 907–33.

(1993b), 'Overvloed of onbehagen? Armoede, armen en armenzorg in 's-Hertogenbosch, 1770-1850', in: Jan van Oudheusden and Gerard Trienekens (eds.), *Een pront wijf, een mager paard en een zoon op het seminarie: Aanzetten tot een integrale geschiedenis van oostelijk Noord-Brabant, 1770–1914* (Bois-le-Duc: BRG), 7–44.

(1994a), 'Goede buren en verre vrienden. De ontwikkeling van onderstand bij armoede in Den Bosch sedert de Middeleeuwen', in: Henk Flap and Marco H. D. van Leeuwen (eds.), *Op lange termijn: Verklaringen van trends in de geschiedenis van samenlevingen* (Hilversum: Verloren), 147–69.

(1994b), 'Verfassungsnorm und Verfassungsrealität in den niederländischen Städten des späten 17. und 18. Jahrhunderts: Die Oligarchie in Amsterdam, Rotterdam, Deventer und Zutphen 1672/75-1795', in: Wilfried Ehbrecht (ed.), *Verwaltung und Politik in Städten Mitteleuropas: Beiträge zu Verfassungsnorm und Verfassungswirklichkeit in altständischer Zeit.* Städteforschung, vol. A/34 (Cologne: Böhlau), 55–83.

(1995), 'Cittadini, abitante e forestieri: una classificazione della popolazione di Amsterdam nella prima età moderna', *Quaderni Storici* 30 (89): 331–57.

(1996), 'Individual, corporation and society: The rhetoric of Dutch guilds (18th. C.)', in: Marc Boone and Maarten Prak (eds.), *Statuts individuels, statuts corporatifs et statuts judiciares dans les villes européennes (moyen âge et temps modernes) / Individual, Corporate, and Judicial Status in European Cities (Late Middle Ages and Early Modern Period)* (Louvain/Apeldoorn: Garant), 255–79.

(1997), 'Burghers into citizens: Urban and national citizenship in the Netherlands during the revolutionary era', *Theory and Society* 26: 403–20.

(1998), 'Armenzorg 1500–1800', in: Jacques van Gerwen and Marco H. D. van Leeuwen (eds.), *Studies over zekerheidsarrangementen. Risico's, risicobestrijding en verzekeringen in Nederland vanaf de Middeleeuwen* (Amsterdam: NEHA), 49–90.

(1999), *Republikeinse veelheid, democratische enkelvoud: Sociale verandering in het Revolutietijdvak: 's-Hertogenbosch 1770–1820* (Nijmegen: SUN).

(2000a), 'The Dutch Republic's city-state culture (17th–18th Centuries)', in: Mogens Herman Hansen (ed.), *A Comparative Study of Thirty City-State Cultures* (Copenhagen: Royal Danish Academy of Sciences and Letters), 343–58.

(2000b), 'Politik, Kultur und politische Kultur: die Zünfte in den Nördlichen Niederlanden', in: Wilfried Reininghaus (ed.), *Zunftlandschaften in Deutschland und den Niederlanden im Vergleich.* Schriften der Historischen Kommission für Westfalen, vol. 17 (Münster: Aschendorff), 71–83.

(2002), 'The politics of intolerance: Citizenship and religion in the Dutch Republic (17th–18th C.)', in: Ronnie Po-chia Hsia and Henk van Nierop (eds.), *Calvinism and Religious Toleration in the Dutch Golden Age* (Cambridge: Cambridge University Press), 159–75.

(2004), 'Moral order in the world of work: Social control and the guilds in Europe', in: Herman Roodenburg and Pieter Spierenburg (eds.), *Social Control in Europe, 1500–1800* (Columbus, OH: Ohio State University Press), 176–99.

(2005), *The Dutch Republic in the Seventeenth Century* (Cambridge: Cambridge University Press).

(2006), 'Corporate politics in the Low Countries: Guilds as institutions, 14th to 18th centuries', in: Maarten Prak, Catharina Lis, Jan Lucassen and Hugo Soly (eds.), *Craft Guilds in the Early Modern Low Countries: Work, Power and Representation* (Aldershot: Ashgate), 74–106.

(2008), 'Painters, guilds and the art market during the Dutch golden age', in: S. R. Epstein and Maarten Prak (eds.), *Guilds, Innovation and the European Economy, 1400–1800* (Cambridge: Cambridge University Press), 143–71.

(2012), 'Urban governments and their citizens in early modern Europe', in: Matthew Davies and James A. Galloway (eds.), *London and Beyond: Essays in Honour of Derek Keene* (London: Institute of Historical Research), 269–86.

(2014), 'Corporatism and social models in the Low Countries', in: Jacques van Gerwen, Co Seegers, Milja van Tielhof and Jan Luiten van Zanden (eds.), *Economic History in the Netherlands 1914–2014*, special issue of *Tijdschrift voor Sociale en Economische Geschiedenis* 11: 281–303.

Prak, Maarten, Clare Crowston, Raoul De Kerf, Bert De Munck, Christopher Kissane, Chris Minns, Ruben Schalk and Patrick Wallis (2018), 'Access to the trade: Monopoly and mobility in European craft guilds, 17th- and 18th-centuries' (unpublished paper).

Prak, Maarten, Catharina Lis, Jan Lucassen and Hugo Soly (eds.) (2006), *Craft Guilds in the Early Modern Low Countries: Work, Power and Representation* (Aldershot: Ashgate).

Prak, Maarten, and Jan Luiten van Zanden (2009), 'Tax morale and citizenship in the Dutch Republic', in: Oscar Gelderblom (ed.), *The Political Economy of the Dutch Republic* (Aldershot: Ashgate), 143–65.

Prevenier, Walter, and Marc Boone (1989), 'The city-state dream', in: Johan Decavele (ed.), *Ghent: In Defence of a Rebellious City* (Antwerp: Mercatorfonds), 81–105.

Price, J. L. (1994), *Holland and the Dutch Republic in the Seventeenth Century: The Politics of Particularism* (Oxford: Clarendon Press).

Przeworski, Adam, and Carolina Curvale (2008), 'Does politics explain the economic gap between the United States and Latin America?', in: Francis Fukuyama (ed.), *Falling Behind: Explaining the Development Gap between Latin America and the United States* (Oxford: Oxford University Press), 99–132.

Puhle, Matthias (2006), 'Die Hanse: Gemeinschaft, Bündnis oder gar Vorläufer Europas?', in: Franz J. Felten (ed.), *Städtebünde: Städtetage im Wandel der Geschichte* (Stuttgart: Franz Steiner), 37–47.

Pullan, Brian S. (1971), *Rich and Poor in Renaissance Venice: The Social Institutions of a Catholic State, to 1620* (Oxford: Blackwell).

(1988), 'Support and redeem: Charity and poor relief in Italian cities from the fourteenth to the seventeenth century', *Continuity and Change* 3: 177–208.

Pult Quaglia, Anna Maria (2006), 'Citizenship in medieval and early modern Italian cities', in: Steven G. Ellis, Gudmundur Hálfdanarson and Ann Katherine Isaacs (eds.), *Citizenship in Historical Perspective* (Pisa: Edizioni Plus), 107–14.

Putnam, Robert D. (1993), *Making Democracy Work: Civic Traditions in Modern Italy* (Princeton, NJ: Princeton University Press).

(2000), *Bowling Alone: The Collapse and Revival of American Community* (New York: Simon and Schuster).

Quast, Jenneke (1980), 'Vrouwen in gilden in Den Bosch, Utrecht en Leiden van de 14e tot en met de 16e eeuw', in: Wantje Fritschy (ed.), *Fragmenten vrouwengeschiedenis*, vol. 1 (The Hague: Nijhoff), 17–27.

Quataert, Jean H. (1985), 'The shaping of women's work in manufacturing: Guilds, households, and the state in Central Europe, 1648–1870', *American Historical Review* 90: 1122–48.

Queller, Donald E. (1986), *The Venetian Patriciate: Reality versus Myth* (Urbana, IL: University of Illinois Press).

Raccagni, Gianluca (2010), *The Lombard League 1167–1225* (Oxford: Oxford University Press).

Rădvan, Laurenţin (2015), 'A winding road: Urban autonomy in the Romanian principalities between the fourteenth and the eighteenth centuries', in: Michel Pauly and Alexander Lee (eds.), *Urban Liberties and Citizenship from the Middle Ages up to Now / Libertés et citoyenneté urbaines du moyen âge à nos jours / Städtische Freiheiten und bürgerliche Partizipation vom Mittelalter bis heute. Actes du Colloque 2009 de la Commission internationale pour l'Histoire des villes.* Beiträge zur Landes- und Kulturgeschichte, vol. 9 (Trier: Porta Alba), 171–99.

Ragin, Charles (1987), *The Comparative Method: Moving beyond Qualitative and Quantitative Strategies* (Berkeley, CA: University of California Press).

Ramos, Rui (2007), 'A tale of one city? Local civic traditions under liberal and republican rule in Portugal (late 18th century–early 20th century)', *Citizenship Studies* 11: 173–86.

Rankin, Mary Backus (1993), 'Some observations on a Chinese public sphere', *Modern China* 19: 158–82.

Ranum, Orest (1993), *The Fronde: A French Revolution 1648–1652* (New York: Norton).

Raphael, Ray (2013), 'The democratic moment: The revolution and popular politics', in: Edward G. Gray and Jane Kamensky (eds.), *The Oxford Handbook of the American Revolution* (Oxford: Oxford University Press), 121–38.

Rappaport, Steve (1998), *Worlds within Worlds: Structures of Life in Sixteenth-Century London* (Cambridge: Cambridge University Press).

Raymond, André (1973–74), *Artisans et commerçants au Caire au XVIIIe siècle.* 2 vols. (Damascus: Institut français d'études arabes de Damas; repr. Cairo: Institut français d'Archéologie orientale, 1999).

(1984), *The Great Arab Cities in the 16th–18th Centuries: An Introduction* (New York, NY: New York University Press).

(1985), *Grandes villes arabes à l'époque ottomane* (Paris: Sindbad).

(1995), 'The role of the communities (Tawa'if) in the administration of Cairo in the Ottoman period', in: Nelly Hanna (ed.), *The State and Its Servants: Administration in Egypt from Ottoman Times to the Present* (Cairo: American University in Cairo Press), 32–43.

(2000), *Cairo*, translated by Willard Wood (Cambridge, MA: Harvard University Press; French orig. 1993).

(2002), 'Urban networks and popular movements in Cairo and Aleppo (end of eighteenth, beginning of nineteenth centuries)', in: André Raymond (ed.), *Arab Cities in the Ottoman Period* (Aldershot: Ashgate), 57–81.

Reckwitz, Andreas (2002), 'Toward a theory of social practices: A development in culturalist theorizing', *European Journal of Social Theory* 5: 243–63.

Ree-Scholtens, G. F. van der (ed.) (1995), *Deugd boven geweld: Een geschiedenis van Haarlem, 1245–1995* (Hilversum: Verloren).

Reich, Jerome R. (1953), *Leisler's Rebellion: A Study in Democracy in New York, 1664–1720* (Chicago, IL: University of Chicago Press).

Reintges, Theo (1963), *Ursprung und Wesen der spätmittelalterlichen Schützengilden* (Bonn: Ludwig Röhrscheid Verlag).

Reith, Reinhold (2008), 'Circulation of skilled labour in late medieval and early modern Central Europe', in: S. R. Epstein and Maarten Prak (eds.), *Guilds, Innovation and the European Economy, 1400–1800* (Cambridge: Cambridge University Press), 114–42.

Resoluties van de vroedschap van Amsterdam, 1490–1550 (1986), ed. by P. H. D. van Iterson and P. H. J. van der Laan (Amsterdam: Bataafsche Leeuw).

Restall, Matthew (2003), *Seven Myths of the Spanish Conquest* (Oxford: Oxford University Press).

Reynolds, Susan (1977), *An Introduction to the History of English Medieval Towns* (Oxford: Clarendon Press).

(2002), *Kingdoms and Communities in Western Europe 900–1300*. 2nd edn. (Oxford: Clarendon Press).

Richter, Daniel K. (2011), *Before the Revolution: America's Ancient Pasts* (Cambridge, MA: Belknap Press).

Riedel, Manfred (1972), 'Bürger, Staatsbürger, Bürgertum', in: Otto Brunner, Werner Conze and Reinhart Koselleck (eds.), *Geschichtliche Grundbegriffe: Historisches Lexikon zur politisch-sozialen Sprache in Deutschland*, vol. 1 (Stuttgart: Klett), 672–725.

Rigby, S. H., and Elizabeth Ewan (2000), 'Government, power and authority 1300–1450', in: D. M. Pallisser (ed.), *Cambridge Urban History of Britain*, vol. 1 (Cambridge: Cambridge University Press), 291–312.

Rijpma, Auke (2012), *Funding Public Services through Religious and Charitable Foundations in the Late-Medieval Low Countries*. PhD dissertation, Universiteit Utrecht.

Ritchie, Robert C. (1977), *The Duke's Province: A Study of New York Politics and Society, 1664–1691* (Chapel Hill, NC: University of North Carolina Press).

Rivière, François (2016), 'Women in craft organisations in Rouen (14th–15th century)', in: Eva Jullien and Michel Pauly (eds.), *Craftsmen and Guilds in the Medieval and Early Modern Periods*. VSWG Beiheft 234 (Stuttgart: Franz Steiner), 93–124.

Robbins, Kevin C. (1997), *City on the Ocean Sea: La Rochelle, 1530–1650: Urban Society, Religion, and Politics on the French Atlantic Frontier* (Leiden: Brill).

Roberts, Keith (1996), 'Citizen Soldiers: The Military Power of the City of London', in: Stephen Porter (ed.), *London and the Civil War* (London: MacMillan), 89–116.

Roberts, Michael (1956), *The Military Revolution, 1560–1660* (Belfast, inaugural lecture) (reprinted in Rogers (ed. 1995a) 13–35).

Robertson, Ian (2002), *Tyranny under the Mantle of St. Peter: Pope Paul II and Bologna*. Late Medieval and Early Modern Studies, vol. 5 (Turnhout: Brepols).

Robertson, John (1985), *The Scottish Enlightenment and the Militia Issue* (Edinburgh: Donald).

Roche, Daniel (1987), 'A pauper capital: Some reflections on the Parisian poor in the seventeenth and eighteenth centuries', *French History* 1: 182–209.

Rodgers, N. (1989), *Whigs and Cities: Popular Politics in the Age of Walpole and Pitt* (Oxford: Oxford University Press).

Roeck, Bernd (1989), *Eine Stadt in Krieg und Friede: Studien zur Geschichte der Reichsstadt Augsburg zwischen Kalenderstreit und Parität* (Göttingen: Vandenhoeck & Ruprecht).

Rogers, Clifford J. (ed.) (1995a), *The Military Revolution Debate: Readings on the Military Transformation of Early Modern Europe* (Boulder, CO: Westview Press).

(1995b), 'The military revolutions of the Hundred Years War', in: Clifford J. Rogers (ed.), *The Military Revolution Debate: Readings on the Military Transformation*

of Early Modern Europe (Boulder, CO: Westview Press; art. orig. publ. in 1993), 55–93.
Rogge, Jörg (1996), *Für den gemeinen Nutz: Politisches Handeln und Politikverständnis von Rat und Bürgerschaft in Augsburg im Spätmittelalter*. Augsburger Forschungen zur europäischen Kulturgeschichte, vol. 6 (Tübingen: Max Niemeyer).
Romano, Dennis (1984), 'Charity and community in early Renaissance Venice', *Journal of Urban History* 11: 63–82.
(1987), *Patricians and* Popolani*: The Social Foundations of the Venetian Renaissance State* (Baltimore, MD: Johns Hopkins University Press).
Rommes, Ronald (1998), *Oost west, Utrecht best? Driehonderd jaar migratie en migranten in de stad Utrecht (begin 16e – begin 19e eeuw)*. PhD dissertation, Universiteit van Amsterdam.
Rommes, Ronald, and Joost van der Spek (2004), *Met hand en hart: Zeven eeuwen smedengilde en St. Eloyengasthuis in Utrecht 1304–2004* (Utrecht: SPOU).
Roney, Jessica Choppin (2014), *Governed by a Spirit of Opposition: The Origins of American Political Practice in Colonial Philadelphia* (Baltimore, MD: Johns Hopkins University Press).
Roodenburg, Herman (1991), 'The "hand of friendship": Shaking hands and other gestures in the Dutch Republic', in: Jan Bremmer and Herman Roodenburg (eds.), *A Cultural History of Gesture* (Cambridge: Cambridge University Press), 152–89.
Roper, Lyndal (1987), '"The common man", "the common good", "common women": Gender and meaning in the German Reformation commune', *Social History*, 12: 1–21.
(1989), *The Holy Household: Women and Morals in Reformation Augsburg* (Oxford: Oxford University Press).
Rosanvallon, Pierre (2007), *The Demands of Liberty: Civil Society in France since the Revolution* (Cambridge, MA: Harvard University Press).
Rösch, Gerhard (2000), 'The Serrata of the Great Council and Venetian society, 1286–1323', in: John Martin and Dennis Romano (eds.), *Venice Reconsidered: The History and Civilization of an Italian City-State, 1297–1797* (Baltimore, MD: Johns Hopkins University Press), 67–88.
Rosenthal, David (2015), *Kings of the Street: Power, Community, and Ritual in Renaissance Florence*. Europa Sacra, vol. 17 (Turnhout: Brepols).
Rosenthal, Jean-Laurent (1998), 'The political economy of absolutism reconsidered', in: Robert H. Bates et al., *Analytic Narratives* (Princeton, NJ: Princeton University Press), 64–108.
Rosenthal, Jean-Laurent, and Roy Bin Wong (2011), *Before and beyond Divergence: The Politics of Economic Change in China and Europe* (Cambridge, MA: Harvard University Press).
Ross, Steven J. (1988), '"Objects of charity": Poor relief, poverty, and the rise of the almshouse in early eighteenth-century New York City', in: W. Pencak and C. E. Wright (eds.), *Authority and Resistance in Early New York* (New York, NY: New York Historical Society), 138–72.
Rosser, Gervase (1989), *Medieval Westminster, 1200–1540* (Oxford: Clarendon Press).
(1997), 'Crafts, guilds, and the negotiation of work', *Past & Present* 154: 3–31.
(2006), 'Big brotherhood: Guilds in urban politics in late medieval England', in: Ian A. Gadd and Patrick Wallis (eds.), *Guilds and Associations in Europe, 900–1900* (London: Institute of Historical Research), 27–42.
(2015), *The Art of Solidarity in the Middle Ages: Guilds in England 1250–1550* (Oxford: Oxford University Press).

Rosswurm, Steven (1987), *Arms, Country, and Class: The Philadelphia Militia and the 'Lower Sort' during the American Revolution, 1775–1783* (New Brunswick, NJ: Rutgers University Press).
Roth, Ralf (1996), *Stadt und Bürgertum in Frankfurt am Main: Ein besonderer Weg von der ständischen zur modernen Bürgergesellschaft 1760–1914*. Stadt und Bürgertum, vol. 7 (Munich: Oldenbourg).
Rowe, William (1984), *Hankow: Commerce and Society in a Chinese City: 1796–1889* (Stanford, CA: Stanford University Press).
(1989), *Hankow: Conflict and Community in a Chinese City, 1796–1895* (Stanford, CA: Stanford University Press).
(1993), 'The problem of "civil society" in late imperial China', *Modern China* 19: 139–57.
(2002), 'Social stability and social change', in: Willard J. Peterson (ed.), *The Cambridge History of China*, vol. 9, pt. 1: *The Ch'ing Empire to 1800* (Cambridge: Cambridge University Press), 473–562.
(2009), *China's Last Empire: The Great Qing* (Cambridge, MA: Harvard University Press).
(2017), 'Urban agency in early modern and modern China', *Urban History* 44: 123–29.
Rowen, Herbert H. (ed.) (1972), *The Low Countries in Early Modern Times*. Documentary History of Western Civilisation (London: Macmillan).
(1978), *John de Witt: Grand-Pensionary of Holland, 1625–1672* (Princeton, NJ: Princeton University Press).
Roy, Ian (1992), 'The City of Oxford, 1640–1660', in: R. C. Richardson (ed.), *Town and Countryside in the English Revolution* (Manchester: Manchester University Press), 130–68.
Rozman, Gilbert (1973), *Urban Networks in Ch'ing China and Tokugawa Japan* (Princeton, NJ: Princeton University Press).
Rubin, Miri (1987), *Charity and Community in Medieval Cambridge* (Cambridge: Cambridge University Press).
Rubinstein, Nicolai (1958), 'Political ideas in Sienese art: The frescoes by Ambrogio Lorenzetti and Taddeo di Bartolo in the Palazzo Pubblico', *Journal of the Wartburg and Courtauld Institutes* 21: 179–207.
Rublack, Hans-Christoph (1984), 'Political and social norms in urban communities in the Holy Roman Empire', in: Kaspar von Greyerz (ed.), *Religion, Politics and Social Protest: Three Studies on Early Modern Germany* (London: George Allen & Unwin), 24–60.
Rudé, George (1964), *The Crowd in History: A Study of Popular Disturbances in France and England 1730–1848* (London: Wiley).
Ruggiero, Guido (1980), *Violence in Early Renaissance Venice* (New Brunswick, NJ: Rutgers University Press).
Ruiz, Teofilo F. (1977), 'The transformation of the Castilian municipalities: The case of Burgos, 1248–1350', *Past & Present* 77: 3–32.
Ruiz Ibáñez, José Javier (ed.) (2009), *Las milicias del Rey de España: Sociedad, política e identidad en las Monarquías Ibéricas* (Madrid: FCE/Red Columnaria).
(2007), *Spain's Centuries of Crisis: 1300–1474* (Oxford: Blackwell).
Ryckbosch, Wouter (2016), 'Economic inequality and growth before the Industrial Revolution: The case of the Low Countries (fourteenth to nineteenth centuries)', *European Review of Economic History* 20: 1–22.

Ryerson, Richard A. (1974), 'Political mobilization and the American Revolution: The resistance movement in Philadelphia, 1765 to 1771', *William and Mary Quarterly* 31: 565–88.
(1978), *The Revolution Is Now Begun: The Radical Committees of Philadelphia, 1765–1776* (Philadelphia, PA: University of Pennsylvania Press).
Sacks, David Harris (1991), *The Widening Gate: Bristol and the Atlantic Economy, 1450–1700* (Berkeley, CA: University of California Press).
(1992), 'Bristol's "wars of religion"', in: R. C. Richardson (ed.), *Town and Countryside in the English Revolution* (Manchester: Manchester University Press), 100–29.
Sahlins, Peter (2004), *Unnaturally French: Foreign Citizenship in the Old Regime and After* (Ithaca, NY: Cornell University Press).
Sarnowsky, Jürgen (2015), 'The "golden age" of the Hanseatic League', in: Donald J. Harreld (ed.), *A Companion to the Hanseatic League* (Leiden: Brill), 64–99.
Sas, N. C. F. van (1987), 'Politiek als leerproces: Het Patriottisme in Utrecht, 1783–1787', *Jaarboek Oud-Utrecht*: 9–42.
Sassen, Saskia (2002), 'Towards post-national and denationalized citizenship', in Engin F. Isin and Bryan S. Turner (eds.), *Handbook of Citizenship Studies* (London: Sage), 277–91.
(2006), *Territory, Authority, Rights: From Medieval to Global Assemblages* (Princeton, NJ: Princeton University Press).
Sauerbrey, Beate (1989), *Die Wehrverfassung der Stadt Braunschweig im Spätmittelalter* (Braunschweig: Stadtarchiv).
Saupin, Guy (1991), 'Les assemblées municipales en Bretagne sous l'Ancien Régime: Quelle participation des habitants ?', in: Daniel Aris (ed.), *La Bretagne au XVIIe siècle* (Vannes: Conseil Général de Morbihan), 165–259.
(1996), *Nantes au XVIIe siècle: Vie politique et société urbaine* (Rennes: Presses universitaires de Rennes).
(2002), *Les villes en France à l'époque moderne (XVIe–XVIIIe siècles)* (Paris: Belin).
(2006), 'La Milice Bourgeoise? Relais Politique Fondamental dans la Ville Française d'Ancien Régime: Réflexions à Partir de l'Exemple de Nantes', in: Bruno Dumons and Olivier Zeller (eds.), *Gouverner la ville en Europe: Du Moyen Âge au XXe siècle* (Paris: l'Harmattan), 73–89.
Schalk, Ruben (2014), 'From orphan to artisan: Dutch apprenticeship during and after the guilds', unpublished paper, Utrecht University.
(2015), *Splitting the Bill: Matching Schooling to Dutch Labour Markets, 1750–1920*, PhD thesis, Universiteit Utrecht.
Schatkowski Schilcher, Linda (1983), *Families in Politics: Damascene Factions and Estates of the 18th and 19th Centuries* (Stuttgart: Franz Steiner).
Schildhauer, Johannes (1975), 'Charakter und Funktion der Städtebünde in der Feudalgesellschaft: vornehmlich auf dem Gebiet des Reiches', in: Konrad Fritze, Eckhard Müller and Johannes Schildhauer (eds.), *Bürgertum – Handelskapital – Städtebünde*. Hansische Studien, vol. 3 (Weimar: Verlag Hermann Böhlau's Nachfolger), 149–70.
Schilling, Heinz (1975), 'Aufstandsbewegungen in der Stadtbürgerlichen Gesellschaft des Alten Reiches: Die Vorgeschichte des Münsteraner Täuferreiches, 1525 bis 1534', in Hans-Ulrich Wehler (ed.), *Der Deutsche Bauernkrieg 1524–1526 Sonderheft Geschichte und Gesellschaft* (Göttingen: Vandenhoeck & Ruprecht), 193–238.
(1992a), 'Civic republicanism in late medieval and early modern German cities', in: Heinz Schilling (ed.), *Religion, Political Culture and the Emergence of Early Modern Society* (Leiden: Brill), 3–59 (orig. 'Gab es im späten Mittelalter und zu

Beginn der Neuzeit in Deutschland einen städtischen "Republikanismus"? Zur politischen Kultur des alteuropäischen Stadtbürgertums', in: Helmut Koenigsberger (ed.), Republiken und Republikanismus im Europa der Frühen Neuzeit, Munich 1988, 101–43).

(1992b), 'The rise of early modern burgher elites during the sixteenth and seventeenth centuries', in: Heinz Schilling, *Religion, Political Culture and the Emergence of Early Modern Society: Essays in German and Dutch History.* Studies in Medieval and Reformation Thought, vol. 50 (Leiden: Brill), 135–87 (transl. of 'Wandlungs- und Differerenzieringsprozesse innerhalb der bürgerlichen Oberschichten West- und Nordwestdeutschlands im 16. und 17. Jahrhundert', in: M. Biskup and K. Zernack (eds.), *Schichtung und Entwicklung der Gesellschaft in Polen und Deutschland im 16. und 17.* Jahrhundert, Wiesbaden 1983, 121–73).

(1993), *Die Stadt in der frühen Neuzeit.* Enzykoplädie der Deutschen Geschichte, vol. 24 (Munich: Oldenbourg).

Schilp, Thomas (2009), 'Westfälische Städte und Rheinischer Bund: Überlegungen zur städtischen Autonomie in der Mitte des 13. Jahrhundert', in: Werner Freitag and Peter Johanek (eds.), *Bünde – Städte – Gemeinden: Bilanz und Perspektiven der vergleichenden Landes- und Stadtgeschichte.* Städteforschung, vol. A77 (Cologne: Böhlau), 41–61.

Schmid, Regula (1995), *Reden, rufen, Zeichen setzen: Politisches handeln während des Berner Twingherrenstreits 1469–1471* (Zürich: Chronos).

(1996), '"Lieb und Leid tragen": Bürgerrecht und Zunftmitgliedschaft als Kriterien der Zugehörigkeit im spätmittelalterlichen Zürich', in: Marc Boone and Maarten Prak (eds.), *Statuts individuels, statuts corporatifs et statuts judiciares dans les villes européennes (moyen âge et temps modernes) / Individual, Corporate, and Judicial Status in European Cities (Late Middle Ages and Early Modern Period)* (Louvain/Apeldoorn: Garant), 49–72.

Schmid, Wolfgang (2003), *Dürer als Unternehmer: Kunst, Humanismus und Ökonomie in Nürnberg um 1500 Beiträge zur Landes- und Kulturgeschichte*, vol. 1 (Trier: Porta Alba Verlag).

Schmidt, Ariadne (2009), 'Women and guilds: Corporations and female labour market participation in early modern Holland', *Gender and History* 21: 170–89.

Schmidt, Georg (1984), *Der Städtetag in der Reichsverfassung: Eine Untersuchung zur korporativen Politik der freien und Reichsstädte in der ersten Hälfte des 16. Jahrhunderts.* Veröffentlichungen des Instituts für Europäische Geschichte Mainz, vol. 113 (Stuttgart: Franz Steiner).

Schmidt, Heinrich Richard (1986), *Reichsstädte und Reformation: Korporative Religionspolitik 1521–1529/30.* Veröffentlichungen des Instituts für Europäische Geschichte Mainz, vol. 122 (Stuttgart: Franz Steiner).

Schmidt-Wiegand, Ruth (1985), 'Die Bezeichnungen Zunft und Gilde in ihrem historischen und wortgeographischen Zusammenhang', in: Berent Schwineköper (ed.), *Gilden und Zünfte: Kaufmännische und gewerbliche Genossenschaften im frühen und hohen Mittelalter* (Sigmaringen: Jan Thorbecke), 31–52.

(1999), 'Genossenschaftliche Organisation im Spiegel historischer Bezeichnungen: Hanse, Gilde, Morgensprache', in: Nils Jörn, Detlef Kattinger and Horst Wernicke (eds.), *Genossenschaftliche Strukturen in der Hanse.* Quellen und Darstellungen zur hansischen Geschichte NF, vol. 48 (Cologne: Böhlau), 1–12.

Schneider, David M. (1938), *The History of Public Welfare in New York State, 1609–1866* (Chicago, IL: University of Chicago Press).

Schneider, Robert A. (1989a), 'Crown and capitoulat: Municipal government in Toulouse 1500–1789', in: Philip Benedict (ed.), *Cities and Social Change in Early Modern France* (London: Routledge), 195–220.

(1989b), *Public Life in Toulouse, 1463–1789: From Municipal Republic to Cosmopolitan City* (Ithaca, NY: Cornell University Press).

Schöffer, Ivo (1975), 'The Batavian myth during the sixteenth and seventeenth centuries', in: J. S. Bromley and E. H. Kossmann (eds.), *Britain and the Netherlands*, vol. 5: *Some Political Mythologies* (The Hague: Nijhoff), 78–101.

Schreiner, Klaus (1996), 'Teilhabe, Konsens und Autonomie: Leitbegriffe kommunaler Ordnung in der politischen Theorie des späten Mittelalters und der frühen Neuzeit', in: Peter Blickle (ed.), *Theorien kommunaler Ordnung in Europa*. Schriften des Historischen Kollegs, Kolloquien, vol. 36 (Munich: Oldenbourg), 35–61.

Schroeder, Klaus-Peter (1991), *Das Alte Reich und seine Städte: Untergang und Neubeginn: Die Mediatisierung der oberdeutschen Reichsstädte im Gefolge des Reichsdeputationshauptschlusses 1802/03* (Munich: Beck).

Schultheiss, Werner (1972), 'Das Bürgerrecht der Königs- und Reichsstadt Nürnberg: Beiträge zur Verfassungsgeschichte der deutschen Städte', in: Mitarbeitern des Max-Planck-Instituts für Geschichte (eds.), *Festschrift für Hermann Heimpel zum 70. Geburtstag*, vol. 2 (Göttingen: Vandenhoeck & Ruprecht), 159–94.

Schultz, Ronald (1993), *The Republic of Labor: Philadelphia Artisans and the Politics of Class, 1720–1830* (New York, NY: Oxford University Press).

Schulz, Knut (1994), 'Die politische Zunft: Eine die spätmittelalterliche Stadt prägende Institution?', in: Wilfried Ehbrecht (ed.), *Verwaltung und Politik in Städten Mitteleuropas. Beiträge zu Verfassungsnorm und Verfassungswirklichkeit in altständischer Zeit* Städteforschung, vol. A/34 (Cologne: Böhlau), 1–20.

(2009), 'Stadtgemeinde, Rat und Rheinischer Städtebund: Das vorläufige Ergebnis des Prozesses der Kommunalisierung und Urbanisierung um 1250', in: Werner Freitag and Peter Johanek (eds.), *Bünde – Städte – Gemeinden: Bilanz und Perspektiven der vergleichenden Landes- und Stadtgeschichte*. Städteforschung, vol. A77 (Cologne: Böhlau), 17–39.

(2010), *Handwerk, Zünfte und Gewerbe: Mittelalter und Renaissance* (Darmstadt: WBG).

Schuttelaars, Anton (1998), *Heren van de raad: Bestuurlijke elite van 's-Hertogenbosch in de stedelijke samenleving, 1500–1580* (Nijmegen: Nijmegen University Press).

Schwarz, L. D. (1992), *London in the Age of Industrialisation: Entrepreneurs, Labour Force and Living Conditions* (Cambridge: Cambridge University Press).

Schwerdhoff, Gerd (1994), 'Die goldene Freiheit der Bürger: Zu den Bedeutungsebenen eines Grundwertes in der stadtkölnischen Geschichte (13.-17. Jahrhundert)', in: Klaus Schreiner and Ulrich Meier (eds.), *Stadtregiment und Bürgerfreiheit: Handlungsspielräume in deutschen und italienischen Städten des Späten Mittelalters und der Frühen Neuzeit* (Göttingen: Vandenhoeck & Ruprecht), 84–119.

Schwinges, Rainer Christoph (ed.) (2002), *Neubürger im Späten Mittelalter: Migration und Austausch in der Städtelandschaft des alten Reiches (1250–1550)*. Beiheft Zeitschrift für Historische Forschung, vol. 30 (Berlin: Duncker & Humblot).

Schwoerer, Lois (1974), *'No Standing Armies': The Anti-Army Ideology in Seventeenth-Century England* (Baltimore, MD, and London: Johns Hopkins University Press).

Scott, D. (1992), 'Politics and government in York', in: R. C. Richardson (ed.), *Town and Countryside in the English Revolution* (Manchester: Manchester University Press), 46–65.

Scott, Tom (2012), *The City-State in Europe, 1000–1600* (Oxford: Oxford University Press).

Seabright, Paul (2010), *The Company of Strangers: The Natural History of Economic Life* (Princeton, NJ: Princeton University Press).

Sen, Amartya (1999), *Development as Freedom* (Oxford: Oxford University Press).

Sewell, William H. (1980), *Work and Revolution in France: The Language of Labor from the Old Regime to 1848* (Cambridge: Cambridge University Press).

(1988), 'Le citoyen/la citoyenne: Activity, passivity, and the revolutionary concept of citizenship', in: Colin Lucas (ed.), *The French Revolution and the Creation of Modern Political Culture*, vol. 2: *The Political Culture of the French Revolution* (Oxford: Pergamon Press), 105–23.

Seybolt, Robert (1918), *The Colonial Citizen of New York* (Madison, WI: University of Wisconsin).

Shapiro, Gilbert, and John Markoff (2001), 'Officially solicited petitions: The *cahiers de doléances* as a historical source', in: Lex Heerma van Voss (ed.), *Petitions in Social History* (*International Review of Social History* 46, Supplement 9) (Cambridge: Cambridge University Press), 79–106.

Sharlin, A. (1978), 'Natural decrease in early modern cities', *Past & Present* 79: 126–38.

Shaw, Christine (2006), *Popular Government and Oligarchy in Renaissance Italy*. The Medieval Mediterranean, vol. 66 (Leiden: Brill).

Shaw, David Gary (1993), *The Creation of a Community: The City of Wells in the Middle Ages* (Oxford: Clarendon Press).

Shaw, Denis J. B. (2006), 'Urban developments', in: Maureen Perrie (ed.), *The Cambridge History of Russia*, vol. 1: *From Early Rus' to 1689* (Cambridge: Cambridge University Press), 579–99.

Shaw, Jo (2007), *The Transformation of Citizenship in the European Union: Electoral Rights and the Restructuring of Political Space* (Cambridge: Cambridge University Press).

Shephard, Edward J., Jr. (1986), 'Social and geographic mobility of the eighteenth-century guild artisan: An analysis of guild receptions in Dijon, 1700–90', in: Steven L. Kaplan and Cynthia Koepp (eds.), *Work in France: Representations, Meaning, Organizations, and Practice* (Ithaca, NY: Cornell University Press), 97–130.

Shiue, Carol (2004), 'Local granaries and central government disaster relief: Moral hazard and intergovernmental finance in eighteenth- and nineteenth-century China', *Journal of Economic History* 64: 100–24.

Shorto, Russell (2004), *The Island at the Center of the World: The Epic Story of Dutch Manhattan and the Forgotten Colony That Shaped America* (New York, NY: Doubleday).

Shy, John W. (1963), 'A new look at colonial militia', *The William and Mary Quarterly* 20: 175–85 (reprinted in Shy, *A People Numerous and Armed: Reflections on the Military Struggle for American Independence*, New York, NY: Oxford University Press, 1976, ch. 2).

Singer, Amy (2008), *Charity in Islamic Societies* (Cambridge: Cambridge University Press).

Skinner, G. William (ed.) (1977a), *The City in Late Imperial China* (Stanford, CA: Stanford University Press).

(1977b), 'Introduction: Urban development in imperial China', in: G. William Skinner (ed.), *The City in Late Imperial China* (Stanford, CA: Stanford University Press), 3–31.

(1977c), 'Regional urbanization in nineteenth-century China', in: G. William Skinner (ed.), *The City in Late Imperial China* (Stanford, CA: Stanford University Press), 211–49.
(1977d), 'Cities and the hierarchy of local systems', in: G. William Skinner (ed.), *The City in Late Imperial China* (Stanford, CA: Stanford University Press), 275–364.
(1977e), 'Introduction: Urban social structure in Ch'ing China', in: G. William Skinner (ed.), *The City in Late Imperial China* (Stanford, CA: Stanford University Press), 521–53.
Skinner, Quentin (1986), 'Ambrogio Lorenzetti: The artist as political philosopher (Raleigh Lecture on History)', *Proceedings of the British Academy* 72: 1–56.
(1999), 'Ambrogio Lorenzetti's Buon Governo frescoes: Two old questions, two new answers', *Journal of the Warburg and Courtauld Institutes* 62: 1–28.
Skocpol, Theda (1979), *States and Social Revolutions: A Comparative Analysis of France, Russia, and China* (Cambridge: Cambridge University Press).
(ed.) (1984), *Vision and Method in Historical Sociology* (Cambridge: Cambridge University Press).
(1995), *Protecting Soldiers and Mothers: The Political Origins of Social Policy in the United States* (Cambridge, MA: Harvard University Press).
Slack, Paul (1988), *Poverty and Policy in Tudor and Stuart England* (London: Longman).
(1999), *From Reformation to Improvement: Public Welfare in Early Modern England* (Oxford: Oxford University Press).
Slokker, Nico (2010), *Ruggengraat van de stedelijke samenleving: De rol van de gilden in de stad Utrecht, 1528–1818* (Hilversum: Verloren).
Smith, Dennis (1991), *The Rise of Historical Sociology* (Cambridge: Polity Press).
Smith, Joanna Handlin (2009), *The Art of Doing Good: Charity in Late Ming China* (Berkeley, CA: University of California Press).
Smith, Pamela (2010), 'Why write a book? From lived experience to the written word in early modern Europe', *Bulletin of the German Historical Institute*, 47: 25–50.
Smith, Rogers M. (2002), 'Modern citizenship', in: Engin F. Isin and Bryan S. Turner (eds.), *Handbook of Citizenship Studies* (London: Sage), 105–15.
Snell, K. D. M. (1985), *Annals of the Labouring Poor: Social Change and Agrarian England 1660–1900* (Cambridge: Cambridge University Press).
Sodano, Giulio (2013), 'Governing the city', in: Tommaso Astarita (ed.), *A Companion to Early Modern Naples* (Leiden: Brill), 109–29.
Soliday, G. (1974), *A Community in Conflict: Frankfurt Society in the Seventeenth and Early Eighteenth Century* (Hanover, NH: University Press of New England).
Solórzano Telechea, Jesús Ángel (2014), 'The politics of the urban commons in northern Atlantic Spain in the later Middle Ages', *Urban History* 41: 183–203.
Soltow, Lee, and Jan Luiten van Zanden (1998), *Income and Wealth Inequality in the Netherlands, 16th–20th Century* (Amsterdam: Het Spinhuis).
Soly, Hugo (ed.) (1999), *Charles V, 1500–1558, and His Time* (Antwerp: Mercatorfonds).
(2008), 'The political economy of European craft guilds: Power relations and economic strategies of merchants and master artisans in the medieval and early modern textile industries', in: Jan Lucassen, Tine De Moor and Jan Luiten van Zanden (eds.), *The Return of the Guilds*, supplement 16 of *International Review of Social History* 53 (Cambridge: Cambridge University Press), 45–71.
Somaini, Francesco (2012), 'The collapse of city-states and the role of urban centres in the new political geography of Renaissance Italy', in: Andrea Gamberini and Isabella Lazzarini (eds.), *The Italian Renaissance State* (Cambridge: Cambridge University Press), 239–60.

Somers, Margaret (1993), 'Citizenship and the place of the public sphere: Law, community, and political culture in the transition to democracy', *American Sociological Review* 58: 587–620.
(1998), 'Conscription: The price of citizenship', in: Robert H. Bates et al. (eds.), *Analytic Narratives* (Princeton, NJ: Princeton University Press), 109–47.
Sonenscher, Michael (1989), *Work and Wages: Natural Law, Politics, and the Eighteenth-Century French Trades* (Cambridge: Cambridge University Press).
Sonkajärvi, Hanna (2008), *Qu'est-ce qu'un étranger? Frontières et identifications à Strasbourg (1681–1789)* (Strasbourg: Presses Universitaires de Strasbourg).
Spaans, Joke (1996), 'De gift aan de armen in Friese steden in de zestiende, zeventiende en achttiende eeuw, toegelicht aan de hand van het voorbeeld Sneek', *Tijdschrift voor Sociale Geschiedenis* 22: 375–93.
Spanninga, Hotso (2012), *Gulden vrijheid? Politieke cultuur en staatsvorming in Friesland, 1600–1640* (Hilversum: Verloren).
Spicer, Joaneath (1991), 'The Renaissance elbow', in: Jan Bremmer and Herman Roodenburg (eds.), *A Cultural History of Gesture* (Cambridge: Cambridge University Press), 84–128.
Spierenburg, Pieter (1991), *The Prison Experience: Disciplinary Institutions and Their Inmates in Early Modern Europe* (New Brunswick, NJ: Rutgers University Press).
Spits, F. C. (1979), 'Unie en militie', in: S. Groenveld and H. L. Ph. Leeuwenberg (eds.), *De Unie van Utrecht: Wording en werking van een verbond en een verbondsacte.* Geschiedenis in veelvoud, vol. 6 (The Hague: Nijhoff), 182–98.
Stabel, Peter (2007), 'Social mobility and apprenticeship in late medieval Flanders', in: Bert De Munck, Steven L. Kaplan and Hugo Soly (eds.), *Learning on the Shop Floor: Historical Perspectives on Apprenticeship* (Oxford: Berghahn), 158–78.
Staeheli, Lynn A. (ed.) (2003), 'Cities and citizenship', special issue of *Urban Geography* 24: 97–184.
Stasavage, David (2003), *Public Debt and the Birth of the Democratic State: France and Great Britain, 1688–1789* (Cambridge: Cambridge University Press).
(2011), *States of Credit: Size, Power, and the Development of European Politics* (Princeton, NJ: Princeton University Press).
(2014), 'Was Weber right? The role of urban autonomy in Europe's rise', *American Political Science Review* 108: 337–54.
Steensel, Arie van (2016), 'Guilds and politics in medieval urban Europe', in: Eva Jullien and Michel Pauly (eds.), *Craftsmen and Guilds in the Medieval and Early Modern Periods.* VSWG Beiheft 234 (Stuttgart: Franz Steiner), 37–56.
Stephens, John N. (1983), *The Fall of the Florentine Republic, 1512–1530* (Oxford: Clarendon Press).
Stercken, Martina (2000), 'Reichsstadt, eidgenössischer Ort, städtische Territorialherrschaft: Zu den Anfängen der Stadtstaaten im Gebiet der heutigen Schweiz', in: Mogens Herman Hansen (ed.), *A Comparative Study of Thirty City-State Cultures* (Copenhagen: Royal Danish Academy of Sciences and Letters), 321–42.
Stollberg-Rilinger, Barbara (2008), *Des Kaisers alte Kleider: Verfassungsgeschichte und Symbolsprache des Alten Reiches* (Munich: C. H. Beck).
Stolz, Otto (1918), *Wehrverfassung und Schützenwesen in Tirol von den Anfängen bis 1918* (Innsbruck: Tyrolia).
Stone, Lawrence (1971), 'Prosopography', *Daedalus* 100: 46–71, repr. in Stone, *The Past and the Present* (London: Routledge & Kegan Paul, 1981).
Stoyle, Mark (1996), *From Deliverance to Destruction: Rebellion and Civil War in an English City* (Exeter: Exeter University Press).

Streecker, Wolfgang, and Philippe C. Schmitter (1985), 'Community, market, state – and associations? The prospective contribution of interest governance to social order', *European Sociological Review* 1: 119–38 (reprinted in Wolfgang Streecker and Philippe C. Schmitter [eds.], *Private Interest Government: Beyond Market and State*, London: Sage, 1985, 1–29).

Streng, J. C. (1997), *'Stemme in staat': De bestuurlijke elite in de stadsrepubliek Zwolle 1579–1795* (Hilversum: Verloren).

(2001), *Vrijheid, gelijkheid, broederschap en gezelligheid: Het Zwolse St. Nicolaasgilde tijden het ancien régime* (Hilversum: Verloren).

Stuart, Kathy (2006), *Defiled Trades and Social Outcasts: Honour and Ritual Pollution in Early Modern Germany* (Cambridge: Cambridge University Press).

Studer, Barbara (2002), 'Frauen im Bürgerrecht: Überlegungen zur rechtlichen und sozialen Stellung der Frau in spätmittelalterlichen Städten', in: Rainer Christoph Schwinges (ed.), *Neubürger im Späten Mittelalter: Migration und Austausch in der Städtelandschaft des alten Reiches (1250–1550)*. Beiheft Zeitschrift für Historische Forschung, vol. 30 (Berlin: Duncker & Humblot), 169–200.

Suter, Meinrad (ed.) (2000), *Kleine Zürcher Verfassungsgeschichte, 1280–2000* (Zürich: Chronos).

Swaan, Abram de (1988), *In Care of the State: Health Care, Education and Welfare in Europe and the USA in the Modern Era* (Cambridge: Polity Press).

Sweet, Rosemary (1998), 'Freemen and independence in English borough politics, c. 1770–1830', *Past & Present* 161: 84–115.

(1999), *The English Town, 1680–1840: Government, Society and Culture* (London: Routledge).

Syrett, David (1964), 'Town-meeting politics in Massachusetts, 1776–1786', *The William and Mary Quarterly* 21: 352–66.

Tabacco, Giovanni (1989), *The Struggle for Power in Medieval Italy: Structures of Political Rule* (Cambridge: Cambridge University Press).

Taillefer, Michel (2000), *Vivre à Toulouse sous l'Ancien Régime* (Paris: Perrin).

Tallett, Frank (1992), *War and Society in Early Modern Europe, 1495–1715* (London: Routledge).

Tallett, Frank, and D. J. B. Trim (2010), '"Then was then and now is now": An overview of change and continuity in late medieval and early modern warfare', in: Frank Tallett and D. J. B. Trim (eds.), *European Warfare 1350–1750* (Cambridge: Cambridge University Press), 1–26.

Tan, Li (2013), 'Market-supporting institutions, guild organisations, and the Industrial Revolution: A comparative view', *Australian Economic History Review*, 53: 221–46.

Tanzini, Lorenzo (2012), 'Tuscan states: Florence and Siena', in: Andrea Gamberini and Isabella Lazzarini (eds.), *The Italian Renaissance State* (Cambridge: Cambridge University Press), 90–111.

Taverne, Ed (1972), 'Salomon de Bray and the reorganization of the Haarlem guild of St. Luke in 1631', *Simiolus* 6: 50–69.

Taylor, Michael (1987), *The Possibility of Cooperation* (Cambridge: Cambridge University Press).

Taylor, Stephen (2013), 'Afterword: State formation, political stability and the revolution of 1688', in: Tim Harris and Stephen Taylor (eds.), *The Final Crisis of the Stuart Monarchy: The Revolutions of 1688–91 in Their British, Atlantic and European Contexts* (Woodbridge: Boydell).

Te Brake, Wayne Ph. (1989), *Regents and Rebels: The Revolutionary World of an Eighteenth-Century Dutch City* (Cambridge, MA: Basil Blackwell).

(1998), *Shaping History: Ordinary People in European Politics, 1500–1700* (Berkeley: University of California Press).

(2003), 'Charles V and his contentious subjects', in: Marc Boone and Marysa Demoor (eds.), *Charles V in Context: The Making of a European Identity* (Ghent: Universiteit Gent), 125–45.

Teeuwen, Daniëlle (2010), '"Vande groote swaricheyt der armen deser Stadt": De reorganisatie van de armenzorg in Utrecht, 1580–1674', *Jaarboek Oud Utrecht*, 48–65.

(2012), 'Collections for the poor: Monetary charitable donations in Dutch towns, c. 1600–1800', *Continuity and Change* 27: 271–99.

(2015), *Financing Poor Relief through Charitable Collections in Dutch Towns, c. 1600–1800* (Amsterdam: Amsterdam University Press).

Temple, Nora (1975), 'The control and exploitation of French towns during the Ancien Régime', in: Raymond F. Kierstead (ed.), *State and Society in Seventeenth-Century France* (New York, NY: Franklin Watts), 67–93 (orig. *History* 51 [1966]: 16–34).

Temple, William (1972), *Observations upon the United Provinces of the Netherlands*, ed. by George Clark (Oxford: Clarendon; orig. 1673).

Terpstra, Nicholas (1994), 'Apprenticeship in social welfare: From confraternal charity to municipal poor relief in early modern Italy', *Sixteenth Century Journal* 25: 101–20.

(1995), *Lay Confraternities and Civic Religion in Renaissance Bologna* (Cambridge: Cambridge University Press).

(ed.) (2000), *The Politics of Ritual Kinship: Confraternities and Social Order in Early Modern Italy* (Cambridge: Cambridge University Press).

Tezcan, Baki (2010), *The Second Ottoman Empire: Political and Social Transformation in the Early Modern World* (Cambridge: Cambridge University Press).

Thijs, Alfons K. L. (2006), 'Religion and social structure: Religious rituals in pre-industrial trade associations in the Low Countries', in: Maarten Prak, Catharina Lis, Jan Lucassen and Hugo Soly (eds.), *Craft Guilds in the Early Modern Low Countries: Work, Power and Representation* (Aldershot: Ashgate), 157–73.

Thompson, I. A. A. (1993), *Crown and Cortes: Government, Institutions and Representation in Early-Modern Castile* (Aldershot: Ashgate).

Thunder, Moira (2004), 'Improving design for woven silks: The contribution of William Shipley's school and the Society of Arts', *Journal of Design History* 17: 5–27.

Tilly, Charles (ed.) (1975a), *The Formation of National States in Western Europe* (Princeton, NJ: Princeton University Press).

(1975b), 'Reflections on the history of European state-making', in: Charles Tilly (ed.), *The Formation of National States in Western Europe* (Princeton, NJ: Princeton University Press), 3–83.

(1978), *From Mobilization to Revolution* (Reading, MA: Addison-Wesley).

(1984), *Big Structures, Large Processes, Huge Comparisons* (New York, NY: Russell Sage Foundation).

(1985), 'War making and state making as organized crime', in: Peter B. Evans, Dietrich Rueschemeyer and Theda Skocpol (eds.), *Bringing the State Back In* (Cambridge: Cambridge University Press), 169–91.

(1990), *Capital, Coercion, and European States, AD 990–1990* (Oxford: Blackwell).

(1993), *European Revolutions, 1492–1992* (Oxford: Blackwell).

(1995), 'Citizenship, identity and social history', *International Review of Social History* 40, supplement 3: 1–17.

(2004), *Contention and Democracy in Europe, 1650–2000* (Cambridge: Cambridge University Press).

Tingle, Elizabeth (2000), 'A city at war: Changing definitions of citizenship in Nantes during the later Wars of Religion 1580–89', *European Review of History* 7: 99–108.

(2006), 'Stability in the urban community in a time of war: Police, Protestantism and poor relief in Nantes during the French Wars of Religion, 1562–89', *European History Quarterly* 36 (2006), 521–47.

Titone, Fabrizio (2009), *Governments of the* Universitates: *Urban Communities of Sicily in the Fourteenth and Fifteenth Centuries*. Studies in European Urban History, vol. 21 (Turnhout: Brepols).

Tittler, Robert (1998), *The Reformation and the Towns in England: Politics and Political Culture, c. 1540–1640* (Oxford: Clarendon).

Tlusty, B. Ann (2011), *The Martial Ethic in Early Modern Germany: Civic Duty and the Right of Arms* (Basingstoke: Palgrave).

Tomkins, Alannah (2006), *The Experience of Urban Poverty, 1723–82* (Manchester: Manchester University Press).

Tomlins, Christopher (1999), 'Why wait for industrialism? Work, legal culture, and the example of early America: An historiographical argument', *Labour History* 40: 5–34.

Torgler, Benno, and Friedrich Schneider (2005), 'Attitudes towards paying taxes in Austria: An empirical analysis', *Empirica* 32: 231–50.

Tóth, Árpád, Gábor Czoch and István Németh (2017), 'Urban communities and their burghers in the kingdom of Hungary (1750–1850): The possibilities databases offer for historical analysis', in: Justin Colson and Arie van Steensel (eds.), *Cities and Solidarities: Urban Communities in Pre-Modern Europe* (London: Routledge), 188–207.

Tracy, James D. (1985), *A Financial Revolution in the Habsburg Netherlands: Renten and Renteniers in the County of Holland, 1515–1565* (Berkeley: University of California Press).

(1990), *Holland under Habsburg Rule: The Formation of a Body Politic* (Berkeley: University of California Press).

(2002), *Emperor Charles V, Impresario of War: Campaign Strategy, International Finance, and Domestic Politics* (Cambridge: Cambridge University Press).

(2003), 'On the dual origins of long-term urban debt in medieval Europe', in: Marc Boone, Karel Davids and Paul Janssens (eds.), *Urban Public Debts: Urban Government and the Market for Annuities in Western Europe (14th–18th centuries)*. Studies in European Urban History, vol. 3 (Turnhout: Brepols), 13–24.

(2008), *The Founding of the Dutch Republic: War, Finance, and Politics in Holland 1572–1588* (Oxford: Oxford University Press).

Trio, Paul, Dirk Heirbaut and Dirk Van den Auweele (eds.) (2002), *Omtrent 1302* (Louvain: Universitaire Pers Leuven).

Truant, Cynthia Maria (1994), *The Rites of Labor: Brotherhoods of Compagnonnage in Old and New Regime France* (Ithaca, NY: Cornell University Press).

(1995), 'Parisian guildswomen and the (sexual) politics of privilege: Defending their patrimonies in print', in: Elisabeth C. Goldsmith and Dena Goodman (eds.), *Going Public: Women and Publishing in Early Modern France* (Ithaca, NY: Cornell University Press), 46–61.

Tump, Janneke (2012), *Ambachtelijk geschoold: Haarlemse en Rotterdamse ambachtslieden en de circulatie van technische kennis, ca. 1400–1720*, PhD thesis, Vrije Universiteit Amsterdam.

(2014), 'The coopers' guilds in Holland, c. 1650–1720: A market logic?', in: C. A. Davids and Bert De Munck (eds.), *Innovation and Creativity in Late Medieval and Early Modern European Cities* (Aldershot: Ashgate), 225–44.

Turner, Anthony (2008), '"Not to hurt of trade": Guilds and innovation in horology and precision instrument making', in: S. R. Epstein and Maarten Prak (eds), *Guilds, Innovation and the European Economy, 1400–1800* (Cambridge: Cambridge University Press), 264–87.

Turner, Bryan S. (1997), 'Citizenship studies: A general theory', *Citizenship Studies* 1: 5–18.

Underdown, David (1985), *Revel, Riot and Rebellion: Popular Politics and Culture in England 1603–1660* (Oxford: Oxford University Press).

Unger, Brigitte, and Frans van Waarden (1999), 'Interest associations and economic growth: A critique of Mancur Olson's *Rise and Decline of Nations*', *Review of International Political Economy* 6: 425–67.

Unger, Richard W. (1978), *Dutch Shipbuilding before 1800* (Assen: Van Gorcum).

Van Bruaene, Anne-Laure, Bruno Blondé and Marc Boone (eds.) (2016), *Gouden Eeuwen: Stad en samenleving in de Lage Landen, 1100–1600* (Gent: Academia Press).

Van Dijck, Maarten F., Bert De Munck and Nicholas Terpstra (2017), 'Relocating civil society: Theories and practices of civil society in late medieval and early modern society', *Social Science History* 41: 1–17.

Van Honacker, Karin (1994), *Lokaal verzet en oproer in de 17de en 18de eeuw: Collectieve acties tegen het centraal gezag in Brussel, Antwerpen en Leuven.* Standen en Landen, vol. 98 (Kortrijk-Heule: U. G. A.).

Van Uytven, Raymond (1980), 'Sociale groepen, juridische en politieke structuren', in: Van Uytven (ed.), *Leuven: De beste stad van Brabant* vol. 1 (Louvain: Stadsbestuur van Leuven), 195–237.

Vanja, Christina (1992), 'Zwischen Verdrängung und Expansion, Kontrolle und Befreiung', *Vierteljahrschrift für Sozial- und Wirtschaftsgeschichte* 79: 457–82.

Vann, James Allen (1984), *The Making of a State: Württemberg 1593–1793* (Ithaca, NY: Cornell University Press).

Velema, Wycher (2007), *Republicans: Essays on Eighteenth-Century Dutch Political Thought* (Leiden: Brill).

Verbruggen, J. F. (1977), *The Art of War in Western Europe during the Middle Ages from the Eighth Century to 1340* (Amsterdam: North Holland Publishers).

Verhulst, Adriaan (1999), *The Rise of Cities in North-West Europe* (Cambridge: Cambridge University Press).

Verkerk, C. L. (1992), *Coulissen van de macht: een sociaal-institutionele studie betreffende de samenstelling van het bestuur van Arnhem in de middeleeuwen en een bijdrage tot de studie van stedelijke elitevorming* (Hilversum: Verloren).

(2004), 'De goede lieden van het gerecht', in M. Carasso-Kok (ed.), *Geschiedenis van Amsterdam*, vol. 1: *Een stad uit het niets: tot 1578* (Amsterdam: SUN), 175–203.

Vermeesch, Griet (2006), *Oorlog, Steden en Staatsvorming: De Grenssteden Gorinchem en Doesburg Tijdens de Geboorte-Eeuw van de Republiek (1570–1680)* (Amsterdam: Amsterdam University Press).

(2009), 'War and garrison towns in the Dutch Republic: The cases of Gorinchem and Doesburg (c.1570–c. 1660)', *Urban History* 36: 3–23.

(2012), 'Professional lobbying in eighteenth-century Brussels: The role of agents in petitioning the central government in the Habsburg Netherlands', *Journal of Early Modern History* 16: 95–119.

Viggiano, Alfredo (2013), 'Politics and constitution', in: Eric Dursteler (ed.), *A Companion to Venetian History 1400–1797* (Leiden: Brill), 47–84.

Vijlbrief, I. (1950), *Van anti-aristocratie tot democratie: Een bijdrage tot de politieke en sociale geschiedenis der stad Utrecht* (Amsterdam: Querido).

Vinson, Ben, III (2002), *Bearing Arms for His Majesty: The Free-Colored Militia in Colonial Mexico* (Stanford, CA: Stanford University Press).

Vives, Juan Luis (2002), *De Subventione Pauperum sive De Humanis Necessitatibus*, libri II, ed. and transl. by C. Matheeussen and C. Fantazzi, *Selected Works of J. L. Vives*, vol. 4 (Leiden: Brill).

Vivo, Filippo de (2007), *Information and Communication in Venice: Rethinking Early Modern Politics* (Oxford: Oxford University Press).

Vlis, Ingrid van der (2001), *Leven in armoede: Delftse bedeelden in de zeventiende eeuw* (Amsterdam: Bert Bakker).

Vos, Aart (2007), *Burgers, broeders en bazen: Het maatschappelijk middenveld in 's-Hertogenbosch in de zeventiende en achttiende eeuw* (Hilversum: Verloren).

Vowell, John, alias Hooker (1919), *The Description of the Citie of Exeter*, ed. by W. J. Harte, J. W. Schopp and H. Tapley-Soper (Exeter: Devon and Cornwall Record Society).

Vries, Peer (2013), *Escaping Poverty: The Origins of Modern Economic Growth* (Göttingen: Vandenhoeck & Ruprecht).

Waarden, Frans van (1992), 'Emergence and development of business interest associations: An example from the Netherlands', *Organization Studies* 13: 521–62.

Wahl, Fabian (2015a), 'Participative Political Institutions in Pre-Modern Europe: Introducing a New Data-Base', unpublished paper, University of Hohenheim, available at http://papers.ssrn.com/sol3/papers.cfm?abstract_id=2498047.

(2015b), 'Participative Political Institutions and City Development 800–1800', unpublished paper, University of Hohenheim, available at http://papers.ssrn.com/sol3/papers.cfm?abstract_id=2562843.

(2016), 'Participative political institutions in pre-modern Europe: Introducing a new database', *Historical Methods: A Journal of Quantitative and Interdisciplinary History* 49: 67–79.

Wakeman, Frederic, Jr. (1993), 'The civil society and public sphere debate: Western reflections on Chinese political culture', *Modern China* 19: 108–38.

Waley, Daniel (1968), 'The army of the Florentine republic from the twelfth to the fourteenth century', in: Nicolai Rubinstein (ed.), *Florentine Studies* (London: Faber), 70–108.

(1991), *Siena and the Sienese in the Thirteenth Century* (Cambridge: Cambridge University Press).

Walker, Mack (1971), *German Home Towns: Community, State and 1648–1871* (Ithaca, NY: Cornell University Press).

Wallace, Peter G. (1994), 'Civic politics and civic values in Colmar, 1648–1715', *French Historical Studies* 18: 907–37.

Wallerstein, Immanuel (1974), *The Modern World-System*. vol. 1: *Capitalist Agriculture and the Origins of the Modern World-Economy in the Sixteenth Century* (New York, NY: Academic Press).

(1980), *The Modern World-System*, vol. 2: *Mercantilism and the Consolidation of the European World-Economy, 1600–1750* (New York, NY: Academic Press).

Wallis, Patrick (2008), 'Apprenticeship and training in premodern England', *Journal of Economic History* 68: 832–61.

Wallis, Patrick, Bert De Munck, Clare Crowston, Raoul De Kerf, Marcel Hoogenboom, Christopher Kissane, Chris Minns and Maarten Prak (2015), 'Barriers to

Citizenship and Trades in Early Modern Europe', unpublished paper, bEUcitizen project, work package 3.
Wallis, Patrick, and Maarten Prak (eds.) (2019), *Apprenticeship in Premodern Europe* (Cambridge: Cambridge University Press).
Walter, Jörg (1971), *Rat und Bürgerhauptleute in Braunschweig, 1576–1604* (Braunschweig: Waisenhaus).
Ward, Joseph P. (1997), *Metropolitan Communities: Trade Guilds, Identity and Change in Early Modern London* (Stanford, CA: Stanford University Press).
Water, Johan van de (1729), *Groot Placaetboek, vervattende alle de placaten, ordonnantien en edicten der edele mogende heeren Staten 's lands van Utrecht, mitsgaders van de borgemeesteren en vroedschap der stad Utrecht, etc.*, vol. 3 (Utrecht: Jacob van Poolsum).
Weber, Max (1968 [1922]), *Economy and Society: An Outline of Interpretative Sociology*, ed. by Guenther Roth and Claus Wittich (Berkeley, CA: University of California Press).
Weikert, Wolfgang (1998), *Erbmänner und Erbmännerprozesse: Ein Kapitel Münsterscher Stadtgeschichte* (Münster: Aschendorff).
Weis, Monique (ed.) (2010), *Des villes en révolte: Les Républiques urbaines aux Pays-Bas et en France pendant la deuxième moitié du XVIe siècle*. Studies in European Urban History (1100–1800), vol. 23 (Turnhout: Brepols).
Welch, Evelyn (1997), *Art in Renaissance Italy* (Oxford: Oxford University Press).
Wells, Charlotte (1995), *Law and Citizenship in Early Modern France* (Baltimore, MD: Johns Hopkins University Press).
(1999), 'The language of citizenship in the French Religious Wars', *Sixteenth-Century Journal* 30: 441–56.
Wensky, Margret (1982), 'Women's guilds in Cologne in the later Middle Ages', *Journal of European Economic History* 1: 630–50.
Werkstetter, Christine (2001), *Frauen im Augsburger Zunfthandwerk: Arbeit, Arbeitsbeziehungen und Geschlechterverhältnisse im 18. Jahrhundert* (Berlin: Akademie Verlag).
Wernicke, Horst (1985), 'Die Bezeichnungen Zunft und Gilde in ihrem historischen und wortgeographischen Zusammenhang', in: Berent Schwineköper (ed.), *Gilden und Zünfte: Kaufmännische und gewerbliche Genossenschaften im frühen und hohen Mittelalter* (Sigmaringen: Jan Thorbecke), 31–52.
Wesoly, Kurt (1985), *Lehrlinge und Handwerksgesellen am Mittelrhein: Ihre soziale Lage und ihre Organisation vom 14. bis ins 17. Jahrhundert*. Studien zur Frankfurter Geschichte, vol. 18 (Frankfurt-am-Main: Kramer).
Western, J. R. (1965), *The English Militia in the Eighteenth Century: The Story of a Political Issue, 1660–1802* (London: Routledge & Kegan Paul).
Westrich, Sal Alexander (1972), *The Ormée of Bordeaux: A Revolution during the Fronde* (Baltimore, MD: Johns Hopkins University Press).
White, Shane (1991), *Somewhat More Independent: The End of Slavery in New York City, 1770–1810* (Athens, GA: University of Georgia Press).
Wickham, Chris (1981), *Early Medieval Italy: Central Power and Local Society 400–1000* (London: MacMillan).
(2014), 'The "feudal revolution" and the origins of Italian city communes', *Transactions of the Royal Historical Society* 24: 29–55.
(2015), *Sleepwalking into a New World: The Emergence of Italian City Communes in the Twelfth Century* (Princeton, NJ: Princeton University Press).
Wiesner, Merry E. (1986), *Working Women in Renaissance Germany* (New Brunswick, NJ: Rutgers University Press).

(1988), 'War, work, and wealth: The bases of citizenship in early modern German cities', in: Merry E. Wiesner, *Gender, Church and State in Early Modern Germany: Essays by Merry E. Wiesner* (London: Longman), 114–26.
(1989), 'Guilds, male bonding and women's work in early modern Germany', *Gender and History* 1: 125–37; reprinted in Merry E. Wiesner, *Gender, Church and State in Early Modern Germany* (London: Longman, 1998), 163–77.
(1993), *Women and Gender in Early Modern Europe* (Cambridge: Cambridge University Press).
(1996), 'Ausbildung in den Zünften', in: Elke Kleinau and Claudia Opitz (eds.), *Geschichte der Mädchen- und Frauenbildung*, vol. 1: *Vom Mittelalter bis zur Aufklärung* (Frankfurt: Campus), 91–102.
Wijngaarden, Hilde van (2000), *Zorg voor de kost: Armenzorg, arbeid en onderlinge hulp in Zwolle 1650–1700* (Amsterdam: Bert Bakker).
Wilentz, Sean (1984), *Chants Democratic: New York City and the Rise of the American Working Class, 1788–1850* (New York, NY: Oxford University Press).
Wilkins, Charles L. (2010), *Forging Urban Solidarities: Ottoman Aleppo, 1640–1700* (Leiden: Brill).
Will, Pierre-Étienne, and R. Bin Wong (1991), *Nourish the People: The State Civilian Granary System in China, 1650–1850* (Ann Arbor, MI: Center for Chinese Studies, University of Michigan).
Wilson, Kathleen (1995), *The Sense of the People: Politics, Culture and Imperialism in England, 1715–1785* (Cambridge: Cambridge University Press).
Winter, Michael (1992), *Egyptian Society under Ottoman rule, 1517–1798* (London: Routledge).
Withington, Phil (2001), 'Views from the bridge: Revolution and Restoration in seventeenth-century York', *Past & Present* 170: 121–51.
(2005), *The Politics of Commonwealth: Citizens and Freemen in Early Modern England* (Cambridge: Cambridge University Press).
(2007), 'Public discourse, corporate citizenship, and state formation in early modern England', *American Historical Review* 112: 1016–38.
(2008), 'Citizens, soldiers and urban culture in Restoration England', *English Historical Review* 123: 587–610.
(2010), *Society in Early Modern England: The Vernacular Origins of Some Powerful Ideas* (Cambridge: Polity).
(ed.) (2011), 'Citizens and soldiers in England, Scotland, Ireland and the wider world', special issue of *Journal of Early Modern History* 15: 3–183.
(2017), 'Urbanization', in: Keith Wrightson (ed.), *The New Cambridge Social History of Early Modern England* (Cambridge: Cambridge University Press), 174–98.
Woltjer, J. J. (1975), 'Dutch privileges, real and imaginary', in: J. S. Bromley and E. H. Kossmann (eds.), *Some Political Mythologies: Britain and the Netherlands*, vol. 5 (The Hague: Nijhoff), 19–35.
Wong, R. Bin (1997), *China Transformed: Historical Change and the Limits of European Experience* (Ithaca, NY: Cornell University Press).
(1999), 'Citizenship in Chinese history', in: Michael Hanagan and Charles Tilly (eds.), *Extending Citizenship, Reconfiguring States* (Lanham, MD: Rowman and Littlefield), 97–122.
Wood, Patricia Burke (2014), 'Urban citizenship', in: Hein-Anton van der Heijden (ed.), *Handbook of Political Citizenship and Social Movements* (Cheltenham: Edward Elgar), 133–53.

Woodward, Donald (1995), *Men at Work: Labourers and Building Craftsmen in the Towns of Northern England, 1450–1750* (Cambridge: Cambridge University Press).
Wrigley, E. A. (1967), 'A simple model of London's importance in changing English society and economy, 1650–1750', *Past & Present* 37: 44–70.
(1985), 'Urban growth and agricultural change: England and the continent in the early modern period', *Journal of Interdisciplinary History* 15: 683–728 (reprinted in Wrigley, *People, Cities and Wealth: The Transformation of Traditional Society*, Oxford: Blackwell, 1987).
Würgler, Andreas (1995), *Unruhen und Öffentlichkeit: Städtische und ländliche Protestbewegungen im 18. Jahrhundert*. Frühneuzeit Forschungen, vol. 1 (Tübingen: bibliotheca academica Verlag).
(2001), 'Voices from among the "silent masses": Humble petitions and social conflicts in early modern Central Europe', in: Lex Heerma van Voss (ed.), *Petitions in Social History* (*International Review of Social History* 46, Supplement 9) (Cambridge: Cambridge University Press), 11–34.
(2008), '"The League of the Discordant Members", or how the old Swiss Confederation operated and how it managed to survive for so long', in: André Holenstein, Thomas Maissen and Maarten Prak (eds.), *The Republican Alternative: The Netherlands and Switzerland Compared* (Amsterdam: Amsterdam University Press), 29–50.
Wyffels, Carlos (1951), *De oorsprong der ambachten in Vlaanderen en Brabant*. Verhandelingen van de Koninklijk Vlaamse Academie voor Wetenschappen, Letteren en Schone Kunsten van België, Klasse der Letteren, vol. 13 (Brussels: Koninklijk Vlaamse Academie voor Wetenschappen, Letteren en Schone Kunsten).
Wyrobisz, Andrzej (1989), 'Power and towns in the Polish Gentry Commonwealth: The Polish-Lithuanian state in the sixteenth and seventeenth centuries', in: Charles Tilly and Wim P. Blockmans (eds.), *Cities and the Rise of States in Europe, A.D. 1000 to 1800* (Boulder, CO: Westview Press), 150–67.
Yi, Eunjeong (2004), *Guild Dynamics in Seventeenth-Century Istanbul: Fluidity and Leverage* (Leiden: Brill).
Yi, Xu, Bas van Leeuwen and Jan Luiten van Zanden (2015), 'Urbanization in China, ca. 1100–1900', paper presented at the XIIth World Economic History Congress in Kyoto.
Yildirim, Onur (2008), 'Ottoman guilds in the early modern era', in: Jan Lucassen, Tine De Moor and Jan Luiten van Zanden (eds.), *The Return of the Guilds. International Review of Social History*, Supplement 16 (Cambridge: Cambridge University Press), 73–93.
Yılmaz, Hüseyin (2015), 'Containing sultanic authority: Constitutionalism in the Ottoman Empire before modernity', *Osmanlı Araştırmaları/The Journal of Ottoman Studies* 45: 231–64.
York civic records. 3 vols. (Leeds) YAS Record Series 98 (1939), 103 [vol. 2] (1941), 106 [vol. 3] (1942), ed. by Angelo Raine.
Zagorin, Perez (1969), *The Court and the Country: The Beginning of the English Revolution* (London: Atheneum).
(1982), *Rebels and Rulers 1500–1660*. 2 vols. (Cambridge: Cambridge University Press).
Zahedieh, Nuala (2010), *The Capital and the Colonies: London and the Atlantic Economy, 1660–1700* (Cambridge: Cambridge University Press).
Zanden, Jan Luiten van (2001), 'Early modern economic growth: A survey of the European economy, 1500–1800', in: Maarten Prak (ed.), *Early Modern*

Capitalism: Economic and Social Change in Europe, 1400–1800 (London: Routledge), 69–87.
(2009), *The Long Road to the Industrial Revolution: The European Economy in a Global Perspective* (Leiden: Brill).
Zanden, Jan Luiten van, Eltjo Buringh and Maarten Bosker (2012), 'The rise and decline of European parliaments, 1188–1789', *Economic History Review* 65: 835–61.
Zanden, Jan Luiten van, and Bas van Leeuwen (2012), 'Persistent but not consistent: The growth of national income in Holland 1347–1807', *Explorations in Economic History* 49: 119–30.
Zanden, Jan Luiten van, and Maarten Prak (2006), 'Towards an economic interpretation of citizenship: The Dutch Republic between medieval communes and modern nation-states', *European Review of Economic History* 10: 111–45.
Zaret, David (1996), 'Petitions and the "invention" of public opinion in the English Revolution', *American Journal of Sociology*, 101: 1497–555.
Zelin, M. (1985), *The Magistrate's Tael: Rationalizing Fiscal Reform in Eighteenth-Century Ch'ing China* (Berkeley, CA: University of California Press).
Zeller, Olivier (2015), *La bourgeoisie statutaire de Lyon et ses privilèges: Morale civique, évasion fiscale et cabarets urbains (XVIIe–XVIIIe siècles)* (Lyon: Éditions lyonnaises d'art et d'historie).
Zimmerman, Joseph F. (1999), *The New England Town Meeting: Democracy in Action* (Westport, CT: Greenwood Press).
Zubaida, Sami, (2008), 'Urban social movements, 1750–1950', in: Peter Sluglett (ed.), *The Urban Social History of the Middle East, 1750–1950* (Syracuse, NY: Syracuse University Press), 224–53.
Zuckerman, Michael (1970), *Peaceable Kingdoms: New England Towns in the Eighteenth Century* (Westport, CT: Greenwood Press).
Zuijderduijn, C. J. (2009), *Medieval Capital Markets: Markets for* Renten, *State Formation and Private Investment in Holland (1300–1550)*. Global Economic History Series, vol. 2 (Leiden: Brill).
Zwitser, H. L. (1991), *'De militie van den staat': Het leger van de Republiek der Verenigde Nederlanden* (Amsterdam: Van Soeren).

Index

As citizenship is the topic of this book, it has not been indexed separately; the entry 'citizenship' refers to formal citizenship only